On a Trail of Southwest Discovery

The Southwest Center Series

Jeffrey M. Banister, Editor

VOLUME 3
of the multivolume work
Frank Hamilton Cushing and
the Hemenway Southwestern Archaeological Expedition,
1886–1889

On a Trail of Southwest Discovery

The Expedition Diaries of Frederick W. Hodge and Margaret W. Magill, 1886–1888

Edited by Curtis M. Hinsley
and David R. Wilcox

THE UNIVERSITY OF
ARIZONA PRESS
TUCSON

The University of Arizona Press
www.uapress.arizona.edu

We respectfully acknowledge the University of Arizona is on the land and territories of Indigenous peoples. Today, Arizona is home to twenty-two federally recognized tribes, with Tucson being home to the O'odham and the Yaqui. The University strives to build sustainable relationships with sovereign Native Nations and Indigenous communities through education offerings, partnerships, and community service.

First paperback edition published 2026

ISBN-13: 978-0-8165-5301-3 (hardcover)
ISBN-13: 978-0-8165-5668-7 (paperback)
ISBN-13: 978-0-8165-5302-0 (ebook)

Cover design by Leigh McDonald
Typeset by Sara Thaxton in 10.5/14 Warnock Pro

Publication of this book is made possible in part by support from the Southwest Center of the University of Arizona.

Library of Congress Cataloging-in-Publication Data
Names: Hinsley, Curtis M., editor. | Wilcox, David R., 1944– editor.
Title: On a trail of southwest discovery : the expedition diaries of Frederick W. Hodge and Margaret W. Magill, 1886–1888 / edited by Curtis M. Hinsley and David R. Wilcox.
Other titles: Frank Hamilton Cushing and the Hemenway Southwestern Archaeological Expedition, 1886–1889 ; v. 3.
Description: Tucson : The University of Arizona Press, 2024. | Series: Frank Hamilton Cushing and the Hemenway Southwestern Archaeological Expedition, 1886–1889 ; volume 3 | Includes bibliographical references and index.
Identifiers: LCCN 2023027616 (print) | LCCN 2023027617 (ebook) | ISBN 9780816553013 (hardcover) | ISBN 9780816553020 (ebook)
Subjects: LCSH: Hodge, Frederick Webb, 1864–1956—Diaries. | Hodge, Margaret Whitehead Magill, 1863–1935—Diaries. | Cushing, Frank Hamilton, 1857–1900. | Hemenway Southwestern Archaeological Expedition (1886–1894) | Anthropology—Arizona—History—19th century. | Anthropology—New Mexico—History—19th century. | LCGFT: Diaries.
Classification: LCC E78.S7 F725 2024 vol. 3 (print) | LCC E78.S7 (ebook) | DDC 979.1/04—dc23/eng/20230907
LC record available at https://lccn.loc.gov/2023027616
LC ebook record available at https://lccn.loc.gov/2023027617

Printed in the United States of America
∞ This paper meets the requirements of ANSI/NISO Z39.48-1992 (Permanence of Paper).

To Victoria and Susan

One More Time

Contents

Illustrations

Map

Figures

Line Drawings

Foreword

The Southwest Center proudly includes in its University of Arizona Press series Curtis Hinsley and David Wilcox's magisterial three-volume study, *Frank Hamilton Cushing and the Hemenway Southwestern Archaeological Expedition, 1886 to 1889*. In the final days of 1886, having secured the financial backing of Boston philanthropist Mary Tileston Hemenway, Frank Hamilton Cushing headed west with a team of assistants to break ground on the Southwest's first large-scale archaeological exploration sustained by private funds. Much of what happened during the next few years would leave an indelible mark on southwestern anthropology. The Hemenway Expedition produced a sizable archive—or perhaps better said, a large documentary record scattered across diverse repositories and sources. Thanks to Hinsley and Wilcox's painstaking collection, curation, and analysis of this archive, we now have a detailed picture of a pivotal moment for our understanding of the region's human history. The authors draw from newspaper articles, personal correspondence, diaries, and a wide array of visual materials to offer a richly layered account of relationships among the diverse expedition team members and board. The fate of the expedition, including its important findings, was deeply shaped by the interweaving of fin-de-siècle cultural and interpersonal politics. With the three Hemenway volumes, Hinsley and Wilcox have made a lasting contribution to Southwest social history and to historiography more broadly.

Jeffrey M. Banister, Director
The Southwest Center

Introduction to the Multivolume Work

In the fall of 1886, Mary Tileston Hemenway, reputedly the most munificent lady in Boston, agreed to sponsor the Hemenway Southwestern Archaeological Expedition under the direction of anthropologist Frank Hamilton Cushing.[1] Hemenway quietly supported many worthy causes, most of them concerned with education and American history, and she was intrigued by Cushing, his Zuni experiences, and his vision for the future of American ethnology and archaeology. Together they dreamed of founding a private institution in Salem, Massachusetts, a Pueblo Museum for the study of American Indians. The artifact collections of the Hemenway Expedition were to form the nucleus of the museum. Accordingly, in late 1886 Hemenway appointed a board to oversee the project, and early the following year Cushing outfitted the expedition and took to the field in Arizona in high hopes of tracing the ancestors of the Zunis and perhaps even solving larger puzzles of aboriginal migration through the Americas.

By the third year of fieldwork, Cushing's persistent illnesses; growing doubts among board members about his integrity, ideas, and even sanity; and Hemenway's own declining health led her son Augustus and the board of the expedition to act. In mid-1889 they fired Cushing and appointed Jesse Walter Fewkes to succeed him as director.[2] For two years Cushing withdrew into serious illness and depression. Without access to his records, in 1891 he nevertheless began a report, a retrospective daily "itinerary" of the expedition. Then, after two years of intermittent effort, in frustration and disappointment he turned wholly to other interests. He never returned to the Hemenway project or the Southwest, and he never again saw the artifact collections, field maps, catalogues, and other materials—or Mary Hemenway. The Pueblo Museum never materialized, and at her death in 1894 Hemenway willed the collections (most of which were in storage in Salem) to the Peabody Museum of Harvard University. Several fragmentary studies from the expedition found their way into print, but Cushing's notes and partial reports were still in manuscript form at his own sudden death at age forty-three in 1900.

Frederick Webb Hodge began his long anthropological career as Cushing's personal secretary on the expedition, and when he married Margaret Magill in 1891 he became Cushing's brother-in-law as well. By the mid-1890s Hodge had become a central figure in both the Smithsonian Institution and its Bureau of American Ethnology, rising to be the head of the BAE from 1910 to 1918. He then moved to George Heye's Museum of the American Indian in New York City (1918–30) as editor and assistant to Heye and from there to the Southwest Museum in Los Angeles, which he directed until the year before his death, at age ninety-two, in 1956. Because of his institutional prominence and long life (he outlived all other expedition participants by at least two decades and Cushing by more than half a century) Hodge had a profound influence on the reputation of the Hemenway Expedition in the twentieth century.

In the 1930s Alfred Tozzer suggested to Emil W. Haury that he write his dissertation at Harvard on the Peabody Museum's Hemenway collections, and Haury produced a classic study of late Hohokam ceramics and material culture.[3] The only archival materials he had at hand, though, were those he found at Harvard and a few illustrations at the Brooklyn Museum. In the course of his research he wrote to Hodge at the Southwest Museum. Hodge responded that he had a "considerable body of Cushing's notes" but that they were "in much of a jumble."[4] He then proceeded, at some epistolary length, to accuse Cushing, his former brother-in-law, of faking an artifact, a turquoise-encrusted toad. Later, in his foreword to Haury's book *The Excavation of Los Muertos and Neighboring Ruins in the Salt River Valley, Southern Arizona* (1945), Hodge recounted more stories about Cushing that made light of him and his ideas, creating a strongly negative image. In Hodge's view, Cushing was "a visionary" who kept few notes, did not hesitate to exaggerate to gain a point, was a slacker, and suffered from "an overwrought imagination and a species of egotism that brooked no opinion adverse to his own."[5] Cushing, he further recalled, had "fiddled away his time in making flags for the tents and other useless trifles" at the expedition's campsites, leaving his field workers without supervision for weeks at a time.[6] He further implied that if there were few archival remains of the Hemenway Expedition it was Cushing's fault. Haury understandably believed Hodge, and so have several generations of anthropologists, archaeologists, and historians.

Today's evidence about the expedition—its roots, practices, results, and reputation—suggests a complex and quite different story. A remarkably large unpublished record of the Hemenway Expedition did in fact survive—and Hodge, ironically, did much to preserve it. Soon after Cushing's death, his close friend Stewart Culin, curator at the Brooklyn Museum, obtained Cushing's personal library and manuscripts from his widow, Emily.[7] In 1921, at a time when his own interests were changing, Culin sent Hodge three crates of Cushing's manuscripts, letter books, and related material.[8] Hodge apparently culled through this material, selecting what he thought was most interesting and depositing it at the library of the Heye Foundation at the Huntington Free Library in the Bronx. The rest of Cushing's material ("in much of a jumble") he took with him to California in 1930, where it eventually became part of the Southwest Museum's Hodge and Cushing collections.[9] In this way the major records of the Hemenway Expedition came to be distributed among the Peabody Museum of Harvard, the Huntington Free Library, the Brooklyn Museum, the Smithsonian Institution, and the Southwest Museum.

After Hodge's death, the Hemenway records that he had kept in his possession for thirty-five years were opened to scholars at the Southwest Museum. Ray Brandes constructed a pioneering 1965 dissertation on Cushing partly from these materials, and Charles Lange and his colleagues, in their multivolume study of Adolph F. Bandelier's years in the Southwest, drew significantly on them as well.[10] Joan Mark, in proposing Cushing as one of the critical figures in the history of American anthropology, recalled Claude Lévi-Strauss's praise for Cushing as a precursor of structuralism, and Jesse Green's annotated edition of Cushing's Zuñi writings, published in 1979, also brought his ethnographic work renewed professional and public attention.[11]

In short, with the increased interest in Cushing's place in the history of American anthropology, students of anthropology and the nineteenth-century Southwest turned to the Hodge-Cushing materials and began to recognize their value and depth.[12] At the same time, other relevant documents surfaced, such as the Hemenway family archives at the Peabody Essex Museum in Salem and Cushing's personal diaries.[13] Still, the Hemenway Expedition remained obscure and puzzling, its meaning lost in the fragments.

Wilcox, an archaeologist, had the opportunity in 1979 to excavate a large portion of a site in Tempe that Cushing, in 1887, had named La Ciudad de los Hornos (City of the Ovens).[14] Curious to learn what Cushing and his party had seen before the Salt River Valley was plowed or covered over by urban landscape, he, too, soon discovered the wealth of archival materials. At the Hayden Library of Arizona State University he discovered a copy of one installment of Cushing's Hemenway "itinerary," the original of which was at Harvard's Peabody Museum.[15] A friend told him of the Southwest Museum's holdings, and another, Gina Laczko, knew of the Hemenway materials archived at the Huntington Free Library in the Bronx. The richness of the Hodge-Cushing collection in Los Angeles astonished Wilcox, and he soon employed it for a report on the Casa Grande ruins, which Hemenway and Cushing had been instrumental in preserving.

After visiting other collections, by 1983 Wilcox could foresee the need for a multivolume work, and he began circulating a proposal. A few months later Raymond H. Thompson, director of the Arizona State Museum, in discussion with Lea S. McChesney of the Peabody Museum, discovered that Edwin L. Wade, Hinsley, and McChesney were thinking along similar lines.[16]

A collaboration seemed natural, and in 1983 Wilcox, Hinsley, and McChesney met at the Peabody Museum. Over the next several years they continued to assemble and transcribe materials, with Wilcox being aided in part by a grant from the Agnese N. Lindley Foundation. Progress was slow, however. In 1988 Hinsley moved from upstate New York to Northern Arizona University in Flagstaff, while Wilcox became head of anthropology at the Museum of Northern Arizona, also in Flagstaff. Soon thereafter, McChesney decided to pursue further graduate work in anthropology, examining the production and marketing of Hopi ceramics.

Our initial goal was to publish only Cushing's unfinished "itinerary," written in the early 1890s—his largest and most unusual unpublished work. In addition to its literary qualities, Cushing's narrative contains valuable and unique archaeological data of relevance to contemporary Hohokam studies.[17] But chance changed these plans. In 1991 Mary B. Davis, librarian at the Huntington Free Library, was inventorying the library's vault. Upon pulling down several books from a high, dusty shelf, she opened them to find, to her amazement, Cushing's distinctive handwriting. Closer inspection revealed that she had found nine letter books totaling more than four thousand pages—virtually the entire official correspondence of the Hemenway Expedition, stored away by Hodge and forgotten for sixty years. Included were all of Cushing's letters to Mrs. Hemenway; correspondence with Sylvester Baxter, the secretary-treasurer of the expedition's board; communications with merchants in Phoenix, Tempe, and Albuquerque; and a wide assortment of other records, including Cushing's instructions to Hodge during the director's long periods of recuperation in California.

Wilcox inventoried the letter books, as well as Hemenway collections at other institutions, and began the enormous task of transcribing selected materials into a computer database. Before the letter books came to light, the Hemenway Expedition existed for us only through fascinating but widely scattered fragments. Now, with the correspondence as a core, the pieces formed a more coherent if still incomplete picture. The Hemenway Expedition puzzle began to make sense, but a larger number of volumes seemed necessary in order to tell the story in all its complexity. This multivolume work is the result: a cultural history of the Hemenway Expedition and early anthropology in the American Southwest, told in the voices of the participants and interpreted by us.

The Hemenway Expedition occupies several critical points in the history of North American anthropology and archaeology. Cushing hoped it would stand as a "rock of ages" for the study of New World prehistory. Despite the largely unpublished nature of its work, the expedition is widely recognized as the foundation of Hohokam studies and a critical base for research into Zuni prehistory as well. Additionally, Cushing brilliantly anticipated modern strategies of multidisciplinary teamwork, with Adolph Bandelier as historian; Washington Matthews, Herman ten Kate, and Jacob L. Wortman as physical anthropologists; Margaret Magill as artist; Sylvester Baxter as publicist; Hodge as secretary/amanuensis; and Cushing himself as linguist, ethnographer, and archaeologist. Most important, perhaps, Cushing's struggle to find a language—a scientific poetics—suitable to his experiential and observational methods reflected a wider struggle between intuitive understanding and disciplined knowledge that continued throughout the twentieth century.[18]

Critically positioned historically, the Hemenway Expedition promises to enlighten current debates over the development of touristic rhetoric and sensibilities in the Southwest, a region that by the 1930s—when Aldous Huxley identified it as the "rest-cure reservation" of his "brave new world"—was already among the most heavily encoded spaces in the global economy and imagination. Frank Cushing's expedition entered the Salt River Valley of central Arizona Territory only a few years after the Atlantic and Pacific Railroad (a subsidiary of the Atchison, Topeka and Santa Fe) completed its main line across northern New Mexico and Arizona en route to Los Angeles. During 1886, too, the last serious Native American armed resistance in the region ended, and local boosters and land speculators were already hastening to alter the territory's image from one of miners, deserts, and wild Indians to a vision of farmers, green orchards, and peaceful pueblos. These were the crucial early years of the dreaming and inventing of the Southwest and of its incorporation into the national imagination.

Through this process, a distinctive regional entity eventually emerged, based on its landscapes, natural resources, and human inhabitants, and appealing strongly to the wishes and projected desires of outsiders. Because the Southwest is an astoundingly rich archaeological field, but also because the acts of digging, removing, and displaying buried artifacts provide ready signs and objects of belonging and proprietary relationship to the land, archaeological exploration and collection came to be central in this cultural exercise of incorporating the Southwest.

Each of these considerations has its place in our project of reconstruction and interpretation. But we return always to the documents, the multilayered and multivocal testimony of a complex endeavor, an enterprise that was at once a scientific exploration, a poetic experience, a financial investment, and a set of convoluted human relationships. The stories and texts come to us on many levels: from Hodge's personal shorthand diary notations of his quiet "portrait" meetings with Margaret Magill under the mesquite trees to Cushing's forty-page letter to Mary Hemenway on the proposed museum; from quartermaster Charles Garlick's invoices for hay and beans to Cushing's stunning, visionary report to the Congress of Americanists in Berlin; from intimate accounts of nausea and delirium to soaring speeches about prehistoric hemispheric connections; and finally from the dreams of 1886 to the misery of sickness and a sense of failure less than three years later. Mistakes, misjudgments, and misunderstandings all played their roles in Mary Hemenway's expedition, to be sure; but so did love, jealousy, and pride. In the end, we argue, a deep conflict of values and aesthetics doomed the expedition in its own time. It is this conflict that must be fully explored and understood if the rich legacy of Mary Hemenway and Frank Cushing is finally to be realized today.

David R. Wilcox
Curtis M. Hinsley

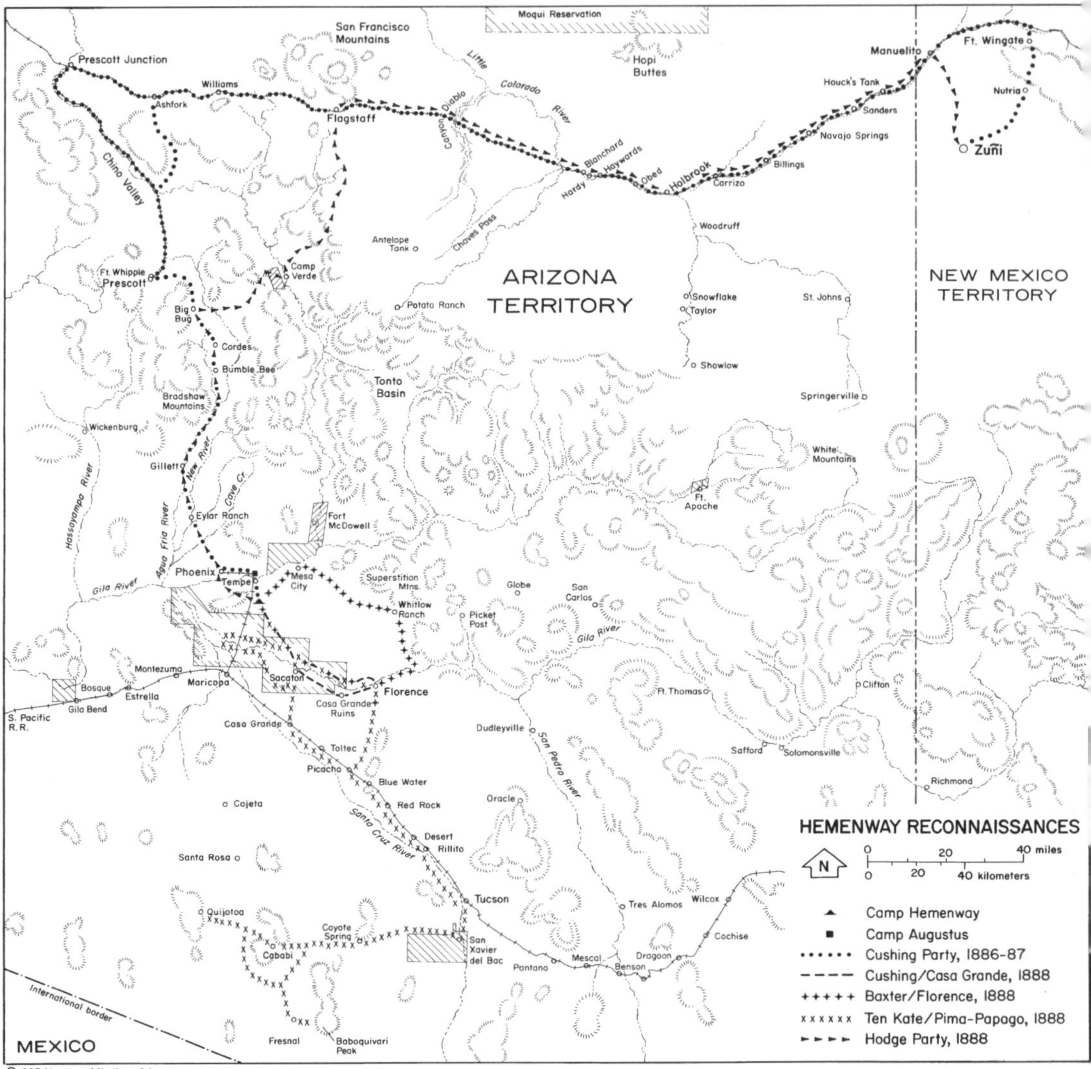

Map 1. Routes of principal reconnaissances conducted during the Hemenway Expedition in the Southwest, 1886–89. *(Map by Jody Griffith, Museum of Northern Arizona)*

Preface to Volume 3

Thirty years ago, archaeologist David R. Wilcox and I planned a multivolume documentary history of the Hemenway Southwestern Archaeological Expedition (1886–89), which was sponsored by Mary Tileston Hemenway of Boston and directed by Frank Hamilton Cushing. The Hemenway Expedition to Arizona and New Mexico was the first sustained, privately funded archaeological enterprise in the American Southwest. From his years living at Zuni pueblo (1879–84), Cushing had come to believe that the ancestors of the Zuni people had migrated northeastward from the Salt River Valley in central Arizona. Hemenway was intrigued by his visions and deeply interested in Zuni folklore as well. With her support and indulgence, his expedition spent sixteen months in the desert outside the small settlement of Tempe, before moving to Zuni pueblo in the summer of 1888. Here they excavated for another six months, then disbanded. Cushing was fired in June 1889. While initially considered a scientific failure and personal catastrophe, the expedition is now recognized as a foundation of Hohokam archaeology. Moreover, through a series of historical accidents it left behind a rich documentary record, dispersed among various archives.

The remarkable archived record of the expedition was largely unknown and unpublished; it includes nearly five thousand pages of correspondence fortuitously discovered in 1991. Accordingly, we fashioned a project goal of presenting a scientific expedition as seen through the eyes of its various participants, as well as through public perceptions at the time. In each volume the historical documents were to be framed by our interpretive essays.

The first volume, *The Southwest in the American Imagination* (1996), introduced the Hemenway Expedition through the writings of Sylvester Baxter, a Boston journalist who served as secretary-treasurer on the expedition's board. A great admirer of Cushing, he wrote the publicity pieces that announced the anthropologist and his undertaking to the world. The second volume, *The Lost Itinerary of Frank Hamilton Cushing* (2002), presented a unique, composite document: Cushing's unpublished, three-part account of the formation of the expedition and the early months of fieldwork in the largely unsettled deserts of central Arizona.

On a Trail of Southwest Discovery, our third and final Hemenway collaboration, sheds new, personal light on the operations and trials of the expedition through the diaries of two principal figures: Frederick Webb Hodge and Margaret Whitehead Magill. Hodge, who was twenty-two when the expedition headed westward in the last days of 1886, was Cushing's field secretary. The expedition was his initial field experience and the beginning of a seventy-year career in American anthropology. Margaret Magill, the youngest sister of Cushing's wife, Emily, was the artist of the expedition. She had lived with her sister and brother-in-law at Zuni pueblo from September 1882 to April 1884, during which time she began sketching and painting. By age twenty-one, in 1886, she was already an impressive artist in watercolor and oil. Cushing appointed her the artist of the expedition. Unexpectedly, she and Hodge fell in love during their first months camping outside Tempe; they revealed their engagement to Frank and Emily in June 1887; and they married four years later. Thus the quartet at the heart of the Hemenway Expedition—Frank and Emily, Fred and Maggie—became family.

Hodge's diary begins in December 1886 and runs without interruption to mid-May 1888, when the Hemenway Expedition was about to move north from the Salt River Valley to Zuni. If Hodge continued his journal during the expedition's final, tumultuous year—which transpired mostly without the Cushings in the field—it has since been lost. The original diary comprises six handwritten notebooks, which are in the Braun Research Library of the Autry Museum in Los Angeles. Wilcox transcribed and digitized the entire diary.

Magill's diary is a typescript document in Cornell University Library's Rare and Manuscript Collections. It runs from February 5 to August 17,

1887, with a gap of eight weeks from April 12 through June 5. At some point the two surviving sections were anonymously typed; the original has not been found. We have interjoined and fully annotated both diaries.

Hodge and Magill often wrote together, in a tent or under a mesquite tree, and occasionally shared their personal jottings; but while there is sometimes overlap, their styles and reflections are distinctive. Magill was a young but strikingly mature single woman adjusting excitedly to life in an archaeological desert camp, while Hodge was an insecure scientific novice who found himself serving a brilliant but erratic—and often ill—superior who was only seven years older than himself. The variant eyes and words of this young, hopeful couple provide us with unique insights into the conditions and challenges of early archaeology in the Southwest.

As we recounted in *The Lost Itinerary*, three years after the collapse of the expedition Cushing began writing an account of the enterprise. Collaborating with Hodge for several months in early 1892, he came to rely on the two diaries, claiming that Hodge's at least was the property of the expedition and that Cushing, as former director, had right of access. Hodge disagreed, and he and Margaret refused further cooperation. Cushing never returned to the project—or the Southwest.

▼

The introductory essay, "Love Among the Ruins," contextualizes the Hodge and Magill diary accounts by relating the broader story of the Hemenway Expedition—its roots in New England, Mary Hemenway's expectations and Cushing's promises, its trail of discoveries, Cushing's illnesses and absences (with Emily and Margaret) in California, the move of the expedition party to Zuni in mid-1888, and its collapse less than a year later. Inevitably the story revolves around the large figure of Cushing, but the essay is equally intended as a study of Fred Hodge's early life, his first experiences in anthropology, and his two most formative relationships: with Magill and Cushing.

The closing essay of the volume returns to Hodge and his long career in anthropology—from the end of the Hemenway Expedition in 1889 to his death in 1956. It is the first extended account of his life. He began as a stenographer in the Bureau of American Ethnology in 1889 and served as its director from 1910 to 1918, when he accepted a position with George Heye's Museum of the American Indian in New York. In the years with

Heye, he undertook six seasons (1917–23) of excavation in the ancestral Zuni village of Hawikku. At sixty-seven in 1931, he resigned from Heye's organization to take on the directorship of the Southwest Museum in Los Angeles. He held that position for another quarter century. Throughout his long and often-honored career, though, the Hemenway Expedition always stayed with Hodge, and the challenge and model of his first mentor and former brother-in-law—who had tragically died in 1900—shadowed him. Fred Hodge died in Santa Fe at ninety-two.

Margaret Magill left Zuni in the spring of 1889, and she never returned to the Southwest. She and Fred had four children, three of whom lived to maturity. At about the time he moved to New York, in 1918, they separated. With her daughter Emlyn, Margaret left Washington for Royal Oak, Michigan, where she lived for ten years. Although she did not make a profitable career of her considerable artistic talent, she continued to paint and study art her entire life. (Her watercolor mentor, William Henry Holmes, also moved to Royal Oak in the 1920s.) She died, aged seventy, at Emlyn's home in York, Pennsylvania, in 1935.

▼

The personal, even intimate aspects of the Hemenway Expedition are endlessly fascinating, but we must also note its wider context and import. Mrs. Hemenway's expedition arrived in the central Arizona desert at a time of settler population explosion—and consequent crisis for the Piman communities of the Salt–Upper Gila River basin. Only forty years before, the Treaty of Guadalupe Hidalgo had transferred sovereignty over virtually the entire Southwest from Mexico to the United States. For the following two decades the Pimas enjoyed economic prosperity, due mainly to relative neglect and minimal American migration during the Civil War years. However, the end of the war brought a flood of settlers from the Northeast and the former Confederacy, whose canal and reservoir infrastructures, land clearing, and wasteful practices rapidly depleted the limited Piman water resources. By the early 1870s an Indigenous irrigation economy that had lasted for centuries had been obliterated. The Hemenway party arrived precisely in the center—chronologically and geographically—of these developments.

The members of the Hemenway Expedition had little sense of this ongoing environmental and economic catastrophe for the people among whom they sojourned. Sadly but understandably, they were much more oriented to the young, rambunctious, multiethnic society of Tempe (and to a lesser degree Phoenix) growing before their eyes. To be sure, Cushing's enterprise was a focus of curiosity and an economic boon to the locals across the river, but he was also aware that the expedition was dependent on local businesses for supplies and support. Further, assuming that the human remains beneath their feet (and too often left to deteriorate on the surface) bore no relationship to the living Natives around them, Cushing and his company generally ignored the small groups of Pimas who approached Camps Augustus and Hemenway. The only exception was Herman ten Kate's two months' anthropometric work among Pima, Tohono O'odham, and Maricopa villages in the spring of 1888—in which Cushing showed little interest. Both Magill and Hodge regretfully noted the clearing and burning of the desert around them, but the terrible effects of settler encroachment on the fragile Native economy and social structure simply escaped them. Those effects were powerful and permanent. The Pimas came to call the period from 1870 to 1910 the "years of famine," during which their lives were reduced to wage labor, social disintegration, and welfare status.[1]

At Zuni, too, the mid-eighties were a time of social and political erosion, as Triloki Pandey and others have documented. Indeed, Cushing believed that his return to the pueblo in the summer of 1888 might help to revive the sagging authority of the Priesthood of the Bow; but as it happened, he stayed only three months and never returned. Under constant pressures from outsiders—religious and military forces, the U.S. government, anthropologists and others—the people of Zuni were entering a spiral of conflict and confusion that would last decades.

If he sensed these dire conditions, Hodge never acknowledged them. Nor, even to the end of his long life, did he ever express second thoughts over excavating human remains. It must be said, in fact, that as he came to see Zuni as "his" ethnographic and archaeological centerpiece and the major source of his professional reputation—not to mention his personal Zuni identity as "Teluli," the little mouse digging in his field—Hodge's actions ultimately contributed to Zuni disruption and division.

▼

David Wilcox passed away in May 2022, after a courageous battle with cancer. David and I first met in 1983. As our Hemenway project now draws to a close, I cannot adequately express my profound respect for my colleague and friend of forty years, a philosopher-archaeologist-historian who showed me what it means to strive to be a person of wide knowledge, deep intelligence, and personal integrity. I am profoundly grateful for our time together.

—*Curtis M. Hinsley*

Acknowledgments

This project owes large debts to the patience and knowledge of directors, librarians and archivists at many institutions. First at the Southwest Museum and then the Autry Museum of the American West in Los Angeles, Kim Walters, Daniela Moneta, Liza Posas, and Marilyn Van Winkle helped us with endless requests over many years. At the Peabody Museum of Archaeology and Ethnology, Harvard University, Patricia Kervick and Laura Costello were unfailingly gracious. Natasha Johnson and Joan Knudson of the Phoebe Hearst Museum of Anthropology, UC-Berkeley, guided David through numerous collections. At Cornell, Eisha Neely of the University Library and Frederic Gleach, curator of Anthropology Collections, assisted us with the vital Hemenway/Cushing materials. Robert Leopold, Caitlyn Haynes, Daisy Njoku, and Gina Rappaport of the National Anthropological Archives, Smithsonian Institution, aided in negotiating relevant documentary and photographic collections.

We were aided as well by Alessandro Pezzati, archivist at the University of Pennsylvania Museum Archives, Philadelphia; Carolle Morini at Peabody Essex Museum in Salem, Massachusetts; Ellen Thomasson of the Missouri Historical Society in Saint Louis; Ray Maxwell at the Archives of Garrett Park, Maryland; Anuja Navara at the Pasadena Museum of History; Kris N. Quist, Monterey Division of California State Parks; Danielle Castronovo of the California Academy of Sciences; Lauren Menzies at the Society for California Pioneers; and Bunny Huffman of the Acequia Madre House and International Women's Study Center, Santa Fe. Joe Cavallo and John Selmer of the Los Angeles Corral of Westerners came to our rescue at a crucial moment. Monica Park of the Brooklyn Museum of Art, Hannah Elder at the Massachusetts Historical Society, and Joshua Ruffler at the Tempe Historical Museum aided our research in important ways as well. Irene Axelrod undertook special research at the Phillips Library of the Peabody Essex Museum in Salem, Massachusetts. We are grateful for these marvelous scholars and public servants.

During the many years of work on this volume David and I were blessed with the friendship and encouragement of many friends and colleagues, among them our dear departed friend Ira Jacknis, Don Fowler, Keith Kintigh, Pieter Hovens, Tom Wilson, Klinton Burgio-Ericson, and, as always, John Hemenway and Gordon Means.

Joe Wilder, the previous director of the Southwest Center of the University of Arizona, and Jeff Banister the current director, strongly supported us for three decades. Their encouragement was absolutely essential to us. At the University of Arizona Press, Allyson Carter, Alana Cecilia Enriquez, Amanda Krause, and Leigh McDonald were unfailingly gracious and efficient in bringing this volume to life. They made it possible.

The Christine Callan Trust in Boston provided significant financial aid, for which we have been especially thankful. We also enjoyed the support, at various points, of the Indigenous Studies Department, the Comparative Cultural Studies Department, and the College of Arts and Sciences of Northern Arizona University, and several administrations and the staff of the Museum of Northern Arizona.

PART I

Love Among the Ruins

Fred Hodge, Maggie Magill, and the Hemenway Southwestern Archaeological Expedition, 1886–1889

"Terrible nightmare. Were the oysters to blame? Falling over precipices and facing revolvers all night and hollowing to the top of my voice (at least so the porter tells me)."[1] Thus twenty-two-year-old Fred Hodge recorded the night of December 5, 1886, on the train from Baltimore to Rochester. The following day he traveled on to the family homestead of Frank Hamilton Cushing near Albion, in western New York State, where he met up with Cushing and his wife, Emily Tennison Magill Cushing (1859–1920), her sister Margaret Whitehead Magill (1865–1935), and three prominent Zuni men, Palowahtiwa, Waihusiwa, and Heluta.[2] Less than a week later the Hemenway Southwestern Archaeological Expedition—named for its Boston patron, Mary Tileston Hemenway (1820–94)—departed for Arizona Territory, with Hodge employed as personal secretary to director Cushing. Hodge had no way of knowing that the next two years in Arizona and New Mexico would become his introduction to the Southwest, to archaeological fieldwork, and ultimately to a half-century career at the institutional centers of American anthropology. He would also learn the risks of life on the edge in America—and the dangers of falling over personal and professional precipices.

Frederick Webb Hodge (1864–1956) was blessed with ninety-two years of life. Born in Plymouth, England, toward the end of the American Civil

Figure 1. Frederick Webb Hodge, 1899. #N.41999, Braun Research Library Collection, Autry Museum, Los Angeles.

War, he passed away quietly in Santa Fe, New Mexico, ten years after the end of World War II. He arrived in America with his parents, Edwin and Emily Webb Hodge, and four siblings in 1872. His father (1831–1919) worked briefly as a coachman before finding a permanent position as a watchman with the U.S. Postal Department; the family soon settled in downtown Washington. Mr. Hodge became a naturalized American citizen in 1882, thereby conferring the same on his family. Emily Hodge (1833–1924) had been trained as a seamstress and taught her first-born daughter, Emlyn, that trade as well.[3] Of the six Hodge children, only the youngest, Charles, was born in the United States. Emlyn and her sister, Evelina, eventually established a real estate and insurance office in the capital. Edwin *fils* went to Yale and Johns Hopkins Medical School, later becoming an army physician and working on yellow fever with Walter Reed. Charles attended Swarthmore and became a businessman. We know nothing of son Ernest. Third-born Fred grew up as a child in the middle, surrounded by family.

When he was fourteen Hodge went to work for the summer at the offices of Henry N. Copp, a Washington lawyer who specialized in the public lands of the American West. His publications—*Copp's Land-Owner: Real Estate and Land Law* and *The American Settler's Guide: A Brief Exposition of the Public Land System*—served as legal guides for investors and settlers regarding the operations of the General Land Office and the Department of the Interior. With his constantly updated manuals Copp stood at the center of the vigorous, often corrupt disposition of the nation's public lands during the swashbuckling post–Civil War decades.[4]

At the end of summer 1878, Fred expected to return to school, but Copp—who was also his school principal—advised him to drop out and continue working: "I think you'll learn just as much in my office here as you would in school. . . . All you're going to have [in school] is word analysis, or something like that," he told the boy. Hodge ended up staying with Copp for five formative years (1878–83). Beginning as an office clerk, he was soon gathering information from federal bureaus for Copp's magazines, editing and proofreading materials, and seeing publications through the entire printing process.[5] In the course of his work the teen also was getting his first close-up look at the daily intricacies of business, publishing, and government practices. But he was developing higher ambitions too. While he never entered high school or finished any formal schooling, Hodge enrolled in night classes: first at Arlington Academy, a one-man operation, then in the "science course" at Columbian University (later part of George Washington University). His main interest was topographic drafting, because he dreamed of fieldwork under John Wesley Powell with the new U.S. Geological Survey, formed in 1879. But he also made time to study the skill that would open his career: stenography.

It was an astute move. Between the end of the Civil War and the turn of the century American corporate life and business practices were undergoing revolutions on every level. Historians have explored in detail the developments in financial, legal, and corporate structures; less attention has been paid to the daily working lives of the thousands of men and women who filled new, obscure niches in office hierarchies. As the industrial economy took hold in the last third of the century, a gap widened between an earlier ideology of independent and productive labor—centered on the image of the self-made, independent male—and the new realities of postwar labor. Most men, it turned out, were to be wage earners or salaried employees of others through their working lives.[6] The new world of office work, with which Hodge had such an early familiarity, was comprised largely of hierarchical male relationships marked by differential status and deferential behavior. As historian Alan Trachtenberg observed some years ago, while postwar America was "dominated by images of personal power, of force, determination, the will to prevail," the actual structures of American business and finance of the time "aimed to diminish risk" by promoting regularity and predictability in the business cycle and commercial relations. Accordingly, "organization and administration emerged as major virtues, along with obedience and loyalty."[7] While an earlier world in which fathers and sons had worked closely in relations of apprenticeship was fading from American life, new forms of filial relationship began to mark corporate bureaucracies.[8]

Accurate, efficient means of communication were vital to business, law, and government in the Gilded Age. Accordingly, a new class of office operatives—bookkeepers, stenographers, and (after the 1870s) typists—arose to meet those needs. Stenography (or "phonography," as it was called) had emerged in the middle decades of the century as a promising pathway to both respectability and manliness for ambitious young men who sought job advancement and secure identity "above the masses."[9] Historian Carole Srole has demonstrated that male stenographers working in corporate structures struggled to find balance between "propriety" (commonly gendered as feminine) and traditionally manly behaviors—by emphasizing sobriety and proper dress, for instance. Often from modest class backgrounds with little education or personal resources, men such as Hodge lived always with the prospect of disrespect, shame, and failure. The road to middle-class respect was gradual, treacherous, and uncertain.[10]

Fred Hodge, child of a hard-working immigrant family, entered the career of stenography as many other young men did at the time: through private early morning or evening instruction squeezed from daytime job responsibilities. He remembered it this way:

> I had been studying stenography at night, and while I didn't finish, I had a pretty fair knowledge of stenography. A neighbor friend and I used to go round to John Irwin's house at five o'clock in the morning to take lessons. Then the lessons came to an end because he accepted a position in Mexico. . . . I had a friend who was a court reporter, and he used to dictate to me, very slowly at first, and I found myself becoming quite proficient after a while.[11]

Since stenographers were in short supply in Washington, they were exempted from the regime of Civil Service exams that began with the Pendleton Act in 1883. Hearing soon afterward of an opening in the catch-all Miscellaneous Division of Powell's Geological Survey, Hodge proceeded to walk in for an interview. He took a rudimentary test from the division head, Joseph Stanley Brown, and passed: "I hadn't made a stenographic line for more than a year, but I managed to get away with the very simple letters he dictated." His first government salary was seventy-five dollars a month. He was nineteen.[12]

In 1884 the offices of the Geological Survey and those of the Bureau of Ethnology—Powell directed both—were located in central Washington. For the next two years Powell was engaged in intense political maneuverings for funding with both Congress and the Smithsonian Institution, and Hodge sat a few feet from his door. The young man shared a small office with Philip Creveling Warman (1859–1908), Powell's personal stenographer and secretary, and divided his own attention between Powell and the next-door office of James C. Pilling (1846–95). Pilling was chief clerk of the survey and Powell's intimate friend (and another fellow stenographer).[13] One of Hodge's favorite stories from this period provides a sense of the close, jocular male office atmosphere:

> One day as I was conferring with Pilling at his desk, the Major came through the slatted door and into Pilling's room. As he often did, Powell went up and down Pilling's room, his armless sleeve held across his back. Stopping for a moment now and then, he looked at Pilling with a smile. Said Pilling:

Figure 2. John Wesley Powell, c. 1900. #64-A-6. National Anthropological Archives, Smithsonian Institution.

"Major, what can I do for you?"

"O, nothing, Jim."

Again the Major stopped and smiled.

"I'm sure there's something I can do for you."

"Nothing at all, Jim. Do you know, Jim, that I'm damned if you're not uglier than I am!"[14]

Personal kidding aside, from their "shabby hand-me-down office" in the Federal District Powell and Pilling were engaged in serious scientific politics.[15] Between 1881 (his first year as director of the survey) and 1885 Powell

Figure 3. James Constantine Pilling. #56–195. National Anthropological Archives. Smithsonian Institution.

increased his annual appropriation from $156,000 to more than half a million dollars—a remarkable amount for a government bureau at the time. Against powerful resistance in Congress and the Coast Survey, he extended the reach of the USGS from the western public lands to embrace all states of the Union. By 1885 the Civil War veteran and explorer of the Colorado River was a major political and scientific force in Washington. For more than two years, from his perch outside Powell's office Hodge observed a steady stream of powerful politicians laugh, smoke, and come to understandings that would revolutionize government science: "I saw practically everyone who came into the Survey who called on Major Powell at that time, because this little room of mine was only two rooms away from Major Powell."[16]

While the Major understandably inspired awe in a twenty-year-old, it was Pilling who modeled Hodge's future in government service. From the

Figure 4. Frank Hamilton Cushing, 1879. #2002–1924, National Anthropological Archives, Smithsonian Institution.

founding of Powell's organizations in 1879 to his death sixteen years later, Pilling worked tirelessly as chief clerk and a member of the Bureau of Ethnology. His personal career project, begun in 1877, was nothing less than complete bibliographies of the literature on all the indigenous languages of North America. He fully realized that the project defied completion: "if I ever print my Bibliography I should like to insert a note telling why the work was never finished," he declared in 1881.[17] Over the years his bibliographic files constantly grew, and he enlisted all of his colleagues in the bureau in this essential Powell program. Pilling scoured private and public libraries in the United States and Canada; when he went to Europe on personal matters he spent most of his time in libraries and bookstores. In the process, he accumulated for the bureau one of the finest ethnological libraries in the world. Brilliant and impatient men could deride his filing-system mentality ("Do you want to do Powell a favor? Poison Pilling," Clarence King, first director of the USGS, apocryphally advised), but Pilling persisted.[18] In all these respects—detail, perseverance, pedantry, reliance on others—he foreshadowed Hodge's future career as stenographer, librarian, Smithsonian bureaucrat, and editor.[19]

Miss Maggie Magill

Having survived his nightmarish oyster attack on the train, Fred Hodge arrived in Rochester safely and continued on to the Cushing farm in Barre Center, arriving in time for dinner on December 6, 1886. Here he was introduced to the family, including Emily's sister: twenty-one-year-old Maggie Magill. Fred was struck: "brim full of fun, fond of a joke, good talker, splendid company, in general appearance reminds me of Isis McMillan (rather better looking), and I am of the opinion that I shall like her very much."[20]

Maggie was the youngest of four daughters of John Whitehead Magill (1830–79), a banker with Lewis Johnson & Co. of Washington, D.C., and Catherine Cecelia "Kate" Myer Magill (1838–91).[21] She attended the Episcopal Female Institute in Winchester, Virginia, until age twelve, when poor eyesight seemed to dictate further education at home—and promptly she became an avid reader. Encouraged by her maternal uncle, Ferdinand F. Myer (1832–1904), she began drawing and painting, later attending the Corcoran School of Art in Washington. Her father died of pneumonia in 1879, the same year that her elder sister Emma (later called Emily) became engaged to Cushing and he departed for Zuni. When he returned with the Zuni priests on their trip to the "ocean of sunrise" in 1882, Frank and Emma were quietly married on July 10 in her mother's house on Q Street. A few weeks later Cushing took his new bride back to Zuni. Emma insisted on bringing along Maggie—and Abram, a Black family cook. The

Cushing party arrived in the pueblo on September 23, 1882, and while the newlyweds set up housekeeping Margaret began sketching life in her strange new environment. When they eventually moved to the new "Cushing house" across the Zuni River in early 1884, they made sure her room had a north light.[22]

Although uncomfortable, Emma worked hard to create a home in her adobe world. Visiting journalist William E. Curtis reported that "Mrs. Cushing does not enjoy life in Zuni as her husband does. She does not and cannot share his fascination for the work in which he is engaged. She hates the uncouth women and the naked children, and despises their filthy ways, but she has made her mud hut a pretty little paradise and has developed the possibilities of comfort even in Zuni." Her sister Maggie, on the other hand, seemed enchanted by pueblo life:

> She has a sister, Miss Magill, with her, who likes the Zunis better than Mrs. Cushing, and is talking of adopting their peculiar dress and joining the tribe. "I would do it," said Miss Magill: "it would be so funny and romantic, but I don't like to cut my hair."[23]

Maggie accompanied Cushing, by foot and horseback, in his explorations of caves, grottoes, farm fields, and sacred places on traditional Zuni lands, and she watched in fascination the dances and women's work in the pueblo. The few surviving pages of her diary from this period evince charm, intelligence, and astute observation. Walking through the pueblo one evening she and Emily "were attracted by singing into a little by-way where we stopped to listen in front of a house":

> The door suddenly opened and a woman came out and seeing us insisted on our going in to visit. When the darkness caused by our entrance cleared away and the light from the small door again shone into the room, I saw eight women kneeling behind eight little flat troughs in the floor, each of which was pared with a large, slanting, flat stone, upon which they rubbed up and down in perfect time as to movement & song. . . . They have queer, shrill, piping little voices which are very attractive to me on account of the novelty. I think it a very wise plan to make a frolic of work, as they do. All their friends are invited to a grinding bee (as we call it).[24]

On the occasion of the highly significant Shalako ceremony in early December 1883, Maggie was enthralled and watchful:

> At sunset we all crowded out on the hills to see the coming of the great Sha la k'o. First a little speck could be seen rising over the distant southern hills which grew as it neared us into a long procession out of which rose six of the most remarkable figures ever seen. They are twice the size of an ordinary man and dressed in long double white blanket skirts embroidered, from under which appear the legs and feet of a man. The masques are green and covered on top and back with bushy black hair, while for the mouth is a long beak, which opens and shuts, making a loud snapping sound.[25]

Magill's sojourn at Zuni pueblo lasted a year and a half, but she was able to enjoy her room with northern light in the new house for only four months before Cushing was recalled to Washington. She spent the next two years in the capital city, during which she contributed artwork to Cushing's remarkable *Zuñi Breadstuff* series. In the fall of 1886, as the expedition took shape, she left Washington and re-joined Emily and Frank at Mary Hemenway's summer home in Manchester-by-the-Sea on Massachusetts's North Shore.[26]

Initially Cushing did not foresee the need for an artist on the expedition, nor, despite her demonstrated skills, did he see Magill as expedition artist. In the original "Programme of Operations and Expenditures" submitted to Mary Hemenway on November 12, 1886, he made no allowance for an artist or photographer, but he did include the following: "A competent Stenographer as Secretary, for reporting of Fieldnotes, Corresponding, etc., etc., . . . An Assistant Secretary or Clerk, for Copying of Manuscript, Keeping of Catalogues, Journals, etc., etc."[27]

After meeting with Powell a week later, Cushing announced that his sister-in-law would serve as the assistant field secretary:

> So far as is practicable, I shall employ her in the use of the type-writer, especially on my manuscripts of the Zuñi folk-tales. As I should wish to have the undivided attention of my secretary for other work, whenever collections are made, and moreover in the labelling and cataloguing of

such collections as I already have in the southwest, I shall employ her as a clerk. . . . I hope you understand fully that it is because she is already well trained in the work, and will, whether employed or not, accompany us for the southwest, and there be more available at less expense than would any one else. No thought of her connection with me influences this proposition.[28]

Powell stressed the importance of an ongoing visual record of what they originally conceived of as a constantly moving reconnaissance: "[Powell] said that while I was doing this work of exploration, I ought to keep a careful and finished itinerary, filled with descriptions and illustrated with abundant maps, sketches and photographs of my explorations . . . the main point being

Figure 5. Mary Tileston Hemenway, c. 1890. Oil painting by Ignaz Marcel Gaugengigl. Courtesy of Gordon Means.

Figure 6. *Mrs. Frank Hamilton Cushing.* Emily Magill Cushing in 1895. Oil painting by Thomas Eakins. Courtesy of the Philadelphia Museum of Art: Gift of Mrs. Thomas Eakins and Miss Mary Adeline Williams. #1929-184-4.

that the work should be finished as it went along."[29] As this advice impressed itself on him in the formative months of 1886, Cushing came to value Magill's artistic skills more highly, and as the expedition ultimately developed, Cushing hired Maggie—"Ikina," his "little sister"—primarily as artist.

The Boston Fascination with Zuni, 1880–1886

In "The White Indian," his tender-harsh obituary of Cushing in *Land of Sunshine* in 1900, Charles F. Lummis (1859–1928) recalled that in 1882 the young ethnographer had been "epidemic in the culture-circles of New England" due to his "personal magnetism, his witchcraft of speech, his ardor, his wisdom in the unknowabilities" of Indian life. The Zuni leaders Cushing had brought to Boston had been "a revelation to the somewhat waterproof East," with the "White Indian" as their impresario. But Cushing was, Lummis qualified, "too much—shall we say, poet. The same acute imagination which enabled him to discover occult things, went on to discovery of things which weren't there." Still Lummis could not deny that the 1882 eastern tour, "so curiously mixed between genuine scholarship and the arts of the showman," had succeeded in its main objectives: to impress the Zunis, and to garner financial support for Cushing's future fieldwork.[30]

Clever, colorful, and jealously competitive as always, Lummis offered a portrayal of Cushing's relations with his New England supporters that ignored the cultural and religious concerns that informed the Hemenway Expedition. Neither Hodge nor his friend Lummis ever grasped those considerations.[31] While Mary Hemenway's broad, coherent philanthropic purposes have been explored, this powerful and serious woman also operated among circles of men and women who shared deeply held suppositions about religious life.[32] These require explication in order to fully understand Cushing's appeal—and thus the Hemenway archaeological enterprise.

Cushing's visit with the Zunis to Massachusetts in early 1882 coincided with two other events of the moment that were of particular importance to some prominent people: the completion of Unitarian minister James Freeman Clarke's magnum opus, *Ten Great Religions* (2 vols., 1871, 1883), and the 1879–83 eastern lecture tour of Omaha chief Standing Bear and his Ponca interpreter Susette "Bright Eyes" La Flesche—a visit that jump-started the Indian reform movement of the eighties.[33] Distinct in origin, the two matters became entwined with Hemenway and Cushing.

Clarke (1810–88), founder of the Church of the Disciples, was the most revered Unitarian minister of Boston, and Mary Hemenway was his devoted parishioner for nearly fifty years. Along with fellow clergyman Edward Everett Hale (1822–1909), Clarke preached Unitarian "practical Christianity": getting out and solving community problems, organizing relief societies and private charities, and saving souls through education and enlightenment. His followers were certain that the coming years would see a moral revolution in America. As William Ellery Channing once confided to him: "Our present stage of society is one which must be passed through. A true civilization lies beyond it."[34]

To this vital end, at the close of the Civil War Clarke undertook a survey of world religious history. In his first volume of *Ten Great Religions* (*An Essay in Comparative Theology*, 1871) Clarke distinguished between what he called the "ethnic religions" of the world—those largely confined to one nation or race of people (e.g., Buddhism, Hinduism, Confucianism)—and universal or converting religions: Judaism, Islam, and Christianity. Only Christianity, he unsurprisingly insisted, was destined to become the universal religion of humanity.

Part of Clarke's appeal lay in his apparent global empiricism and the fact that he embedded his arguments in notions of both historical evolution and divine design. During the 1870s, though, new scholarly attention to Indigenous peoples led Clarke to expand his scope, and in the 1880–81 lectures that became his second volume (*A Comparison of All Religions*, 1883) he added a new category:

> If we look at the facts we shall immediately see that the less highly developed organized religions, which show an undeveloped ritual, priesthood, and creed, without sacred books, with no religious architecture or music, and which exercise little influence on the worshipers, belong to the undeveloped races,—those whom we usually call *savages*. I do not like the word savage, for it carries with it a touch of contempt and the absence of sympathy. Let us call them *childlike* or *primitive races*. They have not yet attained to national existence; they exist in tribes.[35]

The reverend's new class of tribal or primitive religions deserved special attention, he said, not only from recent writings—pointing to Edward B. Tylor, Daniel G. Brinton, and Hubert H. Bancroft—but also from the young fieldworkers of ethnology: among tribal peoples "human nature is in its cradle, and the cry of the infant is the same all over the world." "We cannot look on any religion with indifference," Clarke intoned. A true "science of religion" would require the broadest embrace and many students in the field.[36]

Today Clarke's suppositions strike us as condescending at best, and certainly outdated. But at the time, to his ardent followers, he seemed to invite exciting new vistas of knowledge and virtuous purpose: the prospect of spreading Christianity and shaping a better world. In this regard Cushing's visit with the Zuni priests in 1882 was made for the moment—replete with occasions of pious ritual, lectures on priestly practices, dancing, and Cushing's gnomic poetics.[37] As historian Caroline Carpenter Nichols recently observed, Cushing's "volatile performance of self" promised New England "an encounter that was both thrilling and slightly dangerous." More specifically, "his immersion in the life of the pueblo was . . . vital to accessing the spiritual knowledge eastern elites craved."[38]

As Lummis recognized, Cushing was indeed magnetic: "the most remarkable part of the exhibition, modest, intelligent, full of emotion and sympathy," in Edward Everett Hale's view. The priestly practices and esoteric language of Zuni, as presented by Tenatsali ("Medicine Flower," Cushing's Zuni name) and his priests, beckoned toward a secretive world of early religion:

> The life and language, the religion of the Zunis, are intensely poetic. With no amount of poetry to which my words or pen may aspire, can I hope to give to the world as I feel it, in listening to the ritual, folklore, or even councils of this innocent people, their imagery and their poetry and their quaintness.[39]

Boston was dazzled. The Zunis had "regular lunches and naps" at Hemenway's elegant Mt. Vernon Street house. Eben Norton Horsford (1818–93), a missionary son and emeritus professor of chemistry at Harvard, had already been talking and writing about Cushing with Adolph F. Bandelier (1840–1914) and Lewis Henry Morgan (1818–81); he now met the young man and immediately took his career and health to heart.[40] Hale was thrilled to have Cushing and the gentlemanly latter-day "Aztecs" (as he called them) to dinner at his home.[41] After his wedding with Emily in July 1882 Cushing was careful to maintain these contacts:

> Two weeks since [Cushing wrote to Hale] I was married to a very brave little girl who has faithfully remembered me through all my long years of exile among the Zunis, and who wishes to share my future life and labors among them. She has read many of your works and loves them as I do; she loves their author [Hale], for the good he has done in the world, and for his friendship toward me,—as I do, she sends that love to [you].[42]

When Frank, Emily, and Maggie returned to Zuni in September, the Boston group decided to send him a small library. Hemenway provided the funds, while Horsford and Hale chose the books, drawn in part from references in Clarke's new volume.[43] Tellingly, the first two books Cushing received from his Boston admirers were the two volumes of Clarke's *Ten Great Religions,* followed by works of Brinton, Tylor, and others. Nor was Emily forgotten: she was reading a Hale novel, *Philip Nolan's Friends,* and asked him for "any more like it."[44] Cushing was especially pleased to get Tylor's *Primitive Culture*: "I am largely his disciple, yet I have not read his books since I was a little boy."[45] Writing again from the pueblo, Cushing was effusively grateful:

> I shall never forget my obligations, Dear Professor Horsford, to you, Dr. Hale, and Mrs. Hemmenway. A new life, with its abundant possibilities, is opened up to me, which otherwise had remained unborn.[46]

The fascination with "primitive" religious practices extended beyond Unitarian circles. At the time of Cushing's visit, Brooks Adams (1848–1927), the youngest Adams brother, was formulating his first book, *The Emancipation of Massachusetts: The Dream and the Reality* (1887). Cushing had a strong impact on Adams, who painted the Puritan theocracy as a secretive priesthood that suppressed and banished dissidents. Adams claimed to see historical parallels between Puritan and Zuni priestly practices, a "clear-cut illustration of a general cultural phenomenon in which a group, set apart by its knowledge, limited the advance of thought and discovery" among its people.[47] In an early reach, Adams claimed that his story of early Massachusetts and its witch trials recapitulated human history writ large: "In an archaic age the priest is likewise the lawgiver and the physician, for all erudition is concentrated in one supremely favored class—the sacred caste."[48]

Emancipation was Adams's first foray into the historical thinking that would eventuate ten years later in a more sophisticated and controversial work, *The Law of Civilization and Decay* (1895). As Adams told Henry Cabot Lodge, he saw his first book as an argument for a historical law: "I do not flatter myself that Cushing and I have sounded the depths of knowledge, but I do think we have hit on a feasible explanation of the necessary working out of certain eras of mental growth which deserves at least a refutation."[49]

Adams and Cushing remained mutually admiring and supportive; they corresponded intermittently over years.[50] And Adams publicly expressed his debt:

> The generosity of my friend Mr. Frank Hamilton Cushing in putting at my disposal the unpublished results of his researches among the Zuñis is in keeping with the originality and power of his mind. Without his aid my attempt would have been impossible.[51]

Cushing's eastern trip and *My Adventures in Zuñi,* his popular three-part series in *Century Magazine,* also overlapped with an extended tour of eastern cities by Standing Bear (c. 1829–1908), Susette La Flesche (1854–1903), and journalist Thomas Tibbles (1840–1928).[52] The primary purposes of the tour were to raise awareness of the dire conditions faced by Native peoples under the new reservation system, and to pressure for legislative changes and Native legal rights. While it is too digressive to review fully here, the instigating story focused on circumstances among the Ponca and Omaha peoples in Nebraska. In 1881 Helen Hunt Jackson (1830–85) had published her exposé of government treaty betrayals, *A Century of Dishonor.* The Standing Bear tour aroused widespread outrage at government policies and led, inter alia, to the formation of the National Women's Indian Association (1879) and its numerous state auxiliaries, the Indian Rights Association (1882), the first annual Lake Mohonk Conference (1883), and a great deal of lobbying.[53] Jackson's popular 1884 novel of colonial California mission life, *Ramona,* added further impetus; in 1887 Congress passed the Dawes Severalty Act in response to this outcry.

The "Indian question" (as it became known) permeated Cushing's support group. Mary Hemenway had joined the Massachusetts Indian Association by 1881 and remained an honorary member for the rest of her life. Her close friends Mary Elizabeth Dewey and Martha LeBaron Goddard were deeply involved in the reform movement—and both were members of the Hemenway Expedition board.[54] Helen Hunt Jackson herself was a close family friend of the Horsfords, especially the daughters. Reverend Hale became an outspoken fixture at the Mohonk conferences. How to educate and improve economic self-reliance among Native peoples, free them from evil and designing Whites, and promote legal protections—these were the persistent questions of the movement they joined.

In this context, too, Cushing's direct experiences carried weight. Hemenway saw her expedition as a way of recovering Zuni history and folklore and incorporating its richness into American culture. Hale celebrated the noble potential (and good table manners) of his Zuni guests and suggested that civilization would come to the pueblo through Cushing's influence—or as he suggestively called it, "infection." Cushing hastened to agree:

> I think with you, that the best agent of civilisation is infection. Practically, for instance, the Zuñis now possess about fifty wagons. When I came here, they had two. Doors and glass windows are now common. When I came here, one too often entered the houses through the roof by light transmitted through selenite or open portholes. Yet, reclaiming savagery either voluntarily or by example is more difficult than the cultivation of a wilderness.[55]

Always aware of his audience, Cushing molded his words in creating his scientific and poetic persona in Boston as elsewhere. Without minimizing his serious, long-term health issues, it is fair to say that from the outset Cushing presented himself as a sufferer, a martyr in the pursuit of rare knowledge—a brilliant but flickering flame of intelligence. This became a career theme. At other points he pushed himself forward with considerable presumption, aggressively fighting real and imagined enemies. The following passage, written when he was twenty-five years old, was addressed to Hale—who at sixty was among the most famous literary figures in America:

> I think I was attempting to tell you of my belief in truth, that she is able to stand against either falsehood or error, and that I have but to tell the truth simply, to refute falsehood, error, or their perpetrators. . . . I have, then, inadequately told the truth about my Zunis; yet I have told the truth so far as my abilities enable me to do, and hence, I do not ask, I command that I shall be believed.[56]

Cushing's supporting cast was small but well positioned, and they were intrigued by his youthful charisma, his insights into the exotic Other, and the promise of a religiously progressive humanity. For the time being that seemed sufficient.

Planning the Expedition, 1884–86

In early 1884, after four and a half years at Zuni, Cushing was recalled by Powell to Washington for reasons of both health and politics. After returning to the pueblo Cushing had exposed and thwarted the attempt by a son-in-law of Illinois Republican senator (and 1884 vice presidential candidate) John A. "Black Jack" Logan to claim eight hundred acres of Nutria Valley. These were traditional Zuni lands that had been mistakenly omitted from the 1877 reservation boundaries. But Logan was also an important congressional supporter of fellow Illinoisan and Civil War veteran Powell. Thus, Powell and Smithsonian secretary Spencer Baird decided to bring Cushing back home out of concern for the young man's deteriorating health and to protect the Bureau of Ethnology's appropriations.[57]

Horsford and Hale played some role in the forced return. Urging Powell to recall Cushing for his health, Horsford advised that "Cushing has repeatedly written me of his terrible suffering from dyspepsia. . . . I see a little of the martyr which alarms me. We cannot afford to indulge in such sacrifice."[58] But Cushing's sponsors and friends were facing the dilemma of anthropology's "salvage" period for fieldworkers and collectors: how to justify office work when there was so much disappearing ethnographic material to be recorded in the field? Still, losing Cushing's hard-earned knowledge of Zuni language, stories, myths, material culture, and social organization was what Horsford, Hale, and Powell were trying to avoid. Powell was explicit about it:

> For some time I have thought it much better that Mr. Cushing should come East and elaborate his material; or, that he should at least spend a portion of each year in Washington, for that purpose. He would thereby be enabled to obtain free access to valuable libraries and by comparing his results with those of other investigators guard himself against error. The adoption of this course would, I believe, result in physical as well as intellectual benefit. It would be better, however, for these suggestions to come from Mr. Cushing. I fear that such an intimation on my part would be construed by him to mean a recall by reason of dissatisfaction with his work. . . . I appreciate with you Mr. Cushing's unfortunate temperament. He fancies he has enemies where none exist.[59]

Cushing delayed for a time, returning to Washington in April 1884 with Emily and Maggie. He was suffering from various gastrointestinal maladies that would plague him for the rest of his life.[60] Over the next two years Powell encouraged his brilliant young protégé to write up the linguistic, mythological, and social insights from his Zuni sojourn. However, in the pattern of promise, illness and procrastination that would characterize his career, Cushing produced only his second publication for Powell—a brief study of pueblo pottery.[61] And yet, while pleading prostration he managed in the same period to write and illustrate, for an obscure Indiana agricultural trade journal, a still remarkable, subtle ethnography on the importance of corn in Zuni life: *Zuñi Breadstuff*.[62]

In summer 1885 Frank and Emily retreated from Washington to his family home in Barre Center, New York, south of Albion. At this point Horsford re-entered their life: they left upstate New York in September and moved to Sylvester Manor, Horsford's summer estate on Shelter Island, at the eastern end of Long Island Sound.[63] There is an engaging glimpse of a day in late September 1885, as the youngest Horsford daughter, attractive twenty-four-year-old Cornelia, related an afternoon soiree to her mother:

> Mr. [Sylvester] Baxter drives me wild, and Mrs. Cushing has a cousin who makes me feel as if I should lose my senses if he came one step nearer. Mr. Cushing is as nice as ever. . . . I painted 12 dinner cards for Mrs. Cushing's birthday & took her photograph.[64]

The autumn of 1885 on Shelter Island was idyllic. Writing from the broiling Arizona desert some months later, Emily held close the memory of the "cool delights" and the "cool quietness" of her short time at the manor.[65] For his part, Horsford hoped for improvement in Cushing's health by the sea and had special stoves installed for their comfort well into November.

Throughout this period—in Washington, Barre Center, and Shelter Island—Cushing wrote often of bringing Zuni informants eastward to work with him, but his health struggled and he could not act on the plan.[66] Toward the end of 1885 he and Emily moved to Horsford's Craigie Street home in Cambridge, where Horsford placed Frank under the care of his personal physician, Dr. J. P. Oliver. "Cushing not well enough to have Indians come east this Fall. Suspend operations," Powell cabled to Zuni pueblo trader

Douglas D. Graham in mid-November.[67] The Cushings remained in Cambridge until the end of February 1886, planning to return to Washington. Baxter confided his concerns to Horsford: "I am sorry Cushing goes back before he is cured. I hope he will find a way to continue Dr. Oliver's method of treatment in Washington."[68]

But the Cushings did not return to the capital. Instead, Hemenway invited them to move to her country house, "Old Farm," near Milton, south of Boston.[69] While the exact timing is unclear, Cushing was soon talking with his new host of bringing three Zuni men across country:

> Mrs. Hemenway came down one morning at Old Farm in the Spring of 1886, and in her characteristic way, announced to me that she thought we must have some of the Zuñi Priests visit us that Summer if Mrs. Cushing and I would go with her to Manchester instead of returning, as previously we had intended, to Shelter Island. . . . For she wished to have the Zuñis as true guests like other visitors whom she also wished to have at Casa Ramona [one of her summer homes at Manchester-by-the-Sea on Massachusetts's North Shore], and that the interest of entertaining them would alone suffice even were no other result to accrue, and that as her daughter and son-in-law [Edith and William Ellery Channing Eustis] were not intending to spend the Summer there, as customarily, she could not, or did not wish to, unless we would go down and stay with her.[70]

By this time a stenographer had become central to their plans for recording language, folklore, and myth, as Cushing told Powell:

> As my physician now says I will be able to work an hour or two every day throughout the summer, Mrs. Hemenway has directed me to secure the services of a trained stenographer, so that as much advantage may be taken of this working time as possible. Having become greatly interested in Ethnographic research (as, in her estimation, bearing on the solution of the Indian question),—she has decided to turn much of the fund she has heretofore devoted to Missionary work, into this, which she now thinks a more rational way of aiding the Indian as well as humanity in general. She therefore has placed a suite of appartments in one of her Manchester houses at my disposal for the use not only of my secretary, but also, for three of the Zuni Indians, whom she has already provided shall be brought

> East whenever I am able to resume work uninterruptedly. May I, by and bye, look to you to aid me in securing a good stenographer, should I be unable to find one here? His expenses for six months, and an ample salary will be allowed.[71]

Plans now took shape rapidly. On the sunny, brisk Friday afternoon of August 13, 1886—after several weeks of travel from New Mexico through Chicago and Albion with Cushing's brother Enos—three Zuni men stepped from a carriage in Mrs. Hemenway's driveway in Manchester-by-the-Sea: Palowahtiwa (Ba:lawahdiwa, a.k.a. Patricio Pino), governor of Zuni pueblo and Priest of the Bow; Waihusiwa, son of one of the chief priests of Zuni and later governor of the pueblo; and the young Heluta, a medicine order priest. The assembled houseguests that day included Rufus B. Leighton (1828–1913), a court reporter and stenographer from Gloucester, Massachusetts, whom Hemenway had likely found through Unitarian circles.[72]

For nearly three months Cushing, Leighton, and the Zuni guests worked on a daily basis together at Hemenway's summer home. Hemenway's close friend Mary Elizabeth Dewey (1821–1910) recalled these autumn days on the wild Atlantic coast:

> The life at Casa Ramona soon took quiet and regular form. Mr. Cushing, with an amanuensis, spent the morning over his papers, with the help of one or more of his Indian friends. An unwritten language was to be put into shape and belted in with vocabulary and grammar, its traditions secured, its historic and religious myths preserved, and its folk lore carefully noted down.

Afternoons were spent with archery contests down in the apple orchard by the ocean, and in the cool evenings all gathered around the fireplace for storytelling:

> The circle forms, and Wai-hu-si-wah begins his recitation in a low voice, sitting very still, and only making a little play with his hands, his arms resting on the arms of the chair. The language has a pleasant, melodious sound, but is of course intelligible only to the interpreter [Cushing] and to the other Zunis, who listen with evident interest and satisfaction. . . . The charm of these stories is quite indescribable. . . . Nothing can give the effect that

Figure 7. *Zuni Chiefs*, 1887. Oil painting by Henry Sandham. Courtesy of the Peabody Museum of Archaeology and Ethnology, Harvard University. #969-8-10/49828.

> this gathering into our very ears these utterance of past centuries had upon us with Wai-hu-si-wah's dark, smiling face, and slight expressive gestures contrasting with his interpreter's highly cultivated intelligence, and both bound together by a common sympathy and appreciation which included us all, men and women, white and Indians, in its great human clasp.[73]

In sessions both workaday and intimate, Leighton took down the stories that would eventually become *Zuñi Folk Tales*, published the year after Cushing's death. Hodge edited the original 1901 edition—with a heartfelt foreword by Powell.[74] While neither Cushing nor Hemenway lived to see their publication, he had been prescient: *Zuñi Folk Tales*, first recorded in Leighton's shorthand at Casa Ramona, has never gone out of print.[75]

By November stenographer Leighton's work was done. In the weeks since mid-August Hemenway and Cushing had laid plans for an ambitious archaeological reconnaissance of the Southwest in search of Zuni origins, for which he would need a field secretary. He placed Emily, Maggie, and the Zuni men on a train to Albion, said goodbye to Boston on November 19, and headed to Washington to obtain Powell's blessing—and find a stenographer.

Figure 8. *Wai-Hu-Si-Wa, a Zuni Chief.* Watercolor by Margaret W. Magill, 1889. Courtesy of the Peabody Museum of Archaeology and Ethnology, Harvard University, 94-36-10/84061a.

Getting There: The First Months

Needless to say, Fred Hodge knew nothing of the foregoing events in New England, and had only secondhand stories of Cushing's life to that point. But in late November 1886, with Cushing searching for a stenographer, they met for the first time in the offices of the Geological Survey:

> I remember my vacation had just closed. Cushing came in and asked Major Powell if he could get a secretary to go into the field with him. He said that Mrs. Hemenway had agreed to have him go to New Mexico to conduct archaeological work. And so I just jumped with joy when the opportunity came. J. C. Pilling . . . told Cushing that I was just the guy he wanted.[76]

Three weeks later Hodge was on a train to the Southwest with Frank and Emily, three Zuni companions—and Maggie Magill.

The railroad route to Arizona Territory in 1886 ran through Chicago, Kansas City, and Topeka, but to most eastern imaginations any place beyond Pittsburgh was the Wild West. En route and through the first weeks in the territory, Hodge clung to home through letters to and from family and friends even as he gradually changed with the landscape—"I look like a 'cowboy' now, to be sure, with my light sombrero and flannel shirt," he wrote. He soon learned to enjoy the antics and stories of his Zuni traveling companions: Waihusiwa singing at the top of his voice in the smoking car, Palowahtiwa mistakenly visiting a woman late at night in her berth. At this point a faithful Methodist churchgoer and temperance man, Hodge also began to develop some flexibility: "Was going to the church in the morning but packed condensed milk for shipment early Monday morning instead," he wrote before leaving Albion. "Not a very nice Sabbath task to be sure, but as I whistled Methodist hymns as an accompanyment to my hammering, my conscience did not smite me." And on this initial trip westward he heard from Heluta, for the first of many times, the tale of field mice scurrying from a hawk which provided him with the Zuni name he would proudly wear the rest of his life: Teluli—"Dig your cellar, dig your cellar."[77]

In Albuquerque, which Hodge recalled as a "little bit of a jerkwater town," the party overnighted while switching from the Santa Fe to the Atlantic and Pacific Railroad to continue west into Arizona.[78] Hotel rooms were scarce, so Hodge ended up sharing a bed—briefly—with Adolph Bandelier, whom Cushing had hired two months before as historian of the expedition. It was a memorable night: Bandelier kicked him out of bed and then talked until five in the morning. It was the beginning of a long friendship.[79]

The last days of 1886 were a whirlwind of activity and new experiences for Hodge. From Albuquerque the expedition party took the railroad west to the military post at Fort Wingate, where Hodge enjoyed his first taste of military life in the West.[80] Hurrying to deliver the Zunis back to their home thirty-three miles southwest of Wingate and participate in a mid-winter ceremonial himself, Cushing pushed on with Hodge and the Indians toward Zuni, stopping for the night of December 20 at Nutria Springs after twenty-two difficult miles. Here Hodge camped for the first time under the stars:

> Mr. C. showed me how to make a camp bed, which I was very willing to learn, as it will doubtless be of great need to me before long. Making a layer of pinon boughs upon the ground, and folding a comforter (letting the fold brace the wind) everything was in readiness to crawl in between the folds and cover myself with a red blanket. I slept well all night, awakening only once or twice. The revelation, upon awakening and seeing the starry sky for your ceiling[,] is peculiarly striking.[81]

On December 21 Cushing entered Zuni for the first time in nearly three years; Palowahtiwa and the two younger traveling Zunis had themselves been gone for about six months. The entire pueblo celebrated, and Hodge felt like a "special guest": "They all arose from the low, stone-like elevation that surrounded the room, and some shook hands, and others embraced me."[82] Like the meeting with Bandelier a few days before, Hodge's introduction to Zuni pueblo at the winter solstice of 1886 marked the start of an enduring relationship of regard and fascination. Hodge would spend much of his professional life studying the pueblos, and Zuni in particular.

The next day he and Cushing retraced their trail to Wingate and camped again overnight near Nutria in bitterly cold weather. On this return trip, his frail health and the weather persuaded Cushing to alter his plan of reconnaissance for the expedition: it would be best to proceed immediately to the warmer valley of central Arizona and eventually work back northeastward to Zuni.[83] He also took up Palowahtiwa's suggestion that two other Zuni men, Siwaititsailu and Weta (brother of Waihusiwa), join the expedition.[84] The new plan would require that the wagons and equipment be packed and shipped from Albuquerque and Wingate Station by train west to Ash Fork, and thence proceed down the freight road to Prescott and the valley of Phoenix and Tempe.

With the new itinerary in mind, the day after arriving back at Wingate Cushing brought on Charles Augustus Garlick (1832/33–1909), a topographer with the U.S. Geological Survey, wheelwright for the army, and brother-in-law of John Wesley Powell. "Don Carlos," as he was fondly to be known, became the indispensable quartermaster of the Hemenway enterprise: "I think he could do almost anything with his hands," Hodge recalled of him.[85] Older, experienced, irascible, and fond of drink, Garlick would also become Hodge's second mentor and close colleague in the field—and in the final months of the expedition, his rival.[86]

From the beginning Cushing recognized Garlick's unusual combination of skills and experiences and viewed him almost as a codirector of field operations. To Hemenway, Cushing enthused that he could not believe his luck in finding Garlick available at Wingate, since the older man had already done topographic work in the Salt-Gila River Valley:

> His experience was far more thorough than Bandelier's single-handed survey, and the information he gives me would lead to immediate results on my arrival in the region his travels covered, if I could secure his services. . . . I can do without guidance throughout all this northern region, as no one has explored it more thoroughly than I have. But down there, during my winter's work . . . I would gain much time and have to make much less exertion by employing Mr. Garleck. . . . His survey began where mine left off on the Verde [River]; and he is such a responsible, well-qualified explorer, surveyor . . . that he could carry on work while I was engaged with Mr. Hodge on the folk-tales and other Casa Ramona material.[87]

While he was officially Cushing's secretary and amanuensis, Hodge now began to take on additional physical tasks. He and Garlick disassembled the wagons and packed gear, food, and animals into railroad cars for shipment to Ash Fork; unloaded them at that terminus while bunking in a "filthy" livery stable; then proceeded southward with mules, horses, and wagons to Prescott. Here the men re-joined Emily and Margaret, who had come forward on trains from Albuquerque and Prescott Junction (near today's Seligman). Not for the last time, in Prescott Hodge was asked whether the expedition was a circus, and where would they be performing?[88] But there

Figure 9. Prescott Junction, Arizona, c. 1880. Courtesy of Sharlot Hall Museum, Prescott, #CITN240p.

was no performance: from Prescott the reconstituted party would now take the rocky and dusty stagecoach-freight road through Big Bug, Bumblebee, Black Canyon City, and New River to the desert settlements of Phoenix and Tempe.

The expedition party started south from Prescott on January 31. With some pride Hodge had already found he was appreciated as a competent camp cook, not only of coffee, bacon, and bread, but of Cushing's special diet of steak and granum: "Mrs. Cushing and Miss Magill called in the afternoon and congratulated me on my success as a cook."[89] The pace was relaxed and the days pleasant as the party enjoyed mild weather and grassy campsites. Hodge joined Cushing and Magill in exploring for sherds of prehistoric habitation; he saw his first desert cacti—"sawaya" and "o-kahtea" (saguaro and ocotillo)—and Margaret made her first sketches of him in camp.[90] The third night they stopped at Bumble Bee Post Office and sent off letters.[91]

At New River they lingered at the large Eylar Ranch of brothers Frank and George Alkire and their mother. Here Margaret began her journal with rhapsodic descriptions of the desert landscape, clouds, and sky—and people as well: she found the Alkires' ranching partner, Joe Singleton, "a splendid man and good to look at."[92] Exploring on horseback with Cushing or on foot with Hodge to the mesa tops in search of sherds and prehistoric formations, Maggie painted with words as well as watercolors:

> On our rest stop, Mr. Hodge and I climbed a mesa when I daubed a little. A delightful day and the distant mountain views lovely. Our desert camp was the prettiest of all with bright cactus fires, the distant blue hills, a moon almost full and a lovely sunset. The cayote barked and howled around much to my delight as the sharp sound through the clear air added the one thing needed to the scene.[93]

The diaries of Hodge and Magill over the next seven months provide contrasting and complementary views of daily activities in the field. Even as they grew personally closer, their styles and concerns often diverged widely, reflecting their sensibilities, interests, obligations, and adjustments to camp life. Generally speaking, Magill was closely observant, curious, and refresh-

Figure 10. Eylar Ranch, New River, Arizona, c. 1887. Courtesy Arizona Science Center, Phoenix (Phoenix Museum of History Collections).

ingly playful; Hodge remained more restrained and dutiful—but with occasional outbursts of joy. Except when exploring, she was rarely far from her sketchpad, pencils, watercolors, and oils. With the hire of a Chinese cook, Dah Yung, Hodge was soon freed of most cooking chores (to his great relief), but dictation from Cushing, typing and mailing letters and reports, and keeping the financial accounts of the expedition were daily, time-consuming occupations in his tent—in addition to considerable physical work in the camp and on excavation sites.

Seven decades later Hodge would recall Phoenix of 1887 (like Albuquerque) as a "little jerkwater town," but at the time he was charmed: "what a town! Adobes, Mexicans, Chinese, Indians (Maricopas and Pimas) all jumbled together and thrown on each side of a broad, cottonwood-shaded thoroughfare which they call the main street. But I like it on account of its quaintness as nothing ever reminded me more of an Asiatic city." Maggie likewise saw a "curious little foreign looking little place" with a mixed population, cottonwoods, palms, and figs—all made possible by the recently rebuilt Arizona Dam and its irrigation canals from the Salt River. Here on "main street," while the others shopped for supplies, Maggie sat in the buckboard and, closely observed herself by curious crowds, sketched scenes, Native faces, and clothing.[94]

After three days the party set off on eight miles of dusty road east and south to a hill overlooking the fledgling settlement of Tempe. Here, on a gravel rise, Cushing established Camp Augustus, named for Hemenway's son. Using his Zuni name (as always), Maggie wrote that "Tenatsali is in ecstasies at the prospect of explorations."[95]

Los Pueblitos, Los Hornos, Los Muertos: Fieldwork and Romance

The establishment of Camp Augustus, overlooking the flowing Salt River toward the young settlement of Tempe, signaled major changes for the members of the Hemenway Expedition. No longer a "traveling circus," Cushing's party found its first home and immediately became a local fascination in the sparsely settled desert. The first visitor to cross the Salt from Tempe and trudge up the gravels to the camp was James Harvey McClintock (1864–1934), editor and chief reporter for Charles Hayden's weekly *Salt River Valley*

News. McClintock's enthusiastic articles in the following months popularized the expedition locally and stimulated his own lifelong fascination with Arizona prehistory.[96] Herbert Ralph Patrick (1854–1924), a topographical engineer for the Phoenix-Maricopa railroad with a ranch several miles east of Phoenix, visited frequently (with, it appears, special interest in Maggie) and shared with Cushing his own surface collections and a considerable knowledge of the ancient irrigation canals of the Salt-Gila region.[97] As Cushing recalled, "more or less during our entire stay in the Salado Valley, we were greatly beholden to Mr. Patrick for assistance and contributions."[98] Local rancher James Cooper Goodwin (1864–1922) talked excitedly of a site three miles south of Camp Augustus that he and some friends took to be an ancient silver and gold smelter but which became Cushing's Ciudad de los Hornos, because of the many pit ovens at the site. Of greater ultimate import, at Goodwin's ranch, eight miles farther south via the Maricopa-Phoenix freight road, Cushing found the extensive array of house and pyral mounds that would fascinate him as La Ciudad de los Muertos—the City of the Dead. And then there was "Mrs. Adams," the pipe-smoking settler whose property on the Phoenix-Tempe road was on the site Cushing named La Ciudad de los Pueblitos. Spying Emily in the buckboard for the first time, she exclaimed to Cushing: "Well, she certainly is a right good-looking woman compared with the likes of you! But you're a good enough chap, and you can go on digging just the same, and as I said before the more the better!"[99]

With the stability of a home base and the prospect of new discovery, the functions of the expedition members, including Magill and Hodge, now became more complex. Each took on many roles, as all pitched into the life of camp, excursion, exploring, and collecting. Weta and Siwaititsailu hunted for ducks and other game, and they helped to construct shading ramadas for the camp and collect artifacts on and in the ground at the excavations. Within a few weeks, and with the advice of locals such as Tempe founder Charles Trumbull Hayden (1825–1900)—who provided boxes and barrels from his store for the initial collections—Cushing hired a small group of Mexican laborers for excavation.

Cushing's priorities now emerged in ways that would have significance for the expedition and its staff. As we have seen, from the beginning he had held forth to his two sponsors, Hemenway and Powell, that he would find time during the reconnaissance to prepare his Zuni stories for publication.

Indeed, Hemenway was hoping "intensely" that publication of the folktales would pique in her son Augustus (1853–1931) an interest in anthropology; while Powell, always under pressure to show results from his congressional allotments, urged his young protégé to do the literary work as soon as possible.[100] To both patrons Cushing had also indicated his intention to keep a running record—an "itinerary"—of his travels, experiences, and discoveries for quick publication. Powell urged this point strongly; indeed, partly for this reason Cushing had insisted on having a stenographer and field secretary. Perhaps he was serious in these intentions, but now that he found himself "in the very oyster of the vast present province," face-to-face with the archaeological allures of the Salt-Gila River valley, he found no time for literary work.[101] The thrill of exploration had once again taken him over. Cushing was like a bee gathering anthropological honey, as he had told a young cousin in 1884:

> A honey-bee cares little where he gets his honey. He may extract it from the downy bloom of colored clover fields, or from the thorn-encircled pollen-dusty flowers of thistles; it matters little to him! What matters more is that he gets the honey, for he must have it even in superabundance. . . . [It] is with me as with the honey-bee. I have to have knowledge of savage life, and it matters less to me where I find it, than it does in what measure I find it.[102]

In other words, the Zuni tales would have to wait.[103] What about the itinerary? When Sylvester Baxter, the expedition's home secretary, inquired about its status, Cushing prevaricated: "With reference to the itinerary: it has to be written up irregularly, although the memoranda for it are steadily kept by Miss Magill. Much of it has been written in pencil, some of it in ink that would not copy, and other in copying-ink. To prepare a copy of it at this [time] would waste much time."[104] There is no evidence that Maggie was actually keeping "memoranda" for an itinerary, though Cushing and Hodge had been recording brief and somewhat irregular "Daily Notes" since the previous November.[105] A few days after Baxter's query, Cushing instructed Hodge to start keeping an expedition narrative, and on March 29 Hodge dutifully began composing a "synopsis" of events since the previous December. That document has been lost, but it is clear that neither Hodge's nor Magill's diary was intended as an impersonal record of exploration and discovery. In the first months at Camp Augustus, most of Hodge's written work involved correspondence and account books. For her part, Maggie's primary purpose was always to aid and accompany Emily. Beyond that, she was kept busy exploring on horseback with Cushing and rapidly filling sketchbooks with watercolor and ink drawings of the artifacts from Los Pueblitos, Los Hornos, and Los Muertos that now began to fill Mr. Hayden's boxes and barrels.

The early months of 1887 in the Salt River Valley were the promising, idyllic phase of the Hemenway Expedition. The weather was generally mild, the sunsets stunning, the scenery and wildlife captivating, and even the routines of camp life seemed novel and exhilarating. Maggie and Fred informally named the camp Cushingville Under the Butte—complete with Cushing Court, Minstrel Avenue, Garlick Corners, and Fly Centre.[106] Maggie reveled in her rides with Cushing through the mesquite groves and cholla-covered hills, basking in his approval:

> We cut across country and came in by the river road and Tenatsali [Cushing] after inquiring if I was tired and receiving a negative reply complimented my riding and said I had been up and down over rough places enough to tire out the average man. We got home in good time for supper while the sun was still high enough to give warmth.[107]

Even Hodge, rarely given to poetics, occasionally grew rhapsodic:

> What a delightful feeling passes over one as he lies in his bed while the sun creeps over the eastern mountains, and the birds are singing their morning carols! Camp-life makes one realize his peace with the world, for his sleep is as peaceful as that of a babe, his appetite large and healthful, and what more could be desired? These were my waking thoughts this morning, and I felt as happy as I could be.[108]

Striking up acquaintance with visiting Pimas, Maggie began informal vocabulary lessons, sketched boys and women, eventually visited a nearby village, and became as much a curiosity to them as they were to her:

> They are very primitive and very poor and there are only very few left of them, all the others living in the Gila. There are apparently only two in-

Figure 11. Camp Hemenway, 1888. Cushing in tam o'shanter, Magill (*center*), and Hodge in white shirt, with Garlick, Wortman, Baxter, and Percy B. Yates. Courtesy of the Braun Research Library Collection, Autry Museum, Los Angeles; #N 22-A8.

> dustries at this season, performed by the women while the men lie around sleeping—they were pottery and basket-making. . . . They showed a mild curiosity about my numerous petticoats and at some of the huts they examined my garments quite as critically as I would allow.[109]

Fred had been taken by twenty-one-year-old Maggie from their first meeting at the Cushing homestead in December. By February they had established a joking relationship mediated by Emily; on the fourteenth the women sent him an "anonymous" valentine. "Even in this wild country Cupid shoots his darts, does he!" Hodge confided to his diary.[110] The growing mutual attraction warmed with the spring weather. Soon Maggie was sketching him at work in his tent. In between the chores of camp life and fieldwork, they spent hours talking, sewing, and reading novels aloud to one another. The sketching grew to regular and sometimes secretive meetings, and after Cushing moved the entire camp south to the Los Muertos site (Camp Muertos, then Camp Hemenway) in early May, the couple established their "sylvan studio" under the deep shade of a mesquite grove. Here

Maggie worked on her Hodge portrait for weeks. At times, he admitted, little work got done under the floating desert trees; on two occasions he retreated in his diary to indecipherable Pitman shorthand.[111]

By this point Fred and Maggie were regularly taking "constitutionals" at dawn to get away from the camp's prying eyes. At Maggie's request, Hodge even resolved to cut his cigarette habit from thirty to six a day. On June 11, sitting in 114-degree heat, they related their "love experiences" to one another; on June 17 they became engaged; and a week later, still hesitant to tell Cushing, they confided their "affair" to Charles Garlick.[112]

It was a safe move, for at this point Garlick and Hodge were close. "Don Carlos," in his mid-fifties and married—to Powell's sister Eliza ("Lida")—and with two daughters, was also a fieldwork veteran who was pleased to take the young couple under his wing.

Everyone relied on Don Carlos, and the older man proved to be deeply loyal to the Cushings. In the meantime, though, he was Hodge's invaluable mentor in the field. Their collaborations began as physical labor but soon extended to regional topography and plotting sites. Relying initially on Herbert Patrick's rough map of the locale, Garlick and Hodge climbed Tempe

Figure 12. Charles Augustus "Don Carlos" Garlick, 1887, with Daniel W. Lord in carriage. Courtesy of the Braun Research Library Collection, Autry Museum, Los Angeles. #N.22499.

(now Hayden) Butte repeatedly to map the course of the Salt River, ranged widely southward to the Gila River in search of ruins and landmarks, and spent many dusty hours together traveling back and forth to Tempe, Phoenix, and the excavations. When Cushing decided to begin plotting out the ruins at Los Hornos and Los Muertos, Garlick showed Hodge how to do it. The relationship would ultimately fray, but in the halcyon early days of camp life Hodge found a vital teacher of the skills he had originally sought. Even by early March Fred was writing of overseeing "my workmen" and noting that Cushing complimented him on his work at Los Muertos.[113]

But summer starts early and the sun shines unforgivingly on the Sonoran Desert. By May, Cushing's chronic gastric problems, aggravated by the searing heat, were becoming debilitating. The steady diet of steak and granum, along with frequent stomach-pumping by Emily and Maggie—and always the promise of new discoveries—buoyed Tenatsali's spirit, but he spent less time at the excavations and more in camp.[114] Much of the summer he experimented with photographic apparatus, but with only minor success and major frustration. In late August, he admitted defeat to Baxter: "[I] cannot photograph now. Even with ice day or night the gelatin melts from the plates before negatives can be developed, and the paper sticks to the negatives in this fierce sun, spoiling them. I cannot, therefore, send you either new or old pictures."[115]

Everyone suffered. The coolest daytime spot in camp was the covered buckboard, where Maggie and Emily spent whole days reading, writing, sketching, and talking; their hairpins burned their scalps in the sun, while swims in the Salt River provided rare, delicious reprieves. Dust storms turned hair and clothing gray. Two Chinese cooks, Dah Yung and Choywuy, came and went, replaced by a man named "Alsatian" Charlie McCall. For weeks on end in June and July Magill and Hodge repaired and "restored" what they came to call the "detestable pottery" from the pyral and house mounds of Los Muertos, diluting their long "jugglery" (pottery) hours with "lemonade and diary" parties, while Cushing began to mark the thousands of specimens on Garlick and Hodge's maps of the ruins.[116] To their chagrin, Mexican laborers hired by local landowners began to clear the mesquite forests around them: "Returned to camp to see the flames ruthlessly gnaw away the mesquite under which we had passed so many pleasant moments!" moaned Hodge.[117] Cushing became incapacitated in the sweltering weather.

By early August, Maggie recorded, "the heat is so great that eggs standing in a metal bucket of salt water boiled almost hard."[118] Emily dreamed of the Horsfords' Sylvester Manor back on Long Island:

> My fancy turns longingly to the cool delights of Shelter Island as I sit in the shadow of our canopy and watch the mercury disport itself up and down between 110° and 120°. Even the nights are hot, so there is little left to the imagination; hence as you may think that faculty lies dormant and rusts, leaving me nothing to think, or talk of—but thermometers. What a poem Dr. Holmes could write about *this* hot season.[119]

August 1887 brought significant changes, personally and for the expedition. One evening in mid-month Emily called for an "interview" with her sister, and the lovers' engagement of two months came "out of the bag."[120] The next day Frank marched them out of camp for a "confidential lecture" with (as Hodge curtly noted) the young couple as audience. We do not know the nature of the "understanding" they reached, but it almost certainly involved matters of propriety, for in the following days Fred and Maggie began making a point of entering and leaving camp separately. Beyond that, Cushing's opinion of the match between his sister-in-law and his secretary is not difficult to deduce. Maggie's father had died in 1879; Catherine Magill never remarried, and there were no brothers. Although sister Eleanor had married George C. Payne in 1884, Cushing was the elder and, therefore, effectively the male head of the Magill family.[121] For Maggie's sake he loyally supported Hodge's professional ambitions and gave his blessing to the marriage four years later, but privately Frank had misgivings.[122] They would eventually surface with some bitterness.

The expedition had long overstayed Cushing's intended sojourn in the Salt River Valley; they should have been moving northeastward toward Zuni before the heat of summer.[123] Explaining his change of plans to Baxter and Hemenway, Cushing stressed the unexpectedly rich discoveries at Los Muertos (which he compared to Pompeii) and the other ruin sites—and his poor health. Alarmed by Cushing's deterioration, on August 15 Hemenway met with Baxter and army lieutenant John Gregory Bourke (1846–96) at Manchester-by-the-Sea and asked Bourke to take charge of the expedition while she sent Cushing to California for recuperation.[124] Bourke demurred

Figure 13. Frank Hamilton Cushing in San Francisco, 1887. Photo by Taber Photographic Studio. Courtesy of the Boston Athenaeum. #AA5.4Cus.f (no. 1).

and suggested instead army doctor Washington Matthews. Likewise an ethnographer and close friend of Cushing, Matthews would, it was hoped, not only watch Frank's health but also curate on site the human remains being unearthed and exposed.[125] Mary Hemenway worked quickly: in a week Secretary of the Army William C. Endicott (a personal friend of Hemenway) had reassigned Matthews to the expedition, and on September 1 the army doctor–ethnographer arrived at Camp Hemenway. A few days later Frank, Emily, and Maggie began packing for San Diego.

California Interlude: September–December 1887

Matthews's arrival marked further changes for the expedition. In the first place, he probably saved Cushing's life by diagnosing for the first time the tapeworm in his patient's system and suggesting surgery in California. As Cushing understated it to Baxter, "there was, it seems, a complication (parasitic) in my disease."[126] (He would spend the next two years expelling the visitor.) The case was extremely serious. Hodge recorded: "Mr. Cushing was so ill this morning [September 5] upon our returning from the washwoman's that we all had little hope of his recovery; constant rubbing of his limbs with alcohol by Mrs. C., Miss M., Ramon [Castro] and myself, and fanning by Mr. Garlick, restored him to consciousness."[127] Matthews became anxious to get Cushing away from "our lively companions of the camp—the flies, mosquitos, scorpions, tarantulas, and rattlesnakes—and take him where he might regain his strength, in the cool breezes of the Pacific."[128]

Although Matthews never took the full control of the expedition that Mary Hemenway had anticipated, in the few weeks that he was actually in camp and caring for his friend he managed to assess the poor condition of the excavated skeletal remains that were scattered about. He searched out whatever paraffin he could locate, applied it to some of the exposed bones, and made plans for future treatments. He found that "no attention had been paid to the collection or preservation of human bones, which were extremely fragile, crumbling to dust upon a touch, and which had been thrown about and trampled under foot by curious visitors, so that but little remained of value from the work which had been previously done."[129]

Cushing's decision to stay at his Salt River Valley excavations through the blistering summer months, rather than head north to Zuni, had greatly endangered his health. It was driven by two considerations. The rich alluvium between the Salt and Gila Rivers was undergoing daily clearing and irrigating for agricultural use—large piles of mesquite were being dragged and then burned at night around the camp—so the window for archaeology seemed very narrow. "It dismays me," Cushing wrote, "when I think how soon not only the treasures but even the traces of Los Muertos will be scattered and obliterated by the plough."[130] He also was determined to protect the excavations and artifacts from the constant threat of pothunters and developers.[131] Henceforth the expedition would give greater priority to skeletal preservation and study—a matter in which Cushing heretofore had had little personal interest.[132] Hodge played a key role in this redirection.

After a false start on September 9 caused by a washout on the Southern Pacific Railway, the Cushing party (Frank, Emily, Margaret, and Matthews) returned to camp for two weeks, then left again for San Diego on September 26. Matthews recalled:

> We telegraphed for a Pullman berth for our sick man, but got for him instead room to lie down on the crowded floor of the ordinary passenger-car. Here he fell into a delirious sleep and astonished the gentle tenderfoot by delivering harangues in the Zuni tongue.[133]

Cushing's detailed instructions to Hodge and Garlick, dictated the night before he left, placed Hodge in charge of the "business operations" of the expedition—purchasing supplies, keeping accounts, writing daily memoranda and reports. He also placed the excavation and preservation work largely in his secretary's hands. In these important instructions, Cushing was explicit in guiding Hodge's first independent fieldwork and showed particular consideration for the younger man's future:

> In thus numbering the sepulchers or lettering the rooms of any ruin, constantly compare the maps with the ruins under consideration, first placing on a stake or wire-standard a tag that has been soaked in corrosive-sublimate, to protect from the ravages of animals, and marked with whatever number or letter is entered on the map for any given sepulcher or room. . . . If important interments should be exposed, either of specimens or of skeletons, see, in conjunction with Mr. Garlick, that the skeletons remain undisturbed, and, as soon after their exposure as possible, be recovered, the place of their occurrence being marked with a tag bearing the running sepulcher number. . . . Should the number of these specially interesting [sepulcher] specimens not be so great as to consume too much of your time, I would advise the writing up, quite fully, of any new or especially interesting exposures which may be made, and also that you give, when clear, your ideas, relative to the meaning of said exposures or deposits. Such descriptive work will be useful for me in any event, and

most excellent training for yourself toward the carrying on, by yourself, of course, of possible future, independent and original researches.[134]

Don Carlos was to have charge of the "active operations" of the expedition—by which Cushing meant oversight of the workmen, responsibility for material conditions of camp, and care of expedition equipment and animals.[135] It was a reasonable division of labor, and Garlick and Hodge worked well together at this time. Over the coming months they daily visited the Los Muertos excavations, overseeing the work, plotting the sites, tagging rooms, marking artifacts, and shifting workers around in the hope of greater "pay-dirt."[136] This period saw Hodge's true initiation into the archaeological and collecting practices of the time. He kept Cushing closely informed of events, visitors, and discoveries; looking on from the Pacific Coast Cushing was deeply pleased with "the happy faculty you seem to be developing for the description not only of specimens, but features and characteristics also."[137]

The California recuperation lasted three months—one in San Diego and two in San Francisco. On arrival at the coast Matthews immediately placed Cushing in the care of fellow army surgeon David L. Huntington, then stayed only four days in San Diego before returning, via Fort Wingate and Navajo country, to Washington.[138] Back at the Army Medical Museum he arranged for anatomist Dr. Jacob L. Wortman to join the expedition in order to treat and preserve the exposed skeletal materials prior to shipping them to the Army Museum for study. Cushing agreed to the arrangement. Wortman arrived in late November and stayed with the expedition for seven months.[139]

Apart for the first time, Fred and Maggie wrote to each other almost every day; "Pearl" (his new term of affection) enclosed California roses in her letters, while he penned dozens of pages at a time. But mail delivery was irregular and Hodge was generally lonely and depressed—as well as ill with various maladies.[140] Heavy rains and winds ripped and flooded the camp in October, followed by sudden cold and an unusual number of curious visitors. It all added to his misery. In the meantime Cushing, despite far more comfortable lodgings, was faring little better in San Diego, suffering repeated relapses in what he called "this most undelectable and misrepresented of places." Dr. Huntington offered him little hope of immediate relief or permanent recovery and suggested a sea voyage to San Francisco to obtain special surgical treatment and supplies.[141]

Hopeful as always, at the end of October Cushing embarked with Emily and Margaret for San Francisco, where they settled into the Occidental Hotel.[142] Working daily with Margaret as his secretarial assistant, Cushing kept close tabs on the expedition work. He expressed pleasure with Hodge's reports on the excavations and bolstered the younger man's spirit with words of encouragement: "The training you are now getting in striving so faithfully to fill my place is the best kind that will ever come to you; neither books nor set instructions fulfilling to an equal extent the mission of scientific education."[143]

Cushing lost no time in making contact with the scientific community of San Francisco to promote both the expedition and his own notoriety. The competitive newspapers followed his activities breathlessly. On November 7, only a week after his arrival, Cushing gave his first lecture to the California Academy of Sciences, reciting his experiences at Zuni and offering "Zuni chants" to a rapt audience.[144] Two weeks later he attended the Chinese Theater with celebrity journalist and visiting lecturer Kate Field—beginning a mutual admiration that lasted until her death in 1896.[145] In an extended interview with *San Francisco Daily Examiner* associate editor Henry B. McDowell (1857–1928), he expounded at length on comparisons he saw between Chinese and Zuni myth and rituals.[146] He repeated and elaborated these musings many times.

Cushing made other important connections. He and Emily met a debonair Catalan civil engineer, Eusebio J. Molera (1846–1932), who had married into Monterey's powerful Cooper family and become a major figure in San Francisco civic circles, including the California Academy of Sciences, whose building he designed.[147] Interested in Aztec and pre-Aztec (Teotihuacan) prehistory, Molera was fascinated by Frank and entranced by Emily (who returned the favor).

Molera became a reliable supporter and sympathetic sounding board for Cushing.[148] At the same time, Cushing's longtime interest in southwestern connections to prehistoric Peruvian cultures also took on new life.[149] His musings about ancient hemispheric migrations down the Pacific Coast, which he adumbrated in his academy lectures, intrigued William Randolph Hearst (1863–1951). The young newspaperman envisioned a South American expedition as a journalistic coup and offered Cushing the use of his private yacht (and all expenses) to extend his inquiries to South America.[150]

Figure 14. Eusebio J. Molera. Courtesy of the Society of California Pioneers. #CO24561-123057.

Peruvian connections became a Cushing obsession in the early months of 1888; the Hearst expedition, however, never materialized.[151]

In early December Cushing appeared again before the Academy of Sciences to lecture on the expedition. This time, looking emaciated, pained, and pale, he fainted onstage but was revived and delivered his talk. He finished again with Zuni chants: "It was like hearing a Chinese song without the unearthly noise of the gong," wrote a reporter for the *San Francisco Chronicle,* "and as the lecturer is possessed of a good voice the effect was rather pleasing."[152]

Cushing had clearly made a splash in San Francisco as a suffering, heroic artist-scientist. Hearst, owner and publisher of the *Examiner* since only the previous March, dispatched editor McDowell immediately to Arizona. When he arrived in camp, Hodge and Garlick (following Cushing's close instructions) gave him a tour of the Los Muertos highpoints. McDowell's "Cities of the Dead"—the first of an ardent series of articles—appeared on the front page of Hearst's paper on Christmas Day.[153]

Full Force at Salado: January–May 1888

By the time Frank, Emily and Maggie rode back up to Camp Hemenway on December 22, 1887, many changes were afoot—some of them according to Cushing's plans, others unexpected. While Hodge and Garlick had kept the fieldwork going through the California sojourn, and Margaret had served effectively as Frank's secretary in San Francisco, new faces now began to appear in camp. Wortman, who had arrived after Thanksgiving in the midst of a weeklong drenching rain, was distraught over the condition of the skeletal materials at the digs. The bones simply fell apart. "I do not remember in my experience in such matters," he told Cushing, "to have undertaken a piece of work which has taxed my patience more than the present." Still, he was anxious to pursue his own paleontological interests by cave hunting in the Southwest, and he urged Cushing to extend the expedition accordingly: he wanted to be the first "to prove the contemporaneity of man with the hairy Mammoth and other well known extinct species."[154] In fact, in mid-December Wortman persuaded Hodge and McDowell to accompany him on a largely fruitless trip to caves in the nearby Superstition Mountains, and a few weeks later he and McDowell went off cave hunting for a week in El Paso. Hodge disliked the bothersome journalist and was happy to see Wortman and "the fat man" absent themselves for a week.

Cushing had not requested Wortman and reluctantly accepted him.[155] On the other hand, with the arrival of Herman F. C. ten Kate, Cushing gained a trusted friend in camp.[156] A globetrotting, polyglot physical anthropologist from Holland, ten Kate had first met Cushing at Zuni in 1883. He had immediately been struck by Cushing's "clear and eloquent discourse," and even more by his physical presence: "Endearing and handsome, with sharp, intelligent features, surrounded by reddish blond hair, he reminds one now of an artist, now of a military man, and although he looks older, he is only twenty-seven."[157] Ten Kate saw Cushing as a "dreamer and poet" as well as a brilliant ethnographer. Still, he judged that Cushing was "only half qualified to lead an expedition": "He is not methodical enough, exerts too little control. To some of the personnel he is too indulgent, too weak"—in addition to which, the Dutchman confided to his diary, "there are too many members on the [Hemenway] council who don't know anything about fieldwork."[158] The personal and scientific admiration between Cushing and ten Kate was fully mutual, and early on Frank had entreated the Dutchman to serve as the expedition's physical anthropologist.[159] He finally arrived in camp on November 18, a week before Wortman, having stopped first in Washington, in Santa Fe to confer with Bandelier, and finally at Fort Wingate for an update from Matthews.

The Cushings thus returned at Christmas to a camp that had grown to eleven tents and a staff that included—in addition to Hodge, Garlick, the two women, a cook, and as many as a dozen Mexican workmen—Wortman, ten Kate, and journalist McDowell.

With the new year an even more consequential guest arrived: Sylvester Baxter, secretary-treasurer of the expedition board (a.k.a. "the Association"). Baxter's purpose was to serve as the patron's eyes and ears on the ground; appearing on January 11, he stayed more than three months. Baxter had been a confidant and acolyte of Cushing since 1881, but his visit was also a sign of trouble.[160] Since the previous summer concerns over Cushing's health had been compounded by doubts about his leadership and management, as Hemenway's investment deepened and few results seemed to emerge—including the long-promised Zuni folktales. In the fall, Hemenway had begun requesting more frequent and detailed reports of progress, and Cushing sensed that the unease was not merely over his precarious health. About to return from San Francisco, he tried to reassure the board members: "You will all yet learn that the work [Hemenway] has given me in trust to do is maturing me. That it and the bitter sufferings I have been through, have pretty nearly wrought the childishness out of me. By and by therefore, you will all feel safer, I think, in relying on my judgment."[161]

Words were fine, but doubts persisted. Bandelier, receiving a monthly salary from Hemenway but operating in Santa Fe with his own agenda, further undermined Cushing's authority through summer and fall by writing directly to Baxter and Hemenway to suggest the need for a leadership council. Despite their long-standing mutual regard, Bandelier's effrontery angered Cushing, and in early February he invited "my old friend and new enemy" to Camp Hemenway. As Cushing told his father, on the afternoon of February 2 he stood before Bandelier, Baxter, ten Kate, and Wortman and reasserted his position as director:

> I then most thoroughly [addressed] every member; showed them my definite, detailed plans for years of work and finally gave them together with the Association their choice of two alternatives:—the acceptance of my authority as director, as simply absolute and [un]conditional, or the acceptance of my resignation! Then, obedience or dismissal. I trust that I shall hear of no more "councils" unless I call them myself!

Cushing then further unburdened himself to his father:

> [A]lthough younger than the others, I know what is to be accomplished for Mrs. Hemenway and her friends, how to accomplish, and that I can accomplish it, in my own way,—which must therefore be the way of those who assist me; nor will I brook interference in this from any one.[162]

Hodge watched all this turmoil from close up. He and Margaret were off in their mesquite retreat on the afternoon of the "council," aware of the issues but not included in the deliberations. Perhaps not surprisingly, the three-month separation had created the couple's own strains. Their reunion at Christmas, Emily editorialized to Molera, had been "a hollow mockery": "He said, 'I'm glad to see you,' she said, 'Thank you.' Mildly exciting isn't it? If my memory serves me aright, it is about what I said to Mr. Cushing after his three years in Zuni."[163]

Perhaps Emily's words were an indication of skepticism about the match. But now the affianced were together again, able to spend hour after hour writing and sketching, reading and talking.

While the lovers were burrowing in, the expedition was branching out. Cushing set up Camp Baxter at Las Acequias, a new site north of Camp Hemenway, and it soon began yielding burial goods for Wortman and ten Kate.[164] Newly intrigued by the famous ruin of Casa Grande to the southeast—"only an other and grander, the more recent Muertos!"—Cushing was now dreaming of buying that site as a winter field school for Mrs. Hemenway's proposed Pueblo Museum in Salem.[165] He undertook two reconnaissance trips there in January, first with Wortman and ten Kate (who had visited the ruin in 1883), then with Baxter.[166] Hodge was not included.

Fred was feeling diminished. "Mr. Cushing and the geniuses held another war-council this ev'g," he moaned to his journal.[167] Reduced to seemingly endless copying and escorting curious visitors around the camp, after the comparative freedom and responsibilities of the fall Hodge was deeply dissatisfied with the new regime; he described to his brother the "present condition of affairs and prospects of my home-returning if no change presents itself very soon."[168] When Cushing became excited about newly unearthed terra cotta figurines that indicated to him the prehistoric presence of llamas ("los guanacos") in the Salt-Gila River Valley—which he wrongly counted as further evidence of Peruvian connections—Cushing's mental meanderings were almost too much for Hodge. He again talked with Margaret of resigning over the "llama affair."[169] Maggie soothed him—and lightheartedly sketched what she called Frank's "llamitos." Hodge stayed on.

The first five months of 1888 were the high point of the Hemenway Expedition in Arizona. At first Cushing's health rebounded. Even as he established new sites—Las Acequias and Los Guanacos—the director began anticipating the final cataloguing and packing of specimens for shipment to Salem.[170] Mrs. Hemenway had bought the land on Batchelder Point for her museum and would soon hire well-known Boston architect S. Edwin Tobey to design it.[171] Journalist McDowell returned to San Francisco while Baxter began writing glowing reports that would soon popularize the expedition in the East.[172] In February ten Kate and Wortman discovered an apparent peculiarity in the hyoid bone (between the tongue and the larynx) of some skeletons at Las Acequias, which led to great excitement and, five years later, the expedition's first major publication.[173] In March ten Kate journeyed southward for two months of comparative anthropometric studies among Pima, Maricopa, and Tohono O'odham settlements.[174] Two young men joined the force: Percy B. Yates, a local amateur photographer, was to help with photo work and cataloguing for two months, and Edward Page Gaston, a twenty-year-old from Illinois, arrived as a volunteer in late February to do cataloguing. He stayed ten months.[175]

In late March two notable visits to the camp occurred. On March 20 Eusebio Molera arrived from San Francisco on his way to Mexico. Cushing erected new poles and flags for the camp in Molera's honor, and Emily drove him between Tempe and Camp Hemenway by herself.[176] Cushing and Molera spent a day surveying and photographing the excavations and ancient irrigation canals, Cushing talked for hours of his theories and plans, and Molera left the next evening.[177]

A few days later Edward Sylvester Morse (1838–1925) appeared in camp. His visit presented a major opportunity and challenge for Cushing. Like Baxter, Morse was a member of the expedition board and had been sent to assess Cushing's work; but he was also an internationally recognized marine naturalist, a fellow of the National Academy of Sciences, and a close adviser to Mary Hemenway. A Salem native, Morse had studied with Louis Agassiz at Harvard and directed the Peabody Museum of Salem (now the Peabody Essex Museum); furthermore, he had done pioneering work in shell-mound archaeology in Japan—where he is still considered the father of archaeology. In 1882 Morse had welcomed Cushing and the Zuni troupe to his Salem home. The two shared an esoteric, lifelong interest in archery and the cultural differences in arrow release; in fact, they had together observed the Zuni chiefs at Casa Ramona in the fall of 1886.[178] In short, Morse's seniority counted, his friendship was critical, and his opinion mattered.

Morse stayed twelve days, and his visit was delightful for Hodge as well as Cushing. Believing he had discovered evidence of metalworking—a copper bell—Cushing organized an exploratory party to a mining region in Cave Creek, north of Phoenix. All the men (Cushing, Hodge, Baxter, Morse, Garlick, Wortman, and Ramon and Raul Castro) were included in a six-day outing that featured daytime "grubbing" for pictographs, ore samples and artifacts, and nighttime campfire hilarity with songs and stories.[179] Morse thoroughly enjoyed himself, as did Hodge:

> After supper we sang many popular songs and then had an "exhibition" by Mr. Baxter who caused a great deal of merriment when bedtime came, Prof. Morse acting [as] interlocutor. After supper a discussion on carnivorous vs vegetarian diet followed, resulting in a new sobriquet for poor Baxter the "vegetarian." A few songs by the "Jasper Glee Club" and bedtime came—[180]

Hodge felt new confidence. Toward the end of the month Cushing talked privately with Margaret, and then Hodge, about the couple's future work in anthropology. Frank came away with a new appreciation of their potential together:

> My health has been so bad [Cushing wrote] that it has been impossible for me to engage in writing; but I have enjoyed the opportunity of a long conversation with Miss Magill, by means of which I am happy to foresee that both she and Mr. Hodge can extend their work in other, more and useful and interesting lines connected with mine and that of the expedition generally than has heretofore been clear to me, or I have had reason to hope for.[181]

The "new lines" Magill and Hodge discussed with Cushing probably concerned the irrigation canals and reservoirs that so occupied Cushing's thoughts at the time. A few weeks earlier he had mentioned that Hodge and Garlick might write up a monograph on the prehistoric canal system of the region; after the talks he again surveyed various canal sites with Emily and Margaret, and Fred began entering in his diary unusually full observations of nearby canal features.[182]

Socially at least, the Cave Creek outing with Morse was a highpoint of the expedition in Arizona. By mid-April Cushing's health was again failing. He determined to quickly finish up the classifying, cataloguing, and packing of the thousands of Salado specimens, ship them by rail to Salem, and close up operations in the Salt River Valley. The plan was to return to California with Emily and Margaret for further medical treatment, leaving Hodge and Garlick to move the expedition northeast to Zuni. Subject as always to his medical condition, Cushing intended to re-join the expedition by early June.[183] (The prospect of South America had temporarily faded.) Accordingly, through April and early May, Fred and Margaret, along with Garlick, Yates, and the rest of the staff—and with a new recruit from Boston, Daniel Walter Lord—worked incessantly to finish the work at Camp Hemenway.[184]

Returning from two months with tribal communities to the south, ten Kate reported to Dutch colleagues that everything was "in rep en roer"—chaos.[185] The cataloguing was largely finished by May 4; over the next ten days Hodge did last-minute mapping and plotting while Garlick assembled and stenciled the shipping crates. On May 12 ninety-three cases addressed to Morse in Salem left on a freight train from Tempe. Two days later a very sick and nostalgic Cushing, with Emily and Margaret, once again boarded the 2 a.m. train for San Diego:

> I feel very, very sad to-day. I have to go at once to California. These are my last hours at Los Muertos, with its store of untouched chambers, and who knows what treasures! A year or two and grain will wave over the highest homes of this ancient City of the Dead. A few bone bits bleaching in the sand, a few sherds of pottery and fragments of sterner stuff, a few whirlwinds and dust-clouds—nothing more will be left of Los Muertos![186]

Once again in charge of operations, Hodge and Garlick oversaw the final measuring and recording of the excavation sites. Margaret and the Cushings arrived in San Diego on May 18—the same day that Hodge, back in Camp Hemenway, closed out his eighteen-month diary. On the first of June the men shipped seventeen cases of skeletons to the Army Medical Museum in Washington, and four days later the wagons of the Hemenway Expedition rumbled northward, beginning a month-long migration to Zuni. Writing from his hotel overlooking the Pacific, and undoubtedly envisioning conquistadors, Cushing called it the "Grand March to Cibola."[187]

Return to Cibola: Summer 1888

The "Grand March" was a grueling, thirty-six-day wagon trip. Ten Kate called it "a long and unsuccessful march of more than 400 miles" marked by broken wagons and a lot of sickness.[188] In addition to Hodge, Garlick, and ten Kate, the Zuni-bound troupe included Gaston, Lord, field excavators Ramon and Rafael Castro, and a new teamster named Moore.[189] In an indication of problems to come, the leadership was not clear. Ten Kate later maintained that he and Garlick were supposed to lead the men, but Hodge made all financial and operational decisions.[190] He originally laid out a twenty-four day trip through Camp Verde and northeast through Winslow, Holbrook, and Saint Johns. For reasons that are still not clear, though, the party took a different, longer route from Camp Verde north to Flagstaff, then east along the Atlantic and Pacific railroad route to Holbrook.

Here Morse's son, John Gould Morse (1870–1951), joined the expedition for a few miserable weeks of vacation.[191] In mid-July they arrived in Manuelito, New Mexico, from which Garlick, Moore, and the Castro brothers cleared a road southeast to Zuni. Hodge stayed in Manuelito (with a rail stop, post office, and telegraph station) to maintain contact with Cushing and arrange supplies. He was most anxious for Cushing (and Margaret) to return: "Your counsel now," he pleaded at one point, "would make all the difference imaginable in the sentiment of affairs at camp."[192] But while Frank and Emily forwarded a new French cookbook to the camp cook, Eduard Haag, and Frank apologized to Daniel Lord for the hard trip, Cushing again pleaded doctor's orders to stay by the ocean.[193] Finally, on August 2—after a ten-week absence, and six weeks later than originally planned—Cushing and the ladies rode once again into Zuni pueblo.

The second California sojourn had again been divided—a month in San Diego and six weeks in San Francisco. Medical treatments in both cities once more failed to remove Cushing's tapeworm, but he clearly felt relief away from the desert, writing from the coast to Mrs. Hemenway of the poetry of anthropology:

> Ethnology *must* be cultivated in the Garden of the Imagination—the lightest, richest loam—and fertilized by the dew of human sympathy. . . . It is not the "science," it is the *Poetry* about my dear subject which makes me love it—better than life, and far better than fame.[194]

Perhaps. In fact, the weeks in San Francisco garnered further public attention for Cushing and his enterprise. After the relative (and deliberate) obscurity during the first year of its work, 1888 had already brought a marked change in public awareness—beginning with McDowell's *Daily Examiner* series at the end of 1887 and early in 1888, and continuing with Baxter's Old New World for the *Boston Herald* in April. A further rash of newspaper and journal notices appeared as the expedition was finishing its Arizona work in May.[195] Within days of arrival in San Francisco, then, Cushing stood once more before the California Academy of Sciences, this time lecturing on "Evolution" and answering questions about his research.[196] McDowell produced in the *Examiner* (June 24–July 15) another long, glowing four-part recap of Cushing's version of his life at Zuni and highlights of the expedition.[197]

Cushing returned to Zuni with one of the best photographers of San Francisco. He hoped Edwin H. Husher (1863–1919) would finally resolve the photographic struggles that had plagued the expedition in the sand and heat of Salt River. Percy Yates had played vigorous tennis in camp but had disappointed as both photographer and clerical assistant; Cushing fired him in May. Husher, by contrast, had already made a name for himself as a fellow of courage and initiative. Arriving in San Francisco in 1886, the Indiana native had immediately joined the prestigious Isaiah West Taber Photographic Studio—and soon achieved considerable notoriety. In a newspaper stunt, William Randolph Hearst sent Husher up in a hot air balloon to take aerial photos of San Francisco; then on June 27, 1887, the twenty-four-old "aeronaut" took the first aerial shots of Los Angeles as well—thirteen fascinating pictures—before landing in a cactus patch in the San Fernando Valley.[198] To lure this "splendid little gentleman" to Zuni, Cushing made a deal: Taber and Hearst would have rights to publish Husher's expedition photos. Cushing also agreed to pay Husher three hundred dollars a month—twice his own salary—and promised to build him a dark room at the Cushing house in Zuni.[199]

Cushing's return on August 1 inaugurated the final, difficult phase of his expedition. To understand the last nine months—the excavations at and around Zuni, Cushing's return to the East Coast in October, the expedition's collapse in rancor and recrimination in the first half of 1889, and Hodge's pivotal role in these tumultuous events—requires a grasp of the complex dynamics that Cushing had embedded in his enterprise by the summer of 1888. As we have seen, the original 1886 plan of the expedition had projected a few months in the Arizona deserts followed by an archaeological survey moving gradually northeast to Zuni—recapitulating the presumed ancient route of the Zuni ancestors.[200] But Cushing had totally altered this plan, staying in the Arizona deserts seventeen months; moreover, his health had required two long absences—more than five months—in California. Cushing had not traveled as intended, and he had not written as promised. Expenses always exceeded monthly projections, even as he repeatedly promised savings. (At one point he bought a cow and her calf for fresh milk in camp.) By the time the party was settling in New Mexico, Mary Hemenway was still moving forward with plans for a Salem museum (including an adjacent house for the Cushings), but patience was thin and concern was growing among her advisers, especially her son Augustus and William

Torrey Harris, chairman of the expedition board.[201] Already forced to create daily reports of his thoughts and discoveries, Cushing was now being strongly encouraged to submit weekly rather than monthly records of progress; and expenditures were being more closely scrutinized by Hemenway's trusted Boston accountant, Rufus Leighton.

Under pressure, Cushing assured his patron that, once settled in the pueblo environment, he could more efficiently produce the long-awaited folktales; for this purpose he hired Garlick's elder daughter, Louella (Ella, Nellie), as a second secretary and even proposed to bring to Zuni a favorite illustrator, Henry François Farny.[202] As it turned out, those efforts were bootless. Farny did not come, and Cushing never finished the Zuni tales.

The return to Zuni had unique complications, too, for in several respects Cushing was coming home. First, he knew that he would immediately be expected to reassume exhausting responsibilities as a Bow Priest and adoptive brother of the governor, Palowahtiwa. This indeed happened,

Figure 15. Zuni Woman with Baby (at Camp Cibola), 1888. Note Cushing-Hemenway house in background. Photograph by Edwin H. Husher. Courtesy of the Peabody Museum of Archaeology and Ethnology, Harvard University, 2004.1.298.5.

and his arrival temporarily gave new vigor to the declining Priesthood of the Bow.[203]

Second, foremost in Cushing's mind was returning to the house he had built in his last months in the pueblo four years before, along with additional rooms for collection storage. Located on the south bank of the Zuni River just across from the modern pueblo, Cushing's house sat on the ruins of Halona:wa South, a rectangular pueblo dating from 1250–1350. Frank, Emily, and Maggie had lived in the building for only a few months before he was forced back to Washington in early 1884, but now their tenting days would be over.[204] He set up a tent camp (Camp Cibola) for Hodge and the other men nearby while he and the women moved into their old Zuni home on "Halona Hill"—with a library, kitchen, and cook.

For the longer term Cushing envisioned his expanded Zuni home as the scientific center for a future Hemenway southwestern field school (as he had similarly mused about Los Muertos and Casa Grande).[205] He planned to

Figure 16. Ruins of Hawikku. Photograph by Edwin H. Husher, 1888. Courtesy of the Peabody Museum of Archaeology and Ethnology, Harvard University, 2004.1.298.21.

dig a well near the house and create a special room for Hemenway's future visits; he also discussed with her constructing a corn-grinding mill for the pueblo. Even before arriving from San Francisco, Cushing directed Daniel Lord and several others to establish a side camp in the cedar forests north of the pueblo, where for seven weeks the men cut and prepared wood for his new construction.[206] On the first of September Cushing reported to Molera that a new cellar for his "mansion" was completed:

> Rafters for the roof are already seasoning in the Sierra, stones for the basements are already quarried below the Southern Mesa, and adobes are drying—without cracking,—on the river-side of Zuñi. A carpenter began to hammer and saw this morning, and a mason will begin building Monday morning . . . and What glorious collections we are making! It is not often that an Archaeologist can "build" like that, is it?[207]

Figure 17. Cushing-Hemenway House, Zuni Pueblo. Photograph by A. C. Vroman, 1899. Courtesy of the National Anthropological Archives, Smithsonian Insitution. #NAA INV 06375800.

As it turned out, because of snow and freezing temperatures the new structures were still not finished the following January, three months after Cushing had left the Southwest for the last time. Having paid for all the new work, the Hemenways later laid claim to the entire house.[208]

Zuni represented an intellectual homecoming as well, recentering ethnography in Cushing's research design. Ten Kate wrote, just before leaving the expedition in late August, that "Zuni is, as five years ago, a paradise for ethnologists. . . . I've never more clearly seen the inseparable bond between ethnology and archaeology than here."[209] Since 1883 Cushing had been debating with Bandelier the historical and archaeological puzzles of the conquistadors' "Seven Cities of Cibola."[210] More convinced than ever that he and Bandelier had finally located the ancient Zuni villages of the Spanish accounts—the central one being Halona:wa—Cushing now pictured the excavations as an unassailable structure anchoring a far-reaching archaeological-ethnological program.[211] As he put it, the Cibola work would stand as a bridge "between the strictly prehistoric and the Historico-Ethnologic branches of our work and subject [that] may be built up into a very strong and perfect structure,

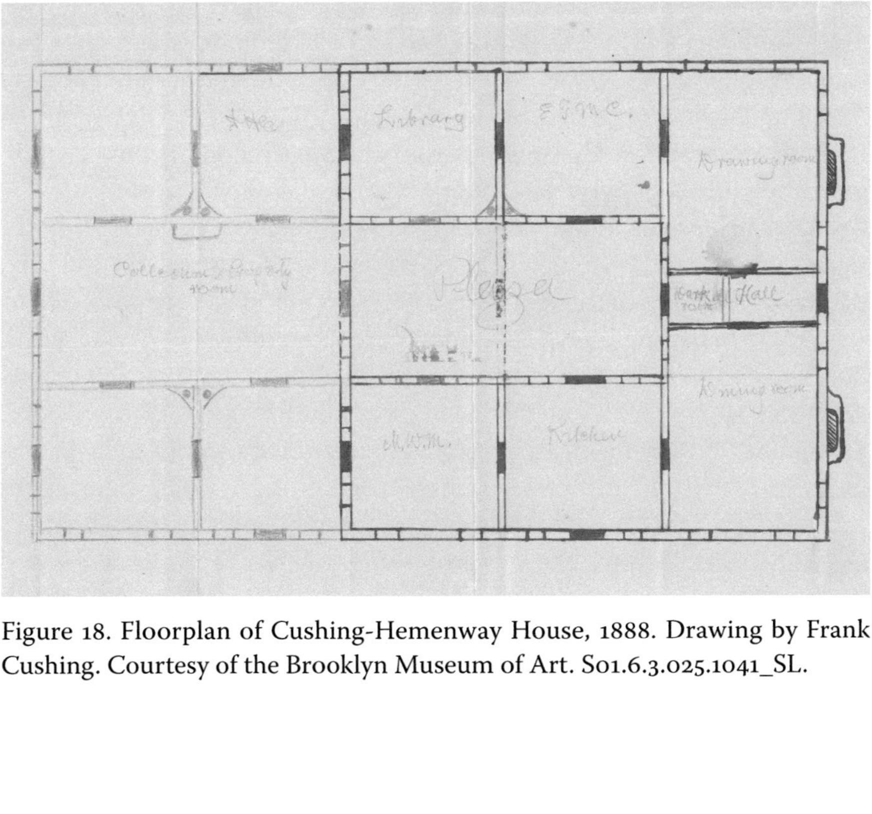

Figure 18. Floorplan of Cushing-Hemenway House, 1888. Drawing by Frank Cushing. Courtesy of the Brooklyn Museum of Art. S01.6.3.025.1041_SL.

capable of bearing the burden of the most ponderous investigation or the current of the most demolishing criticism!" To Baxter he expanded the metaphor of the seven-piered bridge:

> This series of remains, as it goes on accumulating, will build [the] complete arch of the bridge with which we may span the period between the far off ancient remains of the further Northwest and Southwest, and the historical remains of this valley and the documents relating thereto, and between the Zuñis themselves as studied by me in the years just passed. Indeed, looking at it now, I cannot conceive how it was possible for me to forget, so long, in the interest of the Los Muertos work, this possible means of building such a bridge with its seven piers, each resting on an ancient city of Cibola.[212]

Day to day, there was little rest. On top of the pueblo duties, the house construction and the Halona:wa South excavations, Cushing soon became feverishly absorbed in preparing the first official scientific presentations on the Hemenway Expedition for the International Congress of Americanists in Berlin in October. The invitation had come in June to Hemenway from Adolf Bastian (1826–1905), director of the Royal Museum of Ethnology in Berlin, and she had accepted; but unaccountably Cushing was not informed for a month or more. The frenetic weeks of August and September were therefore consumed with selecting materials from Los Muertos and Las Acequias for display at the Congress (and final deposit at the Berlin Museum); arranging the writing of three papers (by Wortman and ten Kate, Bandelier, and himself); and settling on Baxter and Morse to represent the expedition in Berlin.[213] In a white heat of dictation to Hodge, Cushing produced the brilliant "Preliminary Notes on the Origin, Working Hypothesis and Primary Researches of the Hemenway Southwestern Archaeological Expedition."[214] Here for the first time he clarified for a public audience the logic connecting his early work at Zuni, the Salt River Valley excavations, and his current archaeological inquiries—complemented by Bandelier's historical research—into the mysterious early pueblos. While he apologized profusely to Mary Hemenway and others for a work he claimed was barely coherent, in truth "Preliminary Notes" was the intellectual apex of the Hemenway Expedition.

It was indeed a tour de force. Cushing explained that he had come to believe that "a people carry through all succeeding environments—relatively unmodified—the impress or the *Idea* of the earliest environment that affected their culture." In the Arizona deserts he claimed to have found the original environment that had shaped the "culture soul," as he called it, of the Zuni people. Accordingly, he felt free to employ his understanding of current Zuni life in interpreting the excavations—an ethnographically informed archaeology.[215]

The search for the central idea within a cultural configuration, he explained, involved two stages, the first of which he had accomplished during his years at Zuni: he had established the sevenfold nature of Zuni life and isolated the search for the Middle (Center) of the World as the organizing principle of Zuni culture history. It now remained for him to trace, he wrote, both the Zunis and their central cultural idea back through time and space to their origins. This had become the central goal of the Hemenway Expedition. He sought a specific historical and migratory sequence, paying special attention to the relationship between people and physical environment through time. In other words, Cushing argued for the tenacity of deep, original ideas: his entire method depended on the assumption of their perseverance. Far from being repeatedly shaped by environment and altered by historical experience, the mental structures of peoples, he argued, give the framework to the world as they perceive it.[216]

Unfortunately, the remarkable accomplishment of the Berlin papers was marred by a bitter disagreement between Cushing and Dr. John Shaw Billings (1838–1913), director of the Army Medical Museum, over control of the Los Muertos and Las Acequias bones that had been deposited in June with Billings's museum. Cushing requested that ten Kate be permitted to select specimens for display at the Berlin Congress and then permanent deposit at Bastian's museum. Billings refused, arguing that the collection was now in the care of the Army Museum, had not yet been properly studied, and in any case should remain intact. He did offer to release select items for display at the Congress with the understanding that they return to Washington.

Cushing chose vigorously to assert himself against Billings. He thereby drew his patron directly into the dispute, since Billings's superior, Secretary of War William C. Endicott (1826–1900), was a native of Salem and a close personal friend of Hemenway—who meticulously avoided publicity and conflict. The matter dragged on for weeks into the fall, involving accusations of favoring "German science" over American, leaving bitter tastes all around, and further raising questions about Cushing's leadership judgment.[217]

Hodge was intimately engaged, at least scriptorially, in all these complications. What did he think of them, his boss, the expedition's future? Toggling between his cold Camp Cibola tent and the nearby Cushing house, Hodge took dictation and copied for hours on end, even as he oversaw the excavations beneath and around the house.[218] Collections of skeletons and their accompaniments had become Cushing's overriding goal; his "collections with souls" had become justification for excessive expenditures and even personnel decisions. But Cushing, now exhausted and sick, was becoming uncharacteristically testy. With his usual enthusiasm he could report to Mrs. Hemenway at the end of September the unearthing of "something like more than four hundred really perfect specimens, many of them very rare and almost priceless," along with, he said, his equally valuable facts about them.[219] However, the persistent questioning of his judgment wore on him, and after only two months back in the field from the Pacific Coast, he requested a personal conference in Massachusetts. He proposed a one- or two-week absence to sort out misunderstandings; overwhelmed and discouraged, he needed a face-to-face meeting with the patron.

Still, even while preparing to leave the field for the East Coast Cushing welcomed Bandelier to Zuni for a visit (October 5–13). It would be their last meeting. The expedition's historian joined Cushing and Husher at El Morro (A'ts'ina, Inscription Rock), where he copied inscriptions for a day; with Emily he visited Hawikku, twelve miles southwest of the pueblo, where Husher photographed; and he and Frank compared notes on possible identities of the ancestral "Cibola" ruins. Some months before, Cushing had decided to excavate at Heshotauthla (Heshotathluptsina), a ruin twelve miles east of the pueblo, as part of what he considered would be, along with Halona:wan, the expedition's "preliminary work" at Zuni.[220] Seeking a "place where uninterrupted work may be done during my absence," the director now instructed Ramon Castro to establish a side-camp there.[221] From the base in Halona, Hodge was to exercise weekly oversight of the Heshotauthla work during Cushing's absence.[222] Margaret would, as usual, sketch the artifacts as they emerged—as well as Zuni scenes. Frank and

Emily left for Massachusetts on October 20; work began at Heshotauthla four days later.

Crisis and Collapse: November 1888–May 1889

Cushing never returned to the Southwest. His departure with Emily set in motion the final, disarranged phase of the Hemenway Expedition: six months of questionable decisions, misunderstandings, and recriminations for which Hodge was partially responsible. Even sixty-eight years later, in the final days of his life, Hodge was silent about this period. As he tersely told an interviewer: "It is just as well not to make public just why the expedition came to an end."[223] Why? What happened?

As we have seen, pressures and doubts had been building for some time. In August Baxter had asked Cushing for a realistic budget for finishing up the expedition's work by the spring of 1889—"in order to have the undertaking well rounded out as a scientific unit; that is, in its 'Southwestern' aspect." His request was the result of meetings at the Hemenway estate in Manchester to discuss the finances and direction of the expedition.[224] Costs had been running at three thousand dollars a month (sixty thousand dollars today), and Cushing projected at least the same for the fall. But Baxter's personal attachment to Cushing made him a poor messenger. Struggling for delicate phrasing, the home secretary managed to suggest both a possible end to the expedition and the ambitious extension that Cushing sought:

> [The southwestern work] would be but a starting point for carrying out lines of research in other equally important directions, but the work in the Southwest would, as you have said, be something complete in itself, while, at the same time, the ensuing investigations would be necessarily under them, for it is a work that, so far as we can see, knows no end. The latter will, of course, in some way be taken care of when the time comes, but the task now before us is to make the first section a definite block in itself and arrange accordingly.[225]

"Arrange accordingly"—perhaps Baxter's ambiguity reflected the board's uncertainty, but it also allowed Cushing to presume that a flying personal visit to Hemenway would open the way for expanding the expedition to

Mexico and South America, as he had long mulled. The Berlin paper would also serve, he hopefully imagined, as a persuasive appeal to the Hemenway circle for his larger hemispheric vision.[226] And he would be able personally to resolve the unfortunate Billings matter and to review the Salt-Gila River collections then being unpacked in a temporary storage structure on the Salem property. Hodge, Gaston, and Husher could oversee the work at Heshotauthla.

Once again, events mismatched Cushing's intentions. The Halona catalog closed out just before he left, and the crew's attention turned to Heshotauthla while Garlick managed the Halona house construction. As a cold November deepened, the Castro brothers and their men, working largely under Gaston's direction, unearthed some 135 skeletons (although Hodge indicated more to Cushing—"as well as some of the finest pottery the collections contain!"). After his weekly visits from Halona, Hodge reported back to Cushing with enthusiastic descriptions of individual artifacts; eventually he made a large map indicating the excavated areas, though without indicating the positions of individual graves.[227] Despite cold and poor winter light in the house, Margaret made dozens of artifact sketches, which Hodge forwarded eastward.[228] Gaston oversaw the dig and kept the Heshotauthla catalog; the last entries were made on December 14, just before he resigned and returned to Illinois.[229] The Heshotauthla camp broke up in January 1889.[230]

Hurrying to return to the East for what he assumed would be a brief absence, Cushing had left field leadership unclear. Unlike the division of responsibilities between Hodge and Garlick the previous year, this time there were apparently verbal understandings rather than written instructions. Jesse Fewkes, writing twenty years later, maintained that Cushing "assigned the continuation" of the expedition to Hodge, with Gaston "in immediate charge of the laboring force."[231] He also maintained that Hodge submitted "full reports of the progress of the work" to Cushing until "snows forced abandonment" of the expedition; he made no mention of Garlick.[232] But in 1931, in accounting to Emil Haury for the disordered condition of the Zuni collections (by then at the Peabody Museum), Hodge threw blame on Garlick with particularly unflattering words:

> Under Cushing's direction all the collections from the Zuñi sites were in charge of Charles A. Garlick, a kind of camp foreman, who paid little

> attention to them even when sober. Whether there was more of a mixup when Garlick packed the collections for shipment, I cannot say; but I well recall that in packing the skeletal material for shipment to Washington, he did not hesitate to discard any bones that did not readily go in the cases.[233]

The crisis came in the last month of 1888, and it directly involved Hodge. Disappointed at the lack of the promised darkroom, Husher decided to take a photographic trip to Mexico City; Hodge wanted to go along, and asked Cushing's permission. In the last week of November—which was marked by a violent, weeklong snowstorm at Zuni—Cushing telegraphed his approval, and the two men began arranging for a departure on Sunday, December 9. Hodge calculated that, with payments to creditors and workers plus his own expenses, he would need an extra $1,000. For two days he chased Cushing from Massachusetts to New York to Washington with telegrams requesting the funds—then withdrew them anyway from First National Bank in Albuquerque and left for Mexico City. The result was a $1,200 overdraft of the Hemenway account—and deep consternation among the board of directors. Cushing attributed it at the time to purchases of grain and hay for the winter months, but an accounting would clearly be necessary.[234]

Husher and Hodge's three-week Mexico jaunt was a fiasco. Mexican customs held hostage Husher's blank photographic plates; both men then spent days in bed with gastrointestinal misery before visiting Teotihuacán. Hodge bravely claimed to be laying the groundwork for the presumed extension of the expedition to Mexico. He wrote that he saw architectural similarities to Los Muertos, and returned with some purchased potteries and hasty pyramid measurements.[235] Unaware of the financial upset, the two travelers returned to Zuni on December 30 with terrible colds. Hodge was in bed on Halona Hill for two weeks. It had been a costly, helter-skelter trip.

Frank and Emily spent much of November and December either at Hemenway's country home in Milton or the Mt. Vernon Street house in Boston. (They also traveled to Washington to see Emily's family.) Frank visited the collections, which were in temporary storage at Salem under the care of Morse. There is no evidence he lectured; he was ill much of the time. Calendar year 1888 ended with the Cushings in Boston, Margaret and Fred huddled at the unfinished Halona house, and the fieldwork stalled.

Annus Horribilis: 1889

At the turn of the year Cushing wrote in his diary: "Had stormy time this morning (but friendly) in readjustment of Expedition affairs. Most dreadful and nearly fatal experience I ever had. Will have to retrench and ultimately withdraw—I fear."[236]

The Hemenway board ("the Association") now seriously tightened control. They informed Cushing that he would have to cut back monthly expenditures by half, to $1,500. Hemenway told him he could not return to the Southwest for at least two or three months—among other things, she needed him to lobby in Washington for protecting the Casa Grande ruin.[237] In a telling blow, Baxter was removed from the board and replaced by Katherine H. Stone, Hemenway's personal secretary.[238] Most significantly, the board insisted that in Cushing's absence Charles Garlick be named acting field director with responsibility for all business and field operations. Hodge, no longer considered financially trustworthy, was to be sidelined pending a thorough examination of the account books. Cushing's New Year's Day letter to his mother recited the "hard work, hard thinking, hard (in the sense of painful) health" that burdened him and would keep him in the East for the foreseeable future.[239] To Hemenway he pleaded that while his scientific work, he trusted, was satisfactory to her, only his administration of the expedition was not:

> While this has been due perhaps, to the fact that I have looked rather *to results and Scientific methods,* than to *current affairs and business methods* (for which latter I humbly and always acknowledge my lack of qualification), still the outcome is none the less to be deplored!

Still, he insisted, his intentions and actions were always honorable and "justifiable."[240]

For six weeks Cushing did not tell Hodge of Garlick's appointment. Noticing but not understanding his new title, Don Carlos reminded Cushing that he had been "only foreman of part of the force, teamsters and Mechanics and laborers about the [Halona] house," and knew nothing of the financial affairs.[241] In the meantime, at Cushing's prodding Hodge began examining accounts going back to the preceding September. Even as the

Heshotauthla camp broke up and the Castro brothers and other workers dispersed, Hodge anticipated Cushing's return and proposed maintaining a staff of about fifteen and basic expenses of about $1,000 per month.

The pressure for financial clarification intensified. Dispatched to Washington to lobby for Mrs. Hemenway's appeal to Congress for Casa Grande, Cushing turned more insistently to Hodge for a report.[242] He assured Hemenway that "none of us has the slightest cause for worry," and added that he was tired of hearing about it:

> I have been *very* plain with Mr. Hodge about this matter, and I know that in his present statements of the case, he is to be *implicitly trusted*. . . . Further allusion to this topic—which has been the bane of my existence during the past two months and the cause of much of my illness,—will be (most) disastrous to the *work*, and to me![243]

Cushing was engaged in lobbying—even meeting with President Grover Cleveland in the White House—and yet frequently prostrate and bedridden in Washington's Arlington Hotel. Finally in mid-February he told Hodge of Garlick's appointment, assuring him that the expedition would be "well grounded in his hands." Then he spelled out the situation to Garlick:

> I do not think that either you or Mr. Hodge seems to understand that you have been appointed, during my absence, to fulfill, so far as may be, my place; in other words, that the designation by which I have addressed you . . . as "Acting Field Director of the Expedition" has had a *functional* as well as a nominal significance. It is and has been for some time the desire of Mrs. Hemenway and her chief advisors that you have absolute control of matters.

It had been impossible, he added, to do other than acquiesce in the decision—which was made "independently of my influence." In short, Don Carlos was "now wholly in charge."[244] However, there was no reason for anxiety, Cushing separately assured Bandelier, Husher, Hodge, and Garlick: he would soon return and the expedition would resume in a matter of weeks.

Alas, it was a brave delusion. Cushing's health, precarious all winter, now began a dangerous downward spiral; in March he moved from the Arlington

Hotel to Garfield Memorial Hospital in northwest Washington.[245] There he would remain for three months, undergoing harsh treatments to expel the tapeworm as well as cosmetic work on his ravaged face.[246]

Unfortunately Hodge's accounting review turned out badly, and then he compounded the errors. Expecting mild discrepancies easily resolved, he was shocked to find unaccounted expenditures of more than five thousand dollars over four months (September–December 1888) from total deposits by Hemenway of slightly more than sixteen thousand dollars. To Cushing he proposed a drastic and dishonest move: "I can see no other way out of the difficulty than by framing labor-vouchers which will make each month's payroll amount to something like seventy employees—a very large number you will readily see."[247] In this letter (marked "Personal") Hodge also argued that the overdraft of early December was due not to him but to the "grossest inadvertence" and negligence of the Albuquerque bank. If he was seeking Cushing's support or acquiescence, he did not receive it. We do not know Cushing's immediate response, but he was deeply disturbed by Hodge's behavior—and by Maggie's growing estrangement from him in support of her fiancé.

Fred and Margaret resigned from the Hemenway Expedition in early March. Confined in the Washington hospital and restricted (by Emily) from reading his mail, Cushing apparently did not see their letters for several weeks. When he did respond, he wrote first to Margaret—his little sister Ikina. In sadness and self-defense (and self-pity) he reminded Maggie that he had acquiesced in her decision to marry Hodge—"one of my own saddest days"—"mainly by thought for *you*," then proceeded to explain the measures he had been compelled to take. Among other things, he explained, Hodge had misconstrued his demand for an accounting: "he was led to imagine (he should have known me better) that I wanted a lot of fictitious vouchers." Hodge's delay in acting had then led to a second investigation, and ultimately to Garlick's appointment. "In all this *I* erred in judgement—as I always do, *on the side of others,*—each and all of whom have misinterpreted me." Hodge, too, had wrongly supposed "all sorts of accusations" by Cushing against him, which, Cushing insisted, never happened. Finally Hodge resigned—in Cushing's eyes a cowardly act. "And in all this, you, little sister, forgetting everything—your *mother*, sisters, your and Mr. Hodge's joint futures, and—well, never mind about me, for that don't matter,—*have encouraged him!*"

Nonetheless, Cushing concluded to his sister-in-law, he had worked to get permanent appointments for her and Hodge on what he still assumed would be the resumption of the expedition. He insisted that he had always worked on her behalf:

> I gained, too, golden opinions of you everywhere this winter, and framed many plans for helping both you and Mr. Hodge; for, although I may be in little things all that is unlovely, in the greater and truer relations and duties of life I have always tried to be as honest[,] kind and good as I could. . . . I want (believe me) only to defend you and Mr. Hodge, for you have both shown yourselves in need of my concern.[248]

The following day Cushing's tone with Hodge was severe. Responding point by point to the letter of resignation (unfortunately since lost), Cushing took Hodge to task for his pettiness, mean-spiritedness toward Garlick, and arrogance. Hodge and Margaret had complained over the previous year that he was not receiving proper recognition for his topographic and observational skills. Cushing dismissed the complaint, reminding him:

> You seem not to remember . . . I called you to me one evening last autumn, and requested you to prepare under your own name a descriptive paper relative to the House & Temple ruins of the Salado, to accompany your maps & field-notes and to be brought out in Bulletin form. . . . There has as yet been no Official Report of the Expedition printed in any form. Who then has dealt injustice to you . . . ? Have you finished recopying those of the maps as you said you wished to do? Have you finished the General Map of Los Muertos? Have you written the paper I instructed you to prepare to accompany all these?

Hodge had complained, too, about his salary ($1,200 the first year, $1,600 the second), to which Cushing responded that it was more than he deserved: "The man who gets that salary is without the slightest injustice to you or reflection on you, a far better Secretary than you are." And then Cushing got to the most sensitive point: the engagement to Maggie. He deeply resented the arrogance and effrontery of his future brother-in-law:

> It is because of your inability to discern such things that I did not—at first—want you to marry my sister. I told you so, when you failed to recognize that it had been my right to expect your confidence in that matter and, when you refused to acknowledge [it] yourself, answered me that you were that which has humbled most of the "Kings of men" before your day! It is because of this same characteristic manifested in other directions, that I have not advanced you to the position which else, your abilities, your integrity and conscientiousness, would have led me to make you *my equal* as regards the Expedition personnel.[249]

Hodge and Cushing both knew they were facing possible disgrace. To young and ambitious men of modest origins and marginal resources, being accused of financial mismanagement or, worse, dishonesty—especially in the eyes of wealthy patrons—was almost too much to bear. "I plainly see now that I am held in some dishonor," Cushing confessed to Baxter.[250] As his health declined through a dismal April and May, Cushing still hoped to revisit Zuni to straighten out affairs, resume fieldwork, and redeem himself, but he also began dreaming of retreat and recuperation at the family homestead in northwestern New York. He longed for the family farm at Barre Center, writing wistfully to his father from the hospital bed: "I see you and mother in the old woods; see the blue rapid smoke shooting, then eddying upward from the burning brush . . . and listen with you to the frogs, jumping into wood-stained pools of our old-fashioned spring-time."[251] He and Emily began the paperwork to mortgage their Washington home to pay off the five-thousand-dollar Hemenway debt, for which he felt acutely responsible. He heard that Hodge had accused him of "criminal dishonesty"; he in turn attributed the humiliating situation to the mistakes of his "foolish secretary." Reflecting the uncertainty of this period, on the first of May Cushing announced to his Boston friend Brooks Adams that "I've cut (or am cutting, temporarily) the ropes of the Expedition tent and shall go to my father's home until better."[252] But he held on.

Cushing had no intimation that Mary Hemenway was also seriously ill. Facing the diabetes that would kill her in five years, she was confined and protected from upset by a watchful circle of family and friends.[253] Her son Augustus, while disgusted at the financial mess, was equally concerned for his mother's health and her reputation as a generous and astute philanthropist. In respectable Boston circles there was beginning to be talk of her scientific gullibility, especially among those, such as Harvard's Charles Eliot Norton (1827–1908), whose eyebrows already arched at the mention of American archaeology. In April Norton's friend Henry W. Haynes (1831–1912), a widely admired professor of Greek and Latin and an archaeological enthusiast with particular interest in the Southwest, was writing an annual review of American archaeology for Norton's Archaeological Institute of America. Though restrained in print, Haynes privately shared with Norton his concerns about "the barrenness of American archaeology & the foolishness of American archaeologists"—and of the Hemenway Expedition in particular:

> Mrs. Hemenway thinks she is doing a valuable service to the cause of American science, & that great benefit will accrue to mankind from her generosity, which I think is being d[amnabl]y abused. . . . Certainly, there has been "great cry and little wool" about the Hemenway Expedition.[254]

Augustus decided to act. The preceding November his mother's close friend, Martha LeBaron Goddard (1829–88), an adviser on the board, had died.[255] Augustus now filled the vacancy with a former Harvard classmate. Jesse Walter Fewkes (1850–1930) had no experience in any field of anthropology, and he had only briefly traveled by train through the Southwest in the spring of 1887. But he was a fellow native of Essex County who was recently widowed, and the Hemenway mother and son had previously underwritten his research in marine biology. Fewkes was also in the midst of a bitter, damaging professional crisis with Alexander Agassiz of Harvard's Museum of Comparative Zoology.[256]

Fewkes's addition to the board began a chaotic month for the Cushings. Having decided to close up Cushing's fieldwork by July 1, Augustus Hemenway sent Fewkes to Washington to confer with Cushing. At one point he even suggested that they return to Zuni together. The night before he and Fewkes met for the first time, Cushing scrabbled together a memorandum of explanations and points for Fewkes. The memo reads in spots like delirium:

Then I went to Tiffanys where, as fasteners for my often lost pocket-book and other little things, I bought the silver chains you see on my table.

You *must* go with me when I am well enough, to the S. W., to see and attest correctness of *my* vouchers and proceedings. Meanwhile will make mortgage spoken of, then deposit to acct Hemenway, the $4823.

By this and other things it was again supposed I was trying to "play into the hands of the Bureau of Ethnology." Have I? Ask the Bureau! It has been supposed I was down here in Washington "playing sick," and (Bureau again) forgetting the Exped. When that worry anxiety about the Exped. was the one thing breaking me down and making me sicker until I am at last almost a mono-thoughtologist—when not so ravingly and alternately, Quijotic or furiously yet futilely indignat that any one of the things should have been tho't of me[.][257]

At the bottom of the sheet Cushing drew a picture of his impossible situation—his "Gordian Knot."

Unaware of Cushing's dire state, Hemenway adviser William T. Harris was writing to him with an outline for a series of reports—the first of many such exhortations from Harris over the next four years. With her husband too ill to write or even read, an exhausted Emily nursed Frank around the clock and dealt with the Hemenway circle, Garlick, and the banks. On June 15 Baxter reported to Horsford that the situation with Cushing was "most disturbing, and with anyone else I should despair, but his will is so strong, and his vitality so great, that I still have confidence that he will come around all right and carry through his work."[258] But the same day on which Baxter wrote these confident words, without warning, Augustus Hemenway ended the Cushing expedition: he appointed Fewkes as the new director. Fewkes left immediately, alone, for Zuni.

Cushing was utterly crushed and confounded, but it was Emily who was left to express to faithful Don Carlos Garlick her deep despair:

No doubt you know by this time all that has happened. That the Expedition is broken up and Mr. Cushing is no longer its director. It all came of Mr. Hodge's failing for so long, in spite of repeated letters and telegrams, to send in the accounts, and, when they were at last sent, his mention of five thousand dollars deficit (possible) frightened Mr. Hemenway and determined him to put a stop to the whole affair. . . .

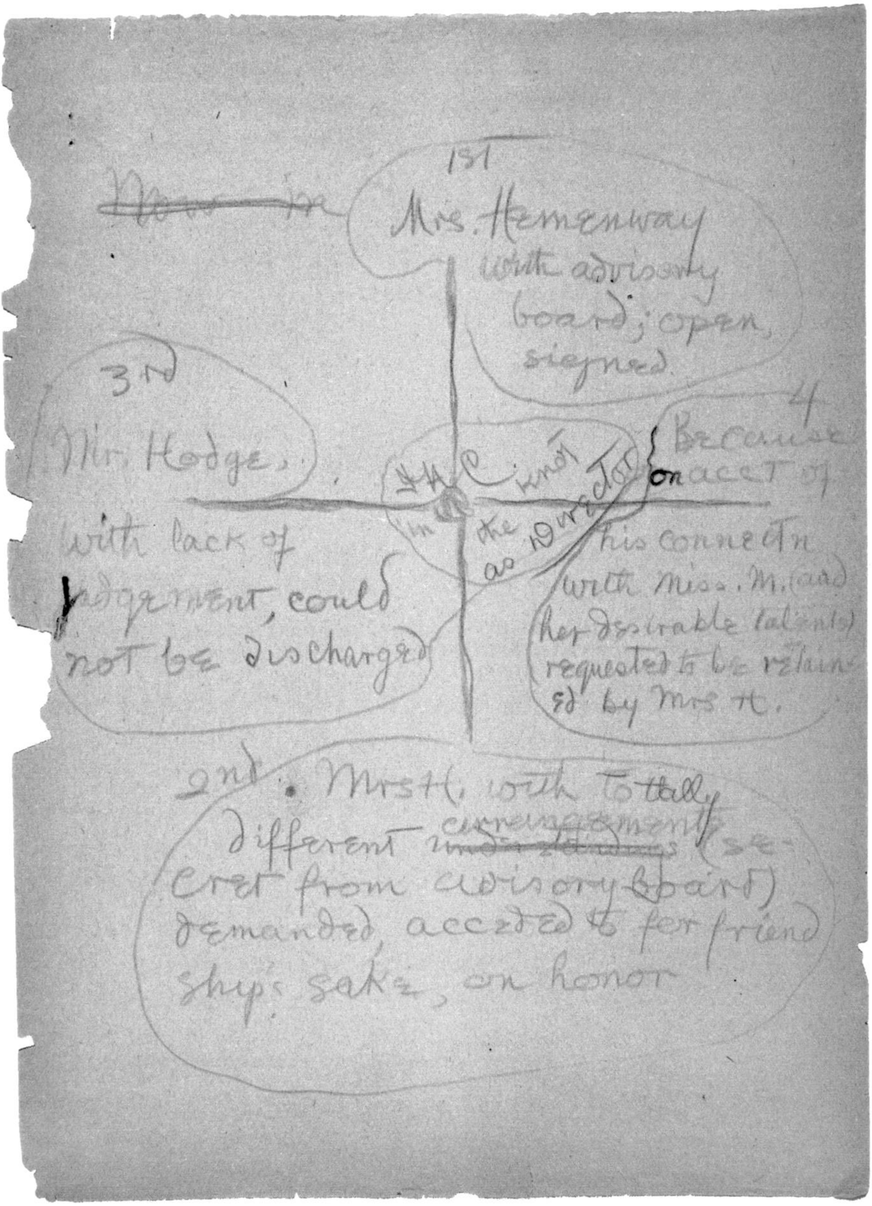

Figure 19. The "Gordian Knot." Cushing Memorandum of 10 May 1889. Courtesy of the Braun Research Library Collection, Autry Museum, Los Angeles; Cushing Collection MS 6, HAE 1.18.

Mr. Hemenway has behaved (to put it *mildly*) with great lack of consideration and official courtesy, and it is due almost entirely to his letters that Mr. Cushing has been ill so long. While he was too ill to leave his bed or to even eat . . . they urged him to go to Zuñi, and now that he has had himself patched up sufficiently to be moved, and had arranged to leave today, they suddenly change their minds, and refuse to defray the cost of the trip. So it must be given up, and Mr. Cushing is made too ill by it to write you as he wished, or even to dictate to me. . . .

My love to you and your daughter. I hope neither of you may ever know anything so hard as the last five months have been to me.[259]

Epilogue

With the breakup of Cushing's Hemenway Expedition, Edwin Husher packed away his ethnologic dreams and set off to photograph Alaska. Bandelier, chiefly concerned as always for his own livelihood in Santa Fe, arranged separately to continue his historical work for a few more months—although he was privately scathing in his judgment of the Hemenway group: "The Lord preserve me from scientific enterprises patronized by old women," he expostulated to Norton. "Never in my life have I seen such people. They simply don't know what they want. I am really glad to get rid of them."[260] At the same time he told Washington Matthews that Cushing should have listened to him:

> I do not wish to be interpreted as "kicking" now after Cushing's downfall, since I directed his attention repeatedly to what I considered weak points in the work performed [in Salt River Valley]. Those remarks were not heeded, and I was even signified, in a polite manner, to "shut up." Again I was assured that everything had been done systematically, whereas the contrary was the case. To anybody but YOU, who are Frank's friend, I would not breathe a word now, but to YOU it is safe to mention such things, as they will not hurt the poor fellow.[261]

Garlick spent the next year negotiating with Fewkes and the Hemenway board over the ownership and disposition of property (both the expedition's and the Cushings'), seeking teamster work, and checking in with Emily. In the early nineties he moved into Phoenix with his wife and daughters.

Frank and Emily immediately left Garfield Hospital for a two-and-a-half-year exile of profound despondency and poverty at the Cushing family homestead in western New York State.[262] They would not move permanently back to Washington until the beginning of 1892, when he re-joined the Bureau of Ethnology as assistant ethnologist.

Following their resignations Fred and Margaret left Zuni in June 1889. On the first of July he joined the Bureau of Ethnology as a stenographer—the position that Cushing had arranged for him—while Margaret worked for two years as an artist with the Geological Survey.[263] Late in July Washington Matthews reported to Cushing:

> The "Codfish" is employed in the Bureau. I met him there a day or two ago. He greeted me in a most friendly and engaging manner. It was hard for me to conquer the impulse that seized me . . . but I reflected that if *you* could forgive him and even help him to get employment *I* ought not to snub him. So I returned his smile—a little stiffly perhaps—and shook hands with him.[264]

In early September 1891, after an engagement of more than four years, Margaret Magill and Fred Hodge were married in Washington.[265] Seven months prior, the Magill girls had lost their sister Katie, who died in childbirth; and a few days after Margaret's wedding their mother, Kate Magill, passed away as well. Kate was fifty-three; Katie was thirty-one. In the face of these terrible losses Margaret's wedding was, Emily told Eusebio Molera, "a very sad one."[266] Cushing did not attend.

PART II

The Hemenway Expedition Diaries of Frederick W. Hodge and Margaret W. Magill, 1886–1888

Editorial Note

At the time we transcribed the Hemenway Expedition diaries of Frederick W. Hodge, they were in the Braun Research Library Collection (SWM MS 7, HAE 2.1) of the Southwest Museum in Los Angeles. The museum is now merged with the Autry Museum of the American West, Los Angeles.

After spending several weeks transcribing on site, with permission we photocopied all six volumes of Hodge's diary and completed the transcription back in Flagstaff. Hodge's handwriting reflects his rapid stenographic style: the words are clear and flow into one another. Reading it was a pleasure. After transcription and digitization we began annotating the diaries. We correlated the letters mentioned in the diaries with the nine volumes of letter press books of expedition correspondence that had recently (1991) been discovered at the Huntington Free Library in the Bronx, New York. (They are now part of the Hemenway Southwestern Archaeological Expedition Papers, 1886–96, in the Cornell University Library's Rare and Manuscript Collections.) This literary cache approaches five thousand pages, a sizable portion of which Wilcox transcribed. He also created a thorough log of the correspondence, which has been added to the Cornell papers. The pressed letters, both typed and handwritten, were considerably more difficult to read, but generally they matched Hodge's diary record.

The Diaries

Saturday, Dec. 4[1]

Make purchases and final preparations for starting. Go to Baltimore.

Sunday, Dec. 5

Stayed in Balto. all night visiting Ed. Very cold and snowing. Coming up in car receive news of burning of Herzog's opera House. Church in the morning. Dinner at Mrs. Baxter[']s where I remained till nearly 3 o'clock; bidding them "good-bye" go home, pack trunk, call on Mr. and Mrs. Wescott with Em. and afterwards Mr. and Mrs. Baldion's. After supper I remain home entertaining in part Mr. & Mrs. Westcott who called and spent the evening with Nettie. Houghton also on hand. Clara Ashley and Nettie Ross also call. Take 10 o'clock train for depot. Em.[,] Evelyn[,] Ernst & Nettie W. accompanying me to the depot. Nearly lose my temper at station agent not letting us all pass through. "Only two on a ticket." Read the "Star" until tired when I retire with orders to porter to awake me at Harrisburg. Harrisburg at last—meet Charlie & Anderson. Talk over old times and discuss an oyster stew each. "Good-Bye" once more and the train rolls out of the depot in which I spent 6 hours waiting only 2 weeks before. Terrible nightmare. Were the oysters to blame? Falling over precipices and facing revolvers all night and hollowing to the top of my voice (at least so the porter tells me.) Breakfast at Williamsport, Penna. 7:15. Dinner at Canandaigua, arrived Rochester 2:20 p.m. and Albion N. Y.[2] C. & H. R. R. 5:50 p.m. Monday, Dec. 6—

Monday, Dec. 6.

Met at Albion station by Mr. Cushing. Proceed to residence of Dr. E. L. Cushing.[3] Supper—retire early.

Tuesday, Dec. 7.

Read Wilkie Collins' "Evil Genius"[4] nearly all day.

Wednesday, Dec. morning, wrote to Mother, Nell, Morsell, Crossman & Seltz.[5] Miss McGill,[6] who is to accompany us on the trip[,] took dinner at the Doctor's. My first impressions—lively, brim full of fun, fond of a joke, good talker, splendid company, in general appearance reminds one of Isis McMillan (rather better looking) and I am of the opinion that I shall like her very much. Mr. Cushing calls in the evening, dictates a letter and asks me to call at Coann's.[7] He looks very much played out, having been out shopping with the Indians all day. After supper I call there, meet Mr. & Mrs. Cushing, Miss McGill. Mr. Cushing dictates a long letter[8] when I return home and again retire early.

Thursday, Dec. 9

Write up notes, go to Coann's for more dictation from Mr. C.[,] which I also write[9] and return to Coann's for his signature. He is napping—Won't have him awakened so I return and write again. Mr. C. calls in the afternoon with the letter signed. Go to depot to meet Mr. C's father[10]—Return to supper after which I continue to read Wilkie Collins and listen to an entertainment by Oscar and "Loey" Ladd. Retire at 10:00.

Friday, Dec. 10

Spend the day at the Doctor's in writing to Ashley, Andy McClure, & Tingley & in finishing "Evil Genius." Mr. Cushing called in the evening and dictated a long letter[,] which I transcribed and mailed.[11] Retired at 10:00.

Saturday, Dec. 11

Everything points to our moving out on Monday for the trip to the Southwest. Will be glad of it, as it is rather tiresome here with nothing particular to do, save an occasional letter to write. Read all day; Mr. Ladd brought in letter from Nell which I read and answered with an 18-page letter after lunch. Had scarcely finished when Mr. Cushing came and I spent about 3 hours in town with him making final arrangements and completing the settling up of local merchants' bills. Got back in time for supper, after which I read and chatted till 11 o'clk.

Sunday, Dec. 12

A mean cloudy day. Was going to church in the morning but packed condensed milk for shipment early Monday morning instead. Not a very nice Sabbath task to be sure, but as I whistled Methodist hymns as an accompanyment to my hammering, my conscience did not smite me. Was going to church in the evening but stayed in and read instead, and at 11 o'clock ate a lunch and retired.

Monday, Dec. 13

Up at 6:40, finished packing milk and my valise and trunk. Went to express office to ship goods to Albuquerque and Washington and to post office where I rec'd letters from Em. and Crossman. Sent trunks to depot and rode down with the 3 Indians. We took the 11:00 train and were off for Zuñi! The trip during the remainder of the day was very enjoyable. The Indians are very amusing and were the centre of attraction during the whole day—some stared at them as though they were inhabitants of another world, while others, whose knowledges were less limited gave them the credit of residing on this sphere. At one station where a stop was made an individual of rather uncouth appearance peered in the door and exclaimed "them must be Indians" with a decided emphasis on the initial letter. I am very much pleased with the Indians[;] indeed, I can sit and devour their droll ways and broad grins by the hour. At night we had *two* stories—one by Wai-hu-si-wa[12] and the other by He-lu-ta.[13] Wa-hu-si-wa's story was about two gods who enticed a number of children to play with them—These gods were of giant strength, and upon arriving at a place where a number of cottonwood trees grew, they took hold of a limb and pulled it gently at first until the topmost branch of the tree was reached—They then told the children to hold on and they would give them a wonderful ride in the air. So they all grasped the tree and were beginning to enjoy swinging up & down when the gods very suddenly loosened their hold on the tree & the children were shot into the air with lightning-like velocity. Their cries were very pitiful and the sounds they made have been ever since thought by the Zuñis to be the crying of "Macmillan's jay." The other folk-tale, which was by He-lu-ta was about the origin of the numerous holes which appear in some of the cliffs near Zuñi. In olden times mice used to frequent the place in large numbers and bored holes in the crevices of the rocks or in the earth. One day one little mouse was busily engaged in digging away when a swallow, which was watching for an opportunity from above, pounced upon the mouse and was about to bear him off when he loudly cried: "Oh, please let me go, and I will give you the turquoise bracelets which I have on my front legs." "Oh," replied the swallow, "have you got bracelets on your fore-legs?" and with the words loosened his hold upon the mouse. He had no sooner released him than he scampered off to the nearest hole, the swallow after him. He had just reached the hole when the swallow grasped him with his beak by the tail, stripping it entirely of fur and skin except on the extreme end. The mouse fortunately escaped, however, and informed the other mice what a narrow escape he had had—The mice, whenever they were at work, used to sing "Dig your cellar", ["]Dig your cellar" "Dig your cellar" "Dig your cellar" and then run away, making a pattering noise with their tiny feet—(which the Indian imitated by saying "t't't't't't't't.["]) The mice which had never had any experience with the swallow were rather loathe to believe the story of the mouse who had been so rudely dealt with. So while at work once more the swallow pounced down for a second time and took his prey off into the air. The mice were very much frightened at this occurrence and soon after abandoned their favorite resort, leaving nothing behind save its "cellars" which they had dug. The descendents of the mouse who first encountered the swallow were all with long fore-legs and without hair on their tails except a little tuft on the tip. This is the origin of the jumping-mouse which frequents that locality as well as the holes which his ancestors inhabited.

After chatting a short while longer we had our berths made up and went to snoozing.

Tuesday, Dec. 14

Breakfast in dining car—Arrived in Chicago at 8:10 Took Indians to hotel made transportation arrangements with C. B. & W. R.R. met Mr. Masson the Gen. Pass. Agent—made a good many purchases in the city, going over rounds in a carriage. Checked baggage again and were off for Kansas City on the C. B. & W. Road at 12:00 p.m. Cold and snowing. (If any of my friends ever visit Chicago, don't fail to see & hear the "usher" in the Grand Central depot. Just "get on" to the way he pronounces Joliet (Jollyette) and his "musical" voice is worth listening to & laughing at—) Dinner on train (best meal yet.) A big blizzard raging—the snow seeming to fall horizontally—Stopped at Galesburg for an hour and in leaving dining-car found our sleeper, Indians &c &c all mixed up on another track. A jolly crowd of gentlemen on board today—Mr. Cushing meets Mr. Watson,[14] son of one of the directors of the road & nephew of the vice-pres't. I met a Mr. Holabird whose father is in the army—well acquainted with Col. Stevenson.[15] They were all very much interested in our aborigine friends and kept us busy in explaining their customs, traits etc. Retire at 10:00 in drawing-room sleeper "Laclede".

Wednesday, Dec. 15

Breakfast on dining-car. Arrive at Kansas City about 8:30—Skirmish around in a very lively manner in re-checking baggage, recurring tickets etc. etc.—Of all the little "hells on earth" give me Kansas City. Take sleeper "Raton" at 10:40 for Albuquerque on the A. T. & S. Fe road—Dinner at Topeka at 1:00 p.m. Wanted badly to call on Howard Brown, Wally Baxter's cousin, but a sick man (Mr. Cushing) on hand. Ladies, Indians, baggage &c. &c. to look after & 20 minutes to stop & do it all was rather out of the question. Fine country is Kansas—level as a billiard-table and miles and miles of corn (stalk) fields. Supper at Florence about 6 o'clock—Wai-hu-se-wa sings in the smoking-room to the top of his voice. Compare notes with Miss Magill after which Wai-hu-se-wa tells another folk-tale—a race story. Retire at 10 o'clock.

Thursday, Dec.16

Fairly good night's rest. Whole party awake with head colds in one form or another—myself with a slightly sore throat. Wild western "scenery" one wide barren plain as far as the eye can reach—Up with the sun. Breakfast at La Junta, Colorado. We soon arrive in sight of the Pikes' Peaks whose snow white prominences form beautiful scenery, so the long monotony of barren plains to which we have now become so accustomed. We are making an up grade of from 100 to 160 feet per mile and by the time we arrive at Raton will have attained an altitude of 12,000 feet. The ground is now covered with snow while this morning not a sign of it was to have been seen. We got out at Hatcher and take a walk—Miss Magill scrambles to get aboard in time. Wai-hu-se-wa has a time with a bleeding nose. Spanish Peaks are now in sight. The atmosphere is so clear that they seem scarcely more than a few miles away, while they are really a great distance. We soon came in view of Fisher's Peak, a huge mass of table-like rock 15,000 feet above sea level & 14 miles from Trinidad. It appears to be but a few feet across the top, but it is 15 acres in open! Mexican mud houses are everywhere about us and I am tempted to believe that we are at Zuñi already. A huge pile to our left is called "Simpson's Rest" named after a man of that name, whose remains repose on its summit, thousands of feet above sea-level—We arrive at Trinidad—quite a thriving place—sombreros decidedly stylish. An hour or two later and we pass decisively through the mountains and at such a clear rate—with two locomotives—that it would not be difficult to keep up with the train for quite a distance at an ordinary running gait. We disembark at Raton for dinner, after which I was chimmed almost to death by an old granger who was death on star-routers and land-grabbers.[16] He told me that no one in the vicinity was without his Winchester & all the law-breakers must "git up and git[.]" Ate my first pinons here in the West purchasing them from a Mexican vendor. The old man also told me that Bob Ingersoll had a log-cabin built in most exquisite style for which he paid his contractor $10,000 and that Stephen W. Dorsey[17] had a "little farm" of 80 × 50 miles square—After leaving Raton we made very fast time, running at a rate of 50 to 60 miles an hour for several hours. Pala-wha-te-wa[18] gives his last night's experience in getting up to take a smoke and in returning getting into the wrong berth in which there was a lady—much to the amusement of Mr. Cushing and to myself after its translation—A most gorgeous sunset this evening. The day seemed inflamed from horizon to horizon—Dinner at Las Vegas. To bed at 10 o'clock.

Friday, Dec. 17

Up at 2:30 dressed and washed "smashed" baggage—went to smoking room where I found Mr. Cushing and Prof. Bandelier[19] chatting and smoking. Prof. B. is historian of the party and is very witty—He gave me what encouragement he could concerning New Mexico, and especially Albuquerque. He gave tin cans and beer bottles as the natural resources of the region from an agricultural standpoint and informed Mr. C. of the whereabouts of several old Wingate[20] friends about whom Mr. C. was very anxious to learn. We arrived in Albuquerque about 3 o'clock and proceeded to a hotel where accomodations for the party were wanting. Going to the Girard House we were safely installed in comfortable quarters. Prof. B. and myself bedded together and he kept me awake spinning yarns until nearly 5 o'clock.[21] Up at 9:15—breakfast. Shave—post office (found letter from Seltz). Wrote letter home. Stayed in hotel most of the day except when doing errands and shopping. Mr. Cushing and myself (anon followed by Wai-hu-se-wa and He-lu-ta) made arrangements with several local merchants towards the purchase of outfitting supplies while in the field. Upon returning to the hotel McNabb was there in an intoxicated condition. We went to the dining-room and filled one table with the exception of one seat which was very soon occupied by McN. He immediately commenced his drunken harangue during the course of which the Indian question, politics and his own eventful career were fully discussed between the "hics." It soon became necessary to remove the ladies to another table and they were soon followed by the "Governor" who could stand his jeers no longer. It looked very bad for a while and his ravings were all the more bloody when he told of the number of outlaws he had killed, and informed us of the whereabouts of others—After supper Mrs. Cushing, Miss McGill and myself called on Mrs. Simmons at the Hotel Armigo where we met Mr. [J. W.] Donnelly, wife and daughter. Mr. Donnelly was formerly Chief Accountant of the Gen'l. Land Office at Washington and it only needed a gentle reminder for him to recognize me. We stayed a short while when we returned with Miss Donnelly to the Grand, as she was very anxious to see the Indians. Miss McGill and myself accompanied her back. I retired at 9 o'clock.

I will not attempt to give my impressions of Albuquerque now. I like the town better than I thought I would, but I have seen so little of the "ins and outs" that I fear an injustice would be done the old town were I to say anything here. Mr. Cushing informs me that rarely a day passes but what a murder is committed.

Saturday, Dec. 18

Mr. Cushing awakes me at 2:20 a.m. in order to take the 3:30 train for Wingate. Prof. Bandelier I learn has already gone to Santa Fé. We take a bus and are soon aboard a sleeper ("Cuba"), the Indians however are assigned to a chair car, which they much prefer, as, strange to say, they have a peculiar dread of a sleeper. Bunked in about 4 a.m. & to-sleep with part of clothing on in "three shakes" etc. Slept well—awake at 8, up at 9, breakfast at Coolidge, N.M. Arrive at Wingate where we are met by Capt. Waterbury[22] with the ambulance. Drive 3 miles to the Fort where I meet Messrs Woodside[23] and Hoblitzell of Balto.[24] Woodside is sutler, post-master etc. etc. and has an excellent business. Hoblitzell is a notary public and a sort of "general counsel" for the soldiers. Am settled in the house of Mrs. Cleghorn in a room lined with cotton but quite comfortable. Stay all the morning and nearly all the afternoon in Woodside's store with the Indians. Mr. Cushing goes back to the Station after the baggage and succeeds in walking home arriving just at dark. Mrs. C. (who, by the way is stopping with Miss Magill at Mrs. Capt. Waterbury's) feels worried so I start down the road to meet him. I come across him near the corral. Went to the "Officers Club room" with Woodside and read the illustrated papers—saw the names of Stanley Brown,[25] "Jack" Hillers[26] &

Ed Oyster in the club's list of visitors. After supper Hoblitzell and I went for a walk, taking in the quarters of the soldiers which were unusually clean owing to the forthcoming inspection drill tomorrow morning. The men were nearly all busily engaged in cleaning up their arms and uniforms; a few making picture frames by glueing petrified specimens on a base made of wood, and one little party occupied in a game of "7-up" (with chips)—We also went to the reservoir pump-house and made a general round of the reservation. Left him at his rooms at 10:00 and returned to my own sanctum where the three Indians were slumbering together on the floor.

Sunday, Dec. 19

Indians are awake ahead of me, but I don't sleep long before awaking myself at their guttural grunts, and grins. Walk around the grounds and return to breakfast. Meet Hoblizell afterwards when we watch the parade of the band and inspection drills of the infantry and cavalry[,] which were excellently well done—Joined by Mr. Cushing. Captain Waterbury introduces me to the officers and I have quite a chat with Capt. Gilman[27] on Washington—Am liking Fort Wingate immensely—about 400 men here in the garrison and the place exceeds my expectations of yesterday morning, when I first arrived. After dinner went to Woodside's. While there the mail came in—letter from Monsell and a combination from Stough, Bailey and Fowle. Went to Capt. Waterbury's in the afternoon where I met Major Parker[28] and Mr. & Mrs. Fornance.[29] Invited to tea but declined as I promised Mrs. Cleghorn that I would return. Returned to Woodside's after supper where I [had] quite a chat with Hoblitzell—adjourned to adjoining adobe where instrumental music was rendered by a quartette from the infantry band. Got pair of blankets from Woodside (as Indians complained of being cold last night) and returned to Cleghorn's where we sang for a while. When Mr. Cushing arrived went to Capt. Waterbury's (about 8:30) to avoid disturbance and was dictated to for 3 hours; returned about midnight to Cleghorn's where I wrote up my notes, finishing them about 4:30 a.m. when I went to bed.

Monday, Dec. 20

Up at 8 o'clock, feeling "rocky" after my 3 hours sleep. Breakfast at 9:00. Mr. C. calls and we repair to Woodside's store-house to unpack, in part, our trunks for the proposed trip to Zuñi to-day. Completing this, I repack my valise for the journey and await in readiness Mr. C's return. I look like a "cowboy" now, to be sure, with my light sombrero and flannel shirt. A rash of some sort has broken out all over my body. I attribute the cause to the alkali water I have been drinking. It feels anything but pleasant, as it itches constantly and has all the likeness to "prickly heat." Another beautiful day, but a few light clouds in view. Towards afternoon it begins to grow breezy, and by 3 o'clock the air is quite cold. All is in readiness by 3:30 when we pull out from Wingate with our 4-mule ambulance (or rather 3 mules and one horse) in-route to Zuñi. Mrs. C. and Miss Magill remain behind.

We had gone but a short distance when we discovered that our team was anything but the best in the country. Constant whipping was the only thing that would keep them going at a jog-trot, as soon as the lash was spared they would invariably lapse into a provokingly stubborn walk. This made our trip all the more laborious, especially as Mr. Cushing was compelled to drive the greater part of the way, the Indians, although their statement to the contrary, being of little service in driving. From Wingate to Nutria Hill the scenery was beautiful; it being like one grand park through this mountainous region, as far as the eye could reach. We covered about 18 miles before dark, and reached Nutria (about 22 1/2 miles from the Fort) about 9 o'clock—pretty good time even though, considering the miserable animals we had in front of us. We formed our camp on the summit of the mountain and built a huge fire[,] which was exceedingly well enjoyed, as our long ride had chilled us completely. While the Governor was building the camp of "pinon["] boughs, the Indians (Heluta and Wai-hu-se-wa) unhitched and fed the horses and assisted in gathering wood for the fire; Mr. Cushing assuming charge of our culinary department. As soon as the fire had burned sufficiently down to permit the broiling of steak on the hot coals, the supper was soon put in first-class shape for eating, which we all did with a will. Besides Mr. C. special diet of granum and steak, we had: pork and beans, tea, bread, maple-syrup and beef-steak. After putting aside the "dishes" we were all in readiness for turning in. Myself, especially having had so little sleep of late. Mr. C. showed me how to make a camp bed, which I was very willing to learn, as it will doubtless be of great need to me before long. Making a layer of pinon boughs upon the ground, and folding a comforter (letting the fold face the wind) everything was in readiness to crawl in between the folds and cover myself with a red blanket. I slept well all night, awakening only once or twice. The revelation, upon awakening and seeing the starry sky for your ceiling[,] is peculiarly striking.[30]

Tuesday, Dec. 21

I crawled out at 7 o'clock—Mr. Cushing was preparing breakfast in which I soon assisted; the two younger Indians were in search of our mules who had taken a peculiar liking to a certain grass plot 15 minutes walk away, and the "Governor" was busily gathering snow to melt for use at breakfast. After the boys returned with the animals we had our breakfast of substantially the same articles of food that we had last evening for supper, with the addition of onions and baked potatoes. Packed up after breakfast and departed for Zuñi about 10:30. The scenery from Nutria is particularly beautiful. The low valley beneath, surrounded by mountains on all sides formed the most beautiful sight in the way of natural splendor I had ever seen. We got to Zuñi about 5 o'clock, and were received by crowds of natives who ascended to the adobe-tops or flicked about the ambulance in wondering curiosity. Children, children, everywhere some in rags, some in bags and some in neater garments looked on as though an American was a new sight. Mr. C. arrived at the house of his adopted parents and after prayer and the usual greeting I was invited in where I was treated, as I thought, as a special guest. They all arose from the low stone-like elevation that surrounded the room, and some shook hands, and others embraced me. Palo-wah-te-wa brought tobacco, and they all gathered around the open fire-place and began to smoke, which lasted for a quarter of an hour. We then departed and drove around the pueblo to the residence of Mr. Graham, the trader, where we had a very hearty supper of beef-steak, mutton, hot-rolls, fried-potatoes, and tea. As soon as the remainder of the Indians learned of the arrival and whereabouts of Mr. Cushing they commenced to flock in and again the forms of embracing and hand-shaking were indulged in. Mr. Cushing went out to visit his family and engaged in some other ceremony and I soon retired. To-day is the greatest ceremonial day of the year. It is called "the day of the New Year Sun"[31] and is observed by strict fasting for 10 days and also the use of fire is prohibited except indoors on this day; not even smoking or the use of fire-arms being allowed outside. This peculiar ceremony is observed in order that the following summer may be attended by abundant rains, thus insuring large crops and successful cattle-raising—

Wednesday, Dec. 22

Up at 8 o'clock, breakfast at 10:30. A beautiful day. This Zuñi sun makes one feel as bright and cheery as nothing else can. Am feeling as comfortable as possible and my appetite is iron-clad. Everything is good to eat now. I can eat bacon, now for the first time in years, and enjoy it too. Our quarters at Mr. Graham's are nearly always filled with wondering Zuñis, who stare at me while I am now writing with the utmost surprise, as I move my pen rapidly across the paper. In the afternoon we make preparation for our return to Wingate and are soon in our ambulance again, this time without our Indian companions. We have a little better success with our animals this time. Mr. Cushing mounts one of the hinder mules and uses the lash frequently while I hold the reins. We get within 8 or 9 miles of Nutria Hill when we camp and make our fire for supper—No bread! Extra supply of granum satisfies me in lieu of the bread, and bacon and beans fill up the remaining gaps. I retire at midnight.

Thursday, Dec. 23

Pass a good night's rest—it being my second in camp. Up before sunrise, Mr. Cushing away tracing up the mules. Mend my pantaloons while in "bed" and assist in preparing breakfast. Arrange our toilets and pack up to be off at 11:30. Reach the other side of Nutria where we partake of a luncheon at 3:30. While so engaged Mr. Graham, with Indian, rides up on burros having started from Zuñi at 10:00 a.m. in route to Wingate where he takes the train home. Stops with us a moment and is off. We finish our meal and after trying our pistols and the rifle are away again. Reach the Fort about 7:30, cold and tired. Supper at Cleghorn's and to bed at 8:30 or 9:00. Pleasant sleep.

Friday, Dec. 24

Up about half past 8. Am disappointed upon going to the post-office and finding no mail for me. Write to the Snovey boys. Go with Mr. Cushing to [Arthur] Watts' camp near the station to return the wagon and team borrowed for the Zuñi trip (Watts had gone to Albuquerque) with the intention of walking back.[32] The man in charge however drove us back to the Post in a buckboard. There is a ball given by one of the Company's to-night, but instead of going remained in my room and wrote a letter of 9 pages home.

Mr. Cushing called about 9 o'clock with the intention of asking me to go over with him, but he found me in bed. This is the quickest Christmas eve I have ever spent. How different from those old times in Washington with Ashley and the rest of the boys (and girls)!

Saturday, Dec. 25 (Xmas)

Christmas day—and who should ever know it in this out-of-the-way place but for the date it bears! Spend the morning in writing to Nell, from whom I received a letter this morning, together with one from Mother. After dinner (turkey and plum-pudding) I go to Waterbury's in order to get a new supply of stationery from our trunk and see Mrs. C. and Miss Magill for the first time since our departure for Zuñi. Return with Mr. C. who dictates some letters which I transcribe on the "Hammond." Finish writing to Nell and retire early. The slowest Christmas ever known to me. Found a little boy dog on my table to-day, a present from one of the ladies in the house.

Sunday, Dec. 26

Overslept myself this morning. Mr. C calls while I am dressing, and expresses pleasure at my sleeping so well. Copy in part, on "Hammond," very long letter to Mrs. H.[33] and after reading a-while go to bed early again.

Monday, Dec. 27

Was awakened by the sound of the bugle, which was evidently blown by some novice, this morning. I could not help laughing to myself at the way he slaughtered his attempted "variations." Finish writing to Mrs. H. this morning.[34] Take clothing to washerwoman, which relieves me somewhat, as I have been wondering where my next clean ones were to come from. Wrote to Roosi directly after dinner, and then took an hour's walk eastward over the rocky hill by the cemetery and returned with several very good specimens of petrified wood. After supper I wrote to Mary Duvall and Eckhardt. When Mr. Cushing came and informed me that he would probably send me to Prescott, Arizona in advance with the two ladies to be followed by him as soon as the papers from Washington and Boston were received. Took a walk around the parade grounds, went in, read a while and retired. The weather has been most charming to-day.

Tuesday, Dec. 28

Awoke after nearly 12 hours sleep to find another beautiful day. Mr. C. dictates[35] and after lunch take a walk in a westerly direction to the wooded hills in search of more specimens, but found nothing of any consequence. On my way over I stopped at a Navajo hogan to watch a woman weave a sash. Hearing the jingling of money within, I lifted aside the fly which covered the entrance and discovered about 10 or 12 of the Indians gambling. Two soldiers were also present. They were playing with cards upon which were engraved peculiar colored figures; but the closest observation could not afford me any clue as to what the game was. Imagine the picture without and within: the woman industriously engaged—the men occupied in wasting the money which she earns! I also see Dougherty[36] who speaks of the country round about, and invites me to take a mule-back ride with him tomorrow to look for some of the crystallized specimens which I have seen in possession of the soldiers. Returning to my room I read for a while and then write to Crossman.

Wednesday, Dec. 29

Arise after another good-night's rest & find snow on the ground, which thaws, however upon the appearance of the sun. Spend the day in doing nothing in particular except straighten accounts in the evening. Mr. Cushing departs for Albuquerque to do some outfitting on 6:40 train. Retire at 9 o'clock.

Thursday, Dec. 30

Up and breakfast at 8 o'clock. Take a walk to the Zuñi Mountains and find several specimens of petrefaction and alabaster. I also practice with my revolver, returning in time for lunch. Hoblitzell has returned from Fort Bayard where he has been for a week. Work on accounts, bills, etc in the afternoon, and after dinner go to officers' club room and read papers. Retire early as usual.

Friday, Dec. 31

My rest was somewhat broken last night. Awoke about 8 o'clock and went out to find that a very slight snow had again fallen. Mr. Cushing being in Albuquerque, and with nothing particular to do, I watched the muster-drill during the morning hours and in watching the feat of putting the bayonet in the scabbard by holding it a certain way, I was approached by one of the privates who introduced himself as Frank P. Chilcote, and who guided me through the quarters of Co. "G" previous to inspection. Chilcote is a young man, who for an ordinary soldier is uncommonly bright and with a pretty good education. During the course of our conversation (which was afterwards continued in the adjutant's office—where he is detailed for clerical duty) I found that he was well acquainted with Hallenbeck, of Ann Arbor University, (Mich Α Φ Κ Ψ). Strange how acquaintances of your friends will meet as in this case! After dinner I walked about 5 miles—going to the mesa to the northward in search of some crystallized petrifaction, but with no success. Retired early as usual for the last day of the year, wondering if the folks at home are holding their usual watch-night meeting.

1887

Saturday, Jan. 1

New Year's day! No calls to-day as has been my custom of previous years. Took a walk to the Navajo camp this morning where I saw some more weaving and the use of the soap-weed[37] for the first time. Came across an old house which had been torn down on account of the death of its occupant, whose body was lying beneath the logs and clay and had been for several weeks. Not a very brilliant New Year's. Mr. Cushing returns from Albuquerque. I receive a letter and some newspapers from home. Play "casino" with the house and retire early to sleep.

Sunday, Jan. 2

Went over to see the Navajo silversmith in the morning and had him make me a pair of sleeve-buttons from four dimes which I furnished him. After dinner I walked to the station to see Mr. Cushing but as he was quite tired he did not dictate. He informed me that he intended going to Zuñi to-morrow, and asked me if I wanted to go. I volunteered, and after eating a very hearty supper returned with the mail wagon. Wrote home in the evening and after beginning preparations for Monday's journey, retired.

Monday, Jan. 3

Awoke early this morning and donned my field-outfit in readiness for Mr. Cushing's arrival from the station. He reached the Fort about dinner time, and after securing commissary supplies we started with our two mules and buckboard for our second trip to Zuñi. In ascending Zuñi mountains Mr. Cushing attempted to walk, while I drove, but had scarcely gone half way when he was so overcome by illness that he was compelled to sit down under a tree and rest until I came up. I handed him his medicine, after taking which he felt considerably better. He then drove while I walked the rest of the distance up the mountains. Our mules made excellent time and only one mishap occurred before we reached camp—we had to return 6 or 7 miles (making a trip of 12 or 14 miles out of our way in consequence) owing to the slipping from under the cover of our buckboard of the bag of meat and bread, which, of course, it was necessary to go after. We camped half a mile of Nutria Hill, and while Mr. C. was preparing supper I led the mules to Nutria spring for watering. It is a beautiful moonlight night, and the mountains in the distance are grander than ever. I returned with the animals, and after supper, which we ate at midnight, retired to sleep as comfortably as I ever slept before.

Tuesday, Jan. 4

Up before sunrise and walked to Nutria spring to fill the canteens. The morning is very cold and my hands were frozen to the canteens as I carried them. Returning to camp I found Mr. C. still sleeping, for as he had had a very sick night of it, he did not retire until nearly 5 o'clock. The whinneying of the mules awakened him, however, and we prepared and ate breakfast and departed about 2:00 reaching Na-ta-te-quin about 4 o'clock, where, owing to a renewal of his attack we were compelled again to camp at the same place as we camped on our return from Zuñi 2 weeks previous. Two Indians who happened to be passing in a wagon were hailed, and after a conversation with Mr. Cushing promised to send back a man upon their reaching Nutria. It was after dark when the native arrived (Hu-la) and we had just crossed legs for supper. It was his intention, at first, to send me on to Zuñi then, but thought it wiser upon a reconsideration to await morning. Mr. C. says the temperature to-night, using his best judgment, is at least 23 degrees below zero!

Wednesday, Jan. 5

Awoke at sunrise and after breakfast, which we eat at 10 o'clock, I proceed with Hu-la in the buckboard to Zuñi. The day is fine, but cold and windy.

We arrive at Zuñi at about 2 o'clock and go directly to Pa-lo-wah-te-wa's adobe. Arriving there some time (meanwhile Wai-hu-se-wa appearing) I call at Graham's establishment to conduct my business with Gibbons[38] who is in charge during Graham's absence in the East. I was somewhat surprised at not finding him home, but a man named James in charge. I made known my business—the purchase of the horse saddle, bridle & rifle—and got as much satisfaction as was possible under the circumstances. Had dinner and returned to Pa-lo-wah-ti-wa's with whom Hula had already made the necessary arrangements under directions from Mr. C. Hula started on ahead while I followed with Pa-lo-wah-ti-wa in the buckboard and Wai-hu-se-wa on horseback. The ride would have been very pleasant were it not so very cold. Reached camp about 8 o'clock, having covered the 16 miles in about 3 hours. Feeling very tired over the journey, I assisted in preparing supper for the 3 Indians and myself and then retired, being lulled to sleep in the moonlight by the chattering of Mr. C. and the Indians, with whom he was holding council.

Thursday, Jan. 6

Lay abed to see the sun-rise, fed the fire and dressed. Our party was increased by the arrival of four more Indians, one of whom was sent afoot by the Zuñi missionaries. After breakfast we started for our return, Mr. Cushing riding the horse which I had secured of Graham. I, myself, driving the mules. Palowahtiwa and Waihusewa returned to Zuñi and Hu-la to Nutria, the four other natives following us. The old man (who was sent by the missionaries) riding with me in the buckboard. We camped at the old place where we stopped for lunch on our return from the first trip to Zuñi. The Indians made themselves generally useful by hauling wood and washing dishes. I retired at 11 o'clock, but Mr. C. remained up nearly all night listening to folk-tales and entertaining the natives without the least consideration for his health!

Friday, Jan. 7

Up at 6:30. Dark as pitch and very cloudy, with a few flakes falling. There is a stir acamp this morning over the losing by Mr. Cushing of a very valuable ring which he was showing to the Indians the night before. The most careful search failed to bring it to light and suspicion is attached to one of the

Indians. We start for Wingate about 10 o'clock. Mr. C. riding horse-back and myself in charge of the mules again, three of the Indians following. The animals make very good time homeward reaching the Post about one p.m. I had great difficulty in descending Zuñi mountains, my brake having become utterly worn out causing the buckboard to almost run atop the mules making them trot down some of the steepest hills. After dinner at Cleghorn's where I was soon joined by Mr. Cushing, I arranged my toilet and looked once more respectable. Visited the Navajo silversmith and got from him my sleeve-buttons and after supper wrote to Mother, Mossell, Crossman, & Seltz. I received my first salary to-day under my new situation.

Saturday, Jan. 8

I woke at 8:00 after a very good night's rest of about 12 hours. Send my check to 1st Nat. Bk at Santa Fe to be cashed and spend my morning in writing up my diary to which I had fallen considerably behindhand on account of my journey to Zuñi. The ground has a white coat on it to-day, it having snowed nearly all night. Received a letter from my friend Fowle and read Washington papers nearly all the afternoon when Mr. Cushing rode up from camp Watts on horseback, but was too tired for dictation. Al-u-san the albino rode in from Zuñi on his burros having started from his home yesterday. He slept with me all night.—or rather on the floor in my room. After writing to the boys I "turned in."

Sunday, Jan. 9

After breakfast this a.m. I walked to the station in the snow, but found Mr. Cushing too much done-up to dictate. About noon I rode the horse to the Post Office for the mail and returned—my letter from Crossman. Repaired to supper at Watt's camp after which I returned to the Post, stabling my horse at Woodside's.

Monday, Jan. 10

Feel very stiff after my yesterday's horseback ride of 9 miles. I work on accounts and bills during most of the morning, when Mr. C. arrives and dictates for an hour. Spend afternoon in writing up my notes and as I could not mail the letter that evening (it being too late) went out with Chilcote and Jackson, who take supper at Cleghorn's. Jackson leaves us early and C.

and I go to the library and then to quarters where I remain until reveille, returning to my room.

Tuesday, Jan. 11

Mr. C. went to Albuquerque last evening leaving me to write up my notes[,] which I do—mailing my letter in time. The train to-day is nine hours late so no letters from home. The weather is very cold now. Remain indoors nearly all day, and retire with Mr. Cleghorn at 9 o'clock.

Wednesday, Jan. 12

Weather is a little milder, but still quite cold. Got letters from Evelyn and Nelly and papers from Em and wrote to Monsell, Crossman and Ashley during the day. At dinner we had fish, and upon my inquiring if it came from the Rio Grande, Mrs. Wicklam innocently replied—"No, it came from Albuquerque"! Pitts spent his after-dinner with me and I learned several little things about the Navajos. Marriage is effected by the prospective "groom" paying to the father—or rather to the family—of his future wife a stipulated sum. If, after marriage, they do not agree, there is no binding force restraining the wife from deserting her husband, or the husband from leaving his wife. If the husband disagree, however, he must leave the children in the care of this mother; and if the wife no longer desires to live with her husband she may take the children with her providing the husband allows it. They are free, after separation, to marry again. In the case of the death of an Indian (Navajo) all his effects are either buried with him or destroyed. If he be alone, and die in his house, he is wrapped in a blanket and the house demolished over his remains, providing the house is in a rather lonely locality. Where the place of his abode is in a more thickly populated settlement he may be tied to his horse and his body deposited in an arroyo or ravine, or hidden amongst rocks—all his effects being deposited or hidden with him, and the horse killed on the spot. Sure death will be the terrible penalty visited by the Gods upon anyone who should touch any of the property of a dead Navajo! These Indians are also very particular about their diet, very few of them eating turkey, although they will kill in order to use their feathers in some of their sacrificial ceremonies. Fish they never touch under any consideration not even if death stared them in the face by reason of starvation. Bear-meat they never taste, nor will they even kill a bear nor tan his hide, for they believe that bears are transfigurations of Navajos who through some misdeed have been prohibited from the pleasures of the "happy hunting grounds." The eagle is supposed to have a world of its own, situated far off towards the sky. This bird is considered sacred above all others. The belief of the Navajo is that he originated in a world beneath or within the earth but as this is a great secret, little information on this subject could be gained for one who divulged it would surely be transformed into a bear! The secret of the connection between this world and the mysterious one beneath, however, is held by certain old men of the tribe, who just before death impart it to their younger brothers thus keeping it extant among a favored few. Pitts and Chilcote spend the evening with me this evening. The Indians[39] arrive from Zuñi and I installed them comfortably in the old adobe on the road and secure subsistence for them.

Thursday, Jan. 13

Got a letter from Mr. Cushing dated at Albuquerque and per instructions contained in it made copy of long letter to Mr. Baxter. Spent part of the day with the Indians, making them understand me as best I could. They call me by my nickname (which I received at Zuñi): Te-lu-li; and I am beginning to get used to it. Went to temperance meeting led by Lieut. Buck[40] in the chapel with Pitts and Chilcote, and afterwards to house of P. Q. S. Stirte where I remained till about 10:30.

Friday, Jan. 14

Slow day for me. Mule sale at the Post—Watts bids on 4 for our outfit. Write to Fowle and sit in my room awaiting return of Mr. Cushing who is due in Wingate this evening. Not arriving. I write to Nell and retire. The weather today has been very agreeable.

Saturday, Jan. 15

Awoke and dressed at 9 this morning. After guard-mount went to call on the Indians, spending the morning with them. After dinner I read the papers received from home by to-day's mail until Mr. Cushing came, when we arranged correspondence and receipts accumulated while on his trip to Albuquerque. Played cards with Chilcote and Pitts in tent near QM's quarters until reveille retreat, when I returned to my room.

Sunday, Jan. 16

Up and at breakfast at 9:30 and witnessed drill and parade. Passed a very quiet Sunday, attending the Roman Catholic Service in the morning and Episcopal in the evening. Mr. Cushing was up during part of the afternoon and dictated a couple of letters.

Monday, Jan. 17

Wrote up letters which Mr. Cushing dictated yesterday in time for evening's mail. Spent the remainder of the day in lounging in the room, visiting the Indians once or twice, attending to their needs. There was a dress-parade this evening which made a very fine display. Letter from Mary Dewall to-day.

Tuesday, Jan. 18

This morning is quite frosty, but as soon as the sun climbed a little higher in the heavens it felt quite warm. I spent the whole day outdoors, enjoying a sun-bath. At night attended the concert given by the band in the chapel, which was well rendered although most of the pieces performed were old to me: selections from the "Mikado", "See-saw" etc. Retired at "taps." Letter from Brother Charlie to-day.

Wednesday, Jan. 19

After breakfast I caught mail wagon and went to station, finding Mr. C. and Mr. Garlick[41] busily engaged in loading up cars. Stayed there until the afternoon seeing Mr. Garlick off for Ash Fork in charge of freight & mules when I had supper (or rather dinner) with Mr. C. and returned to the Post. While packing up my effects for our departure to-morrow morning Mr. Cushing arrived and we hustled around finishing up supply-gathering. After supper went to quarters of Company G and had the luxury of bathing. Played whist with Chilcote, Mr. Price and Sargent —— in tent of Mr. Price, until tattoo when I retired to my room and sewed on my cavalry pants which I purchased from one of the men of Troop K for $1.50. To sleep at 10:30 or 11:00.

Thursday, Jan. 20

Up early and while at breakfast mail driver came when I assisted him with my baggage and we departed for the station. Upon arrival of the train, which was an hour late, we bade good-bye to Palowahtiwa and Waihusewa and boarded the sleeper meeting Miss Magill and Mrs. Cushing who had this morning started from Albuquerque. Amused ourselves during the day as much as possible, enjoying the scenery, especially Cañon Diablo, immensely. Took dinner at Winslow at 2 o'clock and supper at Williams about 7:00. After supper I enjoyed a game of casino with Miss Magill until we arrived at Ash Fork when I disembarked with the Indians, meeting Mr. Garlick who had engaged a room for me at the "section-house." Ash Fork is not as much of a place as I thought; it consisting of but the station, blacksmith shop, store, and two or three dwellings. After knocking a quarter of an hour to wake up the land-lady I was ushered to a room 7 x 7 with this bed of shuck mattress and straw pillow. But feeling so tired I did not mind this and soon fell asleep.

Friday, Jan. 21

Up at 9 o'clock and went to the station, returning immediately after to breakfast. After breakfast went again to the station just in time for western train's arrival with Mr. C. aboard, who had gone with the ladies as far as Prescott Junction[42] and returned in order to arrange matters with regard to our freight which had not all arrived. Mr. Garlick and I spent all the morning in unloading car and putting wagon together, while Mr. Cushing went with Indians and mules to find grazing-grounds and water for them. Unloaded Car No. 2 in the afternoon and put two buckboards together. Twisted my back in the effort, it paining me quite sincerely all the evening. Started to put up a Sibley tent which we finished by dusk and had our first camp in a driving snowstorm with wind directly from west. We had just become amply settled when this unexpected storm arose, which necessitated our turning out and putting our outfit under cover. This being done we returned to our tent and went to sleep while the storm howled and finally stopped.

Saturday, Jan. 22

Up rather late again and while preparing breakfast were joined by a Chinaman (Ah Yung) who had just arrived from California. Mr. Cushing immediately engaged him for our trip to Prescott and he at once set to work cooking bread at the "section-house"—where there was another Chinese cook employed—spent the day in cleaning camp and arranging outfit for starting tomorrow. The Indians make themselves very useful by capturing 7 rabbits with their rifles while grazing mules[,] which our newly acquired celestial cooks in palatable style for supper. Have great trouble in keeping wind and dust out of tent so built a wind-break in front of door. After a smoke all around me retired earlier than usual. Was awakened at an unseemly hour to-night by shouting outside. Mr. Cushing let the stranger in who proved to be a young man about 24 years of age, from Montreal, and who had just arrived here at Ash Fork, having jumped baggage-car about 50 miles east. After warming him up we divided bedding and again settled down, but scarcely had the rest begun to snore when I heard another noise, resembling the rattling of pans and tearing of canvas. Guessing the cause of the disturbance, I untied the door-sheet, and, armed with sticks and stones, drove off the midnight-marauding mule and returned to my bed, feeling none the better for my chase in naught but underclothing and in my bare feet.

Sunday, Jan. 23

Was up long before sunrise and surveying the damage done by our long-eared visitor last night. The tearing open and eating of a portion of a bag of corn was all the wrong he did, but what might have been the result had I not driven him off may better be imagined. Enjoyed the breakfast which Ah Yung cooked this a.m. very much, as I always do when not acting cook myself. Would never have known it was Sunday were it not for this diary which considerately acts as calendar too. We packed our wagon and two buckboards to their utmost capacity, and at sundown were ready to start. Mr. Garlick managed the large wagon, myself the covered buckboard, the Indian (Ce-wah-ti-tei-lu) the other, while Mr. Cushing went on horseback in advance to find a suitable camping place for the night, and We-ta drove the extra animals in the rear of the "caravan." We made but four miles this evening when we came upon Mr. Cushing who had selected a good campground. I felt very much fatigued (as did, in fact, our whole party) after my long days work in packing and the like, so after unhitching my mules, I made up my bed and was soon in dream land.

Monday, Jan. 24

Up at 7 o'clock, and, after our Chinese breakfast, packed and were on the road again at 9:30. The day was long, and the road very rough and dusty, while the amount of sand which had accumulated during this dry season rendered the work of our animals very laborious, and especially as they had no water for 24 hours. I was very glad when we arrived in camp for the animals' sakes as well as my own, for I was exceedingly tired and thirsty. The mountain scenery for part of to-day's route is very beautiful especially in one of the canons through which we pass. The Indians continue to make themselves useful, We-ta having killed a good-sized rabbit and a falcon, the latter being very valuable on account of the use to which the feathers could be put for sacrificial purposes. Made up my bed early again and was once more fast asleep.

Tuesday, Jan. 25

Awoke this morning from the sound of "Te-lu-li; Te-lu-li" issuing from Mr. Cushing's lips. Was soon out and at breakfast, which we had before daylight, and hitching up and packing for our procedure. Mr. Cushing rode to the railroad about a mile away in time to catch the Prescott train and at 9:30 Mr. Garlick and myself were pushing out from camp. We covered 16 miles to-day, over a very dirty road, and the sun poured down upon us until we are all very sunburnt or freckled. Made camp again about 4 p.m. rather early in the day, but we had no better opportunity for we would have been compelled to travel 14 miles more before reaching wood or water had we continued. So watering our horses and mules and making our camp in a very poor place in the Little Chino Valley (for want of a better one) had our cook get supper and after washing my face for the first time in two days, chatted a while with the inn-proprietor, and turned in. Ah Yung gives me some little troubles this evening, getting dissatisfied over some trifle, and giving vent to his spite by handling the dishes very carelessly. I remonstrated with him when he declared his intention of returning to Ash Fork, but seeing that I cared but little, he soon quieted down, and when ready to crawl under his own blanket was again as "sweet as pie".

Wednesday, Jan. 26

Was awake at 3 o'clock, after passing a very uncomfortable night's rest, it being so cold, which was partially accounted for as we had no camp-fire, wood being out of the question except for our purpose of cooking. Yung offered more insolence this morning but I soon tamed him after threatening to send him back. At 9 o'clock we were on the road and made 21 miles arriving in Prescott at 3 o'clock. Drove our teams to the "O K" Yard[43] and camped ourselves in a sort of "teamster's rest" in a corner of the yard. The place is not so very inviting, as the sky peers in through the roof and walls and the place is very dirty. But we set to work and soon have it cleaned up and cook a supper in the open grate. At seven o'clock we "turn in", with six others in this filthy little hole and are all so sound asleep that we think little of our surroundings. One of the hostlers here asked me, just after I had driven into the yard, if we were "a circus", and also where we were "going to perform"! Mrs. Cushing, Miss Magill and Mr. Boyd (one of the gentlemen whom I met on the train on my way out from Wingate and who happened to be stopping at the same hotel with them) visited us while at supper this ev'g.

Thursday, Jan. 27

Did not arise very early this morning, feeling quite tired after our trip. Got breakfast for the crowd over which we all expressed satisfaction, and I felt very proud over my success. Got my check cashed and sent the money orders for which I have been waiting so long. Kept the party in dinner and supper and in the afternoon had a good bath, after which I put on some better clothing and felt much better. Had a chat with Mr. Garlick in the evening and were entertained with songs by the Indians who have been busy all day at sewing new clothing. Prescott beats Albuquerque for gambling dens, for it seems that every other building is devoted to that purpose, otherwise the city is very nice and pleasant.

Friday, Jan. 28

Spent to-day in and around our camp, cooking for the crowd and purchasing for our trip south. Mrs. Cushing and Miss Magill called in the afternoon and congratulated me on my success as cook.

Saturday, Jan. 29

Things look as if we would move out to-morrow. Went with Mr. Cushing this morning to Fort Whipple and returned with a buck-board load of supplies. Boyd also accompanied us and I met several of the officers at the Post. After cooking dinner I assisted Mr. Garlick in packing and at night visited the most important of the gambling houses with Boyd, which was run without attempt at concealment. It is quite cold to-night and after chatting a while on a corner left Boyd and returned to rest.

Sunday, Jan. 30

I arose quite early and cooked breakfast this morning with the hope of packing our mess-chest in a respectable time for departing, when Mr. Cushing (who had just returned from the Post where he had been reporting to obtain our supply of forage, but owing to the day was unable to do so) reported the news that it should not start until to-morrow, we packed what we could during the day, and spent the evening very pleasantly with Boyd, who called just after supper.

Monday, Jan. 31

The day has at last come when we are to start southward. We finish packing early in the afternoon and I went ahead with the buckboard to the hotel after Mrs. C. and Miss M. followed by Mr. Garlick with the four muled team and Newton wagon. Burgess[44] (a new acquisition who wanted to work his way home to Phoenix) the Indians Weta and Siwatitailu who drove the buckboard and extra animals, respectively, and Mr. Cushing on horseback—all forming quite a formidable calvacade, making me think no wonder we were taken for a managerie. The ladies were in waiting when I arrived at the hotel and we departed upon Mr. C.'s coming up a few minutes after. The distance which we expected to cover to-day was but four miles, as it was merely the intention to "make a start" rather than to go any great distance. I did not drive long when Mr. Cushing offered to exchange places and allow me to ride "Douglass". I rode for four or five miles when we made a halt and I surrendered the horse to Mr. C. when he searched for a good camping place before we ascended the mountain with the team. He started up the road, and while we awaited his return Miss Magill amused herself (and us too) by sketching the mules. Having found a suitable place for a camp Mr. C. returned and again delivering the horse to me bade me await the rest of the party while they went on. Mounting the horse I retraced the road for half a mile, reaching the summit of the hill which we had just descended, in time to see the outfit on an entirely different road. I left the road and galloped my horse as fast as possible across country in a direct line for overtaking them. It was almost sunset when I rode up to Mr. Garlick and informed him that he was on a different road, and he explained that he took it as he was informed by a man, whom he had met on the way, that we had gone that way. He suggested that I return and tell Mr. Cushing to proceed for five miles further when our road would meet his. I returned as directed and found Mr. C. and the ladies warming themselves by a fire which they had built and informed him of the whereabouts and intentions of the remainder of the party. So whipping up the mules we drove along to the forks of the road, and finding no suitable place for camping, continued the drive until we reached Agua Fria, stopping only long enough on the way for Mr. Cushing to pop at jack rabbits and cotton-tails with his rifle. There being no hope for wood or water if we proceeded, and as it was now getting late, we camped in the stock yard of Thomas' ranch and were soon joined by the rest of our little party. We pitched the ladies' tent first, and after they were comfortably fixed, got supper and spent the evening in chatting. After all the others were snoozing I assisted Mr. Cushing in rustling camp-logs and while seated around our fire he very kindly suggested a ranching scheme after the Expedition terminated, which delighted me fully. We continued our conversation until nearly two o'clock when I unrolled my bed and went to sleep. The meat was lost from the wagon to night, necessitating the return of the Ind's on horseback to hunt same.

Tuesday, Feb. 1

Was awakened early by the Indians. Got breakfast and assisted generally, but it being our first camp we did not start until noon. We made about 15 miles today over a good road and made a most perfect camp in a very charming valley. Trees afforded shade, which we now begin to relish in this warm Arizona sun, while short but thick grass gave us a smooth carpet to our camp-ground. While getting supper Mr. Cushing and the Indians amused themselves by hunting quail on the mountain slope, securing five or six of them. We all retired early, building a large cottonwood camp-fire before nestling under our blankets.

Wednesday, Feb. 2

We are all so delighted with our camp in this beautiful spot that Mr. Cushing decides to remain over a day in order that we may rest and enjoy ourselves as well as to do several little things that this start upon the road has brought to light. We are very glad of this, for it is like one grand picnic—our camp in this beautiful valley. While at breakfast Miss Magill calls attention to my bed[,] which is on fire. I succeed in extinguishing the smouldering brand which had alighted from the fire and examined its result which was a very large hole in the center of each piece of bedding except one blanket. After breakfast Miss Magill made a sketch of the camp which I thought very good, and early in the afternoon Mr. C., Miss M. and myself went out for a little archery. While away Mr. C. returned to camp after his moccasins and I arched with Miss M. being quite successful in my practice. Mr. C. soon returned and we went to the top of a mesa, about half a mile distant in search of ruins, but without success. After Mr. C's return home on account of illness Miss M. and myself continued our research, but with no better success. We continued on until we found the road, when we returned to camp, dusty and tired. While I prepared the supper, Miss M. kindly repaired the damage done to my bedding this morning. Bunked in early preparatory to an early rising for starting. The night air is very chilly and a heavy dew is falling.

Thursday, Feb. 3

Up before sunrise, but we did not get started until nearly one o'clock. Our ride to-day for 8 miles was through a most charming country. The roads were all very good and comparatively level, and the vegetation along the way assumed a more tropical aspect. The huge cacti—known as "sawaya"[45] and the tree cacti—"o-kahtea" makes its appearance for the first time, the former being from a foot to twelve feet or more in height, according to age, and probably 18 inches in diameter. We made camp at Bumble Bee P. O. about sundown and went to bed almost immediately after supper.

Friday, Feb. 4

Arose about four o'clock this cold morning and had such difficulty in lighting the fire that I almost swore, it extinguishing itself four or five times, which can easily be accounted for by the green mesquite and palo verde wood with which I had to kindle it. Got breakfast and we were all ready to start at 9:30, after writing letter sheets home. I enjoyed the ride to-day more than any previous one on account of the gorgeous scenery along the way. We crossed the mountains through the Black Cañon and the roads were so rough and steep that it kept myself and the brake busy in checking the buck-board during the steep descents. Weta joined us in the afternoon, having gone in search of a deer which he wounded the evening before, but which the coyotes had devoured. We made camp in the bed of Squaw Creek with every prospect of a rain storm arousing us before morning. Sat for Miss Magill while she sketched me by camp-fire light to-night and at 10:30 made my bed in the sand and was soon soundly slumbering.

Saturday, Feb. 5

A few drops of rain falling upon my face this morning at 4:15 this saved Mr. Cushing from his customary calling of me. So dressing quickly and rolling up my bed to keep it dry, I went to the creek-bed to find Mr. C. about to kindle the fire. We had early breakfast and we[re] off on the road at a respectable hour. The ride to-day, while not quite so enjoyable as that of yesterday (the road being very sandy) was very pleasant. The cacti are more enormous and abundant than I have yet seen them, and the giants loom up like huge trees divested of their foliage.

We make camp near the "Eyler Ranch"[46] close by the banks of New River—which, in the East, would form a respectable spring stream—as the weather was cloudy we pitched two wall tents for our shelter in case of rain which we afterwards found to be quite a wise movement as no small quantity fell during the night. Mr. Alkire[47] one of the young men who "ran the ranch" called in the evening and invited us to the ranch in case of rain, but as we were very comfortably situated it was not necessary to accept his invitation. We unrolled our beds and slept under cover of our tent to-night.

Sunday, Feb. 6

Mr. Cushing decided to remain over to-day on account of the threatening appearance of the weather and in order to visit some supposed ruins in the neighborhood of camp about which he had learned from Mr. Alkire. Looked over some letters after breakfast and took a good wash, which, from lack of opportunity and facilities, I felt badly in need of. The ladies went to the ranch with flour and made a bushel of biscuits which we found very acceptable as we were entirely out of our supply of bread. It rained during a portion of the day, but cleared up sufficiently to allow us to make a trip to the top of the mesa at whose foot we were camping, where we found several specimens of ancient pottery—all in pieces—and evidences of habitations.

The view from the mesa is superb, the distant lofty mountains being covered with snow. We retired as early as usual, the rain beating against our tent quite heavily.

Sunday, Feb. 6[48]

Rained in the night a little and though cloudy this morning allowed us to eat a dry breakfast— x x x Mr. Alkire[49] (the people at the ranch are named so) came early after Tenatsali[50] and gave us another invitation to his home in his mother's name, also offered us anything we wished, that they could give. We told him we would call on his mother and as they were so kind and our bread all given out, we would borrow their kitchen to make some biscuit in—He seemed delighted and rode off, to return again immediately with a loaf of delicious bread. It poured all the morning but in spite of weather Tenatsali and Mr. Alkire went off relic hunting while Mr. Garlick drove Em and me in the buckboard to the ranch. x x x

We stayed to lunch with them and afterward till 4 P.M. when Mr. Garlick called for us with the buckboard. Em went with him but as the rain had stopped and the clouds looked promising—at her request—I stayed and walked back to camp with Mr. Alkire and the two gentlemen. While we were in the tent Tenatsali and the other son returned and at a proposal from the latter we all walked up the mesa, to see the ruin on top but scarcely had reached it when (the clouds had been gradually gathering again) the lightening flashed, the thunder rolled, the sky grew inky black and the rain dashed down in torrents—all around us, but only enough where we were to give us a good surface wetting. We found several very pretty little wild flowers (one like a Michaelmas daisy of lilac) and pieces of pottery as well as bits of obsidian and imperfect arrowheads of ——[not identified] such as I found yesterday.

Mr. Alkire the elder is an interesting man, a great reader—who told me a lot of things worth remembering—explained how the wretched cactus that I thought like pussy willow and which I have made acquaintance with—Managed to get through shoe leather and stay when it got there. Its points turn when they have pierced anything and refuse to be drawn out till they are wetted which shrivels them—We set fire to one (which burned like fire-works) then descended the mesa in the twilight which had come on so rapidly.

When I reached camp I found no supper had been prepared and that Tenatsali was very sick, so had to rustle about at a lively rate for something to eat. The men were eating theirs and had left neither hot water or fire for ours and Em and I neither felt very amiable when these things were added to our usual tasks. Mr. Hodge seemed sorry for them and tried to atone by cutting us some wood and holding a piece of burning paper for me to see the granum cooking by. All was done in the rain[,] which is a melancholy adjunct to camp life. Rain poured all the evening with intervals of struggling moonshine and I could only regret that no sketch was made today while Tenatsali slept and Em and I worked over a puzzle—by candle light in the tent.

Slept little as the place was warm and did not sleep till late—

Monday, Feb. 7

The clouds having "rolled by" leaving the beautiful sky above us, we also rolled out this morning, though not very early, and after a long ride over a sandy road, reached the 27-mile descent where we camped at night-fall. Mr. Alkire and his co-partner and friend Mr. Singleton[51] joined us in the morning and went, with Weta, in search of a deer trail, but without success, as they joined us on the road later in the day (at a specified arroya, before starting) where, while we were awaiting their appearance, Miss Magill and I ascended a volcanic mesa in order that she might make a sketch of a large cactus. We were compelled to leave before it was quite finished as our "horsemen" rode up and we were ready to resume our seats in the buckboard. The night is perfect—the sun setting and moon rising almost simultaneously. Miss Magill made another pen-sketch after my sitting this evening when, feeling rather fatigued, pitched my bed beside the wagon and was fast asleep.

Monday, Feb. 7

We were all delighted to find the sun shining when we awoke this morning and all were singing about their work in camp—preparing for departure when I emerged from the tent—rather late I must confess. Mr. Singleton had already arrived upon the scene of action and assisted us with the breakfast—[he] is a splendid man and good to look at. Mr. Alkire 1 and 2 came to make their adieux and the mother made us a long visit.

I made a sketch after my preparations were made. Weta went off deer hunting with the two young men for whom he is lost in admiration. We got started at 12.30 P M. and went 18 miles making camp in the desert at 5.30 through which our way lay today after leaving Eyler Ranch.

Meeting the huntsmen soon after the start Tenatsali joined them and they accompanied us till almost 4 P.M. On our rest stop, Mr. Hodge and I climbed a mesa when I daubed a little. A delightful day and the distant mountain views lovely. Our desert camp was the prettiest of all with bright cactus fires, the distant blue hills, a moon almost full and a lovely sunset. The cayote barked and howled around much to my delight as the sharp sound through the clear air added the one thing needed to the scene.

Tuesday, Feb. 8

Was aroused by Mr. Cushing at 4:30 when I proceeded immediately to cook breakfast which we were eating at sunrise. Miss M. assisted me in washing dishes and at 9 o'clock we were ready to start. No water at all yesterday for the mules owing to our desert camp. Our ride to day—about 22 miles—was rather uninteresting. Were enabled to water our horses from the Arizona Canal.[52] Met Mr. Alkire when about 6 miles from Phoenix who assured us in securing a camp on ranch of Mr. Osborn.[53] While I was getting supper, Mr. C. and the ladies went to town for provisions with our buckboard, and returned very much pleased with the town. Pitched our beds (Garlick and myself) beside the wagon and after Mr. C. handed us our checks for January were moved to sleep by a saw-sharpening voice of some female singing "In the Sweet" (Ladies brought lots of mail from P. O.)

Tuesday, Feb. 8

All up at 4 A.M. and breakfast over by sun rise. x x

Tenatsali and I determined to ride horseback together so Douglas was saddled for me but he is so high that Mr. Garlick (when he went to lift me up) raised my left foot too suddenly and with great force and I was in great pain for some time but soon recovered enough to be lifted on the horse and started off with T. ahead at 9.30 A.M. The ride today not all so pretty as yesterday but the mountain views the same— x x

In the afternoon on the edge of the desert we came to the new irrigating canal[,][54] which has not long been finished through 40 miles of country when our patient animals had their first drink since yesterday noon. Met by Mr. Alkire. The approach to Phoenix is beautiful like a Boughton landscape[55]—pale green and white cottonwood trees against the most transparently blue sky I ever saw. We stopped two miles from town and made camp in the yard of a picturesque tumbled down old adobe house where a sign beside the road said "horsey for sale", which we thought a good sign. While the tent was being pitched Em, Tenatsali and I with Mr. Alkire riding beside us went off to town. It is a curious little foreign looking little place, full of Mexicans, Indians and Chinese. Streets are lined with cottonwood trees like the roads and there are numbers of palm and fig trees in the yards. The gutters are running with water, some of which is rather green and unwholesome looking. The whole place was a desert a few years ago and this abundant vegetation is all due entirely to irrigation. The trees are budding and the fields are covered with emerald green grass. Mr. Alkire pointed out a tree which was large and heavy and only seven years old.

Wednesday, Feb. 9

Did not arise particularly early, but was the first one about camp. Rode to town with Mr. Osborn where I met Mr. Garlick and we dissipated on fruit and candies. Phoenix—what a <u>town</u>! Adobe's, Mexicans, Chinese, Indians (Maricopas and Pimas) all jumbled together and thrown on each side of a broad, cottonwood-shaded thoroughfare which they call the main street. But I like it on account of its quaintness as nothing ever reminded me more of an Asiatic city. Returned to camp and cooked supper about sunset. Camped in the wall tent with Mr. Garlick this evening, having pitched our Sibley for Mr. Cushing and the ladies in the morning.

Wednesday, Feb. 9

Mr. Garlick and Mr. Burgess took Em and me to Phoenix where we visited the laundry, butcher and baker—that is they did while I sat in the buckboard and sketched the street.

The Sibley tent was put up today and is delightfully large and comfortable. Cloudy all day[56]

Made sketch of camp. We including Mr. Hodge went to town with the buckboard and Douglas. Met Mr. Alkire who went off about town with Tenatsali. All went off shopping and left me sketching in the buckboard—

Tenatsali introduced us to Mr. Davis who knew Mama and Papa before they were married.[57] Lovely all day but cooler than yesterday.

Thursday, Feb. 10

Was up and had fire kindled before the rest were out. Rode horse to town. Mr. C. and the ladies riding in the buckboard. Made several purchases of camp articles, and was stared out of countenance by the town idlers which number many. Returned to camp with the ladies and got dinner. Talked with Mr. C. and Mr. Garlick in our tent, when I was again prepared for a snooze[,] which I took. Mr. C. cashed my check today.[58]

Friday, Feb. 11

Arose in time this morning to witness a beautiful sunrise. After breakfast dressed and went to town with Mr. C. and the ladies, where I sent money orders home, took a bath and went shopping with the others. Upon our return to camp I unhitched the mules,—or at least partly did so—our "Thistle" kicked me almost over while pulling the bridle over her ears. Luckily I was quite close to her[,] which warded off the full force of the blow or the kick may have been more serious. Wrote to Mary Duvall after supper when I retired singing "Come Johnie" after the air of "Tit Willow."

Friday, Feb. 11

Warm and sunshiny all day.

Made a sketch after which Mr. Hodge, Tenatsali, Em and I went to town in the buckboard where we stayed till after 4 P.M.

Waiting in store while the others shopped. There were crowds of people coming in and out all the time.

Mexicans, Indians[,] Chinese, Gypsies—Monguls and Maricopa Indians. They have little lines on their faces pricked in India ink—one or two on either side of the mouth extending from the corner down the chin and from the corners of the eyes around the temples to the roots of the hair which, by the way, hangs in little ropes down their backs.

One was standing so temptingly near me in the store that I touched a rope of his head but he did not seem to resent the liberty at all.

Em and Tenatsali at last arrived with the welcome news that Jo Gunn[59]—the grand Mogul among the Chinamen here—had [procured us] a cook whose name was Dah Yung, which pronounced in American style sounds unpleasantly like Die Young.

Saturday, Feb. 12

Mr. Cushing awoke me and when I came out of the tent he was kindling the fire. After getting breakfast we commenced to break camp to move farther southeast of Phoenix on the road to Tempe where the party could be in closer proximity to important ruins in that locality.[60] At noon we started in our buckboard, leaving the wagons to follow (Mr. C. having gone on ahead on horseback). Thank the Lord we have at last secured a Chinese cook, and how relieved I do feel for I was never more tired of anything than I am of cooking for the party. After leaving the P. O. and while waiting for Mr. Cushing, the rest of the outfit came up and the Zuñis were the centre of attraction, for soon the whole street was crowded by envious lookers-on, and even vehicles drew up in order to catch a glimpse at our "circus". After driving eight miles over a very dusty road we camped on a knoll overlooking Tempe and the surrounding valley of the Salt River. The outlook is very pleasant, and our camp elevated (and consequently dry) and clean makes us comfortable, notwithstanding the gravelly bed beneath us. This first permanent incampm't has been styled "Camp Augustus", in honor of Mr. Hemenway.[61] Our celestial's first meal is a perfect success, and after partaking of it we unroll our beds and sleep in the open air.

Saturday, Feb. 12

The warmest day we have had since the start. Rode without wraps. Our landlord Mr. Osborn took me out and showed me that the fig tree was budding, inviting us most cordially to drive in in fruit season and get some of his. We left camp at little before noon and had to stop in town a while where everybody gathered in a crowd around Tenatsali and a number were introduced to us. Doctor Mitchell[62] invited us in to a reception for the Bishop at his house on Tuesday evening and pressed us to come in to service at 11 A.M. or 7 P. M. tomorrow.

A perfect mob of Maricopa Indians gathered around our Zuñis of whom they seem immensely fond, but the feeling is not reciprocal. Dah Yung joined us at Phoenix and at sight of him my hopes of a picture faded away, as his pig tail was neatly tucked up under a broad brimmed straw hat and his body clothed à la American—He is a business like gentleman. Came up to Tenatsali, greeted him politely and asked where he should put his bundle (his bed and valise). T. asked him which wagon he would like to ride on. No matter which answered Dah Yung. The buck board may be best said T. That's good replied the celestial[,] proceeding to tie on the bundle in question. This accomplished he added "We go way from town now and stay over night?" Yes. "You got yeast cakes with you?" "No." "Well two bits buy you plenty." The yeast cakes purchased, he put on a striped seersucker jacket, took his seat without more ado and there sat quietly, till we reached our destination—camp at about 5 P.M.

We found several ruins on the way and Tenatsali is in ecstasies at the prospect of explorations. This side of Phoenix all like the desert with more sand, sage bushes and water. I picked up several nice specimens of pottery at one big ruin[63] in the midst of 28 which Tenatsali counted from his horse.

Made camp in some beautiful hills opposite Tempe and the prospect is permanency which pleases at least the Cushings since there are ruins and sketch subjects in plenty in the neighborhood.

Our new cook gives satisfaction. The Indians invaluable and invariably good tempered.

Mr. Garlick being older than the others, feels a little important and takes the liberty of grumbling. Mr. Hodge listens and is sometimes affected thereby. Mr. Burgess our volunteer is at his journey's end—ergo not so useful as formerly.

Sunday, Feb. 13
Camp Augustus, Tempe
To-day is quite a busy one in camp. We arrange our tents about the camp in the best way imaginable, and we now look as though we had a formidable array of military quarters around us. The H-wall tent is devoted to my use, and I fix it up as best I can, with a straw-carpeted floor, and using my trunk, with a plank across the top, as a writing desk. I make use of it during the day by writing to Nelly B, Ashley and Mary Duvall, after the more arduous tasks are completed, such as cutting tent-pins and doing several camp-chores to make our surroundings respectable. Mr. Garlick spent the evening in the tent with me, and we chatted and wrote together.

Sunday, Feb. 13
This morning after breakfast while camp was making its details I went relic hunting and found two pieces of decorated pottery on one hill just below camp which by the way is called Camp Augustus in honor of Mr. Hemenway.

I went to the ruin on [a] hill top in sight[64] and found here some black stone knives and pottery scraps mostly red and much smutted by burning on [the] sides. One piece had sharp curve showing that the jar was broad thus and red painted solid. Other pieces of cooking pots very thick and of a dark color. Walls enough of large loose stones were still standing to show the outlines or rather proportions of four small rooms on the summit of the hill.

Near by a sacrificial mound traced and built of loose stones, small piled up. In the top were sacrifices. Neither ancient or very modern as they showed signs of moderate age, being weather beaten; they were solely a bunch of red arrows, pointed, at one end and notched at the other, all pointing westward and held in place by a couple of large stones laid on them. A string of blue glass beads was laid among them. On the side of this mound I found two pieces of white pottery decorated in black; one dec. side out curving showing shape of water jar and other curving in showing eating bowl—painted plain red outside.[65] Also found pottery tool used in making jars, a piece of broken pottery ground smooth at edges for shaping inside.

Several Pimas visited camp today with faces grotesquely painted and lines of dark blue pricked in the flesh of both faces and arms. Two sat here some time and Tenatsali offering them cigarettes with Zuni formulae of smoking to the six regions, discovered that they also had the custom of inhaling deep breaths when accepting cigarettes from a friend. I learned from them that hals ar means broken bits of pottery and oni with an inward breath means yes, as with the Moquis [Hopi].[66] Sketched some specimens found at New River.

Monday, Feb. 14

The camp still shows a continuation of industry. Walk to the butte directly north, and with great difficulty climb into natural cave near the summit, expecting to find evidences of a shrine, but was disappointed. Returned to camp and took another walk, with Miss Magill, visiting a sacrificial altar on an adjacent hill, which, from all appearances is modern. Hauled marsh poles and a poplar trunk with Burgess to make platform for Die Yung's "kitahen." We also arranged wagon covered over poles, forming a tent which now have filled with stones.

The Indians herd the stock to-day thus making themselves very useful in that way. Wrote to Eckhardt to night in answer to his recent letter. Mr. Cushing called while Mr. Garlick and I were talking, bringing a "letter" from the ladies in the form of a valentine, (for this is St. Valentine's day) and was very comical, having two hearts at the top pierced by an arrow, while beneath were written two or three sentimental verses of the "Roses are red, violets are blue" fashion. Even in this wild country Cupid shoots his darts, does he!

Monday, Feb. 14

Walked again to ruin with Mr. Hodge. My knee better. A lovely day. All the tents up and various improvements and conveniences for permanency. Helped to mend Sibley tent, two patches where falling sparks had burned it.

More visits from Pima Indians. Three women came first. They are poor looking, their clothes made entirely of American calico, low necked and short sleeved, showing arms somewhat tattooed. They are all barefooted without exception and carry their children on their backs like the Zunis but hold them up with one hand as they are wrapped only in their calico capes instead of blankets which probably owing to the warmth here, I have not seen them use at all.

They wear strings and strings of little colored glass beads around their throats, fitting tightly like a broad collar. Two young men came in afternoon and I sketched them in water colors. One did not object, but the other turned his face away when I attempted to draw him. He had his legs entirely bare and only a breach clout on. A striped gauze shirt and vest of American make on his body. They both wore bunches of feathers tied in their hair (at the back of the head) which streams wildly without regard to sex. They both carried little flutes of hollow cane with four holes burnt in them for notes and painted around at the joints with colored stripes. They made sweet sounds with them but refused to play flatly when I asked them to do so. They are not at all polite and the Zuni are very scornful of them.

Tuesday, Feb. 15

I arise after an excellent night's sleep to find the weather cloudy and windy. Help Mr. Garlick haul a load of mesquite for the tarantula, and one of water from the river. We take Burgess to Tempe this morning where he leaves us to go to Mesa City, and while there we do several errands and bring back milk, meat & hay. The wind increased during the early part of the afternoon and every thing was full of dust. We still continue to arrange camp, making things look thoroughly ship-shape. We have frequent visits from the Pima and Maricopa Indians who gaze at our doings with awe, and finger everything they see like a lady at market.

Tuesday, Feb. 15

Made water color sketch of specimens found in hill. Also gathered many pieces of pottery as well as imperfect axe from this hill just below camp.

An awful day—dark clouds and sand blowing thickly everywhere obliterating the western hills. I walked to top of rocks N. E. and found some curious little caves or holes in them large enough for a man to lie down in. Others stood alone in shape like a Zuni oven. In one a wood rat had made his hole and filled [the] front so thickly with choyers i.e. cactus spines that nothing could approach too near. I have seen several other examples. It is done to prevent cayote, etc.—from digging them out.

Wednesday, Feb. 16

The wind has abated, the rain stopped, and there were brighter prospects of a clear day when I arose. But after breakfast it began to cloud up again and rain all the more. Mr. Garlick went to Phoenix with the large wagon after hay and provisions and while gone Mr. C. and myself pegged his tent in the rain[,] which continued during the remainder of the day. I spent most of the time in my tent writing and in the evening Miss Magill called and asked if I would take a few letters from dictation from Mr. Cushing. I followed her to the tent where I remained all the evening, chatting on current and past topics (after finishing my stenographic work).[67] Returning to my tent I went to bed and was lulled to sleep by the music of the rain beating against the canvas—a sound which always greeted me with a most comfortable sensation.

Wednesday, Feb. 16

Poured rain all day— Mr. Garlick went to town for supplies[:] Phoenix. We get milk and cream from Tempe just across the river. The Indians took the animals off to pasture all day and have great fun visiting the Pimas.

The natives are all calling daily on Tenatsali and showing or rather telling where the ruins and inscriptions rocks lie in the neighborhood. Did not see the others in camp except Dah Yung till late afternoon when the sky cleared and all emerged from dry nests. I was out this morning in gossamer while it rained but no one else except Tenatsali who is always busy about something. This morning ditching the tent around and loosening guy ropes—Tenatsali went exploring this afternoon as usual. After supper he had Mr. Hodge take dictation in our tent so we all spent the evening together.

Thursday, Feb. 17

Got up at sunrise and went to the post office on white horse. Returned and had breakfast and went at work with the writing up of my notes.[68] While so engaged Mr. Garlick came bringing mail from Phoenix among which I found a Tam O'Shanter from home. This created a great deal of merriment among the party who poked fun at my wearing it. Mr. Cushing and Miss Magill went horse-back riding this afternoon and returned with an ancient wooden corn-planter—a very excellent specimen—which they found in a cave which had partly been burned by someone who wanted badly to see a rat's nest afire. The Indians herded stock to-day and came to camp in the evening with a beautiful white crane, whose feathers I utilized for my pillow, which I am engaged in making.

Thursday, Feb. 17

Mr. Hodge rose early and rode across to Tempe to mail T's letters. Since the advent of Yung he has taken on once more secretarial duties only once more. A lot of Pimas came today all with faces grotesquely painted but would not let me sketch them—Would run when I brought out my pencils, which we find a good way to clear the camp, when they become too clamorous for food or tobacco which are their daily demands. The day has been balmy and the sky cloudless.

Tenatsali and I went for a long exploring ride to the hills about 12–30 after Mr. Hodge groomed "Daisy" Mule (which T. rode) and I Douglass who was very steady—My knee almost well and dont hurt at all in the saddle. We rode North taking red sandstone hills in regular order.[69] In all were curious little shallow hollows or caves which we examined without success—The cacti grew thicker and thicker as we went till we were in a perfect forest. In the top of a very tall one Tenatsali's sharp eyes discovered an old arrow which had been shot into it and grown over—to get it down he had to cut down the cactus which fell like a great tree in reality. In one rock was a perfect tunnel through the solid sandstone[,] which we could walk through by bending slightly, at another was a great niche in which was an opening at which we could sit as at an open window and view the country for miles around. It was on the top of an immensely steep hill which our animals could scarcely climb and as we approached we saw two little Indian boys throw big stones through a hole which also was in the ceiling of the niche,[70] but at [the] sight of us, like little frightened rabbits, they disappeared among the rocks and we saw them no more. We rode up into this wonderful place and Tenatsali discovered what no one else would have noticed, that several little hollows in the rock were not natural, but hollowed by friction and used by the ancients as paint pots when they came thither to make pictographs. The choyers grew so thickly that we could scarcely make our way among them but our animals got off with only one each—Douglass let me laborously pull the spines from his leg one by one, without moving a muscle and looked at me so thankfully when it was done. He is so lovable and gentle that my affections are daily more engaged.

At the last hill we dismounted and spent some time and discovered a little cave which had been burnt out. There were a great many little hollows all with the mouths filled by the wood rats with choyers as well as large stones lying loosely in the hills where they had made them nests and scattered them so thickly that we could not step without their clinging to our clothes and piercing our shoes so we had to stop every few moments to relieve each other from the pests. I found some bits of pottery on the hill side—the common red sort which must have been sacrificed there as there was no sign of ruins. Tenatsali made two valuable discoveries, one a sacrifice of antelope head with antlers propped up by rocks and a very ancient tool lying on the side of the mesa evidently thrown from the cave by vandals—It is of wood and stuck full of choyers at the ends showing hard service. These last (Choyers) grew so thickly on the southern side of mountain as to be impossible so we had to burn a pathway and wait for it to cool before we could get down from our perch. We cut across country and came in by the river road and Tenatsali after inquiring if I was tired and receiving a negative reply complimented my riding and said I had been up and down over rough places enough to tire out the average man—We got home in good time for supper while the sun was still high enough to give warmth—

Weta shot a crane this evening—a beautiful white Heron.

Friday, Feb. 18

Another beautiful summer-like day after our cold night. Assisted Mr. Garlick in getting a load of mesquite this morning. Wrote letters nearly all day for transmission of checks in payment of Expedition accounts. Indians herded cattle, returning with a wild-duck. Mr. Garlick keeps busy with his mechanical work, making camp-stools, framing my "secretary" and other wood-workings. Mr. Cushing is not so well again. He has an attack this evening which so weakens him that I have to hold him up in his bed while using the stomach-pump. Sit in my tent this evening and pass the time in reading.

> *Friday, Feb. 18*
> A beautiful day, calm and warm. I sat out and basked in the sun all the morning with Mr. Hodge, drawing a little and giving him a lesson with the pencil. Some little Pima boys came by, with their bows and arrows which led to a little shooting and broke all our bows (but one) as this dry air has made them brittle. Tenatsali was taken very sick this afternoon which prevented our ride. He had to pump out twice with which Mr. Hodge helped us and was very good. I commenced an oil sketch of the sand stone hills North this afternoon. Mr. Hodge went over to Tempe for the mail—

Saturday, Feb. 19
Am up with the sun and ride the big mule—"Daisy"—to Tempe, with the mail. After breakfast we brand the animals and have quite a lively time about it, some of them taking it quite coolly, others kicking and prancing before I touched them. Mr. C. and I spent almost the remainder of the day in unpacking the library and manuscript boxes and in repacking such books as needed no further camp reference. This occupied some little time. I have some of the books on the top of my secretary, which form both useful reading to me as well as an ornament to my tent[,] which now has a very literary appearance. Spend the evening, after supper, in Mr. Garlick's tent, reading.

> *Saturday, Feb. 19*
> About thirty young Indians from Pima—bare legged, going hunting with bows and arrows—passed by this morning and on Tenatsali's suggestion had a shooting match in Camp for nickels. As they still use bows as their only weapon the shooting was fine and very exciting. The arrows were beautifully feathered (some with two feathers and other with three), but the ends only sharpened to a point with

a knife. They fancied ours very much and I exchanged two of mine for theirs. One had a head on it chipped of glass which Tenatsali eagerly brought in as a trophy as we did not suppose there existed Indians primitive enough to use such today.

One with a pleasant face and manner and understanding a few words of English remained after the others and taught us to count up to ten in Pima as well as a number of other words with which I surprised a couple of their women a half hour afterward till they clasped my hands and said I was a Pima, asking me by signs to come home with them and marry into the tribe. Made sketch of Douglass which I put into the racing picture.

Sunday, Feb. 20

For a wonder, this Sunday has come upon us with our being prepared! This is accountable, I believe, mostly for the reason that we have been less busy this week than usual, and partly because we have been settled in one spot which makes things seem more like civilization than it has been with our gypsy-camps—going out coming, day by day, seldom resting and less frequently knowing one day from another as a consequence. After washing up my towels I took the shotgun and went in search of some game; but whether I know not how, or else it was a bad time of day, I got nothing. Read the "Century" all after-noon—the numbers containing Mr. Cushing's article "My adventures in Zuñi",[71] which I found intensely interesting, and especially (since I had been to Zuñi myself and knew the principal characters of his story) was it so, as everything seemed as natural as life. We had visits to-day from 38 Indians who had great sport at shooting with their bows and arrows at a target which Mr. Cushing arranged for them. They seemed highly elated whenever they struck it, because, perhaps, of the half-dime which fell to their lot as a prize for their brilliant marksmanship. Read the evening away with Mr. Garlick in his tent by the fire.

Sunday, Feb. 20

Another lovely day, cooler than yesterday. Spent morning sitting among the bales of hay in the sunshine reading Lady with the Rubies till my metal dress buttons grew hot enough to burn me. At 2.15 Tenatsali and I sallied forth in search of ruins, he on the mule Daisy and I on my good old Douglas who was as fresh as a lark—dancing just enough to be becoming and safe at the same time. We went to the ruins "Ciudad de Los Puebletas"[72] which cover an immense area. The houses are situated a short distance apart—a Mound of sand in the center and ruined walls of stone around it. The ground is literally covered with pottery pieces glistening in the sun and we also found some metata stones finished and unfinished and two perfect stone axes, as well as various small rough knives and arrow heads. The decorated pieces of pottery showed great delicacy and beauty of design. We also found some pieces of shell as well as polishing stones etc. Some little digging had been done and in one hole was the side of a wall several feet high and yards long—smooth and polished like hard cement. There were, we found on close observation, figures of antelope etc. scratched in this wall tho whether done by the Indians themselves or the Mexicans or [illegible] after the ruins were deserted and before filling up with sand, Tenatsali could not determine at once. Among the ruins were various arroyes, all were dry. With the design of visiting and digging soon again, we reluctantly left as the sun was sinking rapidly and we were about six miles from home, but the little mounds and broken stone walls stretching away as far as the eye could reach were alluring. The houses indicated by the fallen walls were small and corresponded exactly with the ruins on [the] hill at Camp Augustus exactly opposite Tempe—Ciudad de los Pueblitos is the same ruins alluded to by Prof. Bandelier in [blank][73] as being three miles from Phoenix, and surrounded by "dry gardens"—by which no doubt he meant the same walls surrounding the sand hills.

The Pimas wear no moccasins (tho' the ground is covered with choyes and they seem to need them badly) only a kind of sandals made with a raw hide sole and buckskin string run through holes in the soles and held on over the two middle toes and wound round the ankle.

Monday, Feb. 21

It was my intention to ride to town early this a.m. in time to catch the stage, but did not go as I was not awake until 7:20—the mail leaving at 7:30. Went to town with Mr. Garlick and while there called at the post-office to mail a letter. Inquiring of the clerk the rate to Algiers, he intelligently asked if that place was in Mexico! Visiting the office of the "News", in order to secure two or three copies of the last issue, which I learned contained an editorial on "the Cushing party,"[74] I asked of the "devil" who was busily engaged in type-setting for Mr. McClintock,[75] the manager, and was told that he had "stepped out". I then asked the price of single copies of the "News", and he "didn't know". "What," said I, "don't you know what to charge when people want to purchase single copies of the paper?" "No sir," replied the devil—"we never sold a single copy." I gave him a nickel, took up two copies, and stalked out. On our return we stopped in the river to fill our four barrels (which still taste of their former contents) an exercise which almost gave me an involuntary bath by the sudden starting of the animals. Mr. Cushing went with the ladies and the Chinaman on a little exploring tour in the forenoon, returning with several specimens. The Indians were again successful to-day while handling the animals, securing a heron and a crane with their rifles. I unpacked the stationery trunk to-day, moving it into my tent, upon which I placed my secretary.

Monday, Feb. 21

This morning the parents of the nice young man from Pima who gave us some words of his language yesterday came up to camp and made us a long visit. I went and sat with her in the hope of learning a few words and was pleased to get her started soon and willingly as instructress and was able to attain 30 new words in addition to those of yesterday. She was much pleased at my wish to learn Pima that after inquiries as to whether I was married, had a mother or no, she made formal offers to Tenatsali of adopting me and having me become unto her a child.

Feb. 21

We started about noon in the buckboard, Emma, Tenatsali, Dah Yung and I for the ruins Ciu-dad de los Pueblitos armed with pick, shovel and hoe and on arriving set to work on one of the hills (was so soft and [blank] underneath in some places I went in to my knees, just in walking over it) and our efforts were rewarded by finding an ornament for necklace, with hole drilled in it of silvery gray stone, a half of shell bracelet and a bone awl, beside[s] quantities of pottery decorated and otherwise as well as unfinished stone implements and quantities of broken shell pieces. Being satisfied as to the expediency of excavating, Tenatsali having a bad stomach we left at 4 P.M. and came home across country up hill and down bouncing along at a gay pace. On approaching the ruin I noticed a pile of bright colored, curiously marked stones, similar to the one on side of hill where stands ruin on hill just opposite Camp Augustus, which Tenatsali said was a shrine.

Tuesday, Feb. 22
Washington's birthday is being celebrated in Washington to-day I suppose. It was not until this evening that I remembered anything about it when I communicated the news to the camp. To-day Mr. Garlick got together a 4-mule team, and with Mr. Cushing, Miss Magill, Mrs. Cushing and myself went about six miles south of Tempe to the old mine about which there has been so much talk.[76] We worked very industriously and found large quantities of unique fragments of unique pottery, and portions of spindle-whorls, bracelets, arrow points, and among other things I discovered a war-club, 2 metate stones and a scraper. We returned to camp well pleased with our day's work and all excited over the richness of the region in which we were located. Spent the evening in Mr. Cushing's tent where he dictated a couple of letters.[77] Miss Magill made me her "victim" (as she calls it) again by sketching me while in the act of writing. A very cold and windy day to-day.

Tuesday, Feb. 22
The morning was bright and pleasant (a few clouds in the sky) so we made ready the four mule team and covered buckboard and all (Mr. Garlick, Mr. Hodge, Emma and I with Tenatsali on horseback) set out for the ruins four miles from Tempe[78] where the excavations made by gentlemen in the neighborhood were stopped when they heard Tenatsali was in the vicinity. Digging enough had been done (beside that in the largest mound)[79] to unearth two great ovens about which there is much speculation and it was to hear Tenatsali's

opinion that operations were suspended. The natives' first supposition was that it was a smelter for precious metals which the Indians were supposed to have mined and some men have formally claimed all gold or silver to be found in that location and placed a paper to that effect in an old stone mortar unearthed from the ruin—for the general public to read. On account of these great ovens Tenatsali named the ruins Pueblo de los Hornos.[80] The use of these same he has not decided yet whether crematories or no—but that they are not smelters for precious metals he is certain as the quantities of broken shell bracelet were proof enough.

We found it a rich place full of relics lying loosely over the ground of which we collected quantities—decorated pottery, of every description, arrow-heads, stone axes and metati stones, a war club and numerous pieces of shell besides a whole bivalve and univalve. It extended as far over the plain as the eye could reach in little mounds which fairly shone with fragments of pottery.[81] After collecting and exploring till late in the afternoon (no digging) we started for home about 4 P.M[.]—but Tenatsali lagging behind made his most brilliant discovery after we left, viz. that sacrificial cave[82] of this ancient race, where there were prehistoric cigarettes of jointed cane, containing tobacco from which the odor has not yet faded and wrapped in [blank] made cotton cloth of their own weaving. These he said resembled in every detail those made even at the present day by the Zunis. All were happy at the finds of the day—especially Tenatsali (tho very sick) who is on track of several more caves. Met Dr. Gregg[83] who took T. in to see his collection and gave him a little article from the ruin, of cement decorated cut lines round the sides /// /// thus which he supposed to be curcelito[?] tho' T. says it is really only a rest for the spindle end. Mr. Hodge came in to take dictation and kindly offered himself as a subject for the pen and ink sketch this eve.

Our first visit to Tempe was made today as we were obliged to pass through it on our way to the ruins. It is an odd little place with rows of cotton wood trees—quite picturesque. The Salado river, which lies between us and Tempe was quite high and the buckboard just escaped the water when we crossed. The river bed is full of large pebbles some curiously marked such as I saw at the shrine's ruin on hill beside us and at Ciudad de los Pueblitos and which I noticed also at the ruin today, Pueblo del los Hornos. I neglected to say that the arrow points found here were the longest and slimmest I ever saw as well as the most delicately chipped. One was White, another obsidian and the third delicately tinted blue and pink, sacred Tenatsali told us. We had scarcely gotten started when the wind blew up a perfect sand storm as well as a little rain which was very cold and disagreeable but cleared soon after we reached the ruin. To add to our discomfort the sun downs and other hats in the top of the buckboard (which is the only place we have to keep them as everything in a tent has to be on the floor) kept falling down repeatedly on our heads and Mr. Garlick grew quite cross at having to stop the mules so often to put them up.

Wednesday, Feb. 23

Wrote up my notes this am. Mr. Cushing went with Miss Magill and the Chinaman to Tempe Butte, where they discovered some pictographs. Mrs. C. and myself watched them through the field-glasses as they climbed the butte. Had another delegation of Pimas to-day, who came to sell their baskets, arrows, bows, etc. After supper I went to Tempe on the white horse to the post office. After returning Mr. C. and I worked on accounts until after 9 when I returned to my tent and retired.

Ash Wednesday, Feb. 23

After copying out my 46 Pima words in a book (I find I have to add an ear as in early to the Zuñi alphabet) I went with Tenatsali and Dah Yung to Tempe. While waiting for Tenatsali outside the store I carefully observed a crowd of Pima Indians, men, women and children who were sitting in the street. One woman opened her dress and nursed her child without the slightest embarrassment in the open town and all scratched their heads (which looked as if they needed a good deal of it!) à la Zuni, by planting in the fingers firmly, slightly buried working with the thumb. The women as well as the men paint their faces grotesquely and all are dressed in ragged American materials such as bandana handkerchiefs in sheets, old table cloths etc. They looked at me and smiled. I am more popular with reds than whites usually, why I cannot tell. Our errands finished Tenatsali and I drove half way up the high Mountain overlooking Tempe [Tempe Butte], descended from the buckboard and tied the mules to a little bush, while we climbed to the top rocks and found many interesting things. The rocks were covered with pictographs—rattlesnakes, dance figures, Mountain sheep, lizards, dragon flies and a mark such as I saw tattooed on a Pima girl's arm. On the way up we found the rocks worn and smoothed in spots which by sitting on them I found to be seats with the stones in front and convenient to the right hand marked as if by the sharpening of some instrument. Tenatsali supposed the place was used in ceremonials, as one to sharpen their weapons at that they might be more powerful. After T. smoked a cigarette we separated, he going round the Mountain on one side and I on the other to explore. I found several chipping stones, pieces of shell and pottery besides a few holes which however contained nothing but rat nests. Tenatsali as he had supposed found a sacrificial cave where he got a few specimens but there were so many cacti choyas at the opening, that he could not get in. We had arranged to meet at the buckboard and I reaching the starting place first, was dismayed to find no sign of mules or vehicle. On [looking] carefully I saw it standing safely down in town. Tenatsali soon joined me and we walked down, found Dah Yung, drove to the P. O. and from there home as it was already quite late.

Thursday, Feb. 24

Our nights are getting a little more pleasant now since the cold snap. We (Mr. and Mrs. C., Miss Magill and myself) went again to the old ruin south of Tempe, and found some more interesting specimens. We felt quite tired after finishing our search and Mr. Cushing suffered another attack of illness during the course of the afternoon necessitating my riding "Douglass" to the nearest ranch for water. Returned through Tempe, where I received a letter at the post-office from Crossman. After supper Mr. C. and myself again worked on the accounts until quite late. Weta shot 11 ducks to-day.

Thursday, Feb. 24
Finished reading "The Lady with the Rubies" by Marlitt.[84] Had numerous Pima Visitors in the morning from whom I bought two large trays. Afternoon Tenatsali, Emma, Mr. Hodge and I went again to the Pueblo de los Hornos ruins, where we found lots of more relics, stone axes, shell ornaments and I found a little turquoise bead such as the Zunis make today, half drilled through. Tenatsali was taken quite sick so could make no discoveries. There is a house near the ruins where Mr. Hodge went for water and on driving out we returned the bucket when the mistress came out and showed us two or three little relics which the children had picked up and which she freely gave us. T. paid the little boy well for their finds. We stopped in town at the P. O. and I received a letter from T——. Wrote Mrs. Coann.[85]

Friday, Feb. 25
Arose about 7:30 and spent the day hard at work with my accounts. Rode to the post-office in the evening, receiving a letter from home. Wrote to Bro. Charlie in the evening and retired about 9:30.

Friday, Feb. 25
Wrote long letter in shorthand to Mr. March. A bright day but rather windy. We spent it by having a general cleaning up and Tenatsali and I changed sides of tent, I keeping the Curtained side. Mr. Patrick[86] called about 5.30 and as supper was getting we invited him to stay and partake and he partook, even remaining till almost ten P.M. He is engineer for the railroad and invited us all to come tomorrow and see his collection at the ranch 4 miles from Phoenix.

Saturday, Feb. 26
Was again occupied to-day in making a statement of the expenditures from beginning of the Expedition to date. Rode to post-office in the evening but found no mail for me. Mr. Garlick went to Phoenix in the morning, returning about five o'clock. Work'd on accounts again after supper & wrote to Bailey.

Saturday, Feb. 26

Mr. Garlick went to Phoenix this morning quite elated as he always is at the prospect of going to town. He intended starting early so he informed us last night but did not get off till after eight when we were all up and ready for breakfast, which he insisted was remarkably early—exclaiming as each one made his appearance that something was surely going to happen that such an early hour should find us up. Thus he excused his lateness but each in her secret soul understood. I made my morning visit to Douglass with Mr. Hodge for audience and fed him some grain.

Another windy day (but sunshiny) till noon when it grew so hot that even Emma had to go out to cool off this aft. I took a good bath and put on a nice dress and collar to see how it would feel after wearing wash net for a month.

Mr. Patrick came about 4 P.M. but we concluded it was too late to start so Tenatsali went alone with him on horseback, while I sketched the line of sandstone hills North, in oils. Mr. McClintock the Editor of the Tempe Newspaper called this morning. He has written a very nice article about Tenatsali—indeed the Cushing party have a notice in his paper every day.[87] Mr. Patrick showed us a new kind of cactus wch. is very small with a root thrice its size, shape of s[weet]. potato.

Sunday, Feb. 27

In order to keep the engagement which Mr. C. had entered into with Mr. Goodwin,[88] all hands with the exception of Dah Yung went to Tempe with the buckboard and a four-mule team and from there to the large ruin which we had already twice visited. Here we searched again most diligently in the sun, for the day is very warm, and with good success in relic-finding. We afterwards went to Goodwin's Ranch, where we examined quite an interesting collection which Mr. Goodwin had made and a number of which specimens he kindly presented to the Expedition. A very large and interesting ruin[89] about half a mile from this ranch we also examined, discovering that the walls were intact and that excavations could advantageously be carried on there. Remained until nearly sunset when we returned toward camp, enjoying greatly our homeward ride in the delightful evening air. We have passed over everything possible for a vehicle to pass over to day—dry sandy and dusty roads; sagebrush clumps, irrigating ditches, wheat fields and anything else likely to appear at first impassable. After supper I spent the evening in my tent conversing with Mr. Cushing who remained until bedtime.

Sunday, Feb. 27
Mr. Burgess came this afternoon (will help with the excavations). Such a day as yesterday—the early morning windy and afternoon hot. Tenatsali had engaged to go with the Goodwins[90] to see ruins near his ranch so about 10 A.M. we sallied forth with four mules to the buckboard pulling Mr. Hodge, Mr. Garlick, Emma and me while Tenatsali rode Douglass, Weta on the [blank]. We met Mr. G. in Tempe stopped at the P. O. to mail some letters. T. was feeling badly so Em gave him some medicine from the b.b. which no expedition starts without, and offered him some wine-rum which he declined. Mr. G. soon returned smelling strongly of peppermints and very amiable in demeanor and we proceeded to our favorite ruin, Pueblo de los Hornos, where we found with Weta's assistance some more valuable relics including an eagle fetich made of flat grey stone—wings spread and claws scratched in, ready to grasp. Tenatsali was taken very sick here and had to lie down under the b.b. I went back to get the hoe for digging and found him without water as Mr. Garlick with his eternal thirst had drunk the last drop from the canteen.

The walk back and relic hunting was oppressively warm and my new shoes extra heavy made felt stiff and uncomfortable in the heat. T. took a vomit after which he felt better so we started on to the other ruin in Mr. Goodwin's place which was eight long miles from Tempe over a dreadful road. We stopped at a ranch half way to water all round as the great heat had made us all thirsty but the water did not mend matters much as it was very salty. At Mr. Goodwin's it was not fit to drink being positively briny. The ruin[91] was according to Tenatsali the best we have seen, being untouched aside from a little digging done by Mr. G. and his brother of wh. he gave us the benefit by presenting a little jar, a stone axe and some spindle wheels of decorated clay. T. gave name, Pueblo de los Muertos.

Monday, Feb. 28

What a delightful feeling passes over one as he lies in his bed while the sun creeps over the eastern mountains, and the birds are singing their morning carols! Camp-life makes one realize his peace with the world, for his sleep is as peaceful as that of a babe, his appetite large and healthful, and what more could be desired? These were my waking thoughts this morning, and I felt as happy as I could be. Have learned the progress of breakfast at the hands of Dah Yung by heart and it only needs following in my minds eye to tell me when it is time to dress. It was Mr. C's intention to go to-day with Burgess and excavate the ruin we visited yesterday, but were so long in getting ready that the project was postponed until to-morrow. Burgess and Mr. Garlick were employed all day in doing "police" duty and now the camp is as clean and smooth as one might desire. I was very busy with my account statement all day, leaving my tent only when the warm air drove me into the breeze, for the thermometer registered 96—the warmest of the season. Read a little at night, wrote to Chilcote at Fort Wingate and after chatting a while with Mr. C. who again visited me this evening, went to bed.

Monday, Feb. 28

Had little fire last night and none this morning as signs of a hot day began to make themselves felt when we first woke. I put on my usual woolen dress but felt so oppressed by the heat that I changed for a jersey which is a degree cooler. Tenatsali and Em with Dah Yung went to Tempe after breakfast. Mr. Garlick & Mr. Burgess brought a load of wood and cleaned up camp. Mr. Hodge busy at reports all day—occasionally emerging from his tent for breathing space. Extracted a choya from Mr. Burgess' finger while waiting for the return of the buckboard—wh. by the way was so late in coming that the proposed trip to the ruins was given up and very well as the heat increased rapidly reaching at 3 P.M. 96 in the shade. I got out my sundown and trimmed it with the antedeluvian red sash and all pronounced it very becoming—comfortable it certainly was, pushed back from my forehead and shading the back of my neck. I called on Mr. Hodge in his tent, then resorted to the buckboard—the coolest spot in camp today and sketched both in water color and oils all the afternoon with two Pima youths as interested lookers on.

Tenatsali quite well all day and Em still tired from yesterday's jolting. While we were still at supper Mr. Hayden[92] the landed proprietor and first settler-founder of Tempe and Dr. Way called and spent half the evening. The poor Indians—who went out early to the ruins in the expectation that we would follow—came in after dark each with a nosebag (which we thus utilize on our expedition) full of relics, but none of special value, but two very pretty arrow heads.

Tuesday, March 1

I remained in camp to-day busily engaged in making out my accounts while the remainder of the party repaired to "Pueblo de las Hornos." Mr. Garlick, assisted by Francisco,[93] dug a trench through two mounds finding one jar and the skeleton of a child with feet toward the west. In camp the weather felt quite warm, the thermometer in my tent reaching 98°.

Sunday [Tuesday], March 1

We got started about noon for the Pueblo de los Hornos with our new workman named Francisco.

Mr. Burgess was called away suddenly to see about his claims so Mr. Garlick dug in his place. We unearthed or rather dug a trench through two mounds. In the first [we] found nothing but broken pottery and a stone war club and in the second [was] part of a child's skeleton with feet turned toward the West, but a coyote had dug a hole there and disturbed the remains & also broken the sacrificial pottery buried with it. Tenatsali on crossing the mound first found a small perfect jar, just below the surface. We also found the collection Weta had made of metati stones etc. and marked with his sun totem in the sand. He made a good find as usual, brought in at night as Si wa-ti tsa lu and he wandered off in search of the other ruin and got almost to the Gila. 98° of heat in the tents today.

Wednesday, March 2

To-day at 9:30 all hands went to "El Pueblo de las Muertos" with Francisco and Jesus[94]—2 Mexican workmen. Towards evening we found 3 jars, containing cremated remains on the south side of the first mound in this Pueblo excavated. Upon our return to camp we found Mr. and Mrs. Hayden[95] and

Mrs. Farmer (wife of Prof. Farmer of the Normal School).[96] After their departure and when supper was had we examined the contents of the jars in Mr. Cushing's tent, where I remained the rest of the evening.

Wednesday, March 2

At 9.30 started for Pueblo de los Muertos—Mr. Hodge, Mr. Garlick, Tenatsali and I in the covered buckboard and Mr. Burgess and two Mexicans to dig in the other and Si'wa ti tsa lu on horse-back. Tenatsali was very sick all day. The place was reached (being 8 miles) only a little before 12 so we ate lunch then the men commenced excavations on the big mound, where they struck a wall and some bones—adult. We then went to a smaller mound which T. had selected and dug a trench half way through and a turn to the side (West) a few feet, unearthing three jars, which were covered by pieces of broken pottery. Started for home at 5.30 taking them with us untouched as to contents for Mr. Goodwin and another man seeing us come and stayed till we left. On arriving at camp quite late (a beautiful moonlight ride) found Mr. & Mrs. Hayden and Mrs. Farmer making a call on us. After supper which was very late all gathered in our tent and examined the contents of the jars which were carefully opened and found to contain cremated bones—human and in one jar some remnants of shell beads such as that Zuni use today—Co ha kwa—showing that sacrifices with the dead were burnt with them. Little pills of charcoal found round the jars and other evidences of firing showed that after the cremated bones were put in the jars they were burned again.

Not so warm as yesterday.

Thursday, March 3

We had an early start for Muertos again this morning, and our day's work was well rewarded with the unearthing of fourteen burial urns, nearly all of which were whole. Mr. Garlick and myself planned the ruin while Miss Magill and Mr. C. made sketches of the pottery. One of to-day's finds was remarkably interesting: Beneath a jar that was covered with broken pottery was another and larger one. The smaller contained the bones of a child—the larger one those of a middle-aged woman—both thoroughly cremated. The conclusion arrived at by Mr. C. was that they probably perished together, and those who buried them, desiring that they should be together in death as in life, buried them one with the other. A few drops of rain were falling as we took the urns from their resting-place as though the heavens, that watched over them as they were interred, could not control its weeping. During our ride home we all witnessed the most gorgeous double-rainbow it had ever been our lots to look upon. It extended from horizon to horizon and the dark clouds and mountains in the distance lent a background that made it appear all the brighter.

Thursday, March 3
Earlier than yesterday the same party including Emma went to the Pueblo de los Muertos, to continue the excavations. Nine jars such as we found yesterday were unearthed—all differing in shape and size and some covered with inverted bowls while others had the broken pottery laid over the mouth of which I made a sketch was a small jar containing bones while on top was a bowl containing adult female bones which in turn had as covering another inverted bowl which was broken as were several of the jars.

Cool and pleasant all day but cloudy and a little rain. Started for camp at 5 P.M. A few drops of rain on the way, just enough to make the lovliest rain bow I ever saw, which with the lights and shadows on the mountains made the ride entrancing. When we reached Tempe the clouds had almost disappeared and the moon was shining brightly. Weta found a remarkably shaped surface jar.

Friday, March 4
I remained in camp again today, working on some correspondence which Mr. Cushing dictated to-me last night.[97] Mr. Garlick started early with the Mexicans and Burgess and they were followed later on by Mr. and Mrs. Cushing and Miss Magill. They found but one jar (which was broken) in the whole day's search, and returned to camp about 8 o'clock.

Friday, March 4
Mr. Garlick went ahead to the excavations, Tenatsali, Mr. Burgess and I following later having an errand and mend to be attended to

at the blacksmith in Tempe. Reached Pueblo de los Muertos about 1 P.M. All at lunch so I immediately made T's granum after eating which he took a nap, having a little headache. Nothing was found all morning but early in the afternoon a little jar Mound I R was unearthed with a long neck which was broken—lying at the side as in sketch p. 8 of sketch book I.[98] Home by moonlight. Mr. Hodge came in to see us in evening.

Saturday, March 5

I remained in camp to-day also. Burgess and four Mexicans accompanied Mr. Garlick with an early start to the same ruin (Muertos). To day was much more successful than was yesterday. On the north side of the second mound of this ruin were found a large drum, drinking dippers (for medicine-water) shell trumpet and sacred black-paint—all used in the ceremonials of the Priesthood of the Bow, at Zuñi,[99] which goes to show, in a great degree, that if the people who inhabited these ruins were not Zuñis they were at least greatly akin to them. On the south side of the same mound were found several ceremonial war-clubs—all too light for actual use. Mr. Patrick called this evening after the party had returned, bringing a map of the Salado Valley which will prove most valuable in our location of ruins.[100]

Saturday, March 5

Spent the day at the ruin again digging at the same mound with two extra Mexicans, making five workmen in all. I went on horseback—Douglass and losing the buckboard (the wagon went abroad early) by riding on first I went half way alone, arriving first. Found five jars had been unearthed before my advent which I was immediately called upon to sketch. After lunch the next mound to the right was begun in II and Tenatsali, true to his instincts, found an estufa in the walls which were immediately struck with a Priest of the bow corner (north, containing a broken sacred drum—a shell trumpet, a drinking shell such as is used for holy water in ceremonials in Zuni today—sacred black paint—and a double headed axe—on the south side of the mound whence the digging was begun Jesus found six ceremonial war clubs. Mr. Goodwin with a friend came over for the afternoon and worried us all by his incessant talking.

Got started for home later than usual. I rode back with Weta in the moonlight (which was lovely and bright) and had a gay time racing and chatting with that larky gentleman. Mr. Patrick (returned from the Gila) came over after tea and stayed till 11 P.M. All spent the evening in our tent. He brought me a lovely little Pima Jar to my surprise. He is as funny as ever with his amazing experiences and pulse warmers. A trip to his house was arranged for tomorrow.

Sunday, March 6

All the folks but myself, Burgess and Dah Yung went in the buckboard to Mr. Patrick's. Mr. Garlick continued on to Phoenix where he spent the day with Dr. Mitchell returning to Mr. Patrick's in time to catch the buckboard on its return trip. I remained in camp during the day "cleaning house," airing my bedding, washing towels and hunting (with no success the latter). Finished reading Mr. Cushing's "adventures in Zuñi" in the "Century" during the evening.

Sunday, March 6

Our escort came promptly this morning—Mr. Patrick—and asked me to ride with him, while T., Em and Mr. G. went in the buckboard. The latter drove in to Phoenix but returned in time to see the relics which were the object of our visit and were displayed after we had inspected the ruin on his ranch.[101] When Em and I found some very nice little specimens—Mr. P. gave T. a few duplicates specimens. Very hot all day. T. taken quite sick. Dust on the road suffocating.

Did not get home till almost sunset. The Indians off all day ruin hunting—returned after dark or rather after night, as the moon made it like day light.

Monday, March 7

With the exception of Mrs. Cushing and Dah Yung we all went to the "Muertos" ruin to-day. Mr. C. went on ahead with the workmen. I accompanied him on the large wagon. Before the others arrived we had discovered a magnificent sacred medicine-water jar, containing two shell dippers which are considerably worn by use. The jar had the "line of life" preserved in its decorations, the same as on the jars made in Zuñi today. Mr. C. and I made plans of this ruin and Burgess and Jesus were put to work on "Ruin No. III" where they excavated three small, but perfectly preserved jars, before the time arrived for us to return to Camp. Goodwin visited us while at the latter mound and told us a very interesting story of an English-speaking Indian and the Mormons at Tempe. This Indian called one day at the house of a Mormon and asked him who lived there. Being told that Mr. Johnson[102] did, he inquired who resided next door, when he was met with the same response. His query as to the person who occupied the adobe across the road was also answered in the same manner, when he finally desired to know who it was living in the house around the corner. "Mr. Jones," replied the Mormon. "Ah" said the Indian "Why is it that a Mr. Johnson doesn't also live there?" "Well", answered the Mormon, "You see, Jones married one of old Johnson's daughters!"[103] Mr. McClintock spent the evening in Camp securing data from Mr. C. in order to write an article for publication in the "Valley News."

With eight workmen I started with Mr. Garlick to "Muertos" reaching the ruin in about two hours. Taking 3 Mexicans and Burgess I continued work on Mound III. Mr. G. with the remaining four men, resuming yesterday's excavations on No. ~~II~~ XIV. I was very successful to-day, my men unearthing about 15 jars etc. nearly all complete. Alone, in the center of our excavation, I found a tolerably well-preserved skeleton of a man, a large portion of the skull being the most complete bone found. During the evening Mr. G. and myself made locations of all the pottery found in my ruin and a plan of the excavation. As working more than the clearing away of debris from the well preserved walls of mound No. II by Mr. Garlick's force nothing in the way of planning his work was done. We had a beautiful moonlight ride home by way of the Maricopa road[104] on account of the bad conditions of the irrigating ditches which we had to cross. Mr. Cushing called on me in my tent this evening as I was lying down, and complimented me on the success of my work to-day. He also spoke at length on our recent finds and future prospects.

Monday, March 7

Had an early start this morning. All went to the ruin Pueblo de los Muertos except Emma and Dah Yung, Tenatsali and I going in the little buckboard (the other being at the Shop mending) and Mr.

Garlick & Mr. Hodge in the wagon with the workmen: 4 Mexicans and Mr. Burgess.

A ruin in Mound II was unearthed (the one which we suspect of being an estufa[)][105] and in it was found a large decorated jar (pg 4, Book I) containing two scallop shells, near which was a large stone used as a loom weight. A diagram of this Mound was made as [were] measurements taken of the walls which were [blank] long and 18 ins. wide. Digging was also done by Jesus and Mr. Burgess in Mound III where four bowls and a little jar were found. All this took quite long so the sun was setting when we got started. A lovely moonlight drive home. Mr. Goodwin in a linen collar and a boiled shirt made us a visit in the afternoon. He told us one of his amusing yarns about an English speaking Indian and a Mormon.

The interesting facts of the day are that the decoration on the jar are pure Zuni. Mr. Hodge found some shell ornaments, such as are used by the Zuni priests of the bow today, and I found part of a clay female figure in Mound II such as is built in the Zuni walls to insure the women in the house where they are that they will be mothers.[106]

Tuesday, March 8

The party for the ruins today consisted of seven Mexicans and Mr. Burgess to dig. Mr. Garlick, Mr. Hodge, Tenatsali, Emma, and I on horseback. Ditches very bad and mud around them heavy and almost impassable. Finds of jars and bowls good in Mound III all of which I sketched. Only one large one F. contained cremated bones. Tenatsali has made the observation that all the burials are made on the South side of mounds.

Mound II was also worked at some but produced nothing but a few specimens of shell beside walls of which the ground plan was carefully continued by Messrs. Garlick and Hodge.

Our only visitors were some travellers from the road, who seeing the workmen came in quest of water. Did not start for home till sunset, but had bright moonlight all the way which was by Maricopa Road reached by means of Gray's Ranch.[107] Had to keep beside buckboard all the time so as the mules trot like "John."

Douglass was obliged to go in like manner or almost trotted me to death—besides groaning occasionally with colic, which he is subject to on account of his drinking propensities. Once upon a time he was almost famished and the memory of that time remains with him so thinking of this as a wise precaution he drinks at every stream—ergo he is colicy.

Water turned into the new ditch by Goodwin's and bad crossing.

Wednesday, March 9

I remained at Camp to-day, busily engaged in working up the accounts. The party at the ruin were not very successful in their finds. Owing to the very bad condition of the roads, by reason of turning on water in several new irrigating ditches, the "excursionists" did not return until 9 o'clock when we had our suppers and retired early.

Wednesday, March 9

The party of yesterday excepting Em & Mr. Hodge went to the ruin this morning. Tenatsali and I in the little buckboard. Went by Maricopa road again and through Gray's and Goodwin's ranches. Ditches worse than ever to cross as the soil around was miry to the extent of the mules thighs and trouble getting them into it.

Mr. Garlick in a bad temper all day. As usual I cooked T's granum and looked after him—tho' he was pretty well today. Finds small.

Had scraper at work cleaning dirt away from the walls of South side of Mound II where only a stone ax, a jar (large) and a drinking (scallop shell) were found. The large mound was commenced and an immense wall about three feet thick was struck.

Left ruins after sunset—later than we have ever before started for home tho' the full moon made it bright as day. After crossing Goodwin's two ditches found man waiting at Gray's ranch to tell us that all was flooded below and impassable—that we would have to go across country and find the Maricopa road—that we would have to cross two more ditches in between but thought we would have no trouble—and we started. The first ditch was fearfully deep so that the water came into the buckboard covering the floor and wetting our feet. Here we parted from the wagon which found the right road and bridge fortunately. We did not and had to cross another ditch which was fearful. The mules sank in to their thighs, then laid down in despair and I thought we were stuck for the night, but they finally got out by much urging. From here we cut again and found the old road on which we proceeded till another overflowing ditch blocked the way, then cut again N. W. and found the Maricopa road after which all was plain sailing as the ditches are all old and firm but we did not get home till 9 P.M.

We decided the excavations could not be continued in Pueblo de los Muertos on account of the water so three Mexicans were discharged and the other four with Burgess engaged to work at Ciudad de los Pueblitos—tomorrow.

Thursday, March 10

Mr. Cushing went with Burgess and four Mexicans to "El Ciudad de las Pueblitos,"[108] about four miles west of camp, on the road to Phoenix. Mr. Garlick accompanied them as far as the ruin and then continued to Phoenix to make purchases. I followed the excavators to the pueblo with the ladies in the buckboard, and Siwahitsialu, Mr. C., feeling unwell, spread his blanket on the ground in the shade of the buckboard and rested while I superintended the work of excavation. The men worked diligently during the hot day and by evening had excavated the earth from about the walls of a three-story ruin about 30 feet long and probably 10 or 12 feet deep. On the interior walls, which were remarkably well finished, were found drawings evidently made by children—and on the floor of the second story, in the middle of the room was found an adobe fire-place, well preserved, and with ashes still remaining in the bowl-like grate. Mr. Cushing told us of the story which resulted in the conversation between him and Mrs. Adams, the wife of the occupant of the land, concerning the ladies and their "Grecian bands" which was exceedingly amusing.[109]

Thursday, March 10

Tenatsali went early with the 5 workmen and Weta to Ciudad de los Pueblitos. Mr. Garlick went on from there to Phoenix for grain etc. Emma, Mr. Hodge and I with Si watitsa lu followed in the buckboard at 10 A.M.

Walls of Mound I[110] were uncovered and found full of pictures scratched on the plastering which looked smooth and black. The building was two stories high and the excavations were begun at the top of the mound. In the 2nd story was uncovered a little fireplace which was hollowed in the floor like a shallow bowl and still contained ashes. The roof line or ceiling of the lower story was very distinct and consisted of a layer of charcoal—charred and between the two layers plastered adobe—floor for 2nd and ceiling for the 1st story. No finds were made but some broken fragments of cooking pot, bones of antelope and bear and a broken shell bracelet. Tenatsali before digging obtained permission from the people named Adams who live in the little house at the base of the great mound and had a most amusing visit. Mrs. Adams was alone when he entered—a lean lank old woman with a pipe in her mouth, which he filled with his best tobacco by way of introduction. In the course of the conversation she said she would have come into Camp to see us yesterday if she had only been sure that the women were at home. She wished to know next if they were his women—then recounted that some women folks from Phoenix came to her house the other day—said they knew all about Mr. Cushing but about the women folks what did they look like? "I just told them" said Mrs. A. "that they was nice looking people—real ladies for they wore the Grecian bend." In going home we stopped a minute while the Mexicans mounted the bales of hay (for we met Mr. Garlick with his load from Phoenix at the road) at the house and Mrs. Adams came out to speak to us. After shaking hands she took a careful survey of Emma then turned to Tenatsali and said with unparalleled candor—"Well, she's a right good looking woman compared with you."[111]

Friday, March 11

Ciudad Pueblitos worked on again to-day. Mr. Cushing dictated to me nearly all the morning as I did not go to the ruin.[112] Mr. Garlick drove the workmen down in the morning and was busy from the time he returned until evening, making preparations on the contemplated trip to Superstition Mountains. A rumor was afloat around Tempe as to an outbreak among the Apaches and in the evening Mr. Cushing rode a mule to town in order to ascertain the truth of the matter. The rumor was substantiated by Mr. Armstrong,[113] the P. M. [postmaster] and several others, who stated that a Lieutenant at San Carlos Agency had been murdered and that five or six renegades had fled to the mountains for safety.[114] They had also taken possession of a ranch and had stolen a number of stock. The ladies were very much excited upon hearing the news and begged Mr. Cushing to defer the trip. The Indians were very busy all day in erecting a "wicky up", of willow poles and arrow-weed to afford shade. The day had been quite warm—the thermometer indicating 100° in my tent.

Friday, March 11

Vicenti [Villa Nueva], one of the workmen, brought Emma and me each a pretty flower this morning. The five laborers went to Ciudad de los Pueblitos and worked alone all day, unearthing the remaining walls of the house, as Mr. Garlick had to come back to get wood. He and Tenatsali went for them at 4.30 P.M. A very hot day. For additional comfort T. (very well all day) and the Zunis constructed a booth à la Pimo in front of the tent—which (four crotches roofed with reeds) gives a shelter from the sun and allowing the breezes full play.

Emma and I spent the day in the buckboard reading and writing. Mr. Hayden called with friends, Mr. Edwards[115] and Dr. Dare.[116]

Mr. Burgess' slight deafness makes him appear more stupid than he really is and the man seems born to misfortune. By no chance does he do the right thing and invariably leaves something wrong when he harnesses the mules. At the Muertos excavations his finds were always the smallest. He dug a whole day at a ditch three feet deep and five long, finding nothing. The next day the Mexicans went to the same place and throwing up a few inches of earth found seven burial jars. On that same day he went to work and had hard luck as usual and when I went over to look after things in the after noon, he said with his melancholy expression and slow drawl that it seemed to him a much easier and quicker way of getting a collection by going to the caves and finding it ready made.

The Cantines have red straps round them so being wet outside to keep the water cool, drip in everything and turn it pink which we call a new shade, cantine pink.

Preparations have been going forward all day for the trip to Superstition Mountain but a shell was fired into camp this evening with the intelligence that the Apaches are on the war path again and have just killed a man in Superstition Mountain so we have been persuading T. not to start. He went to Tempe after supper to find out how much truth there was in the report. He returned doubting the report.

Saturday, March 12

Notwithstanding the rumor of the Apache troubles and its substantiation by the Tempe citizens, Mr. Cushing, Mr. Garlick and Weta started for the range (Superstition) the two former in the small buckboard and Weta on his horse (which we are all fond of calling "The Rat"). I drove Mrs. C. and Miss M. to Ellingson's[117] where we put "Douglass" in pasture, leaving the Mexicans at work removing the "wicky up" which the Indians had built and erecting two larger ones—which they completed before our return to camp. We have now quite a shady camp. The larger "wickyup" is about 25 × 15 feet and the smaller one about 7 × 10. How we enjoy sitting under them in the cool of the evening, chatting of past experiences and probable ones! Was seated in my tent this evening, reading, when I heard the approach of footsteps. Going out I saw a man, coming on a white-horse which was walking very slowly. After the customary greetings he inquired where he would find the Phoenix road. Informing him, he was about to move off, when, seeing that his horse was very nearly "played out," I invited him to rest for a while. He accepted my invitation (and some supper too which I had Yung prepare for him) when a general conversation ensued. He stated that he had been on the road from McDowell[118] all day which led me to inquire about the Apache trouble. He also stated that the rumor was true and that a detachment of soldiers and scouts had been ordered from McDowell to suppress the "reds." After telling some more of his experiences in the section, where he had spent most of his time since the war, I asked him if he would not like to put his horse up for the night and remain himself. He was very glad of the opportunity, as dividing blankets with him and giving him room in Mr. Garlick's tent he signified his appreciation by numerous thanks and we both retired.

Saturday, March 12
Tenatsali and Mr. Garlick started about 11 A.M. for Fort McDowell in the buckboard with Weta on horseback, in spite of Apache story.

Mr. Hodge drove Emma and me in afternoon out to pasture where we left Douglas. The Mexicans stayed today and built us two "wicky ups" (or ram[ad]a as they call them) which will give us shelter and breeze too—

Tired traveller came by from Fort McD—says Apaches are out and troops after them. Stayed all night and we gave him supper and fed his horse.

Sunday, March 13
Got up late this morning and immediately after breakfast shouldered my bag and gun and strolled out over the hills to the north of camp. Seeing nothing worth shooting I returned to camp early, finding that the ladies had gone to Tempe calling. After a bite of lunch I again went hunting, securing 2 doves. While at supper I was much surprised at seeing We-ta gallop up, who informed us that the remainder of the party were on the way to camp and were expected every minute. It was not long before Mr. C. and Mr. Garlick came up. They had been to Fort McDowell where they learned from the authorities there all about the Apache affair, which was substantially the same as I have already noted.

Sunday March 13
Our visitor still here this morning but left about 9.30.

Painted specimens till 3 P.M. 4 P.M. drove to Tempe with Em. to pay visits. Mr. Burgess & Dah Yung went. Called on Mrs. Hayden and Miss Grace Ashley[119] and Mrs. Farmer. The last lives a mile from town in the fine house and is evidently considered "quality folks" by the other inhabitants. Our "wicky up" a great comfort all day during the heat—which was very great—100 in the tent and we all still wearing thick clothes which are none too thick for the evenings, always cool.

Came home from our visits engaged for a day spent at Mrs. Hayden's. Had visits from two store [?] young men from Phoenix while we were away.

Mr. Hodge killed two doves. While we were at supper Weta came dashing in much to our surprise and Mr. Garlick and Tenatsali soon followed.

Had been to F. McD. and learned that there is no danger in the trip to Superstition Mountain so came home for to-night to reassure us and to start tomorrow morning. After supper Mr. Hodge and I made a pyrotechnic display in honor of the returned ones by going up the hill burning choyas and savoyas [saguaros], which looked lovely in the darkness.

Monday, March 14

For the second time the party (Mr. C., Mr. G. and Weta) started for the Range as before, via Mesa City. I dressed up in my dark suit, derby hat and "boiled shirt" and went to Phoenix with the ladies and Dah Yung. I make a note of my appearance as it is the first time I looked like a gentleman since leaving Wingate, nearly two months ago! The nine miles' drive was very dusty and our dark clothes had transformed to gray ere we reached the town. I bustled around, making purchases and attending to other errands for about two hours when we again were on the road "home." I spent an hour in cleaning the dust from my clothing upon returning to camp, and before supper went to the river and took a bath. Bathing in March! Who would think it? Miss Magill very kindly gave me notes for my diary (which I had unavoidably neglected to keep posted during the past week) by the light of a candle, reflected by a canteen, under the "wickyup."

Monday, March 14

Mr. Garlick and Tenatsali with Weta on horseback started out as before for the mountain at 10 a.m. At same time Emma, Mr. Hodge, Dah Yung and I went to Phoenix.

All met at P. O. then at b.b. [buckboard] and started for home at 2, arriving completely covered with dust at 4–5 P.M. After supper we all sat in Indians tent a while then I gave Mr. Hodge some diary points and to bed.

Tuesday, March 15

Soon after breakfast went hunting, with but a single quail for my luck. The ladies spent the day in Tempe, visiting, while I remained in camp working on accounts and so forth, until the heat in my tent became so unbearable that it was impossible for me to continue it. Went out under the "wickyup" and assisted Siwatitsailu in shell-working, where I cooled off sufficiently to resume my "intent" labors. Retired quite early this evening.

Tuesday, March 15

We have the mess chest outside so eat under the "wicky ups" and keep delightfully cool. To be sure the food does too for the breezes flowing constantly dispels all heat—but as long as we keep comfortable we drink lukewarm beverages and eat cold food without complaining. Mr. Hodge says one advantage "they will tally". He has in his [diary] "killed two doves." The next morning I have in mine "ate two doves." So any one wishing to know what became of the game has only to look on my menu where they are accounted for. I had quite a joke on Em this morning. She has been keeping an empty pistol (is afraid to keep one loaded) and box of cartridges beside her bed since Tenatsali left in case of danger. Wishing to have a little target practice after breakfast we got out both pistol and ammunition to discover that the former is 38 and the latter 44 caliber. We fired a dozen loads at a box 12 × 24 due west 20 ft (missing every time) all of which caused Yung to appear much afraid. While Mr. Hodge declared he would put-up an umbrella for they were coming in his direction 50 yds due north.

About 11 A.M. we started for Tempe where we had promised to spend the day with Mrs. Hayden. Mrs. Webster[120] and Mrs. George[121] were invited to meet us and quite startled us by their finery. The latter had on a silk dress and all the jewelry possible for one woman to carry. At dinner three gentlemen were added to the party—the first Mr. Webster was introduced all round to the oldest ladies first but by the personal way in which Mrs. Hayden presented the two others first to me I knew they were single. One was Mr. Peters[122] and the other Mr. [blank], Mrs. Hayden's cousin. I took my knitting so was amused all day, but it was not bad taken all together as Mrs. Hayden is a splendid, whole-souled woman. Mrs. George [is] a great talker, earnest, Southern and very amusing, while Mrs. Webster is a nice little thing. We talked all day and the latter and I became great friends, making arrangements to ride horse back and bathe in the river when my bathing suit arrives. We started for home about five in spite of entreaties to spend the evening. Promised to come again and were promised in turn a dance at the town hall as soon as Mr. Peters returned from Pinal. Found Mr. Hodge had been hunting today so I had a nice little quail on toast for supper at my place.

It just occurred to me that I must have looked pretty dirty in town yesterday as the polite young man at the store who entertained me on a former occasion, offered me a whisk broom, a basin and a towel when I first alighted. Sat in Si'watitsa lu's tent talking till quite late as Mr. Hodge joined us.

Wednesday, March 16

Until driven out by the heat I spent the morning in my tent at work on accounts. Went hunting, caught two quail and a night-hawk, the latter being valued by the Indians very much on account of his feathers which they use for sacrificial purposes. Returned to camp very tired, warm and thirsty as tramping up and down hills and through arroyas is likely to make one. Went to town with the ladies to make purchases and post our mail. While at supper we spied a four-mule team crossing the river which proved to be our excursionists—Mr. C. and Mr. G. They had lots to tell about the "Superstitions" and what they saw there. Weta returned shortly afterwards bringing part of a deer which he had killed—the remainder arriving with the buckboard. Apaches: Mr. G. tells me that they had gotten into a nest of Apaches, Mr. C and Weta having seen two. They pulled the buckboard up in front of the door of an abandoned cabin, and, with their revolvers and rifles closely clasped to them, slept with one eye open listening to the Apaches' calls and their distant answers. They were somewhat alarmed but passed the night in comparative comfort and safety, notwithstanding they expected more exciting times at any moment.[123] While crawling in bed to night I experienced the unpleasant sensation of coming in contact with a lizard. I got up, struck a light, and by the aid of a pair of shears succeeded in beridding myself of an unpleasant bedfellow.

Wednesday, March 16

Under our new canopy this morning it is breezier than ever, the salt and sugar would blow away over the edge of the cup wh[ich] was to be seasoned and we had to pin our napkins to our laps. Yung who is very frugal felt obliged to cut down our allowance of food. When Mr. C. went away tho' he eats nothing that we do. The coffee was so shadowy that it had no taste and Emma asked Yung if he had'nt forgotten to put any in or boiled it over yesterday's leavings. He only chuckled under his hat brim and came slowly towards the table—etc.

Our travellers Tenatsali, Mr. Garlick and Weta returned from Superstition Mountain at 6-30 P.M.

All spent the evening talking over the trip together under the canopy.

Thursday, March 17

Was up in time for breakfast which I ate and returned to my tent to work on the February accounts which have not yet been forwarded to Boston. Weta went hunting early in the morning but, without the mountain sheep he expected to find, returned about 9 o'clk in the evening. He, however, brought to camp a very interesting bird fetich which he had found in one of the ruins. Mr. Garlick spent the day in Tempe at work fixing the buckboard, while Burgess, Siwatitsailu and two Pimas were employed in hauling reeds from the river-bank for making a floor for the larger "wickyup." While so engaged Burgess was attacked by a huge rattlesnake, which he killed and brought to camp. It measured 52 inches and was the longest I had ever seen. Spent the evening in my own and the Indians' tents. Siwatitsailu gave me my "lesson" in Zuñi, managing to learn a few words more through his instruction.

Thursday, March 17

Cool this morning and cloudy—a lovely day for anything.

The photographic outfit was opened and a cane floor made by our Pimo friend to the wicky up. In the meantime he gave me a lesson in his native language.

Tenatsali read aloud to us all the evening—Bayeux Tapestry.[124]

Friday, March 18

The party went to-day to "El Pueblo de las Hornos," leaving me in camp where I was busy all day in finishing up the February accounts, the completion of which greatly relieved me. The weather continues warm, the thermometer registering 96°; but I would not mind this so much were not the flies such an infernal nuisance. They become so annoying at times that my only relief is to rush from the tent and give vent to my wrath by seeking the life of some poor quail or dove which happens to encroach too closely upon the bounds of camp. The "mound-excavators" returned soon after dark securing very little in the way of specimens save a few arrow-points and other less important articles. Remained in my tent, all the evening, reading, retiring quite early.

Friday, March 18

Excavations at Pueblo de los Hornos, four Mexican laborers, Jesus [Arros], Vicenti [Villa Nueva], Rosalina and a new one in place of Francisco who could'nt come. Digging done in three mounds but nothing found excepting a little slate and a small oven such as the Zunis used for baking corn. It was in shape exactly like a funnel, the bottom filled with small stones—the sides smooth and of cement and about four feet deep. All went but Mr. Hodge and Dah Yung. Sketched some of Mr. Patrick's specimens. Had awning put up—were comfortable all day. T. read at night to us.

Saturday, March 19

Was in camp all day today preparing a map of the "Salado Valley" from one furnished by Mr. Patrick of the Maricopa & Phoenix R.R. in order to properly locate any ruins which we might discover in our reconnaissances. The rest of the camp (except Dah Yung and the Indians) went to the same ruin as yesterday ("El Pueblo de las Hornos") returning before sundown. They did a good deal of excavating, having four Mexicans, with Burgess, along but were unsuccessful in their finds. The Indians busied themselves all day—Siwatitsailu in grinding shell for beads and Weta in making a pair of stirrups. Received papers from home which I read during the evening, retiring quite early. Purchased decorated flute to-day: 68¢.[125]

Sunday, March 20

Today was one of the pleasantest I have thus far spent in camp. While the weather was warm, there was a refreshing breeze, and after "cleaning house," which is now a regular Sunday performance of mine, I reclined on my bed and read Cozzin's "Three Years in Arizona and New Mexico,"[126] arising only once or twice to shoot at quail and doves which came in sight of my tent. Miss Magill and Mr. Garlick went soon after breakfast in search of a hand satchel which Miss Magill lost yesterday, containing her diary, paints and other valuable articles. They succeeded in finding it, much to Miss Magill's delight, and returned to camp in about two hours. In the evening I wrote to Harry Smith for the first time since last seeing him, and remained chatting with Mr. Garlick in his tent, until 11 o'clock.

> *Sunday, March 20*
>
> Mr. Garlick and I went early this morning to the Buttes in the little b.b. and by following the wagon tracks of yesterday found my bag and the contents all safe. We got some very pretty wild flowers which I copied in my sketch book on reaching camp.
>
> The flies and mosquitoes have developed within the last few days too and the frogs and crickets crook and chiriup like summer time. Mr. Burgess took his leave today.

Monday, March 21

I remained in camp at work in preparing the map of the Salado Valley. Several Pimas called and I caught one little fellow and painted his face until it has the appearance of "Jacob's coat of many colors." Mr. and Mrs. C. instead of going to the ruin, went to Phoenix to make purchases. Mr. Garlick accompanied by Weta, also went and Weta as usual was the center of the town's attraction, being surrounded in the plaza by a host of Pima women who desired that he should give his turquoise (thliakwa) to them. He returned safely, however, and related his adventure at evening in the most amusing manner. Miss Magill remained in camp all day, busily engaged in writing and sewing. Feeling "headachy" I retired quite early.

Monday, March 21

Tenatsali and Emma went to Phoenix for the day in the buckboard to make various purchases.

Jesus & Vicenti worked all day on a ramada—kitchen. Mr. Hodge and I exchanged visits during the day for company and our Pima friend came and gave me another lesson.

Tuesday, March 22

I was awakened last night by a fearful wind which threatened to rent the tent asunder. As the dust was accumulating in my tent quite rapidly I arose with the sun to remedy the evil. The whole party went to the ruin to-day, Mr. Garlick taking his bed for a few days' stay with the Mexicans, at excavating. The wind continued all day, blowing the dust in all directions. From the appearance of the valley as far as my eye could reach I was confident that the party must have a very unpleasant journey to "Las Muertos," and when they returned and their stories [were] related I was glad I remained in camp at work on the map (which I commenced on Saturday) and which I completed. Mr. Garlick's tent blew completely down and Dah Yung and myself amused ourselves in repitching it. I received through the Tempe post-office a little "poem" on the "Flute" which the ladies afterwards admitted of writing and mailing to me. The joke was in my playing a Pima flute which I purchased of an Indian only a few days ago. Wrote to Mary Duvall whose letter I received last evening and another to Crossman, replying to two of his just received.[127]

Tuesday, March 22

Digging again today at Pueblo de los Muertos—but no finds. Mr. Garlick and the Mexicans have made side camp there to remain several days and continue excavations more advantageously. Mr. G., Vicenti and Francisco went first in the wagon while Jesus remained to drive us as Tenatsali was very ill all day. The dust perfectly suffocating so when we reached P. de los M. the color of my dress was indistinguishable and my hair perfectly blond. The ditches too were bad as several new ones on the road had been filled and we had hard work getting the mules through but by going beyond the Goodwin ranch on the homeward way, avoided all difficulties. Surface finds pretty good.

Em found a perfect gray stone fetish.

A fearfully windy day.

Wednesday, March 23

Mr. Cushing, not feeling very well to-day, concluded not to go to the ruin. We remained in camp until about two o'clk when I, with Miss Magill drove over with the little buckboard, Weta following behind with the "Indian" horse and mule which we put to pasture. We had just arrived at Goodwin's Ranch when we heard the distant rumbling of a wagon which Miss Magill concluded was Mr. Garlick who had just started from his camp for Camp Augustus. She was perfectly correct in her supposition for when we arrived at the ruin we discovered that Mr. Garlick had gone. Dropping the hay and provisions which we had brought for the camping party, I turned the horses' (or rather, mules') heads homeward, overtaking Mr. Garlick on Goodwin's Ranch road. We did not return to the ruin, but continued on, finding Weta awaiting us on the road. We got to camp just after dark, a tired and dusty trio.

Wednesday, March 23

Grand cleaning in camp today so the start was put off so late that Mr. Hodge and I had to set out alone in the little buckboard at 3 P.M. to carry Hay, meat etc. to P. de los M. Reached there over the new road above Goodwin's at 4–45. Found Mr. Garlick in wagon just started. Left things (without going to excavations) and followed him. Overtook him in time and learned that digging[s] in Mound [blank] were productive of good results. Jars etc. found numbering 22 and lettered to [Mound] V.

We took Weta to Pasture with Zuni animals, left him at Pueblo de los Hornos and brought him back with us when we returned.

Lovely day. Wrote my 1st Spanish lesson.

Thursday, March 24

We all went to the ruin to-day, starting about 10 o'clock. Stopping on the road for cottonwood poles was the only interruption in our journey until we reached Goodwin's Ranch Road. There several men were busy in irrigating their ranches from the new ditches into which water had a week ago been turned. A portion of the ditch running along the road had overflowed, covering the roadway for some distance with water, which, when we reached there, was apparently dry. Before it was noticed the mules "put their feet into it", going under the surface about a foot. Fearing, perhaps that they were going to pay our antipodes a visit against their will, they became excited, and, instead of pulling straight through, became unmanageable and turned to the side where they went under the full length of their legs. I jumped from the seat of the buckboard and tried to quiet the struggling animals, one of which had now become almost exhausted. Loosening their traces and collars again excited their ambitions to free themselves, but they became all the more entangled. By this time two of the men came up and we extricated them from the mire, a sad and muddy plight. Putting their harnesses on them again we examined the damages which we found to be a broken double-tree and several breakages in the harness and moved on to "Pueblo de las Muertos." There we found Mr. Garlick with the Mexicans in camp at luncheon. After partaking of ours (and roasting myself in trying to make Mr. Cushing's granum thicken over the fire) we went to the excavations and saw the result of the work. About 30 burial urns or jars had been unearthed, in one mound being but a foot or two apart and but a few inches below the surface. Miss Magill made sketches of all the specimens and we were then ready to return. We were sure to avoid the overflows this time so made a road through the mesquite woods, to the south of the overflowed portion. Gopher-holes and sage-brush were the principal obstacles to the progress of the mules, and sharp branches of thorny mesquite to the discomfort of ourselves. We reached the road in safety however and returned to camp soon after dark. Mr. Garlick returned to camp this evening with the large wagon. I spent the most of the evening in his tent conversing principally on the finds made during this week.

Thursday, March 24

Emma, Tenatsali, Mr. Hodge and I started for Pueblo de las Muertos at about 10:15 A.M. and arrived a little after noon—with much difficulty on account of mud, for tho' we went by way of the new road which we thought safe, some ditches by Goodwin's had overflowed making the ground very soft so the mules mired down (as they say out here) till they were helpless and the wheels in to the hubs.

Finding we could not move Tenatsali and Mr. Hodge got out and began to unharness but scarcely had Susan's trace been unhooked when she began to plunge and crossed to the opposite side, tangling the harness, breaking the whiffletree and worst of all using good "Tricy" for a stepping stone, walking all over her head till we thought she must be dead. The kind young man with an old one came and helped us out, (in time to prevent Tenatsali's shooting Susan whom he thought was killing "Tricy") by unharnessing, taking the mules out first, then pulling the buckboard after them by the wheels. We got off with little damage and the basket of eggs which we carried came through the ordeal without injury. On arriving at the ruin our good Mexicans hurried around to make us comfortable as usual and Mr. Hodge relieved me of the granum cooking. I made sketches of the finds which occupied me till the start at 4-30 P.M.

Mound VIII was worked on (as yesterday) till the jars became too numerous to walk around—then they returned to the walls of [Mound] II much disgruntled at finding nothing. A lovely day. Avoided mud by skirting Goodwin's Ranch and going among the mesquite.

Mr. Garlick came home to camp for the night and Mr. Patrick spent the evening.

Friday, March 25

We all remained in camp to-day, except Mr. Garlick, who returned to the diggings. Just after breakfast I went with him to Tempe, where he purchased grain, and boxes for packing specimens. To-day has been a busy one in camp. We took down my tent, which has been assigned to Miss Magill, and pitched it just east of the Sibley for her use. Then taking the new one we pitched that in the place occupied by the other, for my shelter and comfort. A Mexican has been busy in cleaning camp and we are beginning to look tidier each day. Went to Tempe in the evening to the post-office and to take the Mexican across the river.

Friday, March 25
All stayed at home today excepting a visit to Tempe for Emma and Tenatsali in the morning and Mr. Hodge in the evening when he drove the Mexican home who has been working here today. I spent my day bathing, knitting—etc. etc. Mr. Hodge's tent transferred to me.

Saturday, March 26
Was up right early, Mr. Cushing likewise. Immediately after breakfast we went to work continuing the rearrangement of camp. Went to town with Mr. Cushing and the Indians where we purchased tent-pins and other articles. Taking Mr. Cushing across the river I returned to town and made additional purchases, and recrossing the river loaded the water cask which Siwatitsailu had filled, and some cottonwood poles which Weta had busied himself in cutting, and then returned to camp. Took down the three wall tents and placed them in a row north and south, facing them east upon what we have named "Minstrel Avenue," in honor of the work of my "Pima flute." "Fly Plaza" and "Cushing Court" also designate distinctive places about camp, and "Garlick's Corners" is not to be forgotten. Our little camp is beginning now to appear shipshape and uniform. Put canvas floor in my tent, "cleaned up" and "moved in" spending a pleasant night's rest after good day's work.

Saturday, March 26
There was another revolution in camp today and a complete one. My tent was finished and I moved in, the 3 wall tents were ranged in a row facing East and a new floor and [?] put in the Sibley. Mr. Hodge and I named the camp Cushingville under the Butte and the streets as follows—

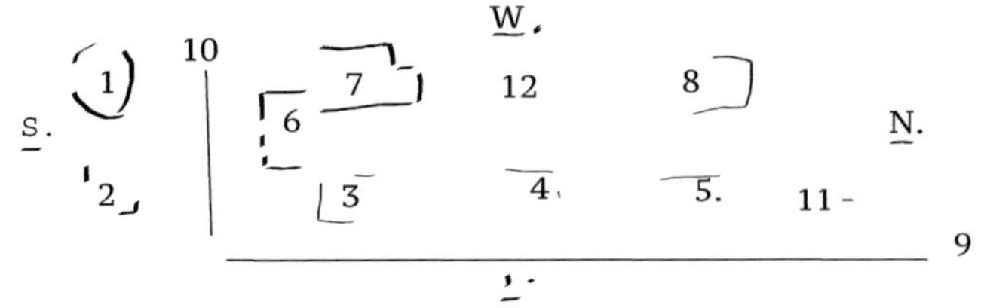

1. Sibley tent.
2. My tent.
3. Mr. Hodge's.
4. Dah Yung & Indians.
5. Mr. Garlick
6. Ramoda.
7. Kitchen - Ramoda.
8. Awning - Pantry.
9. Minstrel Avenue.
10. Cushing Court.
11. Garlick Corners.
12. Fly Centre.

The same Mexican worked here again today and everybody else was busy too so the ruin trip was given up and Mr. Garlick left to superintend alone. He came back before dark bringing the Mexicans (as far as Tempe) and a cute little pitcher which had been unearthed—the first of its kind. He says the finds since our visit have been only six in number. He says also that on Wednesday night they had ice inside camp at Pueblo de las Muertos, tho' the day was suffocatingly warm. Curious weather here—etc.

I cannot give a rule, but it is very delightful tho' the nights are cold enough for us to sleep under five blankets.

Sunday, March 27

Cleaned house this morning as my usual Sabbath occupation, and when that was finished accompanied Mr. Garlick to Ellingson's Ranch, where the animals were in pasture and found that all were doing well. Weta made me a very nice pair of moccasins (mo-kwa-we) to-day, which I immediately put on and strutted about camp like a game-cock. Wrote to Em. in the afternoon, and spent the evening in writing, reading and joking with the Indians.

Sunday, March 27

Tenatsali and I have been at cross purposes all day but the storm blown over this eve; beside writing my letters I helped Emma mend some of the excavated jars and spent the afternoon sketching in oils at the rocky hills East of Camp and then back to the old red sand stone hills North. Mr. H. had a partial engagement to walk to the Pima village with me but forgot and went off to pasture with Mr. Garlick. He apologized very humbly this evening etc.

Monday, March 28

Went to Tempe soon after breakfast and spent the morning there in collecting bills and making out vouchers for March accounts. Getting tired of awaiting the return of Mr. Garlick, who had gone after Cottonwood poles with the wagon, I begged passage across the river east of the usual place for fording on an ox wagon driven by a boy. I had great difficulty in reaching camp, being almost mired in the swamp on the north bank of the river. I earned my way through a dense undergrowth of arrow-weed however and returned in time for lunch. The Indians were busily engaged in making an adobe oven which they finished by evening. Worked in my tent on accounts during the afternoon with the thermometer indicating 110°! The warmest yet, although when we "turned out" this a.m. it registered but 35°. Rec'd a letter from Warman this evening who speaks of Mr. Pilling[128] accompanying Prof. Thompson[129] this season as his Disb'g Agent.

> *Monday, March 28*
> Sketched little flowers and went to the hills to sketch the Northern red rocks. Studied Spanish lesson.
>
> Two Mexicans all day at work on camp improvements and three for the afternoon—108° in tents today—Heat oppressive. Went for refreshment to the river and dabbled my feet in the water. Cold at night and till sunrise in the morning.

Tuesday, March 29
After finishing work on accounts to-day I commenced a synopsis of the doings of the party, from the time we reached Albuquerque, to-date, upon which I was occupied the remainder of the day. Went to town after supper to take Mexicans across the river and to settle some accounts. Mexicans have been working in camp all day, and we are at last "fixed." Received a letter from Mr. Baxter this evening.[130]

> *Tuesday, March 29*
> The five Mexicans here at work again today finishing the awning for trunks which has been enlarged.
>
> Spent day between sewing on my seersucker dress, knitting and helping Tenatsali put eyelets in last fly. Went to my old chestnut sketching place as usual at sunset. Up till 12.

Wednesday, March 30
Worked on my "synopsis of events" this morning. Went hunting in the afternoon bagging four doves and returned to camp to work with Mr. C. in making fly and awning for my tent, upon which we were engaged until dark. Got a stone-bruise in jumping in an arroya to-day with my moccasins on, while hunting, forgetting that the soles are not so thick as those of my shoes. What they lack in weight they fully make up in comfort, however,

especially in hunting, and I find that I can gain stealthily on a dove or quail now, a distance that would surely frighten them off did I wear shoes. Went to town after supper, got Mr. Cushing's watch and called at P. O. finding there papers from home. Among other news was the account of the extinction of Chautauqua by fire.[131]

Thursday, March 31

Mr. Cushing and myself were kept busy all day making a fly for my tent, which we completed and erected, allowing a lap back and front, forming a sort of verandah about my doorway. I wrote a few verses in reply to the "poem" which the ladies had written about me and the flute, this morning, intending to mail it to-morrow.

> *Thursday, March 31*
>
> Day spent as yesterday without the sketching. No Pima visitors—yesterday an immense crowd all day. We put up an awning over Mr. Hodge's tent today that he might write with more comfort.
>
> Weta gone all day after the elusive beaver again and in a visit to the Pima village. Two trips to Tempe today; I stayed at home with Mr. Hodge in the morning but went in the evening. There was a folk tale told under the canopy after supper. I studied my Spanish lesson.

Friday, April 1

Went with Siwahtitsailu after water this morning. Mr. Garlick going to Tempe to make box for a dark-tent. I worked in reciting accounts during the day and with Siwahtitsailu went bathing in the canal in the evening. Mr. and Mrs. Hayden, Prof. [O]. S. Fowler, the phrenologist,[132] Dr. Goodfellow[133] and Major Earl[134] called, spending about an hour. At night we attended a lecture on "Phrenology" by Prof. Fowler, in Tempe: Mr. Cushing was made a subject by the Professor and his scientific revelations were very complimentary to him (Mr. C.). The ladies played "April Fool" well to-day by sending me a "blank" letter, which I supposed to be one from Mr. Warman, they having entered my tent in the morning and taken therefrom an envelope addressed to me by Mr. Warman, which they successfully forged, thus effecting their well-played trick.

Friday, April 1

A courier came to camp about noon to see if we were at home and soon after two carriage loads of visitors, Mr. and Mrs. Hayden, Prof. Fowler the great Phrenologist, Major Earle(?), Dr. Goodfellow and Miss [blank].

Prof. Fowler is an old man past ninety and wonderfully vigorous for his great age. Has very small eye, a large red nose and his hair and beard are Iron white. He is going to give two lectures at Tempe—Tonight in Phrenology and its uses and tomorrow on love and marriage. It has been a very hot day. The Pima chicken wh. Yung bought and put in a box laid an egg today, much to the delight—etc.

T., Em, Mr. Hodge and I went over to the lecture this evening (Mr. Hodge and I first went for the mail[)]—but arriving late had to take our own chairs up with us, getting them at the store—etc.

After the lecture two heads were examined, Tenatsali's (he was called up first) and some other man whom the Prof. designated in his examination as a "stubborn old mule." T made a very nice little address when his examination was concluded.

Saturday, April 2

I spent the day at leisure, driving to town in the ev'g with Miss Magill for the mail, and mailing my "poem" to the ladies which I wrote last Thursday. The day has been oppressively warm, and the flies numerous and tantalizing. Purchased Pima baskets (three).

Saturday, April 2

Tenatsali was quite sick all day so we did not get to Tempe to call on the Prof, have our heads examined or go to the lectures. I had a delightfully refreshing bath in the midst of which Miss Ashley and Miss Johnson called etc. etc.

Mr. H. and I drove over for the mail; lovely moonlight night. After he (Mr. Patrick) left Em and I straggled around out of doors a long time as we did last night with Tenatsali walking to the top of the hill.

Sunday, April 3

After cleaning up my tent thoroughly I read part of the morning away in Bunner's "Story of a New York House" in Scribner's,[135] but the heat drove me from camp before noontime with gun in hand and game-bag and canteen over my shoulder. Went over the northern buttes about three miles in search of quail or dove, but I found but few and secured but one dove. Returned to camp in about 2 hours finding that Mr. Garlick and Miss Magill had gone to Pima village on a sight-seeing tour. I read again in the afternoon and we spent the evening in chatting, under the large wicky-up.

Sunday, April 3

Juan the Pima Indian and children came this afternoon and put up here—all going to work for T.

Mr. Hodge out gunning all the morning. Mr. Garlick took me in the little buckboard to the Pima village.[136] In [the Pima village] I noted some very interesting facts. They are very primitive and very poor and there are only very few left of them, all the others living in the Gila. There are apparently only two industries at this season, performed by the women while the men lie around sleeping—they were pottery and basket-making.

The former is crude work and made with a flat pebble inside the jar and a wooden patty outside (both wet) such as butter merchants use. Their great common red jars for cooling water are admirable. We use them in camp covered with sacking and suspended by rope and cooled by evaporation—as they are very porous.

The baskets are made of willow splints wound around and over several in a bunch forming the center and each row is finished through the work as it is at the top. An awl is used in making a hole between the two stitches in the last line for the splint forming the [hole] to pass through.

The splint ends are not fastened off and all the work [is] kept wet while in progress. The black ones are colored only on one side, showing that the yellow sticks are dyed before [being] stripped. There was only one grinding stone in each house, propped up loosely on four small stones with the muller on top. A perfectly natural stone except where it had been worn in grinding.

Gourds too I found; the long necked kind with holes in the narrow end used as water bottles and corked with a corn cob. Their paint boxes and mortars are similar to those used in Zuni[—]stones with hollows rubbed in them.

The houses are simply hollow mounds with doorways about two feet high, all opening to the east. The fires are made in the middle of the rooms in the floors and as there is no outlet whatever for the smoke the rafters and framework are smoked perfectly black inside till they shine. The walls are of brush wattled on to these and plastered over with mud. The beds are made of sand with straw mats on them and the dogs and chickens live quite comfortably with the rest of the family within doors.

Our hen is essentially Pima—she is allowed to go loose now and insists upon staying in the Sibley tent and laying her eggs there for she laid another one this morning.

Only in one Pima house did I find food prepared and was relieved that their politeness failed to ask me to partake for it was most unappetizing to look at and necessarily more so to eat, consisting of a wheat gruel and something else which looked more like very greasy dish water than anything else. At only one house a woman offered to shake hands and no where were we asked to sit down or come in. They showed a mild curiosity about my numerous petticoats and at some of the huts they examined my garments quite as critically as I would allow.

In the village were some frail-looking square structures made of wattled brush, but all of these were closed with great logs piled against the doorways, hence I could not see into them. Most of the inhabitants were sitting or lounging in ramadas, where they evidently pass most of their time in summer. I noticed a number of little three-quarter circles built of logs and branches, about three feet in height, in the center of each of which was a pile of ashes and several large stones. As the women were making pottery in them, and as several new jars were standing around, I assumed that they were also burned there. In the firing of their pottery the Pima women use wood, not dried sheep-dung as do the Zuñis, from whom they differ widely, too, in other things, especially in the matter of politeness, for they are rather surly than otherwise.[137]

Monday, April 4

Mr. Cushing is very ill to-day—so much so that it is necessary for him to remain in bed the entire day, bringing his cot out under the wickyup. Was sent by Mr. C. under guidance of Juan, a Pima, who had been under instruction at Hampton Indian School, Va., to a ruin[138] which he had discovered in a dense mesquite forest, about 2 1/2 miles northeast of the Pima village.[139] We started out on horses, reaching our destination about noon. We passed near one of the villages and through a smaller when we reached the woods. We found everything in virgin state—untouched, and perhaps before unseen by the eyes of a white person. The ruin is about 90 × 80 feet, with a garden the whole length of the ruin, and about forty feet wide, extending from its east wall. All the walls had, undoubtedly, been constructed of cement,[140] as large quantities of the same, containing gravel were all that remained of them. Bringing a specimen of the cement, a couple of stone knives and a chipping stone and placing them in a saddle pocket one turned campward, this time passing through the larger village, which contains about 25 houses. The women were all busy in weaving baskets, while the men whiled away their time in attitudes of laziness. We stopped about 10 minutes at one house, without dismounting, where Juan learned of the murder of a Pima, in Phoenix, by white men. When we were again on the road he informed me in broken English of the news, and of the ill-feeling of his people toward the Americans in consequence, a story in which I, of course, fully concurred. Went with Miss Magill to "Pueblo de los Muertos," where we examined the work done by the Mexicans last week and returned toward camp with our two Zuñis who had been in charge since Saturday. We reached camp about 8 o'clock.

Monday, April 4

Mr. Garlick and T. making dk. box all morn. Mr. Hodge and I went out in the buckboard this aft. to Pueblo de los Muertos and brought home the Indians—Siwatitsa lu and Weta—who had been there since Sat. evening when they went to watch the collections (left undisturbed in mound VIII to be photographed) after the Mexicans left.

Tuesday, April 5

Mr. Garlick went with the Mexicans to the ruin this morning, after they had worked around camp for an hour or two. Miss Magill tried her hand at driving the 2-mule buckboard to town with Mrs. Cushing. Mr. C. dictates a long letter to Mr. S. Baxter and one to Prof. Jn. Fiske[141] and I spend the afternoon in writing up notes. Wrote to N. B. in the ev'g. Beautiful moonlight night.

Tuesday, April 5

Mr. Patrick came again this morning and stayed so long that it evoked the question from Dah Yung as to what he was coming here so much for. Em and I with Mr. Garlick went off to Phoenix (and left him here) to do some shopping, returning in the afternoon very dusty as the roads are perfect dust heaps and suffocating when stirred up. It was very hot. I got some beautiful wild flowers to paint on the road but all were quite faded when I reached camp.

Juan has told T. of another ruin which he (Juan) and Mr. Hodge both rode out to see yesterday. This morning he, his nephew and daughter went off provisioned by us—to dig there the rest of the week. It is about five miles from here, has walls still standing. Juan last night sang an incantation to Tenatsali and asked to sing more as T. has been confined to his bed for three days but Weta was so much disturbed at the thought, fearing that some witchcraft might be practiced that T. gave up the idea to please him and let Juan tell him only a Pima tradition which is very sacred and will be dictated to me tomorrow. Both the Zunis went also to the ruin. The little Pima dog got left here and made life hideous for us and roused the echoes by howling a long time over the hills.

The hen is getting quite domesticated, returning of its own accord to its box where it slides down between the boards in top and goes to roost. A lovely moonlight evening which I spent in Mr. Hodge's tent teaching him Zuni.

Wednesday, April 6

Finished writing up my notes this a.m. and spent the afternoon in writing to Tom Anderson and in reading.

Wednesday, April 6

Em and I drove to Tempe in independent style this morning with Tricy, Sue and the buckboard to do some shopping, but being persuaded went to the Armstrong house[142] and had a very pleasant little visit with Miss Armstrong, Miss Ashby and Mrs. Austin.[143] Mr. Austin is very pleasant and took a great deal of trouble to fix some flowers in a potato to show me how to keep them fresh [but] they were all faded when we reached home.

Very hot. Three Mexicans went to the ruin Pueblo de los Muertos this morning with Mr. Garlick (who returned in the eve.) to stay the remainder of the week.

A lovely moonlight night but shifting clouds to mar its brightness and threaten rain.

Thursday, April 7

To-day was not a busy one, so I commenced to read Reade's "Foul Play"[144] and whiled the time away pleasantly in camp by hunting, etc. Siwahtitsailu brought a lamb to camp this ev'g which he found near the river.

Thursday, April 7

A blustering, dusty day. Mr. Garlick went to Phoenix in the morning for ruby glass for photographic dark box. Em and I sewed all the morning while T. read aloud Thackeray's Barry Lyndon.[145] In the afternoon I made a sketch of the camp from East side.

Juan the Pima returned to our dismay this evening with his daughter who is very sick with headache, fever[—]so I expect to dream all the diseases in the world tonight—too cloudy for moonlight.

Friday, April 8

Read "Foul Play" after returning from P. O. (where I went immediately after breakfast finding a letter from N. B.). Wrote N. B. in the morning, hunted around camp in afternoon shooting some doves. Mr. Hayden called in the afternoon to press his invitation to attend the ball in Tempe this ev'g. Ladies prepared to go after supper and I drove them over about 9 o'clock but did not stay myself.

About quarter to ten o'clk I went again with buckboard as Mrs. C. owing to illness decided not to remain longer than ten. Waited a few minutes listening to the orchestra which consisted of a brass cornet and squeaky fiddle (to all outward appearances), play selections from the "Grand Duchess," and to a man who was tongue-tied and with a bad-cold call out the figures.

Presently Mrs. Cushing appeared and answered that Miss Magill would remain longer so we returned to camp. Miss Magill reached the camp at 2 a.m. accompanied by Mr. Peters.[146]

> *Friday, April 8*
> Mr. Hodge went to Tempe early this morning. Mr. Hayden came over this afternoon to make sure that we would come to the dance at night.
>
> In some unaccountable way the canes of the ramada floor took fire, burning quite a hole also in the duck floor cover, but it was extinguished in time to prevent much damage.
>
> It has been dreadfully windy all day and dust flying every way so we were obliged to take our lunch in doors. I finished my gingham dress while T. read aloud more from Barry Lyndon. T. was too sick to go to the dance and Mr. Hodge backed out because he had no dancing shoes but he drove us (Em and me) over and fortunately it cleared by evening and the moon shone gloriously. It was 9-15 when we reached Tempe, etc etc.

Saturday, April 9
The Pima maidens flocked around my tent again to-day to sell their wares. What's the attraction I wonder! Read in tent all day, finishing Foul Play at bed time. Mr. Cushing taken very ill again, this evg.

> *Saturday, April 9*
> Stormy looking clouds all day with heavy winds and a little rain in the evening. Painted some of Mr. Patrick's specimens when the dust would admit.

Sunday, April 10
I spent the early morning in scouring my pantaloons and "calsomining" myself ready for Phoenix where Mr. Garlick and myself decided to go to attend Easter service. The ride was very dusty and the weather threatening. Before we reached the town we were gray with the dust but by the thoughtfulness of Mr. G. we were enabled to make ourselves presentable with a clothes-brush which he took with him. The service was led by Dr. Mitchell

and another older gentleman and about 150 persons were present. A lady sang "Nearer My God to Thee" with splendid effect and the organ was well played. We both enjoyed the service very much. After it was dismissed we took our dinner at Joe Gunn's Restaurant and started toward camp. A few drops of rain fell and a stiff wind blew on our way back, covering us completely with dust. Changed clothes immediately after reaching camp and shot three doves in hunting. Wrote a little in the evening and retired about 8:30 with a wild wind blowing.

Easter Sunday, April 10
Mr. Hodge and Mr. Garlick went to church at Phoenix. I discovered a cactus in bloom within twenty yards of my tent. The wind quite cold and blowing a perfect gale all day, sending tin pans from the culinary department flying all over the place as well as anything else loose—shaking tents and flapping canvas at a dreadful rate. In the morning some Pimas were here and gave me a nice lesson in their language. Tenatsali read Barry Lyndon all aft. and finished it. Mercury fell to 50° in my tent by nine o'clock.

Monday, April 11
Awoke about 4 o'clock with a tempest raging without. The wind blew so wildly that I expected every moment to be left without a tent over me, and the rain fell in torrents. Mr. Cushing was up and looking at things about camp. The subsiding of both rain and wind allowed me to sleep until breakfast time when I got up and found it still raining and the air quite chilly. Donned my "rough-weather suit" and heavy shoes and went around camp to survey the damage but found everything intact except the larger buckboard which had gone on a trip toward the eastern arroya. Spent most of the day in my tent reading Conway's "Family Affair,"[147] taking hunting tours between the showers for quail. Retired about 8 o'clk.

Easter Monday, April 11
The rain poured in torrents in the middle of the night, waking me by the noise on my tent wh. was also swaying so that I thought it must go down every minute for the wind was blowing a perfect hurricane. Every one in camp was awake straightening things up and

tightening guy ropes, tho' elaborate preparations were made yesterday evening for the storm which gave warning of its approach. I got up hurriedly and held to my tent poles to steady them in the fiercest wind but partly from fear and partly from cold I had a shaking chill which sent me back to bed, where however I lay awake till the storm lulled somewhat. This morning I was awakened by digging just outside my tent and found Mr. Hodge was kindly digging a trench around my tent to drain off the water which however did not come in at all and I found my fears in the night had been groundless for the pegs were all firm. I put on my waterproof and overshoes and made the usual circuit of the camp to visit the mules etc. and included this morning an inspection of the cacti near us in search of blooms (two of which I found) as all were so much brightened by the rain. Two Mexicans came to start for the ruins this morning but it began to rain again so hard that they gave it up and Mr. Garlick went alone in the big buckboard to bring back the Zunis who have been at Pueblo de los Muertos since Saturday evening watching the finds which were very good for last week only three days and a half of which the Mexicans were at work. They dug in the large Mound, unearthing some skeletons showing great age, beside each of which stood a piece of decorated pottery. They also describe the uncovering of a curious place in the floor about seven feet across which T. thinks a crematory at last.

At noon today the mercury reached 62° in my tent when the sun shone quite brightly at short intervals through rifts in the clouds. It clouded again however by evening and poured rain again. I spent the evening in the Sibley tent sketching Tenatsali while he read aloud to me the life first of Guido and then Walter Scott. Em. was sick all day with a headache so I mustard plastered her. Tchuli[148] has a great fondness for my tent where she makes herself quite at home whenever the opportunity presents itself. The Superstition Mts., Sunflower, and four peaks are thickly covered with snow.[149]

Tuesday, April 12

The day opened warm and brightly but was visited by rain at intervals throughout the day. I remained in my tent nearly all day shooting quail around camp "between the acts."

Wednesday, April 13

It rained again last night and continued during intervals throughout the day. I put on my heavy coat and moccasins and went hunting on the road for quail, capturing 5. Upon returning to camp I had lunch and read while the rain beat against my tent in the afternoon. When the rain would allow I shot at quail and doves that came into camp and secured 12 in all which Yung made into a pie for supper.

Thursday, April 14

Photographed the camp in the morning and about 11 o'clk started in buckboard for Muertos. The roads were much more pleasant than they have been recently having been smoothed by rain. We arrived at the ruin and found the Mexicans at work. They had exposed the walls of the largest ruin and unearthed the skeletons of three adults and a child each accompanied with the usual jar or bowl and all incysted in adobe. They were found well preserved considering their age, but when touched the bones would crumble. They exhibited no evidences of having been burned. After photographing these remains and also the group of bowls, and examining an ancient threshing ground we returned to camp, arriving at dusk.

Friday, April 15

Another day in which rain fell at intervals. Remained in camp until evening (doing nothing particularly) when I went to town with Yung and made purchases for Mexicans at "diggings" which I sent out by We-ta who accompanied us on mule-back. After having my hair cut I awaited the return of Yung who had gone to visit his Chinese friends, when we returned to camp in time to avoid another shower. After supper I went in the buckboard again to town, where I found letters from Ed and Nell. The rain fell very fast on my way back to camp and the night was one of cimerean [*sic*: cimmerian] darkness. The mules lost the road which compelled me to get out and lead them into it again when they kept it safely to camp. After changing my clothing and moccasins I wrote to Nell. Mr. Garlick has been busy in working on a tool-chest and Mr. C. in developing negatives.

Saturday, April 16

Read in morning; after lunch went with Miss Magill to "Hole in the Wall" as the butte two miles northwest of camp is called[150]—While there a shower threatened so we remained until the "clouds rolled by," when we returned to camp. On our way we found some choyas and saguaros in blossom which we secured. Received letters from nobody this evening but wrote myself to Chautauquans.

Sunday, April 17

With Mr. Garlick I went to town this morning to make some purchases. Upon returning to camp Miss Magill and myself got ready and with canteen and camp-stool went to the "Hole in the Wall" where she made a very pretty oil sketch of the place. I took a book and passed away the time pleasantly in reading and watching the progress of Miss Magill's painting. While there a gentleman with his wife, son, and daughter drove up, and climbing up to the hole examined it and viewed the scene for the first time. They spoke very pleasantly, and, after seeing the sights, departed. When the sketch was finished we returned to camp but Mr. and Mrs. Cushing had not returned from "Pueblo de los Muertos" whither they went this morning. Retired early this evening.

Monday, April 18

A day of leisure. Remained in camp all day. Mr. Cushing made views of camp and developed negatives of photographs.

Tuesday, April 19

We all went to ruin today, starting about 11 o'clk. Owing to overflow we were compelled to go a distance out of our way in order to get to "Muertos." Arriving there where the Mexicans were at work at excavating and removing the earth with a scraper to which they had two mules attached, we saw the results of their work. Besides the four skeletons already unearthed was found an olla similar to the fire-place discovered at "Ciudad de los Pueblitos." After Mr. C. and Miss Magill photographed the finds we returned to camp arriving soon after sunset. Mr. Garlick is busy all day on tool-chest.

Wednesday, April 20

I worked to-day on the "itinerary" until lunch-time. In the afternoon Miss Magill commenced an oil sketch of me in front of my tent. Mr. Cushing experiments in photography to-day.

Thursday, April 21

Mr. Cushing and the ladies went to the ruin to-day. Taking advantage of the absence of the latter I laundered my flannel shirt and underclothing and returned to my tent and defied the heat (while clothed in my wet undershirt) to disturb me in my work at plotting the ruins of Muertos from Mr. Garlick's notes.[151] Weta painted my face in true Zuñi fashion. Went bathing early in afternoon in the canal, and enjoyed a good wash. After supper I layed down on my bed and dozed away until everything was dark and still around camp when I undressed and retired for the night. Mr. Garlick worked on the tool-chest all day.

Friday, April 22

Weta, with his war-paint and new head-band went to Pima early this a.m. leaving us with the parting words that with his gay decorations he was "too good" for us. Mr. Cushing spent the day in more photographic experiments. After I completed plotting all the ruins I could today I spent an hour sitting in front of Miss Magill's tent where she gave me a lesson in drawing. After supper this ev'g I napped a while, and before settling down for the night strapped on my revolver and took a walk about half-way to the first northern butte.

Saturday, April 23

While in my tent this morning I was surprised at hearing Dah Yung, our cook, complain to Mr. Cushing of Mr. Garlick and myself poking fun at him and condemning his cooking, saying he was lazy, etc. etc. The trouble grew out of a request this morning by Mr. Garlick to Yung that he make the hash without onions, a suggestion that Yung seemed to resent as a reflection on his abilities as chef. I was working on the plotting of ruins at the time and had occasion to see Mr. Garlick a few minutes when Mr. Cushing came up and after talking a few minutes on the subject of the plotting invited us out of hearing distance of camp, where he asked us what the trouble was. Mr. Garlick explained, and Mr. C. at once thought that it was Dah Yung's excuse to cause trouble in order that he might leave the camp to go elsewhere. I am inclined now to the belief that he took the joke which I gave him a few days ago (that he would be compelled to go 12 miles every morning before breakfast for water when we arrived in Zuñi) in earnest. However Yung has resigned, the resignation to take effect upon the appointment of his successor. Good riddance to bad rubbish! Finished plotting to day. Mr. Garlick put finishing touches on the tool-chest which now presents a very fine appearance. Mr. Cushing and the ladies went to Phoenix about 3 o'clock, returning shortly after 7. Weta walked to the ruin (9 miles) and back, missing the wagon which left before he to gather a load of wood for camp. Finished and mailed Chautauqua letter this afternoon.

Sunday, April 24

Immediately after breakfast this morning I wrote my weekly letter to Nell. While writing, Mr. Cushing asked me whether or not I would like to go to Phoenix. Mr. C. and the ladies had decided yesterday to go this morning, so after they had started Mr. Garlick and myself with Dah Yung went in the large buckboard and drove to town arriving about 12 o'clock. After dinner I went to Tauton and Kellner's[152] and purchased a jersey shirt and necktie, and a towel and was soon ready to return to camp. Mr. Cushing had already made arrangements for another cook to succeed Dah Yung, and we brought him back with us, Dah Yung also returning. On our return Mr. Garlick and myself discussed our proposed trip for the location of the ruins in the Salado Valley. As soon as we reached camp we took the Indians and drove to Tempe to take our clothes to laundry, returning immediately to camp. While writing to Mary Duvall, Miss Ashley and Mrs. Davis[153] called, and upon my informing them that the ladies were in Phoenix they decided to return to town but were afraid to descend the hill at the foot of our camp in their buggy, so I accompanied them to the hill where they got out of the buggy and I saw them safely to the bottom. While they were leaving with the expression of "many thanks for your kindness" etc, Mr. and Mrs. Webster drove up and I was obliged to give them a "send off" too. Returning, I finished my letter to M. D. and sent her a small Pima basket and a pair of dove's and red-tipped blackbird's wings. After supper, which our new cook had a hand in[,] we spent an hour under the large "ramada" chatting in the dim light of a new moon.

Monday, April 25

Mr. Cushing went to "Muertos" this a.m. with the ladies intending to remain there a few days in order to experiment with his camera and in developing his plates, having met with no success in camp.[154] Mr. Garlick and myself left in the covered buckboard immediately afterward overtaking them in Tempe and later on near Ellerson's Ranch, where we were going for the two horses and a pair of mules that were in pasture. Here he instructed us to follow the new cut canal to Petersen's Ranch[155] to find some skulls that had been excavated by the workmen. We failed to find them but discovered a large metate and several stone knives which we placed in the buckboard. After returning with the animals (which we had the greatest difficulty in capturing) we made locations of Tempe Butte with compass and returned to camp. Received a letter from Hough[156] this ev'g. The ladies returned from the ruin alone. Weta went with the Mexicans to the ruin also, this morning.

Tuesday, April 26

Ladies went to Tempe this morning and spent the day in visiting. Mr. Garlick and myself started from camp at 9 o'clk and during the day located all the principal peaks in sight. We finished about 5 o'clock and returned to camp feeling quite tired.

Wednesday, April 27

Not feeling quite satisfied with the accuracy of our work of yesterday, when the time came this morning to place our locations upon the map, we started for Double Butte and made relocations of all the points located yesterday, returning to camp for lunch and plotting. About 2 o'clock—the warmest part of the day—we ascended Tempe Butte and took bearings of all the principal points in view. We were followed to the summit by seven Pimas who kept up their jabbering until we could scarcely hear each other talk. After the work here was completed we descended and went to "Adams' ruin,"[157] on the road, (the ruin of "El Cuidad de los Pueblitos"), and from there to the township line a mile north of the Italian's half-way house where we also took angles on certain points. The ladies went to the ruin this morning and returned, with Mr. Cushing in the evening. Weta and Jesus also returned to camp in the large wagon.

Thursday, April 28

We were obliged to climb Tempe Butte again this morning, having found that the river, as located on Mr. Patrick's map, was in the wrong course. We took angles from the summit on all the river bends in sight and when we descended went to Double Butte where we took the bearing on other points. In climbing Double Butte we discovered a cave that extended for 10 or 12 feet into the side, under the rocks, but as it contained a hornets' nest I did not venture to explore it for sacrifices. In returning to camp for luncheon we met Mr. Cushing who was on his way to Muertos, with "Douglas." He informed us that the horse had behaved very badly while mounting him and that he attempted to throw him, before leaving camp. After we had taken our luncheon we repaired to the ruins on Mr. Patrick's land[158] and after locating them went to Phoenix, meeting the ladies, on the road, returning to camp. After supper I wrote to Nell and with Miss Magill and Mr. Garlick spent a pleasant hour in chatting & in petting the mules!

Friday, April 29

After we had finished plotting this morning we went to the large ruin on the Pima Reservation,[159] where I went with "Juan," the Pima Indian, about a month ago. We did not have much difficulty in finding it again. While there we made a ground plan of the ruin proper as nice as of the smaller mounds, and also of the two reservoirs or ditches adjacent to the main ruin.

After finishing our work here we returned to camp and had our dinner. Mr. Patrick called this evening and related his love affairs and early experiences in this country which were remarkably dry and funny.

Saturday, April 30

Immediately after breakfast I went to Tempe to collect bills contracted during April, for payment, returning to camp by lunch-time. The ladies leave camp quite early for "Muertos" where Mr. C. is still at work with the Mexicans. In the afternoon Mr. Garlick and myself drive to "El Ciudad de los Pueblitos" where we locate the principal ruins of the group and from there to Patrick's where we make locations of all the mounds on his place.

After our work here is completed we go to Phoenix where I collected all the bills outstanding. After supper I wrote letters in settlement of accounts and made checks for payment. Mr. and Mrs. C. and Miss M. returned from the ruin this evening.

Sunday, May 1

This morning I copied with sketch book the townships in the Gila Region from Mr. Patrick's roughs in order to use on trip to the Gila Valley where we go on Tuesday. In the afternoon Miss Magill paints some more on her oil-sketch for which I sat as the "model young man." Mr. Cushing has decided to go to Muertos and remain for a week with the ladies and will start to-morrow.

Monday, May 2

While Mr. Cushing and the ladies were preparing for the Muertos camp, Mr. Garlick and myself started for Hornos where we expected to finish locating all the ruins there and then continue to Muertos and map the ruins at that point; but after reaching the former place we did not locate the 65 ruins we found there until after 5 o'clock, when it was too late to go to the other pueblo.

With Weta who had come out with the white horse to pasture, we returned to camp. Spent the evening in finishing the copying of Patrick's township plots.

Tuesday, May 3

Were awakened about 5 o'clock by Choy-Wuy, who beat upon a tin pan for fully three minutes. He gave as his excuse for calling us so early that his clock was too fast, so being once up we ate breakfast immediately after which Weta started for a walk to the river (distance 9 miles). After packing up we went to Tempe Butte which we climbed (for the third time) and made locations of the Superstition, Estrella and White Tank Ranges of Mts. After lunch Jesus and Weta came to camp from the ruin, in the large wagon, for provisions. About 2 o'clock we started for Phoenix, reaching there shortly after three. Mr. Patrick met us and informed us of the earthquake the Phoenixites had just experienced.[160] During the evening ever[y]body had something to say concerning it, and as it was the first visit of old Sei'smos to the town the citizens were somewhat excited. Spent the evening with Mr. Patrick, in his office and with the young man in Tauton & Kellner's store and at 9 o'clock bunked in with Mr. Garlick in Gibson's stable.[161]

Wednesday, May 4

Got up as the clock on the court-house was striking six and after eating breakfast at the Chinese Restaurant[162] we made a few purchases and were ready to start for the Gila by 8 o'clock. The ride during the entire day was the warmest, longest and dustiest that I have thus far experienced. We stopped for lunch under the shade of a mesquite about one o'clock and after resting an hour proceeded on our journey, stopping every few minutes to form trail or triangulation stations. We arrived at Adams Ranch, 35 miles from Phoenix, at 5:30, where we camped in a very pretty spot on the north bank of the Gila under the spreading branches of the largest mesquite tree I have yet seen. After supper the moon shone brightly—and we chatted the evening away until about 9 o'clock when the cool air drove us to our blankets.

Thursday, May 5

We awoke at 6 this beautiful morning and after preparing breakfast were off on the road in good season. Governor Powers' Ranch[163] was reached by 12:30 where we cooked lunch and spent the remainder of the day. The "Governor" (who earned his title while provisional governor of the southern states) was not at home, but spending his time in Phoenix having become disgusted with the Gila Region after spending a small fortune in irrigating ditches which proved useless on account of overflows from the river. Mr. Garlick worked diligently all the afternoon in plotting and I amused myself by walking and in fighting the pigs which persisted in rooting around our camp. The long ride in the sun caused my head to ache considerably so I turned in quite early.

Friday, May 6

After taking some sights this morning we "pulled out" in good season (about 8 o'clock) for an extension of our trip southward, taking our sights and forming triangulations and trail stations on the way. About 7 miles out we found on a butte of black-rock, which we occupied as a station, some very interesting pictographs, which I busied myself in making sketches of. Leaving this place, which we appropriately named "Pictograph Point" we proceeded, locating several ruins along the lines of our journey, in one of which I found 2 axes and the portion of a worked shell-ornament. We stopped at Hall's Ranch where we cooked lunch and allowed the mules a roll and a rest both of which they seemed to fully enjoy. Proceeding, we reached the ranch of Charly Walz, a young man who lives alone on a very pretty place which he has himself beautified with a substantial as well as neat adobe house, fences, shrubbery, etc. Upon inquiry we learned that we would probably find some ruined battlements or forts in a mountain pass which he pointed out to us. Taking advantage of the opportunity we started for the pass which we explored for 2 1/2 miles without success. We returned and made camp at

Powers' Ranch about 8 o'clock, after the dustiest ride either Mr. Garlick or myself ever experienced. The mules were out of our sight with the dust, and we were both blinded and choked for a time.

Saturday, May 7

We started at 7:45 from Powers Ranch this morning, reaching High Bank in time for lunch and to allow our mules an hour's rest.[164] We continued after lunch was over, over this dry sand desert and with the sun journeying down until my nose and wrists were blistered by the heat. The time passed rapidly during the afternoon as I read Conway's "Living or Dead"[165] during the journey. We camped on the bank of a bayou of the river Gila and passed the evening quietly in wondering at the beautiful sunset and the weird light on the water from the full moon. The cattle were lowing in the distance and everything around was perfectly still save now and then the buzzing of a mosquito, the scampering of a field mouse or the faint whisper of the wind as it breathed on the cottonwoods under which we were camped.

Sunday, May 8

Were awakened by a German who rode up on horseback inquiring if we had seen a young Mexican with a gang of cow-boys. Stating that we had seen such a person yesterday he rode off with the remark that "he was the —— —— * was after". We made use of what few provisions we had left, gave the last of our hay to our almost famished mules and were on the road to Phoenix by half-past-seven. The time passed as it did yesterday—I finished the novel which I started although my eyes, as well as my patience, were tried when we came to a rut that elevated me a foot from my seat. We arrived in Phoenix at noon and after corralling our mules proceeded ourselves to clean out a Chinese restaurant. We remained in town for almost three hours and in the meantime I went to the post office where I found a letter from W. B. awaiting me. Returning to camp we found that Mr. Cushing and the ladies had not yet returned from Los Muertos. Wrote to Nellie in the ev'g.

Monday, May 9

Went to town with Mr. Garlick this a.m. where I found letter from Ashley, a box of candies from Em. and several papers. The papers, when I returned to camp, I read, while Mr. Garlick plotted notes of our recent field-work. The ladies drove in in the afternoon and as it has been a week since seeing them we were glad they came. Went to Muertos in the ev'g with Mr. Garlick where we found Mr. C., the ladies and the Mexicans snugly fixed in camp—

After supper (we having ours before we left our camp), we were entertained by Mr. Cushing who read a portion of Irving's "Knickerbocker's History of New York,"[166] which was quite laughable.

Tuesday, May 10

After the Mexicans had breakfasted we ate our "bacon" and were shown around by Mr. Cushing and Miss Magill to inspect the work that had been progressing so favorably. A great many ruins had been excavated and numbers of jars (of all shapes and in all styles of decoration) together with several skeletons, were exhumed. I saw and we captured our first "Gila monster" while going our rounds—an ugly reptile but very "beautifully decorated" as Mr. Garlick remarked. Weta insists that it is a "rattlesnake with legs".

We returned to camp reaching it by noontime. Mr. G. went to Phoenix in search of our red mule which had broken her halter at "Muertos Camp" but did not return this evening. Wrote to Ashley in the shade of the "ramado" in the afternoon taking an occasional shot at doves. Made my best shot to-day, killing three "at a blow" with a shot cartridge and Weta's rifle.

Wednesday, May 11

While waiting this morning Mr. Cushing came to camp from "Muertos" and gave directions for the removal of the camp to that place, to-morrow. Went to town in the evening where I met Mr. Garlick who had returned by Phoenix and Maricopa road. Returned with him to camp and spent the evening in reading.

Thursday, May 12

We were busy all day in sending two loads to "Camp Muertos"—or as it is now called, "Camp Hemenway",—one by Mr. Garlick and the other by Jesus. The ladies also called and returned with a load of their effects in the buck-board. With Weta, I remained in camp all night, going in the evening to town after the mail, receiving another box of candies—this time from mother, and a letter from Nell. While in Tempe I saw Doctor Goodfellow who had just returned from Sonora on seismologic duty. Not feeling well this evening—too many stewed prunes I suppose. Woke up in the night to arrange my blankets—for, notwithstanding the hot day just past the night is quite cool.

Friday, May 13

Spent the morning in reading Twain's "English as She is Taught," in the Century.[167] Enjoyed it hugely and laughed heartily at the guileless saying of the youngsters. Weta seemed to be as much amused as I was, for when anything I read that was particularly funny he would drop the moccasins that he was making for his Pima mask and ask me to point out the words over which the laughter occurred as though the letters themselves were imps with wry faces and contorted bodies, then, with renewed bursts of laughter he resumed his work—Mr. G. and Jesus came with the two wagons in the early afternoon and after loading them and the buckboard (which I drove) we bade adieu to Camp Augustus—I put on the odometer at Tempe and when I arrived at Camp Hemenway it lacked very little to make 9 miles—Our new camp is well-arranged and its location in a clearing at the edge of a mesquite woods. Bunked in with Mr. Garlick as my own tent had not been unpacked.

Saturday, May 14

Pitched tent and mounted fly this forenoon. Find by raising the rear of my tent at the bottom a draught is created which keeps it delightfully cool. Camp looks very clean and comfortable and its arrangement is made with great taste. The following is something of a plan:

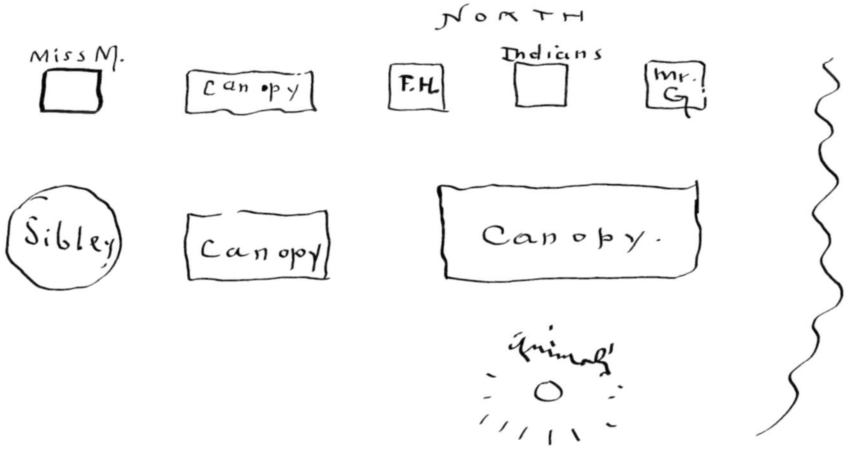

Although in the midst of the mesquites it is a much cooler camp than was Camp Augustus.

Sunday, May 15

Cleaned house and wrote to N. B. Miss Magill called in the afternoon spending a couple of hours in pleasant conversation. Mr. Garlick and Mrs. Cushing also called and we had a great deal of amusement from the reading of Mark Twain's "English as She is Taught."

Monday, May 16

Mr. Cushing dictated to Mr. Baxter during the morning and I spend the afternoon in working up in part my notes.[168]

Tuesday, May 17

Finish writing to Mr. Baxter, and to others, and make our April accounts which took me the remainder of the day. Mr. Cushing called in evening and signed letters.

Wednesday, May 18

Mr. C. had arranged with Mr. Goodwin to-day to go to an ancient canal which ran only about 1 1/2 miles east of "Camp Hemenway", but as Mr. C. was obliged to finish a letter to Mr. Baxter which he had commenced while we were at Gila Bend, Mr. Garlick, Mr. Goodwin and myself started in advance. We struck the canal as expected, but Goodwin, who started on ahead as guide missed it, until we arrived at the Tempe Ditch some four miles north. As Mr. Cushing failed to appear here, Goodwin returned to camp and Mr. Garlick and myself continued along the Tempe Ditch, discovering and locating two ruins, returning for a late lunch. On the way out I found a very beautiful frog fetich which Mr. C. was much pleased about.

As we arrived at camp, Mr. C., Mr. Goodwin and Weta were about to start for the canal which we missed. I pressed the letters and with Miss Magill went to Tempe. Found letter there from Eckhardt—Returned just after sunset. Answered Eck's letter in the evening.

Thursday, May 19

Mr. Garlick and myself in one buckboard, the ladies in the other, and Mr. C. on horseback started for the canal which Mr. Cushing and Goodwin traced out yesterday. Found it to be very extensive. Noted a peculiar feature: that of chipping-stones appearing along the banks of the canal, having been thrown there by the ancients after sharpening their rude stone tools. Leaving the rest of the party at a large pueblo where the ladies wanted to "grub," as they call it, Mr. Garlick and I followed the canal to where it crossed the Tempe and Mesa City road. Finding that we had no pencil, we continued our journey to Tempe where we secured a pencil and purchased a lunch. Returned on same road and ran a meander of the canal within about two miles of our starting point. Got to camp about six o'clock feeling quite tired.

Friday, May 20

Went to town (Tempe) this morning with Mr. Garlick for commissaries. Created a sensation with my tam o'shanter which Miss M. has kindly made for me. Had my hair clipped as closely as possible, which, if not enhancing my "beauty" at least keeps my overtaxed brain from dementing. Returned to camp about two o'clock and spent the remainder of the day resting—if an apology for loafing may be called such. Wrote to Ed Hodge this evening.

Saturday, May 21

All the camp with the exception of myself (the cook and the Indians) drove to Phoenix this morning with the buckboard and four. I remained in camp superintending the work of the Mexicans at their excavation. After the folks had departed I took a tub-bath and wrote to Nell passing the morning thus, and read most of the afternoon away. Folks returned at 2 o'clock with Dr. Goodfellow of Tombstone. The ladies, in appreciation of my remaining in camp during the day and being a "good boy", brought me a package of chewing-gum, a candy watch, stick of candy, "tabby on a stick" and a heart upon which had been impressed "smile again dear!" We had a great amount of laughter over the presents and spent the evening accordingly.

Sunday, May 22

Remained in camp during early morning and went hunting just before lunch-time bringing in 4 quails & 4 doves—Read and wrote away the afternoon hours. Mr. Cushing and Doctor Goodfellow visited all the ruins during the day. Mr. McClintock and Mr. Goodwin called in the evening and had supper. Mr. McC. collected data for another article in the "Salt River Valley News"[169] and they left about 10 o'clock—Miss Magill & Mr. Goodwin drove to Mesa City in the morning, returning in the evening, and Mr. Garlick went to Phoenix from whence he was to proceed to New River to get the red mule which had strayed from camp. Spent the ev'g in my tent napping until bed time arrived.

Monday, May 23

Started this noon for Phoenix with Dr. Goodfellow, driving buckboard & two mules. The day is one of the warmest we have yet had and the ride all the way a very dry, sandy and warm one. Dr. G. was guide during the trip and having forgotten the road by which he came to camp we were led astray at a forked road, which made our ride a longer one. After three hours we reached Phoenix where we went to the Commercial Hotel[170] at which the Doc. was staying, and then to the Natatorium where we had a delightful swim. After attending to several errands the Doc. invited me to supper for which he gave special order at "Joe Gunn's" restaurant. By the time we had finished the sun had set and I gathered in my lines and steered toward camp. Took the new road this time and although the night was dark and I was misinformed as to the destination of the road by a wayward traveler, I reached camp about 10:30 very tired and dusty.

Tuesday, May 24

Went this morning with one of the discharged Mexicans and while there did chores. Mr. Goodwin and Miss Magill drove in in the afternoon and as she afterwards informed me (though I didn't see them) caught me flirting with a Pima maiden!—giving her candy, etc.

Wednesday, May 25

The Prodigal—red mule returned to-day, secured by 2 halters and as many ropes, and looking like a sulky dog. Mr. Garlick arrived with him by midday, having driven from Phoenix. Mr. Cushing busied himself all day at pottery mending and restoring.[171]

Thursday, May 26

Started for Tempe this morning and had gotten as far as Goodwin's ditch when we struck a road that was submerged from an overflow. Before either of us knew it the mules were struggling for their lives—and dry land—in the mire, into which they had sunk up to their bodies. Miss Magill went to Goodwin's where she prevailed upon a man to help me extricate the mules from their predicament and while he was coming—much against his will—I had succeeded in pulling them out. They were certainly a sorry plight. Spent one hour in washing them and their harnesses and with the aid of a rope to the end of which we hitched our team, drew the buck-board to terra firma. Went to town, purchased a lot of bad candy and returned without mishap by another road—

Friday, May 27

Miss Magill went to Tempe to-day with Goodwin—who continued to Phoenix—and returned about dark. Mr. Garlick and myself started for locating ruins but returned and made a lot of wires to which we attached labeling-tags for marking the mounds. Took us the afternoon to do this so no locating direct was attended to. Mr. C. busily engaged in restoring pottery.

Saturday, May 28

Mr. Garlick went to Tempe to-day. Goodwin pays us his usual daily visit. After lunch went with Miss Magill to a neighboring mesquite under the branches of which we sat for a couple of hours, continuing the painting of my "mug" which she declares "looks less and less like the original every day". After the sitting was over I tried my hand and the result was a picture which Mrs. Cushing says looks like a Washington Jewess of Seventh Street.

Sunday, May 29

Goodwin calls early and drew off in pencil a map of the ancient canals which he has recently been tracing.[172] Miss Magill spent nearly the entire day in coloring it, and when it was completed presented quite a professional air. After the mapping was finished Goodwin bored us all to death with his "ranch" talk interspersed with bad Spanish and accompanied by odious comparisons among which was the resemblance he made between Miss Magill and a "go-deviller". The folks all went off to the mounds and while they were away Goodwin contradicted Mr. C. on a scientific subject of which he knew nothing, causing something of a tilt between them.

Monday, May 30

Mr. Garlick and myself started for the ruins this morn'g and succeeded in locating and measuring the ground-plan of an immense house-mound with the accompanying pyrial-mound when it became so warm that we were compelled to return to camp where I sought the cool of my fly-protected tent and plotted our morning's work. Miss M. paid me a visit in the evening and we had another "Lemonade-picnic" and chatted away in ignorance of the flight of time for it was half-past ten before we "broke-up" our meeting.

Tuesday, May 31

I went to Tempe this morning where I spent the greater part of the day in collecting bills of May expenses for payment. Returned to camp in the afternoon and whiled away the evening in sipping lemonade and eating ginger-snaps with Miss M. and Mr. Garlick. The Fowler Bros.[173] & Mr. McClintock paid the camp a visit to-day.

Wednesday, June 1

The camp this morning presented quite a deserted appearance for Mr. and Mrs. Cushing & Mr. Garlick went to Phoenix where they spent the day. Wrote to Ashley in the morning & spent the remainder of the day in pleasant conversation with Miss M. with whom I took lunch and supper. We worked at restoring pottery for a while during the evening when the Phoenixites returned. After supper we paid the ruins a moonlight visit—

Thursday, June 2

Worked up accounts this a.m. and Mr. Garlick feeling very unwell we did not venture in the hot sun to locate ruins, but awaiting the breaking of the heat of the day, went to Tempe on errands returning about dark. Received letters from Nell and Eckhardt. Spent greater part of ev'g with Mr. and Mrs. C. and Miss M. under the canopy where we cracked jokes while Mr. C. restored pottery by combined moon- and candle light. New tent purchased yesterday was pitched this a.m.

Friday, June 3

Arose this morning with the sun and awaking Mr. Garlick we ate breakfast and were with the ruins before six o'clock, but before ten had arrived it became so hot that we were forced into camp. Read papers which I received from home last evening and had a short call from Miss Magill before luncheon. Had a lemonade feast in the kitchen with Miss M. and Mr. Garlick where we remained until sundown and the Mexicans returned from their work. Mr. C. has been busy restoring pottery all day—

Saturday, June 4

Went to Tempe this a.m. and made several purchases. Before starting we had one of our "lemon-ade picnics" which we generally intersperse with stale ginger-snaps or "nic-nacs". Got back from Tempe about 8:30 enjoying the moonlight ride very much. Letters from Eck and mother to-day.

Sunday, June 5

Bathed in tent this a.m. and after cleaning up. After lunch we had our early lemonade and ate chocolate cake which Choy Wuy made very nicely—Mr. Kemp[174] and his wife called in the afternoon as well as Mr. Goodwin. Went with Miss Magill to our "sylvan studio" where she worked upon my mug again this time coming out in a more encouraging manner. Goodwin took Mr. Cushing riding, afterwards Mrs. Cushing and when we returned to camp Miss Magill. He displayed some more of his brilliancy by informing Mr. Cushing of what he knew about the "carbony-ferous" age.

> *Sunday, June 5*
>
> . . . from Phoenix & some others I did not see.[175] Mr. Goodwin spent the day with us & in the aft. took first Em then Tenatsali for short drives. Mr. Hodge gave me another sitting for the portrait.

Monday, June 6

Went with Mr. Garlick soon after sunrise to the ruins where we took notes of ground plans. Sweltered with the heat and ran our feet wild over hundred and eleven different gopher-holes. Returned and read the Duchess' "Phyllis"[176] all the afternoon falling to sleep from hard work and was awakened by our celestial crying "bleckfus leady;" a summons which he invariably applies to each meal—Miss Magill went to our studio in the woods spending the afternoon in letter-writing while Mr. Cushing worked industriously in restoring damaged pottery.

Monday, June 6
I sketched specimens & sewed & wrote letters. Tenatsali read some from Pendennis[177] to us. The doves are with us all day & night.

Tuesday, June 7
Located ruins this a.m. with Mr. Garlick until about 10 o'clock when we returned to camp. After luncheon I started for Tempe and had a very warm and dusty trip all the way. My face, hair, and clothing appear completely bleached with the dust and while half-way on the road was hailed by a freighter who, after I stopped my mules, approached me in the most mysterious way and very confidentially inquired if I had "left any dust in Maricopa". I answered that "it was raining very hard down there" and drove on. Met Patrick in town who invited me down to the corner-stone laying of the railroad station and asked if Mr. Cushing would write an essay for depositing in the stone. I told him I did not think he would but if he would except an article which I was preparing on "The Poisoned Gumdrop as the Lover's Revenge" I would finish it and allow him to use it on the occasion. He laughed at this and asked if I had any poisoned gum-drops around camp to leave them where Goodwin would be likely to get hold of them—Got back to camp by dark and entertained Mrs. Cushing and Miss Magill the entire evening while Mr. C. was developing negatives in the new tent.

Tuesday, June 7
I was occupied with specimen painting today. Mr. Hodge went to Tempe for mail.

Wednesday, June 8
In accordance with an agreement which Miss Magill and myself made last evening, I was up before sunrise, and whistling, received a reply in the same manner. We took the shotgun and went north of camp where I managed to bag four doves. Miss Magill following closely but declining to try a shot since the "last one taken by Mr. Cushing almost dislocated his shoulder"—Returned to camp in time for breakfast after which Mr. Garlick and myself worked on locating until 10:30. Read "Phyllis" and "entertained" Miss M. who paid me a visit in the morning and continued it after luncheon. Went with Mr. Cushing in the afternoon to photograph the ruins taking a hand at

it myself. Miss Magill joined us later, and when Mr. Cushing went to superintend the excavations we experimented with the camera ourselves—Got back to camp just after sundown and after supper I read until 9 o'clock and with Mr. Cushing went to the photo-tent and developed negatives until half past one.

> *Wednesday, June 8*
> I went hunting with Mr. Hodge about five this morning & the result was four doves & a pleasant walk. I cleaned house then went to sewing. During the latter operation Tenatsali read aloud from Pendennis, but in the afternoon was busy with his photographs. Mr. Hodge doing topographical work all day.

Thursday, June 9
Felt very tired this morning when I arose from lack of sleep last night. Went with Mr. Garlick after breakfast to ruins working on locating until about 10 o'clock. Returned to camp, put tent in order and read "Phyllis" until lunch time. After luncheon read more and enjoyed a short nap. Miss Magill called, followed by Mrs. Cushing soon after, and by two o'clock Miss M. and myself repaired to our "studio" under the mesquite where we spent the remainder of the day acting the "model young man" again while Miss M. worked on my portrait. Miss M. called in the evening to get her inkstand filled and in filling it spilled some ink down the front of my prettiest flannel shirt which is the pride of the ladies who use all-endearing terms in speaking of it. Retired about 11:00. Mr. Cushing has been busy to-day in photoing & developing—

> *Thursday, June 9*
> Em & I sewed while Tenatsali read Pendennis. Mr. Hodge gave me another sitting for the portrait. Em & I spent the evening in his tent.

Friday, June 10
Haven't gotten over my sleepiness yet, it seems for I took a nap this a.m., after Choy Wuy awoke me at breakfast-time. As Mr. Garlick started for Phoenix we did no locating so remained indoors reading "Phyllis". Mrs. C. and Miss M. called and we racked our brains in poetizing on Goodwin, Patrick and Camp life in general, but without finishing any of our attempts.

Read Harper's in the afternoon. Mr. C. and Miss M. going to the ruin with the camera. Went with Miss M. to walk in the evening, intending to see Goodwin's "header" at work, but as it was operating at the other end of the ranch we concluded not to go that far, so lingered a while to pluck wild-flowers when we returned to camp. Mr. Garlick returned from Phoenix, via Tempe in time for supper, bringing with him letters from Nell, Chilcote and Mr. Wescott. Answered Nell's this ev'g and paid Mr. Cushing a visit in the photo-tent,—where I remained with him until about 10:30 assisting in the development of negatives. Weta paid me a midnight visit and after smoking a cigarette of peace I retired.

> *Friday, June 10*
> Mr. Garlick went to Phoenix 2-day returning about 7 P.M. with mail. Em, Mr. Hodge & I amused ourselves writing Camp verses & in the aft. He & I went by invitation to see Mr. Goodwin's header, but finding it about 1 1/2 miles down in the field determined 2 wait till it came nearer.

Saturday, June 11
Feeling quite sleepy this morning I did not have the courage to get up until after breakfast was over. At 8 o'clock Mr. Garlick and myself were at work with the ruins and at 10 returned again to camp,—Worked on accounts and correspondence the rest of the morning and a portion of the afternoon, and Miss Magill called and used the "quiet" of my tent to write. Talk over matters in general and relate love experiences. In the afternoon Mr. and Mrs. C. and Miss M. go to the ruins and take more photos, and before supper Miss M. continues her visit with me. Read Harper's the remainder of the evening and retire about 11 o'clock—

> *Saturday, June 11*
> Tenatsali quite sick this morning so stayed in the tent reading "Pen" aloud while we girls sewed. After dinner we three drove about the ruin labelling specimens & brought some back with us assisted by Ramon Castro.[178] Yesterday & 2-day equally hot, the thermometer registering 114° degrees of heat in tents; the evenings are delightfully cool.

Sunday, June 12

Remained in camp all morning and read. Goodwin calls and takes Miss M. to Mesa City per last week's engagement. Major Earl and a Mr. Stowe spent an hour or two in camp taking dinner. Lots of Mormons came over from Mesa to see the ruins and I did the "honors" by guiding them around. Mr. Cushing in the evening develops negatives in the photo-tent, and Mrs. Cushing and Miss M. spend the evening in mine, the former reading aloud "Alice in Wonderland."

> *Sunday, June 12*
>
> Los Muertos has become a popular Sunday resort & to day we had innumerable visitors beside Mr. McClintock & his Mother & Maj. Earle & Mr. Howe who took lunch with us—I mended jars this morning & in the afternoon drove to Mesa City with Mr. Goodwin & in the evening with Em sat in Mr. Hodge's tent where we read Alice in Wonderland aloud. All retired at 10,30.

Monday, June 13

Went with Mr. Garlick after breakfast-time and located the specimens in pyrial mound XXa. Returning to camp I plotted them and spent the remainder of the morning making up May expense accounts. In the afternoon I went to Tempe, taking Weta and Siwahtitsailu as far as Ellingson's where they got the remaining animals—two horses and two mules—from pasture. Returned to camp soon after dark after having a very dusty ride from town. Read papers which I received from home—

> *Monday, June 13*
>
> Cooler than yesterday but still warm enough—The Zuñi animals, white mule & "Cafè", came from pasture. I painted jars & sewed. Mr. Hodge went to Tempe & Tenatsali read aloud from Martin Chuzzlewit.[179]

Tuesday, June 14

Was up so late that I ate breakfast alone and afterwards went with Mr. Garlick and located pyrial-mound specimens and an ancient-ditch. Returning to camp I cleaned my tent and Mr. Cushing called and dictated a long letter to Mr. Baxter,[180] which I transcribed in part and was interrupted to go to Tempe, having a repetition of my yesterday's dusty ride. Got labels for specimens and blue-prints by express, and a letter from Mr. Baxter for Mr. Cushing. Returned to camp before dark finding Miss Magill holding pre-emption over my tent in carrying on her correspondence—Had a chat in which she told me

Mesa City. After supper Miss Magill called again and while we were chatting Mrs. Cushing came with "Alice in Wonderland" from which she read for nearly an hour when she retired. Miss Magill continued her visit, remaining until about eleven o'clock when I retired.

> *Tuesday, June 14*
> Mr. Hodge went again to Tempe and again Em read Alice in Wonderland aloud to us in his tent at evening. A cold night.

Wednesday, June 15
Was up quite early after a poor night's rest and went immediately to work in transcribing the remainder of my notes which I finished by ten o'clock. Miss M. called, bringing her sewing, and we had a mutual entertainment.—which indeed is always the case for she considers herself as much of a hostess as I take it upon myself to be host of my abode—and so much the better, for she is my best friend (next to my dear Ashley) and I enjoy every moment of her frequent visits. Mr. Garlick went to Tempe after dinner, returning [at] supper-time. Ladies went in the evening to one of the pyrial-mounds and brought back two loads of pottery for restoration and labeling—I accompanied them with load number two and assisted in packing the specimens in the buckboard—After supper Miss M. called on me and we spent another evening most enjoyably—

> *Wednesday, June 15*
> Painted specimens again—Mr. Garlick went to town & brought mail. Very cold again at night.

Thursday, June 16
Was up quite early and after breakfast and house-cleaning posted my May acc'ts in Ledger and read "Barry Lyndon" the rest of the morning. Miss

Magill called in the afternoon and we spent two or three hours together most pleasantly—not to say profitably on my part at least, for I made resolution to reduce my cigarette-smoking from nearly 30 to 6 a day. We went in the evening with the buckboard to one of the pyrial mounds, bringing back with us the remainder of the specimens—Stayed in my tent during the evening and read "Barry Lyndon" until about 10-o'clock—Mr. Garlick departed for Phoenix this a.m. to purchase additional mules and wagon—

> *Thursday, June 16*
> The warmest day we have felt. Mr. Garlick went to Phoenix & brought back new mules Pete & Barney— I took a long walk among the ruins with my sketch book, & drew jars until the sun's heat drove me back to camp where I mended specimens. In aft went in buckboard with Mr. Hodge to bring in jars from excavations—

Friday, June 17

This morning, while sitting under canopy with Miss M., we made an engagement to go sketching, so after lunch departed for our prickly "studio" under the mesquite. I posed here for a while for the portrait which she is painting and

Mr. Cushing came while we [were] about to return to camp and Miss M. went with him in the buckboard to one of the ruins, returning with a load of pottery. Mr. Garlick returned this evening with a pair of new mules—"Barney" & "Pete"—and a new Bain wagon. Mr. Goodwin called in the evening.

> *Friday, June 17*
> Mr. Hodge & I mended jars all morning & had a short sitting for the picture after lunch—then Em & I went to mound—where we collected burial urns for cataloguing—Mr. Goodwin called in eve, offering to take me to Phoenix in the morning.

Saturday, June 18

Was up at 5 o'clock and ~~we~~ took a walk with M. for a short distance down the Mesa City road and back. After breakfast we went to work at restoring pottery continuing our filing, scraping[181] and painting all day. Mr. Goodwin came again this evening having been to Phoenix to-day. M. paid me a short visit during the evening. The railroad reached Tempe to-day.

> *Saturday, June 18*
> We mended jars industriously all day—Mr. Goodwin call'd in eve, having been to Phoenix & performed some commissions for us.

Sunday, June 19

Took another "constitutional" this morning at 5 o'clock with M. going as far as Goodwin's Ditch (which we have christened "Lover's Leap" although we both admit the impropriety of such a name). With the ladies I worked on the restoration of pottery until the afternoon. Goodwin called and Miss M. went riding with him in the buggy to Mesa City. We rearranged all the pottery under the canopy on and under a temporary table made by placing boards on large packing-boxes, giving our array of specimens quite the appearance of an ethnologic museum. After supper, M. having returned from her ride, we took a short walk and returned again to restore pottery with Mr. and Mrs. C. and Mr. Garlick, continuing in our occupation until after 10 o'clock.

> *Sunday, June 19*
> The days are so warm we take our walks now before & after sunshine. We mended pottery all day except a little while in aft—when I drove to new railroad station with Mr. Goodwin, who with his brother were [the] only visitors 2-day—The railroad has reached Tempe at last. In the evening we all restored pottery again in the ramada which has been arranged like a museum with shelves for the specimens, or as Tchny Wai says—"all e same e store."

Monday, June 20

Were up at 5 and took our walk, returning to camp before the rest of the campists were up. Mended pottery again to-day. Mr. Cushing who had been busy with photographing and developing for the last few days called in the evening and dictated letters to Prof's [A. H.] Thompson and Fiske which I finished transcribing by 12 o'clock and went to the kitchen for the signature of Mr. Cushing who was busy on Mrs. Hemenway's letter. After he had completed it I press-copied and had all the mail in readiness for Mr. Garlick to take to Phoenix to-morrow. Retired at 2 a.m.

Monday, June 20
Mending pottery again all day. Mr. Garlick went to Tempe. Mr. Cushing dictated all the evening to Mr. Hodge. He reads Martin Chuzzlewit after each meal.

Tuesday, June 21
Miss M. and I were up and took our regular stroll at 5 o'clock. Returning we drank coffee and chatted together and after regular breakfast proceeded to the restorations again at which we worked until evening when, with the ladies I went to Ruin XXVa where we secured the rest of the mound specimens that had been excavated. News of more Apache outbreaks on the one hand and smallpox among the Pimas on the other. These unpleasantries, coupled with the intense heat, which has now grown to an almost unendurable pitch, make our surroundings anything but comfortable. Mr. Garlick went to Phoenix again to-day, purchasing another mule—"Bob." A very interesting specimen in the shape of a tiny snake—about 2 inches in length—was found in the ladies' canopy this morning. Goodwin called and spent a short time talking "ditch" and "header" to Mr. Cushing. M. called in the evening and Mr. Garlick soon followed when we revealed the "affair" to his confidence.[182]

Tuesday, June 21
Mr. Garlick went to Phoenix & brought little mule Bob as match for Mary. Mr. Goodwin made us another visit. Little snake just out of egg in Camp.

Wednesday, June 22
As Mr. C. was up and at work on developing photo-negatives at 5 o'clock M. and I thought it inadvisable under the circumstances to take our customary early walk. We worked very hard all day in the canopy at the pottery-restoration. Mr. Sherman, Sup't of Instruction of the Territory,[183] and Mr. Adams, a grand mogul among the Territorial Methodists and owner of the land upon which we are now camped,[184] paid us a visit in the afternoon. In

the evening M. and myself went to Goodwin's ranch to see the thresher in operation, but did not get there in time to see it work as the sun had just set. We rode to camp with Mrs. Cushing who had started out to collect specimens from the mounds but who got only as far as the ranch, where she went for water for the team, when a terrific gust of wind struck our neighborhood filling everything completely with dirt, and frightening Mrs. C. half out of her wits. While Mr. C. was at work in the photo-tent this evening the ladies made me a call and Mrs. Cushing read "The Looking Glass" one of the "Alice in Wonderland" series—a very ingenious little fairy tale.

Wednesday, June 22
Specimen mending all morning interspersed with readings from Martin Chuzzlewit—Mr. Adams, the owner of this land & Mr. Sherman from Phoenix came to camp. Mr. Garlick went to Phoenix. Mr. Hodge & I went to Goodwin's in late aft 2 see threshing machine and returned in buckboard with Em. A wind storm which made things very disagreeable & dusty.

Thursday, June 23
Despite the early rising of nearly all the camp before 6 this a.m. M and I paid our usual visit to a place a short distance down the mesa road where we spent a short time under the shade of a mesquite-tree, for the sun had become so warm, even so early in the day, that its rays were decidedly uncomfortable. The weather during all this week and last has been all but unbearable—candles melt and run in the sticks; the tools with which we work become so warm that they can scarcely be handled without first melting, even in the shade, and the ladies complain that their hairpins become so hot during the day as to burn their heads. In the afternoon M. and I went to our little retreat where we remained until sundown. The portrait looks at each sitting more and more like Teluli. After supper I threw myself on my bed and was soon asleep. Awoke at 10 o'clk or thereabouts, helped M. to draw water when I retired for the night.

Thursday, June 23
Mending of jars still in progress nearly all day—Mr. Hodge & I had a sitting for the portrait in afternoon.

Friday, June 24

Was up at six o'clock and after breakfast we worked all day on the specimens in restoring them. In the evening M. and myself went to Va mound bringing in the specimens in the buckboard.

> *Friday, June 24*
>
> Mended jars all day together—In evening Mr. H. & I went in buckboard & brought in specimens from Mound Va.

Saturday, June 25

Went with M. at 5 o'clock a.m. to mound VIIIa where we got a load of burial urns, bowls etc. Spent the day in mending these specimens and in the evening took a walk with M. Mr. Garlick went to Tempe to-day returning with letter from home. Mexicans went to town tonight to remain over Sunday.

> *Saturday, June 25*
>
> A very hot day—118°. Went at 5 30 A.M. with Mr. H. & got specimens from Mound VIIIa which we spent the day restoring—Mr. Garlick went to Tempe for mail & Ramon Castro has gone to stay over Sunday. The Zuñis who have been digging this week with the other men "struck" to day on account of the heat.

Sunday, June 26

The Indians who had been at work excavating all the week "struck" to-day on account of the heat. Went out to Goodwin's this morning and bathed in his ditch, returning to camp in his buggy with him. After dinner M. and Mr. G. went to Mesa City—I spent the afternoon in reading "Judith Shakespeare"[185] and in writing to Ashley—M. returned just after dark and she spent a short while in my tent during the evening.

> *Sunday, June 26*
>
> There were several visitors to day in spite of heat which daily increases—All metal things too warm to handle & even the hair pins in my head are quite hot. Water standing in a metal bucket in my tent during the heat of the day I can scarcely bear my hand in. Mr. Goodwin took me for a third drive to Mesa City.

Monday, June 27

Went walking with M. at 5 this morning—returned to mend jars all day. Goodwin came in the evening and took M. to Tempe returning soon after sundown. Mr. Cushing has been busy in arranging and restoring specimens and in photographing during the past few days. Dictated letter to Baxter this ev'g. M. called on me.

> *Monday, June 27*
>
> Mended pottery with Mr. Hodge all during the forenoon and went after lunch with Mr. Goodwin in his buggy to see the thrashing machine and header at work in his fields [and] then to Tempe where I made a little stay at the Armstrong's. On our return home Mr. Goodwin took a late supper with me and stay'd quite late in the evening as this is his last day before going East.

Tuesday, June 28

Went walking with M. at 5:00 returning to transcribe my notes of last evg's dictation after breakfast—After lunch took the new mules "Barney" and "Pete" and with Siwahtitsailu went to Tempe—Got as far as Farmer's where a train was on the track. Finding myself on the wrong side of the road and being unable to cross the ditch I attempted to back and turn my team when I found that it was impossible to do so without taking their bridles and forcing them back. A sudden backward plunge of one of the mules broke the neck-strap, causing the yoke to strike me very forcibly across the face cutting my nose very severely and knocking me senseless for a few seconds. I proceeded to town masked and court-plastered the injured member and was soon collecting the month's accounts and doing the necessary errands to the ridicule of all my acquaintances who inquired if I had been "chopping wood" and wondered if the Fourth of July had come already at Camp Hemenway—After a visit to the slaughter-house in a very severe sandstorm in order to secure a sheep and a hide the Indian and myself turned toward camp—For two or three miles along the road evidences of a heavy rain fall were visible; not only the dust being settled and converted into mud, but spare water remaining in the wagon tracks. While in the town and at camp no rain fell whatever—M. called after supper and sympathized with my lacerated nose—Bathed and retired about 11 o'clk—

Tuesday, June 28
I divided my day (which was very hot) between mending pottery and sewing. Mr. Goodwin came to say goodbye as he goes home this evening & does not expect to find us here on his return. Mr. Hodge went to Tempe and had quite an accident when passing the cars on the Maricopa road. When trying to back the mules a strap broke causing the breast yoke to fly up and strike him in the face. He lost consciousness for a second but in the end suffered no more serious injury than a badly skinned nose. Martin Chuzzlewit is finished & the Virginian[186] begun.

Wednesday, June 29[187]
Up at 5 and in half an hour was out walking with I-ki-na[188] returning before the "family" were up. Mended pottery during the greater portion of the day and had a "lemonade and diary party" in the afternoon. After supper I read "Peppermint Perkins"[189] for which Miss M. had sent to Washington and retired at a respectable hour.

Wednesday, June 29
Mended pottery all day—Tenatsali read aloud from the Virginian—There was a lemonade party in camp to day in spite of the rain which was accompanied by very heavy clouds & much dust & thunder & lightning.

Thursday June 30
Went walking this morning as usual. Restored pottery all day and in the evening was with Mr. Garlick, entertained by the Mexicans who sang and danced in a very pleasing manner. Met M. in "carpenter shop" where we had a chat and then returned to my tent to read "Peppermint Perkins" for a short time. "Jim" Goodwin started for his home in Mo. on Tuesday and this evening his brother called and made a short stay—Wrote to Eck to-night.

Thursday, June 30
Took the usual early morning walk for exercise and restored broken specimens all day—Mr. Goodwin Jr. called on us in his brother's absence.

Friday, July 1, '87
Second month of summer begins to-day and we are still in the Salado sweltering with the heat! Pottery again all day after our usual walk in the morning before breakfast. In the afternoon went with Miss M. to the "studio" where I sat for my portrait until nearly sundown.

> *Friday, July 1*
> Mr. Garlick went to Tempe for barley & mail. There was a sitting for the portrait.

Saturday, July 2
Same thing every day—like Mark Twain's, my diary is assuming the same stereotyped aspect; but instead of "getting up, dressing, eating & going abed", it is "taking an early morning 'constitutional' and returning to mend pottery all day["]—what monotony! Enjoy the walks awfully though. Saw rattlesnake yesterday morning and almost walked on it while it lay in a dormant state in the path which we have wound in and out [of] the sages. Got pottery from mound XXIIIa with Miss M. before breakfast this a.m. and from md. XIVa before sunset this evening. After supper chatted with Mr. Garlick for a while on the wagon seat and after he left me gazed at the moon in a very ungraceful but decidedly comfortable attitude soon falling asleep and remaining in that state until about 10 o'cl'k when I returned to my tent and retired—

> *Saturday, July 2*
> Cooler than yesterday— Mr. Hodge & I went in buckboard to Mounds XXIVa and XIVa & brought in specimens which we restored during the day. Are invited to the Webster's for 4th of July festivities but have declined. News that the Apaches are still at large on the road we wanted to take to Zuñi, so it is thought best for us to return via Prescott. Tom Goodwin went to Phoenix and undertook some commissions for us, and distinguished himself by mailing a letter addressed to himself containing a check. Bright moonlight again. T. read Virginian aloud all evening.

Sunday, July 3
Worked during a part of the morning in restoring specimens of pottery and in the afternoon went with Miss M. to sit for portrait and were compelled

to return to camp very hurriedly on account of a sand storm which arose without warning [and] gave the appearance of an immense column of dust in the distance that was rapidly approaching us—Mr. Garlick went to Phoenix this afternoon.

Sunday, July 3

Took a constitutional before breakfast and painted mended jars all morning. We were visited by a Mormon family of seventeen members who came to see the collections, and looked quite formidable coming in single file. Mr. Hodge showed the sights & when they saw the first skull the Mother exclaimed "what is that"! & on being told it was a skull turned to one of her brood & said "Sallie, thems the kind of bones you've got in your head". Mr. Garlick went to Phoenix and Ramon to Tempe for mail. Tenatsali read Virginian till early bed time. A heavy wind storm came up about supper time making camp very uncomfortable by blowing sand & straws into the food, & leaving the sky cloudy made the night so warm that sleep was almost impossible & I was up & down half a dozen times. It finally cleared & the moon shone so brightly that one time on waking I thought it was morning & got up. Jack, who has been cultivating a taste lately for biscuit & breakfast bacon, broke his halter strap in the night & made a visit to the Kitchen tent in search of his favorite viands, but being caught in the act by Em & Tchny Wai allowed himself to be led back to the manger & tied with out a protest.

Monday, July 4

Hurrah for the "Glorious Fourth"—not so glorious in camp for we worked hard on the inevitable pottery until dinner time. Had a few visitors from Mormontown in the afternoon who were decidedly "confectionery" with each other, the "fellers" placing their arms around their sweethearts with impunity notwithstanding the fun which Miss M. and I silently made at them from my tent. Had two "lemonade parties" in honor of the day (and our thirst) and in the afternoon went to our retreat where very little was accomplished in the way of painting. Were driven back to camp by a terrific wind storm, shortly followed by a drenching rain which threatened to blow or wash away everything in camp—The ladies took refuge in my tent during the storm where we spent the evening pleasantly peering out into the darkness for one minute and bright moonlight another—the rain descending in torrents all the while. A very peculiar phenomenon occurred to night—that of a rainbow by moonlight—the first I had ever seen—Mr. Garlick returned about 2 o'clk this afternoon from Phoenix, bringing letter from Evelyn in which she announces her engagement with C. A. Ramon went to Tempe to-day but did not return until after the storm had subsided, which was quite late.

Monday, July 4

The fourth was spent very quietly in camp until an influx of picnicers came in the afternoon—lots of country girls in all their finery and their beaux with vests but no coats. We commenced mending pottery, but operations were not very brisk as Mr. Garlick did not return from Phoenix with the glue till 2 o'clock and Ramon who always pounds the papier masher was away. I painted on the mended specimens most all day and Tenatsali read from Virginian. In honor of the day Mr. Hodge made lemonade & passed it around, after Mr. Garlick's arrival. Another storm came up at supper time which drenched camp & the wind blew furiously till late in the night so I was afraid 2 go to bed. Em & I were sitting in Mr. H's tent when it commenced to rain & could not get back to our own tents till rubber shoes were brought & boards spread down as the entire camp was like a great lake. It was the most awful & beautiful storm I ever saw & we sat watching the sky till quite late—half of which was black as ink & the other half perfectly clear with moon shining brightly & making against the clouds the first lunar rainbow I ever saw. When I retired to my tent I found a great puddle of water had settled in the middle of the floor, so being afraid to go to bed while the wind blew so heavily I sat on my little camp stool, with rubber shoes on & skirts tucked up out of the wet, trying to read, till far into the nt.

Si wa titsa lu & Wai had high words to day during which the latter drew a knife & threatened to kill Si wa titsa lu which so excited him that he determined to start for Zuñi at once. He packed all his goods, saddled his mule & started off, but nobody worried much about it knowing his mild disposition, & sure enough when the storm was at its worst he came hurrying back very much frightened [and] crept into his tent & nothing more was heard of the quarrel.

Tuesday, July 5

Owing to the rain last night we did not take our morning walk. Viewed the pottery over and saw that a number of the restored specimens had been pretty badly damaged, which took us until 3 o'clk in the afternoon to repair to their former shape. The second storm visited Hemenway this evening but it did not rain. The wind was very severe, and notwithstanding yesterday's heavy rain everything was filled with dust. After supper took a moonlight walk and returned to my tent to answer Evelyn's letter. Siwahtitsailu took a notion to raise a row with Choy Wuy yesterday morning, drawing a knife on him. After being reprimanded by Mr. C. he saddled his mule and started for Zuñi. Got as far as Tempe and the storm appearing caused him to return very speedily to camp very much to Weta's enjoyment and in accordance with our predictions. Ramon went to Tempe to-day returning in time to avoid the wind-storm.

> *Tuesday, July 5*
>
> Ramon went again to Tempe today to send money to his brother Rafael[190] who is engaged for our service. Em, Mr. Hodge and I mended pottery all day and in the evening sat in the secretary tent reading Peppermint Perkins together. Another storm came up this evening, but found us all prepared—with deep ditches dug all around every tent which leaves the camp high & dry—This time it was principally sand & wind which was perfectly suffocating.

Wednesday, July 6

Walked this morning with Miss M. Labored and perspired over the detestable pottery until late in the afternoon when we made preparations for the wind storm which we expect now almost every day. The wind blew very fiercely but was accompanied by no rain. Mr. Garlick went to town today. Brought letter from Will Stuart. Ladies visited me during the progress of the wind this ev'g and Mrs. Cushing amused us with more "Peppermint Perkins". Took bath to-night and returned about 10:30.

> *Wednesday, July 6*
>
> "Jugglery" all day and at evening another heavy sand storm during which Em, Mr. H & I again sat together reading Peppermint Perkins' letters. Mr. Garlick went to Tempe for mail. Our sur-

rounding tract of land is illuminated every night by the burning Mesquites.

Thursday, July 7

"Constitutional" at 5:30. After breakfast went with Mr. Garlick and relocated and plotted walls of certain ruins which took us the greater portion of the day. Worked on the pottery for a short time and about 4:30 went with Miss M. to our "studio" but were soon compelled to remove by the gang of Mexicans who are at work clearing the land. Not much painting accomplished. Returned to camp to see the flames ruthlessly gnaw away the mesquite under which we had passed so many pleasant moments! Mr. Cushing is still busy with the labeling. Spent ev'g in the buck board with Mr. Garlick and retired about 10. Very warm night. Have broken out with prickly heat—

Thursday, July 7

Jar mending occupied the greater part of the day & I have commenced to use oil paints to color the mended places. Mr. Hodge & I had another sitting for the portrait but to our surprise, found the studio Mesquite tree in flames & that part of [the] tract almost cleared so had to find another shady place for the continuation of the work. Mesquite beans are ripe & very pleasant to the taste.

Friday, July 8

Walked this morning. Located and plotted walls of ruins all the morning and restored pottery in the afternoon. Miss M. called and while having a "diary party" Mrs. C. came and asked if we could drive to Gray's Ranch for eggs—We <u>walked</u> to the ranch, secured the eggs and returned to camp just at dusk after a very pleasant walk. [Saw] Mr. Garlick returning from Tempe on our way over and, notwithstanding our combined whistling and shouting, failed to attract his attention. Read papers from home—noticed acc't of the burning of Crossman's house.

Friday, July 8

Mr. Hodge & Mr. Garlick were away until dinner time locating ruins while Em & I copied specimen labels. In afternoon Mr. G. went to

Tempe and the rest of us devoted our time to jar mending until just before tea when Mr. H. & I went for Em to Gray's to get eggs—The Mesquite trees are getting very sparse. Another very hot night.

Saturday, July 9

After walk this morning went in with a will and with Ramon Castro's assistance arranged pottery for cataloguing. Mr. C. and the ladies have been very busily engaged with labeling. Mr. Garlick goes to Phoenix at 5 this morning and returns at noon—quick trip. All hands turn in to work on the pots & jars at 9 o'clk to-night and we are aroused by a coming storm to pack the specimens under wagon-canvas for protection. Bathed and retired at 12 o'clk.

Saturday, July 9

Mr. Garlick went to Phoenix at 5 A.M. and returned at noon. The entire day & even until late at night cataloguing specimens was in progress in which all took part. Very hot all day.

Sunday, July 10

Did not walk this morning so remained abed until late breakfast. With Mr. Cushing I spent the entire day at cataloguing etc. pyral specimens—Ladies also busy all day in copying labels—Very hot day. Mr. Garlick goes to Phoenix again to-day, "on his own hook" and returns in evening with two folding chairs—one intended as wooden wedding present to Mrs. Cushing (which they celebrate to day) and the other for Miss M. Retired early this evening for an early rising if Choy Wuy doesn't forget to awaken me.

Sunday, July 10

Mr. Garlick went again to Phoenix & brought back with him two camp chairs—Mr. Cushing's anniversary present to Em. We all intended celebrating their wooden wedding but were disappointed in doing so. Cataloguing was continued to day.

Monday, July 11

Walked this morning as usual and during the day continued cataloguing. When evening came chatted with Mr. Garlick in the buckboard and retired very early.

Monday, July 11
Cataloguing again occupied the day to the exclusion of everything else but a walk before breakfast—

Tuesday, July 12
After walking this morning we set to work at pottering (Miss M. and myself), Mr. Cushing feeling too ill to work much on the labeling. It rained a little during the morning and the weather is now much cooler. Palm fans and handkerchiefs are not brought so much into use and our nights are much more pleasant.

Tuesday, July 12
Mr. Cushing too ill to catalogue to day—is reading aloud Stephenson's [*sic*] Treasure Island. Mr. H. & I spent day mending pottery. Pouring rain this afternoon and an influx of Mormons.

Wednesday, July 13
Awoke about 5. Raining very hard so did not arise—Mr. Cushing continues ill all day and Mrs. C. spends most of her time in nursing him. Miss M. and I potter again all day under the ramado. Choy Wuy becomes insubordinate and is discharged. Mr. Garlick taking him to Tempe and himself continuing to Phoenix. I wash my "booz-boozies" and launder chiefs and hang them out making quite a "wash-day" appearance of our camp—. Jerked mutton on another line completes the aspect! Lemonade party this aft. with Miss M.

Wednesday, July 13
We awoke to find it raining & showers continued at intervals all day, during which we mended jars. Tchny Wai grew impertinent this morning & was discharged. Mr. Garlick took him to Phoenix & Adolfo the Mexican[191] was installed as cook. More Treasure Island—more Mormon visitors.

Thursday, July 14
Arose at 4:30 and awoke Miss M. [and] had a walk. Cataloguing and labeling all day and visits by a myriad of Mormons. Mr. Garlick returns from Phoenix bringing letter from Nell.

Thursday, July 14
Mr. Cushing better so cataloguing continued. Mr. H & I wrote labels & blanks at the same time from Mr. C's dictation. Mr. G. returned from Phoenix with mail.

Friday, July 15
To-day after our morning stroll—we spend in cataloging and labeling interspersing our work with the more congenial "dobeying". More Mormons!

Friday, July 15
Cataloguing & labeling all day & Mr. Garlick packing specimens. More Mormon visitors.

Saturday, July 16
With checks and vouchers I depart for Tempe this morning to "pay-off". (of course we had our customary constitutional) Took the new road in and made town about two o'clk, ordering dinner. Got some green figs and plums (the first green-figs I had ever eaten) and was in such a hurry to return to camp that figs, plums, honey, shoes and paint-powders were all one before I arrived. Goodwin called this ev'g and brought some more figs for Miss M. Went to carpenter shop and lying on an improvised board couch was soon fast asleep. Awoke in an hour or so and retired.

Saturday, July 16
I mended jars alone all day—as Mr. Hodge had writing to do for Mr. C. & then went to Tempe. On his return he brought us our first fresh figs—some of which Tom Goodwin also gave us later. The Mormons sometimes bring us grapes & mellons when they visit camp.

Sunday, July 17
Walked before breakfast and worked with Mr. Cushing and M[iss] M. <u>very</u> hard all day in labeling and cataloguing, being constantly interrupted by Mormons[,] and Mormons who though very bothersome are very considerate in bringing us fruit of their own raising—their grapes are very delicious, and make most acceptable additions to our <u>cuisine</u>.

Sunday, July 17
The busiest day we've had as Mr. Cushing is feeling well enough to resume the catalogue work. Mr. Garlick went to Phoenix in search of a cook in evening. For readings Rider Haggard's "Jess"[192] has succeeded Treasure Island. After long & faithful efforts I have succeeded in getting the red mule to eat from my hand & old Jack now comes across camp for a biscuit when I call him.

Monday, July 18
Up and off for Gray's Ranch with Miss M. at 5:30. Get eggs and return about half past seven. Catalogue and labels as usual to-day making us all feel tired by ev'g. Mr. Garlick does not return to-day from Phoenix. Took walk towards s.e. of camp with Miss M. after supper returning at dark. Wrote mother this evg.

Monday, July 18
Mr. H. & I walked to Gray's ranch for eggs before breakfast & cataloguing occupied the rest of the day—No sign of Mr. Garlick yet.

Tuesday, July 19
We walk at 6 and return to breakfast at 6:30. Finish up cataloguing and labeling of all the pyral-specimens that have been taken from the mounds and arrange for cataloguing the house-collections—Mormons innumerable continue their visits "to see the sights"—One family presented "that tir young fellar" with a water-melon as compensation for his services as guide. Mr. Garlick returns from his two days' visit to Phoenix, bringing Charlie McCall, our new cook, who proves himself at supper to be a decided success. Patrick sends to Miss M. two boxes of "Salado Valley fruit" (grown in <u>California</u> by the by, with a little billet within each box). At four we go to our little retreat which we find much to our gratification has not been <u>burned</u> after all. Receive another letter from Nell and papers from Ed. this ev'g, thro Mr. Garlick which I spend the evg in reading, retiring at 10 o'clk.

Tuesday, July 19
All united in labelling house mound specimens—Mr. Mc.Clintock spent the morning with us and Mr. Garlick returned bringing mail and an American cook named Charlie Mc.Call who promises well.

Mr. Patrick sent me two boxes of beautiful fruit and two corresponding billets—

Wednesday, July 20

Walk a short distance with Miss M. this morning, returning to[o] late [for] breakfast. Work on painting restored jars during the morning and in the afternoon until about 4 o'clk when I dress and with Miss M. start for Tempe by shortest road. Got there all right though one bad mud-hole sent our wheels in up to the hubs—Left Miss M. at Austin's, where she visited Miss Ashby, while I drove into the town to make necessary purchases for camp. Went to Murphy's where I got a box of fruit as present to the ladies, and returning to P. O. found Miss M. awaiting, with Miss Ashby. Went past Austin's, taking Miss A. with us—three on a seat—on way to slaughter-house. Returned with butcher whom we met on route to town, where we were obliged to remain until after sundown before starting for camp by way of Maricopa road, on account of the mud which we encountered on our way to town. Reached camp by 10 o'clk, without other mishap than missing the road a couple of times in the darkness. Got letters from Evelyn and Mary Duvall in town—Mary sending me a few crumbs of "an old beau's wedding cake" to dream on.[193] After my late supper I read some papers from Wash. and retired about 11.

Wednesday, July 20

Mended pottery all the forenoon and after dinner Mr. H. & I drove to Tempe where I made several visits. We were much delayed & did not get home till 9 P.M.

Thursday, July 21

After walking I painted for while. Miss Magill sketched the decoration of a water vessel. Then we took turns in painting each others portraits—or, rather characteristics—Went to ruin IIIa where we got specimens and returned with them to camp—Read papers during ev'g and after a short visit from Mr. Garlick bathed and blanketed—

Thursday, July 21

Spent day copying pottery designs while Mr. Hodge painted a finished jar. In afternoon went with buckboard to Mound III and brought in remaining specimens.

Friday, July 22
Had our customary constitutional this morning and went to work on jars during part of forenoon. While Miss M. and I sought the coolness of my tent for a few minutes, Mr. Cushing asked me to accompany him to the ruins where we located the specimens-finds in House Mounds I and X. The day is very hot and the hot winds blow over the plains as though from the mouth of a blast furnace. Went to "retreat" in the afternoon, and finding that it had at last been burned sought another, much less shady and pretty. Miss M. spent the ev'g with me and we had a very enjoyable chat. Mr. Cushing celebrates his thirtieth birthday today. Mr. Garlick goes to Phoenix in the morning, returning in the ev'g.

> *Friday, July 22*
> Mr. Garlick went to Phoenix. This is Tenatsali's birthday which was spent very much like other days—He has been mapping & and the rest of us arranging specimens.

Saturday, July 23
Birthday celebrations fall thick and fast—Miss Magill announces hers to day and we make enough of a holiday of it as our little jar-mending will allow by walking in the morn'g, eating candy and plastering with "adobe" at the same time, and in the afternoon finding a very pretty and shady nook half a mile north of camp, where I had my last sitting for my portrait, which is now pronounced by all to be a good piece of work, both as to likeness and coloring,—the latter being exceptionally excellent—Reach camp soon after sundown and spent the ev'g in my tent—Mr. Cushing has been employed for last two days in plotting specimens on map-sheets. Flys are very troublesome and every device which the genius of the camp can improvise for the extermination of the pests which hover around the ollas or any other cool spots which they can find, are now in operation, including honey-besmattered spring boards, soap-bottles, mosquito-nettings, etc. etc.

> *Saturday, July 23*
> Arose very early this morning, had a walk and was variously congratulated on my birthday—Mr. Garlick hoping I would live as long as I wanted to—Mr. Hodge sent home for some fine candy but it didn't come in time so some was gotten from Phoenix in honor of

the occasion. Mended specimens all day—Every body is exercising his ingenuity inventing machines for killing flies which are so bad we can hardly stand them.

Sunday, July 24

Up at 6 but was too late to walk as breakfast was then almost ready—Set to work on "dobeying" pottery under canopy continuing till lunch-time, when Miss M. spread her blanket, and feeling drowsy, took a nap. Started about 3:30 for our new "studio" where we spent the reminder of the day, glad to get away from the monotony of the camp to the shade of the few remaining green mesquites. Mr. Cushing has busied himself again to-day by plotting specimens. Mr. Garlick drove to Phoenix in the morning. The hottest day yet I think. Retired early but was awakened by a wind-storm which blew down the large ramado. Dressed hastily and being still somewhat unconscious, tried to draw my flannel shirt over my legs, thinking them pantaloons—Going out into the moonlight I saw that Mr. C. and Miss M. were already up and we were soon joined by Mrs. C. and the two Castros. The Indians were still fast asleep, but they too were called, Weta first appearing on the scene clad in a breech-clout. We re-erected the canopy, making it fast with ropes and returned to our chambers about 2 o'clk after an hour-and-a-half's hard work. Mr. Garlick, being ill, did not arise. Ramon cut his toe very badly against a tent-pin.

Sunday, July 24

Very warm all day. Mr. Garlick went to Phoenix again and Mr. Tom Goodwin came & brought Em & me some grapes & figs from Mr. McClintock. Dreadful hot wind came up in night blowing down specimen tent and every one was up helping put it up & save specimens but Mr. G. who made himself sick in town, Charlie McCall who sleeps through anything & the lazy Indians who do nothing helpful. Old Pima Juan inflicted himself on us again to day but made himself useful in the night's mishap.

Monday, July 25

Went to Ruins IX and XI this a.m. early with Miss M. but owing to wrong instructions as to the mounds to be visited found no specimens. Returned to camp and after breakfast had a short visit from Miss M. who brought her knitting, and a bag of grapes which were very delicious. Went with Rafael

Castro and located specimens in pyral-mounds XVIa and XVIIa returning in time for lunch and to see about 20 visitors from the Tempe vicinity under the tutelage of Dro. Gregg.[194] They remained until after lunch-time, having a repast of their own in the shop-canopy. Mr. C. entertained the gentlemen of the party, Mrs. C. the ladies and Miss Magill managed the girls, one of whom inquired of her "who that 'ere man is—I have seen him so often" (meaning myself). Located XVIa in the afternoon, and I thought I should be overcome by the heat, so intense was the sun. When I returned to camp Miss M. and I went to our trysting-place where we remained until sundown, spending the afternoon in chatting & sketching. Took a five-minutes walk after supper and after reading "Miles Standish"[195] for an hour retired. I shot my first rabbit this ev'g, picking him off the ground with Weta's rifle.

Monday, July 25
Went with Mr. H. to Mounds IX & XI where there were supposed to be specimens but there were none. He did writing & located specimens in XIIIa to day. I did some jar mending which was interrupted by a party of sight seers—about twenty—including Dr. Gregg who spent almost the entire day here.

Tuesday, July 26
Got up early and went with Miss M. to Mound III where we gathered the remainder of the specimens in that place, returning to camp before breakfast-time. Mended and restored pottery until about 4 o'clk when we went into the woods, remaining there until nearly sunset. Read during the ev'g and retired quite early.

Tuesday, July 26
Went before breakfast with Mr. H. to Mound III where we got all the specimens—burial urns—brought them to camp & mended them during the day.

Wedsnesday, July 27
Went with Miss Magill to pyral mounds XVI and XVII this a.m. before breakfast. Repaired pottery until 4 o'clk when we walked to mesquites south of camp and sat until late in afternoon. Miss M. took her sewing and we read aloud by turns Haggard's "She".[196] Took a short walk by moonlight with

Miss M. after supper and retired at a respectable season—Ramon went to Tempe to-day and brought letters from mother, Crossman, Mr. Fox, U.S. Consul at Plymouth, and Eckhardt, which I read and bunked in early.

> *Wednesday, July 27*
> Mr. H. & I went in early morning to Mounds XVI & XVII for specimens which we mended during the day. Ramon went to Tempe for mail which brought us news of Mr. J. C. G. Kennedy's murder.[197]

Thursday, July 28
Went to mound XIIIa (pyral) this morning with Miss M. to get in specimens as usual—which is now getting to be second nature with us. Worked on pottery-repairing and restoring during the day and in evening went to our little retreat where we read "She" and chatted for a couple of hours—

> *Thursday, July 28*
> To day with Mr. H. brought two loads of specimens from XIIIa & mended them—Went to Goodwin's to water mules—

Friday, July 29
Got another load of pyral-specimens from XIIIa this morning with Miss Magill which we mended during the day until ev'g when we went into woods to read, rest and enjoy the coolness of the shade. The day has been somewhat cloudy and consequently cooler to-day than it has been for some time past, the weather recently being almost unbearable. Took a very short moonlight walk after supper and returning to camp read papers which I received from Em. together with "Century" for July—Worked on accounts for June until about 11:30 when I retired, prepared for an early rising.

> *Friday, July 29*
> Again to XIIIa for another load of specimens & mended them. Ramon went to Tempe for mail.

Saturday, July 30
Went with Miss M. to pyral mound XIIIa this morning and brought in the last of the specimens which we spent the early part of the day mending. About 5:30 we repaired as usual to the retreat to enjoy the shade till supper-

time and returned to find "Pat" snugly ensconced at Camp for the night—bed, cantina, "babies" & all. After tea there [was] a game of Euchre in the ramado in which Miss Magill & Mr. Patrick playing against Mrs. Cushing and myself, were victorious—

> *Saturday, July 30*
> To day with Mr. H. finished bringing in specimens from XIIIa & the mending occupied us till 3. P.M. Mr. Patrick came for the night bringing with him his bed—cantine & "babies." We spent the evening playing eucher—Mr. P. & I against Em & Mr. H.

Sunday, July 31
Took a short walk with Miss Magill before breakfast. Mr. Patrick spent the entire day with us and made himself at home to an extent that amazed the camp, even taking a nap during his enjoyment of which I read the news to Miss M. then repaired alone to the nearest shade tree and read "Judith Shakespeare" in the grateful shade. At half past five Mr. P. left us for good—(he is going to San Diego) when I went with the above mentioned young lady to the mesquite grove and chatted in the cool till tea time.

> *Sunday, July 31*
> Mr. Patrick spent the day with us until after five—making himself thoroughly at home even to the extent of lounging about, removing his shoes & taking a nap, at which point I retired from the scene & read papers with Mr. Hodge. Adolfo returned this evening & brought Em a little mocking bird.

Monday, August 1
Spent the day, after walking early this morning, in making a statement of outfit-rental for the Expedition authorities. Went for a short walk in the evening with Miss Magill and returned to camp when Ramon came from town but there was no mail for <u>me</u>.

> *Monday, August 1*
> Ramon went to town & Weta & Si wa titsa lu went to the Gila relic hunting. I rose at 5 A. M. & went mapping ruin XIV with T. before breakfast. The sun on the paper perfectly blinding—

Tuesday, August 2

Got ready with vouchers etc. after our morning's walk and after writing to Mr. Baxter and to Patrick Hamilton of Phoenix, Sec'y Maricopa Co. Immigration Union, on behalf of Mr. Cushing, went, with Miss Magill, (and using Weta as footman) to Tempe where we remained until dark; I attending to accounts, collecting bills, etc. while Miss M spent the ev'g with Mrs. Armstrong's, where we took supper and drove toward camp in the moonlight reaching it by 9:30 or 10:00 o'clock.

> *Tuesday, August 2*
>
> Afternoon went with Mr. Hodge to Tempe with Weta in behind whom we drove to the slaughter house to get raw hide. After attending to our purchases we were invited to the Armstrong's to tea when I was presented with the handsomest bunch of grapes I ever saw—& when Mr. Smith the syndicate gardener made me go with Mrs. A. to the garden & get a basket of figs & pomegranates. The moon almost full—which made the ride home beautiful.

Wednesday, August 3

After working up accounts this a.m. (our morning walk we had, of course.) I commenced work on the catalogue and had described 45 specimens when Mr. Cushing suggested a new plan of procedure. Miss M. spends nearly all day in my tent in writing letters while I am at my work, seizing the opportunity for a few moments [for] occasional chat. After supper we took a walk by the light of the full moon. Mr. Garlick went to Phoenix this morning and returned without looking at but one side of his memorandum of purchases to be made and consequently came home with but half his load. We joke him a good deal about this, saying "too much bull-fight" etc. etc. which he takes with good cheer.

> *Wednesday, August 3*
>
> Mr. Garlick went to Phoenix. The heat is so great that eggs standing in a metal bucket of salt water boiled almost hard.

Thursday, August 4

Went to house ruin II with Miss M. and brought in buckboard load of specimens before breakfast. Worked on acct's during morning and in afternoon commenced copying catalogue cards into m.s. form, finishing 75 during the time I worked. Miss M. brought in her knitting and sat in my tent while I was engaged with my work, stealing a few moments for conversation with her and in sipping lemonade. Weta had an accident this ev'g which nearly lost him his life. While unhitching the animals to drive them to water, "Chub" became somewhat lively in his old age, and thinking himself loosened ran off carrying part of the manger with him, striking the Indian a very severe blow across the back of the head, knocking him senseless. Arnica and a little Zuñi doctoring at the hands of Siwahtitsailu soon brought him around again however. Took moonlight walk with Miss M. and returning received letters from Ashley through Ramon and Rafael who went to town to-day. Wrote to Bancroft for gold pen and retired quite early.

> *Thursday, August 4*
> Early this morning Mr. H & I went to XXIIIa & house mound II for remaining specimens—mending them & arranging for cataloguing later in the day beside other work—writing, etc. Weta was kicked by Chub & Ramon & Rafael went to Tempe.

Friday, August 5
Got up early and went with Miss Magill to Ruin I for the specimens which remained. Mrs. Cushing also arose early and drove to Gray's for eggs. Worked on July accounts all day while Miss Magill mended pottery and in ev'g went to woods, meeting Miss M. who had gone in advance. Remained there until supper time and then returned to camp. Ramon went to town for provisions etc. and forage. Mr. Garlick spent the day in fixing wagons, plane-table, etc. After supper took moonlight walk with Miss M.

> *Friday, August 5*
> Went with Mr. Hodge to Mound I for remaining stone specimens then returned to jar mending for the rest of the day. Ramon went to Tempe for animal feed & mail & Mr. Tom Goodwin came to tell us his brother would return on Sunday.

Saturday, August 6
Did not walk this morning, but arose quite early, cleaned-up, and started to work on acct's. Miss M. works on pottery all the morning and spends after-

noon with me in my tent, bringing her knitting. Some Pimas, on their way to Sacaton to-day, left a black-shaggy dog of the Newfoundland-fox-hound type. Miss Magill captured its affections immediately, using porterhouse-steak and water as bait. It stayed around all day, following at her heels at every step she took, and persisted in going into the tents. Went to retreat for a short while, meeting Miss M. who had gone on before me—I being quite busy with my accounts. Mr. Cushing spent about two hours in my tent today, talking over accounts, future plans, etc. I made an estimate of expenses for the past 4 months under separate headings, which Mr. C. wants to use in submitting estimates of future expenses—Mr. Garlick spends the day at tinkering, getting ready for our next month's move to Superstition Mts.

Saturday, August 6

Mr. H. very busy about other work so I mended pottery alone. Little half starved Pima dog strayed into camp which I fed & gave water, for which it seemed to be so grateful that I have adopted it & call'd it a "shema" on account of his hungry looks. By night we had become such good friends that I could not keep him out of my tent & had to use a switch very sharply—& even this failed to keep out an insinuating black nose which was constantly thrust between my tent flaps. Growing tired of the scratching & whining I finally got up & went out in the campus to try & find some way of disposing of my new pet, & finding Em also wandering about trying to catch Pete who had gotten loose, we hunted together for bits of rope which we carefully tied together & picketed the dog out by a tent peg—I returned to bed with a feeling of relief—not even taking the precaution of fastening up my tent securely—but had scarcely settled myself when the puppy rushed into the tent having chewed his rope deliberately in two. I got up again & tied him more securely than at first, but when the operation was repeated I hunted up my shawl strap & gave him such a thrashing that he quieted down & lay on my doormat till morning without a murmur.

Sunday, August 7

Got up in time for breakfast. After finishing which gave my tent a thorough cleaning and did some laundering. Bathed and primped. Miss Magill worked on finishing pottery during morning, while I looked lazily on. Mr.

Johnson, Mr. Murphy[198] and a couple of their Tempe friends called, and greatly enjoyed inspecting the remaining specimens which are still uncatalogued and unpacked. Shortly after dinner (1:30) Miss M., the dog (our "mascot") and myself went to the retreat where we remained until sunset. Amused myself by increasing the india ink decorations on my left arm. Ramon went to Tempe to-day for provisions—brought letters from Mother on his return to camp. Mr. Cushing has busied himself to-day by restoring a shell which was originally inlaid with mosaic.[199] Miss M. spent the ev'g in my tent. Goodwin came home from the East to-day.

Sunday, August 7
I finished & painted six jars this morning & in the midst of my labors received calls from Mr. Goodwin just returned—his brother & two young men friends who came with him from Missouri. In spite of the slapping last night my dog is very affectionate & follows my every footstep like a shadow. The aft. being very warm Mr. H. & I sat out under the Mesquites reading until supper time. Ramon Castro went to Tempe for meat, ice & mail. Wind blew furiously all the evening.

Monday, August 8
Up at breakfast time, and made memorandum of purchases for Goodwin to make, who with several new acquisitions to his ranch (in the form of open-mouthed and staring-orbed country-louts whom he brought with him from the East) intend to make a trip to Phoenix to "do" the town in our buckboard. Wrote letters to Mr. Baxter & Prof. Bandelier in the morning, Miss Magill spending the time in my tent with her writing desk. After cataloguing in the afternoon, we went for an evening ramble to the "retreat" where we remained until supper-time as usual. Mr. Cushing held a camp-meeting in my tent this evening for the purpose of exhibiting a very handsome shell frog-fetish which he has been engaged in restoring during the last few days.[200] After the others had adjourned Miss M. continued her visit for a short time longer and then retired to her own tent.

Monday, August 8
My dog is in good training already & gave me no trouble last night. Mr. Hodge busy all day writing. The Goodwin crowd borrowed our

buckboard to go to Phoenix to day. Cloudy all day so very close & warm in consequence.

Tuesday, August 9

Did not walk this morning, so did not arise until breakfast was ready. The burning of all the trees around camp makes the morning strolls so less pleasant than they used to be that we have abandoned them for a while. Miss M. went to "dobeying" soon after breakfast, and I to cataloguing. Went in the ev'g to our retreat, spending a very cool and pleasant spell from the heat of camp.

Mr. Garlick still "tinkers" in fixing up things in readiness for our departure. Goodwin calls at camp this ev'g and tells us of his Phoenix adventures, including the run away, and the breaking of the buckboard which Mr. Cushing loaned to him ~~day~~ yesterday. A storm came up during the evening and we had to bustle to get things under cover. Miss Magill calls on me with rubbers and gossamer in hand and spends the evening in my tent. (I write to Ashley after supper.)

Tuesday, August 9

Mended pottery all day—Mr. Goodwin had a dreadful tale to tell about the trip to Phoenix yesterday when the horses ran away and broke the buckboard so badly it had to be left for repairs. He took tea with us & sat until a heavy storm coming up scattered the party to close tents & make ready. It poured rain all night & thundered & lightened dreadfully. The dog was a perfect nuisance—trying to get into my tent—scratching & whining & kept me awake half the night.

Wednesday, August 10

After cleaning house this morning I entertained Miss M. until breakfast-time when I went east of camp for a walk. Picked up several specimens on my way and discovered new site for a "retreat". Miss M. spent greater part of morning with me in my tent and after dinner went to Ruin XIV with Rafael Castro to put in walls, and found it necessary to make a relocation of the entire ruin owing to additional excavations that had been made since first plotting. Went in the evening to retreat with Miss M.—after having a "lemonade party". After supper M. called on me and I read "She" aloud while she crocheted on a little bag which she is making for my handkerchiefs, etc. Mr. Garlick went to Phoenix to-day[201] and Ramon to Tempe. Wrote Bancroft for stationery (paper and envelopes). Weta almost ends his life by accidentally drinking a cup of lye.

> *Wednesday, August 10*
> Another cloudy close day. Mr. Hodge made a map of ruin XIV, Mr. Garlick went to Phoenix & Ramon to Tempe.

Thursday, August 11
Up in time for breakfast. Went to work on catalogue when Miss M. called and said Mr. Cushing would like us to go to Phoenix. Pulled out from camp about half-past-nine and intended to take shortest road across country, but after reaching Gray's and discovering that the road had overflowed we took the route to Tempe, securing mail there and continued on. Arrived in Phoenix about 1 o'clock, leaving Miss Magill at post-office while I went to blacksmith-shop to get "Thistle's" shoe set and new rim on buckboard hub. Returning to Tauton & Kellner's Store, where I was engaged in making some purchases, Miss M. came in with Mr. Patrick (shirt sleeves). Left them there while I transacted further business in the town, and returned to start. Ice-cream suggested—accepted—ate—enjoyed immensely! Left town about 4 o'clock—reached Tempe where I got hair cut while Miss M. visited Mrs. Hayden—got back to camp by dark. Miss M. spends ev'g with me and we retire comparatively early for a fair rising.

> *Thursday, August 11*
> Mr. Hodge had business in Phoenix & took me with him. An overflowed ditch at Gray's made it necessary for us to go via Tempe—Arriving at Phoenix we separated to attend to our various errands. I met Mr. Patrick & treated him to soda water—& on our way out of town Mr. H. & I visited the Vienna bakery to get ice cream. Little Carlos[202] who has opened a fruit stand here brought me some beautiful grapes & grew indignant when I offered to pay for them. Reached Camp at dark.

Friday, August 12
Miss M. spent a short time with me after breakfast while I worked on catalogue of specimens. Mrs. C. and Miss M. spend remainder of morning

in making fringe for the buckboard which Mr. Garlick has overhauled. In afternoon, after working again on catalogue for a couple of hours, we went to the retreat, remaining till sundown. M. spent ev'g in my tent working on the handk'f bag which she is making for me.

> *Friday, August 12*
> Emma & I made fringe for the new buckboard lining.

Saturday, August 13
I worked on catalogue to-day while M. spent her time with me in finishing up the bag which she presented to me in the ev'g. In the afternoon we have a little misunderstanding in regard to my not getting a letter which blew out of the tent in a sudden gust of wind, but a short walk after supper ended the difficulty most favorably. While we were walking we witnessed a peculiar phenomenon in the way of a very beautiful meteorite which lit up the heavens with day-light brilliancy for a few seconds. M. spend remainder of ev'g with me. Mr. C's health does not improve.

> *Saturday, August 13*
> The sky cloudy & very threatening this eve, but we saw the most beautiful meteor which for a few seconds made everything as bright as twilight.

Sunday, August 14
A cloudy morning with very little rain. Did not arise very early. M. spends morn'g with me (after Goodwin calls) sketching the mules from my tent-door. In afternoon, after dinner I go to mesquites (with hatchet)—about half mile east of camp and spend about an hour in cutting sages and mesquite-boughs and making a new retreat. Return to camp and spent the rest of the afternoon with Mr. Garlick, while Miss M. is away to Mesa City with Goodwin, from whence they return about sundown. M. and I take short walk after supper, and returning, spend the ev'g in my tent eating grapes.

> *Sunday, August 14*
> Spent morning sketching the animals & after noon went with Mr. Goodman [*sic*] to Mesa City where we got quantities of grapes.

Monday, August 15

This morning I was at work on catalogue when M. called with her sketch-book and sketched the new shell bracelet and the frog fetiches of "Muertos". In the afternoon Mr. Cushing invited me to go to the Salado Mtn's in search of caves with him, but feeling head-achy I begged excuse and he had Mr. Garlick go in my stead. Mrs. Cushing spent a while with M. and myself reading newspaper humor. When she departed M. and myself went to our new retreat which I made yesterday and she was quite surprised that it had been made so shady by the mesquite and sage which I brought to the spot. M. also spent ev'g with me and while I was reading "She" Mrs. Cushing called her for an interview, the result of which "lets the cat out of the bag" in regard to our engagement. She returns, tells me briefly the subject of the "confidence" and I retire wondering what the next day may bring forth.

> *Monday, August 15*
> Sketched Los Muertos frog & specimens to-day.[203]

Tuesday, August 16

Ramon called me at 4:30 this morning and we went to XIV to plot division walls, remaining there until breakfast-time. Mr. C., Miss M. and myself go to our retreat where we have a confidential lecture, M. and I constituting the audience. After arriving at an understanding[204] we return to camp, partake of dinner, after which Mr. Garlick and myself go to Tempe where I settle accounts. Owing to delay in getting mules shod and in securing meat (for which we had to await the capture and slaughtering of a steer) we did not get to Camp until after 10 o'clock, finding Mr. Cushing quite ill again. The men, at work on the new excavations (XXII) to-day were very successful, the "Coyote"[205] (our minstrel Mexican) finding three perfect "comales" or tortilla cooking platters,[206] showing the impressions of the moulding mats on their bottoms, besides several axe-heads, shells, and another arrow-shaft straightener. M. had retired before we returned to camp.

> *Tuesday, August 16*
> Mended pottery with Mr. H. after which he & I had a long talk with Tenatsali regarding our matrimonial plans—for which purpose we went out to the retreat. Immediately after lunch Mr. Hodge & Mr.

> Garlick went to Tempe while Mr. C. and I went out to the diggings & found that 3 fine comalis had been unearthed. Later he & Em drove all around the ruins while I made painting of inlaid frog[207]—then we went in buckboard together to Goodwin's to water the mules. The wagon did not return from town till 10 P.M.

Wednesday, August 17

Feeling quite tired after yesterday's long day, I did not arise until after breakfast-time. Goodwin calls, while breakfast is in progress as usual, and spins more of his ranch yarns. Work on catalogue and join Mr. Cushing at Ruin XXII. While there a large decorated bowl, a large water vase and a gigantic olla (6 ft. in diam. 22 in. high) are found. The excitement ~~of it~~ caused by the unearthing of these mammoths brings the whole camp to the spot, including the ladies, who seem especially overjoyed. In the afternoon M. and I mend the rim of the large olla and Mr. C. and Mr. Garlick rivet the cracks in its side. While M. is trying to snatch a nap I spend an hour in attempting the reparation of a "hard-case" cooking vessel. We got away from camp by four o'clock, and soon sought the shade of retreat No. 3 where we remained until sundown. While on our way to camp a wind storm arose, almost blowing us away. After supper Mr. Garlick and myself chat in the buckboard, being joined for a few minutes by "Ikina." Retire at nine o'clock.

> *Wednesday, August 17*
>
> Another comali was found to-day (broken) & the "Coyote" is jubilant over his success, as a reward is given to the finder of valuable specimens. We all went out in a body to see the largest jar which has yet been found—measuring 6 ft 3 in—(in circumference[])—A dreadful sand storm in night.[208]

Thursday, August 18

Was awakened before sunrise by Ramon and by the time we had got to Ruin XIV the sun was peeping over the Superstitions and illuminating the Salado and Estrella Ranges with glittering splendor. Worked away at plotting for two or three hours and returned to camp for breakfast after which I went to work on restoring my "hard-case" jar spoken of yesterday. M. joined me and we labored industriously together until lunch time. While lunch was in progress a whirl-wind paid us a visit making a dart of the dining canopy. We saw it coming and made a break for the open campus with plates in hand to avoid the dust and refuse which it bore in its course. Worked with Ikina, after luncheon, on the jar again and were compelled finally to abandon it as worthless. Repaired the large water-vase and after we had finished gluing M. sketched it and the large olla with myself as an indicator of their immense size. Mrs. C. suggested that we take our walk to the retreat and return before the Mexicans came from work which we do, going to the old retreat (No. 2). Ikina spends ev'g with me. Mr. Garlick also calls for a short while. I retire about 9:30.

Friday, August 19

Ikina called on me after breakfast and remained for a short while, listening to a couple of chapters of "She" which I read aloud.[209] She retired to the "ramado" where she spent the rest of the morning in sketching "Muertos" arrow-points. Went in the evening to Retreat where we remained until six o'clock, returning to camp before the Mexicans returned from the diggings. After supper, M. spent an hour or two in my tent. Rec'd letter from Mother which I answer.

Saturday, August 20

M. made a short call this morning and we both went to specimen-canopy to "dobey" the large jar and water-bottle. Mr. and Mrs. C. took an hour's ride to the ruins while we were at work. Stopped an hour before luncheon and M. read "She" aloud while we leisured away the time. Just after lunch Mr. Cushing dictated part of the letter which he is writing to Mr. Baxter concerning plans of organizing Arch. & Eth. Museum, which I transcribed[210] while M. again called and remained until Goodwin came, when she assisted in his entertainment. Go to XXV with Mr. C. and Miss M. in buckboard and after returning to camp go to retreat where we read more "She" until 6 o'clock. "Gossiped" with M. in my tent until after nine, and after she had departed Mr. C. called and related his story of Weta's confession as to taking the inlaid bracelet while excavating in X. Read papers, wrote to Mrs. Enos Cushing and retired.

Sunday, August 21

McCall awakened me at breakfast-time. Sunday house-cleaning. Call on Mr. Garlick in shop afterwards follows Miss M. Mr. Cushing's summons sends me to town with Indians to make purchases of presents for them and to cash check. Got them shirts, shoes, vests, headbands, calico, tobacco, etc. On way back stop at Francisco Ruellas' for Weta's saddle and can of honey which he had left there last night after selling his horse. Ate watermelon and cantaloupe, picked up the "Coyote" alias "Comale" (Adalpho) who has walked from Camp to Phoenix (18 miles) to "blow in" his week's wages and was on his way back. The return to camp was a very hot and dusty ride, but reached there about 4:30. Washed, dressed and went to retreat, where I met Ikina. She having left note on my desk signifying her whereabouts. Returned to camp sundown. After supper Goodwin called, and when he departed M. and myself took a short walk and then returned to spend a while in my tent. Mr. Cushing pays visit with the Indians and I make checks for payment to them on behalf of presents and purchase of Siwaitsailu's mule, and also for purchase of "Douglas" from Mr. Graham, at Zuñi. Got Ikina's water and retired—

Monday, August 22

Mr. Cushing has been busy to day in preparing for a trip by rail to Maricopa in order to ship the Indians home, but owing to a wind storm which arose in the ev'g, blowing the large canopy over and compelling the whole camp to concentrate its force in holding the remainder of our canvas in place. Went in afternoon to retreat with Margaret.[211] Ramon went to Tempe. M. and I finished reading aloud "She" in the ramada in the morning. After supper we took a stroll and returning to my tent we had visits from Mr. Cushing and Mr. Garlick, the former dictating instructions to R.R. officers for the Indians to take with them. Transcribed and retired.

Maricopa and Camp Hemenway, Tuesday, August 23

This morning we mended a decorated jar—one indicating great age—and made quite a nice job of it. In afternoon went to new retreat which we christened "The Horseshoe" from a shoe which M. found on our way over. Read papers aloud while there and returned to camp about sundown, when

Mr. Cushing told me that he would like me to accompany him to Maricopa. After supper, Mr. C, Mr. Garlick, the Indians and myself drove to the station (Kyrene) on the M. & P. [Maricopa & Phoenix] R.R. (indicated by two freight cars on a side track). Struck across country and after laboring with gopher-holes and sage-brush for two miles reached the track. Waited for half an hour and when train approached I signaled it with lantern. Reached Maricopa and after awaiting for incoming train on Southern Pacific bade our Indian friends adieu with the customary ceremony and went to teleg. office to forward telegrams to Station Agents along route of our Zuñis. Returned to car about 1:30 a.m. and after hearing the experiences of a Mr. Noonan from Gila Bend who spoke in a very comical way in regards to Mr. Garlick and Paul Halman when in his neighborhood a year or so ago, stating that they had traveled all the way from Yuma (180 miles) in search of prehistoric remains without any success, when he took them to his back door and showed him so many that it took them a full week to work them up. This story as to how a number of bones (which he had excavated from an ancient cemetery, while ditching) had "melted" was also very amusing. Stretched out on two seats and napped until the train rolled out of Maricopa at 3 a.m.

Wednesday, August 24

Slept nearly all the way from Maricopa to Kyrene at which latter station we arrived 4:30 a.m. and after waiting about an hour and a half for Mr. Garlick, spending the time in pleasant conversation spread out on the ground on our blankets, we returned to camp about 7 o'clock. Pottered a little with M. in the morning and before lunch time took an hour's nap. Went to the retreat in the afternoon and in the ev'g M. called on me.

Thursday. August 25

Worked on accounts this morning and M. came in afternoon and remained for a while in my tent with me. Mr. Cushing dictated in the afternoon letter to Lieut. Gilman which I transcribed.[212] After supper M. and I took a walk and she spent remainder of ev'g with me in my tent.

Friday, August 26

The whole force of men were put to work in policing the camp to day, but were interrupted in the ev'g by a fierce rain and wind storm which almost blew my tent away. Bed got wet, and letter which I wrote to Lieut. Gilman yesterday also. As storm was passing over M. and myself sat in ramado. After supper we took a short moonlight stroll and spent rest of ev'g in my tent, until Mr. Cushing called me for a dictation which lasted until 1:30 a.m. (on letter to Mr. Baxter: organization of Eth. Museum Institution).[213] New acquisition to the camp equipage to-day in the form of a cow and calf.

Saturday, August 27

Wrote up, this morning, the notes of my last night's dictation, in the rough and with M's assistance commenced to transcribe on typewriter. In the ev'g we took a short walk and M. remained with me until about ten o'clock.

Sunday, August 28

With M. reading from the rough, I transcribed further on letter to Mr. Baxter during this morning. After dinner we went to retreat—and remained during rest of day. Mr. Cushing dictated till 10. o'clk. Mr. G. brings letters from Ashly, Evelyn & Mother.

Monday, August 29

Force of men working under Mr. Cushing's directions in making large wall ramado-tent. M. and I spent morning in my tent at type-writer until the fly was taken off for repairing when we sought the breeze of the shop for our work, remaining until afternoon. I unconsciously took canvas and sat upon it leaving M. the base boards. She speaks to me after lunch—explanations follow and repentance remanded by forgiveness. Write in my tent on type-writer during afternoon with M. and after dinner we sit in buckboard until about 10 o'clk, while Mr. C. is at work on canvas. Go into my tent to burn two or three midnight candles in working on accounts and spend the rest of the night in a nightmare! The Mexicans have fixed up a little "bunco" of their own and their "blowing-in" can now be done in camp.

Tuesday, August 30

Was up quite late this a.m. Finished copying letter to Mr. Baxter as far as dictated. M. continuing to read to me to the end. In afternoon we have a little "lime-juice party" and adjourned to retreat where we remained until supper-time, chatting mainly on our little difficulty of yesterday. M. called on me in the ev'g and we read of "Stanley Brown's Romance" from the "N.Y. Sun".

Wednesday, August 31

Up late again and after breakfast I dissected type-writer (which has suddenly failed me) and with Mr. Garlick attempted to repair it, but without success. M. aided me in correcting type-written ms. of the Baxter letter. Went in ev'g to retreat. M. spends ev'g with me. Indians' old tent pitched for Doctor Matthews.[214] Carlos comes to work again.

Thursday, Sept. 1

Late at breakfast again. Charlie gets into a dilemma by taking shotgun apart and not being able to restore it. I come to the rescue and while so doing Murphy, of Tempe, drives up with Doctor Matthews, although Mr. Garlick went to town early with buckboard to meet him. Spend a short time with Ikina in shop sharpening knife, scissors and erasers before the Dr. comes. Write to Mother, Ed., and to San Fran. jeweler about ring. Mr. Cushing extremely ill. M. smuggles me a note on way to Ruin XXV to sketch and I join her in roundabout way and return to camp alone. Mr. C. and Dr. M. take short ride to mounds before supper. M. calls for a minute with some peaches. Mexicans continue work on large new tent. Mr. Garlick brings me another letter from Mother. Papers speak of deaths of Prof. Baird[215] and of Prof. Fowler the Phrenologist. Write to Cash'r Nat. Savings Bank depositing $5.00.[216]

Friday, Sept. 2

Spend the morning <u>very</u> leisurely and after dinner M. and I start for Tempe via Maricopa Road. Roads very bad from overflows. Collect bills in town while M. visits Mrs. Webster and Mrs. Armstrong. Get an early start back and are detained by Gray's Ranch on acc't of water being turned on in new ditch. Take out mules, making them jump across and then attempted, with assistance of Mr. Cartledge[217] and others from Gray's, to pull the buckboard to the other side, but owing to our load got stuck in the mire. Hitched mules again and in attempting to ford broke double-tree very badly. Cartledge gets another and after attaching it we return to camp to supper by eight o'clk. Got new shirts and socks from home by mail.

Saturday, Sept. 3

Mr. Garlick and Dr. Matthews take early start for Phoenix to-day. Am at work on accounts when M. calls and spends morning with me. Lunch, lemonade party, and we go to retreat to remain until 5 o'clock. Mr. G. and Dr. M. return soon after dark. Ramon goes to Tempe early in afternoon and brings letter to me from Em, which I answer with 16 pages before retiring. McCall brings me the 10 rattles which he pulled from a snake killed in kitchen this evening.

Sunday, Sept. 4

Weekly "house-cleaning", laundering, and bath. Heavy sand-storm in camp all day. Goodwin and McClintock call in morning, spending their time in "shop." After dinner I go to retreat—followed in an hour by M. who sketches sage-brush during most of the afternoon. M. leaves first and I follow to camp in short while by circuitous route. Large tent finished and erected this evening—quite a mammoth! Spend ev'g in my tent and retire early.

Monday, Sept. 5

After breakfast this a.m. went with shotgun on a stroll in mesquite woods north of camp in search of quail, but found none. Returning to camp I went with M. to "Dinky's" the laundress's near Gray's Ranch, and returning from thence read Eth. Rep. '79–'80—Powell article on N. A. Mythology.[218] M. called with Mrs. Cushing for a few minutes in the ev'g. Goodwin brings letters from Charlie (Hodge) & Will Stuart, also receive photos of "V" disaster from Houghton's cousin. Answer Charlie's letter and retire—Note: Mr. Cushing was so ill this morning upon our returning from the washwoman's that we all had little hope of his recovery, constant rubbing of his limbs with alcohol by Mrs. C, Miss M, Ramon and myself, and fanning by Mr. Garlick, restored him to consciousness and by ev'g he was much relieved.

Tuesday, Sept. 6

Mr. C. is improving this morning and is taken in his cot into the shade of my tent for half an hour. After breakfast, Ikina called and after I had harnessed we drove to Mesa City for butter and eggs—securing only the latter, and returning to camp just after lunch-time. Went alone to retreat in afternoon and remained until sunset trying to pass the time pleasantly by reading "Judith Shakespere". Read Scribner at night before retiring. Mr. Garlick went to Tempe to-day taking mules to pasture.

Wednesday, Sept. 7

Read some Powell's Mythology this morning and soon after dinner heard discussion between Mr. C. and the "Coyote" as to over-payment of wages, and ending in his leaving. Mr. Cushing dictates portion of letter to Mr. Baxter while in bed without the "ramado". Read, and write to Ed. during ev'g—rec'd letter from Ed this ev'g per Mr. Garlick who went to Phoenix and returned with new buggy.

Thursday, Sept. 8

M. and Dr. Matthews drive to town this morning to attend to railroad matters concerning trip to Cal'a, returning about 3 o'clk. I transcribe my notes taken last ev'g and Mr. C. works on their revision at intervals during the day. Read papers and write to Stuart during remainder of morning and until M's return from town in the afternoon when I went to retreat where M. soon followed. We returned by opposite routes. Got letter from Mother this ev'g from Dr. Matthews which I answered before retiring.

Friday, Sept. 9

Busy day in camp to-day on account of the elaborate preparations of our "tourists" for their California trip. I am busy all the morning in assisting Mr. Cushing, getting accounts arranged, packing stationery-case and typewriter and in making memoranda for his finishing Mr. Baxter's letter while away. Mr. Garlick went to Tempe. In afternoon Ikina and myself went to retreat and remained an hour. Mr. C. & Dr. M. went for a short drive in ev'g. Mr. C. feels much better. Party started from camp about 8 o'clock with three buckboards en-train, Mr. Garlick lead, accompanied by Dr. Matthews; Mr. Cushing and the ladies came second and myself, Yescas and Ramon followed in the rear. Had some little difficulty with the ditches but reached the road in ample time being joined en route by Mr. McClintock who is on his way to Dakota. Bade hasty goodbye and our little party were off. Rode back part way with Mr. Garlick and partly with Ramon, reaching camp about 11 o'clk.

Saturday, Sept. 10

Was up quite early after passing a restless night being awakened several times by the rain which lasted during the greater portion of the ~~day~~ night. The day is cloudy and comfortably cool though murky. Wrote to Mr. Baxter[219] in morning and hunted quail a short time but with no success. After dinner went with Charlie to Tempe over a very heavy road. Paid accounts for August while Chas. "painted the town" and returned towards camp about 5:30 in the rain. Went about a mile above Farmer's ranch when McCall suddenly signified his intention of returning back to town; so stopping the team I continued my journey, the rain by this time pouring down in torrents. The last I saw of McCall was a form in the railroad track moving his hands frantically but moving neither towards me nor town. Reached camp soon after dark after a couple of hours very hard drive.

Sunday, Sept. 11

The rain awoke me about six o'clk so I got up, donned my "wet day garb" and sauntered forth to inspect damage. Ramon was about ditching the large tent and Sibley and Carlos was devoting his labor to the Doctor's tent. The tents were comparatively dry at this time but the water was fast rising so I reenforced Ikina's ditches, her tent seeming most in danger of flooding. The rain fell faster and the water in camp rose until there was a miniature lake from Ikina's tent to the wood-pile. The Sibley had already filled and Ikina's well in the road. Mr. Garlick appeared and spent his force on the Sibley while I removed the things in the "little dog tent" to the cot where they were soon high and dry. The photo tent caused a good deal of trouble, the manuscripts stored there becoming dampened. I removed them from the box to the plane-table for drying and went into my tent to write to Margaret. The rain passed over for a short period and a worse state of affairs followed by a stiff wind arising drawing tent-pins from all the canvas and keeping us very busy in restoring them. The kitchen and photo-tent blew down and the mss. in the latter were scattered over the floor into the water which keep me employed with Carlos' assistance in restoring them to a box and carrying them into my tent. Tent-pins were tightened all over camp and things made as firm as the soggy earth would permit. No breakfast to-day but a late dinner was heartily partaken of. Yescas playing cook in McCall's absence. Murphy from Tempe drove out in afternoon, while I was working on accounts, with note from Dr. Matthews who, with rest of party were compelled to return to Tempe on account of washout on S. P. R.R. and asking for vehicles to be sent for them. I reply stating condition of camp and telling them to remain in town until to-morrow. The Mexicans are put to work at digging a cistern for drainage, and although about 4 1/2 feet deep and ten feet in diam. a single shower fills it while we are at supper, and again floods the Sibley and my own tent slightly. Am very glad to hear of the folks return as no one knows how lonesome I have felt during the last couple of days.

Monday, Sept. 12

Am up quite early but the swampy condition of camp prevents Yescas from cooking a very early breakfast. Had men to work soon afterwards and raising walls of all the tents commenced to reinforce the ditches and scrape the camp level and clear. Mr. Garlick accompanied by the Castros started for Tempe with the two buckboards and large wagon to bring back our "California tourists" and their luggage. Worked very hard all day and not feeling very well it goes rather hard with me. McCall returned in time to get dinner, looking rather the worse for "painting the town". Mr. G. returns from Tempe about sundown bringing baggage and news that our party will remain until Wednesday. He hands me two letters from M., one of them written from Maricopa on Saturday. Spend the ev'g lying flat on my face as relief from an attack of hemorrhoid. Night spent in wakefulness, notwithstanding dose of quinine. The men deserve commending for their zeal to-day. The camp this morning was a veritable mudhole—this ev'g it is as neat as it ever was.

Tuesday, Sept. 13

We continue our camp-cleaning to-day, the men working on the removal of the dirt from the stable. I am so sore from my attack of hemorrhoids that I walk with the greatest difficulty and cannot sit at all! Mr. Garlick goes to Tempe to get hay—as the road to Cartledge's, where we have been in the habit of getting it recently, is so bad that is impassable—and to take medicine to Mr. C. which came by express on Sat'y. I wrote a note to M. and sent also the letter which I wrote on Sunday. Retire early and bathe, nearly all night, the affected portion of my anatomy with ice-water.

Wednesday, Sept. 14

Am on my back nearly all day but find time, after Mr. Garlick goes to town for Mr. C. and party, to take out canvas flooring of M's tent, which I dry thoroughly, fill up tent with three inches of dry earth, and replace. Ramon goes to town for meat later in the day, and Rafael and Yescas to Ellington's to pasture two mules and to bring four to camp. Carlos puts finishing touches on cleaning camp and after the men return from pasture they scrape the dung piles from stable, making that part of camp clean and healthful. The "Californians" return to camp at 6 o'clock and all expressing pleasure at the appearance of camp. Mrs. C. and M. have very bad colds and quinine is in great demand. Retire quite early.

Thursday, Sept. 15

Spent nearly all day lying on my bed—M. is quite ill too and she remains in her tent most of the day. Mrs. Cushing prescribes for my malady in the morning. Smuggle note to M's tent and receive one under disguise of sketch-book shortly after. Correct some ms. for Mr. C. who spent the day on letter to Mr. Baxter and filled in the gaps by reading Eth. Report '79-'80. Mr. Garlick went to Tempe in the morning. Spend evening stretched out on my back in the kitchen on a bench, conversing on various topics with Mr. Garlick and McCall—including "diamond hitch", "mules" etc. etc.

Friday, Sept. 16

Lay around camp to-day and at intervals when my condition would allow, inserted notes on the "Museum-Institution" letter for Mr. Cushing. In the evening we went to retreat (M. and I) north of camp, remaining but a short time. Sat in ramado a few minutes with M. after supper and retired early. Mr. Garlick went to town with Dr. Matthews on acc't of Miss Ashby's illness.

Saturday, Sept. 17

Third monthly "anniversary" to-day![220] Worked quite steadily all day in the insertion of notes in the M-Inst. letter, which I finished and partly press-copied in the evening.[221] Dr. M. and Mrs. Cushing drove to town to-day and M. spent most of the time during their absence with me, while at work. In ev'g we sat together by hay-rick, Margaret sketching "Charlie." Two "quarrels" and customary "kiss-and-make-ups."

Sunday, Sept. 18

M. went this morning with Goodwin to Mesa City for fruit, returning by noon. During her absence I made my toilet and commenced the continuation of the second Baxter letter which Mr. Cushing had already partly completed. Worked on this letter all the afternoon and in ev'g followed M. to Ruin 23 where she was sketching. Remained short while when we returned to camp by different routes. In the ev'g I continued work on the letter, M. paying me a short visit. Mr. Garlick went to Tempe this morn'g mailing "Mus.-Inst." letter—at last!

Monday, Sept. 19

M. remains in her tent the greater part of the day and I in mine. Mr. Cushing continues work on letter to Mr. Baxter, preparing the rough. Men work in ploughing and scraping out the large ditch north of camp, preparatory to threatening storm. Mr. Garlick went to Tempe for additional shovels etc. for the extra force of men at work. Large snake caught by Mexicans—5 ft. 6 in. which I skin and dry—

Tuesday, Sept. 20

Write all day on letters to Mr. Baxter which I press-copy ready for mailing. Mr. Garlick went to Tempe. Men engaged in excavating on ruin XXI. Dr. M. parafines skeletons for shipment. M. and I went to retreat in afternoon and also had visit from her at ev'g. Trains between Tucson and West are now running for the first time in eleven days—

Wednesday, Sept. 21

Work some on August accounts to day. Mr. Garlick went to Phoenix today. M. and I go to nearest mesquite and with gossamer and sage-brush manage to make sufficient shade to allow us to read aloud Tylor's Anthropology.[222] Myriads of flies infest camp driving us almost insane. It is impossible to remain in the tents at all and swarms and swarms are killed by fly-pads, but the numbers are not missed. Pail after Pail are hourly swept from the large tent. Mosquitoes are also extremely troublesome and night fires of sage-bush seem to have no effect towards diminishing the pests. Ten workmen were engaged on XXI to-day and several sepulchers and their accompaniments were unearthed.

Thursday, Sept. 22

The long table for the reception of specimens was completed by Mr. Garlick today, and in afternoon, assisted by Ramon Castro, arranged specimens thereon ready for cataloguing. M. called with bucket of iced lemonade which we drank together with such enjoyment, when she left for our little retreat near camp. Storm came up and necessitated our deferring operations on the specimens over which canvas was spread and then lashed down. Reinforced my ditches preparing for the rain which did not come. Wind very fierce—ramado blew down and with the Mexicans' assistance I re-erected it. Mr. Garlick went to Tempe for commissaries. Was at the retreat all the morning with Miss M., working on accts. Work prosecuted at XX and XXI. Mr. Cushing accomplishes some photographing and in ev'g develops plates while M. and I spend ev'g in my tent.

Friday, Sept. 23

Remained at retreat all day with Margaret, writing on long letter to Mr. Baxter. Was out mapping on Ruin XIV before sunrise. Men work on XX. Mr. C. develops negatives and M. spends ev'g with me.

Saturday, Sept. 24

Spent nearly all day to-day with M. at the retreat, working on continuation of letter to Mr. Baxter. Got up early this morning and at sunrise was at work on Ruin XIV in mapping. Quite warm all day. Flies still hold the fort—mosquitoes not so bad.

Sunday, Sept. 25

Mr. Cushing called quite early this a.m. (after I had returned from mapping on Ruin XIV and had breakfast) and brought remainder of MS. of Mr. Baxter's letter which I copied in part in my tent, from whence I was driven to the retreat on account of a myriad of flies. M. went to the Mesa Ruin[223] this morning with Goodwin, to "grub," and returned by dinner time joining me for a moment before and spending the afternoon entirely, reading "Tylor's Anthropology" part of the time. Mr. Cushing called and informed us that Mr. G. and Dr. M. had returned from Tempe and that they [the Cushing party] would start for California to-morrow night. Remained at retreat until sundown and returned to camp. Goodwin called to bid adieu and we all sat on the campus chatting over the coming departure and Mr. G. and myself receiving instructions from Mr. C. for conducting Expedition during his absence. Mr. G., Miss M. and myself were left alone when we spent the remainder of the evening in cracking biblical and kindred jokes.

Monday, Sept. 26

Russled about all the morning in arranging things, drawing checks, etc., before Mr. C.'s departure for Cal'a. Received dictation of instructions for Mr. Garlick and myself,[224] and letter arranging the honoring of my drafts, to Armstrong. In afternoon went to retreat meeting M. and remaining until sundown. The dear little girl gave me a lovely silver match-safe for a birthday gift. In the morning M. assisted me in press-copying the long letter to Mr. Baxter while the Dr. and Mr. Garlick went to town, and after finishing went over to "Dinkey's" for laundry in the new "carrawacky" as Mr. G. calls it. Everything is industry in camp this evening preparing for the trip. The large wagon goes to Kyrene first with trunks, followed shortly by the two buckboards. Mr. G, Dr. M, Ramon and myself in the first and Mr. C. and the ladies in the rear. Reached Kyrene and waited half an hour for the train, the wagon with baggage in meantime arriving. Walked track with M. and in a short time all parting was over. The ride back to camp was very lonely and when we arrived (about 11 o'clock) everything was desolate. Did not waste much time in retiring.

Tuesday, Sept. 27

Mr. Garlick went to Tempe this morning for meat. Brought letter sheet from Ikina dated Maricopa. Fix up instructions (transcribing notes written yesterday) press-copy, and send, with letter, to Mr. Cushing. Write to M. also in the ev'g.[225]

Wednesday, Sept. 28

Mr. Garlick goes to Phoenix to-day. Yescas works on tentage and remainder of men on Ruin XX (excepting Carlos who "chores" about camp) 5 skeletons found with accompanying vessels of burial. Get up August accounts during the day and transmit with letter to Mr. Cushing in the ev'g. Write also to Margaret and after spending short time with Mr. Garlick retire. In getting in my cot to-night, which I have appropriated to my own use from the Doctor's tent, I turn a backward somersault in the most unexpected and ungraceful manner, caused by the unaccustomed "luxury"—"bucking". I gathered myself up again crawled abed and went to sleep with a very broad grin on my face. What a lonely day it has been!

Thursday, Sept. 29

Took bath and made change of attire & started to Tempe, by Mr. Garlick's new road, to collect September bills. Remained nearly all day, receiving letter from M. while there dated from Maricopa and announcing their delay until Tuesday night at that Station. Returned to camp before supper—which on account of the myriad flies we postpone until dark. Wrote M. to-night.

Friday, Sept. 30

Worked up September vouchers to-day and enclosed with letter to Mr. Cushing for payment. Mr. Garlick took Jesus and Juan[226] to Armstrong's Ranch for cottonwood poles for corraling hay (268 bales) purchased at Cartledge and which has just been baled. Go to Ruin in the morning and afternoon (#XX) where Ramon and Rafael continue excavations. In the morning I bring to camp small water-jar and two bowls for mending and storing in specimen tent and in ev'g tag the spots where found. Mr. G. and the men return from the Ranch in the afternoon bringing letter from M. written from Colton, Cal'a. In the evening I read paper from home which I received some days ago but left at "retreat" while there with M. last week. Pay off men. The "Coyote" surprises us by appearing in camp to night.

Saturday, Oct. 1

Felt too tired this morning when McCall awoke me at 5 o'clock to go to ruin. Slept a while longer, but after breakfast went to XIV and remained until nearly dinner time finishing the plot excepting a few excavation lines to be placed on pyral mound. Mr. Garlick went with all the men (but Carlos) to Cartledge's Ranch to pile the hay and were compelled to stop for 1/2 hours to assist Goodwin in building his ditch-bridge before they could pass. After dinner I wrote long letter to M. (16 pp.)

Sunday, Oct. 2

With Mr. Garlick I went to Phoenix this morning, arriving there about noon and taking dinner at Chinese restaurant. Walked about town for a couple of hours and spent a while in Geo. Price's cigar-store, where he presented me with a meerschaum cig. holder. Saw Patrick "spreading himself" with a team and double-buggy and four ladies. Gave order to tailor for corduroy pantaloons. Mr. Garlick got meat and ice and we were ready to start about 5 o'clock. Reached camp about eight and was disappointed at not receiving mail from Margaret though Ramon who, with Rafael, Yescas and Jesus went to town early this a.m. Ate supper and afterwards wrote to M. and read papers—

Monday, Oct. 3

Cleaned out tent thoroughly this a.m. and then took bath. Put Carlos to work making wire-standards for tagging rooms and sepulchers in ruins. Mr. Garlick, with the other men, finished stacking the baled-hay and in the afternoon roofed it with chaff and fenced in. Went to Tempe in the afternoon for mail and provisions. Am more and more disappointed at not receiving word from M. Listen to a public minstrel show in front of Davis' by a white man and a darkey, who performed on the bones and banjo very well. Reached camp soon after dark, worked a little, and wrote to Ikina.

Tuesday, Oct. 4

Went to the ruin (XX) this morning after cleaning house. The Mexicans had just unearthed a large decorated water-jar, some large "dipper" shells, and a mosaic amulet; and while I was there two pendants—one in representation of lizard, but fragmentary—were found, also two more large metates of tufa. Brought in the valuables to camp and mended the jar. McCall went to town (Phoenix) by rail early this morning so Carlos has been playing cook to-day. After dinner saddled Mary and went to Tempe—got letter from M. and box of fine candy from Em. Feel very sore after my return to camp from my 18 mile ride after so long a while and to-night am quite tired as well. Answered M's letter and retired early.

Wednesday, Oct. 5

After Mr. Garlick started for Tempe this morning I went to Pyral Md. XIV and finished plotting the excavations made therein on the map. Spent a good deal of time at the Ruin (XX) in the afternoon looking after the work, but nothing of moment was found. Mr. Garlick returned but brought no letter from M. much to my disappointment. Wrote to M. at night however. McCall has not yet returned from Phoenix.

Thursday, Oct. 6

Went to ruins early with Mr. Garlick and after inspection decided to keep the men on XX for a while longer. Went to XXV with Rafael as my assistant and succeeded in relocating and plotting the ruin before dinner-time. Went again in the afternoon. Rafael holding the large umbrella over me while I "inked in". After returning to camp I went to the ruin again and remained until nearly supper time. Nothing of importance has been found to-day save a shell finger-ring. Wrote to M. in the evening while awaiting Mr. Garlick's return from Phoe. & Tempe, hoping to receive a letter from her.

Friday, Oct. 7

Went to the ruin (XXV) quite early this morning with Rafael. The morning is crisp and windy and I have some difficulty in keeping my paper fast to the plane-table—the clouds however afford plenty of pleasant shade for outdoor work and by dinner-time the plotting is finished. Went to town in the afternoon for provisions, but found no letter from Margaret. The wind increased and after sunset the weather grew much colder. As I had no coat with me and but slippers on my feet I felt the need of warmer clothing ere I reached camp, cold and dusty. The men are huddled around the fire and with coats and mufflers try to keep off the sudden chill. Write to M. in the ev'g and retire quite early.

Saturday, Oct. 8

Mr. Garlick and myself visit XX soon after breakfast and although nothing of importance has been found since Thursday we decide to keep them excavating this ruin the remainder of the day. Go to Ruin I and with Rafael's assistance tag the rooms and sepulchers found therein. In the afternoon Mr. Garlick goes to Tempe, returning with letter from M. which I answer after supper. During his absence Goodwin and his friend call and spend an hour with me in my tent. Work on accounts during remainder of the afternoon.

Sunday, Oct. 9

Right after breakfast this a.m. rode over to Goodwin's on lame "Charlie" with telegram (concerning October deposit for Mr. Cushing) as he was getting ready for a drive to Tempe. The wind has been blowing quite fiercely all day, keeping me in my tent at work on accounts and in writing to Mr. C. and M. Sent over to Goodwin's by Rafael in evening to inquire for mail but nothing comes to hand. Am consequently disappointed and spend a very blue ev'g.

Monday, Oct. 10[227]

Mr. Garlick goes to Phoenix this morning for meat, ice, and provisions. As Ruin XX has had no output of "pay-dirt" for two days we decide to transfer force to XVIII. Retaining Rafael to assist me in locating Ruin XX, I set the other men to running outer wall trenches in prospect of finding outlying walls, but none were discovered. Nothing of interest was found during the day. Wind-storm came up in the evening blowing things around in a very lively way. Detail Yescas and Carlos to prepare for rain and they do good service in holding our canvas down. Mr. Garlick returns from Phoenix about 8 o'clock in the rain bringing a Telegram from Mr. Cushing requesting type writer instruction book and reporting good spirits of party, but no letter from M. to whom I write, and retire with the rain pouring in torrents upon my tent.

Tuesday, Oct. 11

Our new flood reservoir was tested by last night's rain—it was the only thing that saved us from another washout, being about half full of water. In the morning, I remap XX, my first plat of relocation being destroyed in last evg's storm. Finished a great deal of the work of inking in before dinner after which I saddled the white horse which Yescas has had in camp for several days and rode to Tempe over one of the heaviest roads I ever traveled. My trip, however, was well rewarded by four letters from M., the last announcing receipt of (at last!) a batch of my own. Men continue at work at XVIII but are discouraged at not making any finds—Write M. long letter in ev'g. Flies terrible once more!

Wednesday, Oct. 12

Have the men run trenches from all the outside walls of XVIII this morning but come across none outside of the walls already excavated. After this is done transfer men to XIII where they work all day with no reward by finds. Mr. Garlick went to Tempe this afternoon but returned with no mail—purpose of his going grain and commissaries. Wrote M. at night. Worked nearly all day on finishing the "inking in" of Ruin XX when I discovered that two pyral mounds were connected with it, the mapping of which my sheet would not allow. Commenced a tracing by corner prickins on a larger sheet and finished walling. Coyotes howl dreadfully in camp to-night but it was too dark to make my revolver more servicable than the notice it made in frightening them off and awaking the camp.

Thursday, Oct. 13

Finish the plotting of XX this morning. Have a visit of Mr. [Frank] Earle and Mr. Helms of Tombstone who bring a letter of introduction to me from Major Earle, father of the former, of Tempe. Show them around the ruins and make it as interesting for them as possible. They stay to Dinner and are off much gratified with what they saw. Drive to Tempe in the afternoon with "Barney" and "Pete" and again meet our morning visitors and drink health with straight lemonade. Two long letters from Pearl[228] seal my happiness and I return to camp aglow with good feeling. Write long letter of 21 pages in the ev'g and also a note to Mr. Cushing.

Friday, Oct. 14

Forgot to note my visit with Ramon to Ruin XIII last night by lantern-light in order to see a very interesting find: Three skeletons were exhumed to-day—two of them forming a double burial. Accompanying one of the remains of the "double" was a medium sized water jar moulded in the form of a duck or goose. Scattered around close by were fragments of charred mescal. Visit the ruin again this morning and watch the work in same rooms: Two large cavities, each about six feet in depth and separated by a substantial adobe wall have been cleaned out. At the bottom of one four small openings in the wall, at the floor, occur, the largest of which extends backward to a distance of about 3 feet. Mr. Garlick went to Phoenix quite early and after dinner I drove to Tempe in hopes of receiving a letter from M—but they were, unhappily, not realized. Returning I lost my whip, and in retracing my road for a mile, saw it hanging in a cottonwood where the snapper had caught in crossing a ditch. Returned to camp before Mr. Garlick (and Yescas who went with him) returned [from] Phoenix upon arriving he handed me a letter from Mr. Baxter who spoke of my "fidelity" to Mr. C. and "admirable work" etc. Wrote to M. and to Mr. Cushing. Yescas did not forget to bring a suspicious looking flask back from town with him, the contents of which kept the other Mexicans in a very boisterous mood during half the night.

Saturday, Oct. 15

Late as usual to breakfast. Went to XVII with Rafael where I made relocation of ruin. From thence to XIII where men are still excavating. A drinking ladle has been found, positioned at the narrower end to protect the hand against burning. Took this specimen and the duck-shaped vessel and brought to camp. Labelled and stored in specimen tent. Plotted my notes of XVII after dinner, and tried my hand at eyeletting new tent for my use. Mr. Garlick went to town in the afternoon but brought no word from Calif. Wrote M after supper and read Washington papers.

Sunday, Oct. 16

After Sunday house-cleaning I had the "Coyote" [clean?] up my clothing. Ramon started after breakfast for Tempe and I spend the morning in anxiety for his return with a letter from M. Write to Eckhardt in the morning and do a little reading before lunch during the progress of which Ramon arrives, bringing two letters from M. and a "Shield" sent by Ashley. Hopes and spirits arise simultaneously. After lunch go to retreat XXV but feel too lonely to remain long. Return to camp and spend afternoon in writing long letter to M. A Pima Indian with two or three associates of his tribe surprise camp this ev'g by stopping and requesting a drink of water in pretty good English. While we are at supper he returns and reports a breakdown of his wagon. Mr. Garlick gives him rope and hatchet and is consequently made happy. Beautiful sunset. Write letter to Mother informing her of my engagement. Give Santos Yescas a lesson in English in exchange for one in Spanish and retire early—9:30

Monday, Oct. 17

A dreary "anniversary." Go early to Ruin XVII and work until noon with Rafael useful assistance in holding wagon umbrella over me while I plot. Finish fieldwork on map and return to camp to dinner. After eating start for Tempe with "Chub" & "Thistle". [John] Mahan hails me for ride to and fro from his ranch. No mail again to-day. Long ride back to camp. Arrive supper-time. Write to M. to-night. Purchased new dirk to-day—also a pipe which I immediately give to McCall upon reaching camp—cigarettes good enough for me! Most still engaged on XIII with no great success—

Tuesday, Oct. 18

Go to Ruin XIII this a.m. where the men are engaged and upon returning plotted pyral-specimens and drew contours on plot of XVII. Mr. Garlick went to Phoenix quite early looking quite stylish with a new suit and a brilliant polish on his shoes—(which undoubtedly surprised them.). After dinner went with Rafael to XXI where I made a relocation of that ruin and made the men at XIII another visit before returning. Wrote Ashley with expectation of going to town but as Chub was lame and no other buckboard team out of pasture postponed trip until to-morrow. Have an attack of neuralgia today which has a great deal to do with my ill feeling. McCall caught a very large tarantula this morning which I have pinned in a life-like position and am drying.

Wednesday, Oct. 19

Rafael and Jesus went to pasture this morning to rope "Bob" mule which had escaped early this morning having been brought to camp yesterday with "Trissy" to relieve Chub & Thistle turned in. Drove to town where I received two letters from Mr. Cushing with checks and vouchers and a letter from M. Paid bills for September and returned to camp after waiting in town about two hours for the arrival of the train. Wrote to M. in the evening.

Thursday, Oct. 20

The men still on XIII, but with no great success—but ordinary relics, such as spindle-whorls, awls, chipping- and other tool-stones, etc, etc. being found. The large specimen-tent was finished and erected yesterday evening. Mr. Garlick went to town (Phoenix) to-day to get meat and ice and take in the fair now in progress. Write to Mr. Cushing in the morning and in afternoon go with "Bob" and "Grissy" to Tempe where I found 4 letters from M. and three from Mr. C. awaiting me—what luck! Had both animals shod, delaying me so that I did not return to camp until it was quite dark. Was writing to M. when Mr. G. returned from Phoenix swearing he would not see the place again for two weeks—probably his rage was the more violent on account of his losing five-dollars on the races at the fair.

Received my La croix papers from town—enough to last me through the Exp'd I believe—

Friday, Oct. 21
Immediately after breakfast I had Yescas assist me in cleaning out my tent for the pitching of the new-one, which, since its erection, looks splendidly. Found it necessary to have Carlos sew a strip on one end of floor-canvas that it might be wide enough. "Moved in" during the afternoon and clean'd up. Neuralgia has attacked the other side of my face making it very painful and to make misery more miserable have an ulcerated throat and a bad cold in general. Write to Margaret in the evening and visit Mr. Garlick, remaining in his tent until 11 o'clock.

Saturday, Oct. 22
Am so ill with my numerous maladies this morning that I felt unable to respond to Mc. Call's summons to breakfast. Got up late and was able to swallow a cup of coffee and small quantity of oatmeal and milk. Idled away the day in reading and lounging in the sun, which is quite warm by the way. Write to M. in the morning and again at evening. The only work I attempted doing at all being the lacing of my tent-corners. Read Haggard's "Allan Quatermain"[229] until tired of the super-humanity he preached, and retired.

Sunday, Oct. 23
Sunday cleaning of house and sunning of beds as usual in camp. Read Haggard's Quatermain during the morning expecting Ramon to return from town by dinner-time but he did not put in an appearance until afternoon when he brought letters from M. and Evelyn and papers from home. Wrote M. and Evelyn both during the afternoon. Mr. Garlick amused himself by roaching the mules' manes. Goodwin called in ev'g taking supper and teaching us what little we do not already know of irrigating-operations in this valley. Read papers and retired early.

Monday, Oct. 24
Was up after breakfast as usual, after eating which wrote quite a long letter to Mr. Cushing who speaks in high praise of the work done. While in Tempe Mr. Garlick erected my new "Coast Survey fly". Took the covered-buckboard

wheels when I went for re-setting. Wrote to M. in the evening a long letter and retired late. A small bowl (plain) and quarter deeper bowl (decorated interiorly) were unearthed to-day.

Tuesday, Oct. 25

Wrote to Mr. Cushing first thing this a.m. sending letter by Mr. Garlick for mailing in Phoenix together with Folk-tale Mss. and inlaid specimens for expressing to him. In the afternoon described specimens recently found and tagged their locations in R'n XIII. Had Carlos make wire standards and tags for marking rooms, specimens and sepulchers. Wrote Mr. C. in reference to accounts in afternoon and in the evening sent letter to Margaret. Mr. Garlick returned by moonlight, 7 oclk. Read a while and retired.

Wednesday, Oct. 26

Soon after breakfast this morning went to Ruin XXI with Rafael and inked the walls and other architectural features, finishing by dinner time. In afternoon drove to town but was disappointed in finding no mail. Wrote to M. in the ev'g and spent an hour chatting with Mr. G.

Thursday, Oct. 27

This morning I finished both field and camp-work on XXI—plotting the pyral excavations and inserting contours. Went to town again in afternoon with Mr. Garlick in large wagon. Took "Allan Quartermain" along and read much to Mr. G's disgust—he expressing the wish that he had a "ten-acre lot of such fellows to ride with." Returned to camp soon after sundown and wrote to M. The evening is beautiful though quite chilly.

Friday, Oct. 28

Plotted the pyral-excavations of XVII this morning and described specimens for tagging in XIII where work is still in progress. My trip to town this morning is unsuccessful as far as any mail is concerned (having made the trip first thing after breakfast) and my birthday is by no means a pleasant one in consequence. Brought out candy which was sent from home a month ago—and which has been in Armstrong's safe ever since—and passed it around among the boys who seemed to enjoy it immensely. Wrote Mr. Baxter a short letter in reference to estimates in reply to me received this morning from him. Went to ruin again in the afternoon and inspected operations. Several small specimens were found among which I saw a mesquite paddle[230] and awl or "prod", a phallic amulet and several others of less importance. Rafael was sent to Cartledge's this ev'g for the "Cafe" which we learn has followed Daisy's example by becoming entangled in a barbed-wire fence. Upon his arrival we see the seriousness of the wounds: two large gouges in the middle of his belly, both apparently exceedingly painful. Wrote to M. again to-night.

Saturday, Oct. 29

Mr. Garlick went to Phoenix to-day for meat, ice, and other subsistence supplies. With Rafael I went to Ruins III & VII and tagged the sepulchres therein, first noting the numbers on my map. Work on XIII continues and a corn-cob (charred) was found at the bottom of one of the three pits lately excavated. Sent Jesus Morales to town (for provisions and mail) on "Barney" and the boys jeered him a great deal when upon leaving camp the red mule stubbornly refused to go, necessitating his leading him. Jesus returned in the evening bringing six letters from M. which made me very happy. Poor "Cafe" has suffered a great deal to-day, screw-worms having embedded themselves beneath the flesh, causing great difficulty in removing them. Ramon spent the entire afternoon in picking them out and I should imagine he removed several hundred. Wrote a long letter to M. this evening and afterwards worked up the bills into vouchers, Mr. Garlick collecting them in Phoenix to-day.

Sunday, Oct. 30

I cleaned up my "house" this morning as customary, and commenced a letter to M. which I finished by installments in the ev'g and at night. Ramon went to town this morning but returned with no mail he however brought the remainder of the outstanding Sept vouchers which I worked up after finishing my letter to Margaret. Keeping me busy until about 2 a.m. We had visitors in the morning—Jones[231] and Herston from Tempe—who took dinner with us and afterwards went the rounds of the ruins under the guidance of Mr. Garlick. While awaiting Ramon's return I read a few pages of "Vanity Fair".[232] Mr. G. & myself went in afternoon to Cartledge's to inspect mules.

Monday, Oct. 31

Made an early start for town this morning where I collected the accounts for October and secured money from P. A. & Co. to pay laborers. No mail from M. but one from Mother, who replies to my letter informing her of our engagement. Found there telegram from Mr. C. announcing arrival in San Francisco. Write to him upon my return as also to Margaret. Am afraid my letters are not very entertaining for failure to receive M.'s letters regularly means utter and uncontrollable discouragement. Did not retire until 2 a.m.—read "Vanity Fair" while abed. (Sent Jesus & Ramon this ev'g for baled hay.)

Tuesday, Nov. 1

Went to town again this morning making another early start and taking Carlos with me, who on account of illness will remain for a few days at the home of his friend, Francisco Ruellas. Paid Hayden's check of $175.00 and got Armstrong's vouchers for September account, for which I was compelled to wait until afternoon, not returning to camp until four o'clock when I immediately set to work in straightening up October vouchers. Mr. Garlick returned from Phoenix (where he went for calomel to dress "Cafe's" wound and to aid in driving out the worms that infest it[)]. Worked again very late to-night, finishing up the October vouchers as far as possible, and forwarding with explanatory letter to Mr. Cushing. McCall signifies intention to resign. Another "nomadie" fit has seized him, nor heaven nor earth could keep him with us I suppose.

Wednesday, Nov. 2

Mr. Garlick went to Phoenix this morning and soon after his departure Rafael and myself went to Ruin VII where I put in the morning in plotting the excavations (made since Mr. Cushing's original map was completed) and in tagging the rooms. In the afternoon, expecting the arrival of Dr. and Mrs. Mitchell and Miss McDermott,[233] I had Adalpho and Rafael assist me in cleaning camp and arranging for the reception of our guests. Wrote to Margaret in the latter part of the afternoon and at sunset our Phoenix visitors arrived. They were overcome with enthusiasm at the arrangement of our camp and with the beautiful scenery and moonlit evening. When the horses had been secured for the night we had a pleasant chat together.

Mr. Garlick entertaining the Dr. & his wife, and myself doing the honors on Miss McDermott's behalf. We sat in the buckboard until the air became quite cool, when we went within the large tent and continued our conversation until bed-time. Little Grace Mitchell seemed to be overjoyed at the prospect of life in camp and examined everything with a critic's eye. No letter from Pearl to-day—the "gayities" cannot comfort my loneliness. Read "Vanity Fair" (after I had retired) until about 11 o'clk when I blew out my candle.

Thursday, Nov. 3

The morning is quite cold but am out early with the intention of going to IX with Rafael to locate. Breakfast being almost ready I was induced by McCall to defer the trip until later. The men were sent out early to XIII (Jesus with the scraper) and Adolpho was retained for finishing up the east new tent. The folks (our visitors) were out bright and early though the crisp desert air compelled them to don their shawls and wraps. Ate a very enjoyable breakfast and soon afterwards all hands went to the ruins, where we spent the greater part of the morning showing the guests the sights. Soon after our return we were joined by Mr. and Mrs. Grant of Wisconsin, and Mrs. G's sister from Chicago, who took dinner with the party. After seeing the specimens in the collection-tent Dr. & Mrs. Mitchell and Mrs. McDermott were ready for departure, so bidding them adieu I went to the ruins, for a second time, to guide our later visitors over prehistoric ground. Had a little lemonade party in the "shop" when we returned to camp and passed half an hour in pleasant conversation. Jesus was sent to town during the morning, returning by dinner-time bringing three letters from Margaret and one from Ashley (also barley and commissaries). Wrote M. long letter (30 pages) in the evening and after reading a little of "Vanity Fair" retired.

Friday, Nov. 4

After a thorough house cleaning this morning I wrote up several "Memoranda of Daily Operations".[234] Mr. Garlick is putting the finishing touches on the newly-painted buck-board and it is beginning to appear quite "gorgeous" with its vermillion wheels and tongue and black uprights and seats. The white canvas top too is whiter still when seen against the brilliancy of the other colors. (But I believe white & black are not colors.) Made a visit in the afternoon to XIII where a wall cyst has been uncovered exposing two small bowls and one large one, also one ollita, all of plain-ware. Jesus went to town after dinner to mail check-book to Mr. Cushing and to bring provisions. Another letter from M. came—oh bliss! Write to her in the evening. Sent tarantula to Charlie Hodge to-day. Adalpho and Rafael have been at work in building an elevated floor of earth for the new kitchen. The "parlor tent" was taken down preparatory to the erection of the new one. Read "Vanity Fair" after retiring until my eyes batted involuntarily when and where the candles and I was soon dreaming of San Francisco.

Saturday, Nov. 5

Went to IX with Rafael this morning to locate, but found the excavations had been carried on so irregularly that I returned to camp first stopping to examine Ruins XI, XII and setting Rafael to work on XIII with Ramon and Jesus. Another large bowl I saw was uncovered being embedded in adobe in a cist-like hole. Mr. Garlick had Juan and Adalpho making another "cuello" for the new salon tent by carrying earth (for the elevation) and ramming and wetting alternately. Went in the afternoon to town where I found letter from M. and telegram from Mr. Baxter announcing Dr. Ten-Kate's[235] departure from Boston via Washington. Brought Carlos from Mexican Town[236] to camp. Mr. G. had the men erect the new kitchen in the evening before supper—it makes a nice appearance in the new position east of Mr. G.'s own—Wrote to M. in the evening and afterwards entertain Mr. G. and McCall in my tent exchanging sunday-school stories. Read "Vanity Fair."

Sunday, Nov. 6

After house-cleaning I read Vanity Fair and wrote to Margaret during the morning. In the afternoon Mr. Scott & sweetheart (?) and Mr. & Mrs. Metz from Phoenix called and I guided them around the ruins. While there, Mr. Goodrich, the Atty Gen. of the Ter'y,[237] called, and seemed very much interested in what he saw. Upon returning to camp we ate a lunch in picnic fashion, spread out on the tool-chest and consisting of sandwiches, cake, pie, crullers, pickles and cheese. Bathed and read some more after the people had departed and in the evening Mr. G. and Charlie spent a couple of hours with me in my tent. No letter from Pearl to-day.

Monday, Nov. 7

Directly after breakfast I wrote orders for Ramon who went to Phoenix for supplies. Mr. Garlick has been superintending the cleaning and erection of the new "salon"-tent which was put in place this evening. Rafael went with me quite early to XVIII which ruin I located and before returning to camp to plot my notes tagged the rooms in XIV and the sepulchres in XIII. In the afternoon Mr. Garlick went to Tempe hoping to find word from Mr. Cushing relative to reception of Dr. Ten-Kate, but none was received. Jesus and Juan went for more hay in the afternoon and Juan & Carlos for water. Carlos also cut and sewed on dust cloth for photo-tent. I was employed from lunch-time on the inking-in of XVIII and the tagging of rooms and sepulchers of III, XVII & XVIII. Wrote to Margaret in the evening from whom I received one (brought by Mr. Garlick) and read a little in "Vanity Fair."

Tuesday, Nov. 8

All hands were at breakfast by sunrise this morning, and soon afterwards I took Rafael to XXII to assist me in the plotting of the excavations that have been irregularly made there. Plotted my notes during the remainder of the morning and in the afternoon went to town where I found long letter from M. Mr. Garlick was employed to-day in making stove-pipe holes of tin in new tents, in superintending the making of corner loops by Carlos and the cleaning also by him of the dust from the new "salon" tent; also making tent-pins and guy-fasteners. The men at the diggings found a portion of a serrated lance head to-day. Wrote to M. in the ev'g & read for a short time Vanity Fair. A terrific [sand]-storm came up while on my return from town. The dust was blinding, choking and otherwise unpleasant and the loosened sage-brush frightened the mules to such an extent that I used all my energy to keep them under control.

Wednesday, Nov. 9

To-day has been a busy one in camp. It has been too windy to work in the field with a plane-table sheet, so I remained in camp and assisted in superintending the work of burning mesquites etc. Mr. Garlick made cots for McCall and myself, cut stove-pipe holes of tin for the cook-tent as well as his own, made ditch-bridges for the new tents, and many other camp items were attended to by him. Sent Jesus to town. Returned by supper time with 2 letters from M. and also paper containing Cushing interview.[238] The men at the ruin find another sepulcher with ladle and water vase accompaniments, and also a portion of a serrated edged lance or spear. In the ev'g I wrote to Margaret and retired quite early.

Thursday, Nov. 10

Adolpho and Juan continued the mesquite-clearing this morning. Jesus and Ramon prosecuted excavation on XIII while Carlos remained at camp at work on dust-cloth for photo-tent. Rafael is assigned to police duty about camp during the morning and in the afternoon assists me in rearranging specimens and cleaning tables in photo tent. Mr. Garlick went to Phoenix this morning for provisions, returning at ev'g with M's photograph![239] Wrote her as usual in the ev'g and went to bed to keep warm—

Friday, Nov. 11

We had two visitors this morning—the Messrs. McGinness—gentlemanly in appearance but Irishmen all over. I showed them around the ruins and upon returning we chatted a while and partook of dinner. McG. the elder very unceremoniously left the table in the midst of our little repast of broiled quail (which they had killed on the road)—and the usual accompaniments. Immediately after dinner they departed without even a "thank you," or a "good-bye"! Mr. Garlick and myself went to town <u>in</u> the afternoon—No mail for me from Margaret—except a paper accounting the Cushing address before the S. F. Academy.[240] Returned, soon after sundown to camp. Wrote a letter (full of disappointment I'm afraid) to M. in the evening and read a little "Vanity Fair".—Adolpho & Juan clear mesquite all day, Carlos sews on dust cloth for new photo tent—the remainder of the force work on Ruin XIII. Sent home 2 Pima baskets.

Saturday, Nov. 12

Mr. Garlick commenced work on my secretary this a.m. putting in partitions and pigeon-holes. Carlos and Rafael assisted in the erection of Dr. ten Kate's tent and in laying new floor-cloth which Mr. Garlick had cut from 10 ft. canvas. Went to town in afternoon, but still no news from M. Am worried. Wrote the little girl again in the ev'g. Carlos finishes the sewing of photo-tent dust-cloth to day. Remainder of the force (including Rafael in the afternoon) work on XIII excavation.

Sunday, Nov. 13

After house-cleaning wrote to Mr. Copp in reply to Mr. Cushing's two letters of yesterday concerning contest of Adams desert claim.[241] Afterwards wrote two letters to Mr. Cushing, one on same subject—other in regard to current affairs,[242] while so engaged was called upon by two young lawyers from Phoenix whom I went with to the ruins. Rafael returned just before supper-time bringing two delightful letters from Margaret. Mr. Garlick and Ramon went with "Charlie" and "Red" to pasture, returning with "Jack" and "Jim", this morning. Poor "Cafe" is convalescent. Wrote M. after supper quite a lengthy letter and sat in tent of Mr. Garlick who boasts a Sibley stove.

Monday, Nov. 14

Mr. Garlick went to Phoenix, returning at evening with letter from M. and Mr. C.—the latter enclosing Oct. checks and vouchers. Adalpho went with him, having passed a sleepless night of groans on account of toothache, and remained in Tempe over night. Carlos finished work upon the photo-tent dust-cloth and Rafael assisted me during the morning in plotting Ruin XXII. Juan was alone in the mesquite-clearing during the day and Ramon and Jesus worked on scraper in XIII. Wrote to M in the evening and warmed up by kitchen fire where the men congregated to do their studying and joke-cracking. Read very little of Vanity Fair and retired rather early but found no sleep—M. tells me of the probability of remaining in S.F. for a longer period than was expected.

Tuesday, Nov. 15

Soon after breakfast this morning I wrote letters to accompany the checks for Phoenix merchants[243] and also long letter to Mr. Cushing. After dinner started for town in the newly-painted buckboard. Paid bills, received letter from M. and returned to camp. Mr. Garlick superintended the work by Carlos and Rafael in removing the old photo-tent and in erecting my old tent for its future use—the other to be occupied by the Mexicans. Mr. G. also got ready the other buckb'd for painting and repairing. Juan continues the clearing of mesquites and Adalpho returns at evening from Tempe (I met him on the road to camp, painlessly and happily trudging along). The men employed by Goodwin have been clearing sage near camp today and to night 20 huge fires illuminate the whole country round about. The men at the ruin—Ramon and Jesus—trace the remaining unexcavated walls preparatory to transferring work to VI to-morrow. Wrote to M. this ev'g in reply to her delightful letter.

Wednesday, Nov. 16

During part of the forenoon the excavators worked on wall-tracing XIII when Mr. Garlick and myself made them a visit transferring work to VI in the running of prospecting trenches. In returning to camp I found what appeared to be a vertebra of some mammoth, lying on the surface about 200 ft. N.W. of VI, and brought it to camp. The men reporting for dinner Ramon informed me that they had come across the first walls and were following them out. Juan & Adalpho worked upon the mesquite-clearing during the day and Carlos and Rafael in making floor for photo-tent and in sewing flaps and pin loops on same. Mr. Garlick went to town in the afternoon returning with letter from M. for me. No news from Dr. ten-Kate. Goodwin's man came over with team to borrow buck-board, awaiting until Mr. G.'s arrival from town. Visited the ruin (VI) again in the afternoon, and made location of Ruins XXIII and XXIV with Rafael's assistance.

Thursday, Nov. 17

Soon after breakfast I went to XXII and with Rafael's aid plotted the walls of the Ruin. Afterwards took Rafael to VI where Adalpho & Juan, having about completed the burning of the mesquites, had joined Jesus and Ramon in the excavating which the now augmented force was pushing rapidly. Took a long walk to the south side of the Section: from thence around to the eastern end, visiting our retreat for a few minutes, on my way across, returning to camp. Mr. Garlick was painting buckboard No 2 with a coat of brilliant red-lead, having, with the assistance of Carlos, already erected the photo-tent (made from my older one). Carlos was busily engaged in cleaning the photo materials and in rearranging them in their order in the new "gallery." Drive to town in the afternoon receiving two letters from Margaret, the latter dated 15" instant and giving very discouraging news of prolonged stay—perhaps through the winter. It was so cold in my own tent this ev'g that I was compelled to seek the warmth of the kitchen stove whi<u>le</u> writing to M. which I am afraid contained bold indications of discouragement. Read a chapter of "Vanity Fair" after crawling between my blankets for the night.

Friday, Nov. 18

Was up by sunrise, donned a "biled" shirt, collar and cuffs and with a cutaway coat, a vest and polished shoes was ready for a trip to Phoenix with Mr. Garlick that I might have my tooth extracted and another filled. Went by way of Tempe calling at the P.O. for word from Margaret but found no letter there. Went to telegraph office hoping to learn the whereabouts of Dr ten-Kate but nothing by way of news was received from him. Continued to Phoenix where I went almost immediately to see Dr. Goodrich[244] the Dentist (and who is also, by the way, a representative in the Territorial Legislature). Visited Mr. Mitchell in the afternoon but remained but a short while, purchasing a turkey for Thanksgiving dinner before we departed. Dr. M. is in Los Angeles booming Phoenix and trying his fortune at drumming up a practice. Miss McDermott has started a kindergarten and Gracie is one of her pupils. Returned to camp by the direct road, meeting Goodwin near "Dinkey's". He had walked up from town to that point when we took him up as passenger. Got to camp when McCall informed us that Dr. ten-Kate had arrived in town this a.m. and not being able to procure conveyance sent a man out with word to send in for him. Ate a hasty supper, had Ramon change the team and started immediately for Tempe arriving about 8 o'clock, having made the 9 miles in an hour and a half. Found that the Doctor was safely installed in the new "Arlington House"[245] and was ushered to his room where I immediately introduced myself and apologized for not receiving word sooner. Chatted together until about 10 o'clock when I secured a room and begged leave of the Dr's presence for the night. Did not have an opportunity to write M. The office was closed and I had neither pen, pencil, nor paper with me, so went to bed with a feeling of disappointment. The mules were coralled soon after my arrival in town. Men worked on XIII to-day.

Tempe, Saturday, Nov. 19

Awoke at sunrise by the jabbering of Chinamen who were busily employed in getting breakfast ready. Arose, and as there were none of the necessary conveniences for arranging the toilet in my room, washed in the basin of the common herd outside the hotel door, and finished my resplendency before "Woody" Armstrong's mirror. Met the Dr. on the verandah and we went to breakfast together, meeting Mr. Webster at the table.

After breakfast walked over to the station and back to the P.O. the mail from Maricopa Station having just arrived. Received a letter from M. and afterwards wrote True one in the Hotel office. Got team from corral and went with the Dr. to Baggage Room at Depot for trunks and found it necessary to walk back to Armstrong's for rope to make them secure. All being ready we started for camp reaching there without incident by 10:30. Cleaned house and commenced long letter to Margaret but was interrupted by the dinner call. Early in afternoon went the rounds of the ruins with the Doctor who was very much pleased with what he saw, but rather distressed at the demolished condition of the skeletons. Finished my letter upon returning from the ruins, and postscripted it after supper when I read a little of Vanity Fair and retired early. Kitchen remado erected to-day.

Camp Hemenway, Sunday, Nov. 20

Ramon and Jesus were sent to town this morning for potatoes, chili, onions, lard and tomatoes. Cleaned house and had Adolpho do my week's washing for me. McClintock and Goodwin called while we were at dinner in which we invited them to join. With the Doctor and Mr. G. they afterwards went into my tent and talked ditches and irrigating until Mr. and Mrs. Marford, Dr. Marford and Mr and Mrs Minse of Phoenix called, when I did the honors by guiding them around the ruins, which they seemed to appreciate very much. Just as they were ready to depart two other gentlemen (one a Mr. Utley[246] of Phoenix—Supt of Schools) came, and this time were shown around by Mr. Garlick. Goodwin and McClintock still clung to my tent apparently insisting that I should not read Margaret's two letters which Jesus and Ramon brought. Dr. ten Kate called for me to go gunning, so we went a couple of miles east of camp, through the sage and mesquite, but game was not abundant and we failed to bag anything. Lost the Doctor in the woods so I returned to camp soon after dark and was soon followed by our Anthropologist. Read M's letters at last and wrote the dear little girl a long letter in the evening, retiring early.

Monday, Nov. 21

Was out rather late for breakfast, being too cowardly to brave the cold! Went while the sun was still in embryo to Ruin XIII (with the Doctor) where we spent the morning in uncovering and removing about ten of the skeletons.

Found three skeletons in Sep 53 instead of two as was at first supposed. After dinner Mr. Garlick stripped the buckboard (No 2) and the Doctor cleaned the bones removed this morning. The men continue the excavation of XIII finding another "defensive stone" in the evening. Rain fell in the evening as I have been trusting it would. Now we have hope of muddy roads instead of those of dust. Mr. Garlick fixed my trunk-till and I rearranged my casas therein. Carlos pieced the dust-cloth of Mr. Garlick's tent to-day. Men hauled water. Wrote to Margaret in the evening—no letter to-day. Mr. G. also made neck-yoke.

Tuesday, Nov. 22

It rained very hard as I got up to McCall's summons for breakfast, continuing during the entire morning and keeping the men in camp. Cleaned my tent out and wrote to Mr. Cushing. After dinner there was a lull in the storm, allowing the men to resume their excavation on XIII. Went out in the afternoon and tagged the locations of recent finds. Mr. G. and Dr. ten-Kate went to Phoenix in the morning returning soon after sundown, having passed through a storm which spent its force at Camp Hemenway making moats around our tents in a few moments. Nothing however was damaged—(thanks to our elevated floors)—and our drainage system which carried off all surplus water. Wrote Ikina this evening though of course I had no way of receiving one from her.

Wednesday, Nov. 23

Rain all last night and until about ten to-day when the men for a short while resumed work on the excavations and I seized the opportunity of driving to town. I had not gone very far however before it commenced to pour with renewed vigor, never ceasing while I was away from camp. Arrived in town about 2:30 (started about 11:30) got commissaries and two letters from M—one from Mr. Cushing—and about 3:00 o'clock started back to camp. The rain beat through the leaky buck-board roof wetting me through, although I had on my heavy "reefer". The road as far as the Tempe Canal was a literal mud-hole when it began to be worse the whole country as far as the eye could see being a perfect laguna. For 6 miles not a square yard of earth could be seen and several times the good "Pete and Barney" were very nearly foundered. I was thankful to be able to reach camp and to get some supper by about 7 o'clock when I wrote to Margaret and sat a while by Mr. Garlick's stove. Of course no work could be done to-day.

Thursday, Nov. 24

A very rainy Thanksgiving Day. After cleaning house I wrote to M. not being able to devote my time to field work on account of the rain. There was a lull in the storm during the latter part of the morning and the men were enabled to work on XIII for awhile. Mr. Garlick seizing the opportunity of constructing a meat box for the kitchen and cutting out "barometer" tent upon which Carlos served. Went to the ruin where the men had found evidences of another cyst, the accompaniments being in situ but I was unable to trace the whereabouts of the remains. Ramon met with a painful accident, having struck his lip with the handle of a shovel, driving a tooth through it. Mr. Garlick made a new band gear for Cafe—the poor animal, by the way, is improving. Had a gorgeous Thanksgiving dinner to-day. Our turkey was put up in gorgeous style by McCall, and all seemed to relish the treat immensely. Wrote to M. again in the afternoon and at evening making quite a lengthy letter in all. Rafael assisted me, just before dinner-time, in tagging the rooms of XX.

Friday, Nov. 25

Raining again! All night it has kept up a constant pattering against my tent and to all appearances it never will stop. Mr. G. with his customary Yankee industry made the poles for harness-ramado and barometer tent and repaired halters and harnesses. The Doctor and myself went to the various ruins between the showers and secured as many of the skeleton-members as possible before further injury by the rain. While writing in the evening (about 3 o clk) Goodwin called and introduced "Mr. Wortman".[247] We sat and smoked, and as usual, talk "rain" and "ditch" for probably 10 minutes before he informed me that he was Doctor Wortman of the Army Med. Museum. The Doc. stated that he had called upon the folks at home before leaving, and that he had brought two pkg's with him in his trunk—presents from them. Of course I am very glad to hear all this for it is like meeting an old friend when one is introduced who has actually seen all that is so dear to a fellow in this "jumping-off-place", such a short time ago! Dr. ten Kate was of course much surprised at Dr. Wortman's early arrival with us as he did not expect him before the beginning of the year at the earliest. Dr. W. had a hard time of it in coming out, having come across country with Goodwin, on horseback. I had a meal prepared for them both which caused the Doctor to remark "Well, this isn't such a bad layout!". After our regular supper the dr. entertained us with an informal little lecture on evolution, paleontology of the teeth and many other little themes which were decidedly interesting. Wrote to M. and retired.

Saturday, Nov. 26

Thank Goodness we have weather worthy of Arizona at last!—a beautiful sunshiny morning. With the two Doctors I went the rounds of the ruins, taking about all the morning as we stopped at I, sat on an adobe wall, and chatted away an hour of the time. Returning to dinner I went in the afternoon with Dr. ten Kate to remove surface bones of sepulchers. Sent over in the evening to Goodwin's, Tom having promised to bring it out with him. Found two letters from Margaret, one from Mother, another from Evelyn with her photograph. Sat in the "Sibley" during the ev'g, with Dr. Wortman, writing to M. while Doc. read Magin. We were soon joined by Dr. ten-Kate and then discussed the work here, its prospects and probabilities, and the advisability of increasing the force. Wrote short letters to Mother and Evelyn and retired about midnight—very cold. Work prosecuted on XIII until the ev'g by Jesus and Juan, when we transferred them to VII to prospect for skeletons, since the severe rains have had a disastrous effect upon the ones uncovered, and those unearthed during the summer are in a very fragile state. Mr. Garlick erected harness shelter to-day, repaired harness and varnished buckboard. Men remove dung-piles.

Sunday, Nov. 27

Soon after breakfast this a.m. started with Dr. Wortman for Tempe. Stiff breeze blowing from mountains, making me miss my coat which I left without taking. Roads fair considering the rain. Letter from M. and box of writing paper. God bless her! Took dinner in cook tent; went to station for baggage of Dr. and returned as far as Goldman's[248] when we found that the blankets I purchased for "Comali", the Dr's valise and the telegram I intended sending to Phoenix for meat were non-ext. River not yet fordable. Got to camp by 3 o'cl'k. Wrote to Margaret in ev'g.

Monday, Nov. 28

Resurrection day in camp. Men are transferred to work on VII (Jesus and Juan) while Ramon & Rafael spend the day in hauling wood, water, & hay (having been obliged to go via McClintock's for the last-mentioned, the road by way of Cartledge's having overflowed). Went with the "Doctors" to inspect the work. I placed the men where prospects for skeleton finds were the most promising I thought and sure enough Jesus reported the discovery of one skeleton when he returned from work at dinner-time. Assisted Dr. ten Kate [to] remove skeletons in the morning, and in the afternoon had Carlos assist me in tagging rooms and sepulchers of XXI & XXII. Dr. W. works upon the uncovering of our newly-found remains and afterwards upon others which Dr. t-K and myself had uncovered during the morning for "fixing". Mr. Garlick went to Tempe in the afternoon—in morning cut and laid new buckboard flooring.

Tuesday, Nov. 29

Carlos made tags and sewed on buckboard boot to-day. Mr. G. cut new canvas flooring for buckbrd and leather-piece for brake-hole. Went to VII in the morning where work is being prosecuted and where Dr. W. is engaged in uncovering skeleton found by Jesus. In afternoon went to Tempe, finding ~~two~~ a letter from Margaret. Brought out sugar and salt. Had hair cut while in town. Wrote M. in the evg. and retired early.

Wednesday, Nov. 30

Mr. Garlick went to Phoenix this morning and I had Carlos assigned to the work of finishing buckboard boot. Remained at VII the greater part of the day inspecting the work. Dr. Wortman very industriously labored upon the apparently discouraging skeleton which has attracted his attention for 2 days past. No mail of course from Margaret to-day. Wrote in evening as usual and sat in the Sibley with the Doctor and the Professor discussing Moki.[249]

Thursday, Dec. 1

Made the rounds of the ruins this morning and wrote short note to Margaret. After dinner went to town where I found two letters from Pearl—answered when I returned. Mr. Garlick worked upon my stove to day, and Carlos was engaged in sewing barometer-tent and doing chores around camp, sweeping, etc etc. The men were transferred to work at Ruin II this morning and during the day had found five skeletons, two of them however, being recoverable. A small decorated bowl, a mesquite pod, stone showing 2d process of arrow-making, and several other specimens were unearthed. Wrote M. in ev'g and retired rather early. (This morn'g I also worked on Nov. vouchers mailing same to Mr. C.)

Friday, Dec. 2

Rain, pattering on my tent-fly this morning, awakened me. After breakfast spent a while by Mr. Garlick's fire when McClintock rode up in a drenching shower, joining us in our conversation, until the storm subsided and the sun again shone, when he took our buckboard and team and drove to Phoenix. Spent a good portion of the afternoon in rearranging my tent. Mr. Garlick having finished making and erecting my stove and hearth. Went again to No II where work progresses but nothing of importance had been discovered. Wrote to Margaret after supper and our Doctors spent an hour or two with me in the discussion of camping experiences and adventures—Retired early—

Saturday, Dec. 3

Soon after breakfast I took Carlos to Ruins VI and XIII and made locations of the walls. Had about finished when I saw McClintock coming in the distance having returned from Phoenix last night. Made for camp where he handed me letters from M. and Mr. C.[250] Wrote short letter to Margaret after dinner, leaving it unfinished until evening. Went to II to inspect the excavating in the afternoon. Dr. Wortman was there working on two skulls in situ and stopped long enough to give me a lesson in patience, should I desire to undertake any of the work in the future. About sundown I went with Dr. ten-Kate (who has spent the day in silicating bones) west of camp into the mesquite-woods between Goodwin's and Cartledge's and in crossing the ditch lost my footing and wetted my mocasined-feet quite badly. Our errand, that of hunting quail and rabbit, was almost fruitless. The Doctor capturing but one of the former and myself nothing. It was dark when I wound my way through the thick undergrowth and proceeded toward camp with-out the Doctor whom I had missed. It happens that he met Goodwin on the way over, who had brought up the mail from town, and I was delighted to find two letters from True, beside my plate, as well as a bundle of papers from home. The roses I found in one of M's letters—how valuable they are to me! Wrote more after supper spreading my letter out beyond twenty pages—and after reading a while by the fireside, retired to rest.

Sunday, Dec. 4

After house-cleaning I wrote up some "Daily Memoranda" of operations, worked a little on accounts, and loafed a while, Goodwin calling in the meantime and taking dinner. After remaining about camp for some time Goodwin and myself went to the woods between Cartledge's and his own Ranch where we separated and hunted doves on our own merits. I had a young man under his employ for use as my "pointer" and succeeded in bagging five doves and a wild-duck—the latter I shot in Goodwin's ditch. Returned to camp without seeing Goodwin again and was accosted by Mr. Garlick who seemed anxious to know how much I "paid" for my game. Dr. ten-Kate had not returned from his trip, on an errand similar to my own, towards the mesquites east of camp; nor indeed did he put in an appearance (bearing two quails as trophies) until after sunset. Rafael returned from town in the evening but brought no news from Margaret. Wrote to her in the evening. What a long day it has been! Played poker with Mr. G. and Dr. W. in G's tent till 11 ocl'k.

Monday, Dec. 5

Worked up accounts for October this morning and in afternoon went to Tempe where I found 2 letters from M. Had "Bob" shod at Hayden's and returned to camp soon after sunset with commissaries. Road from camp at Florence-Junction very badly overflowed from Tempe Canal. Wrote long letter to Margaret in ev'g. Men continued work on II this morning for a short while when Jesus, Ramon and Adolpho were transferred to IX—Two skeletons found during the day. Mr. Garlick worked on topographic map of the valley to-day.

Tuesday, Dec. 6

Work on IX to-day with full force and by evening 7 skeletons were found, with several accompaniments, including the cream-tint ware pitcher. I plotted my notes of VI and XIII and in afternoon located the walls of the former ruin with the assistance of Carlos who spent the morning lakering[251] and in helping the cook. Felt very lonely towards night when I foresaw no prospect of hearing from M. Walked toward our retreat #1 before supper and watched the sage burning by Adams' Mexicans. Returning to my delight I found that Goodwin had brought up the mail from town including a letter from M. and a telegram from Mr. Baxter. Mr. Garlick worked upon the valley map again to-day and also repaired some harness and put the buckb'd upon its wheels. We had a delegation of visitors from California about noon who went the rounds of the ruins with Dr. Wortman. Wrote M. long letter in the evening.

Wednesday, Dec. 7

Commenced quite early this morning to take lessons from Dr. Wortman in "boning", spending a while in the Sibley with our professors, warming up from the effects of a cold night, (the thermometer at 7 a.m. was at 30°), just after breakfast-time. Went to XX with Dr. W. and assisted him in cleaning a very frail skull. Were joined by ten-Kate and proceeded to IX where Ramon had made an excellent job of uncovering a newly-formed skeleton. Remained at IX until dinner hour when we returned to camp with some of the new specimen-finds which I spent part of the afternoon in repairing, being interrupted in my work by more visitors, Mr. and Mrs. Lount[252] of Phoenix (dealers in artificial ice) and the most indecent, ill-mannered pair I have yet had to entertain. Went to the ruin again in the evening (IX) as also to VI and VII for the purpose of tagging rooms and new specimen-finds. Mr. Garlick returned from Phoenix with letter from Margaret and telegram for himself from Mr. C. who authorizes hiring of add'l men and requires Garlick to meet McDowell[253] at Tempe to-morrow morning (McD. of the S.F. "Examiner"). After change of mules he makes his departure in order to be on time for early train in morning. The Doctors call on me, followed by the "Coyote" who gives us some of his experiences while in the Mexican army as well as a lesson in Apatah-Yaqui and Pima. Write to Margaret and retire early. Rafael & Juan haul hay.

Thursday, Dec. 8

Look with anxiety for news from our newly-expected arrival, Mc. Dowell, who did not come until nearly midday, Mr. Garlick having driven him around by way of the ancient canals east of camp. In afternoon we went about over the ruins. Mr. Garlick commenced the making of a new stove from sheet iron he brought yesterday from Phoenix. Men work on IX—two extra on force. Letter from Margaret and answered in the evening.

Friday, Dec. 9

Wrote letters sending accounts to Phoenix merchants with checks this a.m. and in afternoon went to town to pay off. Upon returning wrote orders for workmens' pay. Men work to-day on IX but with few finds. The Doctors are still at work on the skeletons and McDowell spends the day in taking notes & in recuperating from a very bad cold which he contracted en-route. No letters from Margaret but I write in ev'g and retire rather early.

Saturday, Dec. 10

Mr. Garlick and Dr. ten-Kate go to Phoenix to-day and return at night, via Tempe, bringing two letters from M! Remained in camp all morning responding to a volley of queries that McDowell shot me with in making his notes. Goodwin called, and gave his views on ancient ditches etc etc. of course. Just before dinner McD. and myself went to IX where work is progressing. Found a large lizard which I brought to camp after a very lively chase. Pickled him in alcohol and noticed that in 15 minutes afterwards, he was still alive. A little excitement occurred this morning when McCall noticed smoke issuing from the Mexican's tent, and suspecting the cause rushed with a bucket of water to find that the flooring of the tent was in flames and the roof threatened. Carlos reinforced us with more water and soon the quarters were beyond damage. No more stove for our Mexican bretheren! Received dictation from McDowell all the afternoon on his first "Examiner article." After supper had a very big discussion on the population of Los Muertos and of the valley, anciently. Wrote Margaret & retired. McCall & Jesus went to town in afternoon.

Sunday, Dec. 11

All day to-day McDowell and myself worked upon his second article for the "Examiner," and in evg. wrote to Ikina.

Monday, Dec. 12

Mr. G. went to town this morning & had five mules shod. Mc. Call & Jesus Morales did not return yesterday as they had promised, & Carlos does the cooking for the outfit. In ev'g the prodigal returns and invites me to make out his time[,] which I very readily do, thus ending the services of our indefatigable, comical McCall! The men work on IX all day. Juan assists Carlos in cooking. McDowell & myself work until evening on the 2d Examiner article when Dr. ten-Kate relieves me; & while writing Margaret I in turn took the pen again drawing the Ms. to completion.

Camp Hemenway (Superstitions), Tuesday, Dec. 13

Was up by sunrise and worked busily preparing for our trip to the Superstition Mtns. While Mr. G. attended to the bedding and our small camping necessaries I packed the mess-chest and got necessary commissaries together. At nine o'clock we were off—McDowell and Wortman in one buckboard and Dr. ten-Kate and myself in the other. Made Mesa City (2 miles) in good time stopping to water animals for last time before reaching the mountains, and in purchasing apples and cheese—Saw the Pomeroy's,[254] the owners of the ranch where we propose going and gained some valuable information in regard to roads—which were pretty good until we reached the mountains proper, when we had many steep, rocky pitches. Rain and hail beating in our faces with great fury caused us to beat a retreat and camp temporarily beneath the shelter of a mesquite. Our buckboard suffered the most being uncovered and as ten-Kate had a waterproof hat, I was the one who received the drenching to the skin. The water dripped from my coat into the leggings I wore and thence found a way into my shoe-tops, making me feel quite uncomfortable. We went on again and again it stormed. Wortman made the fat man drive while he sought the dryness of our pile of bedding beneath the canopy of their buckboard and laughed at our discomfort! Mt. Diablo was a marvel to look upon. A huge red mountain of rock with pillars surmounting it and supporting crags and rocky caves covered with ice from the rain and hail-fall and a streak of western sunlight breaking through the blackest of clouds and lending a most gorgeous spectacle to the whole scene. In descending our last rocky hill—the roughest road I ever traveled (and one which threatened to overturn us at every step the mules took) we had great difficulty in holding the animals back since our break was in a very bad condition allowing the buckboard to run against the mules, forcing them down the steep banks on a sort of jog trot. Reaching the little stone cabin at Pomeroys ranch we found that two cowboy's were in charge, one of whom was shoeing a horse—the other being out on the range at the time of our arrival. After feeding the mules, which were quite tired after our 32 mile drive, we got supper and soon threw our beds on the ground outside the hut, with feet toward the fire, and slept pretty well until morning beneath a very threatening sky.

Pomeroy's, Superstition Mountains, Wednesday, Dec. 14

Were out quite early, and had a breakfast of "Rocky Mtn Stew" engineered by Wortman. Soon after sunrise we hobbled our mules and were off up the canon (toward the south) in search of caves, we proceeded about four miles, following the course of a pretty little stream that rushed over the huge boulders, cutting a gorge between the lofty volcanic peaks on either side. Separating into pairs, Wortman and myself continued eastward, the other two going toward the west of Mt. Diablo. Our half of the little party climbed many buttes that were very steep and rocky. In one we examined about 30 small caves, and a foot beneath the floor of one of these we unearthed two large pot-sherds. Resting a while we proceeded on our journey which led us into a little valley between a very precipitous mesa-like mount, and Mt. Diablo. Here we found many more caves, examining all that were within reach. Wortman yelled out a find of a rope or cord of a sort of cane, and soon afterwards I discovered several little rolls of yucca-fibre that had evidently been chewed, also a couple of pieces in its natural state as well as a deer's rib. A voice from the summit of Mt. Diablo attracted our attention and there we saw a small speck, waving its arms frantically and yelling something that we were unable to understand. McDowell, it seems, had lost the Doctor, and found his way to the place where we saw him. He succeeded in joining us after descending the mountain-side with the utmost difficulty—in one step going 15 fifteen feet (on his back) farther than he expected. Soon we returned to our camp by circuitous route covering about six miles. McDowell kept continually in the rear, and when the sight of Wortman & myself was lost he would climb the nearest butte after much needless exercise, and shouting to the top of his voice to attract our attention proceeded in following us. Once I heard a very pathetic ejaculation from our "Examiner" and turning saw him midway between the base and summit of a hill trying to extract a cholla from his knee. I shouted instructions to get rid of it when another attacked him from the rear! We reached camp before sunset. Ten-Kate joined us an hour later when I got a supper of "Superstition hash" and wrote to Margaret inside the little stone hut with its cactus-mud roof.

Before finishing my letter I moved my bed outside thinking the rest would like to retire. I was soon asleep, but during the night awoke from the noise "Bob" was making about camp, having broken his halter-strap.

Camp Pomeroy, Superstition Mountains, Thursday, Dec. 15

Up early again after a cold, windy, cloudy night. Wortman and myself got breakfast and leaving McD. & t-Kate to wash the dishes, we drove the mules over the nearest hill where we hobbled them in the grass. Wortman continued onward that he might examine some quartz deposits of which the cowboys (who left for Mesa City yesterday morning) spoke. I returned to camp and with the others went in a north-easterly direction, crossing a beautiful little round basin in which some stock were feeding. After exploring some deep canons opening on the south side of this basin we crossed a basalt-ridge and viewed the valley beyond. Here I fell and cut my hand while carrying a pair of deer antlers which I found while crossing the field. Then descending we recrossed the basin and entered another canon to the northward, exploring it for a distance of three or four miles. As I went ahead down the canon I discovered, to my amazement, a moccasin footprint in the sand, and all sorts of dread about Apaches whirled through my mind. The other two had taken the trail before coming upon the print so did not see it. I continued for half a mile and joined them again farther below. Here we separated, McDowell going in another direction from ten Kate and myself who climbed a hill overlooking the most beautiful canon I ever saw. That I might get a better view I reached another point where I could see a silver streamlet curling around the steep embankment of red rock. I fired my pistol and the roar echoed and re-echoed for fully ten seconds. We again met in the canon in half an hour and retraced our steps up the same canon we descended. When we reached the little green basin I called the attention of Dr. ten-Kate to a little mound covered with stone off the end of a basaltic cliff. We crossed the valley and found it to be the ruins of a stone fortification and around it were several low-lying mounds rising from the natural level of the grass-covered soil. I found here a shell pendant and a piece of tufa different from the surrounding formations. Much fragmentary pottery was scattered about, plainly indicative of an ancient habitation. Partly satisfied with finding at least these evidences we returned to camp where we found Wortman enjoying a repast of crackers, cheese & salmon in which we heartily joined. Wrote to Margaret after supper while the others were hotly engaged in a scientific-artistic discussion which lasted without cessation for fully three hours. We went to bed (myself outside again to watch the animals) and were soon sleeping in a very frosty air.

Superstition Mountains & Camp Hemenway, Friday, Dec. 16
I was the first one out this morning, Dr. ten-Kate following me soon afterwards. While I fed mules Dr. brought wood, made fire and awoke the slumberers. At 9:00 we were off up the rocky incline the mules fresh and spirited and ourselves all aglow with anxiety to reach Hemenway. Stopping long enough at Mesa City for water we continued onward reaching Camp by 2 o'clk. Mr. G. was in Phoenix and the men at work on I and IX. Made them a visit and returning wrote to Margaret from whom I found two letters awaiting me.

Saturday, Dec. 17
"Anniversary Day". Cleaned house and with McDowell started for Phoenix arriving about noon. A Circus captures the town. Mormons & Mexicans rampant. Get new shoes, pants & hat, and make myself lustrous by shaving and hair-clipping while McD. enjoys the luxury of a bath. Witness the parade which consists of an elephant, a camel mounted by a "coon", three or four closed cages, a couple of clowns and yawning females in burro-carts and that's all. Admission one peso. Reach camp by dark having been followed across one arm of the river by a little dog which found it too cold to go farther. Mr. Garlick on hand with two more letters from M. which I answer and am joined by McD. & Wortman—Play poker 5-c ante until 1 am.

Sunday, Dec. 18
Clean house thoroughly & write Mr. Cushing in the morning. The Goodwins call[,] Jim bringing me letter & rose from M. In afternoon write to Pearl & at ev'g Wortman & McD urge me into a game of poker.

Monday, Dec. 19
Mr. G. and Dr. W. go to Tempe this a.m. and I visit the work going on in I and IX. Another double skeleton found in pretty good condition. Write

up notes of trip in morning and in aft. have a visit from Mr. Miller[255] who "prenologizes" me quite favorably. Tag specimens in Ruin IX (i.e., skeletons) McD. writes on third "Examiner" article. Mr. G. & the Dr. return with letters from M. & Mother. A little more poker.

Tuesday, Dec. 20

Finish writing up notes and spend nearly all the remainder of the day in cataloguing specimens-recent finds. Work continues on I and VII but nothing startling is found. No news from Margaret today as nobody goes to town. Write in ev'g and soon after 8 retire.

Wednesday, Dec. 21

Write up daily mem.n [memoranda] all morn'g and after dinner start for Tempe via Maricopa road as Goodwin's recent advancement in civilization—the cultivation of the tract east of camp, makes the road impassable by reason of flood. Meet Woody Armstrong coming on horseback with telegram from Mr. C. requesting teams to be sent to-morrow morning. Was never as happy at receiving news in my life! Face the cold north blast and enter town half frozen. Make purchases of commissaries and add'l blankets and return to find the new ditch west of camp filled with water compelling me to unhitch the mules, ride them to camp, and send back for buckboard. Break the joyful news to the campists who are gathered around the fires trying to keep warm. Dr. Wortman & Mr. McDowell have a "set-to" on the Chinese-Zuñi mythic comparison[256] and its practical utility and upon their leaving my tent I retire to get very little sleep. Thanks to the mind it has at last abated and I can once more lie down without the prospect of my stove-pipe falling on me. Four letters from M. today!

Thursday, Dec. 22

Was awake nearly all night, dreaming of today's anticipation, with my eyes open. Was up and out to breakfast when Carlos called me, after which I spent the rest of the morning in superintending the cleaning of camp. Carlos and Juan worked busily in the rejuvenation of the kitchen and Rafael & Ortiz in general cleaning about camp. I watched the roads incessantly all the afternoon after the train went past and soon espied the little white-topped buckboard dodging in and out of the mesquites toward the east. Ten minutes more and Mr. and Mrs. C. and my long-looked-for M. drove up to camp and for the first time in nearly three months am really happy. M. spent the greater part of the afternoon in my tent and just before supper took a short walk to the ruins (XX). Spent an hour in the Sibley with Mrs. C. and Margaret where I was allowed to see some very pretty Christmas presents which they had purchased. Mr. C. and Dr. ten-Kate took a walk for the purpose of holding a "council of war" and when they returned I departed and retired. A very cold night.

Friday, Dec. 23

Was up just before sunrise after a poor night's rest and after breaking the ice off my wash-basin washed and breakfasted. Wrote daily mem. for Mr. Garlick and checks for Phoenix expe's as this is "town-day" for Mr. G. and Dr. t-K. Wrote up long teleg. for "Examiner" McDowell and shortly after had visit from M. followed by others during the afternoon after I had gone the rounds of the ruins with Mr. C. and Mr. McD. M. was again with me during the evening for a short while when I was invited to call by Mrs. C. remaining with her and M. until about ten o'clock. Mr. C. and the geniuses held another war-council this ev'g in the Sibley.

Saturday, Dec. 24

Did not do much in the line of work to-day. Went with Mr. Cushing to the ruins and was followed by McDowell who forced an "interview" until we were joined by about a dozen Phoenix visitors, when he left disgusted. Our visitors were nearly all young men and among them was a very intelligent Japanese. They seemed to enjoy the interesting explanations of the features of the ruins that Mr. C. made and I was very glad to see how pleased he was with the discovery of a series of post-holes in an adobe wall of Ruin I. Returning to camp I spent a short while with Margaret when we both assisted Mr. Cushing in making candy for Christmas. Had a further chat with the visitors when they came to inspect the specimens in the collecting-tent and here I found the first Phi Psi since I have been in the west—Randolph of Washington & Lee Univ., Virginia. Made candy all afternoon in kitchen with Margaret and Mrs. Cushing. Spent most of ev'g alone and afterwards went at request of Mrs. C. into her tent where she and Margaret were putting together the Xmas presents for the men in which I assisted until nearly midnight when I left taking the things with me for an early distribution in the morning.

Sunday, Dec. 25

Was out and in the kitchen before sunrise, while the Mexicans were at breakfast. As soon as they had finished I was ready to distribute to each a silk bag of candies, a silk handkerchief and a bon-bon, and to some volumes of Spanish novels. Ramon received a very nice pen-knife—all from Mr. & Mrs. Cushing. Afterwards, the camp was more thoroughly astir and I handed in to Mrs. Cushing's tent with some hot water, a card-case for Mr. C., a hdk'f for Mrs. C. and the little gold Virginia Creeper pin for Margaret (M. has spent two nights in the large tent owing to the lack of a stove in her own). Before arising, I espied a couple of mysterious-looking packages tucked under my tent-flap, and getting out of bed found them to contain a beautiful little crescent-pin, set with seven pearls, a little French calendar, and a hand-painted chamois pen-wiper all from Pearl; a laundry list & pincushion from Mrs. Cushing as well as a little Japanese basket of candy, and a very nice leather and nickel traveler's ink-stand from Mr. C. After breakfast we (the ladies and myself) went into the kitchen and for several hours spent our time in preparing for the Christmas dinner, which was not ready however until after four o'clk. M. made occasional visits with me to my tent and after dinner took a short walk north of camp. Upon returning we found the Mexicans rushing wildly about and turning the corner of the kitchen saw a blaze issuing from the top of the Sibley. I rushed to my tent and seizing my water pail assisted in saving the destruction of the tent. Dr. Wortman was within inspecting damages, the upright being still on fire but I extinguished this with a few handfuls of water. Spent part of the ev'g in the Sibley with Mr. C., Drs. W. & t-K and Mr. McD, and a few minutes with Mr. Garlick. Retired after a very pleasant day.

Monday, Dec. 26

Mr. C. made me a late visit last night instructing me as to making out of plan of operations for Dr. Wortman who proceeds with McDowell to El Paso, Texas, via Tempe and Phoenix, where they will make a reconnaissance of the region of the Diablo Mountains, for the purpose of investigating the caves supposed to contain human and animal remains. Write up instructions for the day and have several little visits from M. during the day. In the evening we go for a short walk together and I have another in the ev'g after supper. Ramon, returning from Tempe, brought me two packages from home containing several pounds of Huyler's, a knitted pea-jacket, some hakf's a little card and a couple of photos of Ed. and Juliet Sewall, playing tennis. Read and sewed buttons for a while and retired about eleven o'clk—Engagement-ring day.

Tuesday, Dec. 27

Good night's rest and early breakfast. Gathered up my washing and also Dr. t-K's & went to Mexican woman's tent south-west of Muertos. Saw the "boozy" there with a couple of pups. Catalogued a few specimens and went to ruins VII and IX to tag their locations. Showed Mr. Cushing our new finds and went with him to XX where we inspected the excavations done during his absence. From thence to I where ten men are pushing work on that very interesting east wall. Ruin VII was also visited, finding there Dr. ten-Kate and Ramon working upon the preserving of a double burial. More visitors we found on our way back to camp. After dinner Mrs. C. and M. took short drive down Maricopa road and upon returning M. made me a visit. Mr. C. in the interim having entertained the Dr. and myself with comparative Italian & Zuñi folk tales. M. and I made our first visits to the retreat this afternoon where we spent a delightful half hour, having been compelled to go and return in a very round-about way by reason of Goodwin's ditch operations. After supper M. spent another hour or so with me relating a Zuñi folk tale ~~on~~ about the "three bashful lovers". Paid M & Garlick a short visit in his tent. Mr. Cushing was there with some Casa Grande photos, which we examined.[257]

Wednesday, Dec. 28

Mrs. Cushing and M. drove to town this morning, returning in the afternoon. Spent morning in cataloguing and tagging a few specimens and in visiting I where work is progressing. Wrote Ashley and assisted in erecting ramado on west end of spec. tent made from Mr. C's fly. Took down my own fly to day that I may get the morning sun. The day is delightful indeed but toward evening it becomes cloudy. M. and I walk out to bridge which our men have been building over Goodwin's Ditch east of camp, and after supper she spent a couple of hours with me in making a pair of cambrie curtains for my tent, and taking a short-hand lesson in exchange for some dictation practice which the little girl gave me.

Thursday, Dec. 29

Commenced soon after breakfast to get out and arrange ready for stamping and folding all letters received, in which M. joined me and we finished by sunset. Mr. Garlick returned from Phoenix, whither he went this morning. Men continue work on Ruin I to-day, Mr. C. photographs and Dr. t-K works on skeletons in VII. After supper M. and myself go for a short walk (to Ruin I) in the moonlight and returning sit together in my tent until after 10. Our little secret night.

Friday, Dec. 30

The day opened cloudy. Went to Ruin I and then to VII with Dr. ten-Kate. After breakfast M. called and we spent the morning together, myself in arranging the letters received, by date, while Pearl wrote letters. It rained during the morning and we had a short visit from Mrs. Cushing. In afternoon I continued my work on the letters, Margaret spending the time with me. Later we went across the new bridge to the XXV retreat and stayed during a light shower of rain. The ev'g we also spent together and made it my secret night. Mr. C. and Dr. t-K went ducking but returned with no luck to report.

Saturday, Dec. 31

Went to the ruin (I) early after breakfast and returning to Camp received a visit from Margaret who spent an hour or so previous to her departure with Mrs. Cushing for Phoenix. After Mr. Cushing's breakfast I received a dictation of instructions for work during his absence to the Casa Grande and Casa Blanca ruins.[258] At noon Mr. C., Dr. t-K, Mr. G. and Ramon & Francisco started with large wagon and buckboard and immediately afterward Mrs. C. and M. pulled out for Phoenix, leaving me alone with my notes which I transcribed, wrote up two days' instructions, visited the work at Ruin I and returned to light my fire and read Howell's "Modern Instance"[259] until bedtime. A very lonely ev'g.

1888

Camp Hemenway, Sunday, Jan. 1

Was awfully lazy this morning so did not arise very early. Missed very much my little morning errand of taking M. the bucket of hot-water. After breakfast went for a while to Ruin XX where I attended to the labeling of a few specimens. Saw Cartledge ride up so returned to camp and after his departure read "Howell's Modern Instance" nearly the entire day. Pinney[260] of Phoenix called with a friend while I was thus engaged and I went the rounds of the ruins with them. Read a while longer after returning and Mrs. C. and M. drove up. Took short walk to I with M. before supper, after which M. spent the ev'g with me.

Monday, Jan. 2

Had a short visit from Margaret after breakfast when I went to Ruin XX to tag some more being joined, after Margaret paid me a very hasty visit, by Rafael. Worked until dinner time when I returned to camp and Margaret and myself went to the retreat and spent the afternoon. We also had the evening to ourselves and chatted over many little "cosas."

Tuesday, Jan. 3

To-day's operations were almost a repetition of those of yesterday. A mild cloudy morning sent me to XX to tag, which I finished by dinner time. In afternoon I also employed myself in this manner making labels for XXI and completing same while Rafael and Ramon Alvarez hauled them all to camp by means of the large wagon. Went in ev'g to the retreat with M. who joined me while at my work on the ruins. Here we remained until nearly supper-time and another evening we had together.

Wednesday, Jan. 4

The day opened windy. M. joined me in my tent remaining till dinner time. In the meanwhile several visitors came, among them Mr. Fly of Tombstone[261] who is temporarily located in Phoenix. I went the rounds of the ruins with him posing for a negative which was taken of the large Citadel wall. In afternoon went to town where I collected Decr. accounts and purchased commissaries. Brought Adolpho to camp—a very windy, dusty and consequently unpleasant drive. Found M. awaiting me and rec'd the news that Mr. C. and party had returned from Casa Grande. After supper M. called and I showed her a calendar that N. B. sent me. Chatted the ev'g away pleasantly.

Thursday, Jan. 5

Sunshine and wind during the morning and clouds and rain at intervals during the afternoon, making the day rather unpleasant. Mr. C. and Dr. t-K.

drove off in the morning to the "Pueblo Antiquos"[262] between the Los Muertos and Mesa groups and there examined the surrounding ruins with a view to transferring part of the force to work at that point. M. spent nearly all day with me. Mr. Garlick went to Phoenix for commissary supplies. McDowell and Wortman arrived at ev'g from El Paso, having walked over from Kyrene Station to Camp. They report the remains which they found in the cave be those of a modern Indian and brought no specimens except a very old fossil jaw of some extinct animal which was presented by the hospital steward at Fort Hancock.[263] Spent the ev'g alone at work on accts, M. remaining in her tent reading.

Friday, Jan. 6

Mr. C, the two Doctors and McDowell went to "Los Antiguos" to-day with 7 men and made rather a successful experiment in working up the mounds about that group. Secured three skeletons—one skull being nearly perfect. M. spent the morning with me and the afternoon with Mrs. C. in giving a trial to the sewing-machine which Mr. Garlick brought to [from] town in the afternoon. Worked up my accounts during the day and after supper, M. again visited me. After leaving I called on Dr. Wortman in the Sibley remaining until about midnight. After returning I found to my utter amazement that my tent was on fire, the candle having burned through a miner's candlestick dropping onto my desk amongst a pile of vouchers and other papers destroying them entirely as well as a quantity of rubber-type, stamps, my new gold fountain pen, tobacco-pouch and several other articles. I extinguished the flames with my hat and after surveying damages, ate a large apple and went to sleep with a cigarette between my lips.

Saturday, Jan. 7

The night was quite cold and when we went to breakfast we saw a very beautiful sight in the north. All the mountains glisten with snow and the dark foreground makes them the whiter. Mr. Garlick went to Phoenix to-day, and the rest of the camp (but the ladies and myself) went to Los Antiguos where they were successful with more skeleton finds. M. spent the afternoon with me while I worked in repairing damages from last night's fire, painting the letter double-lobed water-jar in the meantime. The ev'g we also spent together playing poker at which I ~~lost~~ won 50¢!

Sunday, Jan. 8

Spent the morning in loafing[,] M. joining me in my occupation of leisure. Was about to start off with sketch-book to make a drawing of the camp when dinner was announced, Mr. & Mrs. C. returning from a short drive in the meantime. After dinner M. spent a short while with me and then left to attempt to sketch a second time. In the interim I "cleaned house," and myself and joined her just east of camp where, mounted triumphantly on a tea-chest her fingers were making <u>each</u> line tell. It became so cold that the sketching was dispensed with and we took a walk to the mesquites south of the section, remaining until sunset. Found letter from Evelyn upon my return to camp which I answered after M. had drawn her evening call to an end.

Monday, Jan. 9

Went to Tempe this a.m. to pay Dec. accounts. Found Ramon there, he having come up from Phoenix whither he went yesterday on some personal errand. Had mule ("Red") shod, secured commissaries and large quantity of express-matter and returned with Ramon to camp. M. spent ev'g with me in my tent. Mr. C. and party went to Los Antiguos again to-day. M. & I play poker to-night in which I lose 66¢.

Tuesday, Jan. 10

Mr. Cushing and myself unpacked the Ms. and type-writer boxes which had come by express from San Diego[264] yesterday and I also superintended the cleaning of the specimen tent and in repacking the stationery and Ms. chests. Experimented a while on the "Hammond" which failed to operate well. Mr. C., Dr. t-K & McDowell went to Los Antiguos in the afternoon. M. spent part of the time with me, Dr. Wortman stepping in occasionally to try his new patent manifolding process on the type-writer but it failed to operate also. Just before supper Dr. Wortman again called and with M. and myself indulged in a game of poker for gun-wads and fun. After supper and until 11 o cl'k M. spent the time with me in my tent. I wrote letters to Phoenix merchants,[265] transmitting checks, this afternoon & did other account work.

Wednesday, Jan. 11

Was off for town immediately after breakfast in order to meet Mr. Baxter[266] who failed to put in an appearance when Mr. Garlick drove [to] town yesterday. Rec'd news that the train was behind time so spent the long wait by visiting Major Earle, taking dinner with Frank, and in calling upon Yates[267] at the Station. While there the train arrived and Mr. Baxter stepping off the platform, I introduced myself. His trunk had not come so we mounted the buckboard [and] drove to the P.O. awaiting the distribution of the mail and from thence to camp reaching there by dusk. M. called and Dr. Wortman followed spending half an hour before supper. Another visit after supper. M. put up a new desk-curtain in place of the one that was burned, also my "Wardrobe" curtains, to-day while I was absent from camp.

Thursday, Jan. 12

Was rather late in getting breakfast this morning. M. called while I was house-cleaning and remained a while. Worked on accounts and daily memoranda of operations during morning and for an hour or two after lunch, M. in the interim going out to sketch camp from the "Tea Box" site. Made her a little visit and returned to work at which she joined me. Mr. C, Dr. t K and Mr. Baxter held a conclave in the morning and in afternoon went to "Pueblas Acequias" where the greater part of the force are employed.[268] Mr. Garlick returned from Phoenix soon after M. and myself returned from a walk to the south of the section and reported the losing of his bed from the buckboard but the workmen, in driving in from the ruins chanced to pick it up much to the gratification of Don Carlos.[269] M. called just before supper, and again after the meal, and we chatted and read "Tylor's Anthropology" a short time.

Friday, Jan. 13

Attended to some official correspondence, worked on the vouchers which I am now duplicating on account of my fire and wrote up memoranda of operations during the morning. M. paid me a couple of visits and afterwards sat in specimen-tent sketching pottery collections. All the men went to "Las Acequias" early this morning. Messrs. Wortman, Baxter and ten Kate following later. After dinner I was left alone as Mr. and Mrs. C. and M. also drove over there. Mr. G. by the way having gone with the rest with large wagon of camp-outfit for pitching a side camp at that point under Wortman and ten-Kate. Spent the aft. in writing up headings for instructions or rather "daily reports" for Mr. C. and Dr. t-K and in chatting away with our new cook, Moore, who is quite a bright fellow having graduated at the Univ.

of Virginia. Mrs. C. and M. returned to camp first and made me a call until Mr. C. and Mr. B. drove up followed shortly by Mr. Garlick, when we went out to meet him but found that he had forgotten the mail. Goodwin rode out from town with him. M. spent the evening with me remaining until about 9:30 when I escorted her home, returning and retired.

Saturday, Jan. 14

Garlick goes with Rafael in big wagon to take provisions etc. to "Acequias" camp and to gather load of wood en-route. Mr. C. and Mr. Baxter follow in buck-board, leaving the ladies and myself alone with the cook until Rafael's return shortly afterward to clean up about stable and to perform other camp duties. M. spent most of the morning with me, while at my work, in attending to correspondence and accounts—also at intervals during the afternoon whenever she could spare the time from her sketching. Mrs. Cushing took a walk alone to XXV, returning seated beside Mr. Garlick in the large wagon. Received letters from Ashley and Crossman. M. spent ev'g with me remaining until quite late.

Sunday, Jan. 15

Margaret has very unpleasant news for me when I take the little bucket of hot water to her tent this morning. "Pete" got loose last night and in chasing the old fellow around camp fell and sprained her ankle. I carry word to Mrs. Cushing who renders aid by applying "H H H", but a day in her tent spoils our little retreat engagement and instead I spend the morning at work in rubber-type setting and in the afternoon I steer a double dose of visitors about the ruins. Mr. Merritt of the "San Bernardino Index" is of the first party that calls.

They encamp beneath one of the burned mesquites and partake of a lunch while I write and smuggle a note into M's tent in reply to one sent me through Mrs. Cushing this a.m. When they depart from the specimen-tent I pilot sight-seers no 2 around and upon returning find a bottle of Burgundy, a large piece of cake and two apples in my tent, all accompanied by Mr. Merritt's card. Spend the evening in reading the papers which I receive to-day, Rafael going off to the ruins in the a.m. and returning via Tempe. Before supper went to Citadel with Mr. Baxter where we played with the camera for awhile. Mr. C. has been down with the pleurisy all day. Garlick is off to Phoenix.

Monday, Jan. 16

M. feels much better to-day and has hopes of being out to-morrow if improvement continues. Mr. C. dictates and I write up instructions for Garlick who goes with Mr. Baxter to "Las Acequias." Work also on accounts.[270] McClintock calls and remains awhile in my tent. Make M. a short visit and am glad to se[e] a decided improvement in her report on the unlucky sprain. After supper assist Mr. Baxter in the development of plates of photos taken yesterday, and to-day at "Las Acequias" but our experiments were not very successful. Write long answer to letter which I receive from Ed. telling him present condition of affairs and prospects of my home-returning if no change presents itself very soon—Retire after midnight.

Tuesday, Jan. 17

Set up type-heading and print instructions—or rather operations blank for Dr. ten-Kate; also get together stationery for Garlick to take to camp with him. ("Las Acequias"). Mr. and Mrs. C. and Mr. Baxter also go, leaving M. and myself alone. Spend nearly all day in M's tent, taking dinner to her when time comes for it. She ventures out in the afternoon to visit me in my tent, spending a short time with me while I am at work in looking over Leighton's[271] accounts. Another visit to the tent keeps me until the return of Mr. and Mrs. C. when I go out to meet them, receiving a letter from Mother which I answer after supper, write to Mr. Wescott, pay M. good night call, return and retire rather early—"Anniversary" day—7 mos.

Wednesday, Jan. 18

Sent order for gold pen for Evelyn's birthday by Mr. Garlick to-day, who with Mr. Baxter went to Phoenix, returning at night with provisions and a little brown spaniel which we all try hard to name, but no other than worn-out "Boozy" attaches itself to the new arrival. Mr. & Mrs. C. drove again to the ruins of "Las Acequias" leaving M. and myself alone in our glory. Work on acct's and correspondence during main portion of the day, M. spending her time with me. Sit together in ev'g as usual.

Thursday, Jan. 19

Nearly the whole camp go to the ruins to-day leaving M. and I alone. We sat together during the morning, Goodwin and a Mr. Wilson calling just before dinner time. They were followed shortly afterward by twenty-one carriage-loads of visitors from Phoenix, most of them being Eastern tourists, particularly from Peoria, Illinois.[272] After M. and myself had taken dinner I was called upon to guide the visitors,—over a hundred in number—taking in first the collection tent where I explained the specimens amid such remarks as "that's good", "quite plausible", "a little louder, please", etc etc. A Dr. Zeller[273] presented me with a very pretty scarf-pin, made from a Mound Builder's arrow-point. Took them then to the ruins and upon returning was thanked "awfully." M. spent the meantime in my tent sketching pottery, being visited by Mrs. Cole—one of the visitors. We spent ev'g together as usual.

Friday, Jan. 20

M. made me a short visit after breakfast after which went to XVII to tag specimens, M joining me afterwards, spending her time in sketching me while I dodged from one room to another. After dinner I erected the large umbrella just east of camp for shelter to M. while she finished her little water-color of "Hemenway" and proceeded to XVIII, then to XIV finishing the labelling of the specms in those ruins. Mr. C. & Mr. G. have been making Gilbert Thompson tent to-day assisted by Mexicans. While sitting in my tent with M. just before supper Mr. Baxter calls and dictates long letter to Mrs. Hemenway which I write out in the rough after supper and spend remainder of ev'g with M.

Saturday, Jan. 21

Drove to town this morning and secured provisions for "Acequias" camp, proceeding to that point to deposit load and spending two hours of waiting for the readiness of Mr. C. and Mr. Baxter to return, having received instructions to leave my team and drive to Los Muertos with them in their buckboard. The camp looks very lively. Eighteen workmen, sixty three skeletons and many nice specimens lend an industrious aspect to the operations at the diggings. Do not get back to Camp Hemenway until dark when we have a late supper with the ladies and M. spends evening in visiting me. Mr. Fowler[274] calls to day.

Sunday, Jan. 22

Commence early to write up on type-writer the letter to Mrs. Hemenway which Mr. Baxter dictated Friday night, M. greatly assisting by reading rough copy to me. The camp teems with visitors all day—Patrick being among the number. After letter is finished go with M. to retreat where we spend greater part of [day] "grubbing" the ruins on our way back. The camp is busy to day—preparations being in progress for a trip to Casas Blancas[275] tomorrow morning. Dr. ten Kate comes over from Los Acequias, having been enlisted to join the party. Spend the evg with M. in my tent.

Monday, Jan. 23

Made an early rising and cleaned my tent as usual before breakfast. Wrote letters for Mr. C's signature before his start with Dr. Ten Kate, Mr. Garlick and four Mexicans for the Casas Blancas about 11 o clk. The ladies followed the reconnoitres in the rear, going to Camp Acequias with articles and letter for Dr. Wortman. Wrote orders for provisions[276] and sent Rafael to town by noontime for commissaries etc. for both camps. Wrote more letters in afternoon,[277] when ladies returned so we had dinner and M. assisted me in type-writing until sunset. After supper we spent together in my tent, Rafael returning in the meanwhile with papers from home, and also a beauty of a chamois tobacco-pouch[,] which M. handed me, from her mother.[278]

Tuesday, Jan. 24

After breakfast wrote a little on type-writer per M's dictation (letter to Mrs. Hemenway by Mr. Baxter[279] which at first was unfortunately written on non-copying ribbon). Left M. alone (having kindly volunteered to assist in the copying) and went to Ruins IV, V, & VI which I succeeded in tagging—also portion of III—before dinner. In afternoon finished III and XXII, having Mexican follow me to secure labels to the specimens. Returned early in ev'g, M. having finished letter, when we read Wash'n "Capitol" together and chatted until supper time. A short visit after supper and I was left alone to write up my "daily memoranda of operations" and to read papers until bedtime when M. came and bade me good night.

Wednesday, Jan. 25

M. and Mrs. C. drove to town this morning. Went to XXV with the three Mexicans to tag the specimens there & to have them hauled to camp when labeling was completed. Made more tags before noon and after diner went to XIII to tag the specimens there, having the three men assist me. It took us all the afternoon. In returning to camp saw the ladies coming in the distance. M. spent evening with me.

Thursday, Jan. 26

After breakfast M. and myself drove to "Las Acequias" where I intended to label the new skeleton finds but found that Dr. Wortman had already tagged them. Went around the ruins with the Doctor visiting the "Sun Temple"[280] and other excavated remains and noticed four or five skeletons peculiarly buried, being "doubled-up"—heads thrown forward and knees almost touching the chins.[281] Returned to Camp Hemenway for dinner. Spent afternoon in my tent with Margaret, also ev'g, when we take a moonlight walk, seating ourselves on the defensive wall of the ruined Citadel. Men spend the day in hauling wood and water.

Friday, Jan. 27

Went immediately after br'kfs't to XXIII and XXV with the men to label specimens. Send two of the men to other camp at noon, retaining Rafael for camp duty. Early in afternoon made box and packed—ready for mailing M's transparency[,] which she received from Mrs. Hemenway. Sat the afternoon in my tent at work in the briefing of letters, while M. made herself at home with me by sketching pottery. We also spent the ev'g together as usual.

Saturday, Jan. 28

The ladies drove to Las Acequias this morning while I went to VII to tag specimens. While there Goodwin and a friend rode up on horseback and we had a chat together. By dinner time the ladies had returned. Sat a short while in my tent with M. and went again to VII where I tagged as many specimens as my limited number of labels would allow. In the evening M. sat with me and we chatted the time away very pleasantly as usual.

Sunday, Jan. 29

The ladies went to "Acequias" again to-day, and during their absence [I] went to VII, and with Rafael's assistance fastened the labels to the specimens and had them brought to camp as a safeguard against a possible influx of visitors.[282] The ladies returned from the Acequias camp quite early and just before dinner a party of six persons, among them Mrs. McDermott, drove up. Mr. Bennett, one of the party, came to my tent and introduced himself when I made them a visit, just beyond camp under a dead mesquite tree. After dinner went with them to the ruins and was photographed several times with the group by Mr. Chase. After their return and departure we (M. and myself) went to our retreat, remaining until sunset and grubbing the ruins on the way back to camp where we spent ev'g together in my tent.

Monday, Jan. 30

Sent Rafael to Town this morn'g, and ten minutes after his departure thought about necessity of ordering meat. Spring upon "Tricy" just as she was standing at the manger and after a mile and a half bare-back ride, with no bridle, overtook Rafael and slipped from the mule, receiving a passing kick near the hip, but luckily nothing of consequence occurred as an effect. Wrote out order for him and returned to camp to sit with Margaret during the day while I worked up accounts and wrote to Ashley. Took walk after supper and sat with M. during the evening.

Tuesday, Jan. 31

Sat with M. during part of the morning while she sketched in my tent. Went to VII to tag remaining specimens with Lazars and Rafael. In afternoon Rafael went to town for provisions etc. The party returned form their eight day's trip to Casa Grande and the Casas Blancas this ev'g and report a very successful & enjoyable trip. The ladies drove to camp Baxter in the morning.

Wednesday, Feb. 1

Mr. G. & Dr. ten Kate went to Phoenix this a.m. Mr. & Mrs. C. drove to Las Acequias (Camp Baxter). Sat during the greater part of the day with M. in my tent (while she sketched specimens) working on accts. etc. In evening went to Ruin IX to tag the rooms there, and was followed shortly afterwards by M. when we walked to south end of section and returning to camp found Mr. & Mrs. C. and Mr. B. there. Dr. t-K. and Mr. G. came from Phoenix this ev'g. At the table they related how somebody unknown had called for our mail. Miss M. remarked that that was "cool"—whereupon the Doctor replied "Yes it is a very cool ev'g." "Where ignorance is bliss" etc. Sat the ev'g with M.

Thursday, Feb. 2

Sat with M. during most of morn'g in my tent. Mr. Garlick went to Tempe via Las Acequias, taking with him as far as the taller point, Dr. ten Kate, who continues the preservation of the skeletons with Dr. Wortman. In afternoon went to Ruin XIII to plot with Rafael, leaving M. in my tent sketching specimens. Upon returning found that she had gone riding with Mr. C. Went to XXII where three men are at work in excavating. Just before supper M. called and gave me a short acc't of the interview she had with Mr. C., followed by a more detailed one after supper. Prof. Bandelier, who arrived this a.m. and came to camp with Mr. Garlick, paid me short visit.

Friday, Feb. 3

Worked in my tent on correspondence etc. during morn'g after returning from IX where I finished tagging specimens there with Rafael. Upon returning, M. made me occasional visits. In afternoon continued plotting at XIII with Rafael's aide and afterwards went to retreat with M. Council held this afternoon.

Saturday, Feb. 4

Margaret sewed on underwaists all morning ([Hodge squiggle]). Worked on Jan'y accts. during morning. Mr. Garlick went with Prof. Bandelier to Phoenix (Prof. B. returns home). Mr. C., Mr. Baxter, Dr. t-K and myself went to Las Acequias in afternoon, Mr. B. and myself in one of the buck-boards and the other two in the other. Busied myself in paying off men by order and in looking over the ruins. Very cloudy and chilly but fortunately got back to camp before the rain set-in. Drove alone. Mr. C. & Mr. B. following but got off the road and did not arrive until several minutes afterwards. Sat with M. during ev'g, the rain leaking through my tent quite badly.

Sunday, Feb. 5

M. and myself spent morning together in my tent, also part of afternoon when Mr. Cushing called and we walked to Ruin XVII together to talk over recent misunderstanding occasioned by McDowell's beastliness. Everything ended with the utmost satisfaction all around. Mr. Garlick returned from Phoenix (whither he went yesterday noon) bringing papers from home. M. and I went to retreat and also spent ev'g together as usual.

Monday, Feb. 6
M. and Mrs. C. drove to town this a.m. returning by dinner time. Worked on accts all day. Sat with M. in ev'g.

Tuesday, Feb. 7
Got my acct's all ready this a.m. for a trip to town in the afternoon. Made out checks, vouchers etc. and after dinner hour was ready to go. M. accompanied me and we took Lazaro[283] our assistant cook as far as 4-mile turn. Paid accounts, got hair cut, purchased provisions, called at Mrs. Armstrong's for M. and returned to camp shortly after dark, picking up Lazaro en-route. We spent ev'g together of course.

Wednesday, Feb. 8
Spent the day in working on November accounts and transmitting same, also in press-copying letters which Mr. Cushing has busied himself in writing. Mr. Baxter is tinkering with articles for the "Herald",[284] and works into the night at photographic developing. M. spends morning with me making pillow cases and indexing press-copy-book for me.—also evening when we read Tylor's "Anthropology". Mr. Baxter drove to Las Acequias to-day.

Thursday, Feb. 9
Was up just before sunrise & took M. her hot water. After breakfast wrote up memoranda of Operations for last three days and also for to-day. M made me short visit and afterwards went to Las Acequias (Camp Baxter) with Mr. Cuh'g, Mr. G. and Mr. Baxter went to Phoenix this morning, returning in ev'g with letter for me from Mr. Wescott. Wrote on type-writer letter to Mrs. Hemenway from Ms. furnished by Mr. Cushing just before his departure for Las Acequias with M. Mrs. C. and myself consequently ate dinner alone. After return of M. she assisted me in folding and stamping some letters received & in comparing Ms. with my type-written letter. Took short walk (out to Ruin IX). Spent a while in kindling-chopping. After supper spent with M. in my tent as usual.

Friday, Feb. 10
Worked on December accounts and Calif'a expenses all day, M. visiting me frequently in the morning and in afternoon bringing in her sewing and remaining until sunset when we walked as far as Ruin I, the poodle following

or walking beneath our feet. We also spent the ev'g together. Rafael went to town via Las Acequias with Mr. Baxter but brought no mail.

Saturday, Feb. 11

Another day of accounts after writing up instructions for the day, per Mr. C's dictation. M. and Mrs. C. spent the day in Tempe returning by sunset. Major and Mrs. Earle, their son Frank and Mrs. Farmer drove out in the afternoon and I went to the ruins with them. Upon the return of the ladies M. and I went for a walk to the Citadel and after supper chatted until bedtime.

Sunday, Feb. 12

Margaret and I spent the morning together in my tent writing letters. I wrote Evelyn and Eckhardt. Drs. ten-Kate and Wortman called at noontime, taking dinner, and afterwards arranged specimens of hyoid bones for M. to sketch. We intended going to the retreat but were detained at camp so long by the presence of the Doctors that but a short walk was the result. We spent the evening together, however, as usual.

Monday, Feb. 13

M. brought in the hyoids this morn'g and spent the day in sketching them, in my tent. While I worked on acct's. & wrote on letter to Mrs. Hemenway from rough. In ev'g M. and I went for a walk to Ruin I. Ate in new dining tent to-day—napkins!

Tuesday, Feb. 14

At breakfast this a.m. in the new shelter-tent each of us found a valentine beneath his plate, made for the occasion by the ingenuity of Mrs. Cushing. Mine was a revival of the flute, the others equally or even more appropriate to the occasion. Wrote on letter to Mrs. Hemenway during main portion of the day, finishing the "rough" as far as it went; also to Mr. Baxter conc'g Feb'y allotment of $2000. In afternoon worked on acct's, M. spending the day (in drawing the hyoid bones found at "Las Acequias") with me. We took a walk as far as the retreat just before sunset, remaining there for a few minutes, the "Boozy" and "Tip" keeping us company. We also spend the evening together. Sent to Zuñi this afternoon for soap and tooth-powder and also an accompaniment to Bancroft's letter[285] (which I sent yesterday for drawing-material for M.) for sealing-wax. Some canned grapes which I ate for supper, nauseate me but my sickness lasts but a few moments.

Wednesday, Feb. 15

Was out quite early this a.m. and lay on my back reading Mr. Cushing's Zuñi pottery-evolution[286] when M. called and remained until breakfast time. After same Mr. C. dictated yesterday's and to-day's instructions which I copied and was working on the briefing of 1888 letters when M. came again with her sewing and remained all day while I continued with the same work. In ev'g the wind, which has been blowing hard all day increased considerably. Dark clouds soon filled the sky and rain threatened, making me erect my tent-fly and rush about camp to place things under cover as Mr. G. had gone to town and Rafael was off for Camp Baxter. Upon the return of Mr. G. I rec'd a letter from Mother who speaks of the illness at home—what a hospital they must have there! M. spent the ev'g with me as usual and we have a very pleasant chat together.

Thursday, Feb. 16

After breakfast Mr. C. dictated daily memoranda and Director's report, which notes I transcribed and afterwards set up heading and printed with rubber-stamp Report-sheets for the Director. M. visiting me in the meanwhile and remaining until dinner I briefed letters and then went to Mr. C's tent where he dictated to me on his daily report (of the 14 Jan'y-subject: "Casa Grande")[287] until ev'g when I went to my tent to lie down. M. called and we went to retreat with the dogs, remaining a few minutes when we missed "Tip"—she had wandered to camp alone and was playing in a very friendly manner with Mr. Baxter when we arrived. Spent ev'g together as usual. The day has been blustering. Mr. Garlick went to town—brought letter from Bancroft containing bill of $2.50 which I never contracted. Mr. Baxter still grinds out manuscript on the type-writer and collects his thoughts by photographing "Douglas"—at night he invariably over-or-under develops his negatives and gives vent to his feelings by seeking his haven of rest in Mr. Garlick's tent to pass the time until morning in snoring.

Friday, Feb. 17

Commenced early to transcribe yesterday's notes which I finished ere Mr. C. returned from the group of ruins between here and Los Hornos[288] whither he went with Mrs. C. and two of the Mexicans—the latter driving one of the large wagons. M. brought in her sewing and sat during the morning with me. After dinner I received dictations of correspondence from Mr. C. Storm arose and we together held down the new dining tent, getting quite wet in payment. M. called soon after my return to my tent, spending until supper-time. Mr. Garlick brought letter from Ernest, also sugar spoon and butter-knife which I have presented to the dining-table. M. and I spend our "anniversary" ev'g together as usual, having missed the retreat by reason of work combined with the storm.

Saturday, Feb. 18

Commenced this a.m. and wrote up my yesterday's dictation of letters which I finished by noon, M. spending the meanwhile with me. We had some visitors after dinner and M. went the rounds of the ruins with them—people from Cleveland whom Mr. and Mrs. Cushing met this morning at the hamlet mounds [Los Guanacos] west of "Los Muertos." Feeling unusual in afternoon laid down until M's return, when we sat together a while and went to the retreat, Mr. and Mrs. C. starting at the same time for another drive to the ruins. We sat together in the ev'g after supper. Mr. Garlick returned from Phoenix via Tempe—Answered Ernest's letter while M. copied from Encyc. Brit. for Mr. C.

Sunday, Feb. 19

M. came into my tent after breakfast and read rough of Prof. Bandelier's letter to me while I made type-writer copy. Finishing, we sat to-gether, M. knitting while I read newspaper-humor until dinner-time (noticed ad. of Hough's marriage[289]). In afternoon M. sketched flowers which Mr. Baxter brought, and also small mythic animal-fetich belonging to Dr. Hart[290] of Tempe, while I read aloud a chapter of Tylor's "Anthropology." Mr. Garlick and Mrs. Cushing drove to town in aft. to meet Dr. Brühl[291] (a very pleasant old gentleman & a native of Germany,) and arrived at camp while I was making corners of new tent for grommeting. Sat with M. before and after supper as customary. Mr. C. had another bad attack this ev'g.—accompanied by a fainting-spell. Pima Juan sings an incantation.

Monday, Feb. 20

Had a hemorrhage at the nostril last night just before retiring, bleeding for almost 1/2 hour or 30 [minutes]. Was out rather early this morning and paid Dr. Brühl, who occupied G. T. tent #1 during the night, and Pima Juan and his family who also spent their night in camp. The morning is unusually chilly, but notwithstanding this I was imprudent enough to walk about camp in a coatless condition. M. drew "llamitas" (as Mr. Baxter calls them)[292] during the morn'g, while I changed ribbon on the type-writer and did some writing. Mr. C. drove Dr. Brühl to the hamlet mounds, returning at dinner time; after which returned with M. to brief letters and to tack, with her assistance, some green baize on my desk. We took a walk to XXV retreat just after sunset, but remained but a few minutes. Mr. Garlick went to Phoenix with Dr. Brühl in the afternoon and Mr. C. and Mr. Baxter to the hamlet mounds again. Rafael rode to town and returned with papers from home. M. and I sit together until bedtime.

Tuesday, Feb. 21

Rather a lazy day for me as far as work was concerned. Briefed a few old letters after breakfast when M. joined me with her drawings of the "llamitos".[293] Mr. Cushing dictated yesterdays and to-day's instructions which I transcribed by dinner time after which sat with M. and spent afternoon in chatting until storm (wind) came up when I assisted in "holding down the camp". After the breeze had subsided took walk to washerwoman's with M. and returning gathered some flowers for the table-decoration to-night as this is Mr. Garlick's birthday and all the camp except myself has been busy in grinding out "poetry" for the occasion. Mr. Garlick returned just before we did (M. and myself—from our walk) and soon the supper-bell rang. The table looked nicely, a large iced birthday cake surrounded by 16 candles (in commemoration of Mr. G's 16" birthday) was the feature. After the repast Mr. G. read his verses and Mrs. C. and Mr. Baxter afterwards re-read them aloud. The old gentleman was much affected—as was also our new cook (Haag) who was a picture of disdain when he discovered that the cake was "sad." M. and myself spent the ev'g together.

Wednesday, Feb. 22

Washington's Birthday opened beautifully. Had a minute's visit from M. in morning before breakfast also after same (while Mr. and Mrs. C. drove to hamlet-mounds n.w. of camp) bringing her knitting—finishing a pretty little red worsted napkin-ring in readiness for use at dinner-time. Read the newspaper humor aloud, Mr. and Mrs. C. returned at dinner-time. In afternoon Mr. Garlick off for Tempe.—Mr. Baxter has Acequias—Mr. C. a ride on "Douglas". Commenced making two copies of the Garlick rhymes. M. stopped her flower-painting to assist me. Go to retreat—spend ev'g together.

Thursday, Feb. 23

The llama affair discourages me and after breakfast signify my intention to M. to resign.[294] Mr. C. calls and dictates day's memoranda which I transcribe; also part of llama article which I write out as well. M. remains during morning with me—Mr. & Mrs. C. going to hamlet diggings. Dr. Wortman & Dr. ten-Kate come to camp just before dinner & remain all day. In afternoon brief letters, 1887, Marg't remaining with me, making experimental drawings of tufa specimens. We have long chat in evening—taking walk to Citadel after supper, by moonlight.

Friday, Feb. 24

Bad night for sleep—20 grs of quinine did it! Mr. & Mrs. C. & Mr. Baxter drove in 2 buckbr'ds to [Los] Hornos, where they set 4 men at work—brought back at dinner-time a very fine carved shell rattlesnake amulet—the Zuñis symbolical "brother of the lightning." Remained in tent all morning attending to correspondence and briefing old letters while M. sketched tufa-specimens. In afternoon Mr. Cushing and Mr. Garlick in buckboard and M. and myself in the "carrowacky" drove to Los Hornos. "Grubbed" together and succeeded in finding very nice arrow-point among other specimens of lesser importance. Mr. C., Mr. G. and the men returned to camp before us. We reached there soon after sunset, stopping on the way to gather some primroses. Took short walk after supper with M—returning spent ev'g together as usual. Things look brighter to-day.

Saturday, Feb. 25

Started day by briefing letters & attending current correspondence, which I continued until Mr. C. returned in ev'g from Las Acequias (with Ramon) where he drove in morning with Gaston[295] who rides out on horseback, having come all the way from Illinois on purpose to see the ruins. M. spends the day with me with her sewing & knitting. In ev'g take moonlight walk and sit together as usual. Mr. Baxter & Mr. Garlick go to Phoenix—no mail.

Sunday, Feb. 26

Had a thorough house-cleaning this a.m.—actually sweeping under my bed! Gaston pays me an early morning visit as does M. just before breakfast-time. Feel somewhat headachy. M. sits with me all morning writing up diary notes while I loaf and read papers. After dinner overhaul "Zuñi" box in rear of tents, in which rats have played havoc by gnawing Mr. C's Indian articles pretty badly. Go to retreat with M. where she sketches my arm. Return by sunset and after dinner take walk by moonlight to Citadel and spend rest of ev'g together.

Monday, Feb. 27

Was kept busy all day in looking up discrepancy in Bancroft Co's bill, sending out orders for monthly statements, receiving dictation from Mr. Cushing on Bandelier letter etc. M. and I commenced our new "arrangement" to-day by her fitting up a little studio in the specimen-ramado. Had a lonely day of it, but things are on the mend. Breaking up of camp at Las Acequias and Doctors men and camp equipage including specimens all came in the ev'g. Mr. C. & Mr. G. drove to El Pueblo del Cameno this a.m.—returned with fragments of sacred green paint-pouch of woolen goods, nicely woven, and with strings and loops attached—all in comparatively good condition.[296] The party reported that [E. W.] Moore had absconded with "Daisy" and a saddle, necessitating the immediate departure of Mr. G. for Phoenix. Fortunately he was compelled to go no farther than Tempe where Rafael, who went down early in afternoon, had secured the mule. Gaston is rearranging the specimens on the plaza preparatory to cataloging. Preacher Adams & wife call to-day—she proves up on the land tomorrow. M. pays frequent flying visits during day. After supper take moonlight stroll and end ev'g with a squabble[,] which we "make up" in the customary way. Flies increase with the heat and are very troublesome.

Tuesday, Feb. 28

Worked up accts etc. ready for afternoon trip to town where I went to collect bills for Sept [*sic*]—returning soon after dark. M. made me couple of visits in morning. Mr. C. drove to Pueblo Cameno (Miller's Ranch)—bringing back green paint in quite large quantity. Sat with M. while in evg when Mr. C. called me and dictated until 11 o clk.

Wednesday, Feb. 29

Wrote up notes of Molera[297] letter to-day. M. remaining with me while it stormed terrifically during entire day. Mr. G. and Dr. t-K drive to Phoenix. Mr. C. goes to Miller's Ranch ruins and Gaston also, to remain at that place. Wrote orders in ev'g for Mexicans' pay. Sat with M during part of evg. Mr. Baxter coming with type-writer I dictated Molera letter from "rough."

Thursday, March 1

Took bath and cleaned house before breakfast after which received dictations of yesterday's and to-day's memoranda which I wrote up before dinner. M calling in meanwhile and remaining during portion of morning, taking leave to sketch axe-head of stone in specimen tent. Mr. C., Mr. Baxter & Mr. G. drove to "Las Guanacos" in afternoon, myself remaining in tent working up preliminary acct's for Feb'y. M calling again for an hour or so. Just after sunset we walked to retreat and back. Rafael returned from town where he went this aftn. but no mail was brought for me.

Friday, March 2

Bathed before breakfast as usual. M. called and remained for awhile, leaving to water-color some axe-heads in specimen-tent. Worked up Feb. vouchers all day. Mr. & Mrs. C. drove to "Los Juanacos" in afternoon—Mr. Baxter to Las Acequias for photographing and to Mahan's ranch for butter. Mr. Garlick remained at camp to remove M's tent on Dr. ten-Kate's old site, and specimen-tent to west of main collection tent. After assisting M. in rearranging her things in her new home we sat together all ev'g—

Saturday, March 3

Another blustery rainy day. Wrote letters submitting checks to Phoenix merchants. M. remained with me during greater part of day spending also evg as usual in my tent. Mr. G. drove [to] Tempe, bringing papers from home.

Sunday, March 4

Mr. & Mrs. C., M. and Mr. Baxter went to Salado Mountains this morning, leaving Dr. t-Kate and myself "alone in our glory". Read papers and wrote to Mother a short letter ready for enclosing M. O. Upon the return of party had dinner and M. and I went nearly to retreat with oil-colors etc. and she sketched until her fingers became so cold that we walked over to our old mesquite and remained until sunset. Spent evg together—

Monday, March 5

M. spent most of morning with me while I worked up some accounts and after dinner drove to Tempe to pay Feb'y checks, stopping at side camp on Miller's Ranch where Wortman, Gaston & the Mexicans are holding sway. Making necessary purchases in town, returned by same route and was taking leave of Dr. W. just as Mr. C., Mr. Garlick & Dr. t k drove in from the Salado Mountains[298] where they had been in search of pictographs. Returning to camp sat with M. a few moments before supper and spent ev'g together as usual.

Tuesday, March 6

Had short visit from M. before breakfast—continued afterwards while I wrote up commissary etc. supply list for Dr. ten-Kate, who with Peralta started for Sacaton on first reconnaissance to work up Pimas and Papagos.[299] After dinner made up, in part, Dec. '87 accts. Mr. and Mrs. C., Mr. Baxter, & Mrs G. going to "Los Guanacos" leaving M. and myself alone. M. brought in her drawing-materials for sketching sacred pencils,[300] and eagle fetich, and after return of party from side-camp drove with her to Goodwin's ditch to water mules. Sat together in evg, Mr. C. calling and dictating instructions for last 4 days—

Wednesday, March 7

Mr. C. dictated daily directions this a.m. and also long "Report of Director" which I transcribed during the day and in evg took walk to XIV where Manuel is at work excavating. M. and Mr. Garlick went to Phoenix this a.m. soon after breakfast. Returning in ev'g brought me new Norfolk jacket, which I find, to my sorrow, much too large. Sat together after supper munching candy. Rafael brought letter from Evelyn announcing death of Mr. Gibson.

Thursday, March 8

Mr. C. dictates daily instructions as usual and also Directors reports of Mond. and Tuesday which I write out in rough for Mr. Baxter to copy on type-writer. M. pays occasional visits during the day. Also spent greater part of afternoon with me (while I briefed letters) in fixing my last summer's straw hat. Spent ev'g together, taking short walk to Ruin XX—and deciphering letter in shorthand written by Mr. March.

Friday, March 9

Mr. C. dictated instructions as well as "Rep't of Director" this a.m.—wrote up notes during day, M. making me visits in meantime. Spent evg together.

Saturday, March 10

M. & Mrs. C. drove to town to-day, where they remained until ev'g. Mr. C. dictates "Daily Report" of yesterday and also mem. of operations. The former contained an account of the cave finds in Double Butte, comprising nearly 600 cane cigarettes![301] Mr. C. & Mr. G. went again to-day[302] returning with more cigarettes, a Destry's string of the smallest stone-beads imaginable, and a small toba. Wortman's force discovered, at Los Hornos, to-day a small beaten copper ornament—the first metal find yet made.[303] M. and I spend ev'g together as usual.

Sunday, March 11

M. visited me just before "rising" was announced by the cow-bell in the kitchen this morning. Sat together during the remainder of the forenoon, M. writing diary-notes while I wrote up letter to Mr. Baxter which Mr. C. dictated this a.m. immediately after breakfast. Ate pound-cake (sent by Mrs. Hayden) and drank lemonade with M, robbing us both of appetites for dinner and calling "soda-mints" into play. Dr. Wortman called just after dinner & as some Phoenix visitors [men] being entertained by Mr. C. bringing with him a very unique copper tinkler found yesterday ev'g at "Los Hornos." M. and I go to retreat in afternoon remaining until sundown. Mr. Garlick brought sample-book and catalogue of Keuffel & Esser[304] also "Capital" from home—in the mail—also "Shield" from Ashly. M. and I spend evening together. Wrote Mr. Hampson immediately after dinner.

Monday, March 12

Worked up and sent Dec. a/c [account] statement to Leighton, straightened up and made statement of Calif'a expenses, and rec'd dictation of daily Mem. and Saturday Director's report from Mr. Cushing in morning. M. spending short time after breakfast with me. Wrote up notes in afternoon while Mr. & Mrs. C. went to Hornos, Mr. Garlick having driven to Tempe in a.m. M. remained with me from time I finished transcribing my notes until return of Mr. and Mrs. C., when we walked to Ruin XIX where three decorated bowls and small decorated water bottle had been found. Took short walk after supper (to "promenade" wall of Citadel) and returning spent ev'g together. Mr. Garlick brought letter from Asa Phillips.

Tuesday, March 13

Mr. C. called while M. was visiting me and dictated daily directions, also instructions for my conducting of the work during absence of himself. Mr. Garlick, Ramon and Francisco Ribas at Telegraph Pass whence they started about 10:30 o'clock. These, together with Director's Sunday report, I wrote up during afternoon, M. paying me frequent visits with her sewing (the pretty little blue calico masquerade dress). Wrote and press copied letters,[305] and while M. and Mrs. C. went to Cartledge's for eggs, Mr. Baxter and I walked to Ruin XIX where Brayton and Manuel had found two nice axes during their day's work at excavating. After supper M. and I took walk to Citadel, remaining for a while to chat on eastern defensive wall.[306] Returning to camp we sat together during remainder of the evening.

Wednesday, March 14

Wrote up my instructions for operations during Mr. C's absence this morn'g, not having time to finish them yesterday. M. sat with me during a.m., going with Mrs. C. immediately after dinner to Tempe in order to attend the masquerade this evg. Soon after their departure went with Mr. Baxter to Las Acequias in order to photograph the stone close[307] in the Sun Temple there, and to secure upon our return a small, rudely-carved paint mortar of tufa-concretion, which Mr. Baxter purchased of the little girl who found it. Upon arriving at camp Edward[308] informed me that Dr. Wortman had just departed after awaiting my return for three hours. The Doctor, however, secured his money from my trunk as I was informed by a note left on my desk. In the evening I read in Mr. Cushing's "Pueblo Pottery", and spending a short time with Mr. Baxter retired early.

Thursday, March 15

Was late in rising this morning. After breakfast with Mr. Baxter went about removing some of yesterday's sand from my head thro the medium of a shampoo. Worked upon accts. for this year during greater part of day, making three trips to ruin in the meantime (XIX) where Brayton had encountered the evidence of what had once been a considerable fire in one of the rooms. Large mesquite poles, a gigantic cook vessel filled with black mesquite ashes and charred corn and stalks, together with a paint slab, pestle and several potters' stones (all broken by the heat) were found in a blackened condition. The ladies returned from the ball in the ev'g, M. and I sitting in my tent discussing the event. Soon afterwards Mr. C., Mr. Garlick and Fran. Ribas returned from Telegraph Pass, reporting a very successful trip. After supper M. and I took walk to Citadel and spent remainder of ev'g together as usual.

Friday, March 16

M. and I sat together this a.m.—respectively preparing for the German tonight in Tempe, and working on accts. Mr. C., Mr. Baxter & Ramon took long walk southeast of "Muertos" where they traced out the bounds of a very large, ancient lake-bed of an artificial nature.[309] After dinner the ladies drive to town, followed by Dr. Wortman and Mr. Garlick and I go to Ruins IV and V where excavation is in progress by the Los Hornos party that arrived at Hemenway to-day. Returning, assisted in laying off the plaza by means of strings into "checker-board" fashion for collection-classification preparatory to cataloging. Worked on correspondence after supper, also made out checks. Yates comes to work to-day. Mr. Garlick brings mail containing papers from home.

Saturday, March 17

"St. Patrick's day in the morning"!—and raining very fast at that. Mr. Garlick awakens me early to inquire for mail for posting in town this a.m. where he went before breakfast. Ladies return to camp about 11 o'cl'k and M. and I sit together with Doctor Wortman who comes in "to get warm" until dinner. Arrange specimen plaza (in readiness for distribution of collections on Monday) with Gaston and Yates. Mr. Hayden, Mr. Blinn[310] and others call in afternoon. Sit during ev'g with M. being visited by Dr. Wortman, Mr. Baxter & Mr. Garlick. Received letter from Eck this evg—men going to town in afternoon.

Sunday, March 18

M. and I sit together in my tent during morning writing (wrote Phillips) and after dinner went to retreat where we remained until sunset. M. sketching the Sacaton Road while we read "Guenn"[311] by turns. Sat together during evening.

Monday, March 19

The wind blew a hurricane all day long, necessitating the pinning down the tents all around. The day was chilly and dusty which added to our discomfort. Worked some on accounts during the morning, M. paying occasional visits. Also framed letter to Mr. Pilling. During afternoon assisted in classifying specimens on the campus and in rearranging pottery etc. in main collection-tent. Sat during ev'g with M. and Doctor Wortman. Men remove property & specimens back of collection tent today. Mr. Garlick moves to his new abode [*sic*: the "carpenteria"] in same place.

Tuesday, March 20

Mrs. C. drove to town this a.m. to meet Mr. Molera. Mr. G., Mr. Yates and Mr. Cushing have spent their time in making and erecting the flag-poles and flags for the camp. One large pole, bearing the colors of Mrs. Hemenway and Mr. Cushing stands in the centre of the campus and smaller Cushing flags wave above the Cushing and collection tents. M. spends greater part of day with me—Mr. Molera arrives in ev'g with Mrs. C.—(& a very nice gentleman indeed). After supper M. and myself take walk to Citadel.

Wednesday, March 21

Mr. Molera photographed the camp this a.m. while Mr. Cushing was dictating the Memoranda and Report to me—all hands turning out. Wrote up my notes during morning and portion of afternoon M. spending part of time with me while Mr. Molera and Mr. C. drove to Ruins IV, V and XXXI where excavations are in progress. In the ev'g went to retreat remaining a short while. Took walk to Temple [Mound] after supper and spent ev'g together, Dr. Wortman calling and expatiating on materialism, spiritualism and religion in general.

Thursday, March 22

Am not feeling very well to day—worse, perhaps, on account of the heat of the day. M. spends part of morning with me and part in her tent spindle-whorl-sketching. Dr. Wortman reads "Dawn" during morning in my tent.

After dinner to Goodwin's ditch to bath and in ev'g with M. to retreat, taking "Tip" with us and remaining until sunset. Took walk after supper and spent evening together in my tent with Dr. Wortman—Mr. G. went to town this a.m. returning with letter form Ashley and Annual Catalogue of O. K. V.—

Friday, March 23

Worked inside all day to day on accounts of Cal'a trip which I finished up and sent off to Leighton of Boston. M. was with me during greater part of day with her sketching. In afternoon we took short walk to retreat and sat together during the evg. Mr. G. went to town returning with shirts from home, also chocolate and marshmallows, and samples of cloth & new corduroys, which M. and I inspected.

Saturday, March 24

Spend morning and part of afternoon in posting Jan'y and Feb'y accounts and sending to Leighton, M. bringing in her sketching materials to paint specimens in meanwhile. Walk up and down camp after supper and read Tolstoy's "Sebastopol"[312] during evg.

Sunday, March 25

Sit with M. in morning in my tent where we read "Sebastopol" and receive visits from Dr. Wortman and Mr. Yates. After dinner go to mesquite east of camp where M. works on her sketch of the Sacaton road while I read Sebastopol aloud until the afternoon's painting is completed when we move our things a little farther towards the south (about 1/4 mile) remaining until sunset. Took walk to Citadel in the evening after supper and spent the remainder of the time in my tent as usual.

Monday, March 26

A dull, dreary, dismal, damp day. Rain sets in soon after breakfast-time and ere long the camp is a sheet of water. Mr. Garlick lays down a plank-walk and visits M. and I in my tent for the purpose of "drying up." Early this morning a stove was erected in the dining tent, where the remainder of the camp spent the morning in trying to keep warm and dry. In the afternoon Mr. C. calls while I am "re-dobeying" my stove-box and takes M. into large tent for a talk, remaining until nearly supper-time, when she returns and broaches the subject to me. Did not take my supper but awaited M's return followed shortly afterwards by Mr. Cushing and Mr. Yates who spend the ev'g with us.

Tuesday, March 27

Soon after breakfast this a.m. went with Mr. Cushing and M. for a walk to the excavations in progress at main ditch that supplied the south-western portion of Muertos (Ruins IV, V, VI and VII) where several interesting features have been revealed. At the point of excavation the canal forks, the main artery continuing southward and the smaller ditch running toward the ruins above named. In the crotch of the forks a post hole was discovered, being, probably, the remains of a sluice-gate or bridge for allowing the passage of rafts or "balsas"[313]—We then traced out more ancient ditches toward the mesquites on the south section and returned to VII where the force will be engaged this afternoon in cleaning out the canal that circles the s.w. corner of this building. M. left us and proceeded to camp while Mr. Cushing and I followed, conversing on subjects which were brought to light yesterday. In the afternoon I drove four-mule team to town with Mr. Baxter, where we sent telegrams for meat and drugs, procured provisions, mail and, on our way back at Johnson's, hay, which by the way, we had difficulty in bringing to camp, the wires failing to remain secure on one of the bales. In crossing the Hemenway bridge by Ruin XXV "Pete" shied, causing what might have been a disaster. Both wheels of the wagon ran over the side of the bridge, compelling me to jump in order to save myself, while Mr. Baxter grasped the reins and held in the mules while I mounted on the barrel-bracket and relieved him. M., Dr. Wortman and myself spent ev'g together in my tent.

Wednesday, March 28

M. made me a short visit this a.m. when Mr. C. called and dictated "daily operations" since last week (Friday). Wrote up my notes in morning and early afternoon when I joined Mr. C., Dr. Wortman and Gaston who were engaged in re-classifying the Muertos stone-implements, working until Dr. White arrived with two other gentlemen claiming Mr. C's attention. Spent short time with M. in Mr. Yates' tent where the latter has been employed to-day in printing blue photos for M. Worked on Bancroft's sadly mixed account for a while when M. called and we walked to the excavations on the ditch that supplied VII (referred to yesterday). The section cut across the north side of the ditch plainly indicates the slow filling-in or leveling process, and small particles of charcoal having blown in from the burned building are distinctly visible. Returning, Dr. W., Mr. Yates and myself "caught-ball" for a short while before supper after which M. and I spent our time in chatting and reading "Sebastopol".

Thursday, March 29

Just after breakfast M. came and we went over K. & E. catalogue together to select drawing-materials for ordering from Bancroft Co. Dr. Wortman afterwards called when Mr. Cushing sent for me to dictate the Daily Memoranda and his daily report for the past week, making 30 pp. of notes which I wrote up in part during afternoon, M. offering me her assistance until the time came for her to go riding with Dr. Wortman. After their return we took a short walk out the road and after supper went to the Citadel returning to spend the remainder of the ev'g together as usual. Mr. Garlick went to Tempe this afternoon for forage etc. The male portion of the camp spent their ev'g at the "club" (dining-tent) where they sang and told "Sunday-school stories" until a rather late hour, receiving a visit from me just before bed-time.

Friday, March 30

Was out of bed at sunrise this a.m. and, taking M her water, found that she was already awake. In a short time she called and we went to the ruins together—first to the excavation of the reservoir west of XIV where a trench the whole length of the same has been cut to a depth of about 5 feet, revealing near the western end the northern continuation of the same canal that passes VII which we visited in the evening of day-before-yesterday for the first time, and then again this morning upon leaving the reservoir. Returning, we stopped at XIII where we examined the sub-architectural pits that I have been thinking seriously of as having been used as cisterns, being fed by an underground passage from the canal a short distance to the west. After our return to camp I wrote up the Daily Memoranda for yesterday and finished after breakfast the transcription of the remainder of the Director's Report for Wednesday. M. and Mrs. C. went to Tempe just after dinner—M. to remain in town over night to attend the ball this evening, and Mrs. C. to meet and return with Prof. Morse.[314] Mr. C. dictated the "Daily Mem". for today and his yesterday's report. Wrote short note to M. which I send by Dr. Wortman & Yates (who also leave camp to attend the ball) together with the little yellow flowers I picked this a.m.; with Mr. C. and Mr. Baxter I went to the XIV Reservoir exc'n and to XIII and while there Prof. Morse came, driven by Mrs. C. Paid Gaston short visit before supper after which listen'd to a very pleasant talk by Prof. Morse who also called our attention to the zodiacal lights which glow quite distinctly. After doing some mending, retired.

Saturday, March 31

Wrote up yesterday's Directions this morning and worked on a/cs [accounts] etc. until dinner time when with "Mary" went to town, Mr. Garlick following with four-mule team. Met Tom Goodwin (on horse-back), who accompanied me. Had check cashed and went to Webster's where I met M. Played lawn-tennis with Mr. Miller and Doctor Wortman for an hour or two when we returned for team and "Mary", stopping at Armstrong residence. M. and I rode back to camp in buckboard, Dr. K riding the mule. Dr. W. & Mr. Yates spent short time with me after supper, M. following later, remaining a few minutes after they had left.

Sunday, April 1

M. spent most of morning with me. Had visit from Mr. Harrison and Mr. Strickland.[315] Went in afternoon with M. to retreat where we finished reading Tolstoy's Sebastopol. Wrote to M. this a.m. also. Spent evening in writing Mr. Hampson, Bancroft Co. & Simpson the Tailor, M. coming in later, chatting until bedtime.

Monday, April 2

Wrote checks and vouchers during morning for payment in town this afternoon. M. made me a couple of visits and Dr. Wortman & Prof. Morse carried on a scientific discussion and interview. Rode "Gypsy" to Tempe after dinner, stopping at Cartledge's to borrow a spur which did not however prevent my "earning my passage". Returned to camp soon after dusk while all were at dinner. M. remained with me during evening taking my measure for suit which I send for to Simpson of Washington. Mr. Cushing calls and informs me that I am to join the reconnoiters who go to Cave Creek tomorrow.

Tuesday, April 3

Mar. remained with me until 10:30, (the camp being busy in meanwhile preparing for the start) when we were ready for our departure. Mr. Cushing, Prof. Morse, Mr. Baxter, Dr. Wortman, Yates, myself, Edmund and 7 workmen. Mr. Garlick led with four-mule team, Amelio following with another, Mr. Baxter and Prof. Morse in rear with buck-board. Day very hot for April. Reached Gray's Crossing by 12:30 where, while waiting for the passage of the team by ferry, Dr. Wortman, Mr. Baxter, Brayton and myself went into the current which was wonderfully refreshing after the warm dusty ride & the pain in my back that attacked me as soon as I awoke this morning, disappeared entirely. Camped for dinner on north bank of Salado, then moved on to Phoenix where I made several purchases, including white Norfolk jacket. Wetted down with the crowd and we were again on the road. Stopped at Grand Canal for watering animals and to fill barrels and canteens. Edward the cook has evidently taken "too much"—so much so that when we pitched camp about 7 miles north of Phoenix in a thicket of grease-wood Brayton and a couple of the Mexicans were obliged to get supper. Were joined by Mr. Strickland, Supt of the Union Mine (who was at camp on Sunday)[,] having lost his way toward the mine. Sat around a while after supper when I retired, soon followed by the rest.

Wednesday, April 4. Cave Creek, A.T.

Mr. Cushing was up at 4:30 this morn'g the rest of us following at quarter to five o'clock. Got away from camp in grease-wood by 8 o clk and proceeded northward, watering animals from ditch leaving Arizona Canal. Upon reaching the Union Mine we stopped to examine some specimens of gold bearing quartz shown us by Mr. Strickland, then proceeded onward until noon camping in a very pretty valley near Cave Creek (normally only a "creek"). While Mr. Garlick overlooked the making of camp, the rest of us went out in different directions in search of ruin prospects. Returned with large mortar of tufa (in which the country here abounds), a mano and some worked stone tools. Mr. Cushing, who went to "Fortification Butte" a mile north of camp,[316] returned by dinner-time with glowing accounts of the stone redoubt there. After dinner we all went to this Butte, Mr. C, Mr. Baxter, Morse, Yates, Ramon and myself going around to the northeastward where we saw some very interesting pictographs among them being that of a llama, in the act of expectorating—a peculiar habit of that animal. Climbing the Butte I saw that Dr. Wortman and Mr. Garlick with the workmen had already made the summit. Here we saw the fortification with our own eyes—an immense structure 303 feet in length by about 108 feet at its greatest width, and built of the basaltic rock of which the Butte is composed. The structure is in a good state of preservation, being from three to 8 feet high, & containing several rooms. The walls are carefully chinked in with small stones without plaster. Mr. Garlick and I measure with tent-rope while Yates made views with camera, Mr. Cushing and Prof. Morse occupying themselves in sketching some interesting pictographs[317] on the rocks within the fortification, afterwards going off with Ramon, Mr. Baxter and the workmen to make a few excavations to the north of the fort where several terraced houses of stone exist. Dr. Wortman & Garlick, Yates & I remained a while longer, then descended and returned to camp. Found that the Gila Monster found this morning had escaped but the substitute was secured when Prof. Morse and Mr. Baxter returned with another, followed shortly after by Mr. C. and Ramon. The men drive animals (11) to water near the Union Mine while we were at supper, after eating which we indulged in singing, being led by Prof. Morse.

Thursday, April 5
Camp at Cave Creek, Arizona

We were later in getting out this morning as camp was not to be moved until later in the day. Took walk towards east of camp into a thick grove of mesquites and palos verdes, crossing an ancient acequia[318] which I afterwards traced north for some distance in the hope of discovering a reservoir of some sort near the base of the fortification butte, but met with no success in this direction, the canal losing itself near a series of rectangular stone structures, only the tops of which penetrated the surface. Returned to camp and joined the whole party except the cook and Mr. Garlick (the latter feeling ill) who were on their way to the butte where so many pictographs exist. Went along

Cave Creek with Mr. C. where he pointed out to me the hieroglyphs that Yates was to photograph. Mr. C. after searching the butte for further pictures, without success, joined Mr. Baxter, Prof. Morse, and Dr. Wortman across the Creek where they went in search of "evidences," taking the men to excavate some pyral mounds there. I remained with Yates until the four designated views were taken when we returned to camp (meeting the others in-route) for dinner. Early in the afternoon we broke camp, Mr. Garlick and Ramon returning to the Union Mine well for water while the rest of us proceeded southwestward to another butte, upon the summit of which Strickland reported further fortifications to exist. Wortman returned to the mine also, by the way, to apologize for Mr. Cushing's failure to return as promised, and to bring back some ore specimens, with instructions to meet us at the above named butte (five miles off). After remaining there for some time and the Doctor failing to put in an appearance, Mr. C. went ahead with Morse, Baxter and Yates, leaving the 2 wagons behind to await Wortman's arrival until such time as he should set up a smoke signal. After remaining at the summit of the butte until about 3 o'clock (no fortifications were found on this summit by Mr. C. who climbed it before the wagons came up) when the looked-for signal appeared. I volunteered to remain until Wortman came up on "Douglass" and suggested to Mr. Garlick to continue onward towards the smoke, leaving me to walk (about 3 1/2 miles). So they very reluctantly proceeded while I waited until nearly sunset, amusing myself meanwhile in trying to digest roasted "nigger-head" cactus and keeping a watch for Wortman from the butte-side. He finally came, and allowing him to continue to the new camp where we saw the signal, I followed for 3 miles on foot, when Emelio[319] returned with "Douglass" which relieved me from walking the remaining distance. It was supper-time when I reached the camp and well it was for I never in my life did more justice to a meal. After supper we sang many popular songs and then had an "exhibition" by Mr. Baxter who caused a great deal of merriment when bedtime came, Prof. Morse acting interlocutor.

Friday, April 6
In Camp 15 mi. N.W. Phoenix, A.T.

We were all out before sunrise and after refreshing drinks all around of deliciously cool water that had been standing in the barrels over night, had breakfast and went to the butte[320] a few rods south of camp, where Yates photographed and Mr. C., Prof. Morse and myself sketched many of the pictographs that are engraved on the rocks there. We also secured two specimens of pictographs that occurred on the smaller stones, bringing them with us. Among the pictures were many symbols that Mr. Cushing immediately determined to be pure Zuñi. The rain, lightning, fallen water and rainbow signs—also the deer, smoke, mountain-goat and many others. Mr. Garlick had the wagons loaded by the time we returned and were ready to start toward Phoenix. Made good time through the sage and grease-wood until we reached the road, stopping once to kill a rattlesnake that Ramon frightened out while running down a lizard for Dr. Wortman. Arriving at Desert Well we stopped for watering the mules, (which had been without drink since yesterday noon) and to wet our own dry throats. The dust on the road from the well to Phoenix was something dreadful, making us all look like ashmen. To increase this unpleasantness, Ramon fell from the load while the wagon was crossing a rut, bruising his hip quite severely. Reaching town, Mr. Garlick gave Emilio directions to continue towards the ferry while we went to town. Procured my dinner, had a shave and a wash, and got the articles which I purchased an hour and a quarter we drove to the ferry with hunger appeased and thirst quenched. Crossing, we overtook Amelio and the other Mexicans a few miles on, who reported that Edward had left them to go to Phoenix. Passing Los "Canopos"[321] and not finding Mr. Cushing and the rest, I took "Douglass" and after fifteen minutes search spied him temporarily encamped on the bank of a ditch, in the midst of the ruins, awaiting us. Riding back to the wagons I informed the rest and we were very soon in our camp in a clump of mesquites that surrounded a large ancient reservoir. After supper a discussion on carnivorous vs vegetarian diet followed, resulting in a new sobriquet for poor Baxter the "vegetarian." A few songs by the "Jasper Glee Club" and bed-time came—

Saturday, April 7
Camp Canapas, A.T. (4 1/2 mi. s.e. Phoenix)
The day opens cloudy and a few drops of rain fell. Men are assigned to excavations. Three pyral burials unearthed before noon. Go grubbing in ruins and find several specimens, among them being a remarkably beautiful and perfect arrow-point. Mr. Cushing is taken quite ill and Yates and I assist him in making up his bed and in moving the tent to east side of reservoir while Mr. Garlick and Amelio go off in search of the two mules ("Zuñi and Red")

which escaped last evening. After the return of "Douglass" with the strayed animals we had dinner and in afternoon went to new place, with the men, to excavate. Found four more skeletons (house burials) the skull of one of which I succeeded, after the greatest care, in securing, only to find, upon calling Dr. Wortman, that it was too fragile for transporting. Went again in search of stray specimens, found another arrow-point, a fragment of bracelet handsomely carved and some other articles including a shell pendant. Mr. C., Mr. Baxter and Prof. Morse, who went to the base of the Maricopa Mountains, brought their coats full of shards, shells etc. some of them beautifully decorated. Just before they stopped work, the men found two very perfect axes of the usual diorite. Rain threatening during the evening we made the necessary preparations by ditching the open tent and erecting the other one (which we have not used since the start on this trip), and well we did for while the evening's story-telling went on the rain fell fast. The air is still quite warm and another hot day is promised to-morrow. Mr. C. tells of the Zuñi Grandmother and her unsophisticated grandson, which creates considerable amusement.

Sunday, April 8
Camp at Las Canopas

The day opened clear and beautiful after the rain last night. After breakfast all hands went on independent "grubbing" excursions but the mounds seem to be exhausted of their surface treasures as we brought nothing of importance to camp. Gathered together the specimens that had been collected & packed them for transportation to Camp Hemenway and immediately after dinner had Emilio saddle "Douglas" which I rode to town for mail and to telegraph for meat. Returned to camp shortly after the party had arrived from "Canopas." Met M. who went with me to my tent for a few moments where to my delight I found everything in splendid order—much differently to the appearance when I left it. The men are busy in unloading the wagons and distributing the bedding and baggage. Take walk after supper and spend evening together.

Monday, April 9
Camp Hemenway, A.T.

The work is piled up on my desk in consequence of my absence during past week. Mr. C. calls me early in day, dictates daily directions and letter to General Hise[322] rel. to the Peralta claim. M. spends morning with me and after dinner goes on "Gypsy" with Mr. Baxter on "Mary" and Ramon with "Pete" to accompany Mr. & Mrs. C. & Prof. Morse in buckboard with two of the workmen to Mesa City where they remain until sunset to work on the ruins in that vicinity. A Pima Indian who strolls through camp is induced to part with his bow, 8 arrows and a lock of hair for $1.50. Take walk with Wortman in order to test "Tips" swimming qualities and to talk over matters of recent interest. After the return of the folks from Mesa City M. and I take walk out the road toward Ruin I and spend remainder of ev'g together as usual.

Tuesday, April 10

Had a visit from Prof. Morse before breakfast, also one a little later from Margaret, who afterwards brought her work and remained with me during the morning assisting me by reading the rough of letter to Gen Hise (spoken of yesterday) while I copied same on Hammond. Made out checks and transmitted same to Phoenix merchants, also briefed several letters of recent date. Wrote to Mother, sending blue-print of camp at "Las Canopas". In afternoon took Ramon and Dolores[323] to XIVa, where I located and marked pyral specimens found yesterday, and returning took walk with M. to retreat where we remained until sunset. Met Yates on way back and walked to camp with him. Read Tylor aloud before supper. Took walk together after same and spent ev'g together.

Wednesday, April 11

Was rather late in getting up this morning as I remained awake until after midnight to attend to some current desk-work. M. came in early with her sketching materials and remained with me until afternoon when she went to sew on machine. Mr. C. dictated yesterday's and today's Directions, also letter to Prof. Morse concerning War Dept transportation of collections which I wrote on type-writer before dinner, Mr. C. reading my "rough" to me. Briefed letters and catalogued same in afternoon and after M's departure assisted Mr. C. in classifying collections in specn tent, also went with Gaston to VII to bring in shards of large sacred water-jar and several "canopas" that comprised an alter-place there. Upon returning went with M. to retreat where we remained a short while—until after sundown—Returning to the camp we killed a horned rattlesnake, which Dr. Wortman supposes is a new genus. Mr. Baxter brings my pantaloons from Tempe (where he went with Prof. Morse who goes home to-day), Mr. Webster having brought them up from Phoenix—Spend evening with M. The day has been very warm and the flys have begun their torturings. Mr. Garlick, Mrs. Cushing and Gaston are on sick list, giving Dr. Wortman his hands full.

Thursday, April 12

Assisted Mr. Cushing to day in classification of specimens of pottery for cataloguing. A windy and very dusty day. Mrs. Cushing continues quite ill. Baxter and Wortman make preparations for Casa Grande and Florence trip to morrow.[324] M. spends most of day in my tent with her work. In ev'g we go to retreat for short while. Spent evg together. Yates goes to town & brings back letter from Bro. Charlie.

Friday, April 13

Another warm and windy day but not so dusty. Dr. Wortman and Mr. Baxter with a party of Mexicans started for Florence and Casa Grande this morning. Mrs. Farmer, Miss Finch and a couple of gentlemen drove out to camp in cool of morning remaining for an hour or so. Assisted Mr. Cushing in the classification of specimens during greater portion of day. M. driving to town with Yates, after dinner, to play tennis. Upon returning—about 8:30—we sat together until bedtime. Ramon also went to Tempe returning with an intelligent young Mexican, Arrandez, who informs Mr. C. of remains near Florence.

Saturday, April 14

Classified more specimens to-day, M. remaining in my tent with her sketching. The day is very warm again and lemonade is in demand. Went in afternoon to XXIIIa with Ramon and brought in pyral specimens after labeling. Found with cremated-contents of one of the burial urns many small stone beads and in another a few fragments of cloth in a very delicate condition. One of Goodwin's men, who was ditching brought to me a Gila monster which I took to camp and presented to M. with whom I took walk to Citadel where we remained until we heard the cow-bell, causing us to hasten towards camp. Sat ev'g together.

Sunday, April 15

To-day is the warmest of the season. Immediately after breakfast unpack specimens from pyral XIIIa that were temporarily boxed for safe-keeping last summer, and arranged with others, on camp-ground, for cataloguing. With assistance of Ramon and Yates I skinned the Gila Monster that was caught yesterday, after M. who spent the morning in my tent, had sketched the reptile. Just after dinner M. and I went to retreat where we spent the entire afternoon, heedless of the visitors (Misses Ashby and Empy[325] and Messrs Woody Armstrong and George). Had a little archery practice at which M. excelled and spent after supper together in my tent on the bales and in walking the camp.

Monday, April 16

Went this morning with Gaston and Ramon to XVIIa, XIXa, IXa, XXIa and IIaa where we marked, and brought to camp, the pyral specimens. M. spent the meantime in my tent with her sketching. At IXa killed a large whip-snake which I brought to camp. After dinner drove to town for provisions, mail etc. and to telegraph for new letter-press in place of the one recently ordered being broken by Express Co. in transportation. Returned to camp before sunset and took short walk out the road with M. being compelled to return on account of my illness which has taken part possession of me to-day. Took no supper but spent the evening on my back, M. and Mrs. C. calling and rendering medical treatment, pronouncing my case one of malaria. Yates afterwards came, remaining with M. and I until I fell asleep—M. remained longer when she departed also.

Tuesday, April 17

Spent greater portion of morning in my tent with M. who occupied her time in painting pottery specimens. Assisted Mr. Cushing in numbering collections and with Yates' aid skinned the whip-snake which I killed yesterday. Just before noon Wortman and Baxter returned with their party from Florence region, reporting pleasant though not entirely successful trip. Wortman secured one Papago skull. About 3 o clk in afternoon M. and I drove to town in "carrawaky" where we separated at Farmer's, M. to visit Phoenix to-night to attend the "Dairy Maid's Convention" with Maj. and Mrs. Earle. Remained in town until nearly dark, on account of the usual delay in the arrival of the meat, taking dinner at Davis's.[326] Reaching camp I remained a while with Mrs. Cushing, Yates calling on me afterwards and remaining until after my weakness sent me to bed. Am feeling better this evening, Dr. Wortman having administered a good round dose of calomel.

Wednesday, April 18[327]

Mrs. Cushing and Dr. Wortman drove to town this a.m. returning at noon with provisions & M. who spent yesterday in Tempe to attend the Mermaids Convention. Mr. Garlick, assisted by Ramon and their workman, continued the packing while Mr. Cushing dictated to me on catalogue and Yates & Gaston assisted with classification etc—I went with Raimundo[328] to ruin II where we located and brought to camp the remaining specimens. Mr. Webster and Dr. Kingsbury visited camp in late morning, accepting invitation to dine with me. Before tea walked out to Citadel with M. and write dictation from Mr. Cushing most all evening.

Thursday, April 19

Men at work on Temple Mound. Mr. G., Ramon, Rayall and Raimundo packing specimens. Gaston wrapped specimens for packing as Mr. C. [?] catalogued them. Red mule died during night. . . . Mr. Kingsbury Jr.[329] and Mr. Rice called at camp. Before tea walked with M. through barley field and afterward into moonlight stroll to citadel.

Friday, April 20

Excavation on Temple Mound—In morning Mr. C. busy on packing—in afternoon he went to Tempe with Miss Magill who is to remain all night to attend dance. Dr. Wortman & Mr. Baxter also went down, the former to start for Fort B[ayard][330] (Dr. will return to camp shortly) while the latter leaves for good, and goes to Boston via California. I spent entire day remarking stone specimens on plaza in the morning to [?] which a fault has been discovered. Mr. Garlick returned in eve with mail, bringing also a note to me from M. in which she states that she will remain in town until Sunday morning. Preparations in eve. for threatening storm. Mr. Cushing assisted by Gaston & Emilio classify & arrange specimens. Zunis not arrived.

Saturday, April 21

Work continued on Temple mound. Mr. Garlick with his usual assistants occupies day packing specimens. Assisted as yesterday in [?]. I complete the remarking of stone specimens on plaza, afterward classifying them as they were brought in by Emelio and Rafail. Mr. C. & Gaston continue cataloguing till afternoon where the latter is sent to town on the usual errand—At night cataloguing is continued, with the assistance of Yates, Gaston and myself.

Sunday, April 22

Immediately after breakfast, I started with buckboard for Tempe to bring back M. Called for her at Miss Ashby's and made return trip to camp in time for dinner. After dinner and before supper we had games of tennis, as Mr. Yates made court in plaza this morning. Afterward went with M. to retreat & spent evening as usual with her & Mr. Yates in my tent.

Monday, April 23

Working on northern portion of Temple Mound. Packing and box making under Mr. Garlick assisted by Ramon & Yates. Took dictation in [?] all day and in evening; during day assisted by Gaston. Rafael went to town for Bailey while Mr. Yates went to remain over night.

Tuesday, April 24

Excavations at Citadel. Packing, classification and cataloguing continues as yesterday with addition of assistance of ladies. Yates returned from Tempe in morning forgetting mail. Cataloguing of Muertos collection finished at night.

Wednesday, April 25

Rafael Espinosa sent to town early in morning for lumber. Ramon went in afternoon. Work on Temple mound. Classification of cave finds and miscellaneous Muertos collection. Packing in morning under Mr. Garlick assisted by Yates and Ramon. Mr. G. sick in aft. Had a few games of tennis before tea and a little walk with M. afterward. Cataloguing of cave specimens and other above mentioned in evening, assisted by all till almost midnight. Very cold night so after all the others had retired Yates and I built a fire back of his tent and warmed up before going to bed.

Thursday, April 26

Excavation on Temple mound and packing by Mr. Garlick, Mr. Gates and Ramon continued. Classification and cataloguing of remaining Muertos & Las Acequias collections all day & night work till a late hour.

Friday, April 27

Excavations on Temple mound. Mr. Garlick assisted by Ramon packs all morning, and in afternoon goes to town for provisions etc. While Ramon & Rafael continue box making. Dr. Wortman returned in eve with Mr. Garlick. Mr. Yates drives to Goodwins' in late afternoon while I go with M. to retreat. Received dictation on Acequias collection all day.

Saturday, April 28

Work on Temple Mound, box making and packing, as is usual. Mr. Walter Lord[331] arrives. I go in afternoon with Alvarez to Guanacos to collect remaining stone specimens. All up after five this morning to play tennis, another game [?] the ladies in which I did not take part on account of my hip.

Sunday, April 29

Sat all morning in my tent where all the youth of Hemenway assembled and took part in the scientific game of "jacks". Soon after dinner a number of visitors including Miss & Mr. Johnson, Mr. Corpstein,[332] Mr. & Mrs. [?] & some Phoenix people came and spent the afternoon in camp. For their amusement we had claret punch and tennis. In the latter, only Yates, Dr. Wortman & I participated. Mr. Cushing was taken quite sick this p.m. so Dr. and I were with him, trying to give relief for some time. Before tea my services were dispensed with, as he was much better, so I took little walk with M. to Acropolis. Rafael Castro returned to night.

Monday, April 30

Dr. Wortman & Mr. Garlick start for Phoenix in morning for supplies & to purchase new mule "Dandy". Yates goes to Tempe in afternoon, taking with him Herman, who is discharged. Rafael Espinosa goes to Florence. With Ramon's assistance I classify Hornos stone specimens. Mr. Cushing in bed all day but sufficiently recovered by night to continue cataloguing which was assisted by all including Mr. Lord, who will probably remain some time. Work on Temple Mound continued.

Tuesday, May 1

Excavation on Temple Mound. Before we had finished breakfast, Mrs., Mr. & Miss Sawson[333] drove up and stayed long enough after visiting the ruins to play a [game of tennis]. Miss M. & Mr. Yates against Miss Sawson & myself. Playing was very hard as a strong sand storm raged all day, and necessitating the closing of tents made us very uncomfortable. Messrs. Lord and Gaston went out snake hunting and brought home a fine large one, which we ate for dinner and found delicious. Took walk with M. to retreat in afternoon. Dr. & Mr. G. returned at noon. Manuel promoted to first assistant cook in Herman's place. Labelling and cataloguing of specimens at night.

Wednesday, May 2

Work on Temple mound. In aft. Mr. Garlick drove the new mule to Tempe for mail, meat etc. and was accompanied by Mr. Lord. Yates arranged & photographed Guanacos-specimens, Mr. Gaston assisted Mr. Cushing in classifying Hornos, Cave Creek, Canopas & other collections and at night portion of Hornos was catalogued by Mr. Cushing, Gaston & myself. All out before breakfast playing tennis—which was attacked again at noon and evening with vigor. Mrs. C. & M. took drive out Sacaton road in aft. Mr. Garlick returned in evening alone, Mr. Lord having gone on to Phoenix for a few days.

Thursday, May 3

Arrangement and classification of remaining specimens this morning—Packing by Mr. Garlick & Ramon in forenoon; in aft. former went to Tempe to have mules shod, get mail etc. & returned with Mr. Lord. Yates took photos & made blue prints. Work on ruin I. Cataloguing at night of part of specimens classified to day, in which all took part, excepting Mr. Yates who printed photos. M. took drive with Mrs. Cushing while we play'd tennis & on his return she walked with me out to Temple.

Friday, May 4

Classification & cataloguing entirely finished this A.M. assisted by the ladies, Mr. Lord, & Mr. Gaston. Mr. Yates blue printing. Excavations continued on Temple Mound. After dinner I went with Mr. Garlick to Tempe for provisions, payment of April bills & to get hair cut. Made arrangements for purchasing barley enough to last while at Hemenway. Returned in time to play game of tennis with M. and Yates. Little rain in aft. Mr. Cushing much better.

Saturday, May 5

Packing—Preparing boxes for book packing. Dr. Ten Kate & suite returned in afternoon from reconnoissance trip to Gila. Mr. Yates went to Tempe in afternoon for mail etc. Little rain in spite of which walked with M. to retreat before tea.

Sunday, May 6

Dolores & Alvarez kept to assist Mr. C. & myself in the marking of specimen boxes which occupied the entire morning. Mr. Garlick and Dr. Wortman went very early to Phoenix returning about sunset. I immediately after dinner had horses (mules) saddled and went with M. for a long ride out Sacaton road. Started early to avoid visitors who are very troublesome on Sundays generally. Returned to find Mr. McClintock at Camp. Had game of tennis before tea and archery practice. Dr. succeeded in procuring two Pima skeletons at Phoenix. With M. made game of anagrams in eve.

Monday, May 7

Excavating still on Temple mound. Car arrived at Tempe for the transportation of collection to Salem.[334] Packing completed as far as practicable. Mr. C. assisted by Alvarez & Peralta finished labelling of boxes. Dr. Wortman & Mr. Lord drive to Tempe, former remaining—latter returning alone with ice etc.—Assisted M. in doing up packages of blue prints, also did up some for myself to be sent home and wrote letter to Mother. Had game of tennis in late afternoon, and a walk with M. to Temple after tea. Spent evening playing anagrams. Received order to finish mapping of Muertos.

Tuesday, May 8

Spent morning looking over old maps and arranging for work. After dinner went to ruin II and with assistance of Lord & Gaston made additions to map of same, completing the work after my return to Camp. First three loads of specimens were taken to Tempe by Mr. Garlick & Mexicans & packed in car. Alvarez & Dolorez at work on Temple mound where they found this afternoon in a niche in the wall of north(?) room an exquisitely carved & inlaid ring of shell & turquoise, the gem of the collection.[335] Went with M. before tea to retreat and spent evening with her in my tent where Mr. Yates joined us and our game of anagrams. Mr. Cushing dictated letter to Lieut. Gilman which I wrote out and copied.

Wednesday, May 9

Mr. Garlick with Ramon, Rafael & Peralta went with three more loads of specimens to Tempe in forenoon. At 1 [p.]m. Mercury at 98°. Spent morning receiving dictation & writing out notes of letter, making order for men & doing preliminary work on map of XXIII. In early afternoon did field work & finished after my return to camp. Mr. Yates photographing all afternoon. In evening went with Mr. Cushing to all ruins to bring in last of specimens remaining there and at night assisted him in classifying same. Dr. Wortman came to camp from Phoenix this evening where he has been for a couple of days. Joined M. and myself in my tent this evening where we had a game of anagrams.

Thursday, May 10

Gaston awoke me at 5 this morning and calling Alvarez we went to XXIV, the latter holding the umbrella, Gaston assisting in tape-line measuring, while I plotted, finishing field-work on same before breakfast and the entire map soon afterwards. M. spent all morning with me, writing up catalogue-cards from my notes. After dinner wrote to Mother, Ashley, and Houghton, as well as official letters. Mr. Cushing numbered the remaining collections that we brought in yesterday and until sunset we were occupied in cataloguing same. M. and I spent ev'g together as usual. Mr. C. and Mr. Garlick went to Los Hornos and Los Guanacos this ev'g where they secured 2 specimens of fire bowls—Dr. Wortman left in afternoon, to the regret of all in camp, & was driven to town by Dr. ten Kate, who returned in evening with mail etc.

Friday, May 11

Dr. ten Kate and Mr. Lord went to Sacaton soon after breakfast, to be gone a couple of days. I was up again at five o'clock to make plot of ruin XXII, with Gaston & Alvarez to assist in measuring. Finished details of map after returning to camp. M. spent morning with me writing out catalogue cards from my notes, and in afternoon again while Mr. Goodwin (who has just returned from trip East) made us a long visit. Walked with her before tea to retreat, and afterward we spent evening together playing our new game—anagrams—in which the others, being interested, took a small part. Am having a good deal of trouble with my eyes on account of reflected light on my mapping paper, and heat, which is daily increasing—mercury standing to-day at noon as 106° in the coolest spot in camp—which is my tent.

Saturday, May 12

In morning with Gaston assistance surveyed walls of temple and in af [Goodwin] (who has just returned from trip East) made us a long visit. [Repeated passage from day before: Walked with her before tea to retreat, and afterward we spent evening together playing our new game—anagrams—in which the others, being interested, took a small part. Am having a good deal of trouble with my eyes on account of reflected light on my mapping paper, and heat, which is daily increasing—mercury standing to-day at noon as 106 in the coolest spot in camp—which is my tent.]

Monday, May 14

In morn left for California.[336]

Wednesday, May 16

Surveyed Ruin XIX with Gaston's assistance.

Friday, May 18, 1888 [Final Entry]

Nearly finished map of Ruin XVIII assisted by Gaston & Dolores. Worked on east wall of Temple where post holes appear.

PART III

The Anthropological Career of Fred Hodge, 1889–1956

A Play in Three Acts

Act One: Washington, D.C., 1889–1918

On July 1, 1889, Fred Hodge joined the Smithsonian's Bureau of Ethnology as a stenographer with a starting annual salary of $1,000.[1] When he had left the Geological Survey thirty months before to become Frank Cushing's field secretary on the Hemenway Expedition, it was agreed that a place would be made for him in government science on his return. John Wesley Powell, director of both the survey and the bureau, kept the promise. For the next five years in the bureau Hodge was engaged almost entirely in clerical and editorial work, while also organizing and enlarging the library. He did not appear in the eleventh or twelfth annual reports (1890–92), and only briefly the following year. He did not go into the field again until 1895.

In 1890 Hodge published his inaugural article in anthropology, a brief account in *The American Anthropologist* of "A Zuni Foot-Race."[2] Cushing had told a version of the same sport in *My Adventures in Zuñi* in 1883, emphasizing its sacred nature, the relationship to planting and rain-gathering, and the excited involvement of the entire pueblo. While drawing on Cushing, Hodge's descriptive and highly colored telling of an event he probably saw in spring 1889 demonstrated good physical observation—runners' feet, betting among wives and families, horsemen, the rough ground—rather than attention to spiritual or ritual meaning. It was a modest but valuable contribution, and a creditable beginning to his hoped-for independent career. In 1893 he followed "Zuni Foot-Race" with the brief study of ancient Salado irrigation that Cushing had urged him to do—based, he pointed out, on observations and notes taken during the expedition.[3] In this piece he approached the canal system as the work of "ancient pueblo peoples" and, in the main, adopted Cushing's Zuni-derived notions—for example, river stones as "water-tamers" that were intended to urge the water toward dry fields. Estimating the canal system at about 150 miles, Hodge marveled at the patience and laborious industry of the ancient people of the Salt River valley: "Their canals are models for the modern farmer to imitate."[4]

While he was nearly invisible in official records, Hodge's chief assignment was Powell's "synonymy" of North American Indian tribes. For ten years Powell had intermittently put his bureau staff to work on the project, which he considered foundational to the new science of anthropology. In essence, it was a constantly updated, ever-expanding card catalogue of all the names historically applied to Indigenous groups. As Powell noted in the 1879 annual report of the bureau, "to follow any tribe of Indians through post-Columbian times is a task of no little difficulty. . . . The scholars of America have a great work before them."[5] Otis Tufton Mason (1838–1908), curator in the National Museum, had started such a catalogue as a personal project in 1873; Garrick Mallery (1831–94) of the bureau soon became actively involved as well. When James Mooney (1861–1921) arrived in Washington from Indiana in 1885, he had brought his personal catalogue of names. It was a turning point for the project, Hodge recalled:

> Mooney came into Washington, and he wasn't well received. He was a funny-looking little man, with his hair hanging down on his shoulders. Not very prepossessing. But he had this synonymy . . . that was a natural for this thing. The next was an account of all the treaties held with the Indians. And next came various bibliographies. These were popular things, you see, for public consumption. The public wouldn't stand these highly technical things. Major Powell was wise enough to know the public had to be served a lot of pap.[6]

For two decades Powell annually promised Congress the results of the synonymy, an undertaking that kept changing names: Dictionary of Indian Tribes, Dictionary of Tribal Synonymy, Tribal Synonymy of the American Indians, Cyclopedia of the American Indians. After his death it became *Handbook of American Indians North of Mexico* (1907, 1910). While every member of the bureau contributed to the project at some point, by 1890 Henry Wetherbee Henshaw (1850–1930), an ornithologist hired and trusted by Powell, had taken primary responsibility for the synonymy. Hodge became his assistant. It was a fortunate circumstance for a young man anxious to be recognized.[7] Henshaw served as right hand to Powell, was his intended successor as director of the bureau, and became a mentor to Hodge. Moreover, Henshaw was centrally positioned as editor (1889–93) of a new journal, *The American Anthropologist,* a respected board member of the Anthropological Society of Washington, and a prominent promoter of Powell's projects in the bureau. As political controversy over the Geological Survey intensified in the early nineties, Powell came to rely more on Henshaw to administer the bureau. But by then Henshaw's own health was beginning to fail, and in 1892 Powell sent him to California for a two-year recuperation. Two years later, Henshaw resigned and moved to Hawaii.[8] With Powell's distractions and Henshaw's departure, Hodge stepped in; he inherited the editorship of *The American Anthropologist* and major responsibility for the synonymy. These were the years when he began accumulating an enviable bibliographic knowledge focused on the Southwest. Additionally, he was serving as Powell's personal stenographer in preparing testimony to congressional committees:

> I worked with Powell night after night for weeks, in the Geological Survey, because he wanted to defend his case. He had to dictate his argument, and he was up before the committee making this inquiry in Congress every day.[9]

In these years Hodge called on Cushing for his Zuni knowledge: names, etymologies and spellings, histories. Unemployed and recuperating in western New York State, and working largely from memory, Cushing responded with equanimity and generosity to Hodge's requests. Gradually the two men reestablished a cautious but cordial relationship. By the time of Margaret and Fred's wedding in the fall of 1891, Cushing's health had begun to recover and he was reentering scientific society. As he told his California friend Eusebio Molera, he had come to appreciate his former secretary and new brother-in-law:

> I am glad to tell you that our little sister, Miss Margaret, is to be married to Mr. F. Webb Hodge, at the close of the first week in September [1891]. I am also completely reconciled to this event, because Mr. Hodge has worked hard in his new position in the Bureau of Ethnology, has in the two or three years which have elapsed since the engagement was announced changed from a boy to a manly and fine and exceedingly competent young fellow. He has worked faithfully for me in appreciation of the situation that, for Miss Magill's sake, I asked for him, and has been promoted already three times. His field work with the Expedition did more for him than I at one time conceived possible, and if for no other reason I would now do as you once asked me to—approve of him, if only because of his own and our little sister's continued happiness in their relationship to one another.[10]

For a time, Cushing could even joke with young editor Hodge about Frank's well-known florid writing style:

> In reference to those ever recurring *Caps* in my writing, you know my taste is old fashioned. I love to have my Gods, pagan or other, my Priests, Protopriests, Chiefs and their Places, Regions, and even Temples in the North, West, South, East, Upper and Under Worlds, and anything they have to do with here in the Midmost Place, *all* capitalized. Still if it is too unsightly, too troublesome, too much of an innovation, or if there be other strong reason for their elimination, do not spare your marks. Make a clean thing of it.[11]

The two men bonded, too, over antipathy to Cushing's successor as director of the Hemenway Expedition, Jesse Walter Fewkes. Cushing detested and distrusted Fewkes for what he perceived as his shallowness and presumption, and these feelings sometimes overrode his disappointment with Hodge.[12] For his part, Hodge wrote derisively of Fewkes: "Dr. Fewkes has gone off to Zuni again. Have you seen his [article on] 'Summer Ceremonials'? He doesn't seem to be setting the Bureau afire with his H. S. W. A. Ex papers!"[13] Asking Cushing for help in reviewing Fewkes's new *Journal of American Ethnology and Archaeology* for *The American Anthropologist*, Hodge redoubled his disdain:

> Dr. F. went to Zuñi some weeks ago, I learn, from Casa Grande and Salado Valley where he spent about a week in *conquering* the archaeology of the region. It will probably be in type before frost comes.[14]

Hodge's published critique of Fewkes's lack of language and misunderstandings of Zuni archaeological sites seemed informed and authoritative; but actually his remarks depended on the historical work of Bandelier, and even more on Cushing's private notes to him.[15] It marked one of his first published forays into Zuni matters—a small career stepping-stone.

Behind the scenes, though, Hodge was careful not to alienate Fewkes. His review of Fewkes's second volume of the *Journal*, which dealt with Hopi fieldwork, was gentler and generally appreciative.[16] Anxious to avoid Cushing, Fewkes now began turning to Hodge as a mediating voice and a well-positioned man of favors.[17] It was an astute move. By 1893 Hodge was curator of the Anthropological Society of Washington and held a key position on *The American Anthropologist*. In that year Fewkes managed to have an article in each quarterly issue of the journal. The two future directors of the Bureau of American Ethnology recognized that they had a specific thing in common: a thin and fragile anthropological résumé. They grew close because they sensed mutual need.[18]

At the same time Hodge's relationship to his brother-in-law frayed and finally snapped. Cushing returned from his upstate New York exile and rejoined the bureau in February 1892, hopeful of writing up the "Itinerary" of the expedition that Harris and Powell continued to urge upon him. For a year he vacillated between determination to do so and deep exasperation with Fewkes and the Hemenway circle.[19] At New Year 1893 Pilling told him to "publish, publish, publish," and he resolved once again to undertake the project.[20] He arranged to have Hodge paid to take his dictation in after-hours. Crucially, he would depend on both Fred's and Maggie's personal diaries—which he, however, considered the property of the expedition. By mid-February he was dictating to Hodge for hours at a time, rediscovering maps, notes, and plans, and finding he might be able to make "a very complete report" after all.[21]

But then, on March 18, 1893, Hodge balked. The diaries, both he and Margaret insisted, were their personal property and they refused further access by Cushing. Although the men continued working for a few weeks, their relationship became badly strained. Cushing stopped the itinerary project and never returned to it. It was his last effort for the Hemenway Expedition. Henceforth the Hodge-Cushing relationship would be little more than civil.

MAKING A NAME: CIBOLA, SIKYÁTKI, MESA ENCANTADA (1895–97)

After five years in the bureau, in 1895 Hodge began to take steps to augment his scientific standing, to move from bibliographic clerk to scientific contributor. Not surprisingly, his first move involved the continuing debate over the "Seven Cities of Cibola"—an issue that had been central to the Hemenway work at Zuni in 1888. His opportunity arose in the following way:

In 1892 George Parker Winship (1871–1952), an undergraduate student at Harvard, began a collection and translation project that became *The Coronado Expedition, 1540–1542*, published in 1896 in the *Fourteenth Annual Report of the Bureau of Ethnology*. Here Winship presented for the first time in English the essential documents of Francisco Vázquez de Coronado's travels in the Spanish Southwest, including the original Spanish text and translation of Pedro de Castañeda's "Account of the Expedition to Cibola."[22] Though he was young, Winship's was a pioneering accomplishment, encouraged and assisted by such Boston literati as Edward Channing, Justin Winsor, and Henry Haynes. It raised the profile of southwestern Spanish studies, once again bringing attention to the issue of Cibola/Zuni and the identities of the Zuni villages at the time of contact. Hodge took notice. Introduced to the young scholar by Fewkes, he edited Winship's work for the bureau and received in turn generous citation credit; in particular, Hodge's article "The First Discovered City of Cibola," a brief 1895 contribution to the question of the Zuni villages, was noted in Winship's sources. Cushing was barely mentioned.[23]

"The First Discovered City of Cibola" was Hodge's 1895 declaration of intellectual independence. As he well knew, Bandelier and Cushing had begun collaborating on the problem of the "Seven Cities" in 1883, and they considered that they had decisively established the identity of the Spaniards' "Cibola" region with Zuni. In the process they were consciously modeling a new form of collaborative scholarship. Drawing on their combined historical, archaeological, and ethnographic work, between 1885 and 1890 the two friends had suggested—in articles, lectures, and letters to one another—close variations on a list of the seven cities. Cushing in particular saw the seven cities question as a central and potentially popular aspect of the Hemenway Expedition, possibly equivalent to the famous work of William H. Prescott a generation earlier. As he explained to Mary Hemenway:

> From the fact that these Seven Cities of Cibola have been discussed and disputed about historically for more than two of our generations, great promise will be given to our works by virtue of the thoroughly triumphant way in which they will set all matters of question at rest, as well as by reason of the romantic nature of what has come down to us regarding the Discovery and Conquest of these Cities of Cibola. We shall be able to write, with the aid of Bandelier's documents—which increase month by month—with the aid of our excavations of ancient streets, homes, and places of assembly, of our observations and superb collections,—for the arts of ancient Cibola were superb—*and, more than all, with the aid of my investigations of the Descendants of the Current Cibolans—the Zunis*—to write a story and a Conquest almost rivaling in interest at least, the story and conquest of Mexico by Prescott.[24]

As indicated in Cushing's hyperbole, a premise of the expedition—and specifically of the Zuni/Cibola question—was the reliability of Native traditional knowledge as historical fact. When combined with archaeology and archival documents, Bandelier and Cushing agreed, Indigenous narrative could triangulate a true picture of the southwestern protohistorical period. It is striking, then, that in his 1895 article not only did Hodge contradict Bandelier's conclusion about the village in which the Black guide Estevan had been killed in 1539—arguing for Hawikku rather than Kyaki:ma—but he did so by questioning the trustworthiness of Indigenous knowledge in general. Bandelier, he claimed, had misread the evidence by placing too much credence on Native stories—which was precisely Cushing's methodological forte. Although Hodge had himself barely visited Hawikku, he appealed to archaeological and geographical evidence within the Spanish record against Native accounts. He repeatedly called the Zunis unreliable.

Hodge was fully conscious, even proud, of the challenge he was raising to Cushing and Bandelier. Writing to Haynes, he accused Bandelier of "slipshod" work: "It seems to me he hurries too much for an investigator, and I think with you that he is most influenced by his latest discovered authority." He told Haynes that he was "preparing a little paper on 'The First Discovered city of Cibola' and wish[ed] to show the untrustworthiness of tradition as historical or scientific evidence"—and then mentioned Cushing.[25]

Hodge's article was a deliberate and presumptuous rebuke to two mentors by a man who had done no fieldwork of his own. Neither responded publicly or, as far as we know, privately. By 1895 Cushing had given up the Hemenway Expedition and southwestern work and was moving on to Florida, and Bandelier had been living in South America since 1892. But Fewkes did respond to his friend: "I have always thought that Cushing either manufactured or was deceived himself when he said that he had legendary evidence that the pueblo on the Thunder Mt. Foothills [Kyaki:ma] was the site of the tragedy [of Estevan's death]."[26] Hodge must have been pleased with the support—and the criticism of Cushing. The former stenographer was staking what would become a long-running claim to Hawikku.[27]

Fewkes encouraged the growing distance between Hodge and Cushing by promoting the piecemeal descriptive work that was becoming his and Hodge's métier. "I wish we could have a dozen ethnologists in the field," he wrote Hodge, "working on the objective side—collecting facts with detailed descriptions and exoteric minutiae. But if we stick to it, *leaving Ethnological pyrotechnics to those who like that sort of thing*, we are sure to fathom the pueblo ritual sooner or later." For good measure he took field ethnographer Matilda Stevenson to task too, advising Hodge that "only by discussion can we get at truth and as long as personality has no place in discussion it is a very good thing."[28]

Exchanged between men who had little imagination themselves, such remarks are revealing. Fewkes and Hodge were embracing a professional style that featured incremental growth in reputation through frequent, small-scale publications of close, factual ("exoteric") observations. To critics—of whom Fewkes had many, Hodge few—these might amount to plodding, derivative careers, but their praxis had one merit that the "pyrotechnics" of the erratic Cushing lacked: predictable, steady output.[29] The effect was that their names appeared frequently in print.[30] From an institutional perspective of this stage of American anthropology, this brought its own rewards.

In 1895, too, a series of events brought Fewkes and Hodge into direct collaboration for the first time. Mary Hemenway had died the preceding March, and her will specified that Fewkes might continue the expedition work after her death; for some months Fewkes apparently made his office in the Mt. Vernon Street home. But her son Augustus soon became disillusioned and impatient. He arranged to move the twenty-five-thousand-piece expedition collection from Salem to the Peabody Museum at Harvard—first as a loan, later as a gift. In late summer 1895, Frederic Ward Putnam, writing to Franz Boas, caught the drift of things:

> Between us confidentially I think there is a little drawing apart between Mr. Hemenway and the Doctor [Fewkes]; and the Doctor is looking to the Bureau for his future. He told me that Powell wanted him, and he thought likely he should close with the Hemenway work as soon as he had finished the arrangement of the collection. You understand the Doctor and you know his methods. I need not say anything more. I only know from what he said that he is expecting a permanent position in the Bureau.[31]

Fewkes had known as early as January 1895 that the Hemenway estate was about to curtail the expedition's work. He began planning.[32] He announced in May that he would complete installation of Hemenway Expedition materials in the Peabody Museum and then move to Washington. As he told Hodge in idiosyncratic Latin: "Expedition Hemenwayamus mortius est sed non ethnologia Fewkesiana spero."[33] Before resigning, though, he managed to lobby successfully for $1,150 of summer fieldwork with the bureau. Spurred on by Matilda Stevenson's recent ethnography of Zia—the first thorough study of a Rio Grande pueblo—he hoped to study the Zia snake ceremonies "so carefully that a mustard seed will not escape us."[34]

Fewkes's lobbying paid off, but not as he had anticipated. Smithsonian Secretary Langley employed him for the summer with reserved bureau funds to collect archaeological materials, "especially pertaining to so-called cliff houses," for the National Museum. It was to be a trial run. Fewkes decided to focus on the five-hundred-year-old First Mesa ruins of Awat'ovi and Sikyátki.[35] At the request of George Brown Goode (1851–96), Assistant Secretary in charge of the National Museum, Hodge joined Fewkes in midsummer at Sikyátki. (Hodge was assigned to take Goode's brother-in-law, James S. Judd, into the field to distract him from the recent loss of his wife.)

Back in the field for the first time since the 1889 Hemenway collapse, Hodge dug avidly in the prehistoric burials: "He was constantly at the excavations, and the majority of the beautiful specimens were taken out of the graves by him," Fewkes reported.[36] Hodge was in heaven: "turning out pottery every fifteen minutes," he told Powell's assistant, W. J. McGee (1853–1912); "the cemeteries are in the sand drifts, are easily excavated, and the burials occur from a few inches to 8 ft. below the surface."[37]

When the Sikyátki collection came to the Smithsonian, Margaret painted watercolors of dozens of the polychrome pots in rich color for Fewkes's report of 1898. Her drawings were the first published images of the stunning designs that would later be associated, controversially, with the "Sikyátki revival" and Hopi-Tewa (Corn clan) potter Nampeyo (1859–1942).[38] Powell was pleased that the bureau was reasserting its presence in pueblo country, and Langley welcomed the impressive additions to his museum. (Nothing was said of skeletal remains.) Having begun with leftover appropriations for a summer's work, Fewkes was now transitioning to the Smithsonian; he would remain with the Bureau of American Ethnology until his retirement in 1928. But it was Hodge whose fingers scrabbled out most of the pots.

Hodge followed up the weeks at Sikyátki by moving on to Oraibi, Zuni, Laguna, Acoma, and his first visits to Rio Grande pueblos in search of "historical and traditional data" on clan names and linguistic terms for the always-growing synonymy. It was a lightning trip in the old survey tradition, and although he would frequently reference this fleeting exposure as part of his pueblo bona fides, Hodge sensed the superficiality: "We are now looking for new worlds to conquer," he told McGee as he requested more funds and support for an additional "four or five months" (which were denied). Reconnaissance of the pueblo world, he advised, was no longer enough.[39]

If Sikyátki and Awat'ovi reintroduced Hodge to southwestern fieldwork, in 1897 Mesa Encantada—Enchanted Mesa, or Katsímo (Kadzima)—two and a half miles northeast of Acoma pueblo, provided Hodge with a modest but lasting taste of notoriety. While visiting Acoma in September 1895 Hodge had collected sherds around the base of the huge, striking red sandstone mesa, and even halfheartedly tried to climb it. He intended to test the truth of an Acoma legend, variously recounted by publicist Charles F. Lummis a few years before, which told of an ancient people who had inhabited the mesa top. In one of Lummis's versions, "The [Acoma] pueblo was once situated on top of the Mesa Encantada. . . . Four hundred years ago or so, a frightful storm swept away the enormous leaning rock which served as a ladder, and the patient people—who were away at the time—had to build a new city." An inveterate storyteller and popularizer, Lummis presented another version in *A New Mexico David* (1891) which concluded: "Scientific expeditions have exhausted the ingenuity of civilization to scale the Rock of Katzimo, and recover its archaeological treasures, but all in vain. The natives shun it, believing it accursed." Yet a third version involved a landslide that had cut off the women and children on top, leaving them to starve. Hodge could not resist the challenge, and although an elder at Acoma whom he interviewed had ridiculed the stories, he determined to return the next summer to climb what Lummis had anointed "the noblest single rock in America."[40]

But another party had also been reading Lummis. Doubting the accounts, in July 1897 William Libbey Jr. (1855–1927), an accomplished explorer and professor of geology and natural history at Princeton University, took a small party, including a journalist of the *Brooklyn Eagle* newspaper, to the mesa. "Equipped with the apparatus of the U.S. Life Saving Service," Libbey shot a strong rope from the service over the mesa and hauled himself up, seated rather awkwardly on a bosun's chair. After a two-hour survey of the sixteen-acre summit Libbey came down and claimed to have found "not the slightest trace" that a human foot had ever touched the top. The widely respected explorer immediately telegraphed his news to the world: Lummis's stories were nonsense.[41]

Predictably, Lummis was furious. Hodge, who had been scooped, felt his own reputation potentially impugned by the Princeton professor. Lummis wanted action; with McGee's blessing, Hodge complied. Fully prepared this time with rope and extension ladder, and accompanied by popular Pasadena photographer Adam Clark Vroman (1856–1916), Hodge hastened to Acoma and scaled the cliff. In a stay of forty-eight hours in September he found several fragments of pottery, a couple of stone ax-heads, a flint arrow-point, and part of a shell bracelet. In contrast to Zuni, it seems, this time the Native stories, via Lummis, were reliable (or at least useful) for Hodge. Descending, he announced that the mesa had indeed been inhabited at some point—confirmation of the Acoma legend and vindication of Lummis. He rushed over to the Laguna telegraph station and tapped out to Lummis: "Just returned Enchanted Mesa; found evidence former occupancy." Sixty years later Hodge still gleefully recalled that "Lummis must have hit the skies when he got that. He started in. And if he didn't play Libbey to the queen's taste, you know!"[42]

Today it is generally agreed that Libbey was right: nobody ever lived on Enchanted Mesa. But no matter. Mainly through his own exertions, Hodge's adventure story circulated widely—in *Century, Harper's,* Lummis's *Land of Sunshine,* and elsewhere—sometimes with Vroman's photographs of the exploring party on the mesa and their small artifact assemblage.[43] The controversy also founded a long friendship with Lummis. In a sketch of Hodge the following year, the Californian (acting as press agent) celebrated Hodge's "careful documentary study, safe mental attitude, and a valuable course of field training" that were making him one of the "earnest and well-equipped young men rising up" to be the next generation of "Authorities on the Southwest."[44] Lummis and his daughter Turbesé ("Sun") visited at Garrett Park (fig. 20), and when Lummis famously met with President Theodore Roosevelt at the White House in 1901, he relaxed with Fred and Margaret at their favorite Pennsylvania Avenue restaurant: Harvey's Ladies' and Gentlemen's Oyster Saloon.[45]

The Enchanted Mesa adventure became the early foundation of Hodge's status as an authority on the Indigenous Southwest. Mary Austin relates in her 1932 autobiography, *Earth Horizon,* that when she first arrived in Los Angeles around 1900, it was not Lummis but Hodge she wanted to meet: Hodge "told her the thing she wanted most to know, the way of collecting and recording Indian affairs." Forget the strange and unusual, he advised: "fix on the usual, the thing that is always done; the way of the tribe; the way of the average; the way and the why of it."[46]

Hodge and the mysterious lost people of Mesa Encantada soon entered southwestern folklore. In 1903 popular travel writer John L. Stoddard included a long account of the dispute in his published lectures on the Southwest. Willa Cather adapted the legend in her 1909 short story "The Enchanted Bluff."[47] And as we have seen, six decades later Hodge was still enjoying his memorable moment of fame.

First Interlude: Under the Vines and Maples of Garrett Park

After Fred and Margaret were married in September 1891, they soon moved to a new development in the Maryland countryside. Garrett Park was the investment brainchild of Henry N. Copp, Fred's boyhood teacher and first employer. The leafy suburb along Rock Creek was platted out in 1888 on the Metropolitan Branch of the Baltimore and Ohio Railroad running north out of Washington; Garrett Park Station (now on the Metro Red Line) would see generations of waving hellos and goodbyes among young government professionals and their families.[48]

According to latter-day memories, life in early Garrett Park was idyllic. Most of the land lay in "forested isolation," having been bypassed by roads and trolley lines over the years. Copp dreamed of a cultural colony, a kind of Chautauqua community, just a half hour's train ride into the country at a safe remove from urban disease and

Figure 20. Fred, Margaret, Paul, and Winifred Hodge, with Turbesé Lummis, Garrett Park, 1901. Photo by Charles Lummis. Courtesy of the Southwest Museum Research Library, Autry Museum. #N43323.

crowding. Mrs. Jason Defandorf, an original resident who died at age ninety-eight in 1961, recalled it as an "old English village" with street names from Sir Walter Scott novels—a perfect middle landscape:

> *The men read their papers and visited on the train, stopped for the mail, found dinner waiting at home and were ready to take solid comfort under their own vines and maple trees by six o'clock in the evening.*[49]

No place could have been more distant from the dusty tents of Camp Hemenway—or downtown Washington. Fred and Margaret bought an acre for $1,000 and decamped to the suburb. (His sisters, who were in real estate, moved in down the street.) They began building a spacious, elm-shaded home at 11013 Montrose Avenue, surrounded by woods and only a half mile from the train station—a residence still known today in brokerage brochures as "The Hodge House, loved by generations of Garrett Park residents."[50] *On June 24, 1892, their first child, Margaret Cecelia, was born after a difficult delivery—"quite lusty, with beautiful square hands and eyes tending to blueness," as her proud uncle Frank commented on his first sight of her.*[51] *Sadly, the child lived only two years. An ivy twig from her grave in Washington's Oak Hill Cemetery grew to cover the main chimney of the home on Montrose.*[52] *A son, Paul Frederick (1894–1948), arrived just a month before his sister died. Two more sisters followed: Winifred Thornton in 1898 and Emlyn Magill in 1905.*

Garrett Park was recalled as a children's paradise:

> *Before automobile days they could go everywhere with nothing to fear. Only a few teams passed over the county road daily. Mr. Kelly's twenty cows going back and forth to their pasture in the "old chestnut" field were eagerly watched by the small boys from the safe vantage of the high banks.*[53]

Hodge reported to a friend in 1900 that Paul and Winifred simply "lived in the woods in the back of the house." The town council, which he joined in 1903, resisted electrification and sewers; the Hodges used an outhouse and oil lamps, with coal and four fireplaces for heating. They had, Emlyn remembered, a huge icebox and the first Victrola in town; on weekends Fred came home with a new stack of records from Group's Music Store in the District. All weekend "the house was just full of people who came to hear the records."[54]

It was also an Episcopalian world. Reverend David Barr, a popular preacher from St. Luke's in Smithfield, Virginia, became the first rector in 1897. Barr had officiated for Fred and Margaret in 1891, and when the time came he did the same for Winifred. When a Bahá'í group moved into town, Margaret was the curious one: "My mother was the kind of person who would look into this, get us out of her hair, and she looked up everything she could find about the Bahais," Emlyn recollected. The Hodges installed a tennis court by the house, near his large rose garden. They raised and showed rabbits and chickens. Margaret took art lessons from William Henry Holmes (1846–1933), the close friend and bureau archaeologist who was also a superb watercolorist; she exhibited at the Washington Water Color Club annual shows and sketched all over town.[55] *Emlyn told the author: "We all saw that she had an unobstructed room and could paint to her heart's content."*[56] *She drew covers for magazines, including* The Craftsman.

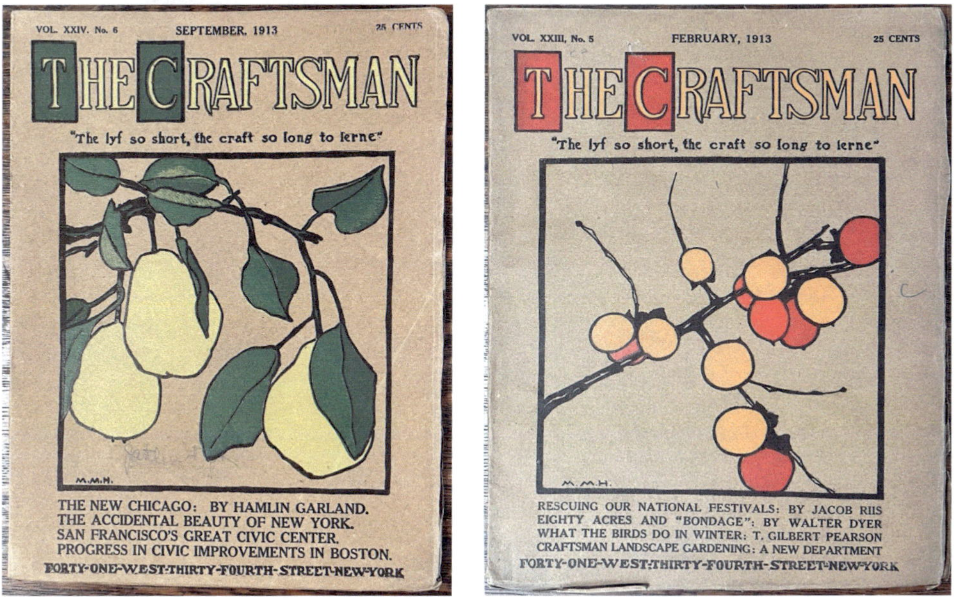

Figure 21. Cover art by Margaret Magill for *The Craftsman Magazine*, February and September issues, 1913.

In 1912 Hodge was elected mayor of Garrett Park, but the following year he and Margaret decided to move back into Washington for a more convenient social life—he was by then ethnologist-in-charge of the bureau. They entertained on Sunday evenings at the new home at 2312 Nineteenth Street Northwest for fellow anthropologists, including Alice Fletcher (with whom Emily Cushing lived for twelve years after Frank's death), Walter Hough, and Sylvanus Morley. Eighty years later Emlyn pictured her father at these events as "terribly insecure" and jealous of her mother, who had the charm of a "natural hostess." At the Sunday open houses, "when people would notice my mother, that's when it showed."

THE DINWIDDIE AFFAIR AND THE DEATH OF CUSHING, 1896–1900

There was one stumble along Hodge's steady career path: an ugly event of 1896–97 that revealed his lasting jealousy and dislike of his brother-in-law. At the 1893 World's Fair Cushing had become close with Robert Stewart Culin (1858–1929) of Philadelphia, where Culin was director of the University Museum. Virtually the same age, the two collaborated for several years on comparative studies of games and other subjects. The Culins and the Cushings—Helen and Stewart, Emily and Frank—remained friends for the rest of Cushing's life.[57] Through Culin and Daniel Garrison Brinton (1837–99), in 1895 Frank entered the small anthropological circle of Philadelphia, which included Dr. William Pepper (1843–98). Provost of the University of Pennsylvania and a powerful social presence in the city, Pepper was deeply interested in archaeology; he was also a respected physician who counted among his patients both Cushing and philanthropist Phoebe Apperson Hearst (1842–1919). Pepper and Hearst had established what her recent biographer has

Figure 22. Margaret Magill Hodge, 1918. Author's collection.

called a "power-working relationship": he advised her on becoming a major archaeological collector and museum founder—both unusual ambitions for even an extremely wealthy woman at the time.[58] Thus came about in 1895–96 her sponsorship of the Pepper-Hearst Expedition to Tarpon Springs and Key Marco on the west coast of Florida, to be directed by Cushing.[59]

Hearst's archaeological enterprise was Cushing's last, controversial success. In two short seasons he produced remarkable results and unique shared collections for the Bureau of American Ethnology and Philadelphia's University Museum. John Wesley Powell visited the Key Marco site in early 1896 and pronounced Cushing's discovery of "The Bayou People" a "work of genius" that was of "world importance" for anthropology.[60] Once again Cushing struggled to produce a final report on his explorations, and his relations with Hearst were soon marred by disputes over salary and division of the collections. Today, though, his work is recognized as a baseline for understanding the prehistory of the Gulf Coast region.[61]

Enter William Dinwiddie (1867–1934), "ethno-photographer" of the bureau. While photographing some of the Florida specimens back in Washington, he accused Cushing of faking a painting on a sun shell and possibly altering other artifacts.[62] He took his concerns to Hodge, for whom he had previously worked.[63] Hodge promptly added, questionably, that Cushing had also faked a turquoise mosaic toad from Los Muertos in order to impress Edward S. Morse and Mary Hemenway. (Although Hodge's own expedition diary does not support this allegation, he would repeat it years later to Emil Haury.)[64] Dinwiddie went so far as to write directly to Augustus Hemenway with the request that he try to substantiate the allegations:

> Mr. F. W. Hodge of the Bureau is one of the men who examined the shell in question and pronounced it a spurious specimen; he also related a definite story in regard to the jeweled frog. . . . It must be said for Mr. Hodge that his peculiarly delicate family relations have kept him silent all these years, and now with a tenure of office to preserve (much official intimidation has been exercised) it will be extremely difficult for him to talk, except before the appropriate investigating committee.[65]

Fewkes and Bureau staffer Joseph D. McGuire (1842–1916) added their weight to the accusations, causing an uproar at the Smithsonian. Cushing noted:

> There has been a conspiracy here—which has ended by creating the worst scientific scandal we have ever known. My integrity has been distinctly questioned by men who professed friendship with me until the last. . . . The Bureau itself—its chiefs Major Powell and Professor [W. J.] McGee—are jeopardized.[66]

The "scandal" lasted for months into 1897 and threatened to end up in the newspapers. In the end Powell and the Smithsonian leadership, as well as Frederic Ward Putnam (1839–1915), director of Harvard's Peabody Museum of Archaeology and Ethnology (where the toad artifact still resides), rallied around Cushing, and the charges were found to be baseless. Cushing was cleared and Dinwiddie was summarily fired. Washington Matthews observed: "So after all the hub-bub the only one to suffer as a result of 'the Cushing slander' is poor little Dinwiddie, with his wife and children, he was only a catspaw for more designing men."[67] Cushing confronted Fewkes, who blamed Hodge. Cushing believed Fewkes: "From first to last he has been deceived by my former secretary Mr. Hodge—who told him among other like falsehoods that to his personal knowledge I had made the [Los Muertos] relic in question," Cushing reported to Putnam.[68]

Recent students of the affair concur that Cushing was wrongly accused.[69] But as he struggled unsuccessfully to organize the Key Marco collections and write a complete report on the Florida expedition, the Dinwiddie-Hodge-Fewkes accusations shadowed his remaining years. In March 1897 Powell and Putnam made a last-ditch appeal to Augustus Hemenway to give Cushing access to the Hemenway Expedition materials for the final Hemenway report. The "Dinwiddie affair" almost certainly was a factor in Hemenway's absolute refusal.[70]

Cushing soldiered on for two years (1898–1900) of fieldwork with Powell in Maine, but a year before his death he expressed to Culin his utter bafflement:

> McGuire is most friendly again. . . . But isn't [it strange] that he should have been so disaffected for so long? Isn't it strange altogether that Hodge, who got his start from me (I have just seen a list of books and studies I recommended to him in the beginning); that Fewkes, who had all my mss—the most important being my "Itinerary of Excavations" of the Hemenway Expedition—in which I told minutely how all Pueblo

finds were to be definitely located by surface indications . . . , and who was thus enabled with ease to become the "Schliemann of America," and again that McGuire who got his archaeologic inspiration and his first lessons in stone-working (as acknowledged by old letters I still have from him regarding my visit to him at his Ellicott City home in 1877)! Isn't it strange and sad too as well as absurd that they should all dispute my authority, and should have questioned and insinuated so much as to the authenticity in the very *source* of their own knowledge? You see I have taken you into my confidence quite unnecessarily. But still these matters may as well be matters of record outside of the papers I personally hold, and moreover I like *you* to know of them anyway.[71]

On April 7, 1900, Cushing swallowed a fishbone during dinner at his Washington home. The bone caused a puncture of the cardial orifice of the stomach and internal bleeding; he passed away in a hospital three days later. Death, after years of physical suffering, suddenly ended a brilliant, controversial career. "From the time that we first went together to Zuñi until the day of his death," Powell said at the memorial service, "he was my companion and friend, and I loved him as a father loves his son." Washington Matthews deplored the loss to anthropology of his irreplaceable knowledge. Culin credited him with stimulating work in Philadelphia and offered a final tribute: "Living in the world and of the world he was utterly disregardful of self. His spirit strayed full often. Even now I think of him, not as dead, but only reunited to that wild brotherhood to whom his heart went out."[72] Hodge, who had known him most intimately, did not speak at the memorial. Rather, he ambivalently advised Lummis to be gentle in his obituary of Cushing in *Land of Sunshine*:

> I would prepare a complete account for you if it were proper that I should do so, but I scarcely think it is. Please be lenient, my dear Lummis; no further harm can be done and I would rather have the good (which you saw more clearly than I) live after him than the (~~bad~~) evil.[73]

A "committee of well-known anthropologists" guaranteed subscriptions for publishing Cushing's long-delayed Zuni folktales, originally recorded by Rufus Leighton at Mrs. Hemenway's Casa Ramona summer home fourteen autumns before. The stories had been hauled in a trunk through Camps

Augustus, Hemenway, and Cibola and elsewhere for years. Now Hodge had them. He edited the volume, which appeared in 1901 with an introduction by Powell—one of the Major's last writings. Emily held the copyright and received the proceeds.[74]

BUILDING A NATIONAL PROFILE, 1897–1902

The death of Cushing accentuates the fact that Hodge's early career in Washington coincided with the passing of the first generation of the Bureau of Ethnology. When Powell lost control of the Geological Survey in 1893, he retreated to his bureau and began a decade of personal decline. Henshaw, his intended successor, moved away in 1894 and was replaced by McGee—a minimally educated but ambitious and arrogant acolyte who had just moved over from the survey. But the greater loss to Powell in those years was the death of Pilling in 1895. Hodge replaced him for a time as chief clerk. Garrick Mallery and James Owen Dorsey (1848–1895), two of Powell's bureau intimates from the earliest days, also passed away in the winter of 1894–95. The brilliant George Brown Goode, Langley's valued National Museum administrator who had served three Smithsonian secretaries since 1873, died suddenly in 1896; he was only 45. That year, too, army lieutenant and Apache ethnographer John Gregory Bourke succumbed at age 50, while army surgeon and Navaho ethnographer Washington Matthews died in 1905. Walter J. Hoffman was gone in 1899 at age 54. To be sure, others soldiered on—James Mooney (1861–1921), Matilda Stevenson (1849–1915), Albert Gatschet (1832–1907), and John N. B. Hewitt (1859–1937)—but none had participated in the camaraderie of the original bureau.

Hodge's annual salary increased by 50 percent from 1894 to 1899 ($1,600 to $2,500). He gained the confidence of both McGee and Samuel P. Langley, a lonely and reticent bachelor with few friends.[75] Beyond the Smithsonian, too, Hodge's star rose with the Anthropological Society of Washington and its journal, *The American Anthropologist.* After Henshaw left as editor in 1893, Hodge joined the new editorial committee and remained on it for the next five years, contributing book reviews, obituaries, and bibliographic notes.[76] In 1898 the society transformed its journal into a national organ of communication for anthropologists. Appointed secretary and managing editor of the new journal (renamed, at his suggestion, simply *American*

Anthropologist),[77] he now worked closely with Franz Boas (1858–1942) in New York and maintained constant communication with every major figure in the field. Hodge seemed to know everyone. His editing experience, going back to his days with Henry Copp, proved invaluable; and like Boas, he was indefatigable. He coaxed and gathered in articles for each issue and conferred with Boas on every aspect of the journal, from the size of pages and typeface to the quality of paper, from length of articles and cost of illustrations to the number of offprints for contributors. The new editorial board was impressive and broadly inclusive, to be sure, but it was the workaholics Hodge and Boas who produced the new *Anthropologist.*

The new national journal and, in 1902, the creation of the American Anthropological Association were major indicators that at the turn of the twentieth century the institutional structures of anthropology in the country were in flux, creating opportunities for both advancement and misstep.[78] Under McGee's lax and rudderless administration, the Bureau of American Ethnology was approaching stillwater,[79] with Powell's vigor faded, his projects lagging, and only piecemeal initiatives—such as Fewkes's work in the Southwest. Langley and Powell were old and cherished friends, but the Smithsonian secretary detested and distrusted McGee. So when the Major died in September 1902, the situation finally exploded into controversy. Within a year McGee was ejected.[80]

As we have seen, for years Langley had been pushing Powell and McGee to produce even a partial "Dictionary of Indian Tribes"—the always-promised synonymy—to mollify Congress. To little avail. Within two months of his old friend's death, Langley decided that the time had come to act, and he had in mind the man who might get the job done: Fred Hodge.

Hodge and Langley were no strangers. The secretary had transferred Hodge over to his own offices at the Smithsonian in February 1901 as assistant in charge of the office and curator of international exchanges.[81] He stayed there four years. It was a bureaucratic, largely clerical position, but it placed Hodge in proximity to Langley and Assistant Secretary Richard Rathbun (1852–1918)—the power center of the Smithsonian. Many tasks were mundane, such as ordering rugs, curtains, and portraits for the regents' meeting room, installing new elevators, hiring messengers, or recommending salary increases for minor employees—even, it seems, contemplating a statue of James Smithson:

> [Hodge:] One of the watchmen recently informed me that many foreign visitors ask to see a statue or portrait of Smithson in order that they may know what the founder of the Institution looked like, and seem surprised that nothing of the sort is on view.
>
> [Langley:] What would you suggest?[82]

Hodge found the period in Langley's office unpleasant and frantic because he was also expected to continue with the synonymy. Langley began to rely on him (and avoid McGee) for advice on BAE research; internal correspondence suggests that Hodge spoke with special favor of Fewkes and Holmes. Then, six weeks after Powell's death Langley formalized Hodge's assignment to the future *Handbook*:

> In accordance with the request of Mr. W. H. Holmes, chief of the Bureau of American Ethnology, and my letter of this date, you are authorized to absent yourself from the institution at one o'clock daily during the present year for the more expeditious preparation of the urgent publication of the Dictionary of Indian Tribes of which Mr. Holmes desires you to assume effective editorship.[83]

The synonymy was now directly in Langley's sight, and for the next three years he took personal interest in it. A week after instructing Hodge, Langley described to Holmes, the new BAE chief, his vision of a two-volume alphabetical handbook under Hodge's editorship. He wanted it out soon, and he expected the entire bureau to cooperate.[84]

ANTHROPOLOGY'S EDITOR, 1902–1910

Langley probably intended the *Handbook* to be a summing-up of Powell's bureau. "A very narrow way of looking at it," Hodge thought. "And showing that he had no idea what ethnology was or the Bureau of Ethnology was about. I don't think he would have cared if the work of the Bureau had been brought to a close then."[85] But by 1902 what had begun as a card catalogue had grown into a vast and enticing body of knowledge. Langley came to grasp the difference, and he saw the politics in it too: "for untechnical work which we hope to get Congressmen to read, it might be better for the immediate purpose to suppress the synonymy altogether, or make it a subordinate feature," he instructed Hodge. "I must be understood to mean not a dictionary of proper names, but a dictionary of Indians and Indian tribes."[86] In fact it was Langley's decision to move from linguistic stock to alphabetical ordering, and he insisted that the broad range of topics be accessible to amateurs—that is, Congress.[87] And, despite Hodge's claim that the secretary foresaw the demise of the bureau, there is some evidence that Langley saw the *Handbook* as its continuing justification. He stated at one point that he wanted a "succinct summary of the Bureau's work in the past, and a promise of its future usefulness."[88]

Still, Langley underestimated the complexity and time-consuming labor of commissioning and editing hundreds of contributions, and his frustration with the *Handbook* grew apace over the next three years. In a moment of exasperation, in late 1904, he exploded to Rathbun:

> From our talk this morning about the Dictionary of Indian Tribes, I realize for the first time that it is almost impossible that the object with which I started it (viz: the preparation of a work which would be primarily, not solely, an abstract of what had already been accomplished by the Bureau, to lay in the form of a hand-book before each Member of Congress at the *last* year's session, and to correct a feeling that great sums were expended on matters of interest only to professional men), could be fulfilled even if another year's time were given. It seems to me as though it has passed away from my primary object into the preparation of a more or less original treatise, demanding the slow labors of individual specialists, and I feel that if I had understood the course that this was to follow, I would not have undertaken it two years ago at all.[89]

A few months later, when Holmes informed him that only the first half of the *Handbook* was ready for printing, Langley again vented his deep disappointment with the entire project:

> I have your letter of the twenty-fourth. I need not enlarge upon the regret I have already expressed that the Dictionary of Indian Tribes has been undertaken in a manner which I had never contemplated. I had understood that it was to be begun in the early part of 1902, with the expectation of

preparing it on such a scale that it could be presented to Congress within a year, but in fact it is now only partly done after three years have elapsed.[90]

In the end Langley would never see even half of the *Handbook*. Preoccupied and frequently absent from Washington with his experiments on flight, he had not realized that his trusted accountant, William Karr, was embezzling tens of thousands of dollars from the Smithsonian. The Karr scandal, discovered in June 1905, blighted the remainder of the secretary's life: humiliated and demoralized, he refused any further salary, suffered two major strokes, and died in February 1906.

The *Handbook of American Indians North of Mexico* was arguably the greatest editorial accomplishment of Hodge's life. He estimated that he gave eleven years to the project, often working late into the night at the Smithsonian and at home in Garrett Park. "The museum man's Bible," as the two volumes came to be called, brought together not only more than two decades of bureau work but the current knowledge of a new generation of anthropologists—in Boston, New York, Chicago, and Berkeley—mostly trained by Putnam and Boas. Beside Hodge, who wrote dozens of the articles, rewrote many others, and proofread them all, the major bureau contributors were Holmes, Mooney, and Cyrus Thomas (1825–1910). But as historian Virginia Noelke noted, "the list of contributors resembles a roll-call of professional and amateur anthropologists in America" at the beginning of the century. Alfred Louis Kroeber (1876–1960) in California was paid one dollar an hour; the young John Reed Swanton (1873–1958)—a Boas student involved in his mentor's linguistic work and just beginning a long career in Washington—told Boas that he could only work for him at night. Washington Matthews was "humiliated" at the notion of working for ten dollars per thousand words, he told Hodge, and preferred to work for nothing on "your dictionary."[91]

In the end it was Hodge, though, who produced the *Handbook*. "Whatever contributions any of us made . . . are incidental to a work which remains a great monument to the industry and intelligent handling of its editor," Swanton wrote.[92] Hodge described the many-years-long process this way:

> Every week we had our contributors, those in Washington, the National Museum, the Bureau, and so on, meet in Holmes' office and we'd discuss

> the articles that had been turned in. I remember I read them [aloud] and if there were any suggestions to offer, they were offered. . . . I assembled all the material, I wrote many of the articles myself. Many of those that bear the initials of others I had to rewrite because they weren't to the standard.[93]

When the first volume finally appeared in 1907, the *Handbook* was wildly popular; both the first and the second volume of 1910 immediately went out of print. In 1913 Congress appropriated funds for a reprint of another 6,500 sets (only five hundred of which came to the bureau). Powell had envisioned it; Langley had insisted on it; and Hodge had shepherded home the *Handbook*. It was the major accomplishment of the bureau's seven years under Holmes.

Hodge's reputation as the editorial concierge of American anthropology solidified in these years, and not only because of the *Handbook*. When the new American Anthropological Association (1902) assumed responsibility for the *American Anthropologist* as the official national organ of the profession, Hodge was the obvious choice to continue as editor. With the exception of the year 1911, he stayed on until the beginning of World War I. The work involved an astonishingly broad correspondence with not only many figures who are still familiar in the history of anthropology—Boas, Kroeber, Putnam, Dorsey, Stevenson, Alice Cunningham Fletcher (1838–1923), Clark Wissler (1870–1947), Bandelier, Fewkes, Edgar Lee Hewett (1865–1946), Aleš Hrdlička (1869–1943), Zelia Maria Magdalena Nuttall (1857–1933)—but dozens of marginal or lesser-known figures.[94]

As George Stocking recounted some years ago, the Boas-McGee dispute of 1902 over the exclusiveness or inclusiveness of the new AAA resolved in McGee's more democratic favor.[95] Under Hodge's editorship its journal reflected as much. "My impression," Richard Woodbury commented, "is that articles in the journal under Hodge's editorship reflect contemporary interests, heavily descriptive and including a good deal that we would now consider trivial."[96] For instance, the *Anthropologist* addressed the nation's fascination with its overseas possessions—Cuba and Puerto Rico (Fewkes), Guam (a five-part series by botanist-linguist William Safford), and the Philippines (William Jones, Albert Jenks, Frances Densmore). It served, too, as a consistent outlet for the enthusiastic young Yale archaeologist George

Grant MacCurdy, and for the wide-ranging reports of David I. Bushnell. Excepting Fewkes and Aleš Hrdlička, the Washington cohort that had dominated the original *Anthropologist* took a back seat to rising centers and independent voices. Hodge's *Anthropologist* was decidedly empirical, welcoming and celebrating a wide geographical and topical range of offerings. As Fay-Cooper Cole (1881–1961) observed in his obituary of Hodge, "In general he was interested in presenting facts and raising problems rather than in dealing with theory."[97] And turnaround time was rapid, providing grateful contributors publication priority and exposure.

As if the *Handbook* and the *Anthropologist* were not enough, in these years Hodge began the longest editorial commitment of his life: Edward S. Curtis's decades-long, twenty-volume *The North American Indian*, a massive photographic and ethnographic project. When Curtis (1868–1952) first approached the Smithsonian with his vision in 1904, only Hodge responded positively; other officials, including Holmes, found the prospect of a grade-school graduate photographing, recording, possibly even filming among eighty tribes simply absurd.[98] But two years later financier J. Pierpont Morgan (1837–1913) agreed to support the project with $75,000 over 5 years. Curtis turned immediately to Hodge and hired him as text editor at the rate of $7 per 1,000 words. Hodge, who was 42 at the start, saw the project through to the end in 1930.

Over 24 years Curtis made hundreds of wax cylinder recordings, took 40,000 photographs, and published 20 volumes of text and portfolio.[99] He and his talented assistant William E. Myers researched and composed nearly all the ethnographic text in the volumes, which Hodge then edited and proofed.[100] Even many years later he was particularly proud of his "intense" indexes for each volume.[101] But, as their archived correspondence shows, Hodge was much more than an editor to Curtis. In the first place, he provided scholarly and institutional credentials against doubters and critics such as Boas and Mooney. He also served as a reliable, patient sounding board and a stabilizing element during Curtis's tumultuous personal and financial adventures. In other words, he not only provided invaluable bibliographic knowledge but calmed nerves, opened doors, and reduced friction from critics. Curtis once admitted to him: "I think it is better to let other people kill your snakes."[102] Sometimes the tight deadlines were punishing—in one year Curtis and his crew produced three volumes—but by this time Hodge was used to living under constant pressure. Only near the end, after Myers had left in 1926, did Curtis and Hodge have a serious disagreement over content or style. Their project was a remarkable and resilient collaboration.

THE BUREAU'S ETHNOLOGIST-IN-CHARGE, 1910–1918

Holmes never wanted to succeed Powell as head of the BAE in 1902, and he found little joy in his seven-year tenure. A weak administrator in the face of more powerful personalities, he permitted the bureau to slide under the supervision of Langley and then Charles Doolittle Walcott (1850–1927), who was an old friend from Geological Survey days.[103] By 1910 all BAE correspondence was passing through the Smithsonian centrum and the bureau offices were relocated to the North Tower of the Renwick Castle. In effect the bureau was subordinated and disciplined to the parent institution, so that "airplane builders and geologists were now making final decisions in the field of anthropology." In her study of the Holmes years, Virginia Noelke further concluded that while Powell "left the BAE without a clear definition or purpose," seven years later Holmes "left a scientific agency which had no important role in either the field of anthropology or in the [government] bureaucracy."[104]

Noelke's judgment is harsh, but to the degree that it is true, it was hardly Holmes's fault. While new researchers were training with Boas and Putnam (and soon with Kroeber and Robert Harry Lowie [1883–1957] at Berkeley), and new energies were being felt in Chicago, Philadelphia, and Santa Fe, the BAE staff was aging. The only new personnel infusion under Holmes was linguist John R. Swanton. Holmes could do little more than regret the situation. As he told one correspondent, the problem was that "few die and none resign in the Government service."[105] With relief he stepped down at the end of 1909, returning to the National Museum as chair of the Division of Anthropology.

Hodge inherited the stagnant condition. The bureau's annual appropriation when he took over in 1910 was $42,000. It was the same eight years later when he handed the BAE on to Fewkes. Secretary Walcott requested quarterly financial updates from Hodge, and any non-Smithsonian publication by a Bureau member required the secretary's approval. Even auctioning off used BAE library shelves went across Walcott's desk.[106] Moreover, as he readily admitted, Hodge was no politician.[107] Annually he recommended to Congress increases and new initiatives; they were ignored. For example, Hodge envisioned building on the success of the *Handbook* with an ambitious program of handbooks of the Indigenous peoples of each state, beginning with Alfred Kroeber on California tribes. But the California work was delayed beyond his time at the Bureau, and Congress provided nothing for the initiative.[108] Two new staff members joined—Truman Michelson (1911) and John Harrington (1915)—while Matilda Stevenson passed away (1915) toward the end of her Tewa work; Hewitt, Mooney, and Francis La Flesche (1857–1932) plugged away on long-term projects, while Boas (BAE "honorary philologist") and his student Leo Joachim Frachtenberg (1883–1930) received maintenance funding for linguistic work. The bureau's annual reports, which had never been issued promptly under Powell or Holmes, fell even further behind in the decade of world war: the 1910 report appeared in 1918; Hodge's final report (1917–18) was not even submitted by Fewkes until 1922, and printed in 1925.

Soon after Hodge became "ethnologist-in-charge" of the BAE, Edgar Lee Hewett proposed a joint project with his School of American Archaeology in Santa Fe. The BAE and the SAA joint program was to embrace linguistics, archaeology, and ethnography of ancient and current pueblo life in the upper Rio Grande Valley, as well as questions of climatic and other influences on Indigenous life. The personal appeal for Hodge lay in the prospect of collaborative excavation in the Jémez region, which he enjoyed in September 1910 and 1911. Though locally influential, Hewett was already recognized and disparaged by some as an ambitious and disruptive player in southwestern anthropology. Alfred Marston Tozzer (1877–1954), a Mayanist at Harvard, deplored his lack of planning and self-aggrandizing emphasis on collections: "with the exception of certain people connected with the Bureau of Ethnology and the Smithsonian [and] . . . personal friends in the west there is not a person connected with a scientific institution in the country which is doing work in American anthropology who approves of Hewett's work," he confided in 1910. The assessment of Alfred Vincent Kidder (1885–1963) was only slightly more balanced: Hewett was in his estimation "a rather consistent limelight hunter, an inveterate politician and lobbyist, a man who would rather wreck a thing than not run it himself.

On the other hand, he *does* get things accomplished." After decades of familiarity and friendship, even Hodge judged the southwesterner to have been a "plodding, hard-working, phlegmatic individual" whose egocentrism sometimes stood in the way of his own protégés.[109]

Hewett was clearly an uncertain element. Still, the BAE/SAA project brought a new, young generation into field collaboration in northern New Mexico—John P. Harrington, Jesse Logan Nusbaum (1887–1975), Barbara Freire-Marreco (1879–1967), Sylvanus Griswold Morley (1883–1948), and Neil Judd (1887–1976), among others. Hewett's overreach doomed the BAE collaboration, though. When he accepted an additional position as director of exhibits at the upcoming Panama-California Exposition in San Diego, Hodge balked. Convinced that Hewett could not possibly give adequate attention to existing priorities, Hodge ended the joint effort after the 1911 season. Hewett's biographer, after reviewing his commitments at the time, concluded that "Hodge had reason to think him overambitious."[110]

A more consequential experiment was Fewkes's work in the West Indies, which brought about the bureau's first arrangement with George Gustav Heye (1874–1957) of New York. As historians have noted, from Heye's first collecting in the late 1890s his relationships with other institutions, such as the University Museum in Philadelphia and the American Museum of Natural History, were ambivalent, even fractious.[111] But after being introduced to him by George Hubbard Pepper (1873–1924) in 1904, Hodge stayed in touch with the wealthy young collector. In 1912 Fewkes traveled to New York to examine Heye's private collection of Antillean artifacts for illustrations in a publication on West Indian archaeology. Further visits led to a joint BAE-Heye expedition to the West Indies the following year.[112]

Fewkes's efforts in turn brought to pass a congenial, mutually helpful partnership between Heye and Hodge. After a bitter public divorce ended his first marriage in 1912, Heye decided to invest his fortune passively in public utilities and devote himself entirely to building a museum of his own in New York.[113] On his second honeymoon, with Thea Page, in the summer of 1915 the newlyweds excavated at Nacoochee mound in northeastern Georgia together with Hodge and George Pepper. Between May and September they unearthed seventy-five burials.

Don D. Fowler has called the Nacoochee dig Heye's "opening gambit" to bring Hodge to New York.[114] Certainly it was welcome fieldwork for Hodge

Figure 23. Fred Hodge and George Heye at Nacoochee Mound, Georgia, 1915. Courtesy of the Braun Research Library Collection, Autry Museum; N43321.

and the beginning of a special friendship between George, Thea, and Fred. Hodge supervised the work, which "disgorged quantities of what Heye loved most: spectacular art, including effigy vessels & a pipe of a raptorial bird whose open mouth served as a bowl."[115] When the summer season was over they traveled to Santa Fe and Zuni, where Hodge confessed his thirty-year dream of excavating the site of Hawikku and introduced the Heyes to the pueblo and his influential friend Hewett. Forty more years later, Hodge still recalled how in the summer of 1888 he had "wept over" his "pet" site: "I saw this big ruin out there; [I thought:] oh, wouldn't I like to dig in there."[116]

George Heye probably saw an opportunity to please his new friend—"I think he was more interested in me than in the ruins of Hawikuh," Hodge later mused—and also collect some professional credentials for his fledgling museum.[117] If so, it worked. Heye tempted Hodge with an expedition of his own and a position at the new Museum of the American Indian (MAI). After spending virtually his entire life in Washington, Hodge was about to make a major personal and institutional change.

Figure 24. Fred Hodge and George Heye on a stroll. Courtesy of the Braun Research Library Collection, Autry Museum; N43322.

Act Two: New York

NEW YORK AND MR. HEYE'S MUSEUM

By 1915 the idyllic Garrett Park years were a thing of the past, and the Magill-Hodge marriage was unraveling. The two older children were moving away from home (Paul was twenty-one; Winifred was seventeen and soon to be married). Late in her life the youngest, Emlyn, still remembered with bitterness that she and her mother saw little of her father after they moved into Washington in 1913, and that at some point he returned from a Mexico trip with divorce papers—which Maggie considered illegal. No matter. Hodge turned his back on his wife, the children, and Washington in response to the appeals of George and Thea Heye, a New York bachelor lifestyle, and archaeological fieldwork.[118]

At fifty-four Hodge was thoroughly tired of BAE office work and desperate to get outdoors. He also found himself attracted to an urban world of parties, drink, fast cars, long dinners at the Heyes' seventeen-room Manhattan apartment, and all-night banquets at the Waldorf.[119] Fred Hodge was becoming a jocular storyteller, and now he had appreciative audiences.

And a new friend. Jess Nusbaum, another recent hire at MAI, strongly encouraged Heye to add him to the staff; he told Heye that "Teluli had a profound knowledge of anthropology—knew practically all of the anthropologists and archeologists—knew them intimately and all about the research they had conducted, and was the ranking man in editing and publishing their related reports." Hodge and Nusbaum soon found a Manhattan apartment together; when Jess married Aileen O'Bryan in 1920, she and her son Deric moved in with them. Although Nusbaum soon grew to despise both of the Heyes and angrily left the museum in 1921, he always treasured Hodge as a professional and a friend. In 1962 he told Watson Smith and Richard Woodbury that Hodge had been "the salt of the earth with much of its sweetness preserved."[120]

Today, more than a half century after his death, George Heye remains enigmatic. The story of his emergence as an anthropological force in the first decades of the century has been often told, usually with various servings of criticism or outrage—and perhaps a slice of envy.[121] *New York Times Magazine* critic William Grimes wrote that he pursued "an aggressive brand of anthropology and archeology that blurred the distinction between artifact and plunder."[122] Challenging established individuals or institutions—notably Franz Boas and the American Museum of Natural History—Heye used his vast wealth to cut his own autocratic swath, focusing on hiring an eclectic, all-male staff and amassing collections with little attention to documentation or provenance. "Heye," wrote another New York reviewer, "was an outsize man with a voracious appetite for the objects of his desire, whether fine food or Indian artifacts."[123] Yet another oft-quoted assessment summed up his passion this way:

> George had absolutely no sense of sin. He didn't give a hang about Indians individually, and he never seemed to have heard about their problems in present-day society. . . . George didn't buy Indian stuff in order to study

> the life of a people, because it never crossed his mind that that's what they were. He bought all those objects solely in order to own them—for what purpose, he never said.[124]

Other judgments have been more circumspect. Curator Ann McMullen recently called for a broader consideration of Heye as a museum builder rather than merely an omnivorous collector, proposing that anecdotal remarks by Heye's contemporaries have too often been taken as harsh verdicts. Furthermore, she has suggested, the narrative of the "crazy white man" has served not only to obscure serious purposes but also to enhance the preferred self-image of the Smithsonian's Museum of the American Indian—whose founding collections exist, after all, largely because of him.[125] Clara Sue Kidwell has noted, too, that "Heye personally catalogued virtually every object in the collection, and despite his critics, he was concerned with accuracy in describing provenance"—even asking Boas's help in naming associated tribes.[126]

Edmund Carpenter observed a few years ago that, if nothing else, "Heye assembled a staff like no other, anywhere, ever."[127] From Columbia he brought Marshall Saville (1867–1935), George Pepper (1874–1924) from Philadelphia, Alanson Skinner (1886–1925) from nearby AMNH, peripatetic Nusbaum from the Southwest, and Boas-trained Mark R. Harrington (1882–1971) from the University of Pennsylvania Museum. But not all of Heye's men were trained, or even semi-trained, in a branch of anthropology. Donald Cadzow (1894–1960) arrived in New York from his uncle's trading post on the Yukon-Alaska border; Charlie Turbyfill was little more than a Carolina farmhand when Heye hired him (at Nacoochee), initially for southeastern archaeology; and "the Chief" brought in Edwin F. Coffin, a former racecar driver, to be the museum's first archaeological photographer.[128]

In what journalist Barbara Braun called the Heye Foundation's "salad days"—1916 to 1928—these men explored, bought, excavated and collected throughout the western hemisphere.[129] At a time when positions in anthropology were few and uncertain, the MAI seemed to them a dream come true; as Carpenter phrased it, they "didn't need to teach or deliver babies or sell insurance."[130] They could do what they wanted—explore, dig, publish:

> His crew had the money to dig up or buy up everything that the rest of us couldn't afford. His archaeologists enjoyed the euphoria of believing they

had lifetime tenure. They allowed Heye to pick their brains, and eventually they were rewarded with the satisfaction of having taught him quite a good deal.[131]

Into this unique and vigorous environment Hodge officially arrived in 1918 as Heye's second-in-command. In the two-floor museum offices, the workforce was divided into the "Heye-Jinks" group upstairs (Heye, Nusbaum, Coffin, Turbyfill, and some others) and the downstairs "Hodge-Podge" (Hodge, Saville, Pepper, Skinner, Cadzow, Harrington). Their internal weekly publication, "The Museum Mustard," cast sophomoric intra-group aspersions. "In these columns," Harrington remembered sweetly, "nobody was spared—shown by the fact that our Director was sometimes called 'Heye, Wide and Handsome.'" Among the milder doggerel were these (from Harrington):

Oh it's Skinner this, and Raymond that
And hustle up, you brutes.
But we're the little horses
Who bring home the buckskin suits.

And:

Oh I went to get my lunch once
And I stayed away an hour,
And what I caught when I got back
Would crush the Eiffel Tower.[132]

Hodge joined this network of boyish camaraderie with two main charges: the museum's ambitious publication program and the promised Hawikku expedition. In 1915 Heye's friend Archer Milton Huntington (1870–1955), adopted son of railroad magnate and industrialist Collis Potter Huntington (1821–1900), gave land in the Bronx and at Audubon Terrace on Upper Broadway for Heye's new museum; three years later he added a $125,000 publication fund.[133] This was to be Hodge's editorial bailiwick—but not entirely so, since both Huntington and Heye took personal, insistent interest in even the physical details (size, margins, typeface) of the museum's publications. Engaged with Hawikku, Hodge tried to slough off the editing chores by suggesting the hire of another editor. After the Notes and Monographs series was launched in 1919 he advised Heye that "any fool can see it through." Heye disagreed and insisted on Hodge's editorial services. And the load was indeed heavy: between 1921 and 1923 alone, the museum prepared or published thirty-seven volumes and pamphlets—more than 2,800 pages. Hodge edited all of them—and every other MAI publication through 1930.[134]

Among the volumes in the Notes and Monographs series that Hodge brought to publication in this period was a reissue of Cushing's *Zuñi Breadstuff*, which had originally appeared serially in 1884–85 and been partially serialized again in 1893–94.[135] In May 1919 Hodge informed Emily Cushing, who had moved to Los Angeles, that since the copyright on *Breadstuff* had run out, he planned to print it as a book, to be supplemented with photographs by Nusbaum from the upcoming season at Zuni. He offered her two hundred copies. While regretting the strange dimensions of the proposed four-by-six-inch volume, she agreed. But Emily died the next year, just as *Zuñi Breadstuff* reappeared.[136]

Hodge's version of *Zuñi Breadstuff* was yet another phase in his awkward, ongoing dialogue with his deceased brother-in-law. He introduced the volume with a passive-voice, unsigned foreword consisting mainly of Powell's 1900 memorial praise of Cushing as a man of intellectual and manual genius. The distinctive and whimsical drawings by Frank and Margaret in the original series Hodge now rearranged, mixing some with the Nusbaum photographs at the back of the book. He also altered and recombined about a third of the nineteen chapters, and editorialized by adding bracketed notes to Cushing's originals—updating and "correcting" the classic work of thirty-five years before. It would not be Hodge's last editing of Cushing.

HAWIKKU, 1917–1923

As early as 1912 Hodge was corresponding with his old friend from Hemenway days, Zuni Dick (Tsinahe), who was by then lieutenant governor of the pueblo, about excavating the ruins of Hawikku. Without consulting the governing council or others, Dick gave permission to excavate the ruin twelve miles southwest of Zuni—but not the burial grounds nearby. After the brief visit to Zuni with George and Thea in October 1915, Hodge returned the following summer armed with permission to excavate from the secretary of the interior—who also had not consulted the pueblo authorities. The expedition was to be jointly sponsored by the BAE and Heye's organization, with collections divided between the National Museum and the MAI. It would be funded by Heye's friend and MAI trustee Harmon W. Hendricks.[137]

Harmon Hendricks (1846–1928) was the scion of a prominent Sephardic Jewish family of New York. His grandfather had established Hendricks Brothers copper mills during the War of 1812, and the metals firm remained in the family for more than a century. By 1912 Hendricks, a childless bachelor, was the sole heir; he had been a friend of Heye's father, and he lived with his sisters in the same building as George and Thea. At his death in 1928 he left $250,000 to MAI—far less than Heye had expected—and the rest of his $4 million estate to nieces and Jewish organizations. During his lifetime, his most famous gifts to the museum were two wampum belts originally presented to William Penn. Both he and fellow bachelor-trustee James Bishop Ford (1844–1928) were devoted to Thea and donated specimens in her name as well.[138]

Hendricks gave about $3,700 for the first season at Hawikku. Why did he agree to support the multiyear expedition? According to Hodge, he simply said, "Very glad to do that":

> He was a very fine man. Not only did he pay the expenses of the field work during all that time—and employing fifteen Indians and running a camp is no small expense—but he was a gentleman, punctilious in all of his dealing with everybody.[139]

Factional disputes within the pueblo prevented initial work in 1916; not until the following April was Hodge able to return and prepare the inaugural season of the Hendricks-Hodge Expedition.[140] But Zuni pueblo was no longer the relatively cohesive community that Hodge and Cushing had known thirty years before. Due mainly to outside agents (traders, anthropologists, missionaries, military and government figures) and their insistent influences in pueblo affairs, the Bow Priesthood that had traditionally regulated both internal and external affairs suffered a precipitous decline in the 1890s. It was the beginning of a "tumultuous era in Zuni history," in the words of anthropologist Triloki Nath Pandey. Matilda Stevenson reported in 1896 that the priesthood comprised only fifteen aging men; by 1916 merely five remained, and by 1921 only four. By contrast, the secular civil government of the pueblo grew steadily in numbers and consequence, with an eleven-member tribal council by 1916.[141] Some have traced the priesthood's decline to the early nineties, when Elder Brother Bow Priest Naiuchi and others had attempted to punish Nick Tumaka for witchcraft. Although Tumaka was widely disliked in the pueblo, American soldiers imprisoned Naiuchi and cut his long hair. This occurred more than once. Diminished and mortified, he quit the priesthood and died in 1904.[142]

At the same time a personal feud between the politically prominent Pino and Eriachos families underlay a decades-long campaign to reestablish a Catholic mission at the pueblo.[143] The personal-political-religious conflict reached a boiling point in 1916, just as Hodge hoped to begin his dig. While the mission proposal was widely opposed and defeated on that occasion, Catholic priests continued to visit and baptize, and in 1922 (through collusion with government agent Robert Bauman) land was given for a chapel and the mission came. In this interim the pro- and anti-Catholic split in Zuni became hardened and bitter, affecting all aspects of the pueblo's politics, even family life. Hodge's excavation project, which was generally accepted (or tolerated) by the Pino anti-Catholic faction (sometimes labeled "Protestant" or "progressive") and opposed by the Eriachos Catholic group, soon became caught in these disturbing currents.[144]

Further complicating matters, Zuni was being confronted with fierce competition among university departments and museums over the ethnography, archaeology, and material cultures of the pueblo world. For example, Stewart Culin of the University Museum in Philadelphia traveled to the Southwest in 1901 with the Chicago Field Museum's George Amos Dorsey (1868–1931)—who, historian Eliza McFeely has aptly noted, "had learned to use the railroad effectively in order to give him an edge in what he perceived as the race to salvage Native American artifacts from the region."[145] Culin first saw Zuni itself the following summer on another collecting trip that was also a pilgrimage to honor his departed friend Cushing. After moving to the Brooklyn Museum he returned in 1903 and 1904, taking advantage of depressed conditions in the pueblo to compete with Matilda Stevenson for traditional and commissioned collections (especially masks).[146] In the same years Pepper was collecting at Zuni for the American Museum in New York.

On his final visit in 1907 Culin found a more prosperous and busy pueblo—a "lively crossroads" of tourism and business, he thought.[147] But a new generation of anthropologists was about to descend upon Zuni. In 1909 Clark Wissler, curator of anthropology at the American Museum, persuaded Archer Huntington to support a new research and collections program focused on the Southwest.[148] Although the significant impact of the Huntington Southwest Survey was to be in archaeology, an initial focus was ethnographic, and Wissler assigned Herbert Joseph Spinden (1879–1967) to pueblo country; he visited Zuni in 1911–12. In 1915 Alfred Kroeber and Elsie Clews Parsons (1879–1941) spent much of the summer in the pueblo, and returned in the autumn of 1918. They were the first wave of Boasians—Leslie Spier, Boas himself, Ruth Leah Bunzel (1898–1990) and Ruth Fulton Benedict (1887–1948)—who would re-focus anthropological attention on Zuni during the 1920s.[149] "It may be," George Stocking once mused, "that Boas' ongoing shift from historical diffusionism to the psychological study of the individual and culture made more attractive an area where the culture seemed still vibrantly 'alive and well.'"[150]

Perhaps. But if so, the scientific visitors failed to appreciate that the community was in fact under severe stress. Popular journalist George Wharton James (1858–1923), staying with governor Tsinahe, wrote in 1918 that he found young Zuni children "healthy, happy, vigorous and naked." Uncritical and nostalgic, James's three-part series in *Overland Monthly* that year seemed to mimic Cushing and Baxter four decades before. While the Zunis might appear "crude, simple, ignorant, and perhaps brutal," he enthused, "what a wealth of poetry, of symbolism, of imagery, of tradition, of folk-lore lies back of those simple and weather-beaten, life-scarred faces."[151] Clearly, the persistent vision of Zuni as a preindustrial, conflict-free world that would further blossom forth in the writings of Ruth Benedict and Aldous Huxley (1894–1963) was already well established in the wartime decade.[152]

Hodge may have been less impressionable and effusive than James, but he was also uniquely influential. Pandey, in his landmark study "Anthropologists at Zuni," remarked that no anthropologist was "more directly involved in Zuni politics" than Hodge—and not in a positive sense. Ruth Bunzel, who first came to the pueblo in 1924, told Pandey that Hodge's Hawikku work had aroused "a good deal of discomfort at Zuni, with their feelings about the contamination of the dead, their fear of ruins, etc."[153] But to the degree that he recognized that he was stepping back into a changed and divided community in 1916, Hodge was prepared to be transactional.

He worked six seasons at Hawikku: from 1917 to 1923. (In 1922 the delayed opening of Heye's museum preempted MAI fieldwork.)[154] The initial season was a joint operation between the BAE and MAI, but after Hodge resigned from the bureau in early 1918 the Heye museum took full control. Art historian Klinton Burgio-Ericson has carefully reconstructed the timeline and foci of Hodge's Hawikku seasons.[155] Hodge began in the burial grounds west of the Hawikku house ruins, uncovering nearly three hundred graves in 1917. The second field season he continued in the burial grounds, bringing the count of opened graves to about a thousand. During the long third season (1919) Hodge's assistant Nusbaum explored the ruins of the seventeenth-century Purísima Concepción mission church while Hodge moved his main force to the housing blocks of the ancient pueblo. In 1920 Hodge continued in the housing and excavated a double kiva beyond. This work extended into 1921; at this point Hodge also undertook his only deliberately stratigraphic work, a trench through the plaza. The trench, in Burgio-Ericson's estimation, produced Hodge's "most scientifically rigorous data."[156]

After the year of hiatus, the 1923 season became a joint venture between Heye's museum and Louis Colville Gray Clarke (1881–1960) of Cambridge University's Museum of Archaeology and Ethnology. In this final season Hodge proceeded with his excavations both in burial grounds and in the pueblo room blocks, while his MAI colleague Samuel Kirkland Lothrop (1892–1965) excavated a few miles to the north at the town of Kechiba:wa (Kechipauan) with the Cambridge group.

Judgments of Hodge's Hawikku work have been mixed. Between 1918 and 1952 he published nearly twenty progress reports and shorter publications on various aspects of the excavations, but never a full report.[157] A year before his death he asked archaeologist Watson Smith to take on the task of compiling a final report and gave him full access to his notes and other materials. Smith was joined by Richard and Nathalie Woodbury (1918–2009), and they wrote up the Hawikku work in the decade after Hodge died. In a thorough and dutiful presentation of the records and data they praised Hodge for his meticulous fieldnotes, but they also noted that a firm ceramic typology and chronology was not possible from his records since, in their estimate, "southwestern archaeology was still in its Age of Innocence" at the time—and in any case Hodge did not systematically save sherds and provided only vague descriptions. Still, in their general judgment "Hodge was a pioneer in the use of stratigraphic chronology in American archaeology."[158]

That assessment has not held. Melinda Elliott, in *Great Excavations* (1995), observed that Hodge's conclusions today seem "obvious and unremarkable," but, she added, he did contribute to understanding the history of the pueblo. Further, since Hawikku has generally proved to be typical of large-pueblo settlements built after the abandonment of Mesa Verde around 1300, Hodge's main legacy, Elliott argued, has been that of data-gatherer for more theoretically inclined successors.[159]

For some time the Hendricks-Hodge Expedition raised mainly quizzical expressions: Why did Hodge not dig down further into an obvious earlier level, to Hawikku's archaeological origins? To what extent were his collections compromised back in New York by George Heye's cavalier, even dismissive approach to mundane sherds? Recently the questioning has become sharper. Archaeologists David R. Wilcox and David A. Gregory, in *Zuni Origins* (2007), noted that the "New Archaeology" that was developing in the 1910s by Nels Nelson in Galisteo Basin, Spier and Kroeber at Zuni, and Kidder at Pecos largely passed Hodge by; in their view he "botched the effort" at Hawikku and his seven-year effort was a "failure."[160] As Burgio-Ericson sees it today, Hodge now appears less a pioneer than a generational holdover who proceeded without a firm research design and adopted the new stratigraphic methods only partially and belatedly. He notes that it was only after Kidder, Earl Morris, and Sylvanus Morley had visited Hawikku in the 1920 season that Hodge began to apply new insights and practices in stratigraphy and dendrochronology. Focused on the time of Spanish contact, still mulling the puzzles that had so fascinated Cushing and Bandelier, and convinced of cultural discontinuity at the site, Hodge narrowed his focus but "retain[ed] the qualities of scale and spontaneity through which his predecessor, Cushing, had performatively created the persona of an archaeologist-adventurer."[161]

The limited scientific results at Hawikku are less censurable than Hodge's manipulative attitude and actions toward the Zunis in a period of disruption and confusion. Gwyneira Isaac and Burgio-Ericson have recently examined the extent to which Hodge and the Heyes bullied, threatened, and possibly bribed Zuni leadership, manipulating religio-political divisions in order to pursue ethnological collecting as well as excavating. Hodge, for instance, led the Zunis to believe that only by digging at Hawikku could he assure that the site would not be taken from the tribe by the Department of the Interior.[162] Working with Tsinahe, Governor Lewis, and the "Protestant" leadership, he hired only Zuni men from that faction.[163] In 1919 Jess Nusbaum ran into resistance when he began photographing not only the site but the pueblo and outlying communities as well—"many wouldn't stand for it," he reported to Hodge.[164] The following season, at Thea's urging and despite demonstrated Zuni reluctance, the first filming of Zuni dances occurred.[165] Fully aware of the Zunis' strong dislike and resistance to exhuming ancestral remains, Hodge persisted nonetheless[166]—even praising his workers for their willingness to overcome their "tabus."

Well supplied with bottled water from Gallup and Albuquerque, chickens and eggs, and a full-time cook, on occasion the Hawikku camp must have resembled a playground for the visits of George and Thea—who once asked Hodge to prepare some partially dug graves with "skellies" (skeletons) for them to unearth fully on arrival.[167] The treasure-trove language of Hodge's reports—"rich" cemeteries with "fine things"—recalled the long letters of Cushing to his patron, Mary Hemenway, dictated to Hodge back in 1887–88. Cushing had boasted then that, unlike other expeditions, his field practices were producing "collections with souls"—that is, artifacts with copious contextual notes and sketches. In robust health and working in far more comfortable conditions than Cushing had, Hodge enjoyed visits to "Camp Harmon" from, among others, the Heyes, Harmon Hendricks, George Bird Grinnell (1849–1938), and writers Mary Austin (1868–1934) and Mary Roberts Rinehart (1876–1958).[168] He aimed to entertain folks and still outmatch the written field record of his first mentor. And he did.

Like the Hemenway Expedition, though, upset and recrimination ended the Hawikku work. In the final season of 1923 Hodge hired Owen Newton Cattell (1898–1940, son of psychologist and *Science* magazine editor James McKeen Cattell) to film at the pueblo. Cattell had recently served as scientific photographer on an expedition to the Amazon headwaters.[169] Heye trustee James B. Ford fully financed the Zuni filming project. Aided by Donald A. Cadzow of MAI and Lorenzo Chavez, Hodge's reliable Zuni foreman, during that summer Cattell used ten thousand feet of film in recording Zuni arts and ceremonies. In the face of Zuni doubts Hodge argued

Figure 25. Zahrah Ethel Preble in Indian Garb, 1915. *Chicago Tribune*, 26 September.

that the films would protect religious observations from federal interference—a major concern in the pueblo at the time. But when Cattell returned in November, unannounced, to film the sacred Shalako drama at the winter solstice, the Hodge project crossed a line. Urged on by Agent Bauman, resisters from the "pro-Catholic" faction forced Cattell to stop filming, his cameras were smashed, and Hodge was banned from the pueblo.[170] Reporting on the filming project in the museum's Indian Notes and Monographs series the following year, Hodge remarked that the moving picture results had been "most successful." He made no mention of his expulsion.[171] Thus ended the fieldwork of the Hendricks-Hodge Archaeological Expedition.[172]

Second Interlude: Zahrah Preble and the Sounds of Zuni

In summer 1927 Fred Hodge was married a second time, to Zahrah Ethel Preble (1880–1934)—"a mighty bully girl from San Francisco," as he described her to Charles Lummis.[173] *The Preble family traced a modest prominence in American history to naval officer Edward Preble (1761–1807), who fought in the Barbary Pirate Wars (1801–5) and after whom six Navy ships were later named. Zahrah's father, Charles Sumner Preble (1855–1939), was a Massachusetts native who became a survey engineer and newspaperman in Reno, Nevada; her mother, Ella Melana Thomson Preble (1851–1929), was an Ohio girl and painter of miniatures. The couple moved to Berkeley in 1887, where they raised four daughters (Sarah/Zahrah, Donna, Hazel, and Amy) and were considered by some to be a pioneer family of the Bay Area.*[174]

The roots of Hodge's second marriage lay, like those of his first, with the Hemenway Expedition—and, more precisely, in the always-

performative life of Frank Cushing. The fascinating story revolves around Zuni music.

During his recuperations in San Francisco in 1887 and 1888, Cushing gave several lectures to the California Academy of Sciences on the Hemenway Expedition and his life at Zuni. He closed these talks by singing his "Zuni chants." By contemporary accounts, Cushing's performing voice was magnetic and the songs, sung in Zuni (whatever their accuracy), were indeed enchanting to his hearers. Journalist Kate Fields, a cosmopolitan and well-traveled attendee, recalled being captivated:

> *Mr. Cushing is never more charming than when chanting the religious and other songs of his dark brothers. The sympathy he feels for a misunderstood race gives to his singing voice a timbre that appeals pathetically to the ear and extorts applause from the most unthinking. They don't know why, but they are delighted. The heart of the man is in his throat.*[175]

Also in the audience was the librarian of the California Academy, a musician and composer by the name of Charles Troyer (1837–1920). "Carlos" (as he preferred after 1885) was a figure who had constructed a deeply dubious autobiography of mystery, adventure, and accomplishment. Born in Frankfurt/Mainz, Germany, as a child he learned violin and piano; he later claimed to have known and played with both Jenny Lind and Franz Liszt—on Liszt's personal piano. After migrating to New York he taught music for a time "to some of the fine old Knickerbocker families," but then sought exotic experiences in the West Indies and South America. After the other three members of his traveling quartet died, Troyer proceeded to track songbirds alone into the Brazilian rainforest. Here, so he claimed, he lived among several Indigenous ("Incan") tribes, risking his life repeatedly but charming the primitives with the sounds of his violin. Finally, "after nine months of captivity he was allowed to depart under promise of return to bring them new and tuneful musical instruments." But the four hundred tribal songs he had supposedly transcribed had been lost with the deposing of Brazil's Emperor Dom Pedro II—whom he claimed as a personal friend.[176] *When the fifty-year-old musician* encountered Cushing in 1887 he was teaching music in San Francisco and serving as librarian of the Academy.[177]

Charmed by Cushing's renditions at the academy lectures, Troyer asked to transcribe the Zuni songs into written musical form. Thus began a thirty-year career in composing, publishing, and performing in the new Indianist music movement. In 1893 he published *Two Zuñi Songs*—a lullaby and a "lover's wooing song." He dedicated them to Cushing. The two 1893 songs are, according to music historian Michael Pisani, "the first known published compositions said to be based on traditional tribal Indian music." On the other hand, Pisani goes on, Troyer's Zuni music "exhibits virtually no trace of indigenous elements." Charles Lummis distrusted Troyer, and Hodge called him "an old faker" who never visited the Zunis or any other tribe.[178] Indeed, Pisani is unsparing of "the German-born con artist who affixed wildly imaginative ritualistic descriptions to his melodramatic fantasies."[179]

But Troyer had his followers. By 1893 the young Genevieve ("Viva") Cummins (1875–1905) had appeared—one of many female singers of "exotic" and "Indian" music to grace private homes, women's clubs, and small stages as the century turned. A precocious San Francisco girl and student of Troyer, eighteen-year-old Viva traveled with her widowed mother to the 1893 Chicago World's Fair to study folk music on the Midway Plaisance—and to hear the Zuni songs directly from Frank Cushing's lips, as he recorded in his diary:

> At noon, went to see Miss Cummins in California Bldg. Her mother was with her. Greatly pleased with meeting me again. Had envied me always more or less she said, my good luck in place of her Husbd's who lost all his work in dying. . . . Had interesting long talk and sang over the two Zuñi songs several times for Miss Cummins.[180]

Following the fair, Viva embarked upon a fast-moving career as a "polyglot chanteuse," performing in various guises and languages and sometimes accompanied by Troyer.[181] In 1894 *Wenner's Magazine*, a popular music review, featured her dressed in Bedouin, "Zuni," and "Muezzin" garb—made for her on the Midway, it was said—and noted her multilingual repertoire.[182] Two years later the

San Francisco Call *celebrated the hometown girl (with slightly raised eyebrows):*

> *Throughout musical and scientific centers in the east a new interest has been created in the weird, fascinating songs of the Zuni Indians through a wholly unlooked-for medium. These same songs had been taken on a phonograph by members of the Hemenway Expedition purely in the interest of science, and so far only one musician [Troyer] has succeeded in transposing them in accordance with the rules of harmony. . . . It remained for a young lady, and a San Franciscan at that, to bring the songs and melodies of these interesting people of New Mexico before the public.*[183]

For a season, Viva was a minor bicoastal phenomenon. Phoebe Hearst met her at the Waldorf in New York and, impressed by her Zuni lullaby, offered her a scholarship to the "Agromonte School of Opera and Oratoria."[184] *In 1896 Viva married a railroad man, Augustus Doan, and her mother, Ella, remarried as well; by 1900 the couples were living together in London. Viva was studying voice and performing as what one journalist called a "race impersonator."*[185] *She attended the Paris Exposition of 1900 and the Saint Louis Fair in 1904. When she suddenly died in New York in 1905, she was only thirty years old.*

By the time of Viva's death the Indianist movement was opening to flower, spurred in part by the earlier presence in America (1892–95) of Antonín Dvořák and, in 1901, the establishment of Arthur Farwell's music publishing house, the Wa-Wan Press.[186] *Troyer added two more songs to his Zuni collection—"Sunrise Call" and "The Coming of Montezuma"—and Wa-Wan Press published the four pieces in 1904 as* Traditional Songs of the Zuñis. *A second series of four followed.*[187] *Cushing having passed away in 1900, Troyer now began to portray himself as ethnographer as well as musician. He falsely claimed to have lived at Zuni for years and to have been instructed into the innermost sacred knowledge of the priests. He accompanied his compositions with imaginative cultural descriptions.*

Troyer soon found another muse for his Zuni fantasies: a second San Francisco woman named Sarah (Zahrah) Ethel Preble. In late 1911 the thirty-one-year-old performed, like Viva before her, at the home of Mrs. James (Sara) Roosevelt in New York, and a few weeks later at the Waldorf-Astoria for a society event of the National Plant, Flower, and Fruit Guild. The New York Times *reported that the "young California girl" who had "lived among the Cliff-Dwellers" of the Southwest interpreted the Zuni lullaby and wooing songs in a "serious and graceful manner." The* Montclair (N.J.) Times *enthused that "Miss Preble's presentation of our native Indian songs and dances is causing a sensation."*[188]

Preble's early life in northern California is largely a blank; we do not know when she and Troyer met.[189] *One account of 1915 told that while attending the University of California in Berkeley she had "begged" a reluctant Troyer to teach her; only after she had sung to him the "Sunrise Call" "with much of the weird charm and primitive fire of the aborigines" did he relent. According to the same report, Zahrah fancied herself a woman of remarkable telepathic power who, when singing Zuni songs, felt she "becomes an Indian in outward appearance as well as emotionally."*[190]

Over the next decade Preble presented Troyer's music along the California coast and in New York.[191] *When popular San Francisco evangelist Bill Stidger discovered that Troyer was in his congregation he arranged the church's first concert in March 1914: "An Indian Concert of Songs and Dances" with Troyer and Preble (advertised as "a sinuous dancer") garbed as a Zuni maiden. The building was decorated with blankets and a tent, Stidger and the boy ushers dressed as makeshift Indians, and the Methodist preacher even tried (unsuccessfully) to get "a real Indian" to make a fire with sticks in the church. His sanctuary was packed for the first time.*[192]

Zahrah Preble performed in costume with Troyer at the Panama-Pacific International Exposition in August 1915, and a few days later they performed at Annie Rix Militz's Metaphysical Headquarters in San Francisco. Shortly thereafter she was pictured performing, in full headdress, as a Zuni mother at the Étude Club in San Francisco. The San Francisco Examiner, which fondly followed her events, suggested that she "has sung Indian songs so long and thought in the Indian way so continuously that she seems almost to have conquered her Scots ancestry and become a primitive."[193]

But telepathic singing and dancing as an Indian brought little income. Always interested in raising and teaching children, in 1917–18 Zahrah served as a high school director of music in Escondido, and in 1919 she spent some time at the Pala Indian School near San Diego—her first, impactful exposure to California Mission Indian life.[194] *In the same years she became devotedly involved with the Camp Fire Girls movement around Stockton, serving for two years as an artistic coach and counselor in the summers. For a short time (1920–21) she served as west coast "special correspondent" for an Atlanta-based trade journal,* The Oil Miller, *reporting on coastal market developments in olive, vegetable, and cottonseed oils.*[195] *But this was unfulfilling and short-lived, for Zahrah's real commitment was to teaching and performing. In January 1921 the* Stockton Daily Evening Record *announced that Preble, "known especially by the Woman's Clubs and Camp Fire Girls organizations throughout the state for her beautiful voice and her artistic rendition in costume of the Carlos Troyer Zuni Indian songs and dances," would be moving to the Panama Canal Zone.*[196] *She soon left to take up a position in the U.S. government's Bureau of Clubs and Playgrounds and to coach high school drama in Balboa.*[197] *She stayed a year.*

After returning from Panama in 1922, at some point she met Hodge in New York (there is no indication they previously knew each other). In late January 1923 she recorded "The Sunrise Call" and "Lover's Wooing" at the Victor Studios in New York.[198] *In June, as the final Hawikku season was organizing, the* Brooklyn Daily Eagle *announced that Preble would accompany the Hendricks-Hodge Expedition for a distinctly non-archaeological purpose: "Seeking New Jazz Music in Archaeology's Oldest Hunting Ground." Referencing the late Troyer's Zuni songs (and repeating the fiction that he had lived three years in the pueblo), Preble informed the public that, after all, "every piece of jazz music . . . is nothing more than the old savage chants dressed up in new clothes."*[199] *While Hodge dug in the dirt, Zahrah would seek among "the oldest city and possibly the oldest race" of North America new sounds and syncopations.*

One could dismiss these remarks, like so much else in the Troyer-Cummins-Preble archive, as puffery. That would be a mistake. No longer a girl in a feathered costume, Preble was by now conversant

Page Five

Seeking New Jazz Music in Archaeology's Oldest Hunting Ground

Zahrah E. Preble Who Plans to Live With the Indians in Order to Find New Jazz Rhythms

Illustrated by James R. Ray

ZAHRAH E. PREBLE, who has appeared in every big city of the country as a singer of Indian songs, is to accompany the F. W. Hodge Expedition of the Museum of the American Indian, Heye Foundation, New York City, when it begins an extensive exploration this summer in and about Hawikuh, New Mexico. But the young woman is not going there for archaeological research, as are the scientists who will make up the party. She is going for a more poetic purpose—that of searching out new rhythms about which new syncopated music may be constructed for the amusement and recreation of the people of this country and the world.

Strange as it may sound the project is wholly a feasible one, for Miss Preble will explain to you that practically every piece of jazz music we hear played is really nothing more than the old savage chants dressed up in new clothes. And, as those clothes are getting a bit frayed, Miss Preble is anxious to find new garments with which to clothe these catching tone waves.

According to Miss Preble, if new music is to be discovered it will have to be found among the descendants of the Zuñis, the Indian tribe which inhabited the famous original seven cities of Cibola. Excavations already made there under the direction of the Museum of the American Indian reveal that this is the site of the oldest city and possibly the oldest race of human beings who inhabited the United States.

Miss Preble says:

"Fifty years ago Carlos Troyer, then a young man, full of adventure, was captured in South America by a roaming band of Indian hunters. These people were presumably of Inca ancestry, and he was kept in their village on a great rocky island in the midst of terrible swamps, far in the interior of Bolivia. There he witnessed a great celebration, in which the drum and flute players and other musicians from twenty or more such villages gathered and gave a musical performance in unison! And this had been a custom of these people for centuries, so they said! 'Go to the Indian, thou American!'

"Carlos Troyer later became an investigator of the music and customs of the North American Indians, and, through a friendship with Frank Hamilton Cushing, was introduced by him into the country of the Zuni Indians, in New Mexico. Here is one of the transcriptions he made of an Apache Medicine Chant, which is a regular pre-Coue treatment for those who are ill:

APACHE MEDICINE CHANT.

Never despair, banish all fear,
Clouds in the sky, soon they pass by.
Watch for the Sunlight with joy and delight,
Mother Sun is our guide.
Never despair, banish all fear,
Be of good cheer, help will be here.

Sing with us, laugh with us,
Telling a funny tale:
Hounds lost a rabbit-trail;
Sing with us, laugh with us,
Watch a bear climb a tree,
Trying to catch a bee.
Bee stings his nose,
Down the bear goes,
Drop, drop, drop.

Cheerful and bright, look for the light,
Hope for the best, take a good rest.
All will be well, doubt and fear you must dispel.
All will be well, all will be well.'

According to Miss Preble, out of some of the beautiful expressions of the legendary life of these people come lovely songs which are never sung out of their proper season or ceremony under any inducements. A few of them have been preserved by Carlos Troyer, who lived for three years with these people in order to record their music, later rendering it into our system of notation, as correctly as possible, and keeping the words and the English translations as true to those used by the Zunis as could be done. When he asked one of the oldest Zunis of the village where they got their lovely music the old man replied: "From our forefathers." And when Mr. Troyer persisted, and wanted to know where his forefathers got it, he replied: "From the sun."

The sincerity with which he said it robbed it of any ridiculous meaning. And in the light of recent investigations in the field of modern music, Julian Carrillo, a Mexican musician of considerable note, claims that the future of music will be based upon a scale split into not only quarter-tones, but even smaller intervals. That our present scale of twelve chromatic sounds will be only a skeleton outline for intermediate intervals of sound so finely tuned that our present sense of hearing will have to develop to be equal to perceiving it. May it not be possible that Senor Carrillo is a descendant of one of those "forefathers" who listened to the sun and then spoke its music?

Perhaps we shall once again return to that period of thousands of years ago, when men did listen to the music of the spheres, and gained their melodies from the rapid vibrations of the sun's bright rays. At any rate, our modern composers are beginning to realize that this Indian music is a mine of musical treasure as yet hardly touched.

In the melodious "Hymn to the Sun," transcribed by Carlos Troyer, the Zunis teach their little children to "listen to the sun" with shells, which they hold over their ears, as they sing and dance the following poetic song:

HYMN TO THE SUN.

Early in the morning we waken, we waken,
When Mother Sun-god rises, we welcome her with joy.
She greets us with a radiant face,
She meets us with a warm embrace, so sweetly.

What a wondrous shower of sounds,
Countless beats in rapid rounds,
Ever changing, ever new,
Constant strains of high and low,
They are messengers of love,
Spirit voices from above,
Bringing light and life and joy,
Telling us of bliss on high.
Listen, just listen!

Glory to the sunlit rays,
Glory to the sun-god's ways,
They command us to endure
To be silent, chaste and pure,
To be faithful, true and brave,
To the laws our fathers gave,
Or harken to the sun-god's voice,
Beckoning your soul to rise,
In radiant light, the source of song,
The origin of thought has sprung;
As light and song in one unite,
Let us forever seek the Light.
Listen, just listen.

When a young maiden looks with favor upon a young man he takes heart, and on a moonlight night seeks her house, and invites her to come down from the housetop (where half the pueblo dwellers spend their time) and walk with him under his blanket, which he will wrap tenderly about her, thus consummating the betrothal to which she consents by this act. This is the song he sings to her:

LOVER'S WOOING.

O, what happiness! How delightful,
When together we neath one blanket walk!
Can it be that my young maiden fair
Sits awaiting, all alone tonight?
Is she waiting for me only?
May I hope it is my young maiden
Sitting all alone and awaiting me?
Will she come then, will she walk with me?
Neath one blanket, we together be?
Will she come?

The Zuni children are sung to sleep with the following mental suggestions, quite similar to those we are now told by psychologists that we should state to our children for their subconscious minds to assimilate during sleep:

ZUNI LULLABY.

Now rest thee in peace with thy playmates above,
Close thine eyes, my baby.
Go join in their happy enjoyments, my love,
Sleep on soundly, sweetly.

Kind spirits will guard thee, and show thee the light,
So open thy vision, thy dreams will be bright
So rest thee, my baby, in peace and in joy,
While I pray for thee, love,
To the Sun-god on high.

Then to the forces of nature which are as beneficent gods to these simple people of the desert, and to the Great Spirit over all, the mother offers a prayer:

Grant, oh Sun-god, thy protection,
Guard this helpless infant sleeping.
Starry guardians, forever joyful,
Faithful Moon-god, forever watchful,
Spirit Living, Spirit Resting,
Guard us, lead us, aid us, love us, forever.

When a Young Maid Walks With a Young Man Under His Blanket, She Thus Consents to a Betrothal.

Figure 26. Zahrah Preble "Seeking New Jazz Rhythms" at Zuni. *Brooklyn Daily Eagle,* June 10, 1923.

with some trends and debates in modern music, specifically experiments in microtonal composition. Citing the work of Mexican composer Julian Carillo (1875–1965), Preble predicted that "the future of music will be based upon a scale split into not only quarter-tones, but even smaller intervals"—requiring adjustments in hearers' sensibilities. "Our modern composers are beginning to realize," she went on, "that this Indian music is a mine of musical treasure as yet hardly touched."[200] Ten years later Preble would likewise champion the eccentric tonal experimenter and instrument inventor Harry Partch (1901–74) in his first Guggenheim applications.[201]

Still, there is no evidence that Preble returned from the final, tumultuous year at Hawikku with new rhythms or intervals for the jazz age. Instead, she apparently spent considerable time with Zuni mothers and children, and came away impressed with their childrearing. In a series of syndicated articles sponsored by the National Kindergarten Association, she challenged American women to learn from the strict but calm and loving mothers of the pueblo Southwest—women of "the oldest cradle," she said, who "had lived nothing but moral and chaste lives" before Whites arrived. Alternately romancing the primitive and censuring lackadaisical White parents, Preble's pieces displayed some experience in observing birthing, bathing, and early child-raising in the pueblo.[202]

But the most intriguing publication from Preble's Zuni summer had nothing to do with music or children. In 1926 appeared in Sportlife *magazine her article on "The Oldest Sport in America: The Stick-Race of the Indians of the Southwest"—her account of a Zuni foot race observed at Hawikku.[203] The article is notable for several reasons. It will be recalled that Hodge's first anthropological publication (in* The American Anthropologist*, 1890) was on the same subject: "A Zuni Foot-Race," in which he had expanded upon Cushing's 1883 description (in* My Adventures in Zuñi*). At times Hodge had borrowed Cushing's phrases.[204] Preble's article was doubly derivative, but also distinctive.*

Cushing had emphasized that Zuni games were sacred, since they were reenactments of the games with which the twin War Gods (Ahayu'da) "had whiled away the eons of time ancient," as he put it.[205] *Coming after the early planting season, the race encouraged rainclouds to follow the sticks home. Runners from competing kivas trained for four days before the stick race, which engaged the entire pueblo and involved a run of twenty-five miles toward Thunder Mountain and back. In Hodge's telling seven years later, by contrast, while the race (which he probably saw in 1889) has "more or less of a religious significance," it is equally an occasion for betting valuables, household goods, even horses. Hodge's description of the race is closer and more elaborate, including the rough topography, the accompanying horsemen, and the excited engagement of observers. But his event is notably more secular than Cushing's, with greater emphasis on the physical challenge.*[206]

Preble's trope of age notwithstanding ("oldest cradle, oldest sport"), from the first line of her account we see a changed Zuni world of 1923. Motoring in the open air with Hodge ("my companion") on the twelve-mile dirt road from the pueblo to Camp Harmon at Hawikku, she espies a boy kicking a stick. Hodge explains to her the traditional game. The scene then shifts to their camp, with several photos of breech-clothed Zuni men, as two rows of runners prepare. One having forgotten his cloth, Preble hunts up a white towel from her trunk. A few wagons of wives and family noisily arrive at camp. At this point it becomes apparent that the race is being sponsored well out of season. And the race is not between kivas but between teams of workers at the two excavation sites of Hawikku and nearby Kechipauan. Indeed, according to Preble, the race—nine miles rather than twenty-five—is the friendly result of the "considerable rivalry between the two gangs of native workmen in unearthing skeletons and rooms with their contents."[207]

Preble's 1926 account borrows heavily from her future husband's of a generation before, but with greater emphasis on the attractive bodies and physical strength of the Zuni men—running "like the native jack-rabbits" through the rough terrain—and the constant "merriment" and "banter" of the betting women. "The instincts for play, for gambling, and for worshipping their gods are equally strong in every Zuñi mind," she offers.[208] *But in the reading it is hard to avoid a sense of dislocation and appropriation. On one hand, Preble em-*

ploys the ethnographic present to suggest an ageless Zuni practice of planting, rain, and a prayerful relationship to the gods; but on the other hand, the event itself seems little more than a gay afternoon outing connected more to a controversial archaeological project than to traditional cultural values: the Zuni men and their families return by wagon to their pueblo homes, while the archaeologists go off to dinner under the ramada. Needless to say, Bow Priests are nowhere to be seen. And in place of secluded days of preparation, blessings, and prayer sticks for rain, we are left with the image of Zahrah's white towel on a Zuni body.

After her Zuni sojourn, Preble moved to upper Manhattan, presumably to be near Hodge. Over the next several years she tried her hand at some pulp fiction.[209] *She and Fred married in 1927 and returned for a brief, apparently bittersweet reunion at Hawikku in the summer of 1928.*[210] *Their Christmas card that year bespoke a new freedom:*

We free our bird from a Zuni jar,
And send him winging near and far–
To speed to you good Christmas cheer,
With wishes best for your new year.[211]

Three Christmases later Fred and Zahrah took Dollar Steamship Lines' President Grant *through the Panama Canal to Los Angeles and Fred's new directorship at the Southwest Museum. They soon settled into a comfortable social life at 1375 Lida Street in shady Pasadena. Zahrah learned how to drive.*[212]

Figure 27. Fred Hodge, Fourth Lake (Adirondacks), New York, 1925. Courtesy of the Braun Research Library Collection, Autry Museum, Los Angeles; N43325.

Figure 28. Zahrah Preble, Fourth Lake (Adirondacks), New York, 1925. Courtesy of the Braun Research Library Collection, Autry Museum, Los Angeles; N43324.

Once settled in southern California Zahrah's lasting interests in education and Indigenous folk coalesced in a writing project for elementary schoolchildren: she planned a series of five booklets on the traditional lifeways of Gabrielino Indian children. The California Jurisdiction Act of 1928 had just recognized the potential standing of long-deferred land claims for the San Gabriel Band of Mission Indians (Gabrielino-Tongva Indian Tribe), whose ancestral lands lay throughout the San Bernardino region. They had been removed some years before to Tejon Pass. Zahrah wrote the first book, Tomar of Siba, *with suggestions from her husband and illustrations by her sister Donna. She introduced it as "a story with an ethnological background designed for the instruction of schoolchildren." Hodge's foreword promised it would counteract "misinformation for juvenile consumption." The little book appeared in 1933.*[213] *Sadly, it was her last publication: after only seven years of marriage and a brief bout with liver cancer, Zahrah Preble Hodge died in the South Pasadena Sanitorium on April 27, 1934.*

NEW YORK AFTER HAWIKKU, 1924–1932

Hodge returned from Hawikku intending to write a full report. Hendricks had provided a small publication fund, which was augmented at his death in 1928 by $15,000. The funds lay largely untouched for more than thirty years.[214] In fact Hodge came to believe, angrily but wrongly, that Heye had spent them for museum operating expenses. The controversy over Hodge's unwritten Hawikku report would sour relations between the two men for the rest of their lives.

In the meantime, though, Hodge resumed heavy editing chores for the reports of ongoing fieldwork and collecting of others. While he barely appeared in the museum's annual reports himself, every year he produced more than a thousand pages of MAI publications, including the popular new Indian Notes quarterly series.[215] The purpose of the generously illustrated Notes was to feature current field activities and recent acquisitions in brief, easily absorbed and well-illustrated pieces contributed by MAI staff. Hodge had always believed in rapid-fire publication of even "preliminary" results, and Notes again served that purpose.

He became involved in various ways, too, with new attention to the museum's library. From the founding in 1916 the MAI library had been housed in the nearby headquarters of the American Geographical Society. By the mid-twenties the collection had grown to more than five thousand volumes and Heye decided to move it to the basement of the Museum. This occurred in May 1927, just a year after trustee Ford had provided the funds for two major purchases: the personal libraries of Hodge ($25,000) and Marshall Saville ($50,000). Each man dated the beginning of his bibliophilia to about 1890, and each possessed many rare books and manuscripts.

Hodge's description of his library is revealing. In addition to 1,200 volumes and 1,600 pamphlets on the Southwest, his accounting of the library included the following:

> [T]he original unpublished manuscripts of Frank Hamilton Cushing; the letters given to the Zuñi Indians by military officers and others connected with the exploring expeditions following the Mexican war; photostat copies of various unpublished Spanish documents from the Archivo General at Sevilla, the archives of the Vatican, and the Library of Congress.[216]

These materials had all been in the Cushing trunk that Emily gave to Stewart Culin in 1903 for safekeeping after Frank's death; in 1921 Culin gave them to Hodge, who incorporated them into his "library." Within, and especially rare, were the papers that Pedro Pino (Lai-iu-ah-tsai-lu), governor of Zuni from 1830 to 1878 and father of Palowahtiwa, had collected and stored in his pueblo rooms over decades, and which Cushing somehow had obtained. "A perusal of Pedro Pino's papers reads like a history of the Southwest," Pedro's biographer has written.[217] The "photostat copies" from Spain and the Vatican had probably been made by Bandelier while working for the Hemenway Expedition.[218] Additionally, although not listed by Hodge, his library included nearly five thousand pages of correspondence, in nine letterbooks, from the Hemenway Expedition.

Finally, Hodge's listing of his library noted "the beginning of an elaborately annotated Bibliography of the Pueblo Indians . . . compiled on several thousand cards."[219] Almost certainly this was the ever-expanding bibliography that he had compiled for nearly three decades at the Bureau of Ethnology—and therefore, presumably, it was government property.

The fates of these materials are not incidental to Hodge's biography. Spurred by the Hodge and Saville acquisitions, in 1926 Heye announced establishment of the James B. Ford Library and a new group, Friends of the Library. The new Ford library was housed in the museum basement, but the move was temporary. Three years later Archer Huntington built an addition to the Huntington Free Library and Reading Room at Westchester Square in the Bronx—formerly Collis Huntington's home. Here he provided room and shelving for one hundred thousand volumes, so in 1930 the Ford Library moved to the Bronx with an endowment from Huntington. The Hodge collection thus had a new home, but with a caveat in the original purchase: that "whatever arrangements may be made should contemplate my retention of the library during my lifetime." When Hodge left for the Southwest Museum two years later, many materials went with him.[220] However, the Hemenway letterbooks—nearly five thousand pages of Cushing correspondence—stayed in the Bronx, undiscovered until 1991.[221]

The Heye Museum's salad days ended abruptly in 1928. In the last week of March Hendricks and Ford, Heye's close friends and generous trustees, died within thirty-six hours of one another. A month later Heye discovered that the millions he had expected from them would be little more than

$300,000. On May 1 he dismissed fifteen people, including Harrington, Cadzow, and the younger Saville brother, Foster. (Marshall stayed on until 1932 with support from Thea.) Over the next fourteen months three more trustees passed away: Walter L. Worrill, William E. Harmon (1862–1928), and Minor Cooper Keith (1848–1929). Hendricks, Ford, and Keith had been with Heye since 1916; he relied on them for their financial gifts, and in the case of Keith—who was vice president of United Fruit—ready access to Caribbean and Central American fields. Thus even before the stock market crash of late 1929 decimated his personal finances Heye suddenly and severely had to cut back. Not surprisingly, this left much bitterness.[222]

Hodge negotiated to stay on at reduced salary, but Heye stipulated that the Hawikku write-up would have to be pursued outside of office time; it was his standard policy toward scientific staff. Hodge reminded "the Boss" that Hendricks had left a special fund for finishing up Hawikku; Heye replied that he needed it for expenses.[223] This was the last straw for Hodge. As the Great Depression deepened and a new opportunity arose in 1931, Fred and Zahrah decamped for the West Coast.

Act Three: Pasadena

THE SOUTHWEST MUSEUM

Mañana flor de sus ayeres—"Tomorrow will be the flower of its yesterdays." Charles F. Lummis's motto for the Southwest Museum reflected his lifelong obsessions with history, its salience for the present, and his own future legacy. He had incorporated the museum in 1907, largely designed its architecture, and opened the Mount Washington campus in 1914 along the Arroyo Seco, between downtown Los Angeles and Pasadena. It was Los Angeles's first museum. To be sure, the Southwest Museum formed only a singular drama in Lummis's operatic life of physical adventure, prodigious literary output, regional and self-promotion, and scandal.[224] But, as Thomas Wilson observed of him, the very force of personality that makes founders successful often creates problematic consequences for their institutions.[225] Lummis was actively involved in the museum of his dreams for little more than a decade, and though, after years of illness, he died in 1928 of a brain tumor, his spirit and influence were still very much alive when his old friend Fred Hodge arrived as director in early 1932.

Lummis and Hodge could never agree about when they first met, but it was probably at Zuni in early October 1888.[226] As we have seen, they enjoyed each other's camaraderie and support over a decade of mutual career growth around the turn of the century. They remained friends, but as Hodge took charge of the BAE in 1910 they were drawing apart, and Lummis was entering a tumultuous period of bitter public divorce and professional (and physical) setbacks from which he never recovered. His museum began existence in Arroyo Seco in 1914 already deeply in debt from its construction—a condition from which it, too, never recovered. Lummis resigned as secretary of the board in 1915 but stayed on as trustee for four more years; in 1917 the museum placed him on a $100-per-month lifetime retainer and returned the Southwest collections and his nearby house, El Alisal, that he had deeded to the future museum in 1910.[227] By 1919 his active relationship with the museum had ended.

Hector Alliot (1862–1919), having served as curator of Lummis's Southwest Society since 1909, became the first director of the Southwest Museum in 1917, but he died two years later. An archaeologist and art historian, Alliot was a familiar civic figure and popular lecturer in the city. He was adviser to the Ruskin Art Club—the first women's club in Los Angeles—and at his passing that club established the museum's Hector Alliot Memorial Library of Archaeology. Alliot held many positions in cultural organizations, including president of the Southern California Academy of Sciences (1907). Under his brief leadership the Southwest Museum emphasized history, archaeology, art, field sciences, and local outreach to students.[228]

After Alliot's passing the museum entered a period of drift as an unfocused, general interest repository of everything from Hispanic and Native American artifacts to butterflies. The first temporary director (1919–21), Milbank Johnson, was a respected physician, and the second director (1921–26), John Henry Comstock (1849–1931), was an entomologist; both faced debilitating financial pressures.[229] In 1926, however, James Augustus Brown Scherer (1870–1944) succeeded them. Scherer had served (1908–20) as the last president of Throop Polytechnic Institute in Pasadena, which became Caltech under his leadership. He then traveled and wrote for six years, increasingly interested in Native American and California history.[230] In his five-year directorship Scherer refocused the museum's programming and collecting on southwestern anthropology, Native American history, and education. He hired an impressive professional staff: Mark Harrington, Charles Avery Amsden (1899–1941), Avery Monroe Amsden (1860–1945), Harold Sterling Gladwin (1883–1983), and Frances Emma Watkins (1899–c. 1987). In 1927 he inaugurated *The Masterkey*, initially a bimonthly (later quarterly) membership magazine that attained national respect over sixty-two years. In 1928 appeared the first Southwest Museum Papers: Monroe Amsden's *Anthropological Reconnaissance in Sonora* and Gladwin's *Excavations at Casa Grande, Arizona*; many more followed. By 1930 the museum was offering public programs for schoolchildren and adults. Of equal importance, Scherer established an advisory council that included Alfred Vincent Kidder, Alfred Kroeber, John Campbell Merriam, and James Henry Breasted, thereby putting forward the Southwest Museum as a national player in anthropology.

Locally and regionally, too, Scherer brought new visibility. The 1920s was a boom decade for Los Angeles, driven by immigration (largely from Mexico), petroleum, and Hollywood. Adjacent Pasadena was enjoying unprecedented prosperity, too, as seen in a spate of new civic building, a boisterous downtown business district, and the first Rose Bowl game in 1922. The bohemian "Arroyo Seco Culture" of Lummis's heyday continued to attract a new generation of artists and Arts and Crafts adherents.[231] New private organizations of history, art, literature, and anthropology—such as the Southwestern Archaeological Federation of 1929 (now the Southwestern Anthropological Association), the Zamorano Club of California bibliophiles (1928), the Huntington Library (1919)—attested to a cultural coming of age for the region.[232] Director Scherer and the Southwest Museum contributed to this southern California energy. Additionally, in 1927 Scherer became one of the original trustees of the new Laboratory of Anthropology in Santa Fe, forging a link that Hodge would value and sustain. (Hodge was on the lab's organizing committee.)[233] Although the coming years brought significant economic strain, Hodge would continue the cultural engagements that Scherer had established.

Scherer's directorship was a long five years for him, and by 1931 he was ready to return to a longstanding fascination with Japanese culture and politics. Perhaps, as one historian observed, "the problems of personnel relations and public relations had been proving more difficult for a man of his temperament than those of scientific organization and research."[234]

Mark Harrington stepped in briefly as acting director, but just as Jess Nussbaum had advised George Heye to hire Hodge in 1916, now Harrington recommended his former MAI colleague to be the next director. There were no competitors. After a series of New York interviews in late 1931, Hodge prepared to move to Pasadena.

When he wooed Hodge in 1916 George Heye had promised raises, but there were none; after 1928 Hodge's salary was cut. Thus, at an age when most men are pondering retirement, and in the early deep trough of the Great Depression, sixty-eight-year old Hodge must have viewed the Southwest Museum appointment as a godsend. It offered a final career option—and perhaps a rejoinder to Heye's frustratingly unscientific museum-building. Though the museum's core of activist supporters had always been small and less wealthy than Heye's trustee circle, they were women and men dedicated to the growth of regional history and culture: lawyers, physicians, businesspeople and developers, educators and artists.[235] Hodge added the missing ingredient: anthropological heft.

LAST WORDS ON THE HEMENWAY EXPEDITION—AND CUSHING

But still there was the Hemenway-Cushing shadow. In the fall of 1931, as Fred and Zahrah were still in New York pondering their upcoming California adventure, a recently arrived Harvard graduate student in archaeology, Emil Walter Haury (1904–92), was casting about for a PhD dissertation topic. Alfred Tozzer suggested that he study the Hemenway Expedition collections from the Salt River Valley, which had been largely ignored since being deposited at the Peabody Museum in 1894.[236] Chasing his personal timeline—two to three years to finish—Haury acted quickly. Concerned about the lack of documentation among the dusty boxes of artifacts, he immediately wrote to Hodge as the sole survivor of the expedition.[237] Hodge responded with alacrity. He all too readily accused Cushing of keeping few notes and relying on his memory in the field, wasting time writing long letters to Hemenway and Baxter that "contained a great deal of bunk." Hodge then rehearsed at length his conviction that Cushing had secretly "manufactured" the controversial turquoise mosaic frog and passed it off to Morse and Hemenway as an authentic artifact from Los Muertos. Hodge also mentioned that he had "a considerable body of Cushing's notes and parts of articles, in much of a jumble" and would look through it: "As soon as I can, I shall try to see what I can find in the mess. If there is anything pertaining to your present quest . . . I shall let you know."[238] Although the Cushing letterbooks were available to him in New York, he offered little of substance and ultimately sent nothing.

Subsequent letters to Haury referred to Cushing's "fanciful report" to the 1888 Berlin International Congress of Americanists conference and his "visions" of waterstones and canal navigation.[239] But Hodge did not indicate the nature or extent of the expedition-related documents that he still possessed in New York (and later, Pasadena). Again, he sent Haury nothing. Years later Haury wrote:

> Hodge had assured me that such records had existed. The irony of it all was that when an inventory was made of Dr. Hodge's voluminous papers after his death, and the collection had been acquired by the Southwest Museum, many documents, some of Cushing's included, were found that related to the Salt River Valley excavations. Had those been available to me, the dissertation would have been far more meaningful.[240]

Haury kept to his timetable. He sent the dissertation draft to Hodge at the Southwest Museum in early 1934, since Hodge had agreed to provide a foreword to the eventual publication. Hodge made no significant suggestions to the draft but, in a series of handwritten notes, further faulted Cushing for his imaginings and laziness:

> Illness prevented Cushing, at times, from visiting the diggings from Camp Hemenway nearby; at other times he fiddled away his time in making flags for the tents and other useless trifles. Sometimes weeks passed without the laborers having any supervision excepting that given by the intelligent Mexican laborer Ramón Castro. Cushing was jealous of note-taking by anyone but himself.[241]

Eight years passed. Hodge promised the foreword but seemed uncertain of an approach. Haury added his own brief history of the expedition to his book manuscript. When Hodge finally delivered his foreword in 1942, it focused harshly on Cushing; as Hodge explained to Peabody Museum director Donald Scott, "I believe that Cushing was entirely responsible for what was or was not accomplished by the Expedition."[242] Scott and Haury asked Hodge to add some paragraphs about the nature of archaeological conditions and praxis in "those pioneering days." Hodge refused by not responding. As published, his three-page foreword repeated the accusations of Cushing's incompetence and visionary meandering: Cushing suffered, he asserted, from "an overwrought imagination and a species of egotism that brooked no opinion adverse to his own." The lack of documentation and the "paucity" of the expedition's results, he said, could be attributed entirely to the director's personality. Sensing perhaps the severity of his words, Hodge added:

> It may be ungracious to thus speak of one who passed away more than forty years ago, yet it seems important to the science of which he was an advocate that this insight into his character and attitude be revealed, since it had a vital bearing on the methods and results of his work, and explains in some degree the lack of information that the operations of the Hemenway Expedition suffered.[243]

Hodge's contribution had little effect on what is recognized today as Haury's classic study of Hohokam archaeology, but it did shape the perception of Cushing for decades to come. Hodge had had his last, belittling public words on his former brother-in-law and the Hemenway Expedition of sixty years before.[244]

FINAL YEARS: MUSEUM DIRECTOR, 1932–1955

A formal photograph of the attendees at the first Pecos Conference in the summer of 1927 shows Fred Hodge standing at the far-right edge of the picture. The symbolism is apt. Along with Fewkes (who did not attend), by 1927 he was the last of a fading generation, an honored historical figure already superseded in southwestern archaeological theory and practice by a new generation of university-trained figures—and their students, such as Haury.[245]

The trustees of the Southwest Museum hired him for other qualities, however. In his 1960 history of the Museum W. W. Robinson caught the reasoning: "Hodge, fond of people, had led an active social life, was a man of pleasant wit, a good story-teller, and delightful as an *ex tempore* speaker."[246] Moreover, he was a national figure with extensive organizational affiliations and a very wide network that had been established, as we have seen, through decades of editorial aid to others. As Heye had earlier appreciated, Hodge seemed to know everyone, and everyone seemed to like him. Approaching seventy, he had begun to fully inhabit the jocose social persona that had first appeared in New York.

In his history of Hodge's years at the Southwest Museum, Thomas Wilson divided the twenty-three-year tenure (1932–55) into three phases: an initial surge of activities to the beginning of World War II; a pause and diminution during the war years; and partial resumption, below prewar levels, in the final decade to 1955. The first years saw a burst of energy in collecting. Hodge drew on long-standing friendships and acquaintances, and knowledge of private collections, to bring new strength to the museum's holdings, especially in southwestern and Californian Hispanic and Native artifacts. His skill and charm in negotiating loans that eventually became gifts were rare. He strongly supported the fieldwork (especially at Paleoindian and Archaic sites) of Harrington, Amsden, and others, much of which was begun under Scherer. As previously in Washington and New York, Hodge leaned heavily on the practice of immediate, frequent, and attractively illustrated publications to announce field results and showcase recent acquisitions, employing not only *The Masterkey* but a new series, Leaflets. (Assistant curator Frances Watkins was especially skillful in producing the latter.) Staff appreciated and donors loved the attention. The collections—archaeological, ethnological, historical, photographs, paintings, and drawings—grew by more than a hundred thousand items over two decades.[247]

True to his bibliophilia, Hodge built an impressive reference library to aid the collecting and research arms of the institution. He emphasized photographic and other visual records, and saw it as a critical legacy. As Wilson summarizes: "He collected, by gift, exchange or purchase, books, serials, manuscripts, broadsheets, prints, pamphlets, maps and other materials within the Museum's focus." At his death the library and photograph archives would also total more than one hundred thousand items.[248]

Space was always a dilemma. The museum building that Lummis had designed, with its striking Caracol Tower rising above the Arroyo Seco, was poorly designed for exhibits and difficult for public access. In the late thirties Hodge renovated and expanded the exhibit spaces, adding a new wing for the exceptional Indigenous basket collection of Caroline Boeing Poole (1884–1932). He also made more effective use of the lobby area and members' room for special exhibitions and the club-like comfort of donors and other guests. As new collections increased from fieldwork and acquisition, though, space limitations became acute. Even after a second rearrangement in 1954 the Southwest Museum's exhibit galleries suffered from poor lighting and labeling and a sense of crowding. One critic, writing in 1956, concluded that Hodge's museum "has not kept pace with museological developments which are common knowledge to museum personnel throughout America and Europe."[249] In contrast to Heye's practices at the Museum of the American Indian, Hodge placed supreme importance on public attendance figures, membership rolls, and the educational outreach of his museum. Neither membership (still less than six hundred by 1954) nor endowment was ever remotely adequate. But always there were the collections—and the large shadow of George Heye. As Wilson perceptively concludes, Hodge "literally charmed the collections out of numerous individuals and pulled out all stops to secure others, yet during the whole period there is little retrospection about the purposes of collecting."[250]

Hodge oversaw or edited an impressive array of monographs in these years. During his tenure the Southwest Museum Papers series included reports by Harrington, C. A. Amsden, Elizabeth Warder Crozier Campbell (1893–1971) and her husband William Henry Campbell (1895–1944), Frances Densmore (1867–1957), S. K. Lothrop, and George Walton Brainard (1909–56), among others. In 1936 Mu Alpha Nu, the anthropology fraternity founded at the University of Southern California three years before, established the Frederick Webb Hodge Anniversary Publication Fund to commemorate his fifty years in anthropology.[251] The first volume, partially supported by George Heye, was Hodge's own *History of Hawikuh* in 1937; five more Anniversary Fund volumes appeared in his lifetime.

Hodge's personal life took another fortunate turn in the Pasadena years. Shortly before Zahrah's untimely death in 1934, a Wisconsin woman interested in textile (cretonne) design visited the Southwest Museum to study the patterns and colors of the eight-hundred-item kachina collection. Gene Patricia Meany (1898–1989) had studied interior decoration in San Diego and New York but had first seen kachina figures at the Milwaukee Public Museum; she was planning a drawing book. She met Hodge as he was repairing some pottery and he took immediate interest in her and her project. Every afternoon (she recalled) he brought her "a cup of strong, bitter coffee" and they drank together. He brought her home to meet Zahrah and the two women became friends. Gene and Fred were married in Santa Fe in August 1936, just as her first book, *The Kachinas Are Coming*, appeared. He wrote the foreword.[252]

Fred and "Genie" Hodge enjoyed a lively Pasadena social life, centering on Sunday afternoon teas at their Lida Street home after museum lectures. She drove him to anthropology conferences and meetings through the Southwest, and they grew increasingly attached to Santa Fe, where he was a trustee of the School of American Research and the Laboratory of Anthropology and a founder of the Indian Arts Fund. Their social circles in both Arroyo Seco and Santa Fe were wide, as Bernard L. Fontana attested:

> I know from close acquaintance of people who knew him that during Hodge's years at the Southwest Museum he was lionized by the Los Angeles intelligentsia. Writers, artists, historians, and virtually anyone in Southern California with an interest in Indians or in anthropological themes generally looked to Hodge as their guru. . . . Although Hodge was already dead by the time I arrived on the Santa Fe scene in the early 1960s, it was also clear he was lionized there as well by a large group of extremely wealthy women as well as by writers (including poets) and artists who had a passion for American Indians.[253]

Among their closest friends in both Pasadena and Santa Fe were Leonora Scott Muse Curtin (1879–1972) and her daughter Leonora Frances Curtin Paloheimo (1903–99)—fondly known as Leonora I and Leonora II. Leonora I's mother, Eva Scott Fenyes (1849–1930), the only child of a wealthy New York City couple, had traveled globally but fallen in love with Southern California and Santa Fe in the 1890s. An accomplished watercolorist, she had helped to finance and served as an early trustee of the Southwest Museum, and had worked with Lummis to restore California missions (which she also painted).[254] Her Pasadena home—where all three women lived from 1916 to 1930—became a center for the early bohemian art community.[255]

Her daughter (Leonora I) became an amateur ethnobotanist, a patroness of the Southwest Museum and, along with granddaughter Leonora II, an enthusiastic supporter of Fred's career and Gene's art. "It was Teluli who kept us all laughing," Leonora II happily remembered.[256] For years Gene Hodge exchanged hand-colored Christmas cards and poems with the Curtin-Paloheimo women.[257] On Hodge's ninetieth birthday in 1954, Leonora II penned a poem that expressed her affection for the Teluli figure that Hodge had become in the eyes of his acquaintances.

Teluli
Today, as yesterday and tomorrow
one tall of spirit stands
High above the field and furrow
On noble mountain slopes.

The eyes of men look skyward, knowing
that sequoias dwell on high
But lo, this humble giant's learning
Is where the seeker gropes.

He bends his lavish hand to raise
and lead the smallest lamb,
While with his chosen words of praise
Can light prolific hopes.

Yet, in those famous pigeonholes, his mind
has stored some billion jokes
So that when it's time to laugh we find
He also knows the ropes.[258]

Curtain Call

Fred Hodge passed away quietly in the evening of September 28, 1956, after an afternoon picnic in the hills around Santa Fe. It was seventy years since he had first met Frank Cushing in Powell's offices of the Geological Survey. He had outlived his brother-in-law by fifty-six years, but he never outran

Cushing's shadow. In fact, the most important lessons of his long career in anthropology—lessons that assuredly conformed to his personality—had been learned in relation and reaction to Cushing. He had absorbed them early and deeply.

Army lieutenant John G. Bourke once called Cushing an "electric light" among a "congregation of penny-dips"—brilliant, charismatic, unique—and a threat to "many an old plug who has grown fat and greasy."[259] Powell, a master of institutional science, considered him an intuitive genius. But in his brief, erratic trajectory Cushing never understood institutions; he used them, depended upon them, but always straddled a border between organized science and his poetic, imaginative freedom. He lived for the moments of discovery but had little time for deadening chores of scientific polish and proof. The flash of brilliance, the promising insight, the far-reaching theory—then Cushing was moving on, leaving the litter of his research strewn for others to pick up, if they could.

As both protégé and brother-in-law Hodge saw firsthand that Frank and Emily Cushing paid a steep price in health and personal welfare for Frank's disinterest in organizational conformity—and he determined to find another pathway. As one art historian has remarked of Thomas Eakins's famous 1895 Cushing portrait: "This is not a man who has happily bridged the gap between the pre-modern and the modern."[260] Radically independent son of a nonconformist country doctor, Cushing neither obtained academic degrees nor trained students; controversy constantly trailed him. His patron relationships—Hemenway, Hearst—were intense and unsteady; only Powell was completely steadfast. The coming world of institutionalized social science was alien and probably unwelcome to the outdoor boy from Albion. And Cushing was chronically, sometimes dangerously ill.

Hodge knew all this intimately, as he had cooked Cushing's special meals and helped many times to pump his stomach and comfort him in desert tents. In strong contrast, Hodge was robust, rarely sick; for decades he could largely count on a steady working pattern over long periods and often deep into the night—whether in camp or in the city. It was a fortune of good health that stayed with him (despite dozens of cigarettes a day) literally to his final hours.

Above all, Hodge understood modern organizational life. Middle child of an immigrant family, he learned early to tread carefully and dutifully through the hierarchical world of men in business, science and politics. From Copp, Pilling, and Powell to Langley, Heye, and Hendricks his career steps were gradual—and remarkable opportunities seemed to fall to him as others moved or died and vacancies appeared. Hodge worked tirelessly, and he never said no. The traumatic ending of the Hemenway Expedition in 1889 was the severest crisis of his early career, as it threatened his still fragile reputation for probity and honesty. From that point he proceeded to embed himself, mainly through editing chores and occasional fieldwork, as concierge and eventual gatekeeper for the new, sometimes slippery profession of anthropology. After all, personal advancement depended on publication—printer's ink was the lifeblood of an anthropological career. A coaxing, helpful editor gained many grateful adherents.

Chiefly interested, like his friend Fewkes, in descriptive accounts of field activities and artifacts, Hodge rarely took a public stance on theoretical or political controversies. Even in the most severe professional flare-up of the early century—the censure of Franz Boas by hostile Washington and Harvard anthropologists in 1919 ("the scientific reaction against cultural anthropology," George Stocking labeled it) Hodge played a quiet and meliorating role, despite close friendships with Boas's archenemies William Henry Holmes and Aleš Hrdlička. In Stocking's words an "easygoing and tractable Washingtonian," Hodge maintained a balance and kept collegial relations with all parties. His correspondence with Boas remained congenial well into the 1930s.[261]

After moving to Pasadena Hodge assumed the role of lovable elder statesman and storyteller. While his mind remained remarkably sharp for some historical details, his preferred mode of recall became the humorous anecdote, or the western tall tale: burros stuck in arroyos, "strange frontier characters I have known," and so forth. His daughter Emlyn recalled him, with distaste, as a "born humorist." Anthropologist Marjorie Lambert (1908–2006) was struck by Hodge's "meticulous mind and memory" but nonetheless judged that by the time she got to know him in the thirties "he was more of a storyteller than anything else." But, she added, "he had such charm that you couldn't forget him."[262] James Frank Dobie (1888–1964), folklorist and "Storyteller of the West," described his friend Hodge as "an ample and noble human being, a great scholar and delightful gentleman, and a companion of rich anecdote."[263] Yet another latter-day admirer, author and librarian Lawrence Clark Powell (1906–2001), attempted in homage to repeat Hodge's 1896 climb of Mesa Encantada but settled for writing a poem as he sat in its shade with a dove, lizard, and butterfly:

> Sky, sun, and water, the Southwest and Fred Hodge.
> These are the immortal elements.
> This is the region we inhabit.
> Here is the man we love and honor.[264]

Figure 29. Frederick Hodge, 1956. Photo by Lonnie Hull. Courtesy of the Los Angeles Corral of Westerners.

In *Old Dan Dubois*, a lighthearted memoir for the Los Angeles Corral of Westerners in 1950, Hodge cobbled together a piecemeal biography of frontiersman, scout, and New Mexican rancher Dubois (Dennis Donovan, c. 1833–1923). In a series of humorous vignettes Hodge emphasized Dubois's many knife and bullet wounds, his infamous love of liquor, and the mystery of his origins. Hodge's sketch was pure western mythmaking—and wildly popular with his California audience. What Hodge did not mention, however, was Dan's long and admiring friendship with Cushing beginning in the early 1880s at Zuni, and Hodge's own introduction to the man: when "Old Dan" served as a teamster for the Hemenway Expedition in the summer of 1888. Anecdote was more palatable than historical fact.[265]

The career that began in 1886 with Pullman car nightmares of western cliffs and revolvers ended on a warm autumn evening in Santa Fe seventy years later. He had asked that his ashes be spread over the ruins of Hawikku. The Zuni world that a young Fred Hodge had first seen on the Hemenway Expedition was to be, he hoped, his final home.

A few weeks after his passing, Fred Hodge returned to Hawikku. Today many will find rich irony, even offense, in the admixture of his ashes to a graveyard from which he had extracted hundreds of Native burials. At the end of his long life, though, Teluli's world saw only its appropriate completion. "His ashes scattered on Hawikuh was a fitting end to the discarded husk," wrote Arthur Woodward (1898–1986), archaeologist and friend of many years. "He was close to the history of the Southwest, especially Zuni and Hawikuh, and now he is literally a part of it. He began his career digging in the dust of ages and now that he has melted into it, the union is perfect."[266]

Abbreviations

AMH	Acequia Madre House (Women's International Study Center), Santa Fe
BR/AM	Braun Research Library Collection, Autry Museum, Los Angeles
CURMC	Cornell University Division of Rare and Manuscript Collections, Ithaca, New York
FWHC	Frederick Webb Hodge Collection, Southwest Museum, Los Angeles
HC	Hemenway Southwestern Archaeological Expedition papers, 1886–96, Collection #9186. Cornell University Library, Division of Rare and Manuscript Collections, Ithaca, New York
HCP	Hodge Cushing Papers, Southwest Museum of the American Indian, Autry National Center of the American West, Los Angeles
HLB	Hemenway Letter Books, Hemenway Southwestern Archaeological Expedition Papers, 1886–96, Collection #9186, Series II, 1–9. Cornell University Library, Division of Rare and Manuscript Collections, Ithaca, New York
MAIA	Museum of the American Indian Archives, Smithsonian Institution, Suitland, Maryland
NAA	National Anthropological Archives, Smithsonian Institution
NYSLA	Edward Everett Hale Papers (1750–1909), Manuscripts and Special Collections, New York State Library and Archives

PEM	Peabody Essex Museum, Salem, Massachusetts
PMH	Pasadena Museum of History, Pasadena, California
RWD	Papers of Ralph W. Dexter, Kent State University Archives, Kent, Ohio
SIA	Smithsonian Institution Archives, Washington, D.C.
SMA	Sylvester Manor Archives, Fales Library and Special Collections, New York University
THS	Tempe Historical Society, Tempe, Arizona

Notes

Introduction to the Multivolume Work

1. Obituary of Mary Tileston Hemenway, *Boston Transcript*, 10 March 1894.

2. Fewkes's career as director of the "Second" Hemenway Expedition is the subject of Wade and McChesney's *America's Great Lost Expedition.*

3. Haury, *The Excavation of Los Muertos.*

4. Hodge to Haury, 5 October 1931, FWHC, no. 138.

5. Foreword to Haury, *The Excavation of Los Muertos*, vii–ix.

6. Handwritten notes from Hodge to Haury, 30 March 1934, X-file 94–36, H-2, Peabody Museum Archives, Peabody Museum of Archaeology and Ethnology, Harvard University.

7. Ira Jacknis, "The Stewart Culin Papers," MS, Brooklyn Museum.

8. Culin to Hodge, 28 February 1921, FWHC.

9. Neil Judd et al., "Frederick Webb Hodge, 1864–1956." The Southwest Museum recently completed a computerized inventory of the Hodge and Cushing Collections.

10. Raymond Stewart Brandes, "Frank Hamilton Cushing: Pioneer Americanist"; Bandelier, *The Southwest Journals of Adolph F. Bandelier, 1880–1882.*

11. Joan Mark, "Frank Hamilton Cushing and an American Science of Anthropology," 484; Green, *Zuni*; Green, *Cushing at Zuni.*

12. See also Hinsley, *The Smithsonian and the American Indian*; Hinsley and McChesney, "Anthropology as Cultural Exchange"; McChesney, "The Vision of Mary Hemenway"; and Wilcox and Sternberg, *Additional Studies.*

13. Eustis, *Augustus Hemenway, 1805–1876.* Cushing's personal diaries were given to Jesse Green by Anne E. Smullen, a grandniece of Cushing's wife, Emily Magill Cushing; see Green, *Cushing at Zuni*, 348.

14. Wilcox et al., *One Hundred Years of Archaeology.*

15. The installments of Cushing's itinerary constitute the second volume of this work.

16. Wade and McChesney's exhibit catalogue *America's Great Lost Expedition* appeared in 1980. See also Hinsley, *The Smithsonian and the American Indian*; Hinsley, "Ethnographic Charisma and Scientific Routine"; Hinsley, "From Shell-Heaps to Stelae"; and Hinsley, "Wanted."

17. Wilcox and Howard, "The Contribution of the Hemenway Expedition"; Wilcox et al., *One Hundred Years of Archaeology*; Wilcox, "Pueblo Grande."

18. See, e.g., Swentzell, "Levels of Truth."

Preface to Volume 3

1. Ezell, "History of the Pima," 158–59.

Part I. Love Among the Ruins

1. Hodge diary, 5 December 1886.

2. Cushing married Emma Magill at her mother's home in Washington, D.C., on 10 July 1882. During her seventeen months at Zuni pueblo (September 1882–April 1884) she adopted a name change, first to Emalie and then Emily. Her husband called her Emalie. Her sister Maggie always referred to her as Em or Emma, never Emalie or Emily.

3. Frederick Hodge's siblings were Emlyn Maria (d. 1943), Edwin Richard (1860–1936), Ernest (b. 1869), Evelyn/Evelina Beatrice (b. 1867), and Charles Gordon (1876–1965). Hodge Genealogy File in author's possession, courtesy of Jenny Pease.

4. Hodge recalled that Copp (1843–1912) "came to our house one night and said he wanted a boy to assist him during the summer," and his father encouraged him to work. Hodge, *Frederick Webb Hodge, Ethnologist*, 7.

5. Hodge, 8.

6. "In terms of liberal economics the age of the entrepreneurial individual was, for the mass of the population, over. America itself changed startlingly, from a largely self-employed and family-business economy in 1870 to one where in 1900 12 per cent of the population owned 99 per cent of the wealth" (Bush, *Halfway to Revolution*, 6). Some years ago, historian James McGovern remarked of this period: "While at the same time the entrepreneurial freedom of American men was being undermined, their economic future being made uncertain, and their working patterns being altered, the test of manliness remained in large measure what it had been—the man's ability as a breadwinner" (McGovern, "David Graham Phillips").

7. Trachtenberg, *Incorporation of America*, 84.

8. Rotundo, *American Manhood*, 194–221.

9. Phonography was also a vital reform movement of the pre–Civil War decades, overlapping with abolition, temperance, women's rights, and Swedenborgianism—each of which promised to usher in a higher phase of civilization. Srole, *Transcribing Gender and Class*, 17–43, 71–77.

10. By the 1870s shorthand was being advertised, Srole argues, "as a means for men to advance beyond the common man or woman by turning to older discourses of respectability and a reframed self-made man." Goals beyond stenography included school proprietor, office supplier, or (as in Hodge's case) publisher-editor. Srole, 72, 74.

11. Hodge, *Frederick Webb Hodge, Ethnologist*, 10.

12. Hodge, 11. Stanley-Brown had similarly modest Washington roots. Born in the slums of the District, educated in its public schools, and self-taught in shorthand and typewriting, Joseph Stanley Brown (1858–1941) became private secretary to President James A. Garfield. He had previously been personal secretary to Powell, who loaned him to Congressman Garfield in 1878. After Garfield's assassination in 1881, Stanley Brown resumed work for Powell until 1885, when he went to Yale, graduating in 1888; that year he married Garfield's daughter Mary ("Mollie") and added a hyphen to his name. He went on to have a career in investment banking. (Hieb, *The Doctor Danced with Us*, 199; Feis, *Mollie Garfield*). On Stanley-Brown's unusual abilities and closeness to the Garfield family, see Millard, *Destiny of the Republic*, 91, 106–7, 146–47.

13. Philip Warman, like Hodge, had attended Columbian University. While still quite young he traveled widely with Powell and was deeply trusted. Warman edited numerous USGS publications until his early death at age forty-nine in 1908. On Pilling's career and friendship with Powell, see Hinsley, *The Smithsonian and the American Indian*, 164–67; and Stegner, *Beyond the Hundredth Meridian*, 263–66.

14. Hodge to Matthew Stirling, 3 January 1955, MS 4372, Folder 15, Aleš Hrdlička Papers, NAA. He added that neither Powell nor Pilling was "a beauty." But Powell treasured Pilling, and at the latter's death in 1895 Powell was despondent in his sorrow: "Through many years of the active life James and I were associated, in the office and in the field. Field work led us into the wilderness of mountain and canyon, of forest and desert, away from the comforts and conv[e]niences of civilization, where life itself was preserved by a constant struggle. In all this experience my boon companion never failed nor faltered" (Powell to Mrs. Pilling, 12 August 1895, reproduced in *James Constantine Pilling*).

15. Stegner, *Beyond the Hundredth Meridian*, 251.

16. Hodge, *Frederick Webb Hodge, Ethnologist*, 13.

17. Pilling to Daniel Shea, 11 April 1881, NAA, cited in Darnell, "The Development of American Anthropology," 63.

18. Stegner, *Beyond the Hundredth Meridian*, 263–64.

19. For Hodge's major editorial contributions to American anthropology see Wilcox, "Going National," 420, 424, 429; and part III of this volume.

20. Hodge diary, 7 December 1886. (Isis McMillan has not been identified.)

21. In addition to Emily the sisters were Catherine Cecelia (Katie, 1861–91) and Eleanor S. (a.k.a. Ellen, Eleanore, Nellie, 1863–1936). Information from U.S. Census for 1880 and 1900.

22. Information in this paragraph comes from the author's interview with Emlyn Hodge (daughter, 1905–99), 5 December 1993. The wedding was announced on 11 July 1882 in the *Washington Evening Star* and the *National Republican*.

23. Curtis, *Children of the Sun*, excerpted in Green, *Cushing at Zuni*, 282. Maggie "loved" life at Zuni, her daughter Emlyn recalled, while Aunt Emily "didn't have much adventure" (author interview, 5 December 1993). Curtis's (and Emlyn's) opinion of Mrs. Cushing's dislike of pueblo life is probably overdrawn. In 1895 Thomas Eakins painted portraits of both Frank and Emily. Samuel Murray, assistant to Eakins at the time, recalled Emily as "a peach" but also "cantankerous": "She hadn't been able to stand the dirt and curiosity of the Indians," wrote Murray, "—she was a 'baby doll'" (McHenry, *Thomas Eakins*, 112). However, art historian Laurie V. Dahlberg, in a remarkably perceptive commentary, is closer to the mark. She considers the Eakins portrait of Emily a "provocative" and underrated work: "The intelligent and sensitive rendering of Mrs. Cushing's head and the prominent treatment of her solid arms contrasts with the delicacy of her dress. . . . It is this contrast between social refinement and physical power that is so striking." Dahlberg concludes: "Eakins portrayed Mrs. Cushing as the patient source of strength behind this emaciated genius; she is also his connection to the white society that Cushing could never completely relinquish" (Wilmerding, *Thomas Eakins*, 126–27). All evidence indicates that throughout their married life—beginning at Zuni, through near-constant illness, controversy and poverty—Emily was a rock of solidity to her husband.

24. Magill, "Margaret Magill's Zuni Diary," 543–44. On pueblo corn-grinding as a trope of early southwestern writing, see Hinsley and Wilcox, *The Southwest in the American Imagination*, 196–205. Magill's 1885 drawing of the Zuni women grinding corn (in both of these publications), initially appeared in Cushing's *Zuñi Breadstuff* (1884–85). At first disturbed by Zunis' treatment of their dogs, eventually she "learned to mind my own affairs & came to the conclusion

that the Zuñis knew best after all how to manage their own animals" (to "Uncle Ferd," in Magill, "Margaret Magill's Zuni Diary," 542).

25. Margaret Magill, "Zuñi Mid-Winter Ceremonial," MS 516, Hodge-Cushing Papers, BR/AM.

26. Magill painted Waihusiwa weaving at the Manchester home on 20 September 1886. Peabody Museum of Harvard, Accession #973-14-10/519447, Bin 67. (The accession is mislabeled "watercolor of Navajo weaver.") For another version of the watercolor see Hinsley and Wilcox, "A Hemenway Portfolio," 556, 563. (It should be noted that by this time Emma had adopted her name as Emily.)

27. Cushing to Hemenway, 12 November 1886, Cushing Collection, MS 6, HAE (Hemenway Archaeological Expedition) 1.28, BR/AM.

28. Cushing to Baxter, 24 November 1886, HLB 1: front insert, pp. 1–9, HC. By 1886 Magill was indeed practicing shorthand and the new office skill of typewriting. See also Cushing to Baxter, 30 November 1886, HLB 1: 14.

29. Cushing to Baxter, 24 November 1886. Powell's model in this respect was probably his second trip down the Colorado River (1871–72), when he took a photographer.

30. Lummis, "The White Indian," 11, 15.

31. Audrey Goodman has demonstrated the persistence of Lummis's romance-over-science view of Cushing, including Hodge's contribution. See Goodman, *Translating Southwestern Landscapes*, 17.

32. Hinsley and Wilcox, *The Lost Itinerary of Frank Hamilton Cushing*, 5–18; and Hinsley, "Two Marys and a Martha."

33. Mathes and Lowitt, *The Standing Bear Controversy*.

34. Quotations are from Clarke, *Autobiography*, 111, 119.

35. Clarke, *Ten Great Religions*, 26. "I have been often called upon to discuss the religions of the primitive or childlike races. . . . The importance and value of researches in this direction have of late years been more fully recognized than formerly" (vi).

36. Clarke, 2, vii. Clarke specifically cited, among others, Tylor's *Researches into the Early History of Mankind* (1870) and *Primitive Culture* (2 vols., 1871); Brinton's *The Myths of the New World* (1868); Rushton Dorman's *Origin of Primitive Superstitions, etc., Among the Aborigines of America* (1881; Dorman was a Chicago book collector); and Hubert Howe Bancroft's *The Native Races of the Pacific States* (1874), which Clarke called "an important work of great extent, and full of valuable information" (xx).

37. For analysis on these points, see Hinsley, "Zunis and Brahmins"; and Hinsley, "Charlatan, Scientist, or Poet."

38. Nichols, "Celebrity and the National Body," 117, 140.

39. Hale to Emily Hale, 25 March 1882, in Hale, *Life and Letters*, 315.

40. See, e.g., Mary Morgan to Horsford, 17 October and 12 November 1882, Horsford Papers, SMA. Horsford was former Rumford Professor of applied chemistry at the Lawrence Scientific School. Immensely wealthy from having developed a commercially successful baking powder, he also had serious interests in Norse or Viking settlements in New England, and in historical and Indigenous place-names. For his part, Bandelier first met Cushing in the spring of 1883 during a two-week stay at Zuni and came away thrilled, telling Mary Morgan that Cushing was the true, brilliant heir to her husband's ethnology: "We must be proud of this remarkable young man; he deserves our pride, our sincere attachment and support" (Bandelier to Mary Morgan, 18 March 1883, in White, *Pioneers in American Anthropology*, vol. 2, 250). It has been suggested that Cushing had met Lewis Henry Morgan, who died in late 1881; I have found no evidence of this.

41. Hale to Emily Hale, 24 and 25 March 1882, in Hale, *Life and Letters*, 314–15.

42. Cushing to Hale, 24 July 1882, Box 20, Folder 2, NYSLA. At this point Cushing's "long years of exile" amounted to thirty months.

43. Horsford to Hale, 4 September 1883, Box 20, Folder 2, NYSLA.

44. Cushing was especially grateful for their "sadly kind consideration of her lonely life" at Zuni. Cushing to Horsford, 23 October 1883, Horsford Papers, Box 58, Folder 35, SMA. (She signed herself "Emalie.")

45. Cushing to Hale, 20 September 1883, Box 20, Folder 2, NYSLA.

46. Cushing to Horsford, 23 October 1883, Horsford Papers, Box 58, Folder 35, SMA. Cushing also reported that he had read the Reverend Clarke's volumes "with avidity" and found them "full of suggestions" for his future work at Zuni.

47. Anderson, *Brooks Adams*, 39.

48. Adams, *The Emancipation of Massachusetts*, 212.

49. Adams to Lodge, quoted in Anderson, *Brooks Adams*, 43.

50. They continued to exchange warm letters at least until 1893. As he was leaving on a six-month tour of Europe in the spring of 1887, Adams expressed his friendship: "Of all the men I know I think I miss you the most [since] I met you" (Adams to Cushing, 12 April 1887, Cushing Collection, MS 6, HAE 1.1, BR/AM). Two years later he visited Cushing in Garfield Hospital in Washington and urged him to come to Europe (Cushing to Adams, 2 April 1889, HLB 6: 168–70).

51. Adams, *The Emancipation of Massachusetts*, prefatory note to the first edition. Adams dedicated the book to Cushing.

52. Cushing, "My Adventures in Zuñi." As a boy Tibbles had fought under John Brown in the antislavery movement. He and Susette La Flesche married in 1881. He was the vice presidential candidate of the Populist Party in 1904.

53. Mathes, *The Women's National Indian Association*; Mathes, *Gender, Race, and Power*; Mathes and Lowitt, *The Standing Bear Controversy*.

54. Hemenway named her Manchester summer estate Ramona.

55. Cushing to Hale, 20 September 1883, Box 20, Folder 2, NYSLA.

56. Cushing to Hale, 16 April 1882, Hale Papers, Box 20, Folder 2, NYSLA.

57. Baird lectured Cushing: "You, of course, are sufficiently aware of Gen. Logan's character—that he is indomitable and relentless; and while he is a most valuable friend, he is a very dangerous enemy." For explanation of the "Logan affair" and Sylvester Baxter's central role (and possibly Cushing's) in its exposure, see Green, *Cushing at Zuni*, 261–66 (quotation on 263); and for a revealing account of the close friendship between James and Matilda Stevenson and the Logan family, see Hieb, *The Doctor Danced with Us*, 198–200.

58. Horsford to Powell, 19 November 1883, cited in Green, *Cushing at Zuni*, 309–10.

59. Powell to Hale, 24 November 1883, NYSLA.

60. Chiefly a deformed stomach and later a tapeworm, which he finally expelled in 1890 with mercury treatments and pickled in a jar as a scientific specimen. Cushing to Washington Matthews, 20 February 1890, HLB 7: 10–14.

61. Cushing, "A Study of Pueblo Pottery." The first was "Zuni Fetiches."

62. For which he was paid well. Cushing told Powell of the outside work in January 1884. Editor/publisher David H. Ranck had proposed the series when Cushing was still at Zuni in 1883 as a way of adding "spice" to make his publication, as he said, more "digestible": "Milling, practically, is a threadbare subject," he confessed (Ranck to Cushing, 4 February 1885, MS 6, BOE [Bureau of Ethnology] 1.37, HCP). For his part, believing that he would live at Zuni long enough to "monograph" the tribe, Cushing in late 1883 began building a house across the river in the pueblo; he was in considerable debt at the time of his recall in January 1884; for *Breadstuff* he received ten cents per line of printed text, in addition to payment for his illustrations. "Cushing received $1248.40 from Ranck for his manuscripts, and an additional $127.75 for his illustrations, equaling the amount he continued to receive as a salaried employee of the Bureau of Ethnology" (Hieb, *The Doctor Danced with Us*, 221).

Zuñi Breadstuff appeared in nineteen installments (January 1884–August 1885) in *The Millstone: An Illustrated Monthly Journal, Devoted to the Advancement of Milling and Mechanical Interests*. Ranck reprinted nine of the installments in another of his publications, *The Corn Miller*, in 1893. In 1920, two decades after Cushing's death, Hodge received permission from Emily to reprint the entire series in book form with additional photos taken at his archaeological dig at Hawikku, outside Zuni. See part III in this volume.

63. Sylvester Manor, one of the earliest settlements on Long Island, is now Sylvester Manor Educational Farm.

64. Cornelia Horsford to "Dear Mamma," 28 September 1885, Horsford Family Papers, Subseries C, Box 92, Folder 57, SMA. Emily Cushing's troublesome "cousin" has not been identified. However, the four-page Sylvester Manor House guest list for 1885 includes the Cushings and Baxter, as well as such luminaries as Sarah Orne Jewett and Mr. and Mrs. Julian Hawthorne (Horsford Family Papers, Box 114, Folder 26, SMA). Emily was twenty-six on 27 September 1885.

65. Emily Cushing to Horsford, 13 August [1887], Box 58, Folder 34, SMA.

66. Cushing's health seemed to improve for a few weeks in September and October 1885, as indicated by a flurry of correspondence between Cushing, Horsford, Powell, and Pilling: "Cushing's digestion has been badly deranged by his life at Zuni, but he is now eating greater variety than when he came here, and promises in time to get his stomach again all right," Horsford reported (Horsford to Powell, 13 September 1885, NAA).

67. Telegram, Powell to Graham, 17 November 1885, NAA.

68. Baxter to Horsford, 2 February 1886, Box 58, Folder 34, SMA.

69. Old Farm, an eighteenth-century farmhouse, was bought by Mary and Augustus Hemenway in 1865; in 1877, the year after Augustus died, she had it renovated to a Queen Anne–style country mansion by influential New England architect William Ralph Emerson—who also designed her homes at Manchester.

70. Cushing to William Torrey Harris, n.d. (c. June 1891), Cushing Collection, MS BAE (Bureau of American Ethnology) 1.45, BR/AM. On Hemenway's "Casa Ramona," see Hinsley and Wilcox, *The Lost Itinerary of Frank Hamilton Cushing*, 15–16; and Lewis, *American Country Houses.*

71. Cushing to Powell, 2 July 1886, NAA. For interpretation of the "Indian question" and Hemenway's work with Indian reform, see Hinsley, "Two Marys and a Martha."

72. On Rufus Leighton and his wife, Caroline Cushing Andrews Leighton (1832–85), see *West Coast Journeys, 1862–1879*, http://www.kouroo.info/kouroo/thumbnails/L/RufusLeighton. As a young man Leighton had been a follower of Unitarian preacher and abolitionist Theodore Parker. He edited Parker's sermons (which he had written down in the 1850s) into *Lessons from the World of Matter and the World of Man* (Boston: American Unitarian Association, 1908). Caroline, who died in 1885 at only fifty-three, was from Newburyport, the home of Mary Hemenway's mother: "This was the Newburyport which Mary Hemenway . . . used to visit as a girl. She was Mary Tileston then . . . and to the last she had a warm affection for the old town" ("Editor's Table," *New England Magazine:*

An Illustrated Monthly new series 22, vol. 5 [July 1900]: 620). In other words, the Leightons were not strangers to Hemenway's social and religious world.

73. Dewey, "Visit of the Zuni Indians," 551–65; quoted passages 561, 563–64.

74. In addition to his stenography skills, Leighton was the accountant for the Hemenway Expedition board of directors. His notes and transcriptions thus became the property of the expedition. After its collapse in 1889, Cushing tried unsuccessfully to retrieve them, since he considered them his property and a source of potential income. He tried in vain to recontact Leighton. The folklore material, Cushing cried to Sylvester Baxter in the depths of 1891, "is the only material I had which was capable of immediate popularization, by which I have hoped, in my dark hours, to sustain myself when able to bring it out" (Hinsley and Wilcox, *The Lost Itinerary of Frank Hamilton Cushing*, 30, 300n89). Cushing's private agonies—"God, show me the morning"—over what he considered an unforgivable scientific trespass are reflected in later diary entries. In particular see those for June 1891, MS 97–28, NAA.

75. An anonymous article in *Saturday Evening Post* in 1909 maintained that Mrs. Hemenway secretly recorded Cushing's Zuni tales: "Every Sunday afternoon . . . Mr. Cushing would go to Mrs. Hemenway's house, drink tea with her and tell her the folk tales of the Zuni. Finding in her an eager listener he was delighted to discourse on the subject that he had studied so patiently. It never occurred to him to suspect that behind a screen near the window was concealed *a young woman* [emphasis added] who took down, in shorthand, every word he uttered. By this means, in the course of many Sunday afternoons, Mrs. Hemenway secured, in the form of typewritten manuscript—transcribed from the stenographer's notes—a remarkably complete account of the myths of the Zuni. Mr. Cushing knew nothing about the matter. After his death the material was placed in the hands of the Bureau of Ethnology, which was delighted to get it, and published it in the shape of a large volume with suitable illustrations" ("Never Knew He Was an Author," 21). The account is unverified and probably apocryphal. Presumably, it would have occurred during the Cushings' sojourn at Old Farm in 1885, or possibly he visited her Mt. Vernon Street home in Boston while staying at the Horsford home in Cambridge that winter. Such a betrayal of Cushing's trust, however, seems totally out of character for Mary Hemenway, and what we know of Leighton's work sufficiently explains how the *Zuni Folk Tales* came about.

76. Hodge, *Frederick Webb Hodge, Ethnologist*, 23. Hodge does not provide a date, but this first meeting occurred in late November or early December 1886. The search for a stenographer had been more complicated than Hodge realized. Several individuals, including a favorite named "Mr. March" in Boston,

turned down the offer to go to Arizona (Cushing to Baxter, 30 November 1886, HLB 1: 14).

77. Hodge diary, 16 December, 20 December, and 13 December 1886. Though the name does not appear in the diary for that day, in his reminiscences Hodge added: "When the story was over I walked down the aisle of the car when Heluta and Palowahtiwa were talking together. Getting behind Heluta, I whispered, 'Teluli! Teluli!.' Whereupon Palowahtiwa said, 'Well, that's a good name for him.' So in that way the Zunis knew me as Teluli ever after" (Hodge, *Frederick Webb Hodge, Ethnologist*, 47; cf. Hodge, "Dig Your Cellar").

78. Hodge, *Frederick Webb Hodge, Ethnologist*, 24. "Mr. Cushing informs me that rarely a day passes but what a murder is committed [in Albuquerque]" (Hodge diary, 17 December 1886).

79. Hodge diary, 17 December 1886. At the Bandelier Memorial Conference in Santa Fe in 1940 Hodge still recalled the night fondly and colorfully: "A convention of some kind caused Albuquerque accommodations to be scarce, but Bandelier and I finally found lodgment in the second story of an adobe bunkhouse [the Girard House], and as we shared the only bed, we became well acquainted in a trice, for Bandelier immediately and literally kicked me out of bed, calling me a 'damned scrub,' which was my pet name forever after." Lange et al., *The Southwestern Journals of Adolph F. Bandelier, 1885–1888*, 470n707. A few months before his own death in 1956, Hodge poignantly recalled traveling to New York City in August 1910 for a small dinner in celebration of the near-blind Bandelier's seventieth birthday:

> "When I came to the door Bandelier himself let me in. At that time he was suffering from double cataract[s] and could merely make out the form of a person. I disguised my voice and said, 'Beg your pardon, but would you like to buy some nice apples?' He slapped me on the shoulder and said, 'Come in here, you damned scrub.'" (Hodge, *Frederick Webb Hodge, Ethnologist*, 213)

80. It was also Hodge's first taste of the air of the Southwest: "I got off the train at Fort Wingate and took a deep breath. It was sage I smelled: *artemesia tridentata*. And then I looked at the landscape. I had never seen such clear air. That was it: the good smell and the pure air" (Powell, *Books West Southwest*, 41).

81. Hodge diary, 20 December 1886.

82. Hodge diary, 21 December 1886.

83. This "new" plan had been Mrs. Hemenway's preferred itinerary for Cushing. See Baxter to Cushing, 18 November 1886, MS 6, BOE 1.6, Cushing Collection, BR/AM.

84. Cushing to Baxter, 10 January 1887, HLB 1: 103. For the various roles of Siwaititsailu and Weta on the Hemenway Expedition see Hinsley and Wilcox, *The Lost Itinerary of Frank Hamilton Cushing*, passim.

85. Hodge, *Frederick Webb Hodge, Ethnologist*, 26.

86. At one point Maggie recorded: "Mr. Garlick, being older than the others, feels a little important and takes the liberty of grumbling. Mr. Hodge listens and is sometimes affected thereby" (Magill diary, 12 February 1887).

87. Cushing to Hemenway, "Christmas night 1886," Cushing Letterbook 1: 86–95, Huntington Free Library/Cornell Special Collections. In the light of subsequent events it is worth noting Cushing's description of Garlick's proposed duties as stated in this key letter: He requested Garlick to "drive my escort team, look after camps, property, collections, etc., and assist me when not otherwise employed in surveying and collecting from the ruins; as well as taking charge of the work during my temporary absence . . . or when I was occupied in literary labors." Cushing sought always to assure his patron that the "literary labors" with Hodge would continue, even in the midst of fieldwork operations; the hire of Garlick was framed accordingly.

88. Hodge diary, 26 January 1887.

89. Hodge diary, 28 January 1887.

90. Hodge diary, 3 and 4 January 1887.

91. Bumble Bee, in the Bradshaw Mountains of central Arizona, was settled in 1863 as a U.S. Army outpost. The post office was established in 1879. With the decline of the stage and of mining in the region, the post office was moved and the site faded. On the establishment of the Phoenix-Prescott stage and freight route through Black Canyon in the 1870s, see Hanchett, *Catching the Stage to Phoenix*, 129–50.

92. For the Alkire brothers, a photo of their "Eylar Ranch" in 1887, and the expedition's days there, see Hinsley and Wilcox, *The Lost Itinerary of Frank Hamilton Cushing*, 125–29; and Wilcox et al., "Delineating Hilltop Settlement Systems."

93. Magill diary, 7 February 1887. In his entry for that day Hodge noted that Magill was sketching a large cactus on the mesa top: "The night is perfect—the sun setting and moon rising almost simultaneously."

94. Hodge diary, 9 February 1887; Magill diary, 8, 9, and 11 February 1887. She remarked in detail on hairstyles, facial decorations, and women's clothing.

95. Magill diary, 12 February 1887.

96. McClintock later became state historian of Arizona. See Hinsley and Wilcox, *The Lost Itinerary of Frank Hamilton Cushing*, 153 and 314–15, nn 73 and 74.

97. Patrick, *The Ancient Canal Systems*.

98. Hinsley and Wilcox, *The Lost Itinerary of Frank Hamilton Cushing,* 219; and Patrick, *The Ancient Canal Systems.*

99. Hinsley and Wilcox, *The Lost Itinerary of Frank Hamilton Cushing,* 236. For Cushing's hilarious account of Mrs. Adams in his Itinerary, see p. 141 as well.

100. Baxter to Cushing, 18 November 1886, Ms 6 BOE 1.6, BR/AM; and Cushing's response of 24 November 1886, HLB 1.

101. Cushing to Baxter, 5 March 1886, HLB 1: 205.

102. Cushing to "Miss Cushing," 16 March 1884. Env. 302, Hodge-Cushing papers, BR/AM. (Slight alterations in punctuation have been made.)

103. *Zuñi Folk Tales* appeared posthumously in 1901. For Hodge's generous review of the volume, see Hodge, "Cushing's Zuni Folk Tales."

104. Cushing to Baxter, 12 March 1887, Cushing Letterbook 1: 222–36, HC. Controversy over responsibility for the itinerary grew after the expedition ended. See Hinsley and Wilcox, *The Lost Itinerary of Frank Hamilton Cushing,* 26–37.

105. Cushing had begun the "Daily Notes" on 15 November 1886. Hodge took over on 17 December in Albuquerque. They were written in pencil on individual sheets. Internal evidence suggests that the "Daily Notes" that now exist from early February 1887 onward were reconstructed, probably at Cushing's request, around 1892–93 from Hodge's diary or other documents since lost. There is no evidence that Margaret ever kept "notes" for an itinerary.

106. Magill diary, 26 March 1887.

107. Magill diary, 17 February 1887.

108. Hodge diary, 28 February 1887.

109. Magill diary, 3 April 1887.

110. Hodge diary, 14 February 1887. "Mr. Cushing called at my tent while Mr. Garlick and I were talking, bringing a camp-made 'valentine' from the ladies to me, with canceled postage stamps affixed and a postmark neatly drawn in the corner" (Hodge, "Daily Notes," 14 February 1887).

111. Entries for 14 and 17 June 1887 (not presented here).

112. Hodge diary, 21 June 1887. Margaret and Fred considered June 17 their engagement anniversary date.

113. Hodge diary, 7 March 1887.

114. Granum was a popular medicinal health food, derived from wheat and mixed with water or milk, that came on the American market in 1877 for invalids and convalescents. It was the staple of Cushing's diet at this time.

115. Cushing to Baxter, 25 August 1887, HLB 2: 228.

116. Hodge diary, 6 July 1887; Magill diary, 6 July 1887. Regarding Cushing's "pyral" mounds: Cushing and his crew had the opportunity to observe the Salt River sites before they had been plowed by settlers, which destroyed the surface

40 cm, leaving intact only the lower portions of a great variety of pits that had been excavated for houses, storage, or cremation. Caliche, a calcium carbonate that accumulates in desert soils, was used as an excellent, cement-like building material (Wilcox and Shenk, *The Architecture of the Casa Grande*; Wilcox et al., *One Hundred Years of Archaeology*). "Pyral mounds" was a term that Cushing invented to describe the mounds of debris he found on the surface, which the occupants of these prehistoric villages (now called the Hohokam by archaeologists) had cleaned out of the pits they excavated to cremate their dead. Often pottery and other artifacts were included when that was done. Afterward, they apparently mixed together the physical remains of cremated bone and artifacts and placed most of that material in an olla capped by a bowl or other object (sometimes with the addition of other artifacts) to be reburied in a nearby "cemetery" (a cluster of "secondary cremation pits"). At some point, they also apparently would clean out what was left in the primary cremation pit and place the residue in a "plural mound" so that the pit could be reused to conduct another cremation ceremony.

117. Hodge diary, 7 July 1887. "Mr. Hodge & I had another sitting for the portrait but to our surprise, found the studio Mesquite tree in flames & that part of tract almost cleared so had to find another shady place for the continuation of the work" (Magill diary, 7 July 1887).

118. Magill diary, 3 August 1887.

119. Emily Cushing to Horsford, 13 August [1887], SMA. The reference is to Oliver Wendell Holmes's 1830 poem "The Hot Season."

120. Hodge diary, 14 August 1887. Fred and Maggie were married in Washington in the first week of September 1891.

121. George Payne's father, Colonel James G. Payne, was auditor of the Supreme Court of the District of Columbia. George graduated from Columbian University law school and was admitted to the bar in 1883. He died in 1901 (*Washington Post*, 16 October 1901, 3, 7; and 17 October 1901, 3).

122. "We just received Akina's [Margaret's] letter telling us that the time for your marriage is chosen! I congratulate you, my dear Mr. Hodge, most sincerely. And tell my dear Margaret that I also congratulate her, affectionately; and that I am so truly glad I can do this as heartily and happily as I do lovingly" (Cushing to Hodge, 17 June 1891, Env. 449, Hodge-Cushing Papers, BR/AM).

123. Siwaititsailu and Weta in particular were miserable and homesick—and troublesome. Cushing paid their way back to Zuni by train on 23 August (Cushing to Douglas D. Graham, 18 August 1887, HLB 2: 104–8). Bandelier advised Horsford: "He should never have remained after the 1st of May. That country is too detestably hot, and with Frank's poor health it was positively dangerous

to stay and to work" (22 August 1887, Box 56, Folder 2, Horsford Family Papers, SMA).

124. Bourke had been a friend and ethnographic colleague of Cushing since 1881 and an acquaintance of Hemenway as well. See Porter, *Paper Medicine Man*, 112–40, 276–77. Bourke's account of his dinner with Mrs. Hemenway and the decision regarding Matthews reads in part: "Mrs. Hemenway asked me to name a suitable man, to take charge of Mr. Cushing's work for one or two months? I answered: 'nothing easier in the world, Madam. My friend, Dr. Matthews, of the Army, is just the man for the place. As an ethnologist, he has no superior in the world. Cushing, of course, in his special field, is approached by nobody, but if anybody can be compared to Cushing, it is Dr. Matthews, whose extended researches among the Navajoes dove-tail in with those made by Cushing among the Zunis'" (Bourke, Diaries, 15 August 1887).

125. Cushing hesitantly accepted the turn of events. He collapsed dangerously the day after Matthews' arrival (Hodge diary, 5 September 1887). For insight into the triangular friendship between Bourke, Matthews, and Cushing, see Halpern and McGreevy, *Washington Matthews*, 7–9.

126. Cushing to Baxter, 4 September 1888, HLB 2: 241–57.

127. Ramon Castro was a young Mexican from Sonora who became Cushing's most trusted and skillful excavator and foreman of the other laborers.

128. Matthews, "The Cities of the Dead," 218.

129. Matthews et al., "Human Bones of the Hemenway Collection," 141. Matthews was in the expedition camp for only 26 days.

130. Cushing to Baxter, 30 August [?]–20 September [?] 1887, HLB 2: 274–328.

131. As with Casa Grande a year later, in these months and in San Francisco Cushing was exploring, with Hemenway's knowledge, options for buying the excavation sites for protection and future work.

132. Cushing readily admitted his lack of focus on the bones, and he welcomed Matthews' interest and expertise. However, as Robert Poor pointed out some years ago, Cushing later faulted Matthews for his attention to physical anthropology, which Cushing felt had narrowed the doctor's scientific thinking (Poor, "Washington Matthews," 45). The most thorough account of Matthews's work with the expedition and his long friendship with Cushing is Merbs, "Washington Matthews." Today, of course, the archaeological practice of exhuming Native burials is widely deplored (see, e.g., Redman, *Bone Rooms*; Fabian, *The Skull Collectors*; and Thomas and Deloria, *Skull Wars*). Nowhere in the documentary history of the Hemenway Expedition is there a single expression of doubt or hesitation concerning the practice. Matthews certainly thought it was an important scientific thing to do, and later produced the first monographic

study about the Hemenway Expedition (Matthews et al., "Human Bones of the Hemenway Collection").

133. Matthews, "The Cities of the Dead," 218–19. Cushing recalled the rail trip in painful detail: "Another wash out had occurred which delayed our train twenty-four hours during which we had to wait in a breathless spare car[,] myself out of food. . . . When our delayed train did arrive there was no sleeper attached, yet every car was crowded to suffocation by cargoes of delayed passengers. I grew frightfully ill before reaching Colton [San Bernardino County, California]. . . . There we were forced to remain over night—awaiting another delayed train on the southern Californian road; but as the accommodations were fairly good, I somewhat mended" (Cushing to Baxter, 2 November 1887, HLB 4: 64–77).

134. Cushing to Hodge, 26 September 1887, Cushing Collection, MS 6, No. 125, HAE 1.21, BR/AM.

135. Cushing to Garlick, 26 September 1887, Cushing Collection, MS 6, No. 107, BR/AM.

136. Hodge diary, 10 October 1887.

137. Cushing to Hodge, 10 October 1887, Cushing Collection, MS 6, No. 126, BR/AM; HLB 4: 20–28, HC.

138. Matthews stayed in New Mexico long enough to observe a Mountainway chant in early October. See Johnson, "Documenting the Multisensory and Ephemeral," 237. For Huntington, see Heitman, *Historical Register and Dictionary*, 558.

139. Jacob Lawson Wortman (1856–1926) was a native of Oregon who worked with Joseph Leidy, Edward D. Cope, and Henry Fairfield Osborn. On his return from the Southwest in the summer of 1888 he reported glowingly on the Hemenway Expedition (Wilson, "The Hemenway Expedition in Arizona"). He became a noted vertebrate paleontologist for the Carnegie Institute and the American Museum of Natural History but eventually abandoned paleontology because he felt he was not receiving recognition. Without his own means, like Cushing he depended on wealthy or well-connected entrepreneurial scientists like Osborn or Powell. He spent the last twenty-five years of his life as a pharmacist in Brownsville, Texas. See Rainger, "Collectors and Entrepreneurs"; Holland, "Dr. Jacob L. Wortman"; and Osborn, "J. L. Wortman."

140. Hodge was rarely ill, but in these weeks his problems included facial neuralgia, an ulcerated throat (he smoked heavily), a debilitating case of hemorrhoids, and a cold.

141. Cushing to Garlick, 16 October 1887, HLB 4: 29–35. The Cushings and Margaret stayed at the Florence Hotel, which advertised the "largest and best

furnished rooms of any hotel in southern California at $2.50 to $3.00 per day" (1889 Florence Hotel postcard, Special Collections and Archives, UC San Diego, La Jolla, https://lib.uscd.edu/sca).

142. The Occidental Hotel was built in 1861 as a luxury hotel catering to wealthy travelers on the west coast. It was destroyed in the earthquake and fire of 1906 (Jocelyn, "The Old Occidental"). Mrs. Hemenway was paying the Cushings' California expenses. His medical treatments in San Francisco were overseen by army surgeon William McNutt.

143. Cushing to Hodge, 18 October 1887, Cushing Collection, MS 6, No. 128, BR/AM; HLB 4: 45–50.

144. "Interesting Address by Mr. Cushing," 6. According to this journalist, Cushing claimed he had lived with the Zunis for ten years.

145. Mary Katherine Keemle "Kate" Field (1838–96) became an admirer of both Cushing and Mary Hemenway. After their initial meeting in San Francisco (where she also stayed at the Occidental), Field and Cushing met there again in the summer of 1888. She noted: "Frank Cushing, whose health is much better than it was a year ago, is again visiting San Francisco. He lunched with me here lately and was delighted with the scenery. If possible, he will come over again and we'll go in search of Indian remains. How lucky he is to be backed by a woman like Mrs. Hemenway!" At Hemenway's death in 1894 she wrote warmly of the patron and of Cushing—to which Cushing responded: "God bless you, my dear Miss Kate Field" (Whiting, *Kate Field*, 463, 494). For Field's remarkable life see Whiting, *Kate Field*; Moss, *Kate Field*; and Scharnhorst, *Kate Field*.

146. McDowell, "The Mythic Drama." Henry Burden McDowell, son of Union general Irvin G. McDowell, studied law, Sanskrit, and Chinese at Harvard (AB 1878). He was a chemist and engineer before pursuing a career in San Francisco journalism that featured special interest in Chinese theater, mythology and religion. Based on his time with Cushing, he published maps of the prehistoric irrigation of the Salt River Valley (Waldman, *Who Was Who*, 809).

147. Regrettably the academy's building collapsed in the 1906 earthquake. For a history of the academy to that time see Leviton and Aldrich, *Theodore Henry Littell's*.

148. Emily's flirtations with Molera were innocent but still striking: "The camp is very stupid now and so am I," she wrote in January. "Mr. Cushing is so much better now that he is off every day directing the men, and while he is gone there is no Adam to come and talk to me and say pretty things. . . . Were you drinking [on New Year's Eve] to the memory of any other Eve?" (Emily Cushing to E. J. Molera, 12 January 1888, Cooper-Molera Papers, Bancroft Library, UC-

Berkeley). For Molera's life, see Troy, "Eusebius Joseph Molera"; for his prominent roles in the academy, see Leviton and Aldrich, *Theodore Henry Littell's*.

149. Cushing had first begun talking of Peruvian connections during the eastern trip with the Zuni priests in 1882. Intrigued, Mary Hemenway gave Cushing a copy of Ephraim G. Squier's *Peru: Incidents of Travel and Exploration in the Land of the Incas* (1877) at Christmas 1887.

150. Cushing later regretted that he had not accepted what he described as Hearst's offer of a $5,000 annual salary, $5,000 for "entertainment," $10,000 for current expenses, and Hearst's yacht with all provisions and staff. Cushing refused the offer, he said, out of honor to Mrs. Hemenway. Cushing to Baxter, 28 April–3 May 1889, HLB 6: 251–64. On Hearst's free-spending braggadocio and his "madhouse" of journalists in this first year of newspaper ownership, see Proctor, *William Randolph Hearst*, 47–53.

151. See, e.g., Cushing to Molera, 28 February 1888, HLB 3: 376–83, for Cushing's detailed outline of the staffing and considerable financial requirements for a South American coastal extension of the Hemenway Expedition. He anticipated working with Molera and Gustav Brühl (1826–1903), a physician, poet, and archaeologist.

152. "City of the Dead: The Ruined Town of Los Muertos," *San Francisco Chronicle*, 18 December 1887; cf. "City of the Dead," *Arizona Weekly Citizen*, 10 December 1887: "He concluded by singing the 'maiden's song' and lullaby. The music has a beautiful rhythm and a wonderfully pleasing construction for a barbaric race." In 1895, when Thomas Eakins was painting Cushing's portrait in Philadelphia, his assistants remarked upon Cushing's voice: "[Charles] Bregler heard Cushing in Eakins' studio giving the Indian war cry in English, and it was like beautiful music" (McHenry, *Thomas Eakins*, 113).

153. McDowell, "Cities of the Dead." See also McDowell, "A Dead Civilization"; McDowell, "Dust"; and McDowell, "The Seven Cities."

154. Wortman to Cushing, 6 December 1887, Cushing Collection, MS 6, No. 150, BR/AM.

155. It should be added, though, that Wortman worked assiduously on the bones at "Las Acequias," the new site north of Camp Hemenway; moreover, on his return to Washington in May he gave a glowing report of the expedition's work. See Wilson, "The Hemenway Expedition in Arizona."

156. In the Cushing Collection in the BR/AM are thirty letters from ten Kate, from 1883 to 1896, testifying to his devotion to Cushing. One of McDowell's *Examiner* articles was an interview with ten Kate.

157. Hovens, "Ten Kate's Hemenway Expedition Diary," 637.

158. Hovens, 647.

159. For ten Kate's relationship to Cushing and his work on the Hemenway Expedition, see ten Kate, *Travels and Researches*; ten Kate, *Over Land en Zee*; Hovens, "Ten Kate's Hemenway Expedition Diary"; and Hovens, *Herman F. C. Ten Kate, Jr.*, 138–50.

160. "I expect to go on a trip of several weeks to Arizona to see Cushing for Mrs. Hemenway and make some arrangements for the expedition" (Baxter to Horsford 22 December 1887, Horsford Papers, SMA). On Baxter's role as Cushing's publicist, see Hinsley and Wilcox, *The Southwest in the American Imagination*.

161. Cushing to Baxter, 12 December 1887, HLB 4: 219–21 (quote on 219).

162. Cushing to Thomas Cushing, 11 February 1888, HLB 3: 298–300. By contrast, Bandelier simply noted in his diary: "Ten Kate, Baxter, Frank, etc., are very kind" and "We had a long and satisfactory conference" (Diary of 2 and 3 February 1888, Lange et al., *The Southwestern Journals of Adolph F. Bandelier, 1885–1888*, 243). Bandelier met alone with Cushing the next morning as well, and left at noon.

163. Emily Cushing to Eusebius Molera, 12 January 1888, Cooper-Molera Papers, Bancroft Library, UC-Berkeley.

164. Initially there was some confusion as to status between the two men, but Cushing ultimately named Wortman as ten Kate's assistant. Partly because of Cushing's vagueness, however, the disposition of the bones—did they belong to the expedition or the Army Medical Museum?—became a contentious issue that embittered ten Kate. See Hovens, "Ten Kate's Hemenway Expedition Diary," 640. For recent archaeological investigations at this site, see Hackbarth and Brunson, *Excavations at Las Acequias*.

165. From the beginning Hemenway and Cushing had planned a private Pueblo Museum in Salem, for which the expedition collections would form the core. Cushing laid out meticulous plans for the structure, staffing, and functions of the museum—including a lecture hall on the site and a winter field school in Arizona—in a forty-three-page letter (typed, with marginal subheadings) to Baxter, written over many weeks (Cushing to Baxter, 2 August–18 September 1887, HLB 2: 169–212). Mrs. Hemenway dispatched her trusted friend Edward S. Morse, the famous zoologist, archaeologist, and director of the Peabody Museum of Salem, to Europe for four months (August to November) to survey display practices and cases in forty-three museums (Morse, c. 1891–93, draft letter [6 pages, handwritten, no addressee], Edward S. Morse Papers, PEM; Wayman, *Edward Sylvester Morse*, 317–33). She purchased thirty acres of prime land on Batchelder Point, Salem, around the same time and later built a temporary storage facility for the collections—"a plain iron one-story building,

50 feet long, windowless, and with only one door" ("Ancient Pueblo Remains: Discoveries in an Arizona Valley," *New-York Times*, 13 May 1888). The land is now Forest River Park in Salem.

166. For the first trip, see Cushing, "Itinerary of Reconnaissance"; for the second see Baxter, "Archaeological Camping in Arizona." The plans for a winter field school never materialized, but Hemenway and Cushing were instrumental the following year in having Casa Grande set aside by Congress as the nation's first federally protected prehistoric site. See Clemensen, *A Centennial History*.

167. Hodge diary, 23 December 1887.

168. Hodge diary, 17 and 18 January 1888.

169. Hodge diary, 23 February 1888. Today these unusual zoomorphic figures of quadrupeds, which continue to be found in Salt River Valley Hohokam sites, are considered to represent dogs rather than South American camelids. They date from A.D. 950 to 1150. See Foster and James, "Dogs, Deer, or Guanacos."

170. The exact location of Cushing's site of Los Guanacos has been debated for more than a century. For a recent assessment see Brunson and Fedick, "Los Guanacos."

171. Tobey became known for the 1887 Romanesque revival building of the S. S. Pierce Company in what is now Copley Square (Sammarco and Buchanan, *Milton Architecture*, 95).

172. Hodge reported with amusement Baxter's mode of composition in camp: "Mr. Baxter still grinds out manuscript on the typewriter and collects his thoughts by photographing 'Douglass' [Cushing's horse]—at night he invariably over-or-underdevelops his negatives and gives vent to his feelings by seeking his haven of rest in Mr. Garlick's tent to pass the time until morning in snoring" (Hodge diary, 17 February 1888). Baxter's sometimes febrile writings are presented in Hinsley and Wilcox, *The Southwest in the American Imagination*.

173. Matthews et al., "Human Bones of the Hemenway Collection." Cushing enthused to Mrs. Hemenway that the discovery might alter the racial classification of mankind.

174. Hovens, "Ten Kate's Hemenway Expedition Diary," 656–82.

175. Yates was a railroad telegraph operator (*Phoenix Herald*, 19 April 1887, 3, col. 2). He and Maggie enjoyed playing tennis in a small court he cleared in the camp. We do not know why Gaston (1868–1956) joined the Hemenway Expedition. Cushing's plans for the Pueblo Museum (noted earlier) did call for providing field opportunities for young men. Gaston arrived in Camp Hemenway on 25 February 1888, and began helping with the cataloguing; he continued to do so in the Salt River Valley and then at Zuni until December 20, when he returned home to Lacon, Illinois. During 1893 he returned to Zuni and later

wrote about Native handicrafts (Gaston, "Among the Red Indian Handicrafters"). He eventually became an international journalist and, with his sister Lucy, a prominent figure in temperance and anti-cigarette campaigns (Blocker et al., *Alcohol and Temperance*, 693).

176. "One large pole, bearing the colors of Mrs. Hemenway and Mr. Cushing, stands in the center of the campus and smaller Cushing flags wave above the Cushing and collection tents" (Hodge diary, 20 March). Nearly a half-century later Hodge recalled this act in ridiculing Cushing as a feckless leader (Hodge, Handwritten notes to Emil Haury, 30 March 1934, X-file 94-36, H-2, Peabody Museum Archives, Peabody Museum of Archaeology and Ethnology, Harvard University).

177. Writing to Molera on 28 February (HLB 3: 376–82), Cushing had detailed his argument that "the greatest at least of all the American cultures [Cushing's "Shiwian" or "Aridian" hemispheric culture] had its origin and infancy in the deserts of North, instead of those of South America."

178. On Morse's life, see Benfey, *The Great Wave*; Hickman and Fetchko, *Japan Day by Day*; Wayman, *Edward Sylvester Morse*; and Howard, *Biographical Memoir of Edward Sylvester Morse*. Morse's account of his history with the Hemenway Expedition is in an undated (c. 1891–93) draft letter to an unknown recipient in the Edward S. Morse Papers, PEM. For Morse's account of the Manchester archery shoot, see Morse, *Additional Notes on Arrow Release*, 6. Popular artist Henry Sandham (Canadian, 1842–1912) produced in autumn 1886 a small oil painting, *Zuni Chiefs*, of the three Zunis practicing archery in the orchard below Mrs. Hemenway's Manchester home. Hemenway descendants presented the painting to the Peabody Museum in 1968 (Shaplin "A Memento of the Hemenway Expedition"). See fig. 7, this volume.

179. The total party was fifteen men.

180. Hodge diary, 5 and 6 April 1888.

181. Cushing Daily Report, 26 March 1888, CURMC.

182. Hodge diary, 27 and 30 March 1888. See Hodge "Prehistoric Irrigation in Arizona."

183. Cushing to Henry François Farny, 30 April 1888, HLB 5: 55:57.

184. Daniel Walter Lord (1854–1922) was a friend of Baxter and a former Harvard student of Charles Eliot Norton. At Norton's suggestion he joined the expedition on April 28 and remained with it until January 1889. Lord had clerked on the Mexican Central Railroad in Mexico City and become interested in archaeology. Lord fell in love with Zuni as Edward Gaston had and could write with a romantic flair like Cushing's: "I have enjoyed Zuñi as much by night as by day. When the moon is obscured, the dark mass against the sky looks like a distant mountain, but in the clearer evenings I can make out the

houses & there are people talking together in low tones on the roofs, & now & then a pleasant laugh,—& among the cells of the honey comb dark forms are busy with their water jars" (Lord to Cushing, 23 July 1888, Cushing Collection, MS 6, HAE 1.35, BR/AM).

In 1923 Miss Mary Patterson Lord donated to the Heye Foundation a collection of 29 ethnographic specimens collected by Daniel Lord while on the Hemenway Expedition. They include 10 Hopi, 4 Zuni, 5 Navajo, 5 Apache, 1 Jicarilla Apache, 1 Ute, and 1 Brulé Sioux items (Mary Davis, personal communication to David Wilcox, 1996).

185. Ten Kate, "Schrijven van Dr. H. F. C. ten Kate," 317.

186. Cushing to Baxter, 14 May 1888, HLB 5: 100–17. On the other hand, Cushing had no love for the Salt River/Tempe residents: "The party cannot leave the Salado Valley too soon. . . . The attitude which the Saladeňos have seen fit to assume toward an enterprise which has done them incalculable good, is one which fills me with inexpressible contempt—of their low, sordid lives, and even causes me to doubt (what I have hitherto held an inviolable article of faith) that their graves only are destined to purify them, and to thus pave the way to a better order of things" (Cushing to Hodge, 30 May 1888, Cushing Collection, MS 6, HAE 1.31, BR/AM; HLB 4: 320–27).

187. Cushing to Hodge, 18 May 1888, Cushing Collection, MS 6, HAE 1.31, BR/AM; HLB 4: 240–45.

188. ten Kate, "Schrijven van Dr. H. F. C. ten Kate," 536; ten Kate, "Eenige Mededelingen de Hemenway Expeditie," 223.

189. Rafael was the younger brother of Ramon Castro, who had sent for him to join the expedition on 5 July 1887.

190. ten Kate, "Schrijven van Dr. H. F. C. ten Kate," 318.

191. Young Morse fell both sick and homesick; Cushing sent him back home after a month (Cushing to E. S. Morse, 13 August 1888, HLB 5: 197–98; PS MC: 337–38).

192. Hodge to Cushing, 11 July 1888, HC.

193. Cushing to Lord, 16 July 1888, HLB 4: 493–94.

194. Cushing to Mary Hemenway, 1 June 1888, HLB 4: 341.

195. See, e.g., "Ancient Pueblo Remains"; "Arizona's Buried City: Lieut. Cushing Describes the Relics of the Past Unearthed at Los Muertos," *Arizona Daily Star*, 23 May 1888; Wilson, "The Late Discoveries of Mr. Frank Hamilton Cushing"; Wilson, "The Hemenway Expedition in Arizona"; Daly, "Recent Geographical Work"; and Leslie, "Cushing Expedition."

196. Cushing arrived in San Francisco on June 12 and attended the special meeting and reception in his honor at the Academy on Monday, June 18. See

Leviton and Aldrich, *Theodore Henry Littell's*, 296; and McDowell, "America's Antiquities"; McDowell, "Tried for Sorcery"; McDowell, "Left in Zuni"; and McDowell, "Zuni Mysteries." Much of McDowell's series, presented as an extended interview, reiterated Cushing's *My Adventures in Zuñi* (1882–83).

197. McDowell, "America's Antiquities"; McDowell, "Tried for Sorcery"; McDowell, "Left in Zuni"; and McDowell, "Zuni Mysteries." Knowing of her aversion to publicity, Cushing strained to explain to Mrs. Hemenway that, while he took no responsibility for the exaggerations and errors of newspaper accounts, they were vital to creating a public audience for the expedition's future work. Indeed, he wrote, "I wonder if it is not my duty to be as accomodating to these newspapermen as possible" (Cushing to Hemenway, 20 July 1888, Cushing Collection, MS 6, HAE 1.280, BR/AM).

198. Kevin, "This May Be the First"; Tinder, *Directory of Early Michigan Photographers*; and *The Photographic Times and American Photographer*. Feared lost on an expedition to Alaska in 1889, Husher went on to an illustrious photographic career in Detroit and Los Angeles, among other things working with the elderly William Henry Jackson and producing the first color photo postcards. Today about three dozen of Husher's photos for the Hemenway Expedition in 1888–89 are extant in four archives: Peabody Museum Photo Archives, Harvard; National Anthropological Archives, Smithsonian Institution; Bancroft Library, UC-Berkeley; and Braun Research Library Collection, Autry Museum, Los Angeles.

199. Cushing to Garlick, 22 July 1888. Cushing Collection, MS 6, BAE 1.35, BR/AM; Cushing to Baxter, HLB 4: 462–72. Adjusted to 2020 dollars, Husher's salary was more than eight thousand dollars a month. The photographic dark room was not built.

200. "It had been my original intention to penetrate eastward though one or the other of these great confluent valleys, into the mountain plateaus, a hundred miles, more or less, nearer to Zuñi, with the object of seeking what I had supposed would prove to be the farthermost remains in that direction of a Zuñi people." Cushing, "Preliminary Notes," 161.

201. William T. Harris (1835–1909), Hegelian philosopher and U.S. commissioner of education (1889–1906), taught at the Concord School of Philosophy every year of its existence (1880–88). He became Hemenway's trusted adviser on matters of educational reform. On his central role in the expedition's governance, see Hinsley and Wilcox, *The Lost Itinerary of Frank Hamilton Cushing*, 28–31. His role as intermediary between Cushing and Hemenway emerges in Harris's diary for the summer of 1888 (in William Torrey Harris Papers, Missouri Historical Society, Saint Louis).

202. Newspaper accounts from the 1890s show that the Garlick family lived in Phoenix, where Charles (d. 1909) was a wagonmaster and Ella (d. 1903) was active in the Woman's Christian Temperance League. The Garlicks had two daughters, Louella (Nellie) and Mamie. Mamie became a high school teacher and Louella taught kindergarten in Phoenix. Louella married J. Sidney Gould in 1895; Mamie married Richard Parsons and moved to Denver. When Charles died at Mamie's Denver home in 1909, the *Arizona Republic* (11 February 1909, 3, col. 2) reported: "Mr. Garlick first came to the valley about 1885 or 1886, with the Frank Cushing expedition, which conducted the earliest and most extensive antiquarian research and exploration of prehistoric matters. Several months, perhaps a year, were spent here in the valley on that business. Some years later, Mr. Garlick came here with his wife and they made it their home for a long time. He was an estimable citizen, highly respected by all who knew him." Interestingly, the following piece appeared in the *Arizona Republican* on 13 October 1895: "The old Hayden house in Tempe narrowly escaped destruction by fire Friday night. A cat and a lamp tipped from a table furnished the cause. Mrs. Garlick and daughter were just in time." (The Hayden house today is the oldest continuously occupied structure in metropolitan Phoenix.)

Henry François Farny (1847–1916), an Alsace-born American artist based in Cincinnati, was a popular illustrator specializing, by the 1880s, in Native American scenes. He had contributed illustrations to Cushing's *My Adventures in Zuni* (1882) and the *Zuñi Breadstuff* series (1884–85); Cushing was proposing that he do the same for the folktales. Most of Farny's illustrations were based upon photographs by Jack Hillers; though he made several trips through the West, it is not clear that he ever visited Zuni. He did meet and sketch the visiting Zuni chiefs in Washington in 1882. For Farny's career, see Appleton and Bartalini, *Henry Farny*; and Carter, *Henry Farny*.

203. Cushing to Baxter, 13 August 1888. JFL HLB 5: 219–38. On Palowahtiwa's central role at Zuni, see Walker, "Palowahtiwa and the Economic Redevelopment"; on the crisis and decline of the Bow Priesthood at Zuni in these years see Pandey, "Factionalism in a Southwestern Pueblo," 131–60.

204. Green, *Cushing at Zuni*, 316, 412n2.

205. Hodge, *Frederick Webb Hodge, Ethnologist*, 51. This had been Cushing's intention from the beginning. In his original program of operations submitted to Mrs. Hemenway in November 1886, Cushing had proposed that the "summer headquarters" of the expedition be located "at my house on 'Halona Hill.'" Cushing to Hemenway, 12 November 1886, Cushing Collection, MS 6, HAE 1.28, BR/AM.

206. Cushing to Garlick, 22 July 1888, Cushing Collection, MS 6, BAE 1.35, BR/AM.

207. Cushing to Molera, 1 September 1888, HLB 5: 335–37.

208. Hodge, *Frederick Webb Hodge, Ethnologist*, 51–52. The "Hemenway House" became a trading post and was demolished in 1971. See Burgio-Ericson, "A:shiwi A:wan Museum and Heritage Center."

209. Ten Kate, "Schrijven van Dr. H. F. C. ten Kate," 537 (21 August 1888).

210. See Cushing, "The Discovery of Zuni"; Bandelier, *The Gilded Man*, 159–60. Jesse Green, *Cushing at Zuni*, reviews the history of Cushing and Bandelier's long, shared fascination with the Seven Cities puzzle. He pointedly notes, too, that on this subject Hodge, in his *History of Hawikuh* (1937) "summarizes the contributions of all [Hodge's] known predecessors—except Cushing" (352n43).

211. On Cushing's changing thoughts about the Cibola ruins, see Green, *Cushing at Zuni*; Kintigh, *Settlement, Subsistence, and Society*; and Cushing to Hemenway, 20 July 1888 (Cushing Collection, MS 6, HAE 1.28, BR/AM), in which he promised her a story equal in historical and romantic interest to William H. Prescott's *History of the Conquest of Mexico* (1843).

212. Cushing to Bandelier, 22 August 1888, HLB 5: 250–60. Cushing to Baxter, 13 August 1888. HLB 5: 219–38.

213. Cushing favored ten Kate to represent the expedition, but Mrs. Hemenway felt that the spokesmen in Berlin should be Americans. Baxter had studied in Berlin and Leipzig as a young man; Morse was an internationally respected and well-traveled scientist who, the preceding year, had examined European museums for two months at Mrs. Hemenway's bidding. Both men communicated effectively and had a broad grasp of the expedition's work.

214. Cushing, "Preliminary Notes." The other papers were Bandelier, "The Historical Archives," and Wortman and ten Kate, "On an Anatomical Characteristic of the Hyoid Bone." Only the latter paper arrived in time to be read at the conference. In addition to the papers, Morse presented an account of the Los Muertos work, and Baxter offered a summary of Bandelier's documentary work. All three papers were eventually published in the congress's *Compte-Rendu*.

215. Cushing, "Preliminary Notes," 191. Although direct influence is uncertain, Cushing's notions of a central cultural "Idea" and a "culture soul" bear strong resemblance to Adolf Bastian's (1826–1905) "folk ideas" (*Völkergedanken*) and a "societal soul" (*Gesellschaftsseele*) in which the individual's mind is embedded.

216. "A primitive people, once having conceived an Idea, rather modify (nominally) a changed environment to suit it, than modify it to suit their changed environment" (Cushing, "Preliminary Notes," 191). Cushing's ideas about a seven-part organization for Zuni were also expressed in two drawings he made that interpreted the architectural structure of the Casa Grande building (Wilcox and Shenk, *The Architecture of the Casa Grande*). This integration of concepts

of the four quarters of the universe with an axis of upper, middle and lower world is well known by ethnographers in West Mexico as an "axis mundi" concept (Coyle, *Náyari History, Politics and Violence*; Liffman, *Huichol Territory*). Wilcox ("The Mesoamerican Ballgame"; "Microcosm and Macrocosm"; Wilcox et al., "Ancient Cultural Interplay") proposes that these basic concepts may go back to the Late Paleolithic period in the Old World and may have been brought to the New World by the population that archaeologists call the "Paleoindians," resulting in a kind of "founder effect" in the cosmology and religious beliefs of all American Indians.

217. The correspondence between Cushing, Billings, ten Kate, Baxter, and Matthews on this matter extended over several months—and became quite personal.

218. "I spent one winter [1888–89] in a tent when snow often covered the ground three feet deep" (Hodge, *Frederick Webb Hodge, Ethnologist,* 30). It is worth recalling that Hodge had stopped keeping a diary six months earlier.

219. Cushing to Hemenway, 27 September 1888, HLB 5: 415–29.

220. Cushing to Baxter, 2 June 1888, HLB 4: 374–404. The Hawikku site has an estimated 800 pueblo rooms dating to AD 1400–1680 and the ruins of a seventeenth-century Catholic church. Heshotauthla is an oval pueblo ruin with an estimated 875 rooms, dating to AD 1275–1385 (Kintigh, *Settlement, Subsistence, and Society*; Gregory and Wilcox, *Zuni Origins*).

221. Cushing to ten Kate, 12 October 1888, HLB 5: 479–84.

222. Cushing to Hemenway, 11 October 1888, HLB 5: 468–75.

223. Hodge, *Frederick Webb Hodge, Ethnologist,* 49.

224. Baxter met in Manchester with Mrs. Hemenway, Morse, and Wortman on 7 August, and with Mrs. Hemenway and William T. Harris on 20 August. Harris, who had conferred with Cushing in San Francisco in July, was particularly concerned about the cost and results of the expedition.

225. Baxter to Cushing, 21 August 1888, Cushing Collection, MS 6, BOE 1.6, BR/AM.

226. Cushing to Hemenway, 1 September 1888, HLB 5: 349–53; Cushing to Hemenway, 27 September 1888, HLB 5: 415–29. Emily also wanted to visit an ailing sister.

227. See, e.g., Hodge to Cushing, 6 November, 15 November 1888, HC; and Hodge to Cushing, 1 December 1888, HLB 6: insert 36–41.

228. At the start of December Hodge reported that "Miss Magill is looking forward with the rest of us to the completion of the house, when, with the large double window and northern light, she will have all the facilities conducive to successive [*sic*] work" (Hodge to Cushing, 1 December 1888, HLB 6: insert 36–

41). Fewkes published five color plates of Magill's 1888 Zuni sketches (Fewkes, "Ancient Zuñi Pottery"). Today her drawings are divided between the collections of the NAA, the Hemenway materials at Harvard's Peabody Museum, and the Braun Research Library Collection, Autry Museum, Los Angeles.

229. A deeply religious man who was awed and moved by Cushing, Edward Gaston remained in touch with Frank and Emily, and returned alone to Zuni pueblo for a prolonged visit in 1893. In September 1889 he wrote to Emily regarding her husband, "that genial and tolerant man": "I think others can truthfully say as do I that the force of that noble and self-sacrificing example will make itself felt in the lives of those with which it came in contact for all time" (Gaston to Emily Cushing, 16 September 1889, Cushing Collection, MS 6, BAE 1.36, BR/AM). In 1893 he considered writing a sketch of Cushing's life (Cushing Diary, 25 March 1893, NAA).

230. Gaston had also shared responsibility with Hodge and Cushing for the Halona:wan catalog. X-file 46–73, Peabody Museum, holds the handwritten entries.

231. Fewkes, "Ancient Zuñi Pottery," 44.

232. Ibid.

233. Hodge to Haury, 5 October 1931, No. 138, FWHC. On the other hand, Hodge told Clarissa Parson Fuller in 1942 that under *his* direction "the work continued until late the next spring" (Hodge to Fuller, 30 October 1942, in Fuller 1943: 89n81).

234. Cushing to "Dear Friend" [Baxter], 15 December 1888, Cushing Collection, MS 6, HAE 1.9, BR/AM.

235. Hodge to Cushing, 24 December 1888, HC.

236. Cushing Diary, undated [end of 1888], NAA.

237. On Hemenway's successful efforts to have Congress set aside the Casa Grande ruin see Clemensen, *A Centennial History*; and Hinsley and Wilcox, "Arizona's First Sacred Site," 136–40.

238. We know little of Katherine H. Stone. In later years she was active in civic affairs in Boston, especially on behalf of children. In 1908 she collaborated with Benjamin Ives Gilman on a brief article on the expedition (Gilman and Stone, "The Hemenway Southwestern Expedition"); her assessment of Mary Hemenway's "marked executive ability" is in Stone, "Mrs. Mary Hemenway," 12.

239. Cushing to Mother, 1 January 1889, HLB 6: 1–2. This letter was not sent until April 17. (Cushing to his mother, 17 April 1889, HLB 6: 208–13.)

240. Cushing to Hemenway, Cushing Collection, MS 6, HAE 1.28, BR/AM. This unfinished and unsigned letter may not have been sent—but nevertheless provides insight into Cushing's psychology (and strategy) at a critical juncture.

241. Garlick to Cushing, 13 January 1889, Cushing Collection, MS 6, HAE 1.21, BR/AM.

242. The Hemenway appeal to set aside the ruin as a federally protected property was the first such site protection in American history. It was presented by Massachusetts Senator George Hoar and passed without debate on February 4. For the full text of Hoar's presentation to Congress and an account of the development of the appeal, see Clemensen, *A Centennial History*, 31–33; and Wilcox and Sternberg, *Additional Studies*, 5–12.

243. Cushing to Hemenway, [4 February] 1888, HLB 6: 55–67.

244. Cushing to Garlick, 17 February 1888, HLB 6: 85–89. A few days earlier he had written to Hodge that Garlick's appointment had been "conferred upon him by our association [the Hemenway board]" (Cushing to Hodge, 10 February 1889, Cushing Collection, MS 6, HAE 1.31, BR/AM).

245. Bandelier to Hodge, 27 March 1889, HC, Br/AM. Garfield Memorial Hospital, located at Florida Avenue and Eleventh Street in northwest Washington, was only five years old in 1889. Funds for the facility had been largely raised by the wives and daughters of members of Congress. It was incorporated to serve indigent people in need of medical care; two-thirds of the patients received free care. The daily cost per patient in 1889 was $1.54 (Williams, "The Mysterious Wrought Iron Gates").

246. At Zuni Cushing had caught smallpox, which (as photographs of the time show) marked his face (McHenry, *Thomas Eakins*, 113). His treatments may have worsened his condition. Emily reported to Eben Horsford in September 1889: "Mr. Cushing has had a little lead poison from a face-remedy given by some of his doctors last winter. I suppose that, along with the *calculi*, is what gives him so much suffering." Photographs between 1887 and 1892 suggest that the treatments may have been worse than the disease. (Emily Cushing to Horsford, 3 September [1889], Horsford Papers, SMA.)

247. Hodge to Cushing, 20 February 1889, HC. The expedition labor force was never more than twenty.

248. Cushing to "I'Ki na" ["Little Sister," Margaret Magill], 30 March 1889, HLB 6: 141–56. The "saddest day" refers to the day they announced their engagement to him.

249. Cushing to Hodge, 31 March 1889, Cushing Collection, MS 6, HAE 1.31, BR/AM. The letter is incomplete and unsigned.

250. Cushing to Baxter, 28 April 1889, HLB 6: 251–64.

251. Cushing to Father, 18 April 1889, HLB 6: 214–23.

252. Cushing to Brooks Adams, 1 May 1889, HLB 6: 235–38. Adams had invited him to travel in Europe.

253. Cushing was never permitted to see Mrs. Hemenway again.

254. Haynes to Norton, 22 April 1889, Papers of the Archaeological Institute of America, Box 4. ("Great cry and little wool" refers to the bleating and shearing of sheep.) Cf. Haynes, "Recent Progress in American Archaeology"; Haynes, "Early Explorations of New Mexico"; and for Haynes's career, Peabody, "Henry Williamson Haynes." While Norton championed Bandelier's work in the Southwest for the Archaeological Institute of America, from his first exposure he never liked or trusted Cushing. "I am a little sceptical as to some of his supposed discoveries" was his initial response to the young man, and it never changed (Norton to Horsford, 26 October 1881, Box 66, Folder 1, Horsford Family Papers, SMA). In 1889 he wanted Haynes to be harsher in print; Haynes declined.

255. On the close relationship of Hemenway and Goddard, see Hinsley, "Two Marys and a Martha"; and Goddard, "A Zuni Religious Service."

256. Judd, *The Bureau of Ethnology*, 27; Stephens and Calder, "The Zoological Career," 259, 264n13. On Fewkes's career in anthropology, see Fowler, *A Laboratory for Anthropology*, 161–71; Browman and Williams, *Anthropology at Harvard*, 291–92; and Wilcox, "Going National."

257. Cushing "Memorandum for Dr. Fewkes tomorrow," 10 May 1889, Cushing Collection, MS 6, HAE 1.18, BR/AM.

258. Baxter to Horsford, 15 June 1889, Horsford Papers, SMA.

259. Emily Cushing to Charles Garlick, 18 June 1889, HLB 6: 333–35.

260. Bandelier to Norton, 13 and 27 December 1889, Box 4, Archives of the Archaeological Institute of America, Boston. Bandelier received his last Hemenway check in January 1890, leaving him without a regular income.

261. Bandelier to Matthews, 28 November 1890, Hodge Papers, MS 7, BAEL (Bureau of American Ethnology Letters) 1.5, BR/AM. To Norton (who much preferred Bandelier over Cushing) he was even more critical of his old friend: "Cushing has sadly miscarried the business, . . . he squandered recklessly, and went away at it without system or method. I know Cushing probably better than most people. He has made some invaluable discoveries, but the sudden popularity and newspaper fame turned his head. As soon as the Hemenways showed such extravagant confidence in him it was "Mr. Director" thereafter, and no longer work as it should have been done" (Bandelier to Norton, 10 October 1889, cited in White, *Pioneers in American Anthropology*, vol. 1, 92).

262. Hinsley and Wilcox, *The Lost Itinerary of Frank Hamilton Cushing*, 26–37. For three months (18 December 1890–18 March 1891) Frank and Emily lived in a convalescent hotel in Buffalo.

263. She also contributed to the Bureau of Ethnology. See, e.g., "Zuni Court, Balcony" in the bureau's *Annual Report for 1892–1893*: 529.

264. Matthews to Cushing, 23 July 1889, Cushing Collection, MS 6, HAE 1.38, BR/AM.

265. There is some doubt about the wedding date. The *Washington Post* noted their marriage license on 31 August; evidence in correspondence suggests that they were married a week later.

266. Emily Cushing to Eusebio Molera, 1 November 1891, Phoebe Hearst Papers, Bancroft Library, UC-Berkeley. Death seemed to stalk the Magill women in these years: sister Eleanor (Ellen, Nellie) and her husband, George C. Payne, who already had a son and daughter, lost two infant boys in 1892 and 1895; Fred and Margaret lost their first child, Margaret Cecelia, at two years old in 1894. George Payne died in 1901, a year after Cushing.

Part II. The Hemenway Expedition Diaries of Frederick W. Hodge and Margaret W. Magill, 1886–1888

1. Book 1 of Hodge's diary runs from 5 December 1886 to 6 May 1887. He misdated the first entry as 5 December; it was Saturday, 4 December.

2. Located in western New York on an Indigenous trail north of Batavia, Albion was a small town on the Erie Canal where Cushing spent much of his childhood.

3. Enos L. Cushing (1850–1937) was Frank's oldest brother; he was a dentist who had traveled to Zuni pueblo to bring three Zuni men to Mary Hemenway's estate in Manchester-by-the-Sea, Massachusetts, in the fall of 1886.

4. The most successful novel by popular English writer Wilkie Collins (1824–89), *The Evil Genius* (1886) deals with deception, adultery, and divorce in the Victorian era.

5. These letters have not been found; we know little of the friends and family to whom Hodge wrote many letters during the expedition.

6. Margaret Whitehead Magill (1865–1935) was Emily Cushing's youngest sister and Cushing's sister-in-law. She was the expedition illustrator with sketchbook, watercolors, and oils; she married Hodge in 1891.

7. Ezra Titus Coann (1829–1900) was a banker in Albion and a close family friend and supporter of Frank and Emily Cushing.

8. Cushing wrote to Major John Wesley Powell (1834–1902), director of the Bureau of Ethnology, Smithsonian Institution on 7 December (HLB 1: 26–32).

9. On 9 December Cushing wrote to James F. Peirce, Rufus Leighton (his former stenographer during the work at Mrs. Hemenway's summer estate), and Percival Lowell (HLB 1: 33–38, 39–43, 44–47).

10. Cushing's father, Thomas Cushing (1827–98), was a physician who had served in the Union army during the Civil War; he retired to a farm in Barre Center, south of Albion, in 1878.

11. On 10 December Cushing wrote to Sylvester Baxter (1850–1927), secretary of the expedition's board (HLB 1: 49–54.)

12. Wai-hu-si-wa, an important Zuni storyteller and religious leader, had been with Cushing at Manchester-by-the-Sea in 1886.

13. He-lu-ta, a Zuni leader, had been with Cushing at Manchester-by-the-Sea in 1886.

14. "Mr. Watson" was apparently connected to the Baltimore & Ohio Railroad.

15. Colonel James Stevenson (1840–88) of the Bureau of Ethnology, Smithsonian Institution, led the Smithsonian collecting expedition to the Southwest pueblos in 1879 that brought Cushing to Zuni. See Hieb, *The Doctor Danced with Us*, 143–236; and Green, *Cushing at Zuni.*

16. "Star-router" was a contemporary term for a corrupt politician, such as Boss Tweed of New York or Senator Dorsey of Arkansas.

17. Stephen Wallace Dorsey (1842–1916), a Republican senator (1873–79) from Arkansas, became secretary of the Republican National Committee in 1880. Accused and acquitted of scandal, he subsequently engaged in cattle raising and mining in New Mexico and Colorado ("Stephen Wallace Dorsey," Wikipedia, https://en.wikipedia.org/wiki/Stephen_Wallace_Dorsey).

18. Palowahtiwa (c. 1832–?) also known as Patricio Pino, was an accomplished silversmith and governor of Zuni pueblo. Cushing had lived in the Pino household through much of his time at Zuni, 1879–84. (Green, *Cushing at Zuni*, passim; Walker, "Palowahtiwa and the Economic Redevelopment," 665–77; Walker and Wyckoff, *Hopis, Tewas, and the American Road*, 45–56.) Palowahtiwa was also at Manchester-by-the-Sea in the fall of 1886.

19. Adolph Francis Alphonse Bandelier (1840–1914) was the historian of the expedition and a close friend of Cushing. In his diary for 16 December 1886 Bandelier reports: "Met Cushing at Lamy [New Mexico], in company with his two ladies, Mr. Hodge, and three Zuñis: Pala-ua-tiua and two young men. Very, very pleasant on all sides. Frank looks rather as usual" (Lange et al., *The Southwestern Journals of Adolph F. Bandelier, 1885–1888*, 187).

20. Fort Wingate, New Mexico, was a U.S. Army military fort near the railroad line and a jumping-off place for Cushing's trips to Zuni Pueblo to the south.

21. Bandelier wrote of this day in his journal: "Reached Albuquerque at 3 a. m., about. Found at last, rooms at the Girard House. Called at Altheimer's, Hunning's, Candelaria's, Father Gentile's, and Father Durante's [He was saying goodbye before an pending trip to Mexico City for the Hemenway Expedition]. All very kind. Cushing says that the Indians of 'Marata' [which lay between Hawikuh and Acoma, in the El Morro Valley] spoke another language than

those of Zuñi. There are still some of them remaining alive at Zuñi. Financially, everything seems all right. Cushing telegraphed for $450—to Boston" (Lange et al., *The Southwestern Journals of Adolph F. Bandelier, 1885–1888*, 187, 471). Lange and colleagues further cite an account by Hodge of his night with Bandelier as follows: "Bandelier and I finally found lodgment in the second story of an adobe bunk-house, and as we shared the only bed, we became well acquainted in a trice, for Bandelier immediately and literally kicked me out of bed, calling me a 'damned scrub,' which was my pet name forever after" (470).

22. Captain William Malcolm Waterbury of the Thirteenth Infantry was born in 1841. He retired in 1895 with the rank of major (Heitman, *Historical Register and Dictionary*, 1007, cited in Lange et al., *The Southwestern Journals of Adolph F. Bandelier, 1883–1884*, 382n197).

23. Woodside was the post trader at Fort Wingate; he died before the Hemenway Expedition returned there in 1889.

24. Fetter Schrier Hoblitzell (1838–1900) was a lawyer from Baltimore who was the (Democratic) Speaker of the Maryland House of Delegates in 1878, served in the U.S. House of Representatives, 1880–84, and was on the Baltimore City Council, 1888–89 ("Fetter Schrier Hoblitzell," Wikipedia, https://en.wikipedia.org/wiki/Fetter_Schrier_Hoblitzell). The Hoblitzell Hodge met probably was his son.

25. Joseph Stanley Brown (1857–1941) had been hired as a secretary by Powell in 1876, and then was "loaned" on Sundays and holidays to James A. Garfield (1831–81); he became Garfield's private secretary during his brief presidency. Stanley Brown helped arrange Powell's appointment as director of the Geological Survey. He married the late president's daughter Mary "Mollie" Garfield in 1888.

26. John K. Hillers (1843–1925) became a boatman and photographer on John Wesley Powell's second (1871–72) trip down the Colorado River, and then for the Bureau of Ethnology, accompanying the Stevenson expedition to the Southwest (Waldman, *Who Was Who*; "John Karl Hillers," Wikipedia, https://en.wikipedia.org/wiki/John_Karl_Hillers).

27. Capt. Benjamin Hidden Gilman (1850–98) graduated from West Point in 1872 and was the regimental quartermaster for the Thirteenth Infantry between 1 September 1886 and 15 March 1889 (Heitman, *Historical Register and Dictionary*, 458; "Benjamin H. Gilman," Bill Thayer's Web Site, http://penelope.uchicago.edu/Thayer/E/Gazetteer/Places/America/United_States/Army/USMA/Cullums_Register/2423*.html).

28. Probably Major Daingerfield Parker (1832–1925), who had become a major in the Ninth Infantry in 1884 (Heitman, *Historical Register and Dictionary*,

769). He graduated from West Point in 1861 and fought during the Civil War at Bull Run, Antietam, Fredericksburg, and Gettysburg (Michael Robert Patterson, "Daingerfield Parker—Brigadier General, United States Army," Arlington National Cemetery, http://www.arlingtoncemetery.net/daingerfield-parker.htm).

29. Probably James Fornance (1850–98) and his wife, Fannie Barbee (d. 1894). The son of a Pennsylvania lawyer who had served several terms in Congress, Fornance graduated from West Point in 1871 and was assigned to the Thirteenth Infantry; in 1884 he was assigned to posts in New Mexico. He died in the battle of San Juan Hill, Cuba, in 1898 ("James Fornance," Bill Thayer's Web Site, http://penelope.uchicago.edu/Thayer/E/Gazetteer/Places/America/United_States/Army/USMA/AOG_Reunions/31/James_Fornance*.html).

30. Crossed out: "I crawled out at 7 o'clock. Mr. Cushing was arranging his toilet, the two younger Indians were in search of our animals, which had strayed away during the night, and the 'Governor' [Palowahtiwa] was gathering snow."

31. The winter solstice.

32. Arthur Watts was in charge of the winter camp of the U.S. Geological Survey at Wingate Station.

33. Cushing wrote to Mrs. Hemenway on 25 December (HLB 1: 86–89).

34. See HLB 1: 86–95.

35. Cushing wrote to Baxter on 28 December 28 (HLB 1: 96–98).

36. Possibly Captain William Edgeworth Dougherty (1841–1915) (Heitman, *Historical Register and Dictionary*, 330, 413; "Gen William Edgeworth Dougherty," FindAGrave, http://www.findagrave.com/cgi-bin/fg.cgi?page=gr&GRid=3525327).

37. Probably *Yucca baccata*, a Yucca soapweed species.

38. Richard Gibbons (1859–1924) was a Mormon farmer and sheep rancher in Saint Johns; he was elected to the Arizona legislature in 1901 (Goff, *Arizona Biographical Dictionary*, 114; see also HLB 1: 114–16).

39. Two young Zunis, Weta and Siwaititsailu, had been detailed to accompany the Hemenway Expedition.

40. Probably William Langdon Buck (1856–1912), who became a first lieutenant in the Thirteenth Infantry Regiment in 1888 (Heitman, *Historical Register and Dictionary*, 258).

41. Charles Augustus Garlick (1833–1909), a brother-in-law of John Wesley Powell, married Eliza Dean Powell (1838–1903) in 1861. He became the majordomo for the Hemenway Expedition ("Eliza Dean (Powell) Garlick (1838–1903)," WikiTree, http://www.wikitree.com/wiki/Powell-4011).

42. Prescott Junction was near today's Seligman, Arizona. For an amusing account of Cushing's stay there, see Hinsley and Wilcox, *The Lost Itinerary of Frank Hamilton Cushing*, 103–7.

43. The "O. K." Yard was owned by Joseph Dougherty near his store on Gurley Street and opposite the central square.

44. James Burgess had joined the expedition at Prescott, and later went on to Mesa City.

45. Saguaro cactus.

46. The Eylar Ranch was just north of today's New River, and at this time was owned by Frank and George Alkire (see Hinsley and Wilcox, *The Lost Itinerary of Frank Hamilton Cushing*).

47. Franklin Tomlin Alkire (1865–1962) acquired the Eylar Ranch in 1887; he became one of Phoenix's most prominent businessmen. His papers are MS 0012, Arizona Historical Society, Tucson, Arizona (http://www.arizonahistoricalsociety.org/wp-content/upLoads/library_Alkire-Frank.pdf).

48. The first part of Margaret Magill's Hemenway diary begins here on 6 February and goes to 11 April.

49. Triangle Bar Ranch was one of the largest in Arizona Territory; where it once stood can still be seen today, north of the New River exit off Interstate 17, a biological reserve where three palm trees stand (personal communication from George Alkire, 1998).

50. Tenatsali was Cushing's Zuni name; it means "medicine flower."

51. Joe F. Singleton was a colleague of the Alkires in the ranching business (*Phoenix Herald*, 14 July 1887, 3, col. 2).

52. The Arizona Canal was completed in 1884 by William John Murphy (1839–1921), who was from Illinois and served under William Tecumseh Sherman in the Union Army. In 1887 he founded the Arizona Improvement Company and proceeded to develop two communities northwest of Phoenix called Peoria and Glendale ("William John Murphy," Wikipedia, https://en.wikipedia.org/wiki/William_John_Murphy).

53. The William Lewis Osborn (1842–1927) ranch and dairy farm was located from Seventh to Fifteenth avenues and Thomas to Osborn streets in Phoenix, two miles north of town on the Black Cañon Road (*Phoenix Directory for the Year 1895*).

54. The Arizona Canal.

55. George Henry Boughton (1834–1905) was an Anglo-American painter who lived mainly in London and was known for the delicacy and grace of his pictures, those of Dutch life and scenery being especially characteristic (*Encyclopaedia Britannica*, vol. 3, 14th ed. [London: Encyclopaedia Britannica, 1932], 959).

56. Crossed out: "Was up and had fire kindled before rest were out of their tents. Mr. C. and the ladies drove to town in buck board, Hodge following on Douglas. Returned to camp with the ladies (Mr. C. spent ev'g in tent of Mr. Garlick and I)."

57. This is apparently the man Cushing describes (at some length) in his itinerary as being "at one time, of great wealth but having been disappointed in love fled away, whilst still comparatively young, into the southwestern wilderness" (Hinsley and Wilcox, *The Lost Itinerary of Frank Hamilton Cushing*, 137).

58. The Magill diary has no entry for 10 February 1887.

59. Joe Gunn was the Chinese-American proprietor of the Commercial Hotel Restaurant in Phoenix (Hinsley and Wilcox, *The Lost Itinerary of Frank Hamilton Cushing*, 136–37).

60. The wagon road to Tempe from Phoenix ran east-west along today's Van Buren Street. Omar Turney's map in *Prehistoric Irrigation in Arizona* shows that it ran just south of his La Ciudad site and north of his Dos Casas and Pueblo Grande sites.

61. Augustus (1853–1931) was Mary Hemenway's only son, named for his father, Edward Augustus Holyoke Hemenway (1805–76).

62. Dr. George H. Mitchell, a former Indian agent on the Pima Reservation, was an Episcopal clergyman who served briefly (1887–88) as the health officer for Phoenix (*Phoenix Herald*, 10 March 1887, 3, col. 2; 4 January 1888, 3, col. 3; *Arizona Gazette*, 6 August 1887, 1, col. 3). Dr. Mitchell also had a prescient conception of Phoenix's future, which he shared with the *San Francisco Examiner* while on the west coast in August 1887: "[Y]ou know, we are having a boom in Phoenix now. Everything is going on in grand style. We shall soon rival California and make Phoenix a second Los Angeles" (*Arizona Gazette*, 5 August 1887, 1, col. 3).

63. Haury interprets Cushing's "La Ciudad de los Pueblitos" as Turney's La Ciudad. Pueblo del Patricio, owned by Herbert Patrick, lay about a mile farther west of where Los Pueblitos is plotted on the Hemenway map (Haury, *The Excavation of Los Muertos*, 186–88, fig. 1). He speculates that Cushing's El Pueblo de los Piedras was Turney's Pueblo Grande, located about five miles east of Phoenix Townsite. The fact that Magill (20 February 1887) identifies it with a site described by Bandelier ("Reports by Adolph F. Bandelier") as lying three miles east of Phoenix confirms this identification. The Phoenix-Tempe wagon road also lay close to the La Ciudad platform mound (Turney, *Prehistoric Irrigation in Arizona*, map). This means that Wilcox's inference, in "Pueblo Grande in the Nineteenth Century," that Cushing's Los Pueblitos was Pueblo Grande must be wrong, and that the tower structure the Cushing party excavated in that site should be assigned to Turney's La Ciudad; perhaps it is the tower-like feature Mound B mapped by Frank Midvale during his work there in the 1920s (Wilcox, *Frank Midvale's Investigations*). Our discussion about the identification of Los Pueblitos in vol. 2, *The Lost Itinerary of Frank Hamilton Cushing*, also must be revised.

64. Haury calls this and nearby sites Los Pueblos Arriba (*The Excavation of Los Muertos*, 189).

65. These were probably Salado polychromes dating to the fourteenth or fifteenth century. The arrows and blue beads, however, were probably early historic Piman or Maricopa. Haury reports Gila Polychrome and Casa Grande red-on-buff from Los Pueblos Arribas but does not mention the blue glass beads (*The Excavation of Los Muertos*, 189).

66. The closely related Pima and Hopi languages are in the Uto-Aztecan language family.

67. On 16 February Cushing wrote to Baxter (HLB 1: 151–56).

68. These were letters to Bandelier and Herman ten Kate, the Dutch physical anthropologist who later joined the expedition (HLB 1: 157–58, 159–61; see Hinsley and Wilcox, "A Hemenway Portfolio").

69. Today this is the Papago Park in east Phoenix.

70. This is "Hole in the Rock" in Papago Park (see Turney, *Prehistoric Irrigation in Arizona*, map).

71. Cushing, "My Adventures in Zuñi."

72. Today this site is called La Ciudad (Turney, *Prehistoric Irrigation in Arizona*; cf. Wilcox, "Pueblo Grande in the Nineteenth Century"), based on the measurement of three miles east of Phoenix Townsite.

73. Bandelier, "Reports by Adolph F. Bandelier."

74. We have not located this editorial in the short-lived *Salt River Valley News*.

75. James Henry McClintock (1864–1934), who graduated from the Tempe Normal School in June 1887, was the editor of the *Salt River Valley News* for about six months that year. He later became a Rough Rider, postmaster of Phoenix, and Arizona historian. His papers are in Special Collections, University of Arizona Library.

76. Cushing named this site La Ciudad de los Hornos, after the large earth ovens that occur there, which James Cooper Goodwin and others had mistaken for slag heaps. The temperature reached in these earth ovens often exceeded 100°C, and thus melted granite rocks used in the cooking process (see Howard, "The Casa Buena Hornos").

77. Dated 23 February, these letters went to W. F. White (Topeka, Kansas) and Major Powell (HLB 1: 184–85, 186–89).

78. Soon called La Ciudad de los Hornos.

79. The "largest mound" was a Classic period Hohokam platform mound; it was taken down by farmers in 1956 before any scientific work could be done in it (Wilcox et al., *One Hundred Years of Archaeology*).

80. For a modern study of this site see Wilcox et al., *One Hundred Years of Archaeology*. While engaged in this work (after Howard brought Wilcox a copy of one installment of Cushing's Hemenway itinerary that he found in the Hayden Library, Arizona State University), one of the seeds was planted that led to this documentary history.

81. A later map by Hodge and Garlick showed that the size of this site is about 480 acres (see Wilcox et al., *One Hundred Years of Archaeology*).

82. Cushing later made extensive collections at this site, known as Double Butte Cave (Haury, *The Excavation of Los Muertos*).

83. Dr. John L. Gregg (1828–96) of Tempe owned a ranch near Pueblo del Monte, a Hohokam platform mound site north of Los Hornos.

84. *The Lady with the Rubies* was an 1885 novel by Eugenie Marlitt (1825–87).

85. Marcia Clement Coann was the wife of Ezra Titus Coann in Albion, New York.

86. Herbert Ralph Patrick (1854–1924) was a civil engineer who surveyed the route of the thirty-six-mile Maricopa-Phoenix Railroad in 1887; he later published a study of Hohokam irrigation (Patrick, *The Ancient Canal Systems*). He also owned the site later called Pat's Ruin and Pueblo del Patricio by Cushing (Haury, *The Excavation of Los Muertos*, Fig. 1); apparently it was a western "suburb" of the site later named La Ciudad by Omar Turney (*Prehistoric Irrigation in Arizona*; Wilcox, *Frank Midvale's Investigations*), and which Haury identified with Cushing's La Ciudad de los Pueblitos.

87. We have not found extant copies of these issues of the *Salt River Valley News*.

88. James Cooper Goodwin (1864–1922) owned part of the site of Los Muertos and showed this site to Cushing. He later became an important local businessman, Rough Rider, and Arizona legislator. He died in an auto accident on the Apache Trail.

89. Cushing's Los Muertos site.

90. Goodwin and his brothers Will, Garfield, and Tom all had prolific careers as Tempe businessmen. Garfield later had a curio store in Tempe.

91. "Los Muertos," where they were to dig for many months (see Haury, *The Excavation of Los Muertos*; Brunson, "The Social Organization of the Los Muertos Hohokam").

92. Charles Trumbull Hayden (1825–1900) established a flour mill at the Tempe crossing where Tempe Butte forced the Salt River to cross a rock ledge. He was the father of Carl Hayden, Arizona's long-serving U.S. representative and senator ("Charles T. Hayden," Wikipedia, https://en.wikipedia.org/wiki/Charles_T._Hayden).

93. Francisco Ruellas was the first of the Mexican laborers hired (26 February) by the expedition.

94. Jésus Arros was the second workman hired on 26 February.

95. Hayden and wife, Sally, were the first citizens of Tempe.

96. Hiram Bradford Farmer (1843–1912), whose wife's name we have not been able to learn, was the first principal of the Tempe Normal School, 1886–88 (Hopkins and Thomas, *The Arizona State University Story*). His Tempe house was later acquired by James Cooper Goodwin and is today listed on the National Register of Historic Places ("Farmer-Goodwin House," Tempe Facility Directory, https://www.tempe.gov/Home/Components/FacilityDirectory/FacilityDirectory/456/).

97. Cushing's letter to Baxter is dated Mar 4 (HLB 1: 197–203).

98. These sketchbooks have not been found.

99. The Priesthood of the Bow at Zuni were responsible for dealing with the outside world; Cushing had been initiated into this priesthood (see Green, *Cushing at Zuni*).

100. This was possibly a draft of the map he later published (Patrick, *The Ancient Canal Systems*).

101. This is the ruin later called La Ciudad by Omar Turney (*Prehistoric Irrigation in Arizona*); it was excavated in the 1920s by Frank Midvale for Dwight Heard (see Wilcox, *Frank Midvale's Investigations*).

102. Since Benjamin Franklin Johnson (1818–1905), one of the close companions of Mormon leader Joseph Smith, brought four of his six wives to Tempe in 1882, this story may be true.

103. In 1882 the extended family of Benjamin Franklin Johnson bought 80 acres from Charles Trumbull Hayden for $3,000 and built a village of 250 people along Mill Avenue between Fifth and Eighth Streets. In 1887 they sold out to the Tempe Land and Improvement Company and moved to an area west of Mesa City, where they built a new settlement called Nephi, later Alma.

104. The Maricopa road connected Tempe to the Southern Pacific Railroad at Maricopa on the Gila River to the southwest of town.

105. *Estufa* is a Spanish term for what in Hopi is called a *kiva*; Cushing thought the room was dedicated to ceremonial uses.

106. Hodge's diary has no entry for 8 March 1887.

107. Gray's Ranch lay west of Los Muertos and east of the site Cushing called Los Guanacos in T 1 S, R 4 E, southeast quarter of section 15, and all but southeast quarter of section 22 (Goodwin Map, Hemenway Collection, Peabody Museum, Harvard University).

108. This was Cushing's name for what today is called Pueblo Grande (see Wilcox, "Pueblo Grande in the Nineteenth Century").

109. For this story, see Hinsley and Wilcox, *The Lost Itinerary of Frank Hamilton Cushing.*

110. This is the tower mound described by Cushing in the third installment of his "Itinerary" (Hinsley and Wilcox, *The Lost Itinerary of Frank Hamilton Cushing*; Wilcox, "Pueblo Grande in the Nineteenth Century").

111. Crossed out: "Watched the moon rise over the hills before supper—"

112. This work appears in HLB 1: 216, 217, 218–19, 220–21.

113. John Samuel Armstrong (b. 1857) was part owner of Petersen, Armstrong & Company, a general merchandise store in Tempe with which the expedition did much business. Armstrong introduced the bill in the Arizona Territorial Legislature that established a Normal School in Tempe (later Arizona State University). See "History of Arizona State University," Wikipedia, https://en.wikipedia.org/wiki/History_of_Arizona_State_University.

114. Lieutenant Steward Mott died 11 March 1887 from injuries received the previous day in an assault by a Native American named Nah-Diaz-Az at the San Carlos Agency, Arizona Territory (Heitman, *Historical Register and Dictionary*, 732; *Phoenix Herald* 13 May 1887, 3, col. 2).

115. Possibly William H. Edwards (b. 1842), who lived in Tempe in the early 1880s in a house halfway between Hayden's store and the James T. Priest house.

116. We have not been able to further identify Edwards or Dare.

117. Mons M. Ellingson (1850–1928) was a Tempe rancher who had immigrated from Norway. His homestead was at Southern and Mill avenues; in 1888 he built the first clay-brick house in Tempe (THS).

118. Fort McDowell was located on the west side of the lower Verde River northeast of Tempe; it was named for Irven McDowell (1818–85), a Union general in the Civil War. After the war he moved to San Francisco where his son, Henry Burden McDowell (1857–1928), became a newspaperman with the *San Francisco Examiner*. On young McDowell's relationship to Cushing and the Hemenway Expedition, see part I in this volume.

119. Grace was the daughter of Mrs. R. J. Ashley (c. 1835–1919). She and Margaret became friends.

120. The wife of A. G. Webster, who was a bookkeeper for Charles T. Hayden and built a house in Tempe in 1885 (THS).

121. The wife of Capt. William L. George, who operated a livery stable business in Tempe.

122. Alfred Jordan Peters (b. 1853) organized the Quijota, Tempe and Phoenix Wagon and Railroad Company in 1884; Benjamin Goldman and John Armstrong were business associates, and he became the buyer for Hayden in 1892 (Bensel Directory Company, *Phoenix Directory for the Year 1892*, 136).

123. For Cushing's exciting account of these encounters, see Hinsley and Wilcox, *The Lost Itinerary of Frank Hamilton Cushing*, 249–51.

124. Possibly *The Bayeux Tapestry* (1875) by novelist Frank Rede Fowke (1847–1927).

125. The Magill diary has no entry for 19 March, probably because the diary fell out of the buckboard—but happily was found the next day.

126. Cozzens, *The Marvellous Country.*

127. Crossed out: "We went over to the ruin 'Camp Pueblo de las Muertos' to-day in the covered buckboard and two mules. Stopped on the road for cottonwood poles which we strapped on the buckboard and took with us to make a canopy-frame at the above camp."

128. James Constantine Pilling (1846–95) was John Wesley Powell's chief clerk and close friend. For his important relationship to Hodge, see part I in this volume.

129. Almon Harris Thompson (1839–1906) was a brother-in-law of Powell and a topographical engineer with the U.S. Geological Survey from 1870. From 1884 to 1895 he was in charge of the geographic work of the USGS west of the Mississippi River.

130. Cushing Collection, MS 6, No. 100, dated 22 March, BR/AM.

131. The Magill diary has no entry for 30 March.

132. Born in Cohocton, New York, Orson Squire Fowler (1809–87) popularized phrenology in America. He was a journal and book publisher who is credited with helping Walt Whitman publish *Leaves of Grass*, advocated for octagonal house design, and for women's and children's rights and temperance. In his diary entry for 1 September, Hodge notes hearing about Fowler's passing ("Orson Squire Fowler," Wikipedia, https://en.wikipedia.org/wiki/Orson_Squire_Fowler).

133. Dr. George Emery Goodfellow (1855–1910) was from Tombstone, where he had become an expert on gunshot wounds; he was in Tempe to check on his investments in the Tempe Land and Improvement Company (Chaput, *Dr. Goodfellow*).

134. Major Frank. S. Earle of California was the superintendent of the Tempe Land Improvement Company, a group of San Francisco and Tombstone investors who bought 240 acres from Charles T. Hayden, as well as land from others, and developed it soon after the Maricopa and Phoenix Railroad arrived in town.

135. Henry Cuyler Bruner (1855–96), *The Story of a New York House*, 1887. Hodge was reading a serialized version in *Scribner's Magazine* (January–June 1887).

136. Crossed out: "where we were disappointed not to find all the trays and things which we expected."

137. Pages 143 and 144 of the diary are missing in the typescript; however, Cushing quoted from them in his itinerary of the expedition (Hinsley and Wilcox, *The Lost Itinerary of Frank Hamilton Cushing*), and we have restored them from his quotation. There apparently was a drawing to accompany the text, but it has not been found.

138. Cushing named the site Pueblo del Juan; it is Turney's Pueblo Ultimo in *Prehistoric Irrigation in Arizona* (Haury, *The Excavation of Los Muertos*, 189)—a platform mound that is still extant on the Salt River Indian Reservation. For more on "Pima Juan" see Hinsley and Wilcox, *The Lost Itinerary of Frank Hamilton Cushing*, 272–73.

139. This places the Pima village about two miles due east of Camp Augustus, just north of the Salt River, and west of a deep gully shown on Turney's 1929 map in *Prehistoric Irrigation in Arizona*.

140. The cement is caliche, a calcium carbonate soil horizon that the Hohokam excavated, mixed with water, and used as an excellent building material.

141. HLB 1: 312–15. John Fiske (1842–1901) was an American philosopher and historian, and an advocate of the philosophy of Herbert Spencer; Mary Hemenway sponsored his writing and lectures at Old South Church in Boston.

142. The house of John Samuel Armstrong, a prominent Tempe merchant.

143. Albert W. Austin (1826–95), his wife, Martha, and their son, Aleppo Granville Austin (1859–1944) were farmers who lived on Mill Avenue south of Thirteenth Street (thus out of town); they owned T 1 N, R 4 E, southwest quarter of section 22 (Bensel Directory Company, *Phoenix Directory for the Year 1892*; Goodwin Map, THS).

144. English writer Charles Reade (1814–84) published his melodramatic three-volume novel *Foul Play* in 1869.

145. William Makepeace Thackeray's (1811–63) *The Memoirs of Barry Lyndon, Esq.* appeared in an 1885 edition of *Thackeray's Complete Works*, which the Cushings may have had with them.

146. Alfred Jordan Peters (b. 1853), a Tempe businessman, became a manager for Hayden in 1892.

147. Frederick J. Fergus (1847–85), under the pseudonym Hugh Conway, published the novel *Family Affair* in 1885.

148. "Tchuli" has not been identified but was possibly the camp chicken. Margaret is not referring to "Teluli" (Hodge's Zuni name).

149. Here ends the first part of Magill's diary; the pages are missing for 12 April to 5 June 1887.

150. "Hole in the Rock" is located in today's Papago Park, Phoenix (Turney, *Prehistoric Irrigation in Arizona*).

151. Haury published the final inked maps prepared by Hodge and Garlick of the Los Muertos site as a whole and its ruins 1–25, although he had to regenerate ruin IX from the original map points and could not find the maps for Ruins VIII, X, XII, XV, XVI and XVII (*The Excavation of Los Muertos*, figs. 2–22, 21, 26).

152. Ernest Frederick Kellner (1849–1914) was a businessman and financier centered in Globe, where his principal business was the New York Store. The George D. Tantau and E. F. Kellner grain warehouse was off the alley between Cortez and Center Streets south of Madison (Sanborn Fire Insurance Maps, Phoenix, January 1889). Kellner had branch stores in many communities and on reservations. He famously "never borrowed a dollar" (Biography File, James H. McClintock Papers, Phoenix Public Library).

W. L. Whepley was also grand master of the Independent Order of Odd Fellows of Arizona (W. Elliott, *History of Arizona Territory*, 294–95; also "Stories from a Reminiscent Pioneer," *Arizona Daily Star*, October 24, 1909).

153. Probably the wife of R. A. Davis, the proprietor of the Tempe Hotel in Tempe.

154. This is a significant point. Although Cushing and Hodge tried taking many photographs, the field conditions for development of the plates defeated these efforts, explaining why there are so few of these photographs extant today.

155. Niels Petersen was a Danish immigrant with large ranching and business interests in Tempe. His house, built later at today's Southern and Priest Streets, still stands and is operated by the Tempe Historical Society.

156. Walter Hough (1859–1935) was just beginning his long career as a Washington anthropologist, having become a copyist for Otis Tufton Mason at the National Museum in 1886 and, in 1887, an aide to Mason. He appears to have already been a friend of Hodge; he wrote Hodge's obituary for the *American Anthropologist* in 1956.

157. That is, to Pueblo Grande.

158. Cushing's Pat's Ruin (Turney's La Ciudad) was located in Phoenix under today's St. Luke's Hospital north of Van Buren on Nineteenth Street (Wilcox, *Frank Midvale's Investigations*).

159. Turney's Pueblo Ultimo, *Prehistoric Irrigation in Arizona*.

160. The Great Sonora Earthquake that occurred about 3:00 p.m. on 3 May 1887, was centered in the Bavispe area of northeastern Sonora; it was one of the strongest earthquakes ever recorded in the mountain west, although the *Arizona Gazette* reported that "in Phoenix it was scarcely felt" (Merrill, *One Hundred Steps*, 153–55). Dr. George E. Goodfellow and photographer C. S. Fly of Tombstone made an official investigation of it on behalf of the USGS (*Science* 11 [January–June 1888]: 162–63; see also Bennett, "An Afternoon of Ter-

ror," 107–20). Both Baxter ("Archaeological Camping in Arizona") and Hodge (in Haury, *The Excavation of Los Muertos*) recounted amusing stories about Cushing's use of this event to support his theory that earthquakes caused the abandonment of the Salt River Valley platform-mound sites. Interestingly, in the Picacho Mountains south of Florence, archaeological evidence of both the Sonoran earthquake and an earlier one were found, the earlier one dating to about the time of the abandonment of the Classic Hohokam sites (Holmlund, "MikkaGlaciaren").

161. J. M. Gibson's stable in Phoenix was located on Washington Street between Yuma and Cocopa (Sanborn Fire Insurance Maps, Phoenix, 1889).

162. Probably the Garden City Restaurant, Tuck Hing, Proprietor, which was in the Goodrich Building, Washington and Center Streets, Phoenix (*Phoenix Herald*, advertisements, 1887).

163. Ridgely Ceylon Powers (b. 1836) was from Ohio. In 1869 he was elected lieutenant governor of Mississippi, and in 1871 became governor. He later moved to Prescott, and from there to the Gila River region.

164. The second book of Hodge's diary (7 May to 28 June 1887) begins with a poem, largely illegible, that appears to be titled: "The Moonlight on the Mountain Top."

165. Hugh Conway [F. J. Fargus], *Living or Dead* (1886).

166. Washington Irving (1783–1859), *A History of New York: From the Beginning of the World to the End of the Dutch Dynasty: Being the Only Authentic History of the Times that Ever Hath Been Published, by Diedrich Knickerbocker* (1809, 1880).

167. Mark Twain, "English as She Is Taught," *Century Illustrated Monthly Magazine* 33, no. 6 (April 1887): 932–36.

168. HLB 1: 366–84, 389–90.

169. A transcription of such an article is in the Arizona Historical Society Library, Tucson, in the Byron Cummings Collection (MS 200, Box 9, Folder 102): "An Arizonian Pompeii," *Salt River Valley News* 2, no. 17 (28 May 1887).

170. The Commercial Hotel was located at the center of Phoenix at the corner of Jefferson and Center streets (Bensel Directory Company, *Phoenix Directory for the Year 1892*, 57).

171. An examination of the Hemenway Collection at the Peabody Museum by Wilcox revealed that many of the painted pots had not only been fitted back together but had also been repainted by the expedition, in the name of "restoration."

172. The Goodwin map (or perhaps a later version) is in the Hemenway Collection, Peabody Museum, Harvard.

173. One brother was Lincoln Fowler (1859–1924), who in 1887 was a Phoenix city councilman (*Phoenix Herald*, 5 May 1887, 3, col. 2). His brothers were Frank P. (d. 1922) and Dr. R. C. Fowler, both of Phoenix, Dr. Henry Fowler of New York City, and Gates M. Fowler of Los Angeles (*Arizona Republican*, 3 September 1924, 12, col. 2).

174. Probably Harry E. Kemp, the owner of the Arizona Hardware Company, and his wife.

175. Magill's diary begins again, in midsentence, and goes from 5 June to 17 August 1887. The beginning page number of this typescript diary section is 23, indicating twenty-two pages are lost.

176. *Phyllis* (1888), by The Duchess [Margaret Wolfe Hamilton, 1855–97].

177. Thackery, *The History of Pendennis: His Fortunes and Misfortunes, His Friends and His Greatest Enemy* (1849–50), in *Thackeray's Complete Works* (1885).

178. Ramon Castro was a young Mexican from Sonora who became Cushing's most trusted and skillful excavator and foreman of the other laborers.

179. Charles Dickens, *The Life and Adventures of Martin Chuzzlewit* (1842–44).

180. Thli-a-kwa was Baxter's Zuni name, meaning "blue medicine stone," or turquoise. He received it on the Zunis' trip to Boston in 1882.

181. The "scraping" probably was to remove a calcium carbonate deposit on the pottery.

182. That is, the "affair" between Hodge and Magill: this is the first explicit admission in Hodge's diary of this development.

183. Moses Hazeltine Sherman (1853–1932) had been the superintendent of instruction for Arizona Territory from 1878 to 1881, and was adjutant general of Arizona, 1883–87, but by this time he was an important businessman in Phoenix, having already been the first president of the Valley Bank. In 1889 he moved to Los Angeles where he became one of the principal developers of that city (Biographical Files, Arizona Historical Society, Tucson; Goff, *Arizona Biographical Dictionary*, 89). James McClintock became one of his close friends.

184. George H. Adams was the superintendent of missions for the Methodist church in Arizona (*Tombstone Prospector* 20 October 1887, 3, col. 3). He bought part of the Los Muertos site, which Cushing schemed unsuccessfully to acquire.

185. William Black (1841–98), *Judith Shakespeare, A Romance* (1884).

186. The reference here is not to Owen Wister's (1860–1938) *The Virginian, A Horseman of the Plains* (1902), which began as a series of articles in 1893.

187. Book 3 of Hodge's diary runs from 29 June to 18 August 1887.

188. Ikina was Magill's Zuni name. It means "little sister" (Parsons, "Mothers and Children at Zuñi").

189. Peppermint Perkins, *The Familiar Letters of Peppermint Perkins* (1886)—lighthearted social commentary on Boston life.

190. Rafael was the younger brother of Ramon Castro, who sent for him to join the expedition in July 1887.

191. Rodolfo (a.k.a. Adolpho, Adalpho) Sanchez was also nicknamed "Coyote" and "Comale" by the Hemenway crew; he was a Yaqui or Mayo Indian of the Chuakualan (Hare-Eaters) clan who as an escaped prisoner served in the *pelones* or punitive troops of the Mexican army (Hovens, "Ten Kate's Hemenway Expedition Diary," 647–48).

192. H. Rider Haggard (1856–1925), *Jess* (1887).

193. A wedding cake in a dream is presumed to be a sign of good fortune and new beginnings. Apparently Hodge had told his marriage plans to his friend Mary Duvall—to whom he had been regularly writing since leaving Maryland.

194. Dr. John L. Gregg was Tempe's first doctor; he owned a ranch southwest of town.

195. Henry Wadsworth Longfellow (1807–82), *The Courtship of Miles Standish and Other Poems* (1859).

196. Haggard, *She: A History of Adventure* (1886).

197. Joseph Camp Griffith Kennedy (1813–87) drafted the bill that created the U.S. Census in 1849. He was the first superintendent of the bureau, and served again in 1860 (*National Cyclopedia of American Biography*, vol. 16, 444). On 13 July 1887 he was murdered by stabbing in the street by a laborer. He was an intimate friend with many of the most powerful men in Washington (*New York Times*, 14 July 1887, 1, col. 6).

198. Possibly James M. Murphy, who in 1884 owned a general store in Tempe and had a house located on a Hohokam platform mound south of Tempe Butte in what Omar Turney called Plaza Tempe in his *Prehistoric Irrigation in Arizona* (Lange et al., *The Southwestern Journals of Adolph F. Bandelier, 1883–1884*, 128, 390n287). However, it seems more likely that it was Edward A. Murphy (d. 1919) who owned the Tempe Livery Stable in 1887–88; he became the second mayor of Tempe, 1896–97 (*Phoenix Herald*, 1887–88, THS).

199. This is likely the turquoise-encrusted toad Hodge later accused Cushing of faking. On August 16 Magill painted an "inlaid frog." On August 8 Hodge again mentions the "handsome shell-frog fetish" which Cushing was involved in "*restoring*" (emphasis added). It is notable that at the time Hodge indicated no reservations. For detailed discussion of the issue, see Wilcox, "Restoring Authenticity."

200. A photograph of the "restored" specimen was later published by Kunz (*Gems and Precious Stones*; see Wilcox, "Restoring Authenticity"). Having seen

the specimen at the Peabody Museum, Harvard University, Wilcox judges that it is a crudely done example of restoration compared to other such toad/frog turquoise-encrusted emblems.

201. Garlick showed the (restored) turquoise inlaid frog/toad to people at the *Phoenix Herald*, which published an account on August 10 (p. 3, col. 2). The account stated that it was made from "a sea shell about 1 3/4 inches wide by 2 1/2 long which had been completely inlaid on the back with small square blocks of turquoise. The back is figured in the shape of a frog and, except one eye of the frog, the ornament is complete as made. The eyes are of some black substance, something like obsidian. The inlaying seems to have been done by first covering the shell with some sorts of imperishable black cement and pressing the stones into it. There have been two or three of these figures found in the ancient ruins of this valley but the one just mentioned is the largest one ever discovered."

202. Possibly Carlos Gonzales, who worked for a time for the expedition.

203. There is a sketch of an incomplete turquoise encrusted toad in the Brooklyn Museum's Culin Collection that might be a drawing by Margaret Magill of the specimen before Cushing "restored" it. Like the purported fake toad, the one in the drawing has a stripe down the back (Wilcox, "Restoring Authenticity"). However, according to Hodge's diary Cushing had begun to restore the specimen as early as 7 August.

204. While the nature of this understanding is not explicit, the secrecy with which Fred and Margaret now began to communicate suggests that Cushing, as the head of the family of which Margaret was a part, insisted that proper Victorian propriety be maintained between them in public. See part I, this volume.

205. "Coyote" was a nickname of Mexican laborer Adolpho Sanchez.

206. Haury discusses these interesting ceramic specimens at some length, calling them "griddles" or "comales" for baking thin tortilla-like bread. He notes that all three were found in one room and that they were associated with several red ware bowls and two Gila Polychrome bowls—which suggests an age in the fourteenth century AD. Ruin XXII on the Hemenway map of Los Muertos lies due south of Camp Hemenway and north northeast of ruin I (Haury, *The Excavation of Los Muertos*, pl. 28, and 109–11, fig. 2).

207. Probably the turquoise-encrusted frog/toad; we have not located the painting of this specimen, but it might be the basis for the color reproduction published in Kunz, *Gems and Precious Stones* (see Wilcox, "Restoring Authenticity").

208. This is the end of the extant Magill diary.

209. Book 4 of Hodge's diary begins 19 August and ends 9 October 1887.

210. This remarkable letter is HLB 2: 169–212, dated August 2 and 30.

211. This is the first time that Hodge in his diary refers to Magill as Margaret.

212. HLB 2: 134–37, dated 27 August.

213. HLB 2: 169–212; Hemenway and Cushing planned to build an ethnological museum in Salem. See part I, this volume.

214. Dr. Washington Matthews (1843–1905) was an assistant curator of the U.S. Army Medical Museum and a close personal friend of Frank Cushing. See Hinsley and Wilcox, *The Lost Itinerary of Frank Hamilton Cushing*; and part I, this volume.

215. Spencer Fullerton Baird (1823–87) was secretary of the Smithsonian Institution from 1878 to 1887 (Rivinus and Youssef, *Spencer Baird of the Smithsonian*). Cushing originally traveled in 1879 to Zuni under Baird's authority and direction.

216. Crossed out: "The Mexicans continue work, under Mr. Cushing's directions, on the large tent to-day. I work on accounts in the morning, and in afternoon write to Mother and Ed."

217. Thomas Grantz Cartledge (b. 1850) was a farmer who, with his wife, Matilda (1852–1903), lived in Tempe.

218. Powell, "Sketch of the Mythology."

219. HLB 2: 161–63; he also wrote to Pilling: HLB 2: 159–60.

220. Fred and Margaret dated their engagement as 17 June 1887.

221. This letter is inserted in the second Hemenway letter book, HLB 2: 169–212.

222. The reference is to Tylor, *Anthropology*. This appears to be the most serious book that Hodge was reading—an indication of his growing interest in anthropology.

223. The only ruins in the vicinity of Mesa City shown on the Hemenway map are called Pueblo de la Mesa, located south of the townsite. On Turney's 1929 map in *Prehistoric Irrigation in Arizona* this is La Casa de Mesa (Haury, *The Excavation of Los Muertos*, fig. 1, 189). In or adjacent to Mesa City there were three other Hohokam villages called Pueblo de Lehi (a.k.a. Mesa Grande), Casa de Nephi, and La Casita by Turney, but the Hemenway Expedition apparently did not map or name them. However, on 12 March 1887, Cushing clearly visited the Mesa Grande site and describes the others from the top of its great platform mound (Hinsley and Wilcox, *The Lost Itinerary of Frank Hamilton Cushing*). Today the Mesa Grande mound is owned by the City of Mesa and there is a fine interpretive kiosk and excellent interpretive trails designed by Jerry Howard and his colleagues.

224. Cushing Collection, MS 6, No. 125 and 107, respectively, BR/AM; see Hinsley and Wilcox, "A Hemenway Portfolio."

225. We have not found the long series of letters exchanged between Hodge and Magill during her stay with the Cushings in California. They went first to

San Diego, where Cushing consulted with a doctor, and then to San Francisco for more medical consultation. See part I, this volume.

226. This laborer was either Juan Yescas or Juan Palma.

227. Hodge's Book 5 runs from 10 October 1887 to 8 March 1888.

228. "Pearl" was Hodge's new pet name for Margaret.

229. Henry Rider Haggard, *Allan Quatermain* (1887)—sequel to *King Solomon's Mines* (1885).

230. See Haury, *The Excavation of Los Muertos*, 183 and Fig. 120; Hodge's account implies it probably was found in Ruin XIII.

231. Edward W. Jones, a liveryman in Tempe (Bensel Directory Company, *Phoenix Directory for the Year 1892*).

232. Thackeray, *Vanity Fair: A Novel Without a Hero* (1883).

233. Meyer's Phoenix Business Directory of 1888 lists Letitia McDermott as a teacher. She was from a Frederick, Maryland, family that dated back 250 years; she married R. Allen Lewis, territorial manager for the New York Life Insurance Company who in 1897 became the Arizona Territorial Adjutant General.

234. Many of these "Memoranda of Operations" and "Directions for the Daily Operations" are now in the Hemenway Expedition Collection at Cornell University. They begin on 23 December 1887 and extend to 10 April 1888. Cushing apparently ordered the new forms in response to the Hemenway Board's request for more regular accounting of field activities.

235. Herman F. C. ten Kate (1858–1931) was a Dutch physical anthropologist who became part of the Hemenway Expedition (see Hinsley and Wilcox, "A Hemenway Portfolio"; and Hinsley and Wilcox, *The Lost Itinerary of Frank Hamilton Cushing*; and part I, this volume).

236. When the land in the town of Tempe was officially platted in 1888, the area of San Pablo was called East Tempe, but the common name became Mexican Town (Scott Soliday, Tempe Historical Museum, personal communication, 1995).

237. Attorney General Briggs Goodrich (1849–88) took the oath of office on 28 April 1887 but soon died of Bright's disease. Alexander D. Lemon (1834–1908) was the owner-operator; he was elected to the Arizona Council in 1883 (Goff, *Arizona Territorial Officials*, vol. 5, 66–67).

238. See "Among the Zunis, Lieutenant Cushing's Life with the Pueblo Indians," *Daily Examiner*, San Francisco, 8 November 1887, 4, col. 3–4.

239. While in San Francisco, Cushing had his photograph taken at the I. W. Taber & Co.; it seems likely that that is where Margaret had hers taken too. Regrettably, we have not found this image.

240. See "Academy of Sciences, Interesting Address by Mr. Cushing, the Ethnologist," *San Francisco Chronicle*, 8 November 1887, 6, col. 2.

241. HLB 4: 88–97 and 98–101. On 13 November (HLB 2: 469–73) Hodge reported to Cushing that he had written to Henry N. Copp (1843–1912) in Washington, saying that he was the "author of several leading works on the public land systems and the laws and decisions affecting it, is a recognized authority on land and mining law. I made the 'mesquite' my point above all others, for what I know about the rulings in contested cases brought up under other land districts, I am more and more inclined to believe that the land is non-desert under the law." Copp had been Hodge's first employer. On the Copp-Hodge relationship see part I, this volume.

242. HLB 2: 460–68 and 469–73.

243. HLB 2: 478–81; these business letters went to Callon Brashers, S. D. Lount (ice company), Tantau & Kellner (grocer), C. S. Eschman Co. (druggist), Kelly & Marlow (butcher) and J. B. Long (hardware), all in Phoenix.

244. Dr. L. H. Goodrich was a dentist in Phoenix who also had many investments in land (*Phoenix Herald*, 23 March, 3, col. 1).

245. Arlington House was a hotel in Tempe run by Charles Salari.

246. *Meyer's Phoenix Business Directory for 1888* lists A. A. Utley as a notary public.

247. Jacob Lawson Wortman (1856–1926) was a paleontologist who at the suggestion of Washington Matthews had been dispatched by the Army Medical Museum to assist with the recovery of human remains by the expedition (see part I, this volume).

248. Benjamin Goldman ran a general merchandise store in Tempe (*Tempe News* advertisements, THS).

249. Moki (Moqui) was a name for the Hopi Indians.

250. HLB 4: 187–89 (to Hodge), 190–200 (to ten Kate), and 201–3 (to Wortman).

251. That is, putting lacquer on human bones to preserve them.

252. Turney credits Mrs. Julia Ackerman Lount and the first Phoenix postmaster, George H. Mowry, with making the first archaeological collection in the valley, which they exhibited in a back room of J. W. Benham's Curio Store (which he styled the "Phoenix Free Museum"; Turney, *Prehistoric Irrigation in Arizona*, 28). She was a member of the Arizona Antiquarian Association, 1895–1901. Samuel David Lount (1835–1901) was the first to manufacture ice in Arizona (in 1877), aided by his brother George. The original plant was at Washington and Pinal streets (Goff, *Arizona Biographical Dictionary*, 63; also McCormick Papers, Phoenix Public Library, Biography). See also *History of Arizona Territory with Illustrations*, 279, 302. By January 1889, the Sanborn Fire Insurance Maps indicate, the ice plant on Pinal Street was closed. Samuel was noted locally for his "eccentricity."

253. Henry Burden McDowell (1857–1928) was an editor of the *San Francisco Examiner* who visited the site and wrote a series of articles on the expedition. See part I, this volume.

254. Francis Martin Pomeroy (1820–82), his wife, Irene Ursula Haskell, and their family of eight children were among the Mormon pioneers of the Mesa Company who founded Mesa City in 1878.

255. According to practitioners of phrenology, an individual's character and abilities could be deduced from the size and shape of various bumps on the head. The "science" was extremely popular by the 1880s in America. Possibly this was a man named Winchester Miller.

256. See McDowell, "The Mythic Drama." While in San Francisco, Cushing accompanied writer Kate Field and McDowell of the *Daily Examiner* to the Chinese theater, where he "was able to establish the closest analogy between the theater of the Chinese and that of the American Zuni" (9, col. 1). He also declared: "My study in this direction [of comparing Chinese and Zuni myth] ought to open up an ethnological field of research which should add greatly to our knowledge concerning the origin, the migration, the relative age and civilization of mankind in the Pacific ocean and in the Far East." These notions he would pursue further in collaboration with Stewart Culin and the study of games (see Lyman, "Stewart Culin," 91–115; and Lyman, "Two Neglected Pioneers").

257. Cushing wrote to Hodge on 17 November (Cushing Collection, MS 6, HAE 1.30, BR/AM; HLB 4: 126–30) that he had secured "a series of views taken twenty years ago [circa 1867] of that magnificent ruin—four of them 18 × 20 inches in size." He was considering transferring the operations of the expedition to that site.

258. Cushing Collection, MS 7, No. 137, BR/AM. For Cushing's account of the reconnaissance to the Casa Grande Ruins, see Hinsley and Wilcox, "A Hemenway Portfolio," 590–604. Haury briefly describes the artifacts recovered (*The Excavation of Los Muertos*, 189–91).

259. William Dean Howells, *A Modern Instance*, 1882.

260. A native of Albion, New York (Cushing's hometown), Daniel Hyde Pinney (1837–1921) was a Phoenix lawyer who served on the Arizona Territorial Supreme Court, 1882–85 ("Daniel H. Pinney," Wikipedia, https://en.wikipedia.org/wiki/Daniel_H._Pinney).

261. Camillis Sydney Fly (1849–1901) of Tombstone had arrived in Phoenix a few days earlier (*Arizona Gazette*, 31 December). Fly was a photographer who had taken a series of famous photographs of Geronimo and his band that were published in *Harper's Weekly* in 1886; a year later he accompanied George E. Goodfellow as photographer on his official investigation of the great Bavispe earthquake of 1887.

262. This is part of what Omar Turney later called (following Cushing) Las Acequias.

263. First established as Camp Rice in 1882 by Tenth Cavalry Buffalo Soldiers, this military outpost on the border with Chihuahua near El Paso was renamed in 1886 for General Winfield Scott Hancock, who had died at the battle of Gettysburg. It was flooded in 1886. A Southern Pacific Railroad depot was built there in 1887, but after it flooded again in 1894 it was abandoned in favor of a site one and a half miles away (which still exists today) ("Fort Hancock, Texas," Wikipedia, https://en.wikipedia.org/wiki/Fort_Hancock,_Texas).

264. The Cushing party returned to San Diego, California, by steamer, from which they took the train back to Tempe.

265. HLB 3: 130–34, to Tantau & Kellner (grocers) and Schaenfeld and Heyman (furniture).

266. Baxter, secretary-treasurer of the expedition, had come to consult with Cushing—and to report back to the Hemenway board. See part I, this volume.

267. Percy B. Yates worked for the Phoenix and Maricopa Railroad as a telegraph operator; he also was a noted amateur photographer whom Cushing later hired on the expedition (*Phoenix Herald*, 19 April 1888, 3, col. 2). See part I, this volume.

268. Las Acequias was located north of Los Muertos and southwest of Mesa City (Turney, *Prehistoric Irrigation in Arizona*). For an account of recent excavations at this site, see Hackbarth and Brunson, *Excavations at Las Acequias*.

269. At this point Hodge begins to call Charles Garlick "Don Carlos."

270. HLB 3: 146–49: to C. A. Kinkner & Co., San Francisco; to Herberger from Cushing; and to Dr. D. L. Huntington, Cushing's doctor in San Diego.

271. Hemenway employed Rufus Leighton in 1886 as a stenographer. See part I, this volume.

272. The tourists from Peoria were quite likely residents of the new community in northwest Phoenix developed by William Murphy and called Peoria.

273. Dr. George Anthony Zeller (1858–1938) was a native of Illinois. He graduated from Washington University in Saint Louis in 1879, joined the army in 1899 and in 1902 became the director of the newly completed Illinois Hospital for the Incurably Insane, later the Peoria State Hospital.

274. On the Fowler brothers see note 173.

275. Casa Blanca lay on the south side of the Gila River south of Los Muertos and west of Casa Grande, where a platform mound is still extant today.

276. HLB 3: 185–86: to Lon Farsee, Tempe; Jones & Helston, Tempe; C. T. Hayden; and Peterson, Armstrong.

277. HLB 3: 190–91, 195–96: to W. W. Newell, Cambridge; and the editor of the *Tempe News*. William Wells Newell (1839–97) was the founder and editor of the *Journal of American Folk-Lore* (1888).

278. On the Magill family see part I, this volume.

279. HLB 3, inserted between pages 177–78.

280. "Sun Temple" is what Cushing called the features today referred to as Hohokam "ballcourts." See Wilcox, "The Mesoamerican Ballgame," 101–25. For further evaluation of these ritual features, see Wilcox et al., "Ancient Cultural Interplay."

281. Such burials might be evidence of violent acts (Wilcox and Haas, "The Scream of the Butterfly").

282. Visitors had become troublesome because some walked on the specimens that had been excavated but left to be recorded later, causing Cushing to write to the newspapers to close the excavations to further visitation.

283. Possibly Lazuro Beyer (or Bijar, or Bejar) or Lazaro mentioned earlier.

284. The *Boston Herald*, for which he was an editor (see Hinsley and Wilcox, *The Southwest in the American Imagination*).

285. HLB 3: 304: to the Bancroft Company, San Francisco, stationers.

286. Cushing, "On the Development."

287. Daily Director's Reports, 14 January 1888.

288. Cushing soon called it Los Guanacos. For recent archaeological work at this site see Mitchell et al., *Ceremony and Symbolism*; and Chenault and Lindly, "Guanacos, Symbolism, and Religion."

289. Walter Hough's marriage; on Hough see note 156.

290. Dr. Fenn John Hart (1859–1935) came to Tempe in October 1887; he opened a drugstore and later became known as a physician and surgeon (*Tempe News*, THS).

291. Dr. Gustav Brühl (1826–1903), a physician from Cincinnati who had been born in Prussia, was a friend of Bandelier with a deep interest in the prehistory of the Americas (Lange et al., *The Southwestern Journals of Adolph F. Bandelier, 1883–1884*, 396n326).

292. These were large quadruped clay figurines found at Los Guanacos that Cushing interpreted as llamas, based on ideas he had begun to have about contact of southern Arizona with Peru (Cushing, "Preliminary Notes"). Today it seems more likely that they are dogs or perhaps deer. See part I, this volume.

293. Magill's drawings of these figurines are in Cushing Collection, MS 6, HAE 3.27, BR/AM.

294. Cushing's llama theory apparently was too much for Hodge.

295. Edward Page Gaston (1868–1956) arrived in Camp Hemenway on 25 February and was hired to help with the cataloguing, which he continued to do in the Salt River Valley and then at Zuñi until 20 December. He returned home to Illinois and became a newspaperman. See part I, this volume.

296. Pueblo del Cameno was apparently another name for Los Guanacos. Haury describes this textile remnant but does not interpret it as a medicine bag, nor does he discuss its associations (*The Excavation of Los Muertos*, 178–79).

297. Eusebio Joseph Molera (1846–1932), a native of Catalonia, was a civil engineer and officer of the California Academy of Sciences whom the Cushings had met the previous November in San Francisco; he was planning an expedition to Mexico and Peru. For more on Molera, see part I, this volume.

298. The Salado Mountains were also called the Salt River Mountains on some 1880s maps, while Cushing called them the Maricopa Mountains. Today they are the South Mountains—south of modern Phoenix.

299. Catarine Peralta (b. 1871) accompanied Herman ten Kate on his reconnaissance of southern Arizona (Hovens, "Ten Kate's Hemenway Expedition Diary").

300. Haury calls these artifacts "green crayons" (*The Excavation of Los Muertos*, 178).

301. See Haury, *The Excavation of Los Muertos*, 193–201 and pl. 87, 88.

302. Beginning with the end of this sentence, Hodge's final Book 6 starts here and runs from 10 March to 18 May 1888.

303. Haury pictures a copper bell with a loop handle from Los Hornos (*The Excavation of Los Muertos*, 183, pl. 85b).

304. Keuffel & Esser (K+E) was a drawing equipment company.

305. These letters included Cushing's 13 December 1887 letter to Mrs. Hemenway (HLB 3: 429–39); and another of 12 March 1888 (HLB 3: 440–42).

306. This was the eastern wall of the massive caliche compound wall around the platform mound, Ruin I. Cushing regarded it as defensive—a hypothesis that has been developed further in Wilcox, Robertson, and Wood, "Antecedents to Perry Mesa," 2001.

307. A "stone-close" is what Cushing inferred a blocked doorway was, believing that the whole could be moved in and out, like a door (see Hinsley and Wilcox, "A Hemenway Portfolio"; and Wilcox and Sternberg, *Additional Studies*).

308. Either Edward Gaston or Edward the cook.

309. This feature is shown as a reservoir on Turney's 1929 map in *Prehistoric Irrigation in Arizona*.

310. Lewis Winship Blinn (d. 1928), from Tombstone, was the president of the Tempe Land and Improvement Company, which was formed in 1887 to

take advantage of the business opportunities created when the Maricopa and Phoenix Railroad established a connection to the Southern Pacific Railroad at Maricopa on July 3 of that year. Mr. Blinn not only sold lots; he had a large lumber company in Tempe as well as other businesses (*Phoenix Herald*, 18 July 1887, 3, col. 2; 25 July 1887, 3, col. 2).

311. Blanche Willis Howard (1847–98), *Guenn: A Wave on the Breton Coast* (1883).

312. Leo Tolstoy's (1828–1910) *Sebastopol* was translated from French by Frank D. Millet, with an introduction by W. D. Howells, in 1887.

313. For Cushing's theory that balsa rafts were used to transport goods on the canals, see Cushing, "Preliminary Notes"; and Hodge, "Prehistoric Irrigation in Arizona."

314. Edward Sylvester Morse (1838–1925), the distinguished zoologist from Salem, Massachusetts, was a respected member of Hemenway's board who came out to inspect the work from 30 March to 11 April 1888. See Wayman, *Edward Sylvester Morse*; and part I, this volume.

315. Strickland was superintendent of the Union Mine near Cave Creek, north of Phoenix. Located about 17 miles north of Phoenix at that time, the Union Mine produced gold-bearing quartz down about 20 to 60 feet. By 1897 Frank Alkire owned the mine; the Union Hills take their name from this mine.

316. This clearly is the site of Fort Mountain [AZ T:8:34 (ASU)]; see Holliday, *Archaeological Investigations*. There are petroglyphs on its northeast side (Todd Bostwick, personal communication, 1998), as Hodge reports on 5 April.

317. Petroglyphs are pecked, thus breaking through the "desert varnish" of the rock surface, exposing a lighter subsurface. Pictographs are painted figures.

318. There was a prehistoric canal south of Fort Mountain (Rodgers, "The Fort Mountain Archaeological Complex").

319. Emilio (or Amelio) Lopera was fired by Cushing on March 23 but reinstated at Zuni later in the year.

320. This is probably Moon Hill, which lies about 14.5 miles north of the Salt River and about 8 miles southwest of Fort Mountain; it still has many petroglyphs on small boulders (Todd Bostwick, personal communication, 1998). Nearby is the Shaw Butte Site, with a defensive wall (van Waarden, "Hilltop Sites in Central Arizona") and petroglyphs and room orientations that correlate well with astronomical azimuths.

321. Cushing's Las Canopas was a large Hohokam village site due south of the Phoenix townsite; the Hemenway Expedition did some testing there (Haury, *The Excavation of Los Muertos*, Fig. 1). On Turney's 1929 map in *Prehistoric Irrigation in Arizona*, this location is a site called Pueblo Viejo, where Warren

King Moorehead (1866–1939) excavated in 1897–98 (*The Oasis*, 26 March 1898, 2, col. 1–2; and Moorehead 1906). The name "canopas" was taken by Cushing from objects in Peru that are privately worshiped, such as oddly shaped stones. Confusingly, in *Prehistoric Irrigation in Arizona* Turney assigned the name Las Canopas to another site located east of Pueblo Viejo at today's Southern and Fortieth Street.

322. HLB 5: 15–16, to General John Hise. Hise (1815–89) was appointed surveyor-general of Arizona by President Grover Cleveland.

323. The only workman named Dolores was Dolores Espinosa.

324. For an account of the Baxter-Wortman reconnaissance, see Hinsley and Wilcox, "A Hemenway Portfolio," 625–34.

325. Ida Empey (b. 1868) was a daughter of Benjamin Franklin Johnson. See notes 102 and 103.

326. This was at the Tempe Hotel.

327. The Hodge diary entries for 18 April to halfway through 9 May are entered by Margaret Magill.

328. Raimundo Balenzuela (a.k.a. Valanzuela).

329. William J. Kingsbury (1858–1934) was a prominent attorney in Tempe who later ran the Farmers and Merchants Bank of Tempe, 1900–23. He had been for a time the immigration commissioner of Texas and was a promoter of immigration to Phoenix. In 1923 he was sentenced to prison for embezzling (*Phoenix Herald*, 22 November 1887: 3, col. 3; THS).

330. Old Fort Bayard was located in western New Mexico just outside of Silver City. Established in 1866, it was a base for Apache scouts and Black Buffalo Soldiers who operated against Apaches until the capture of Geronimo in 1886 (http://www.silvercity.org/stilltheoldwest/historic_fort_bayard.php).

331. Daniel Walter Lord (1854–1922), a friend of Baxter and a Harvard student of Charles Eliot Norton, arrived in Camp Hemenway on 28 April 1888, and remained with the expedition until mid-May 1889. See part I, this volume.

332. Peter Corpstein (b. 1857) managed a lumber yard in Tempe for the Blinn Lumber Company.

333. We have not identified the Sawsons.

334. The packing slip for the transport of the Hemenway Salt River Valley collections is at the Phillips Library, Peabody Essex Museum, Salem, Massachusetts.

335. Haury treats it as special, but does not note the significance of its provenience, that is, its being found in a niche in a room associated with the main mound, Ruin I, which Cushing regarded as a Temple Mound (*The Excavation of Los Muertos*, frontispiece item C, 158).

336. Frank, Emily, and Margaret departed for California on 14 May. They rejoined the expedition ten weeks later, when Hodge, Garlick, and the others had moved the expedition northeastward to Zuni. Hodge left no entries for Tuesday, 15 May, or Thursday, 17 May.

Part III. The Anthropological Career of Fred Hodge, 1889–1956

1. BAE Personnel Records, NAA. He later claimed to have begun as an "assistant ethnologist." Hodge testimony, 1903 Barnett Investigation, Box 304, Folder 5, 285, NAA; cf. Hodge, *Frederick Webb Hodge, Ethnologist*, 56.

2. Hodge, "A Zuni Foot-Race." Hodge had presented the paper at the Anthropological Society of Washington; it was printed in entirety in *Evening Star*, 24 May 1890, 13, cols. 5–6.

3. Hodge, "Prehistoric Irrigation in Arizona."

4. Hodge, 324.

5. *First Annual Report of the Bureau of Ethnology (1879–80)* (Washington, D.C.: Government Printing Office, 1881), 76.

6. Hodge, *Frederick Webb Hodge, Ethnologist*, 78–79; cf. Hinsley, *The Smithsonian and the American Indian*, 156–58.

7. On Henshaw, see Nelson, "Henry Wetherbee Henshaw."

8. After ten years Henshaw recovered and eventually returned to head the U.S. Biological Survey (today's Fish and Wildlife Service).

9. Hodge, *Frederick Webb Hodge, Ethnologist*, 82. Without a right arm, lost in the Civil War battle of Shiloh, Powell could neither write easily nor type.

10. Cushing to Molera, 27 August 1891, Cushing Collection, MS 7, no. 333, BR/AM. Cushing overstated: Hodge had had two raises (from $1,000 to $1,500 per year). His title changed in 1893–94 to ethnologist, with a raise to $1,600 (BAE Personnel Records, NAA). The Hodge-Magill wedding day was probably 5 September 1891.

11. Cushing to Hodge, 8 September 1892, Hodge Papers, MS 7, BAEL, 1.29, BR/AM.

12. Hinsley and Wilcox, *The Lost Itinerary of Frank Hamilton Cushing*, 26–37.

13. Hodge to Cushing, 26 April 1891, HC. "A Few Summer Ceremonials at Zuñi Pueblo" appeared in the first volume of the Hemenways' *Journal of American Ethnology and Archaeology*, edited by Fewkes (1–61).

14. Hodge to Cushing, 25 May 1891, HC.

15. Cushing to Hodge, 29 May 1891, HLB 7: 192–216; cf. Hodge, "Review of *A Journal of American Ethnology and Archaeology, Vol. 1*." Cushing encouraged him to publish: "The best and fullest report you can make should rather precede than follow any of mine. *The changes that have come about in our relations,*

mutual aid with others as well, make, it seems to me, no difference" (emphasis added). Isolated in Albion, Cushing privately reacted to Fewkes's publication with disgust and pain: "Good description some, but worthless full of error & Zuñi parts rubbish. The most dishonorable trespass on a scientific work, this on mine by the Hemenway Expedition & Dr. Fewkes I have ever known of and hard, so hard to hear from friends at one time. God, show me the morning. I seem broken by it!" (Cushing Diary, 4 June 1891, NAA).

16. Hodge, "Review of *A Journal of American Ethnology and Archaeology, Vol. 2.*"

17. Fewkes was especially anxious to mollify Cushing by convincing him that he had no desire to steal work or credit. (Cushing was not persuaded.) See, e.g., Fewkes to Hodge, 5, 21, and 30 January 1892, Hodge Papers, BAEL 1.38, BR/AM. In the Hodge papers at BR/AM, Fewkes's fifty letters to Hodge (1890–95) are cordial—and careful.

18. Yet their pathways to success diverged: Fewkes became one of the most prolific authors in the early *American Anthropologist,* while Hodge remained behind the scenes as editor and administrator.

19. The stops and starts of the itinerary work, 1890–93, are recounted in detail in Hinsley and Wilcox, *The Lost Itinerary of Frank Hamilton Cushing,* 26–37.

20. Cushing diary, 31 December 1892, NAA.

21. Cushing diary, 15 and 17 February 1893, NAA.

22. Winship, "The Coronado Expedition." The full title is *The Narrative of Castañeda: Account of the Expedition to Cibola which took place in the year 1540, in which all those settlements, their ceremonies and customs, are described.*

23. Fewkes to Hodge, 16 February 1893, BR/AM; Hodge, "The First Discovered City of Cibola." In his acknowledgments Winship named Bandelier, Augustus Hemenway, Fewkes, and Hodge, but not Cushing.

24. Cushing to Hemenway, 20 July 1888, Cushing Collection, MS 6, HAE 1.28, BR/AM. Emphasis added.

25. Hodge to Haynes, 24 February 1894 and 2 March 1895, Haynes Papers (MS N-44), Box 4–5, Massachusetts Historical Society. This attack was but the opening salvo on the factual reliability of native oral traditions. As the "new archaeology" declared by Clark Wissler in 1917 gained traction, a broader consensus emerged about the untrustworthiness of Native oral traditions that is only recently, with the passage of NAGPRA (Native American Graves Protection and Repatriation Act), begun to be completely reassessed (Wilcox and Fowler, "The Beginnings of Anthropological Archaeology"; Wilcox, "Looking for Middle Ground").

26. Fewkes to Hodge, 24 February 1895, BR/AM. Recent scholarship has again suggested that Kyaki:ma was the first site seen not by Vázquez de Coronado but by the earlier Spanish explorer Marcos de Niza. The recent archaeological discovery of crossbow bolts at Hawikku further confirms it was the site of a battle described in the Coronado accounts (Cordell and McBrinn, *Archaeology of the Southwest*).

27. Hodge mentioned Cushing only in passing. While protesting his high "personal regard" for Bandelier (and blaming the editor of Bandelier's *The Gilded Man* [1893]), he took the historian severely to task. Hodge, "The First Discovered City of Cibola," 152.

28. Fewkes to Hodge, 9 March 1895, 21 March 1895, Hodge-Cushing Collection, BR/AM.

29. On the relationship between Fewkes's earlier training in zoology and his role in archaeology, see Hinsley, "Ethnographic Charisma and Scientific Routine." For a recent, fair-minded assessment of Fewkes, see Fowler, *A Laboratory for Anthropology*, 161–71. Another measure of Fewkes's eventual scientific reputation was his election to the National Academy of Sciences in 1914.

30. In the three years of 1896–98, Fewkes published eleven articles in *The American Anthropologist* alone—more than any other individual. (For a comparative study of who published in the *AA*, see Wilcox, "Going National.")

31. Putnam to Boas, 25 August 1895, Boas Papers, American Philosophical Society.

32. Fewkes to Reginald Gray (Hemenway attorney), 24 May 1895, M122, Hemenway Papers, PEM; Fewkes to Hodge, 22 January 1895, Hodge-Cushing Collection, BR/AM. Fewkes finished labeling the exhibit the following November (Fewkes to Gray, 12 November 1895, M122, Hemenway Papers, PEM).

33. "The Hemenway Expedition is dead but not, I hope, Fewkes' ethnology" (Fewkes to Hodge, 19 May 1895, Hodge-Cushing Papers, BR/AM). Thanks to Peter Pilles for this reference. The Hemenway materials were exhibited in six new cases; Fewkes finished the installation in November and left immediately for Washington. Fewkes to Gray, 12 November 1895, M122, Hemenway Papers, PEM.

34. Fewkes to Hodge, 22 March 1895, Hodge-Cushing Collection, BR/AM. It is notable that Fewkes habitually used "we" and "us" in writing to Hodge of professional matters. On Fewkes's critique of Stevenson's snake ritual account and her response, see Miller, *Matilda Coxe Stevenson*, 94; and Fewkes, "A Comparison."

35. He also dug at Awat'ovi in the 1895 season.

36. Fewkes, "Archaeological Expedition," 527.

37. Hodge to McGee, 3 August 1895, BAE Letters Received, 1888–1906, Box 104, Hodge file, NAA.

38. On Fewkes's relationship to Nampeyo and the Sikyátki "revival," see Fowler, *A Laboratory for Anthropology*, 166–68; and Wade and McChesney, *America's Great Lost Expedition*, 11–12. Fewkes greatly exaggerated the influence of his unearthed wares on Nampeyo and other potters (Kramer, *Nampeyo and Her Pottery*).

39. Hodge to McGee, 14, 18, 25 August and 12 September 1895, BAE Letters Received, 1888–1906, Box 104, Hodge Folder, NAA.

40. Lummis, *The Man Who Married the Moon*, 263; Lummis, *A New Mexico David*, 53; Hodge to McGee, 18 August 1895.

41. Libbey, "How He Climbed"; Libbey, "A Disenchanted Mesa." For an account of the episode from Libbey's viewpoint, see Cook, *Immortal Summer*, 117–18. He came to regret the entire enterprise, which caused him "untold humiliation"—although ultimately he was correct.

42. Hodge, *Frederick Webb Hodge, Ethnologist*, 126. The entire episode is well told in Vroman, "Katzimo, the Enchanted Mesa." Lummis was unsparing, writing in the *San Francisco Chronicle* (23 July) that "the most notorious and sensational confounding of a would-be scientist in the annals of American scholarship befell a college professor who 'spoofed' a tradition of the people of Acoma" (Cook, *Immortal Summer*, 117). In his late-life paean to Hodge, "Sky, Sun, and Water," Lawrence Clark Powell called it Hodge's "most brilliant" exploit and quoted Lummis's contemporary judgment: "Mr. Hodge, whose patient, prudent, competent work has gained him substantial reputation wherever there are scientists, earned it by years of arduous experience in the field, on top of all the study required." L. C. Powell approached the rock himself and sat "in the shade of a juniper bush, content to take Hodge's word for it that the mesa had once been inhabited" (Powell, "Sky, Sun, and Water," 165; cf. Powell, *Books West Southwest*, 57).

43. Hodge wrote at least six Enchanted Mesa articles himself: Hodge, "Katzimo the Enchanted"; Hodge, "The Enchanted Mesa," *National Geographic Magazine*; Hodge, "The Cairn of the Enchanted Mesa"; Hodge, "The Enchanted Mesa," *Century Magazine*; Hodge, "The Enchanted Mesa," *Science*; Hodge, "Die Erforschung der Verzauberten Mesa."

44. Lummis, "Authorities of the Southwest," 146.

45. Thompson, *American Character*, 210.

46. Cited in Powell, *Books West Southwest*, 45–46. Austin and Hodge maintained a warm relationship until her death in 1934. In Hodge's New York period, they socialized with (and financially supported) Bandelier's second wife, Fanny (1875–1936).

47. Stoddard, *Lectures, Volume 10*, 129–34; Cather, "The Enchanted Bluff."

48. The development was named after Robert Garrett, president of the Baltimore and Ohio Railroad at the time.

49. Defandorf, "Memories of Garrett Park," 4.

50. "For Sale: The Hodge House: A Piece of Garrett Park History Built in 1898," website of Tamara Kucik, Realtor, Tower Hill Realty. The home sold for $900,000 in 2017. Their architect was Victor Mindeleff (1860–1948), a friend from the bureau, who published a classic BAE report, "A Study of Pueblo Architecture: Tusayan and Cibola," *Eighth Annual Report of the Bureau of Ethnology* (Washington, D.C., 1891).

51. Cushing Diary, 17 July 1892.

52. Emlyn Hodge, interview, 15 March 1988 (transcript 1993), Archives of Town of Garrett Park, author's possession, courtesy of Ray Maxwell.

53. Defandorf, "Memories of Garrett Park," 7.

54. Information in this paragraph is from Emlyn Hodge interview, 1988.

55. *Washington Post*, 10 May 1891, 30 November 1902, 29 November 1903. Thanks to Phil Kovinick for references.

56. Emlyn Hodge, interview with author, 5 December 1993.

57. On the Culin-Cushing relationship see Wilcox, "Anthropology in a Changing America." After Frank's death Emily entrusted Culin with his papers and Zuni costume.

58. Nickliss, *Phoebe Apperson Hearst*, 247–48: "Hearst described Pepper as 'the friend who saved my life, and whose wise council and judgment helped me to solve many serious problems.'"

59. Cushing, "Exploration of Ancient Key-Dweller Remains." Pepper and Hearst first asked Clarence Bloomfield Moore (1852–1936), who was already working in Florida, to undertake the expedition; he declined. On Hearst's relationships with Pepper and Putnam, see Jacknis, "Patrons, Potters, and Painters," 142–44. The most thorough account of the Pepper-Hearst Expedition is Gilliland, *Key Marco's Buried Treasure*; but see also Gilliland, *The Material Culture of Key Marco*; and Kolianos and Weisman, *The Lost Florida Manuscript*; and Kolianos and Weisman, *The Florida Journals*.

60. Powell to Sara Stevenson, 3 February 1899, cited in Wilcox, "Restoring Authenticity," 109.

61. "We have no end of difficulties with Cushing. . . . *He is* a hard case," Sara Yorke Stevenson (1857–1921), a leader of anthropological work in Philadelphia, told Hearst. "We must exact regular reports from these men—and arrange for the full control of objects, plans, drawings, photos, and scientific notes—& all rights to control of publications, etc." (Stevenson to Hearst, 9 June 1899, Sara Stevenson Letterbook 3, 1895–99, University of Pennsylvania Museum Archives).

On Stevenson's role and relationships in Philadelphia anthropology, see Danien and King, "Unsung Visionary." For detailed studies of Americanist archaeology in Philadelphia, see Fowler and Wilcox, *Philadelphia and the Development.*

62. Wilcox, "Restoring Authenticity," 92.

63. *Fifteenth Annual Report for the Bureau of American Ethnology, 1893–94,* 40, 45.

64. Hodge to Haury, 5 October 1931, MS 7, HAE 1.4, BR/AM.

65. Dinwiddie to Hemenway, 16 November 1896, MS 122, Hemenway Family Papers, PEM.

66. Cushing to Pepper, November 1896, MS 6, PHE (Papers of Hemenway Expedition) 1.21, BR/AM.

67. Matthews to Cushing, 21 January 1897, Hodge-Cushing Papers, BR/AM. Dinwiddie went on to a notable career as a war correspondent and photographer.

68. Cushing to Putnam 21 November 1897, cited in Gilliland, *Key Marco's Buried Treasure,* 101. However, as Gilliland points out (101–2), to others (notably Augustus Hemenway) Fewkes continued to protest his own innocence—"I was in the Southwest at the time"—but still questioned Cushing's veracity in the whole affair. In March 1897 Putnam took the toad, at the Hemenways' request, to be studied in Washington. Putnam's secretary, Frances Mead, told his daughter Alice: "They perhaps begin to feel that they have been unjust [to Cushing] and wish to find out the truth if possible. . . . [Your father] is more inclined to favor Mr. C. than Mr. F. in this matter" (Mead to Alice Putnam, 24 March 1897, RWD).

69. Wilcox, "Restoring Authenticity"; Gilliland, *Key Marco's Buried Treasure,* 99–101. Wilcox (personal communication, 2021) stresses that "beyond a reasonable doubt" is his standard of judgment: Cushing's claim that he "restored" the artifact, which was an original find, is plausible. But admittedly the reconstruction is crudely done, as Haury well saw.

70. Powell to Putnam, 24 March 1897, and Putnam to A. Hemenway, 6 April 1897, Hemenway Papers, PEM; Putnam to A. Hemenway, 3 May 1897, UAV 677.38, Harvard University Archives, Cambridge, Massachusetts. The Powell-Putnam proposal was to have the artifacts studied at the Peabody and the documentary work done at the Bureau of American Ethnology. Powell assured Hemenway that he could keep relationships between Fewkes and Cushing "harmonious" in the process.

71. Cushing to Culin, 17 February 1899, Culin Archival Collection, Brooklyn Museum.

72. McGee et al., "In Memoriam," 367, 376–77.

73. Hodge to Lummis, 4 May 1900, MS 1.1.2085B, BR/AM. In his tribute, "The White Indian," Hodge's friend inaugurated the criticism of Cushing as

overly imaginative and untrustworthy: "Cushing was too much—let us say, poet. The same acute imagination which enabled him to discover occult things, went on to the discovery of things which weren't there" (Lummis, "The White Indian," 15).

74. Hodge, "Cushing's Zuni Folk Tales," 125; Hodge to Matthews, 22 November 1901, Washington Matthews Papers, Wheelwright Museum of the American Indian, Santa Fe. In her introduction to the 1931 reprint of *Zuñi Folk Tales,* Mary Austin suggested that Cushing died "chiefly of overwork and under-appreciation." Perhaps, she mused, he was indeed "a changeling, a throw-back to the mysterious little people" who have access to a world of "fairy-lore" (Cushing, *Zuñi Folk Tales,* xxviii–xxix).

75. Hinsley, *The Smithsonian and the American Indian,* 237; Adler, "Samuel Pierpont Langley." There is no full biography of Langley.

76. Richard Woodbury to David R. Wilcox, 30 May 1996, personal communication.

77. Hodge to Boas, 23 January 1899, F. W. Hodge Correspondence, Boas Papers, American Philosophical Society.

78. The outstanding analysis of the period is Darnell, *And Along Came Boas.*

79. In 1894 the Bureau of Ethnology became the Bureau of American Ethnology.

80. Hinsley, *The Smithsonian and the American Indian,* 262–92. Langley appointed William Henry Holmes, not as director, but as chief of the BAE. McGee took a job as head of the Anthropology Program for the Saint Louis World's Fair of 1904, but when a new natural history museum like that which had emerged from the 1893 World's Fair in Chicago (the Field Museum) did not happen in Saint Louis, he gave up his leadership position in American anthropology. He returned to Washington, where he helped his old friend President Theodore Roosevelt with irrigation and other issues until cancer took him in 1912. Franz Boas moved into the leadership vacuum he left (see Fowler and Parezo, *Anthropology Goes to the Fair*; Wilcox, "Creating Field Anthropology"; Wilcox, "Going National").

81. Again, Hodge was replacing a man who had recently died, William C. Winlock.

82. Langley to Hodge, March 1901, 11 November 1901, 29 January 1902, Records of Secretary Langley, 1866–1927, No. 7, Box 34, Folders 20–22, SIA.

83. Langley to Hodge, 1 November 1902, Group 34: Secretary, 1891–1907, Outgoing Correspondence, Ethnology, Box 23, Folder 4.5 (1/9/1900–12/15/1902), SIA.

84. Langley to Holmes, 8 November 1902, Group 34, Box 23, Folder 4.5, SIA.

85. Hodge, *Frederick Webb Hodge, Ethnologist,* 87.

86. Langley to Hodge, 16 December 1902, Group 34: Secretary, 1891–1907, Outgoing Correspondence, Ethnology, Box 23, Folder 4.6 (12/15/1902–4/21/1905), SIA.

87. Noelke, "The Origin and Early History," 239–40.

88. Quoted in Noelke, 240.

89. Langley to Richard Rathbun, 11 October 1904, Group 34, Box 23, Folder 4.6, SIA. Could we not get just a *sample* printed, Langley pleaded.

90. Langley to Holmes, 28 January 1905, Group 34, Box 23, Folder 4.6, SIA.

91. Noelke, "The Origin and Early History," 241, 242 (quote); Matthews to Hodge, 25 January 1905, Washington Matthews Papers, Wheelwright Museum of the American Indian, Santa Fe.

92. John R. Swanton, "Notes Regarding My Adventures in Anthropology and with Anthropologists," File 4651, NAA, quoted in Noelke, "The Origin and Early History," 243.

93. Hodge, *Frederick Webb Hodge, Ethnologist*, 90.

94. The Boas-Hodge letters for these years in the Boas Papers, American Philosophical Society, number in the hundreds.

95. Stocking, "Franz Boas and the Founding."

96. Woodbury to David R. Wilcox, personal communication, 30 May 1996.

97. Cole, "Frederick Webb Hodge," 520.

98. Egan, *Short Nights of the Shadow Catcher*, 86–87.

99. Over the years the number of Curtis's phonograph cylinders has been greatly exaggerated. The total was probably about 500 or 600—not 10,000, as is often cited. For a careful analysis see Jacknis, "A Chamber of Echoing Songs."

100. Myers resigned and was replaced for volumes 19 and 20 by Stewart Eastwood (recommended by Hodge and a Boas student, Frank Goldsmith Speck [1881–1950]). Graybill and Boeson, *Edward Sheriff Curtis*, and Egan, *Short Nights of the Shadow Catcher*, provide detailed accounts of the project. See also Anne Makepeace's multiple-award-winning film, *Coming to Light: Edward S. Curtis and the North American Indian* (2000). For a sardonic view of Curtis, see Wiggins, *The Shadow Catcher*.

101. Hodge, *Frederick Webb Hodge, Ethnologist*, 104.

102. Quoted in Graybill and Boesen, *Edward Sheriff Curtis*, 84.

103. For a sympathetic biography of Walcott, see Yochelson, *Charles Doolittle Walcott*.

104. Noelke, "The Origin and Early History," 232, 322.

105. Holmes to G. Stanley Hall, 25 April 1905, NAA, quoted in Noelke, "The Origin and Early History," 313.

106. Hodge to Walcott, 13 April 1912 and 30 November 1914, Folder 3 (Hodge-Holmes), BAE Letters Received and Sent, 1909–50, NAA.

107. Although as a council member and then Mayor of Garrett Park, Hodge may have been better at politics than he here admitted—although in those cases the interactions were probably quite personal.

108. Kroeber went on to publish *Handbook of the Indians of California* in 1925.

109. Hinsley, "The Problem with Mr. Hewett"; Hinsley, "Edgar Lee Hewett," 227–28; Hodge, *Frederick Webb Hodge, Ethnologist,* 227. Ego notwithstanding, Hewett highly estimated Cushing's contributions: "I have far more confidence in the work of such transcendently gifted men as Cushing than I have in all the critics put together. It has always been difficult for those of limited ability to understand how such streams of mythology as came out of Zuni under the magic wand of Cushing could be genuine." By 1930 he also considered Hodge the "final authority" on Zuni archaeology. Hewett, *Ancient Life in the American Southwest,* 184, 331.

110. Fowler, *A Laboratory for Anthropology,* 269–72; Snead, *Ruins and Rivals,* 143–47; Chauvenet, *Hewett and Friends,* 99. Wilcox ("Going National"; "Anthropology in a Changing America"; "How Emil Haury (Gradually) Broadened the Horizons"; and Wilcox and Fowler, "The Beginnings of Anthropological Archaeology") observes that Hewett and his longtime colleague and friend Byron Cummings were both trained as professors of education, Latin, and Greek; believed strongly in outdoor education; and were old-fashioned antiquarians who saw collections ("relics") as art (Snead, *Ruins and Rivals*). They formed a strategic alliance with Mitchell Carroll, the secretary of the Archaeological Institute of America, and a fellow classicist, around the journal *Art and Archaeology.* Its time ended in 1934. A year later a new strategic alliance was formed with the creation of the Society for American Archaeology and its journal *American Antiquity,* which proclaimed the findings of the "new archaeology" based on time-relations, typologies, and scientific "culture history" (Wilcox and Fowler, "The Beginnings of Anthropological Archaeology"). Both groups sought to attract readers of like mind ("avocationalists") who shared or could be persuaded to share their values. Any modern evaluation of Hewett must consider that he founded enduring institutions, including what started out as the School of American Archaeology (now School of Advanced Research), the anthropology departments at both the University of New Mexico and the University of Southern California, the Museum of New Mexico, the Art Museum of New Mexico, and the San Diego Museum of Man (now San Diego Museum of Us). He also wrote the federal Antiquities Act of 1906. When the western branch

(now Pacific Division) of the American Association for the Advancement of Science (AAAS) was founded in 1920, Hewett was its first president—Cummings followed.

111. E.g., Carpenter, *Two Essays*; Force, *Politics and the Museum*; Wallace, "A Reporter at Large."

112. See, e.g., *Annual Report for the Bureau of American Ethnology, 1914–15*, 17.

113. Heye married Blanche Agnes Williams (1874–1924) in 1904. She died tragically in 1924 ("Wealthy New York Woman Found Dead in Bathtub at Home," *San Antonio Light*, 17 November 1924). They had two children: Larry, who died at age twenty-two in an auto accident in 1932, and Mildred, who died in 1941. Heye saw little of either child (Carpenter, *Two Essays*, 85–86).

114. Fowler, *A Laboratory for Anthropology*, 301. Charlie Turbyfill, a North Carolinian who became Heye's treasured curator, recalled that "Heye organized a big expedition to Georgia, and stopped in Atlanta to marry his second wife, and we all went on the honeymoon trip to White County, where we dug that famous big Nacoochee mound. Books were written about it afterward; we made a killing" (Wallace, "A Reporter at Large," 109).

115. Carpenter, *Two Essays*, 20; cf. Hodge, "The Nacoochee Mound in Georgia."

116. Hodge, *Frederick Webb Hodge, Ethnologist*, 131–32; *Albuquerque Morning Journal*, 7 October 1915, 6, col. 4. Surviving 1888 Hemenway Expedition records do not indicate that Hodge had particular interest in the site.

117. Hodge, *Frederick Webb Hodge, Ethnologist*, 131.

118. The Hodges were separated in 1919. Margaret moved with Emlyn to Royal Oak, Michigan, where she lived until 1928. She died at age seventy in York, Pennsylvania, on 19 October 1935.

119. Fowler, *A Laboratory for Anthropology*, 301; Carpenter, *Two Essays*, 24.

120. Nusbaum to Smith and Woodbury, 30 March 1962, OC 157, Folder 2, NMAI Archives.

121. See, e.g., Wallace, "A Reporter at Large"; Carpenter, *Two Essays*.

122. Grimes, "The Indian Museum's Last Stand," 69.

123. Braun, "Cowboys and Indians," 32.

124. Wallace, "A Reporter at Large," 107.

125. McMullen, "Reinventing George Heye," 72–74.

126. Kidwell, "Every Last Dishcloth," 252.

127. Carpenter, *Two Essays*, 58—where the author also provides a list of twenty-eight men.

128. It should be noted, too, that Heye supported graduate students, such as Frank Speck, with salaries and field expenses at the University Museum. See Kidwell, "Every Last Dishcloth," 238–39. Junius Bird described the hiring

of Coffin as follows: "One year George lost his rapport with Rolls-Royce and Locomobiles, and switched to Pierce-Arrows. The Pierce-Arrow people sent him one of their products equipped with a kind of mechanic-in-residence, an ex-racing driver named Ed Coffin, who shortly developed into one of the best archeological photographers anywhere and was running digs for George" (Carpenter, *Two Essays*, 44).

129. Braun, "Cowboys and Indians," 32. When the Hawikku expedition began in 1917, for instance, Heye was also sponsoring excavations and collecting activities in Guatemala, Peru, the West Indies, Arkansas, Vermont, Alaska, and southern California (Annual Report of the MAI Board of Trustees for 1917–18, 5–7).

130. Carpenter, "Three Chapters," 5.

131. Wallace, "A Reporter at Large," 105. (Quotation from an anonymous archaeologist, identified in Carpenter, "Three Chapters," as Junius Bird [1907–82].)

132. Harrington, "Memories of My Work," 4–6, and handwritten notes. Heye was also known as "Heyewatha." Mark Harrington, who later worked with Hodge at the Southwest Museum, was among the few who remained forever grateful to Heye. "You never broke a promise to me," he wrote in 1936, "and when I was in trouble or sorrow, and needed counsel, sympathy, or tangible aid, you NEVER failed me" (Harrington to Heye, 5 January 1936, Box OC [Official Correspondence] 149, Folder 2, NMAI Archives). He named his son Johns Heye Harrington. (Both of Heye's children had died young.)

133. The gifts from Heye's supporting millionaire friends ("the boys")—Huntington, Harmon Washington Hendricks (1846–1928), and James B. Ford (1844–1928)—can only be guessed from the poor records that were kept. Estimates of the principle of Huntington's publication fund range from $62,500 to $165,000.

134. Grimes, "The Indian Museum's Last Stand," 69; Carpenter, *Two Essays*, 36; Hodge, *Frederick Webb Hodge, Ethnologist*, 172.

135. See part I, note 24, this volume.

136. Hodge to Emily Cushing, 5 and 20 May 1919; E. Cushing to Hodge, 14 May 1919, Box OC 125, Folder 10, NMAI Archives. David H. Ranck, the editor of both the original and the partial series, had held the 1884 copyright.

137. Heye and Hodge undoubtedly intended to blunt the ambitions of Clark Wissler (1870–1947) and the American Museum of Natural History regarding Zuni archaeology. See Snead, *Ruins and Rivals*, 117; Fowler, *A Laboratory for Anthropology*; and Wilcox and Fowler, "The Beginnings of Anthropological Archaeology."

138. Carpenter, *Two Essays*, 32–33; *New York Times*, 26 June 1931, 15, col. 1.

139. Hodge, *Frederick Webb Hodge, Ethnologist*, 133.

140. Burgio-Ericson, "'Plainly Read, Like a Book,'" 135–36. Hodge preferred to call it the Hendricks-Heye Expedition.

141. Pandey, "Factionalism in a Southwestern Pueblo," 94, 97. In Pandey's words, the Bow Priests "had an ambivalent function consisting of both protection and coercion" (Pandey, "Anthropologists at Zuni," 325).

142. Stevenson followed Naiuchi's family to his burial plot and later paid his son twenty-five dollars to unearth Naiuchi's most sacred possession: his war pouch. She presented it to the National Museum (Hinsley, "Collecting Cultures," 17; Miller, *Matilda Coxe Stevenson*, 133; and *Twenty-Third Annual Report of the Bureau of American Ethnology (1901–02)* (Washington: Government Printing Office, 1904), 317).

143. Pedro Pino (Lai-iu-ah-tsai-lu, 1788–c. 1884; governor 1830–78) and his son Patricio Pino (Palowahtiwa/Ba:lawahdiwa, governor 1879–c. 1890) headed the most prominent political family in Zuni in the late nineteenth century; Jesus Eriachos was a multilingual Yaqui/Mexican who had been captured by Apaches as a child and sold to Zuni. As Burgio-Ericson and Isaac point out, linguistic ability aided greatly in relations with outsiders, including anthropologists ("Teluli's Melancholy Picnic," 8).

144. According to Burgio-Ericson and Isaac, the terms "Protestant" and "Catholic" referred not to religious beliefs but to "differing strategies of political alliance" ("Teluli's Melancholy Picnic," 9). See also Pandey, "Factionalism in a Southwestern Pueblo," 205, who writes: "The division of Zuni into Catholic and Protestant factions does not represent an ideological split but is simply based on the personalities of the people supporting one group or another."

145. McFeely, *Zuni and the American Imagination*, 144.

146. Consequentially, too, Zuni was still reeling from the smallpox epidemic of 1898–99, which had killed two hundred people (of a total population of less than 1,500). For Culin's collecting at Zuni see Fane, "The Language of Things," 21–27; Fowler, *A Laboratory for Anthropology*, 229–32; and McFeely, *Zuni and the American Imagination*, 120–44.

147. "Culin encountered the market all around him," and was surprised by what he called a "general air of prosperity" (McFeely, *Zuni and the American Imagination*, 136–37).

148. Huntington was a new trustee of the AMNH, brought on by board chairman Henry Fairfield Osborn (1857–1935). See Fowler and Wilcox, "The Beginnings of Anthropological Archaeology."

149. Fowler, *A Laboratory for Anthropology*, 332–40. For an account of the Huntington Southwest Survey and the intense rivalry between Wissler and Hodge over Zuni archaeology, see Snead, *Ruins and Rivals*, 97–123. Snead sug-

gests that "control of the archaeological resources of the area in the interests of professional and institutional politics were often more critical than scientific motivations" (117).

150. Stocking, "The Ethnographic Sensibility," 220.

151. James, "With the Zunis," 112, 255.

152. Benedict, *Patterns of Culture*; Huxley, *Brave New World*. Huxley had read his Cushing: both "Palowahtiwa" and "Waihusiwa" appear on the "Savage Reservation" in *Brave New World*.

153. Pandey, "Anthropologists at Zuni," 331.

154. Although Heye's museum was officially established in 1916, World War I intervened. The army requisitioned the new museum building and "military cartographers soon were at work in its galleries" (Force, *Politics and the Museum*, 10).

155. The following discussion relies on the analysis in Burgio-Ericson, "'Plainly Read, Like a Book.'"

156. Burgio-Ericson, 137.

157. See, e.g., Hodge, "Excavations at Hawikuh"; Hodge, *Turquois Work at Hawikuh*; Hodge, *Circular Kivas near Hawikuh*; Hodge, "The Six Cities of Cibola"; and Hodge, *History of Hawikuh*.

158. Smith et al., *The Excavation of Hawikuh*, 7.

159. Elliott, *Great Excavations*, 100–101. For analysis of the "new archaeology" proclaimed in 1917 by Clark Wissler in the AMNH's *Natural History* magazine, in which stratigraphic excavations were a key feature, see Wilcox and Fowler, "The Beginnings of Anthropological Archaeology."

160. Gregory and Wilcox, *Zuni Origins*, 4. See also discussion of the larger AMNH program orchestrated by Wissler with funding from Huntington in Wilcox and Fowler, "The Beginnings of Anthropological Archaeology."

161. Burgio-Ericson, "'Plainly Read, Like a Book,'" 148.

162. Burgio-Ericson and Isaac, "Teluli's Melancholy Picnic," 16.

163. Richard Hart cites the following passage from an investigation by the Bureau of Catholic Indian Missions at Zuni in 1924: "[A] great many of the Indians objected [in 1917] to Hodge excavating here. Even at the present time there is a strong sentiment against it. The people do not think it is the right thing to dig up the dead. It was necessary for Hodge to have the local officials with him to do that. The Indian Office gave a permit to Mr. Hodge to excavate, provided it was approved by the Indian officers. The officers here were supposed to talk to the people about it. Hodge hired quite a few to work for him" (Vertical file "Zuni," Museum of New Mexico, Santa Fe, cited in "Factors Relating to Zuni Land," 178n40).

164. Hart, 43n133.

165. Burgio-Ericson, "'Plainly Read, Like a Book,'" 136.

166. Burgio-Ericson and Isaac, "Teluli's Melancholy Picnic," 15.

167. Heye never seriously considered Indigenous opposition to unearthing or collecting human remains. Supporting Aleš Hrdlička's outrage at having a skeleton-collecting party canceled in 1933, he commiserated: "I am truly sorry anybody in the world can be irritated by scientific work" (Redman, *Bone Rooms*, 255–56). Hodge was more circumspect but never expressed second thoughts.

168. For Rinehart's delightfully wry account of her 1921 summer tour of the Southwest, see *The Out Trail*. Her stay at Zuni was very brief.

169. Hart notes that Owen Cattell was accompanied by one of his three brothers: McKeen, Ware, and Jacques ("Factors Relating to Zuni Land," 178). Cattell produced ethnographic films for the Heye Foundation from 1912–27 with the assistance of Hodge, including the Zuni films of 1923. At the time of his death he was assistant editor of *Science* and manager of Science Press; he served as director of exhibits for AAAS conventions (*New York Times*, 28 March 1940, 29). He and a fellow Columbia University student were convicted of conspiracy to obstruct U.S. conscription laws during World War I (Gruber, "Academic Freedom").

170. The Shalako conflict was a traumatic event at Zuni, leading to a transfer of power to the "Catholic" faction and a permanent political split. See Burgio-Ericson and Isaac, "Teluli's Melancholy Picnic"; and Wenger, *We Have a Religion*, 185–87. It led eventually to a "prohibition against photographing ceremonial activities in Zuni that has been sustained to the present" (Holman, "Curating and Controlling," 114; cf. Colwell-Chanthaphonh, "Sketching Knowledge"). For the serious political consequences in the pueblo over the next decade, see Hart, "Factors Relating to Zuni Land," 178–88.

171. Hodge, "Motion Pictures at Zuni," 30. The article is not attributed but is almost certainly by Hodge. On the subsequent fate of the films, see O'Neal, "Going Home."

172. It should be noted, however, that the Heyes and Hodge formed sincere and longer-term friendships with specific Zuni individuals of the "Protestant" circle. In early 1923 Lorenzo Chavez and Waihusiwa—the teller of Cushing's folklore tales back in 1886—traveled to New York City as part of a Pueblo contingent to testify against the Bursum bill before John Collier. Both men stayed in the city for more than a week afterward, living in the Heyes' apartment, while Chavez had surgery on a damaged eye. The surgery was successful, avoiding blindness. The Heyes paid all expenses, and the visitors were escorted and hosted around town—from the zoo to museums to private clubs and a luncheon on the S.S. *Mauritania* (sister ship to the *Lusitania*). It was Waihusiwa's

second and final trip to the East Coast (after the memorable sojourn at Mary Hemenway's Manchester estate in 1886). The most revered man at Zuni, "Father Waihusiwa" died in 1930.

Thea Heye continued to send Christmas packages to Zuni for another decade. See "Letters to George and Thea Heye from Lorenzo Chavez and Other Zuni Indians," Huntington Box 9, Folder 1, CURMC.

173. Hodge to Lummis, 28 May 1928, Box 7, Folder 17, Charles F. Lummis Papers (MS 297), University of Arizona Library Special Collections. Born Sarah, she adopted "Zahrah" as her public name.

174. *Berkeley Daily Gazette*, 6 May 1929.

175. Field, *Kate Field's Washington*, 1893, 128. In a flyer announcing a Cushing lecture on 10 December 1890, the Buffalo Society of Natural Sciences noted that "Mr. Cushing fully acquainted himself with . . . the love-songs of their young men and maidens, and the quaint and curious lullabies of the Zuni mothers, with which his lectures are illustrated." One month before he died, Cushing ended his final lecture at the Pratt Institute in New York—possibly the last of his life—by singing "The Song of the Corn Maiden" and a Zuni lullaby, which he had sung in San Francisco and many times since (*Pratt Institute Monthly*, May 1900, 163).

176. However, Dom Pedro II was not deposed until 1889.

177. Cadman, "Carlos Troyer," iii–v. The story of Troyer's life as told by Cadman also widely circulated in newspaper accounts.

178. Farwell, *"Wanderjahre of a Revolutionist,"* 113n7.

179. Pisani, *Imagining Native America in Music*, 361n15, 257; Farwell, *"Wanderjahre of a Revolutionist,"* 113–15. Farwell maintained, inter alia, that Troyer solved Cushing's stomach problems and thereby "prolonged his life" (113n7).

180. Cushing Diary, 3 September 1893, NAA. He later noted: "Had a sweet note from Mrs. Cummins in reference to her daughter's singing of the Zuñi songs and costumes etc." (12 November 1893). The father, Adley H. Cummins, had been a lawyer, philologist, and amateur ethnographer who died at age thirty-nine. Viva's mother, Ella Sterling Cummins (1853–1934), a writer of autobiography (as Amora Esmeralda) and California scenes, later married novelist and editor Philip Mighels. See Esmeralda, *Life and Letters*; and "Mighels, Ella Sterling, 1853–1934," accessed 2 September 2017, http://socialarchive.iath.virginia.edu/ark:/99166/w62b91xt.

181. "Town Talk," *San Francisco Daily Times* 9 (n.d.): 6.

182. "Wenner's Magazine Reception for Prof. and Mrs. Robert Irving Fulton," *Wenner's Magazine* 16 (May 1894): 191. On this occasion she sang "the blanket wooing of a brave, and a cradle song by a squaw."

183. "Weird Melodies of a Strange New Mexican People, Now the Fad in Music Circles," *San Francisco Call*, 9 August 1896, 8. This five-column account of the Cushing-Troyer-Cummins story deserves fuller quotation for a sense of the colorful inflation by the *Call* reporter: "[In 1887–88 Cushing] sang the wonderful songs that were until then unknown to civilized ears—songs he had studied and imitated in the dreary, sunburned homes of the Zunis. Nothing like these melodies had ever been heard before. It was not strange that the depth of mystery, the singular force of expression and the absolute novelty of this music fascinated [Troyer]. . . . The tones it seemed were largely taken from nature—possibly the sigh of the wind that somehow tells us a mournful story as it passes through the trees or house, now swelling into a full volume of sound, and again fading away to an almost inaudible whisper, still retaining its quality. Then it would take on the color of a joyful bird song, or at least indicate that influence; but over all there appeared like streaks of light, a ring of true feeling, intensely human, often pathetic. . . . 'It is impossible,' was the exclamation of the eminent archeologist, on being told that the Zuni songs could be recorded [on paper]. But the musician persevered. . . . They were played for [Cushing's] benefit, and at once Dr. Cushing proclaimed them perfect."

184. Cuban musician and voice teacher Emilio Jacobo Agromonte Pina (1844–1918) established his School of Opera and Oratorio in New York City in 1893. He returned to Cuba in 1903.

185. Griffith, "Singing in Twenty Languages." This article includes photographs of Viva performing as "squaw," "Hindoo," Javanese, Spanish, Hungarian, "Muezzin," Bedouin, and "Little Big Thunder."

186. Browner, "'Breathing the Indian Spirit'"; Crawford, *The American Musical Landscape*. Browner points out Crawford's distinction between the ideals of authenticity and accessibility in the Indianist phenomenon—that "making songs accessible to the general public required changing them to fit into the Western musical system. Thus accessibility contributed to the degradation of authenticity, the very reason composers sought out Native songs in the first place" (280).

187. Troyer, *Traditional Songs of the Zuñis*. The later set included a "sun dance," a "rain dance," and a "ghost dance."

188. *New York Times*, 16 January 1912, 13; *Oakland Tribune*, 12 October 1911, 38; *Montclair Times*, 13 January 1912, 7. In first announcing her upcoming performance, the *Times* (24 December 1911, 4) introduced Zahrah, imaginatively, as one who had "studied the music and folklore of the Zuni Indians and visited the Indian tribe with which she had been familiar since childhood."

189. The first program in which Troyer and Preble appear together took place before a very large audience at the University of California in 1909, but on this

occasion she sang Tchaikovsky's "Don Juan's Serenade" and he played "The Sunrise Call" (*San Francisco Call*, 3 May 1909, 4).

190. "A Sister to the Indians," *Chicago Tribune*, 26 September 1915, 524. The first paragraph of this article ("A Sister to the Indians") provides the flavor: "A woman anthropologist might be expected to savor of the bluestocking type; but there is nothing to indicate the strong-minded woman in the personality or appearance of Miss Zahrah E. Preble, who has elected to devote herself to the study of the human species in general and of the famous Zuni Indians of New Mexico in particular. Anthropologists agree that these Indians show the highest intellectual development of any of the native redmen."

Between 1904 and 1920, when Troyer died at eighty-three, many women performed his Zuni compositions in public events and private homes, sometimes in generic "Indian" costume and with the composer accompanying on piano. An interesting example is Enid Watkins (1890–1971). A founder and co-chairperson of the Los Angeles Philharmonic Orchestra, and a soprano, between 1917 and 1932 Watkins sang with opera companies in New York, San Francisco, and Paris. But in 1914, when she was twenty-four, the *Musical Monitor* reported that "Enid Watkins, a California girl who has made a study of the Zuni tribes [*sic*] of the Southwest, sang a group of Indian songs in costume at the Plaza, New York." The previous year she had sung with Troyer at a teachers' convention (*San Francisco Call*, 11 July 1913, 3). A photo of her in costume can be found on Wikipedia at wikipedia.org/wiki/Enid_Watkins. Cf. "Miss Watkins in Indian Songs," *New York Times*, 11 January 1917, 13.

191. See, e.g., *New York Times*, 9 March 1913; *Western Journal of Education* 22 (1916): 22; *Music Magazine/Musical Courier* 80 (22 April 1920): 53.

192. Hyland, *Evangelism's First Modern Media Star*, 34–36. "Of course we're Methodists! But these Indian dances are ceremonial dances," Stidger reminded the dissenters in his congregation.

193. *Pacific Coast Musical Review* 28 (1915): 6, 8; "Clubhouse Walls Bar Storm from Gay Music," *Oakland Tribune* 25 January 1916, 8; *San Francisco Examiner*, 27 June 1915, 8. Annie Rix Militz (1856–1924) was a prominent spiritual leader in the turn-of-the-century New Thought/Christian Science movement. Less impressed, music historian Amanda Cannata has labeled the Troyer/Preble performances at the 1915 Exposition "exoticizing and racist musical ventriloquism" (Cannata, "Articulating and Contesting Cultural Hierarchies").

194. Preble's "Interesting Westerners" column for *Sunset Magazine* that year was a vignette of the government teacher at Pala, Ellen Lawrence. Photographs from that visit are in the Zahrah Preble Collection at BR/AM.

195. Preble, "Jottings from the Pacific Coast."

196. *Stockton Daily Evening Record*, 10 January 1921, 6.

197. *Musical America* 33–34 (1921): 44, stated: "Her work will take her to the twelve villages in the Canal Zone where Government employees are stationed, and in addition to her own interpretations, she will coach for dramatic and musical performances." See also *The Zonian* 12 (1921), Balboa High School Yearbook.

198. Discography of American Historical Recordings, Matrix No. 1923-01-27-03.

199. *Brooklyn Daily Eagle*, 10 June 1923, 84. Perhaps in anticipation of the outing to Zuni, the previous October Preble had published an instructive article on "Simple Camp Cookery."

200. *Brooklyn Daily Eagle*, 10 June 1923.

201. Preble to Leonora Curtin, 9 November 1933, Curtin/Paloheima Archives, AMH. On the debates that began in the 1890s over the tonal qualities of Indigenous American music (including Zuni recordings), see the recent discussion in Walden, "Pitch vs. Timbre."

202. Preble, "Child Cultures Oldest Cradle"; Preble, "A Tip from Pueblo Indian Mothers"; Preble, "Teacher Versus Mother."

203. Preble, "The Oldest Sport in America."

204. Hodge, "A Zuni Foot-Race"; Cushing, "My Adventures in Zuñi," 102–3.

205. Cushing, "My Adventures in Zuñi," 101.

206. Hodge's account was soon followed by John G. Owens's more detailed and contextualized account of the stick-race, which he called "the great national game of Zuñi," as popular as baseball. Owens had spent eight weeks of the summer of 1890 with Jesse Fewkes at Zuni (Owens, "Some Games of the Zuñi," 44).

207. Preble, "The Oldest Sport in America," 30.

208. Preble, 29, 78.

209. Preble, "Catching Motion on the Wing."

210. For analysis of Hodge's 1928 revisit, see Burgio-Ericson and Isaac, "Teluli's Melancholy Picnic."

211. Hodge Christmas card, December 1928, Box 59, Folder 2, Scrapbook, 25 A–B, PMH.

212. Zahrah Preble Hodge to Leonora Curtin, 3 April 1932, AMH; F. W. Hodge to Leonora Curtin, 14 December 1931 (telegram), Box 59, Folder 2, Scrapbook, PMH.

213. Preble, *Tomar of Siba*; *Pasadena Post*, 28 April 1934, 3. In 1940 Donna Preble (1882–1979) illustrated and published the second book in her sister's series (Preble, *Yamino-Kwiti*). In her last year Zahrah also published a short piece on San Ildefonso potter Maria Martinez (Preble, "Maria Martinez, Indian Master-Potter") and may have been planning a larger study.

214. In some letters Heye made mention of a "Hawikuh Suspense Fund" and withdrew from it to support Hodge's salary in 1930 and 1931. Further information on these monies has not been found.

215. Not to be confused with the Indian Notes and Monographs series (10 vols.). The MAI publications also included Contributions to South American Archaeology (2 vols., 1907 and 1910); Contributions from the Museum (9 vols., 1913–25); Leaflets (5 vols., 1920–26); and Miscellaneous (43 vols., 1920–27). It is not immediately obvious how items were assigned to one series or another. Among the Miscellaneous publications were, by 1927, seven editions of the List of Publications and two editions of the "Aims and Purposes" of the museum. Archer Huntington's substantial publication endowment enabled constant output under Hodge's oversight.

216. Hodge to Heye, 25 February 1926; and Hodge to Ford, 3 March 1926, Box V-E, Folder 9, MAIA.

217. Hart, *Pedro Pino*, 126.

218. Although the Photostat brand and technology of copying did not appear until 1907, other methods were available as early as the 1870s.

219. Hodge to Heye, 25 February 1926, Box V-E, Folder 9, MAIA.

220. Hodge to Heye.

221. While inventorying the library vault, librarian Mary Davis discovered the letterbooks and, recognizing Cushing's distinctive handwriting, contacted Hinsley. He and Wilcox traveled to the Bronx, where Wilcox inventoried all the letters. This discovery directly led to a commitment to a documentary history of the Hemenway Expedition. The letterbooks are now in the archives of Cornell University Library—with much else from the Huntington Free Library.

222. Accounts vary concerning these events. Remarks here are based on Carpenter, *Two Essays*, 84–85; and Jesse Nusbaum to Smith and Woodbury, 30 March 1962, Box OC 157, Folder 2, MAIA. Not all were bitter: Mark Harrington, who immediately found a lifelong home at the Southwest Museum, always felt warmly toward Heye—and named his son Johns Heye Harrington.

223. Hodge recalled: "When you consider all the work done at Hawikuh, I didn't even finish the study of the artifacts. Heye, you know, said, 'Why bother about that? Costs money and what's the use?' Of course I was eager to get away from there; it's devastating to members of the staff to have that sort of thing to contend with" (Hodge, *Frederick Webb Hodge, Ethnologist*, 230).

224. Thompson, *American Character*, is an insightful biography; see also the excellent essay on Lummis in Goodman, *Translating Southwestern Landscapes*, 3–34.

225. Wilson and Falkenstien-Doyle, "Charles Fletcher Lummis," 96.

226. Lummis to Hodge, 15 September 1923, MS 1.1. 2085K, BR/AM.

227. According to Thompson, Lummis bequeathed the house and his southwestern artifacts to the museum foundation in order to protect them from his estranged wife, Eve, in the divorce. In 1924 the museum bought the house and collection back from Lummis, who by then was destitute (Thompson, *American Character*, 280).

228. Alliot was a nephew of French anthropologist Paul Broca (1824–80). He had excavated at the ruins of Tyre in 1891 and was director of the popular cliff-dweller exhibit at the Chicago World's Fair of 1893, which so fascinated Cushing (Setchell, "In Memoriam," 1919; Robinson, *The Story of the Southwest Museum*, 18–20; and Hinsley and Wilcox, *Coming of Age in Chicago*).

229. Robinson, *The Story of the Southwest Museum*, 21–22.

230. Drury, "James A. B. Scherer."

231. Starr, *Inventing the Dream*, 107–8: "Arroyo Pasadena . . . lived on the edge of the wilderness; for the rocks and chapparal of the Arroyo Seco brought the ecology of the untamed interior right into the suburbs." Bohemian residents of the Arroyo gloried in "Southern California's resistant, elemental texture" (108). See also Starr, *Endangered Dreams*, 123–25.

232. See, e.g., Dixon, "The Origin and Development"; Zamorano Club, *The Zamorano Club Programs, 1928–91*. Henry Edwards Huntington was the nephew of Collis and cousin of Archer Huntington. He married Collis's widow, Arabella, combining two-thirds of Collis's prodigious estate. Having made his own fortune in electric railways in Los Angeles, he and his wife devoted themselves to art, books, and their wonderful gardens, long gloriously open to the public in San Marino, California.

233. Fowler, *A Laboratory for Anthropology*, 366–71; Stocking, "The Santa Fe Style."

234. Robinson, *The Story of the Southwest Museum*, 24.

235. Robinson. Through ex-officio appointments, by 1960 the museum's board included the heads of ten Southern California universities and the Henry L. Huntington Library.

236. Haury, "Wherefore a Harvard Ph.D.?"

237. Not strictly true: Margaret was still alive, living with her daughter Emlyn in York, Pennsylvania; she died in 1934.

238. Hodge to Haury, 5 October 1931, X-file 94-36, H-2, PMA.

239. Hodge to Haury, 14 October 1931, and 2 March 1932, X-file 94-36, H-2, PMA. Hodge had accepted the water stones theory in his early article on Salado ancient irrigation (Hodge "Prehistoric Irrigation in Arizona").

240. Haury, "Wherefore a Harvard Ph.D.?," 722.

241. Hodge to Haury, handwritten "memoranda," 30 March 1934, X-file 94-36, H-2, PMA. As mentioned in Hodge's diary, on one occasion (20 March 1888) Cushing made tent flags in honor of Eusebio Molera's visit to the camp.

242. Hodge to Scott, 2 April 1942, X-file 94-36, H-2, PMA. Donald C. Scott (1879–1967) was a son-in-law of Mary Hemenway's daughter Edith Eustis.

243. Haury, *The Excavation of Los Muertos*, vii–ix. See also Haury, "Wherefore a Harvard Ph.D.?," an essay about his Harvard experience and writing his dissertation. Judy Brunson has recently also written a dissertation ("The Social Organization of the Los Muertos Hohokam") discussing her analysis of the Hemenway Salt River valley collections at the Peabody Museum, which adds more detail about its scientific significance.

244. But not his last private words. In 1942 Clarissa Parsons Fuller, a history graduate student at the University of New Mexico, was writing her MA thesis on Cushing at Zuni and on the expedition. Hodge responded twice (30 October and 8 December 1942) to her queries. Hodge's letters to Fuller are lost, but she reported in the thesis: "Hodge said that Cushing's failure as an administrator brought about the end of the Expedition. The fieldnotes and reports of the Expedition, containing the troubles it was having, are in Peabody Museum at Harvard and were not available to me" (Fuller, "Frank Hamilton Cushing's Relations," 89n82). As with Haury, Hodge misled Fuller regarding the records.

245. Woodbury, *Sixty Years of Southwestern Archaeology*, 81, fig. 3.1. Woodbury writes that Hodge did not attend the 1927 conference, but also presents the photograph with Hodge (75, 81). Woodbury also makes the point that "the first Pecos Conference was not made up of patriarchs," the average known age being forty-one (73). Hodge was sixty-three.

246. Robinson, *The Story of the Southwest Museum*, 26.

247. Wilson, "F. W. Hodge and the Southwest Museum," 6, 8–9.

248. Wilson, 10.

249. Cited in Wilson, 14. "Hodge used temporary exhibitions to great effect to attract donations of objects to the Museum," Wilson observes (15).

250. Wilson, 25.

251. Mu Alpha Nu chapters were established in several American universities. The brainchild of Edgar Lee Hewett following the death of William Henry Holmes in 1933, it appears to have been a movement to retain relevance by the old *Art and Archaeology* crowd in American anthropology, making Hodge their new iconic symbol for their values.

252. G. Hodge, "A Brief Account of My Life," 241–42. *The Kachinas Are Coming* is still in print, as is her *Four Winds: Poems from Indian Ritual*.

253. Personal correspondence to the author, 11 July 1995.

254. Hundreds of her charming, delicate mission paintings are in the Eva Scott Fenyes Collection in the Braun Research Library Collection of the Autry Museum in Los Angeles.

255. Nelson, "The Evolution of Eva Fenyes." Eva Fenyes's artwork is also in the Fenyes Family Papers at the University of Minnesota.

256. Leonora Paloheimo, interview with the author, 11 November 1992.

257. On the three generations of women, see Weideman, "Three Wise Women." Thanks to Ms. Bunny Huffman for courteous research assistance. The Fenyes-Curtin-Paloheimo home on Acequia Madre in Santa Fe is now the Women's International Study Center.

258. Author's collection, courtesy of Genevieve Pease.

259. Bourke to Cushing, 30 September 1884 and 7 June 1882, HCP. "Penny dips" were cheap candles; "plug" referred to chewing tobacco.

260. Clark, "The Iconography of Gender," 17; cf. Truettner, "Dressing the Part"; and Braddock, *Thomas Eakins*. Braddock calls the Cushing portrait "one of the grandest and most extraordinary visual tributes ever painted by [Eakins]" (174). A second portrait of Cushing by Philadelphia painter William Hovenden is less known but should be compared to the Eakins image. It shows a more sensitive and even shy Cushing, not the harsh, manly, and assertive character seen by Eakins. (For the portrait see Hinsley and Wilcox, *Coming of Age in Chicago*, xxviii.)

261. Stocking, "The Scientific Reaction," 283. The sponsoring committee of the Hodge Anniversary Publications Fund in 1936 is indicative in this regard. It included Boas, Hrdlička, Kidder, Kroeber, Tozzer, Edward Sapir, Elsie Clews Parsons, and Edgar Lee Hewett, among others—virtually a who's-who of American anthropology at the time.

262. Author interview with Marjorie Lambert, November 13, 1992. "He had a technician's mind," she said, recalling that he once told her: "I just love to restore pottery."

263. "J. Frank Dobie," *American-Statesman*, 14 October 1956, MS 7, SWM 6.1B, BR/AM.

264. Powell, "Sky, Sun, and Water," 165.

265. Hodge, *Old Dan Dubois*; cf. Taylor, *Looking for Dan*.

266. "Tribute to Fred Hodge," *Branding Iron* (newsletter of the Los Angeles Corral of Westerners) 36 (December 1956): 2.

References Cited

Adams, Brooks. *The Emancipation of Massachusetts: The Dream and the Reality*. Introduction by Perry Miller. 1887. Reprint, Boston: Houghton Mifflin, 1962.

Adler, Cyrus. "Samuel Pierpont Langley." In *Smithsonian Institution Annual Report for 1906*, 515–33. Washington, D.C.: Government Printing Office, 1907.

"Ancient Pueblo Remains: Discoveries in an Arizona Valley." *New-York Times*, 13 May 1888.

Anderson, Thornton. *Brooks Adams: Constructive Conservative*. Ithaca: Cornell University Press, 1951.

Appleton, Carolyn M., and Natasha S. Bartalini. *Henry Farny, 1847–1916*. Exhibit Catalogue. Austin: Archer M. Huntington Art Gallery, University of Texas at Austin, 1983.

"Arizona's Buried City: Lieut. Cushing Describes the Relics of the Past Unearthed at Los Muertos." *Arizona Daily Star*, 23 May 1888.

Bandelier, Adolph F. *The Gilded Man (El Dorado) and Other Pictures of the Spanish Occupancy of America*. New York: D. Appleton, 1893.

Bandelier, Adolph F. "The Historical Archives of the Hemenway Southwestern Archaeological Expedition." In *Congrès International des Américanistes, Berlin, 1888*, 449–59. Berlin: W. H. Kühl, 1890.

Bandelier, Adolph F. "Reports by Adolph F. Bandelier on His Investigations in New Mexico during the Years 1883–1884." Appendix in *Fifth Annual Report of the Executive Committee, Archaeological Institute of America*, 55–98. Cambridge, Mass.: Archaeological Institute of America, 1884.

Bandelier, Adolph F. *The Southwest Journals of Adolph F. Bandelier, 1880–1882*. Edited by Charles H. Lange and Carroll L. Riley. Albuquerque: University of New Mexico Press, 1966.

Baxter, Sylvester. "Archaeological Camping in Arizona, Parts 5 and 6." In "A Hemenway Portfolio: Views and Voices from the Hemenway Archaeological Expedition, 1886–1889." Edited by Curtis M. Hinsley and David R. Wilcox. Special issue, *Journal of the Southwest* 37, no. 4 (1995): 605–24.

Baxter, Sylvester. *The Old New World: An Account of the Explorations of the Hemenway Southwestern Archaeological Expedition in 1887–88, Under the Direction of Frank Hamilton Cushing*. Salem, Mass.: Salem Press, 1888. Reprinted from the *Boston Herald*, April 15, 1888, in Curtis M. Hinsley and David R. Wilcox, *The Southwest in the American Imagination: The Writings of Sylvester Baxter, 1881–1889*, 113–44. Tucson: University of Arizona Press, 1996.

Benedict, Ruth. *Patterns of Culture*. Boston: Houghton Mifflin, 1934.

Benfey, Christopher. *The Great Wave: Gilded Age Misfits, Japanese Eccentrics, and the Opening of Old Japan*. New York: Random House, 2003.

Bennett, E. Fay. "An Afternoon of Terror: The Sonoran Earthquake of May 3, 1887." *Arizona and the West* 19 (1977): 107–20.

Bensel Directory Company. *Phoenix Directory for the Year 1892*. Phoenix: Bensel Directory Company, 1892.

Blocker, Jack S., David M. Fahey, and Ian R. Tyrrell, eds. *Alcohol and Temperance in Modern History: An International Encyclopedia*. Santa Barbara: ABC-CLIO, 2003.

Bourke, John Gregory. Diaries, 1872–96. U.S. Military Academy Library, West Point, N.Y.

Braddock, Alan C. *Thomas Eakins and the Cultures of Modernity*. Berkeley: University of California Press, 2009.

Brandes, Raymond Stewart. "Frank Hamilton Cushing: Pioneer Americanist." PhD dissertation, University of Arizona, Tucson, 1965.

Braun, Barbara. "Cowboys and Indians: The History and Fate of the Museum of the American Indian." *Village Voice* 31 (8 April 1986): 31–40.

Browman, David L., and Stephen Williams. *Anthropology at Harvard: A Biographical History, 1790–1940*. Cambridge: Peabody Museum Press, 2013.

Browner, Tara. "'Breathing the Indian Spirit': Thoughts on Musical Borrowing and the 'Indianist' Movement in American Music." *American Music* 15, no. 3 (Autumn 1997): 265–84.

Brunson, Judy. "The Social Organization of the Los Muertos Hohokam: A Reanalysis of Cushing's Hemenway Expedition Data." PhD Dissertation, Department of Anthropology, Arizona State University, Tempe, 1989.

Brunson, Judy, and Scott L. Fedick. "Los Guanacos: One Hundred Years Later, Recent Documentary and Archaeological Research Concerning a Prehistoric Hohokam Site First Investigated by the Hemenway Expedition of 1887–1888." Presented at 53rd Annual Meeting of the Society for American Archaeology, Phoenix, Ariz., 1988. doi: 10.6067/XCV8402854.

Burgio-Ericson, Klinton. "A:shiwi A:wan Museum and Heritage Center." Society of Architectural Historians Archipedia, 2017. https://sah-archipedia.org/buildings/NM-01-031-06161-03.

Burgio-Ericson, Klinton. "'Plainly Read, Like a Book': The Place of the Hendricks-Hodge Expedition in Archaeological History." *New Mexico Historical Review* 95, no. 2 (Spring 2020): 131–58.

Burgio-Ericson, Klinton, and Gwyneira Isaac. "Teluli's Melancholy Picnic: Zuni Resistance to the Hendricks-Hodge Archaeological Expedition amidst Assimilation-Era Politics." *New Mexico Historical Review* 97, no. 2 (2022). https://digitalrepository.unm.edu/nmhr/vol97/iss2/1.

Bush, Clive. *Halfway to Revolution: Investigation and Crisis in the Work of Henry Adams, William James and Gertrude Stein.* New Haven: Yale University Press, 1991.

Cadman, Charles Wakefield. "Carlos Troyer: A Biographical Appreciation." In Carlos Troyer, *Indian Music Lecture: The Zuñi Indians and Their Music.* Philadelphia: Theo. Presser, 1913.

Cannata, Amanda. "Articulating and Contesting Cultural Hierarchies: Guatemalan, Mexican, and Native American Music at the Panama-Pacific International Exposition, 1915." *Journal of the Society for American Music* 8, no. 1 (February 2014): 76–100.

Carpenter, Edmund Snow. "Three Chapters from an Unfinished, Two-Volume Study of George Heye's Museum of the American Indian." *Native American Studies* 15, no. 1 (2001): 1–12.

Carpenter, Edmund Snow. *Two Essays: Chief and Greed.* North Andover, Mass.: Persimmon Press, 2005.

Carter, Denny. *Henry Farny.* New York: Watson-Guptill, 1978.

Cather, Willa. "The Enchanted Bluff." *Harper's Magazine* 118 (April 1909): 3–15.

Chaput, Don. *Dr. Goodfellow, Physician to the Gunfighters, Scholar, and Bon Vivant.* Tucson: Westernlore Press, 1996.

Chauvenet, Beatrice. *Hewett and Friends: A Biography of Santa Fe's Vibrant Era.* Santa Fe: Museum of New Mexico Press, 1983.

Chenault, Mark L., and John M. Lindly. "Guanacos, Symbolism, and Religion During the Hohokam Preclassic." In *Religion in the Prehispanic Southwest*, edited by Christine S. VanPool, Todd L. VanPool, and David A. Phillips Jr., 115–34. Lanham, Md.: AltaMira Press, 2006.

"City of the Dead." *Arizona Weekly Citizen*, 10 December 1887.

"City of the Dead: The Ruined Town of Los Muertos." *San Francisco Chronicle*, 18 December 1887.

Clark, William J. "The Iconography of Gender in Thomas Eakins' Portraiture." *American Studies* 32, no. 2 (1991): 5–28.

Clarke, James Freeman. *Autobiography, Diary and Correspondence.* Edited by Edward Everett Hale. Boston: Houghton Mifflin, 1892.

Clarke, James Freeman. *Ten Great Religions, Part I: An Essay in Comparative Theology.* Boston: James R. Osgood, 1871.

Clarke, James Freeman. *Ten Great Religions, Part II: A Comparison of All Religions.* Cambridge, Mass.: Riverside Press, 1883.

Clemensen, A. Berle. *A Centennial History of the Nation's First Prehistoric Preserve: 1892–1992.* U.S. Department of the Interior, National Park Service. Washington, D.C.: Government Printing Office, 1992.

"Clubhouse Walls Bar Storm from Gay Music." *Oakland Tribune*, 25 January 1916, 8.

Cole, Fay-Cooper. 1957. "Frederick Webb Hodge, 1864–1956." *American Anthropologist* 59, no. 3: 517–20.

Colwell-Chanthaphonh, Chip. 2011. "Sketching Knowledge: Quandaries in the Mimetic Reproduction of Pueblo Ritual." *American Ethnologist* 38, no. 3: 451–67.

Cook, Mary J. Straw. *Immortal Summer: A Victorian Woman's Travels in the Southwest: The 1897 Letters and Photographs of Amelia Hollenback.* Santa Fe: Museum of New Mexico Press, 2002.

Cordell, Linda S., and Maxine E. McBrinn. *Archaeology of the Southwest.* 3rd ed. New York: Routledge, 2016.

Coyle, Phillip E. *Náyari History, Politics and Violence: From Flowers to Ash.* Tucson: University of Arizona Press, 2016.

Cozzens, Samuel Woodworth. *The Marvellous Country: or, Three Years in Arizona and New Mexico, the Apaches' Home.* Boston: Shepard & Gill, 1873.

Crawford, Richard. *The American Musical Landscape.* Berkeley: University of California Press, 1993.

Curtis, William E. *Children of the Sun.* Chicago: Inter-Ocean, 1883.

Cushing, Frank Hamilton. "The Discovery of Zuni or the Ancient Province of Cibola or the Seven Cities." Handwritten MS, 1885. Frank Hamilton Cushing Manuscript Collection, MS 6, BOE 4.5. Southwest Museum, Autry Center, Los Angeles.

Cushing, Frank Hamilton. "Exploration of Ancient Key-Dweller Remains on the Gulf Coast of Florida." *Proceedings of the American Philosophical Society* 35 (1897): 153.

Cushing, Frank Hamilton. "Itinerary of Reconnaissance to Casa Grande Ruins, December 31, 1887, to January 4, 1888." In "A Hemenway Portfolio: Voices and Views from the Hemenway Archaeological Expedition, 1886–1889." Edited by Curtis M. Hinsley and David R. Wilcox. Special issue, *Journal of the Southwest* 37, no. 4 (1995): 590–604.

Cushing, Frank Hamilton. "My Adventures in Zuñi." *Century Illustrated Monthly Magazine* 25 (1882–83): 191–207, 500–11; and 26 (1883): 28–47. Reprinted with introduction by Oakah L. Jones. Palo Alto: American West, 1970.

Cushing, Frank Hamilton. "On the Development of Industrial and Ornamental Art Among the Zunis of New Mexico." In *Report of the 54th Meeting of the British Association for the Advancement of Science, Montreal, August–September, 1884*, 914–15. London: John Murray, 1884.

Cushing, Frank Hamilton. "Preliminary Notes on the Origin, Working Hypothesis and Primary Researches of the Hemenway Southwestern Archaeological Expedition." In *Congrés International des Américanistes, Berlin, 1888*, 151–94. Berlin: W. H. Kühl, 1890.

Cushing, Frank Hamilton. "A Study of Pueblo Pottery as Illustrative of Zuni Cultural Growth." In *Fourth Annual Report of the Bureau of Ethnology, 1882–1883*, 467–521. Washington, D.C.: Government Printing Office, 1886.

Cushing, Frank Hamilton. "Zuñi Breadstuff." *The Millstone: An Illustrated Monthly Journal, Devoted to the Advancement of Milling and Mechanical Interests* (later *The Millstone and the Corn Miller*) 9–10 (January 1884–July 1885). Reprint, *Zuñi Breadstuff*. Edited by Frederick W. Hodge. Indian Notes and Monographs 8. New York: Museum of the American Indian, Heye Foundation, 1920.

Cushing, Frank Hamilton. "Zuni Fetiches." In *Second Annual Report of the Bureau of Ethnology, 1880–1881*, 9–45. Washington, D.C.: Government Printing Office, 1883.

Cushing, Frank Hamilton. *Zuñi Folk Tales*. Reprint with introduction by Mary Austin. New York: Alfred A. Knopf, 1931. Reissue, Tucson: University of Arizona Press, 1986.

Daly, Charles Patrick. "Recent Geographical Work of the World." *Journal of the American Geographical Society of New York* 20 (March 1888): 1–38.

Danien, Elin C., and Eleanor M. King. "Unsung Visionary: Sara Yorke Stevenson and the Development of Archaeology in Philadelphia." In *Philadelphia and the Development of Americanist Archaeology*, edited by Don D. Fowler and David R. Wilcox, 36–47. Tuscaloosa: University of Alabama Press, 2003.

Darnell, Regna D. *And Along Came Boas: Continuity and Revolution in Americanist Anthropology*. Amsterdam: John Benjamins, 1998.

Darnell, Regna D. "The Development of American Anthropology, 1879–1920: From the Bureau of American Ethnology to Franz Boas." PhD dissertation, Department of Anthropology, University of Pennsylvania, 1969.

Defandorf, Mrs. Jason F. "Memories of Garrett Park." *Montgomery County Story* (newsletter) 16, no. 3 (1973): 1–13. www.montgomeryhistory.org.

Dewey, Mary E. "Visit of the Zuni Indians to the Summer House of Mrs. Mary Hemenway in 1886." 1886. Reprinted in "A Hemenway Portfolio: Voices and Views from the Hemenway Archaeological Expedition, 1886–1889." Edited by Curtis M. Hinsley and David R. Wilcox. Special issue, *Journal of the Southwest* 37, no. 4 (1995): 551–65.

Dixon, Keith A. "The Origin and Development of the Southwestern Anthropological Association: The First Thirty-Four Years (1929–1962)." *SWAA Newsletter* 22, no. 2–3 (1983): 1–5.

Dobie, James Frank. "J. Frank Dobie." *American-Statesman*, 14 October 1956.

Drury, Aubrey. "James A. B. Scherer, 1870–1944." *California Historical Society Quarterly* 23, no. 1 (March 1944): 92–93.

Egan, Timothy. *Short Nights of the Shadow Catcher: The Epic Life and Immortal Photographs of Edward Curtis*. New York: Houghton Mifflin Harcourt, 2012.

Elliott, Melinda. *Great Excavations: Tales of Early Southwestern Archaeology, 1888–1939*. Santa Fe: School of American Research Press, 1995.

Elliott, W. W. *History of Arizona Territory with Illustrations*. Phoenix: W. W. Elliott, 1884. Reprint, Flagstaff: Northland Press, 1964.

Esmeralda, Amora [Ella Sterling Mighels]. *Life and Letters of a Forty-Niner's Daughter*. San Francisco: Harr Wagner, 1929.

Eustis, Frederic A. *Augustus Hemenway, 1805–1876: Builder of the United States Trade with the West Coast of South America*. Salem: Peabody Museum, 1955.

Ezell, Paul. "History of the Pima." In *Handbook of the North American Indians*, vol. 10, *Southwest*, edited by William C. Sturtevant and Alfonso Ortiz, 158–19. Washington, D.C.: Smithsonian Institution Press, 1983.

Fabian, Ann. *The Skull Collectors: Race, Science, and America's Unburied Dead.* Chicago: University of Chicago Press, 2010.

Fane, Diana. "The Language of Things: Stewart Culin as Collector." In *Objects of Myth and Memory: American Indian Art at the Brooklyn Museum*, edited by Diana Fane, Ira Jacknis, and Lise M. Breen, 13–27. Brooklyn: Brooklyn Museum, 1991.

Farwell, Arthur. *"Wanderjahre of a Revolutionist" and Other Essays.* Rochester: University of Rochester Press, 1995.

Feis, Ruth Stanley-Brown. *Mollie Garfield in the White House.* New York: Rand McNally, 1963.

Fewkes, Jesse Walter. "Ancient Zuñi Pottery." In *Putnam Anniversary Volume: Anthropological Essays Presented to Frederic Ward Putnam in Honor of His Seventieth Birthday*, edited by Franz Boas, 43–82. New York: G. E. Stechert, 1909.

Fewkes, Jesse Walter. "Archaeological Expedition to Arizona in 1895." In *Seventeenth Annual Report of the Bureau of American Ethnology, 1894–95*, part 2, 519–744. Washington, D.C.: Government Printing Office, 1898.

Fewkes, Jesse Walter. "A Comparison of Sia and Tusayan Snake Ceremonials." *American Anthropologist* O.S. 8 (1895): 118–41.

Fewkes, Jesse Walter. "A Few Summer Ceremonials at Zuñi Pueblo." In *A Journal of American Ethnology and Archaeology*, vol. 1, edited by Jesse Walter Fewkes, 1–61. Boston: Houghton, Mifflin, 1891.

Fewkes, Jesse Walter, ed. *A Journal of American Ethnology and Archaeology*, vol. 1. Boston: Houghton, Mifflin, 1891.

Fewkes, Jesse Walter. "Reconnoissance of Ruins in or near the Reservation." In *A Journal of American Ethnology and Archaeology*, vol. 1, edited by Jesse Walter Fewkes, 95–133. Boston: Houghton, Mifflin, 1891.

Field, Mary Katherine (Kate) Keemle. *Kate Field's Washington.* Washington, D.C., 1890–95.

Force, Roland W. *Politics and the Museum of the American Indian: The Heye and the Mighty.* Honolulu: Mechas Press, 1999.

Foster, Michael S., and Steven R. James. "Dogs, Deer, or Guanacos: Zoomorphic Figurines from Pueblo Grande, Central Arizona." *Journal of Field Archaeology* 29, no. 1–2 (Spring 2002–Summer 2004): 165–76.

Fowler, Don D. *A Laboratory for Anthropology: Science and Romanticism in the American Southwest, 1846–1930.* Albuquerque: University of New Mexico Press, 2000.

Fowler, Don D., and Nancy Parezo. *Anthropology Goes to the Fair: The 1904 Louisiana Purchase Exposition.* Lincoln: University of Nebraska Press, 2007.

Fowler, Don D., and David R. Wilcox, ed. *Philadelphia and the Development of Americanist Archaeology.* Tuscaloosa: University of Alabama Press, 2003.

Fuller, Clarissa Parsons. "Frank Hamilton Cushing's Relations to Zuñi and the Hemenway Southwestern Expedition, 1879–1889." Master's thesis, Department of History, University of New Mexico, 1943.

Gaston, Edward Page. "Among the Red Indian Handicrafters." *Windsor Magazine* 13 (February 1901): 335–38.

Gilliland, Marion Spjut. *Key Marco's Buried Treasure: Archaeology and Adventure in the Nineteenth Century.* Gainesville: University of Florida Press, 1989.

Gilliland, Marion Spjut. *The Material Culture of Key Marco, Florida.* Port Salerno: Florida Classics Library, 1989.

Gilman, Benjamin Ives, and Katherine Ham Stone. "The Hemenway Southwestern Expedition." *Journal of American Archaeology and Ethnology* 5: 229–35. Boston: Houghton Mifflin, 1908.

Goddard, Martha LeBaron. "A Zuni Religious Service at Manchester-by-the-Sea." In "A Hemenway Portfolio: Voices and Views from the Hemenway Archaeological Expedition, 1886–1889." Edited by Curtis M. Hinsley and David R. Wilcox. Special issue, *Journal of the Southwest* 37, no. 4 (1995): 566–70.

Goff, John S. *Arizona Biographical Dictionary.* Cave Creek, Ariz.: Black Mountain Press, 1983.

Goff, John S. *Arizona Territorial Officials V: The Adjutants General, Attorneys General, Auditors, Superintendents of Public Instruction, and Treasurers.* Cave Creek, Ariz.: Black Mountain Press, 1991.

Goodman, Audrey. *Translating Southwestern Landscapes: The Making of an Anglo Literary Region.* Tucson: University of Arizona Press, 2002.

Graybill, Florence Curtis, and Victor Boesen. *Edward Sheriff Curtis: Visions of a Vanishing Race.* New York: American Legacy Press, 1976.

Green, Jesse. *Cushing at Zuni: The Correspondence and Journals of Frank Hamilton Cushing.* Albuquerque: University of New Mexico Press, 1990.

Green, Jesse. *Zuni: Selected Writings of Frank Hamilton Cushing.* Lincoln: University of Nebraska Press, 1979.

Gregory, David A., and David R. Wilcox, ed. *Zuni Origins: Toward a New Synthesis of Southwestern Archaeology.* Tucson: University of Arizona Press, 2007.

Griffith, Margaret Dinorben. "Singing in Twenty Languages." *Royal Magazine* 5, no. 29 (1901): 432–36.

Grimes, William. "The Indian Museum's Last Stand." *New York Times Magazine*, 27 November 1988, 46–77.

Gruber, Carol Signer. "Academic Freedom at Columbia University, 1917–1918: The Case of James McKeen Cattell." *AAUP Bulletin* 28, no. 3 (1972): 297–305.

Hackbarth, Mark R., and Judy Brunson. *Excavations at Las Acequias*. Technical Report 96, no. 4. Flagstaff: Northland Research, 1997.

Hale, Edward Everett, Jr., ed. *The Life and Letters of Edward Everett Hale*. Vol. 2. Boston: Little, Brown, 1917.

Halpern, Katherine Spencer, and Susan McGreevy, eds. *Washington Matthews: Studies of Navajo Culture, 1880–1894*. Albuquerque: University of New Mexico Press, 1997.

Hanchett, Leland L., Jr. *Catching the Stage to Phoenix*. Phoenix: Pine Rim, 1998.

Harrington, Mark Raymond. "Memories of My Work with George G. Heye." Archives of the National Museum of the American Indian, Box OC (Official Correspondence) 88, Folder 2.

Hart, E. Richard. *Pedro Pino: Governor of Zuni Pueblo, 1830–1878*. Logan: Utah State University Press, 2003.

Hart, Richard. "Factors Relating to Zuni Land, 1900–1951." In *Zuni Land Claims: Hearing Before the Subcommittee on Indian Affairs of the Committee on Indian and Insular Affairs, 12 September 1976*. House of Representatives, 94th Congress, 2nd Session: 156–222. Washington, D.C.: Government Printing Office, 1976.

Haury, Emil Walter. *The Excavation of Los Muertos and Neighboring Ruins in the Salt River Valley, Southern Arizona*. Papers of the Peabody Museum of American Archaeology and Ethnology, Harvard University, 24, no. 1. Cambridge, Mass.: Peabody Museum, 1945.

Haury, Emil Walter. "Wherefore a Harvard Ph.D.?" In "A Hemenway Portfolio: Voices and Views from the Hemenway Archaeological Expedition, 1886–1889." Edited by Curtis M. Hinsley and David R. Wilcox. Special issue, *Journal of the Southwest* 37, no. 4 (1995): 711–33.

Haynes, Henry Williamson. "Early Explorations of New Mexico." In *Narrative and Critical History of America*, vol. 2, *Spanish Explorations and Settlements in America from the Fifteenth to the Seventeenth Century*, edited by Justin Winsor, 473–504. Boston and New York: Houghton Mifflin, 1886.

Haynes, Henry Williamson. "Recent Progress in American Archaeology." In *Tenth Annual Report, 1888–1889*, 95–105. Boston: Archaeological Institute of America, 1889.

Heitman, Francis Bernard. *Historical Register and Dictionary of the United States Army, 1781–1903*. Vol. 1. Washington, D.C.: Government Printing Office, 1903.

Hewett, Edgar Lee. *Ancient Life in the American Southwest.* 1930. New York: Tudor, 1948.

Hickman, Money, and Peter Fetchko. *Japan Day by Day: An Exhibition in Honor of Edward Sylvester Morse.* Salem: Peabody Museum of Salem, 1977.

Hieb, Louis A. *The Doctor Danced with Us: Jeremiah Sullivan and the Hopi, 1881–1888, and Other Essays.* Los Ranchos, N.Mex.: Rio Grande, 2018.

Hinsley, Curtis M. "Charlatan, Scientist, or Poet? Frank Hamilton Cushing's Search for a Language of Experiential Knowledge." In *Anthropology, History, and American Indians: Essays in Honor of William Curtis Sturtevant,* edited by William L. Merrill and Ives Goddard, 55–58. Smithsonian Contributions to Knowledge 44. Washington, D.C.: Smithsonian Institution Press, 2002.

Hinsley, Curtis M. "Collecting Cultures and Cultures of Collecting: The Lure of the American Southwest, 1880–1915." *Museum Anthropology* 16, no. 1 (1992): 12–20.

Hinsley, Curtis M. "Edgar Lee Hewett and the School of American Research in Santa Fe, 1906–1912." In *American Archaeology, Past and Future: A Celebration of the Society for American Archaeology, 1935–1985*, edited by David J. Meltzer, Don D. Fowler, and Jeremy A. Sabloff, 217–36. Washington, D.C.: Smithsonian Institution Press, 1986.

Hinsley, Curtis M. "Ethnographic Charisma and Scientific Routine: Cushing and Fewkes in the American Southwest, 1879–1893." In *Observers Observed: Essays on Ethnographic Fieldwork,* edited by George W. Stocking Jr., 53–69. Madison: University of Wisconsin Press, 1983.

Hinsley, Curtis M. "From Shell-Heaps to Stelae: Early Anthropology at the Peabody Museum." In *Objects and Others: Essays on Museum and Material Culture,* edited by George W. Stocking Jr., 49–74. Madison: University of Wisconsin Press, 1985.

Hinsley, Curtis M. "The Problem with Mr. Hewett: Academics and Popularizers in American Archeology, c. 1910." *History of Anthropology Newsletter* 7, no. 1 (1980): 7–10.

Hinsley, Curtis M. *The Smithsonian and the American Indian: Making a Moral Anthropology in Victorian America.* Washington, D.C.: Smithsonian Institution Press, 1994.

Hinsley, Curtis M. "Two Marys and a Martha: Three Massachusetts Women and Indian Reform in the 1880s." In *Gender, Race and Power in the Indian Re-*

form Movement: Revisiting the History of the WNIA, edited by Valerie Sherer Mathes, 55–81. Albuquerque: University of New Mexico Press, 2020.

Hinsley, Curtis M. "Wanted: One Good Man to Discover Central American History." *Harvard Magazine* 87, no. 2 (November–December 1984): 64A–H.

Hinsley, Curtis M. "Zunis and Brahmins: Cultural Ambivalence in the Gilded Age." In *Romantic Motives: Essays on Anthropological Sensibility*, edited by George W. Stocking, Jr., 169–207. Madison: University of Wisconsin Press, 1989.

Hinsley, Curtis M., and Lea S. McChesney. "Anthropology as Cultural Exchange: The Shared Vision of Mary Hemenway and Frank Cushing." Paper presented at the joint meeting of the American Ethnological Society and the Southwestern Anthropological Association, 1984.

Hinsley, Curtis M., and David R. Wilcox. "Arizona's First Sacred Site: The Mystique of the Casa Grande, 1848–1889." *The Bilingual Revue/La Revista Bilingüe* 25, no. 2 (May–August 2000): 129–45.

Hinsley, Curtis M., and David R. Wilcox. *Coming of Age in Chicago: The 1893 World's Fair and the Coalescence of American Anthropology*. Lincoln: University of Nebraska Press, 2016.

Hinsley, Curtis M., and David R. Wilcox. "A Hemenway Portfolio: Voices and Views from the Hemenway Archaeological Expedition, 1886–1889." Special issue, *Journal of the Southwest* 37, no. 4 (1995): 519–742.

Hinsley, Curtis M., and David R. Wilcox. *The Lost Itinerary of Frank Hamilton Cushing*. Tucson: University of Arizona Press, 2002.

Hinsley, Curtis M., and David R. Wilcox. *The Southwest in the American Imagination: The Writings of Sylvester Baxter, 1881–1889*. Tucson: University of Arizona Press, 1996.

Hyland, Jack. *Evangelism's First Modern Media Star: The Life of Reverend Bill Stidger*. New York: Cooper Square Press, 2002.

Hodge, Emlyn M. Interview, Archives of Town of Garrett Park, 15 March 1988. Typescript, 1993. 40 pages, unpaginated. Author's possession, courtesy of Ray Maxwell.

Hodge, Emlyn M. Interview with author, 5 December 1993. Notes in author's possession.

Hodge, Frederick Webb. "The Cairn of the Enchanted Mesa." *Science*, n.s., 6, no. 153 (1897): 846.

Hodge, Frederick Webb. *Circular Kivas near Hawikuh*. Contributions from the Museum of the American Indian, Heye Foundation, 7, no. 1. New York: Museum of the American Indian, 1923.

Hodge, Frederick Webb. "Cushing's Zuni Folk Tales." *Records of the Past* 1, no. 4 (1902): 122–25.

Hodge, Frederick Webb. "Die Erforschung der Verzauberten Mesa (La Mesa Encantada)." *Globus* 75 (March 1899).

Hodge, Frederick Webb. "Dig Your Cellar." *Masterkey* 11, no. 1 (1937): 20–21.

Hodge, Frederick Webb. "The Enchanted Mesa." *Century Magazine* 16, no. 1 (1898): 15–31.

Hodge, Frederick Webb. "The Enchanted Mesa." *National Geographic Magazine* 8, no. 10 (1897): 273–84.

Hodge, Frederick Webb. "The Enchanted Mesa." *Science*, n.s., 6, no. 157 (1897): 994–95.

Hodge, Frederick Webb. "Excavations at Hawikuh, New Mexico." In *Explorations and Field Work of the Smithsonian Institution in 1917*, 61–72. Smithsonian Miscellaneous Collections 68, no. 12. Washington, D.C.: Government Printing Office, 1918.

Hodge, Frederick Webb. "The First Discovered City of Cibola." *American Anthropologist* 8 (1895): 142–52.

Hodge, Frederick Webb. *Frederick Webb Hodge, Ethnologist: A Tape-Recorded Interview*. April 1956. Unpublished typescript, 1957. Author's possession.

Hodge, Frederick Webb. *Handbook of American Indians North of Mexico*. Bureau of American Ethnology Bulletin 30, Parts 1 and 2. Washington, D.C.: Government Printing Office, 1907 and 1910.

Hodge, Frederick Webb. Handwritten notes to Emil Haury, 30 March 1934. X-file 94–36, H-2. Archives, Peabody Museum of Archaeology and Ethnology, Harvard University.

Hodge, Frederick Webb. *History of Hawikuh, New Mexico, One of the So-called Cities of Cibola*. Publications of the Frederick Webb Hodge Anniversary Publication Fund 1. Los Angeles: Southwest Museum, 1937.

Hodge, Frederick Webb. "Katzimo the Enchanted." *Land of Sunshine* 7, no. 6 (1897): 225–36.

Hodge, Frederick Webb. "Motion Pictures at Zuni." *Indian Notes* 1, no. 1: 29–30. New York: Museum of the American Indian, Heye Foundation, 1924.

Hodge, Frederick Webb. "The Nacoochee Mound in Georgia." In *Smithsonian Miscellaneous Collections*, vol. 56, 375–82. Washington, D.C.: Government Printing Office, 1916.

Hodge, Frederick Webb. *Old Dan Dubois*. Los Angeles: Los Angeles Corral of Westerners, 1950.

Hodge, Frederick Webb. "Prehistoric Irrigation in Arizona." *American Anthropologist* 6 (July 1893): 323–30.

Hodge, Frederick Webb. "Review of *A Journal of American Ethnology and Archaeology, Vol. 1*, Edited by J. Walter Fewkes." In *American Anthropologist* 4 (July 1891): 289–94.

Hodge, Frederick Webb. "Review of *A Journal of American Ethnology and Archaeology, Vol. 2*, Edited by J. Walter Fewkes." In *Science* 20, no. 501 (1892): 152–53.

Hodge, Frederick Webb. "The Six Cities of Cibola, 1581–1680." *New Mexico Historical Review* 1, no. 4 (1926): 478–88.

Hodge, Frederick Webb. *Turquois Work at Hawikuh, New Mexico*. Leaflets of the Museum of the American Indian, Heye Foundation, 2. New York: Museum of the American Indian, 1921.

Hodge, Frederick Webb. "A Zuni Foot-Race." *American Anthropologist* 3 (1890): 227–31.

Hodge, Frederick Webb, and C. Hart Merriam. "Henry Wetherbee Henshaw." *American Anthropologist* n.s. 33 (1931): 98–105.

Hodge, Gene Meany. "A Brief Account of My Life and How I Met Dr. Hodge." In *Frederick Webb Hodge, Ethnologist: A Tape-Recorded Interview*. April 1956. Unpublished typescript, 241–43. 1957.

Hodge, Gene Meany. *Four Winds: Poems from Indian Rituals*. Santa Fe: Sunstone Press, 1972.

Hodge, Gene Meany. *The Kachinas Are Coming: Pueblo Indian Kachina Dolls with Related Folktales*. Los Angeles: Steller-Millar, 1936. Reprint, Flagstaff: Northland Press, 1967.

Holland, W. J. "Dr. Jacob L. Wortman." *Annals of the Carnegie Museum* 27 (1926–27): 199–201.

Holliday, William G. *Archaeological Investigations in the Cave Creek Drainage, Tonto National Forest, Arizona*. Archaeological Report No. 1. Albuquerque: USDA Forest Service, Southwestern Region, 1974.

Holman, Nigel. "Curating and Controlling Zuni Photographic Images." *Curator: The Museum Journal* 39, no. 2 (1996): 108–22.

Holmlund, Per. "MikkaGlaciaren: Bed Topography and Response to 20th Century Climate Change." *Geografiska Annaler: Series A: Physical Geography* 68, no. 4 (1986): 291–302.

Hopkins, Ernest J., and Alfred Thomas Jr. *The Arizona State University Story*. Phoenix: Southwest, 1960.

Hovens, Pieter. *Herman F. C. Ten Kate, Jr. (1858–1931) en de Antropologie der Noord-Amerikaanse Indianen.* Meppel, Netherlands: Krips Repro, 1889.

Hovens, Pieter. "Ten Kate's Hemenway Expedition Diary, 1887–1888." *Journal of the Southwest* 37, no. 4 (1995): 635–700.

Howard, Jerry B. "The Casa Buena Hornos: A Study in Morphology, Typology, Function, and Formation Processes." In *Excavations at Casa Buena: Changing Hohokam Land Use Along the Squaw Peak Parkway 1*, edited by Jerry B. Howard, 145–200. Soil Systems Publications in Archaeology 11. Phoenix: Soil Systems, Inc., 1988.

Howard, L. O. *Biographical Memoir of Edward Sylvester Morse, 1838–1925.* National Academy of Sciences Biographical Memoirs 17, no. 1. Washington, D.C.: National Academy of Sciences, 1935.

Huxley, Aldous. *Brave New World.* New York: Harper & Brothers, 1932.

"Interesting Address by Mr. Cushing, the Ethnologist." *San Francisco Chronicle*, 8 November 1887, 6–7.

Jacknis, Ira. "A Chamber of Echoing Songs: Edward Curtis as a Musical Ethnographer." In *Return to the Land of the Head Hunters: Edward S. Curtis, the Kwakwaka'wakw, and the Makings of Modern Cinema*, edited by Brad Evans and Aaron Glass, 99–127. Seattle: University of Washington Press, 2014.

Jacknis, Ira. "Patrons, Potters, and Painters: Phoebe Hearst's Collections from the American Southwest." In *Collecting Native America, 1870–1960*, edited by Shepard Krech III and Barbara A. Hail, 139–71. Washington, D.C.: Smithsonian Institution Press, 1999.

James, George Wharton. "With the Zunis in New Mexico." *Overland Monthly*, 1918, 105–12, 254–60, 285–99.

James Constantine Pilling. Privately printed, 1895.

Jocelyn, Stephen P. "The Old Occidental." *California Historical Society Quarterly* 2, no. 1 (March 1953): 57–64.

Johnson, Adam Fulton. "Documenting the Multisensory and Ephemeral: Navajo Chantway Singers and the Troubles of a 'Science' of Ceremonialism." *Journal of the History of the Behavioral Sciences* 55 (2019): 230–51.

Judd, Neil Merton. *The Bureau of Ethnology: A Partial History.* Norman: University of Oklahoma Press, 1967.

Kevin, Roderick. "This May Be the First Aerial Photo of LA." LA Observed, 2013. Accessed 28 May 2018. www.laobserved.com/archive/2013.

Kidwell, Clara Sue. "Every Last Dishcloth: The Prodigious Collecting of George Gustav Heye." In *Collecting Native America, 1870–1960*, edited by Shepard

Krech III and Barbara A. Hail, 232–58. Washington, D.C.: Smithsonian Institution Press, 1999.

Kintigh, Keith W. *Settlement, Subsistence, and Society in Late Zuni Prehistory.* Anthropological Papers of the University of Arizona 44. Tucson: University of Arizona Press, 1985.

Kolianos, Phyllis E., and Brent R. Weisman, eds. *The Florida Journals of Frank Hamilton Cushing.* Gainesville: University Press of Florida, 2005.

Kolianos, Phyllis E., and Brent R. Weisman, eds. *The Lost Florida Manuscript of Frank Hamilton Cushing.* Gainesville: University Press of Florida, 2005.

Kramer, Barbara. *Nampeyo and Her Pottery.* Tucson: University of Arizona Press, 2003.

Kunz, G. F. *Gems and Precious Stones of North America.* New York: Scientific Publications, 1890.

Lange, Charles H., Carroll L. Riley, and Elizabeth M. Lange. *The Southwestern Journals of Adolph F. Bandelier, 1883–1884.* Albuquerque: University of New Mexico Press, 1970.

Lange, Charles H., Carroll L. Riley, and Elizabeth M. Lange. *The Southwestern Journals of Adolph F. Bandelier, 1885–1888.* Albuquerque: University of New Mexico Press, 1975.

Leslie, Frank. "Cushing Expedition." *Frank Leslie's Illustrated Newspaper* 66 (12 May 1888): 195.

Leviton, Alan E., and Michele L. Aldrich, eds. *Theodore Henry Littell's The California Academy of Sciences, 1853–1906.* San Francisco: California Academy of Sciences, 1997.

Lewis, Arnold. *American Country Houses of the Gilded Age.* New York: Dover Publications, 1982. Revised reissue of George William Sheldon, *Artistic Country-Seats: Types of Recent American Villa and Cottage Architecture with Instances of Country Club-Houses.* New York: D. Appleton, 1886–87.

Libbey, William, Jr. "A Disenchanted Mesa." Unknown publication, 21 August 1897. In Princeton Scientific Expeditions Collection AC# 102, Mudd Library, Princeton University.

Libbey, William, Jr. "How He Climbed the Mesa Rock: Professor Libbey's Own Story of His Perilous Ascent to Its Top." Unknown newspaper, 31 July 1897. In Princeton Scientific Expeditions Collection, AC# 102, Mudd Library, Princeton University.

Liffman, Paul M. *Huichol Territory and the Mexican Nation: Indigenous Ritual, Land Conflict, and Sovereignty Claims.* Tucson: University of Arizona Press, 2011.

Lummis. Charles F. *A New Mexico David.* New York: Charles Scribner's Sons, 1891.

Lummis, Charles F. *The Man Who Married the Moon.* New York: Century, 1892.

Lummis, Charles F. "Authorities of the Southwest: Frederick Webb Hodge." *Land of Sunshine* 6, no. 4 (1897): 146–47.

Lummis, Charles F. "The White Indian." *Land of Sunshine* 12 (1900): 8–17.

Lyman, S. M. "Stewart Culin and the Debate over Trans-Pacific Migration." *Journal for the Theory of Social Behavior* 9 (1979): 91–115.

Lyman, S. M. "Two Neglected Pioneers of Civilizational Analysis: The Cultural Perspectives of R. Stewart Culin and Frank Hamilton Cushing." *Social Research* 49, no. 3 (1982): 690–729.

Magill, Margaret Whitehead. "Margaret Magill's Zuni Diary, 1882–1883." In "A Hemenway Portfolio: Voices and Views from the Hemenway Archaeological Expedition, 1886–1889." Edited by Curtis M. Hinsley and David R. Wilcox. Special issue, *Journal of the Southwest* 37, no. 4 (1995): 535–50.

Mark, Joan T. "Frank Hamilton Cushing and an American Science of Anthropology." *Perspectives in American History* 10 (1976): 449–86.

Mathes, Valerie Sherer, ed. *Gender, Race, and Power in the Indian Reform Movement: Revisiting the History of the WNIA.* Albuquerque: University of New Mexico Press, 2020.

Mathes, Valerie Sherer, ed. *The Women's National Indian Association: A History.* Albuquerque: University of New Mexico Press, 2015.

Mathes, Valerie Scherer, and Richard Lowitt. *The Standing Bear Controversy: Prelude to Indian Reform.* Urbana: University of Illinois Press, 2003.

Matthews, Washington. "The Cities of the Dead." *Land of Sunshine* 12 (1900): 213–21.

Matthews, Washington, J. L. Wortman, and John S. Billings. "Human Bones of the Hemenway Collection in the United States Army Medical Museum." *Memoirs of the National Academy of Sciences* 6, Memoir 7 (1893): 141–86.

McChesney, Lea S. "The Vision of Mary Hemenway." Paper presented at the 87th annual meeting of the American Anthropological Association, 1988.

McDowell, Henry B. "America's Antiquities: Interesting Discoveries Among the Ruins of Buried Zuni Cities." *San Francisco Daily Examiner*, 19 June 1888, 4.

McDowell, Henry B. "Cities of the Dead: Marvelous Discoveries in the Arizona Desert." *San Francisco Daily Examiner*, 25 December 1887, 1–2.

McDowell, Henry B. "A Dead Civilization: Remains of a Great People in the Deserts of Arizona." *San Francisco Daily Examiner*, 30 December 1887, 1–2.

McDowell, Henry B. "Dust: Digging Out Skeletons at Los Muertos." *San Francisco Daily Examiner*, 1 January 1888, 1–2.

McDowell, Henry B. "Left in Zuni: Frank Cushing Tells the Story of His Life in That Pueblo; Their Strange Worship; A Great Epic Poem—Belief in the Analogies." *San Francisco Daily Examiner*, 1 July 1888.

McDowell, Henry B. "The Mythic Drama: Cushing Compares the Chinese Theater with the Ka-Ka of the Zuni." *San Francisco Daily Examiner*, 20 November 1887, 9.

McDowell, Henry B. "The Seven Cities: Important Discoveries Made in the Ruins of Los Muertos." *San Francisco Daily Examiner*, 22 January 1888, 9–10.

McDowell, Henry B. "Tried for Sorcery: Frank Cushing Describes his Trial for Witchcraft by the Zunis; His Narrow Escape; Some of the More Recent Discoveries Made by Him at Los Muertos." *San Francisco Daily Examiner*, 24 June 1888.

McDowell, Henry B. "Zuni Mysteries: How they Hunted for the Exact Middle of the World; A Great Epic Poem; Visiting the Moquis; Questions Which Have Long Disturbed the World's Intellect." *San Francisco Daily Examiner*, 8 July 1888.

McFeely, Eliza. *Zuni and the American Imagination.* New York: Hill and Wang, 2001.

McGee, William John, William H. Holmes, J. W. Powell, Alice C. Fletcher, Washington Matthews, Stewart Culin, and Joseph D. McGuire. "In Memoriam: Frank Hamilton Cushing." *American Anthropologist* New Series 2, no. 2 (1900): 354–80.

McGovern, James R. "David Graham Phillips and the Virility Impulse of the Progressives." *New England Quarterly* 39, no. 3 (1966): 334–55.

McHenry, Margaret. *Thomas Eakins, Who Painted.* Privately printed typescript, 1946.

McMullen, Ann. "Reinventing George Heye: Nationalizing the Museum of the American Indian and its Collections." In *Contesting Knowledge: Museums and Indigenous Perspectives*, edited by Susan Sleeper-Smith, 65–105. Lincoln: University of Nebraska Press, 2009.

Merbs, Charles F. "Washington Matthews and the Hemenway Expedition of 1887–88." *Journal of the Southwest* 44, no. 3 (2002): 303–35.

Merrill, W. Earl. *One Hundred Steps Down Mesa's Past.* Mesa, Arizona: Privately printed, 1970.

Millard, Candace. *Destiny of the Republic: A Tale of Madness, Medicine and the Murder of a President*. New York: Anchor, 2011.

Miller, Darlis. *Matilda Coxe Stevenson: Pioneering Anthropologist*. Norman: University of Oklahoma Press, 2007.

Mitchell, Douglas R., John M. Lindly, and Mark L. Chenault. *Ceremony and Symbolism at Los Guanacos: Excavations at the Salt River Project Kyrene Generating Station*. Flagstaff: SWCA Environmental Consultants, 2003.

Morse, Edward S. *Additional Notes on Arrow Release*. Pamphlet. Salem, Mass.: Peabody Museum, 1922.

Morse, Edward S. Draft letter (6 pages, handwritten, no addressee). n.d. (c. 1891–93). Edward S. Morse Papers, Peabody Essex Museum, Salem.

Moss, Carolyn J., ed. *Kate Field: Selected Letters*. Carbondale: Southern Illinois University Press, 1996.

Nelson, Amber. "The Evolution of Eva Fenyes." *Pasadena Magazine*, 2017. Accessed 29 July 2018. https://pasadenamag.com/artsandculture/the-evolution-of-eva-fenyes/.

Nelson, Edward William. "Henry Wetherbee Henshaw: Naturalist." *The Auk: A Quarterly Journal of Ornithology* 49, no. 4 (1932): 399–427.

"Never Knew He Was an Author." *Saturday Evening Post*, 27 November 1909, 21.

Nichols, Caroline Carpenter. "Celebrity and the National Body: Encounters with the Exotic in Late Nineteenth-Century America." PhD dissertation, Department of American Studies, College of William and Mary, 2008.

Nickliss, Alexandra M. *Phoebe Apperson Hearst: A Life of Power and Politics*. Lincoln: University of Nebraska Press, 2018.

Noelke, Virginia Hull McKimmon. "The Origin and Early History of the Bureau of American Ethnology, 1879–1910." Unpublished PhD dissertation, Department of History, University of Texas at Austin, 1974.

O'Neal, Jennifer R. "Going Home: The Digital Return of Films at the National Museum of the American Indian." *Museum Anthropology Review* 7, no. 1–2 (2013): 166–84.

Osborn, Henry Fairfield. "J. L. Wortman: A Biographical Sketch." *Natural History* 26, no. 6 (1926): 652–53.

Owens, John Gundy. "Some Games of the Zuñi." *Popular Science Monthly* 39 (May 1891): 39–49.

Pandey, Triloki Nath. "Anthropologists at Zuni." *Proceedings of the American Philosophical Society* 116, no. 4 (1972): 321–37.

Pandey, Triloki Nath. "Factionalism in a Southwestern Pueblo." PhD dissertation, Department of Anthropology, University of Chicago, 1967.

Parsons, Elsie Clews. "Mothers and Children at Zuñi." *Man* 19 (1919): 168–73.

Patrick, Herbert R. *The Ancient Canal Systems and Pueblos of the Salt River Valley, Arizona.* Phoenix: Phoenix Free Museum Bulletin 1, 1903.

Peabody, Charles. "Henry Williamson Haynes." *American Anthropologist* 15, no. 2 (1913): 336–46.

Phoenix Directory for the Year 1895. Phoenix: Arizona Directory Company, 1895.

The Photographic Times and American Photographer: An Illustrated Monthly 19 (1889): 523–24 (letter).

Pisani, Michael V. *Imagining Native America in Music.* New Haven: Yale University Press, 2005.

Poast, Florence M., comp. *Bibliography of Frederick Webb Hodge, 1890–1916.* Washington, D.C.: Privately printed [New Era], 1917.

Poor, Robert Marshall. "Washington Matthews: An Intellectual Biography." Master's thesis, Department of Anthropology, University of Nevada, Reno, 1975.

Porter, Joseph C. *Paper Medicine Man: John Gregory Bourke and His American West.* Norman: University of Oklahoma Press, 1986.

Powell, John Wesley Powell. "Sketch of the Mythology of the North American Indians." In *First Annual Report of the Bureau of Ethnology, 1879–1880,* 17–56. Washington, D.C.: Government Printing Office, 1881.

Powell, Lawrence Clark. *Books West Southwest: Essays on Writers, Their Books, and Their Land.* Los Angeles: Ward Ritchie Press, 1957.

Powell, Lawrence Clark. "Sky, Sun, and Water: The Southwest of Frederick Webb Hodge." *Southwest Review* 39, no. 3 (1954): 157–65.

Preble, Donna Louise. *Yamino-Kwiti: Boy Runner of Siba.* Caldwell, Idaho: Caxton, 1940. Reprinted as *Yamino-Kwiti: A Story of Indian Life in the Los Angeles Area.* Berkeley: Heyday, 1980.

Preble, Zahrah Ethel. "Catching Motion on the Wing." *Complete Novel Magazine* 7 (November 1926): 107–12.

Preble, Zahrah Ethel. "Child Cultures Oldest Cradle: What America's Oldest Indian tribe Can Teach the Modern Mother on the Secret of Properly Rearing Children." *Brooklyn Daily Eagle,* 24 June 1923, 11.

Preble, Zahrah Ethel. "Jottings from the Pacific Coast." *Oil Miller* 12–13 (October 1920–January 1921).

Preble, Zahrah Ethel. "Maria Martinez, Indian Master-Potter." *Southern Workman* 62, no. 5 (May 1933): 213–15.

Preble, Zahrah Ethel. "The Oldest Sport in America." *Sportlife: The National Magazine of Sports and Recreation* 74, no. 4 (April 1926): 28–30, 78.

Preble, Zahrah Ethel. "Simple Camp Cookery." *American Cookery* 27, no. 3 (October 1922): 180–82.

Preble, Zahrah Ethel. "The Sunrise Call" and "The Lover's Wooing." Victor Recordings, New York, 27 January 1923. http://adp.library.ucsb.edu/indes.php/talent/detail/17858/Preble_Zahrah_E.vocalist_soprano_vocal.

Preble, Zahrah Ethel. "Teacher Versus Mother: A Discussion of the Responsibility for the Survival of Spoiled Children in American Homes." *Sunset Magazine* 52 (January 1924): 31.

Preble, Zahrah Ethel. "A Tip from Pueblo Indian Mothers." *Child Welfare Magazine of the National Congress of Parents and Teachers* 2, no. 9 (1924): 565–66.

Preble, Zahrah Ethel. *Tomar of Siba: The Story of a Gabrielino Indian Boy of Southern California*. Los Angeles: Schoolhouse, 1933.

Proctor, Ben. *William Randolph Hearst: The Early Years, 1863–1910*. New York: Oxford University Press, 1998.

Rainger, Ronald. "Collectors and Entrepreneurs: Hatcher, Wortman, and the Structure of American Vertebrate Paleontology Circa 1900." *Earth Sciences History* 9, no. 1 (1990): 14–21.

Redman, Samuel J. *Bone Rooms: From Scientific Racism to Human Prehistory in Museums*. Cambridge: Harvard University Press, 2016.

Rivinus, E. F., and E. M. Youssef. *Spencer Baird of the Smithsonian*. Washington: Smithsonian Institution Press, 1992.

Robinson, William Wilcox. *The Story of the Southwest Museum*. Los Angeles: Ward Ritchie, 1960.

Rodgers, James B. "The Fort Mountain Archaeological Complex, Cave Buttes, Arizona." In *Limited Activity and Occupation Sites: A Collection of Conference Papers*, edited by Albert E. Ward, 147–163. Contributions to Anthropological Studies 1. Albuquerque: Center for Anthropological Studies, 1978.

Rotundo, E. Anthony. *American Manhood: Transformations in Masculinity from the Revolution to the Modern Era*. New York: Basic, 1993.

Ryan, Joseph. *The Ruskin Art Club: A History*. Los Angeles: Ruskin Art Club, 1997.

Sammarco, Anthony Mitchell, and Paul Buchanan. *Milton Architecture*. Chicago: Arcadia, 2000.

Scharnhorst, Gary. *Kate Field: The Many Lives of a Nineteenth-Century American Journalist*. Syracuse, N.Y.: Syracuse University Press, 2008.

Setchell, William Albert. "In Memoriam: Hector Alliot, 1862–1919." Los Angeles: Southern California Academy of Sciences, 1919.

Shaplin, Philippa. "A Memento of the Hemenway Expedition." Buried Treasures of the Peabody Museum 4. Cambridge, Mass.: Peabody Museum Association, 1971.

"A Sister to the Indians." *Chicago Tribune*, 26 September 1915, 524.

Smith, Watson, Richard B. Woodbury, and Nathalie F. S. Woodbury. *The Excavation of Hawikuh by Frederick Webb Hodge: Report of the Hendricks-Hodge Expedition, 1917–1923*. New York: Museum of the American Indian-Heye Foundation, 1966.

Snead, James E. *Ruins and Rivals: The Making of Southwest Archaeology*. Tucson: University of Arizona Press, 2001.

Srole, Carole. *Transcribing Gender and Class: Masculinity and Femininity in Nineteenth-Century Courts and Offices*. Ann Arbor: University of Michigan Press, 2010.

Starr, Kevin. *Endangered Dreams: The Great Depression in California*. New York: Oxford University Press, 1996.

Starr, Kevin. *Inventing the Dream: California Through the Progressive Era*. New York: Oxford University Press, 1985.

Stegner, Wallace. *Beyond the Hundredth Meridian: John Wesley Powell and the Second Opening of the West*. Boston: Houghton Mifflin, 1954.

Stephens, Lester D. and Dale R. Calder. "The Zoological Career of Jesse Walter Fewkes, 1850–1930." *Archives of Natural History* 37, no. 2 (2010): 255–73.

Stocking, George W., Jr. "The Ethnographic Sensibility of the 1920s." In *Romantic Motives: Essays on Anthropological Sensibility*, edited by George W. Stocking Jr., 208–76. Madison: University of Wisconsin Press, 1989.

Stocking, George W., Jr. "Franz Boas and the Founding of the American Anthropological Association." *American Anthropologist* 62 (1960): 1–17.

Stocking, George W., Jr. "The Santa Fe Style in American Archaeology: Regional Interest, Academic Initiative and Philanthropic Policy in the First Two Decades of the Laboratory of Anthropology." *Journal of the History of the Behavioral Sciences* 18 (1982): 3–19.

Stocking, George W., Jr. "The Scientific Reaction Against Cultural Anthropology." In *Race, Culture, and Evolution: Essays in the History of Anthropology*, edited by George W. Stocking Jr., 270–308. New York: The Free Press, 1968.

Stoddard, John L. *Lectures, Volume 10: Southern California, Grand Cañon, Yellowstone Park*. Boston: Balch Brothers, 1903.

Stone, Katharine H. "Mrs. Mary Hemenway and Household Arts in the Boston Public Schools." *Journal of Home Economics* 21, no. 1 (January 1929): 7–12.

Swentzell, Rina. "Levels of Truth: Southwest Archaeologists and Anasazi/Pueblo People." *Contact: Southwest Region Interpreter's Newsletter* (1992): 11–13.

Taylor, John Lewis. *Looking for Dan: The Puzzling Life of a Frontier Character—Daniel DuBois*. Indianapolis: Dog Ear, 2014.

Ten Kate, Herman F. C. "Eenige Mededelingen de Hemenway Expeditie" [Some News Concerning the Hemenway Expedition]. *Tijdschrift van het Koninklijk Nederlandsch Aardrijkskundig Genootschap* Series 2, Vol. 6, Part 1 (1888): 216–24.

Ten Kate, Herman F. C. *Over Land en Zee: Schetsen en Stemmingen van en Wereldreiziger* [Over Land and Sea: Sketches and Moods of a World Traveler]. Zutphen, Netherlands: W. J. Thieme & Cie, 1925.

Ten Kate, Herman F. C. "Schrijven van Dr. H. F. C. ten Kate aan de Redaktie" [Letters to the Editor from H. F. C. ten Kate]. *Tijdschrift van het Koninklijk Nederlandsch Aardrijkskundig Genootschap* [Journal of the Royal Dutch Geographical Society] Series 2, Vol. 5, Part 1 (1888): 316–17 (28 February); 317–18 (9 May); 536–37 (21 August); Series 2, Vol. 6, Part 1 (1888): 105–6 (10 December).

Ten Kate, Herman F. C. *Travels and Researches in Native North America, 1882–1883*. Edited by P. Hovens, L. A. Hieb, and W. J. Orr. Albuquerque: University of New Mexico Press, 2004.

Thomas, David Hurst, and Vine Deloria Jr. *Skull Wars: Kennewick Man, Archaeology, and the Battle for Native American Identity*. New York: Basic, 2000.

Thompson, Mark. *American Character: The Curious Life of Charles Fletcher Lummis and the Rediscovery of the Southwest*. New York: Arcade, 2001.

Tinder, David V. *Directory of Early Michigan Photographers*. 2013. William C. Clements Library, University of Michigan. Accessed 27 May 2020. https://clements.umich.edu/files/tinder_directory.pdf.

Trachtenberg, Alan. *The Incorporation of America: Culture and Society in the Gilded Age*. New York: Hill and Wang, 1982.

Troy, D. Q. "Eusebius Joseph Molera." *California Historical Society Quarterly* 11, no. 1 (1932): 94–95.

Troyer, Carlos [Charles]. *Indian Music Lecture: The Zuñi Indians and Their Music*. Philadelphia: Theo. Presser, 1913.

Troyer, Carlos [Charles]. *Traditional Songs of the Zuñis, Series 1 and 2*. Newton Center, Mass.: Wa-Wan Press, 1904.

Troyer, Carlos [Charles]. *Two Zuñi Songs*. San Francisco: Sherman, Clay, 1893.

Truettner, William H. "Dressing the Part: Thomas Eakins' *Portrait of Frank Hamilton Cushing*." *American Art Journal* 17 (1984): 50–52.

Turney, Omar. *Prehistoric Irrigation in Arizona*. Phoenix: Arizona Historian, 1929.

Tylor, Edward Burnett. *Anthropology: An Introduction to the Study of Man and Civilization*. London: Macmillan, 1881.

van Waarden, Nora. "Hilltop Sites in Central Arizona: An Analysis of Their Functional Relationships." Master's thesis, Department of Anthropology, Arizona State University, Tempe, 1984.

Vroman, A. C. "Katzimo, the En-chanted Mesa." *Photo-Era: The American Journal of Photography* 7, no. 2 (1901): 140–45.

Wade, Edwin L., and Lea S. McChesney. *America's Great Lost Expedition: The Thomas Keam Collection of Hopi Pottery from the Second Hemenway Expedition, 1890–1894*. Phoenix: Heard Museum, 1980.

Walden, Daniel. 2019. "Pitch vs. Timbre." In *The Oxford Handbook of Timbre*, edited by Emily Dolan and Alexander Rehding. Accessed 6 October 2019. www.oxfordhandbooks.com.

Waldman, Carl. *Who Was Who in Native American History*. New York: Facts On File, 1990.

Walker, Willard. "Palowahtiwa and the Economic Redevelopment of Zuni Pueblo." *Ethnohistory* 21, no. 1 (1974): 65–75.

Walker, Willard, and Lydia Wyckoff. *Hopis, Tewas, and the American Road*. Middletown, Conn.: Wesleyan University Press, 1983.

Wallace, Kevin. "A Reporter at Large: Slim-Shins' Monument." *New Yorker* 36 (19 November 1960): 104–46.

Wayman, Dorothy Godfrey. *Edward Sylvester Morse: A Biography*. Cambridge: Harvard University Press, 1942.

"Wealthy New York Woman Found Dead in Bathtub at Home." *San Antonio Light*, 17 November 1924.

Weideman, Paul. "Three Wise Women: The Life and Legacy of Eva and the Leonoras." *Pasatiempo* (June–July 2013). Accessed 20 April 2021. https://www.santafenewmexican.com/pasatiempo/three-wise-women-the-life-and-legacy-of-eva-and-the-leonoras/.

"Weird Melodies of a Strange New Mexican People, Now the Fad in Music Circles." *San Francisco Call*, 9 August 1896, 18, cols. 1–5.

Wenger, Tisa. *We Have a Religion: The 1920s Pueblo Indian Dance Controversy and American Religious Freedom*. Chapel Hill: University of North Carolina Press, 2009.

"Wenner's Magazine Reception for Prof. and Mrs. Robert Irving Fulton." *Wenner's Magazine* 16 (May 1894): 191–92.

White, Leslie A. *Pioneers in American Anthropology: The Bandelier-Morgan Letters, 1873–1883*. 2 vols. Albuquerque: University of New Mexico Press, 1940.

Whiting, Lilian. *Kate Field: A Record*. Boston: Little, Brown, 1900.

Wiggins, Marianne. *The Shadow Catcher: A Novel*. New York: Simon & Schuster, 2007.

Wilcox, David R. "Anthropology in a Changing America: Interpreting the Chicago 'Triumph' of Frank Hamilton Cushing." In *Coming of Age in Chicago: The 1893 World's Fair and the Coalescence of American Anthropology*, edited by Curtis M. Hinsley and David R. Wilcox, 125–52. Lincoln: University of Nebraska Press, 2016.

Wilcox, David R. "Creating Field Anthropology: Why Remembering Matters." In *Curators, Collections, and Change: A History of Field Museum Anthropology*, edited by Stephen E. Nash and Gary M. Feinman. Chicago: Field Museum of Natural History, 2003.

Wilcox, David R. *Frank Midvale's Investigations of the Site of La Ciudad*. Arizona State University Anthropological Field Studies 19. Tempe: Arizona State University, 1987.

Wilcox, David R. "Going National: American Anthropology Successfully Redefines Itself as an Accepted Academic Domain." In *Coming of Age in Chicago: The 1893 World's Fair and the Coalescence of American Anthropology*, edited by Curtis M. Hinsley and David R. Wilcox, 413–58. Lincoln: University of Nebraska Press. 2016.

Wilcox, David R. "How Emil Haury (Gradually) Broadened the Horizons of the AAHS." *Glyphs: The Newsletter of the Arizona Archaeological and Historical Society* 67, no. 5 (2016): 8–11.

Wilcox, David R. "Looking for Middle Ground: Archaeology on the Colorado Plateau Today." In *The Colorado Plateau: Cultural, Biological and Physical Research*, edited by Charles Van Riper III and Kenneth Cole, 11–18. Tucson: University of Arizona Press, 2004.

Wilcox, David R. "The Mesoamerican Ballgame in the American Southwest." In *The Mesoamerican Ballgame*, edited by Vernon Scarborough and David R. Wilcox, 101–25. Tucson: University of Arizona Press, 1991.

Wilcox, David R. "Microcosm and Macrocosm in Southwestern Archaeology." In *Archaeology of the Great Basin and American Southwest: Papers in Honor of Don D. Fowler*, edited by Nancy J. Parezo and Joel Janetski, 260–79. Salt Lake City: University of Utah Press, 2014.

Wilcox, David R. "Pueblo Grande in the Nineteenth Century." In *Archaeology of the Pueblo Grande Platform Mound and Surrounding Features*,

Vol. 1. Introduction to the Archival Project and History of Archaeological Research, edited by C. E. Downum and T. Bostwick, 43–71. Pueblo Grande Museum Anthropological Papers No. 1. Phoenix: Pueblo Grande Museum, 1993.

Wilcox, David R. "Restoring Authenticity: Judging Frank Hamilton Cushing's Veracity." In *Philadelphia and the Development of Americanist Archaeology*, edited by Don D. Fowler and David R. Wilcox, 88–112. Tuscaloosa: University of Alabama Press, 2003.

Wilcox, David R., and Don D. Fowler. "The Beginnings of Anthropological Archaeology in the North American Southwest: From Thomas Jefferson to the Pecos Conference." *Journal of the Southwest* 44, no. 2 (2002): 121–234.

Wilcox, David R., and Jonathan Haas. "The Scream of the Butterfly: Competition and Conflict in the Prehistoric Southwest." In *Themes in Southwest Prehistory*, edited by George R. Gumerman, 211–38. Santa Fe: School of American Research, 1994.

Wilcox, David R., and Jerry B. Howard. "The Contribution of the Hemenway Expedition to Hohokam Archaeology." Paper presented at the 87th Annual Meeting of the American Anthropological Association, 1988.

Wilcox, David R., Jerry B. Howard, and Reuben Nelson. *One Hundred Years of Archaeology at Ciudad de los Hornos*. Soil Systems Publications in Archaeology 16. Phoenix: Soil Systems, Inc, 1990.

Wilcox, David R., Gerald Robertson Jr., and J. Scott Wood. "Antecedents to Perry Mesa: Early Pueblo III Defensive Refuge Systems in West Central Arizona." In *Deadly Landscapes: Case Studies in Prehistoric Southwestern Warfare*, edited by Glen E. Rice and Steven A. LeBlanc, 141–94. Salt Lake City: University of Utah Press, 2001.

Wilcox, David R., and Lynette O. Shenk. *The Architecture of the Casa Grande and Its Interpretation*. Arizona State University Archaeological Series 115. Tucson: University of Arizona Press, 1977.

Wilcox, David. R., and Charles Sternberg. *Additional Studies of the Architecture of the Casa Grande and Its Interpretation*. Arizona State Museum Archaeological Series 146. Tucson: University of Arizona Press, 1981.

Wilcox, David R., Judith Rowe Taylor, Joseph Vogel and J. Scott Wood. "Delineating Hilltop Settlement Systems in West-Central Arizona, A. D. 1100–1400." In *Enduring Borderlands Traditions: Trincheras Sites in Time, Space, and Society*, edited by Suzanne K. Fish, Paul R. Fish, and Elisa Villalpando, 195–229. Tucson: University of Arizona Press, 2007.

Wilcox, David R., Phil C. Wiegand, J. Scott Wood, and Jerry B. Howard. "Ancient Cultural Interplay of the American Southwest in the Mexican Northwest." *Journal of the Southwest* 50, no. 2 (2008): 103–206.

Williams, Paul K. "The Mysterious Wrought Iron Gates at 11th and Florida Ave NW Revealed!" *The House History Man* (blog), 17 January 2017. http://househistoryman.blogspot.com/2017/01/the-mysterious-wrought-iron-gates-at.html.

Wilmerding, John, ed. *Thomas Eakins, 1844–1916, and the Heart of American Life*. Exhibition catalogue. Washington, D.C.: Smithsonian Institution Press, 1993.

Wilson, Thomas. "The Hemenway Expedition in Arizona." *Nature* 38 (25 June 1888): 629–31. Reprinted from *American Naturalist*, June 1888.

Wilson, Thomas. "The Late Discoveries of Mr. Frank Hamilton Cushing in Arizona." *American Naturalist* 22, no. 255 (1888): 271–75.

Wilson, Thomas H. "F. W. Hodge and the Southwest Museum, 1932–1955." Los Angeles: Southwest Museum, 1994. www.academia.edu/23044465.

Wilson, Thomas H., and Cheri Falkenstien-Doyle. 1999. "Charles Fletcher Lummis and the Origins of the Southwest Museum." In *Collecting Native America, 1870–1960*, edited by Shepard H. Krech III and Barbara A. Hail, 74–104. Washington, D.C.: Smithsonian Institution Press, 1999.

Winship, George Parker. "The Coronado Expedition, 1540–1542." In *Fourteenth Annual Report of the Bureau of Ethnology (1892–93), Part 1*, 378–607. Washington, D.C.: Government Printing Office, 1896.

Winsor, Justin. *Narrative and Critical History of America*. 8 vols. Boston: Houghton, Mifflin, 1884–89.

Woodbury, Richard B. *Sixty Years of Southwestern Archaeology: A History of the Pecos Conference*. Albuquerque: University of New Mexico Press, 1993.

Wortman, Jacob L., and Herman F. C. ten Kate. "On an Anatomical Characteristic of the Hyoid Bone of Pre-Columbian Pueblo Indians of Arizona, U. S. A." In *Congrès International des Américanistes, Berlin, 1888*, 263–72. Berlin: W. H. Kühl, 1890.

Yochelson, Ellis. *Charles Doolittle Walcott, Paleontologist*. Kent, Ohio: Kent State University Press, 1998.

Zamorano Club. *The Zamorano Club Programs, 1928–91*. Los Angeles: Zamorano Club, 1992.

Index

Note: Page numbers in *italics* indicate illustrations.

About the Editors

Curtis M. Hinsley is Regents' Professor Emeritus of history at Northern Arizona University. He received his PhD from the University of Wisconsin–Madison in 1976. He has written widely on American cultural history. He is co-editor with David R. Wilcox of volumes 1 and 2 of *Frank Hamilton Cushing and the Hemenway Southwestern Archaeological Expedition, 1886–1889*, which includes *The Southwest in the American Imagination: The Writings of Sylvester Baxter, 1881–1889* (1996) and *The Lost Itinerary of Frank Hamilton Cushing* (2002). His most recent work is *Coming of Age in Chicago: The 1893 World's Fair and the Coalescence of American Anthropology* (University of Nebraska Press, 2016), which he again co-authored with David R. Wilcox. His most recent book is *Zuni, Hopi, Copan: Early Anthropology at Harvard, 1890–1893* (2023). Hinsley has received numerous grants and awards for his work, including from the National Endowment for the Humanities, the National Science Foundation, and NAU's Distinguished Professor of the Year award for Humanities.

David R. Wilcox was an independent scholar at his passing in 2022. He had previously been curator of anthropology and a senior research anthropologist at the Museum of Northern Arizona. He also served as an adjunct professor of anthropology at Northern Arizona University. He received his PhD in anthropology from the University of Arizona in 1977. A prolific writer, he produced more than 100 peer-reviewed publications, including 16 books, 3 special journal issues, 76 book chapters, and 20 journal articles. He co-edited, with Curtis M. Hinsley, volumes 1 and 2 of *Frank Hamilton Cushing and the Hemenway Southwestern Archaeological Expedition, 1886–1889*, as well as *Coming of Age in Chicago: The 1893 World's Fair and the Coalescence of American Anthropology* (2016).

The Southwest Center Series

Jeffrey M. Banister, Editor

Ignaz Pfefferkorn, *Sonora: A Description of the Province*

Carl Lumholtz, *New Trails in Mexico*

Buford Pickens, *The Missions of Northern Sonora: A 1935 Field Documentation*

Gary Paul Nabhan, editor, *Counting Sheep: Twenty Ways of Seeing Desert Bighorn*

Eileen Oktavec, *Answered Prayers: Miracles and Milagros Along the Border*

Curtis M. Hinsley and David R. Wilcox, editors, *Frank Hamilton Cushing and the Hemenway Southwestern Archaeological Expedition, 1886–1889*, volume 1: *The Southwest in the American Imagination: The Writings of Sylvester Baxter, 1881–1899*

Lawrence J. Taylor and Maeve Hickey, *The Road to Mexico*

Donna J. Guy and Thomas E. Sheridan, editors, *Contested Ground: Comparative Frontiers on the Northern and Southern Edges of the Spanish Empire*

Julian D. Hayden, *The Sierra Pinacate*

Paul S. Martin, David Yetman, Mark Fishbein, Phil Jenkins, Thomas R. Van Devender, and Rebecca K. Wilson, editors, *Gentry's Rio Mayo Plants: The Tropical Deciduous Forest and Environs of Northwest Mexico*

W. J. McGee, *Trails to Tiburón: The 1894 and 1895 Field Diaries of W. J. McGee*, transcribed by Hazel McFeely Fontana, annotated and with an introduction by Bernard L. Fontana

Richard Stephen Felger, *Flora of the Gran Desierto and Río Colorado of Northwestern Mexico*

Donald Bahr, editor, *O'odham Creation and Related Events: As Told to Ruth Benedict in 1927 in Prose, Oratory, and Song by the Pimas William Blackwater, Thomas Vanyiko, Clara Ahiel, William Stevens, Oliver Wellington, and Kisto*

Dan L. Fischer, *Early Southwest Ornithologists, 1528–1900*

Thomas Bowen, editor, *Backcountry Pilot: Flying Adventures with Ike Russell*

Federico José María Ronstadt, *Borderman: Memoirs of Federico José María Ronstadt, edited by Edward F. Ronstadt*

Curtis M. Hinsley and David R. Wilcox, editors, *Frank Hamilton Cushing and the Hemenway Southwestern Archaeological Expedition, 1886–1889*, volume 2: *The Lost Itinerary of Frank Hamilton Cushing*

Neil Goodwin, *Like a Brother: Grenville Goodwin's Apache Years, 1928–1939*

Katherine G. Morrissey and Kirsten Jensen, editors, *Picturing Arizona: The Photographic Record of the 1930s*

Bill Broyles and Michael Berman, *Sunshot: Peril and Wonder in the Gran Desierto*

David W. Lazaroff, Philip C. Rosen, and Charles H. Lowe Jr., *Amphibians, Reptiles, and Their Habitats at Sabino Canyon*

David Yetman, *The Organ Pipe Cactus*

Gloria Fraser Giffords, *Sanctuaries of Earth, Stone, and Light: The Churches of Northern New Spain, 1530–1821*

David Yetman, *The Great Cacti: Ethnobotany and Biogeography*

John Messina, *Álamos, Sonora: Architecture and Urbanism in the Dry Tropics*

Laura L. Cummings, *Pachucas and Pachucos in Tucson: Situated Border Lives*

Bernard L. Fontana and Edward McCain, *A Gift of Angels: The Art of Mission San Xavier del Bac*

David A. Yetman, *The Ópatas: In Search of a Sonoran People*

Julian D. Hayden, *Field Man: The Life of a Desert Archaeologist*, edited by Bill Broyles and Diane Boyer

Bill Broyles, Gayle Harrison Hartmann, Thomas E. Sheridan, Gary Paul Nabhan, and Mary Charlotte Thurtle, *Last Water on the Devil's Highway: A Cultural and Natural History of Tinajas Altas*

Thomas E. Sheridan, *Arizona: A History, Revised Edition*

Richard S. Felger and Benjamin Theodore Wilder, *Plant Life of a Desert Archipelago: Flora of the Sonoran Islands in the Gulf of California*

David Burkhalter, *Baja California Missions: In the Footsteps of the Padres*

Guillermo Núñez Noriega, *Just Between Us: An Ethnography of Male Identity and Intimacy in Rural Communities of Northern Mexico*

Cathy Moser Marlett, *Shells on a Desert Shore: Mollusks in the Seri World*

Rebecca A. Carte, *Capturing the Landscapes of New Spain: Baltasar Obregón and the 1564 Ibarra Expedition*

Gary Paul Nabhan, editor, *Ethnobiology for the Future: Linking Cultural and Ecological Diversity*

James S. Griffith, *Saints, Statues, and Stories: A Folklorist Looks at the Religious Art of Sonora*

David Yetman, Alberto Búrquez, Kevin Hultine, and Michael Sanderson, with Frank S. Crosswhite, *The Saguaro Cactus: A Natural History*

Carolyn Niethammer, *A Desert Feast: Celebrating Tucson's Culinary Heritage*

Gary Paul Nabhan, editor, *The Nature of Desert Nature*

David Yetman, *Natural Landmarks of Arizona*

Michael Chiago Sr. and Amadeo M. Rea, *Michael Chiago: O'odham Lifeways Through Art*

David Wentworth Lazaroff, *Picturing Sabino: A Photographic History of a Southwestern Canyon*

David Yetman and Alberto Búrquez, *Mexico's Valleys of Cuicatlán and Tehuacán: From Deserts to Clouds*

Curtis M. Hinsley and David R. Wilcox, editors, *Frank Hamilton Cushing and the Hemenway Southwestern Archaeological Expedition, 1886–1889*, volume 3: *On a Trail of Southwest Discovery: The Expedition Diaries of Frederick W. Hodge and Margaret W. Magill, 1886–1888*